Indian Epigraphy

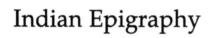

SOUTH ASIA RESEARCH

Series Editor

Richard Lariviere

A Publication Series of
The University of Texas Center for Asian Studies
and Oxford University Press

THE EARLY UPANIṢADS
Annotated Text and Translation
Patrick Olivelle

INDIAN EPIGRAPHY
A Guide to the Study of Inscriptions in Sanskrit, Prakrit,
and the Other Indo-Aryan Languages
Richard Saloman

A DICTIONARY OF OLD MARATHI
Anne Feldhaus

DONORS, DEVOTEES, AND DAUGHTERS OF GOD
Temple Women in Medieval Tamilnadu
Leslie C. Orr

INDIAN EPIGRAPHY

A Guide to the Study of Inscriptions in Sanskrit, Prakrit, and the Other Indo-Aryan Languages

Richard Salomon

New York Oxford
Oxford University Press
1998

Oxford University Press

Oxford New York
Athens Auckland Bangkok Bogotá Buenos Aires Calcutta
Cape Town Chennai Dar es Salaam Delhi Florence Hong Kong Istanbul
Karachi Kuala Lumpur Madrid Melbourne Mexico City Mumbai
Nairobi Paris São Paolo Singapore Taipei Tokyo Toronto Warsaw

and associated companies in
Berlin Ibadan

Published by Oxford University Press, Inc.
198 Madison Avenue, New York, New York 10016

Library of Congress Cataloging-in-Publication Data
Salomon, Richard. 1948—
Indian epigraphy : a guide to the study of inscriptions in Sanskrit, Prakrit, and the other Indo-Aryan languages / Richard Salomon.
p. cm. — (South Asia research)
Includes bibliographical references and index.
ISBN 0-19-509984-2
1. Inscriptions, Indo-Aryan. I. Title. II. Series: South Asia research (New York, N.Y.)
CN1150.S25 1996 491'.1—dc20 95-31756

3 5 7 9 8 6 4 2
Printed in the United States of America
on acid-free paper

Dedicated to the memory of Professor D. C. Sircar

Preface

This book is intended to provide a general survey of all the inscriptional material in the Indo-Aryan languages. This is a vast body of material, comprising tens of thousands of documents over a chronological range of more than two millennia and a geographical range including not only "India" in the broadest traditional sense of the term but also much of southeast, central, and other parts of Asia. The range of the material is equally broad in terms of languages, scripts, style, and content. I have attempted to survey the entire corpus of inscriptions in all the Indo-Aryan languages and to present it in such a way as to make it accessible not only to specialists in the field but also to nonspecialists, whether they be Indologists working in other subfields (e.g., South Asian historians) or scholars involved in epigraphic and related studies in other regions of the world. I have therefore tried to strike a balance between the needs of the nonspecialist, who may be less interested in technical details, and the desire to present a complete and accurate picture of this complex subject; where it proved necessary to choose between the two, I preferred to err on the side of completeness.

This book is intended to supplement rather than to supplant previous general studies of Indian epigraphy, especially *Indian Epigraphy* by D. C. Sircar, whose expertise in this subject no one could hope to exceed or even equal. Nonetheless, I have felt it worthwhile to attempt a more up-to-date survey (that of Sircar being now more than thirty years old), one which will present the field from a somewhat broader and less specialized point of view.

It seems advisable to state clearly at the outset the limits which have been set for this study. This is, first of all, a book on epigraphy, not paleography; that is to say, it is mainly concerned with the study of inscriptions and their contents rather than with the forms, varieties, and historical development of the scripts in which they are written.[1] The term "inscription" is interpreted in the loose sense in which it is traditionally used in Indic studies, including documents written in ink on such surfaces as clay, wood, or skin (the German *Aufschrift*) as well as inscriptions proper, that is,

1. The terms "epigraphy" and "paleography" are used here in the senses in which they are traditionally employed in Indic and Semitic studies (see G. S. Gai, *Introduction to Indian Epigraphy*, 1–3, and Joseph Naveh, *Early History of the Alphabet: An Introduction to West Semitic Epigraphy and Palaeography* [Jerusalem: The Hebrew University, 1987], 6) rather than as they are used in classical studies, wherein "paleography" is generally used to refer to the study of texts written in ink, as opposed to those engraved on hard surfaces.

writing carved into hard surfaces such as stone or metal *(Inschrift)*. Also following traditional Indological usage, which is convenient if not strictly logical, I have included inscriptions on seals and sealings but not those on coins, the latter falling into the province of the related but separate field of numismatics. And although paleography as such (in the sense just defined) is not a major focus of this book, it seemed undesirable, indeed, impossible to discuss inscriptions without any reference to writing at all. I have therefore limited myself to a general discussion of the history and development of Indian writing and scripts (see chapter 2), without attempting to trace in detail the historical development of the many Indic scripts. (For further information on paleography proper, the reader is referred to the various sources mentioned in section 8.2.1.)

As for the epigraphic materials to be treated in this book, it should be emphasized that the limits are linguistic rather than geographical or chronological. Any and all inscriptions in Indo-Aryan languages, whether ancient or recent, from India[2] or from other lands, are treated as relevant to this study. Indian inscriptions in languages of other families—mainly Dravidian languages—are not treated in detail, although I have not felt constrained to apply this exclusion too rigidly since the fields of Indo-Aryan and Dravidian epigraphy are closely related and even overlap to a considerable extent (for example, in the many bilingual Indo-Aryan/Dravidian inscriptions). This limitation is admittedly primarily one of convenience; although a complete study of Indian inscriptions ideally would cover material in Indo-Aryan, Dravidian, and other language groups, from a practical standpoint the material involved is so vast that it would hardly be possible to do it justice in one volume. In any case, I am not qualified to treat Dravidian inscriptions adequately. In point of fact, most previous studies of Indian epigraphy have similarly concentrated on one or the other of the two major bodies of material, namely, Indo-Aryan or Dravidian, presumably for similar reasons, though they have usually not explicitly admitted that they are doing so.

I have followed a similar course with regard to the study of the still undeciphered writing of the Indus Valley civilization; that is to say, I have mentioned it only in passing (see sections 2.1.2, 2.2.3.1, and 2.2.3.3) insofar as it may relate to the scripts of the historical period. Should the language represented in these inscriptions eventually turn out to belong to the Indo-Aryan (or Indo-European) group, they would of course have to be added to the present corpus, but for the meantime they must be treated as a separate body of unidentified material.

I have benefited from the assistance of so many individuals and institutions that it is impossible to give them all the credit they are due. Those individuals who have made particularly important contributions include Gérard Fussman (Collège de France), Oskar von Hinüber (University of Freiburg), Jason Neelis (University of Washington), K. R. Norman (Cambridge University), David Pingree (Brown University), Rosane Rocher (University of Pennsylvania), and David Shulman (Hebrew University). They either read the entire manuscript or substantial portions and freely shared

2. The term "India" is used here as elsewhere in this book (cf. 4.3.7) to refer to traditional India, roughly corresponding to the modern nations of India, Pakistan, and Bangladesh.

of their erudition in their respective specialties, thereby remedying, in part at least, my own shortcomings. Dr. Nalini Balbir of the Institut National des Langues et Civilisations Orientales (Paris) provided very helpful comments on Jaina materials. Especially important were the contributions of William Arraj (Seattle), who read the entire manuscript with scrupulous care and offered many valuable suggestions. Timothy Lenz (University of Washington) skillfully assisted in the preparation of the maps. I wish to express my sincere graditude to them and the many other persons who helped me—and to apologize for being unable, in some cases, to make full use of their suggestions due to limitations of space, time, and my own abilities, but certainly not as a result of any disregard for their assistance.

Among the many libraries whose resources facilitated the preparation of this book, special mention must be made of my home institution, the University of Washington, several of whose staff members went to great lengths in assisting me in various ways and whose skill and patience vastly facilitated the entire undertaking. Deserving of special thanks are Irene Joshi, South Asia librarian; Marie Noelle Deseilligny, reference librarian; and the entire staff of the interlibrary borrowing service.

I must also express my sincere appreciation to the institutions which saw fit to support the research for this book: the John Simon Guggenheim Foundation, the National Endowment for the Humanities, and the Graduate School Research Fund of the University of Washington. To these institutions, and to all of the individuals who have assisted or expressed interest in this project over the many years it has taken to complete, I am also grateful for their patience.

Finally, a word of thanks to my friends and colleagues in the Department of Asian Languages and Literature, University of Washington, who helped in so many ways in this project, not least of all by their long-lasting interest, support, and patience.

Seattle, Washington R.S.
April 1996

Contents

Abbreviations

AI	*Ancient India*
AP	Andhra Pradesh
AR	*Asiatic(k) Researches*
ARASI	*Annual Reports of the Archaeological Survey of India*
AR(S)IE	*Annual Report on (South) Indian Epigraphy*
ASI	Archaeological Survey of India
ASI(A)R	Archaeological Survey of India, (Annual) Reports
BEFEO	*Bulletin de l'École Française d'Extrême-Orient*
BHS	Buddhist Hybrid Sanskrit
BIP	G. Bühler, *Indian Paleography*
BPLM	G. H. Ojhā, *Bhāratīya Prācīna Lipi Mālā*
BS	O. von Hinüber, *Der Beginn der Schrift und frühe Schriftlichkeit in Indien*
BSO(A)S	*Bulletin of the School of Oriental (and African) Studies*
C	G. Coedès' number for Campā (i.e. Vietnam) ins.
CII	Corpus Inscriptionum Indicarum
DIP	A. H. Dani, *Indian Palaeography*
DKS	C. C. Das Gupta, *The Development of the Kharoṣṭhī Script*
EC	*Epigraphia Carnatica*
EHS	Epigraphical Hybrid Sanskrit
EI	*Epigraphia Indica*
EINES	D. C. Sircar, *Early Indian Numismatic and Epigraphical Studies*
ESIP	T. V. Mahalingam, *Early South Indian Palaeography*
EZ	*Epigraphia Zeylanica*
GD	J. Brough, *The Gāndhārī Dharmapada*
HBI	E. Lamotte, *Histoire du bouddhisme indien*
HGIP	M. A. Mehendale, *Historical Grammar of Inscriptional Prakrits*
IA	*Indian Antiquary*
IAAR	*Indian Archaeology: A Review*
IC	L. Renou and J. Filliozat, *L'Inde classique*
ICTWI	J. Burgess and Bh. Indraji, *Inscriptions from the Cave-Temples of Western India*
IEBHA	F. Asher and G. S. Gai, eds., *Indian Epigraphy: Its Bearing on the History of Art*
IEG	D. C. Sircar, *Indian Epigraphical Glossary*

IESIS	C. Sivaramamurti, *Indian Epigraphy and South Indian Scripts*
IGI	*Imperial Gazeteer of India*, vol. 2
IHQ	*Indian Historical Quarterly*
IIE	G. S. Gai, *Introduction to Indian Epigraphy*
IIEP	D. C. Sircar, "Introduction to Indian Epigraphy and Palaeography"
IIJ	*Indo-Iranian Journal*
ins(s).	inscription(s)
IVMD	N. Karashima, *Indus Valley to Mekong Delta: Explorations in Epigraphy*
JA	*Journal Asiatique*
JAHRS	*Journal of the Andhra Historical Research Society*
JAIH	*Journal of Ancient Indian History*
JAOS	*Journal of the American Oriental Society*
JAS[B]	*Journal of the Asiatic Society* [*of Bengal*]
JBBRAS	*Journal of the Bombay Branch of the Royal Asiatic Society*
JB(O)RS	*Journal of the Bihar* (*and Orissa*) *Research Society*
JESI	*Journal of the Epigraphical Society of India*
JIABS	*Journal of the International Association of Buddhist Studies*
JIH	*Journal of Indian History*
JNSI	*Journal of the Numismatic Society of India*
JOI	*Journal of the Oriental Institute* [Baroda]
J(P)ASB	*Journal* (*and Proceedings*) *of the Asiatic Society of Bengal*
JRAS	*Journal of the Royal Asiatic Society*
JUPHS	*Journal of the United Provinces Historical Society*
K	G. Coedès' number for Khmer (i.e., Cambodia) ins.
KI	A. M. Boyer, E. J. Rapson, and E. Senart, *Kharoṣṭhī Inscriptions Discovered by Sir Aurel Stein . . .*
KS	F. Kielhorn, *Kleine Schriften*
l(l).	line(s)
MASI	*Memoirs of the Archaeological Survey of India*
MI	H. Lüders, *Mathurā Inscriptions*
MIA	Middle Indo-Aryan
MP	Madhya Pradesh
MRE	Minor rock edicts (of Aśoka)
NIA	New Indo-Aryan
NWFP	North-West Frontier Province (Pakistan)
OBS	S. P. Gupta and K. S. Ramachandran, *The Origin of Brahmi Script*
OHRJ	*Orissa Historical Research Journal*
OIBA	G. Bühler, *On the Origin of the Indian Brāhma Alphabet*
OKA	G. Bühler, "Origin of the Kharoṣṭhī Alphabet"
PIP	R. B. Pandey, *Indian Palaeography*
RIE	K. V. Ramesh, *Indian Epigraphy*
SAI	H. Falk, *Schrift im alten Indien*
SI	D. C. Sircar, *Select Inscriptions . . .*
SIE	D. C. Sircar, *Indian Epigraphy*
SII	*South Indian Inscriptions*

SIP	A. C. Burnell, *Elements of South-Indian Palaeography*
SITI	T. N. Subramanian, *South Indian Temple Inscriptions*
StII	*Studien zur Indologie und Iranistik*
UP	Uttar Pradesh
v(v).	verse(s)
ZDMG	*Zeitschrift der Deutschen Morgenländischen Gesellschaft*

Note on Citation and Bibliographic Form

Individual inscriptions referred to in the text are cited with a brief reference (e.g., abbreviated title of journal, volume, page numbers); detailed references are given in the Index of Inscriptions Cited at the end of this book. Similarly, references to books are given in shortened form (author and title) if the books are listed in the bibliography; otherwise they are cited in full. (For criteria of inclusion, see the note at the beginning of the bibliography.) This system has been adopted in the hope of striking a compromise between convenience of reference and cumbersome detail in the main text. It also permits the Index of Inscriptions Cited and the bibliography to function simultaneously as documentation for this book and as general compilations of important inscriptions and epigraphic publications, respectively.

Where appropriate, brief bibliographic summaries of specialized literature relevant to a particular section are added after the heading.

References to page numbers in other publications are given using only numbers (e.g., EI 1, 1–10); citations with "p(p)." refer to pages of this book. But a few exceptions to this are made in the bibliography and the Index of Inscriptions Cited, where necessary for clarity of reference. Cross-references within this book are generally by section number, but in the case of longer sections, page references are added.

The transliteration employed for words in Indic and other languages follow, as far as possible, the standard modern scholarly systems. Toponyms (i.e., names of villages, towns, etc.) are generally cited in transliteration according to the local pronunciation, but it is impossible to achieve complete accuracy and consistency due to lack of reliable documentation, local variations, and similar factors. In doubtful cases the toponym is cited as given by the editor(s) of the relevant inscription. Names of places for which a nontechnical English spelling is standard and familiar, including the names of all Indian districts and states, are given as such rather than in scholarly transliteration (e.g., Delhi rather than Dillī; Bombay rather than Mumbaī).

Indian Epigraphy

1

The Scope and Significance of Epigraphy in Indological Studies

Though it has been frequently stated, the importance of epigraphy in Indology can hardly be overemphasized. The primary reason for the particular importance of epigraphy in the study of traditional India (as compared, e.g., with that of classical Europe or China) is the extreme paucity, especially in the ancient period, of the type of historical data from literary sources which is available for other major civilizations of the ancient and medieval world. This situation is a reflection of what might be called the "ahistorical" orientation of traditional Indian culture. Traditional India, with its strongly idealistic and theoretical orientation, had little interest in what we in the modern world think of as "history," and except for a few outstanding exceptions Sanskrit and classical literature include little in the way of "historical" texts in the stricter sense of the term. As a result, the history of ancient and early medieval (i.e., pre-Islamic) India must for the most part be reconstructed from incidental sources; that is, sources whose original intent was something other than the recording of historical events as such. Such sources include many branches of literature, both secular and religious, but these typically give us little more than tantalizing tidbits of historical information, often distorted, and out of context at that. Far more revealing are the archaeological sources, including not only the results of formal stratigraphic excavations but also numismatic and above all epigraphic materials.

It has been authoritatively estimated[1] that something like 80 percent of our knowledge of the history of India before about A.D. 1000 is derived from inscriptional sources.[2] Without inscriptions, for example, we would have only the vaguest notion of the history of the Gupta dynasty, the greatest northern Indian empire of the classical period. But the importance of epigraphy goes beyond historical studies in the narrower sense of the term, that is, political history. The modern study of most aspects of the cultural history of traditional India, such as the arts, literature, religion, and language, are also heavily indebted to inscriptions for their basic chronological and geographical framework. Again reflecting the non-historical

1. D. C. Sircar, EINES 91.
2. For further details, see section 7.1.

orientation of traditional Indian culture as a whole, traditional literary and cultural relics typically seem to exist in a chronological vacuum; for example, the date of original composition of literary texts, especially in the earlier centuries, is rarely recorded in the works themselves (although later manuscript copies are often dated). Thus the dates and even the relative chronologies of major cultural developments are often uncertain or totally unknown. But here again inscriptional material, with its vast volume and diversity of contents, frequently comes to the rescue. In the history of literature, for example, inscriptional allusions to and imitations of great classical poets, as well as original compositions preserved in epigraphic form, provide a bedrock of evidence for the chronological development of Sanskrit poetic literature.[3] The same holds true, to a greater or lesser extent, for nearly all branches of Indology;[4] in the words of D. C. Sircar, "there is no aspect of the life, culture and activities of the Indians that is not reflected in inscriptions."[5] Thus epigraphic materials, directly or indirectly, provide almost the only solid chronological foundation for modern historically oriented studies. This is true primarily because inscriptions, unlike literary sources, which almost always come to us only after being copied and recopied through the centuries, are inherently datable, either by an explicit date or by paleographic estimate.[6] A reference to a particular legal principle, religious sect, philosopher, poet, and so on, in an inscription thus gives at least an approximate terminus ante quem for a person or event whose date might otherwise (i.e., from literary sources alone) be impossible to determine even in the broadest estimate.

It is mainly for these reasons that epigraphy is a primary rather than a secondary subfield within Indology. Whereas in classical studies or Sinology, for example, epigraphy serves mainly as a corroborative and supplementary source to historical studies based mainly on textual sources, in India the situation is precisely the opposite. There, history is built upon a skeleton reconstructed principally from inscriptions, while literary and other sources usually serve only to add some scraps of flesh here and there to the bare bones. There are, of course, some exceptions to the rule, most notably in Kashmir, where unlike nearly everywhere else in India a sophisticated tradition of historical writing flourished, best exemplified by Kalhaṇa's *Rājataraṅgiṇī*. Nonetheless, the general pattern remains essentially valid for political, and to a lesser extent for cultural, history.[7]

The paucity of historical materials in the usual sense for India is balanced, as it were, by the relative abundance of inscriptions.[8] According to Sircar, "About 90,000

3. For further discussion, see section 7.2.

4. For examples and details, see sections 7.3–7.

5. EINES 102.

6. See section 5.4.

7. In this respect, the study of the history of traditional India is methodologically more comparable to the study of the early urbanized cultures such as those of Egypt and Mesopotamia, for which the principal sources are epigraphic rather than literary, rather than to that of the contemporary classical cultures of Europe and the Near and Far East.

8. The abundance of inscriptions in India may be attributed, in part at least, to the desire of the issuing authorities to preserve their records in a form which would survive the rigors of the Indian climate, where documents on perishable materials such as palm leaves or paper tend not to last more than a few generations. In particular, the widespread practice of recording land grants and other transactions on copper plates seems to reflect such concerns (see section 4.1.2).

inscriptions have so far been discovered in different parts of India."[9] These estimated 90,000 inscriptions come from virtually every corner of India and from every century from the third (or possibly fourth) century B.C. up to modern times, though their distribution is by no means equal in terms of antiquity and geographical and linguistic distribution. For example, early inscriptions, that is, those from before about the beginning of the Christian era are relatively rare, and inscriptions only become very common in medieval times, from about the eighth century onward. In general, the bulk of inscriptions in the later period are from southern India and the majority of these are in Dravidian languages.[10]

Sircar's estimate of 90,000 inscriptions from India presumably does not include inscriptions in the neighboring South Asian countries of Pakistan, Nepal, Bangladesh, and Sri Lanka, which would add many thousands more to the total. Inscriptions in Indian languages, moreover, are also found in large numbers over a vast area of Asia and even beyond Asia, for instance, in Africa.[11] The comments made earlier about the prime importance of Indian inscriptions apply equally to these extra-Indian inscriptions, many of which constitute our principal, sometimes even our sole, source for the historical study of the Indianized civilizations of ancient Southeast and central Asia.

The number of known inscriptions, moreover, is constantly growing as new records, including many of considerable importance, continue to be discovered within and outside of India every year.[12] A complete history of India written today, taking into account all recent epigraphic discoveries, would be significantly different from and more complete than one written, for example, only twenty years ago; there is no reason to think that this pattern should change in the foreseeable future. Moreover, as also noted by Sircar,[13] a great many of the estimated 90,000 inscriptions already found in India have not yet been published. While it is true that many of the still unpublished records are either of minimal importance or too badly damaged to be deciphered, no doubt some of them will, when they are finally published, add significantly to our historical and cultural knowledge. Sircar thus decries the incorrect notion "that all important inscriptions have already been discovered and utilized in the reconstruction of the lost history of ancient India and that there is little else to do."[14] Epigraphy is indeed still a living and developing field, even if it has in recent years suffered something of a decline in standards in India[15] and a general neglect elsewhere.[16]

The decline of Indian epigraphic studies may be attributed, in part at least, to the special difficulties and problems involved in this field.[17] Not only is the material vast,

9. EINES 91. It has recently been estimated that some 58,000 Indian inscriptions have been published (R. Garbini, JESI 19, 1993, 64).

10. According to Sircar (EINES 91), "the largest numbers come from the Tamil- Kannada- and Telugu-speaking areas—about 35,000, 17,000, and 10,000 respectively."

11. On Indian-language inscriptions from outside of South Asia, see section 4.3.7.

12. Cf. EINES 91 and SIE 13.

13. EINES 91.

14. EINES 109; cf. also 91.

15. See EINES 91–2.

16. Cf. SIE 13 n. 1: "The study of Indian inscriptions . . . is no longer popular among European scholars." But see also section 6.5.

17. EINES 92.

voluminous, and inherently difficult; it also requires a command of a range of languages, dialects, and script forms far greater than that needed for epigraphic studies in most other parts of the world. The inscriptions include materials in virtually all the major languages of the Indo-Aryan and Dravidian families and also involve several non-Indian languages of Southeast Asia and other regions. The variety of scripts is enormous, these being subject to the same pattern of extensive local and chronological variation as are Indian languages and dialects. Indian epigraphy is thus a subject of vast complexity which requires many years of study, but its inherent importance and the rewards to be gained from it more than justify the effort.

2

Writing and Scripts in India

2.1 General Introduction

The history of writing in India, insofar as it applies to the material treated in this book,[1] is essentially coextensive with the history of the Brāhmī script and its many derivatives, and of the Kharoṣṭhī script. While the latter, though important in its day, was a regional script which died out without any descendants, the former is the parent of one of the major script families of the world, comprising not only all of the indigenous scripts of South Asia (as opposed to those of Perso-Arabic or European origin) but also several other major scripts of central and especially Southeast Asia. While the processes of development of these scripts will not be presented in detail in this book (this being, as explained in the preface, primarily a work on epigraphy rather than paleography), the general outlines of these developments, particularly as they relate to epigraphy proper, are presented in the context of a general discussion of the history of epigraphic writing in India.

2.1.1 Writing in traditional India

On the whole, traditional (i.e., pre-Islamic) India was much less oriented toward the written word than many other ancient and traditional cultures such as those of classical China and Japan or of the Islamic world. From Vedic times on, and even to the present day in some cultural contexts, it is oral rather than written learning that has always been esteemed in India as true knowledge, an attitude reflected in such proverbs as *pustakasthā tu yā vidyā parahastagataṃ dhanam*, "Knowledge in a book [is like] money in someone else's hand."[2] There is a pervasive, if unspoken, attitude

1. As explained in the preface, the protohistoric Indus Valley writing itself will not be discussed here except insofar as it relates to the study of the writings of the historical period.

2. Quoted by Ojhā, BPLM 14 n. 6 (attributed to the *Cāṇakya-nīti*). The esteem accorded to the spoken as opposed to the written word should not, however, be overstated. In this connection, Kālidāsa's *Raghuvaṃśa* 3.28cd, *liper yathāvadgrahaṇena vāṅmayaṃ nadīmukheneva samudram āviśat*, "As one enters the ocean through the mouth of a river, so did [Raghu] enter into literature by learning to write correctly," has been cited (e.g., in PIP 4 and Falk, SAI 252 n. 2) as an indication of the respect accorded to the written word, at least in the classical (as opposed to the Vedic) tradition. This status is also reflected in the attribution of the invention of writing to Brahmā himself (see later discussion).

that the written word is essentially a reflection rather than a true manifestation of language, and this may explain the relative lack of attention to the aesthetic aspects of writing in traditional India (2.5.3), as well as the carelessness and imprecision which characterize many, though by no means all, of the written documents, both epigraphic and non-epigraphic, of ancient India (2.5.1).

This same orientation no doubt also explains the paucity of descriptions of writing as such in Sanskrit and related literatures. Discussions of the origin and history of writing, its varieties, styles and methods, and practical instruction therein are surprisingly rare in Indic texts, though we do find a few more or less incidental references in some relatively late texts to the invention of writing by the creator god Brahmā.[3] This tradition is also reflected iconographically, Brahmā and also his wife (or daughter) Sarasvatī, the goddess of learning, being regularly depicted in sculpture with a book in hand. But beyond legendary accounts such as these, the literature of the Brahmanical-Hindu tradition has, on the whole, little to say about writing as such; this, in striking contrast with its profound fascination with (spoken) language and grammar.

The picture is somewhat different in the heterodox traditions of Buddhism and Jainism, which (especially the former) exhibit a higher esteem for the written word.[4] Moreover, it is only in the texts of these traditions that we find lists of Indic scripts. Most important among these is the list in the tenth chapter (*Lipiśālāsaṃdarśana-parivarta*) of the *Lalitavistara*[5] of the sixty-four scripts (*lipi*), beginning with Brāhmī and Kharoṣṭī [*sic*], which the future Buddha knew as a child.[6] The historical value of

3. E.g., *nākariṣyad yadi sraṣṭā likhitaṃ cakṣur uttamam / tatreyam asya lokasya nābhaviṣyac chubhā gatiḥ*, "Had the Creator [Brahmā] not invented writing, the supreme eye, the course of this world would not have gone well" (Richard W. Lariviere, ed., *The Nāradasmṛti*, University of Pennsylvania Studies on South Asia, vol. 4 [Philadelphia: Department of South Asia Regional Studies, University of Pennsylvania, 1989], I.78); and a verse attributed in several sources (e.g., Mitramiśra's *Vyavahāraprakāśa*; see BIP 1 n. 3 and PIP 3 n. 2 for further references) to Bṛhaspati: *ṣāṇmāsike' pi samaye bhrāntiḥ saṃjāyate nṛṇām / dhātrākṣarāṇi sṛṣṭāni patrārūḍhāny ataḥ purā*, "Because men forget things within six months, of old the Creator invented letters [to be] set down on leaves."

4. It is thus not a coincidence that the art of calligraphy is more highly developed in Buddhist and Jaina manuscript traditions than in Brahmanical circles.

5. The *Mahāvastu* (I.135 in E. Senart's edition [Paris: L'Imprimerie Nationale, 1882]) also has a similar list of thirty-two scripts.

6. The list, according to the edition of S. Lefmann (Halle: Verlag der Buchhandlung des Waisenhauses, 1902), I.125–6 reads:

(1) Brāhmī (2) Kharoṣṭī (3) Puṣkarasārī (4) Aṅgalipi (5) Vaṅgalipi (6) Magadhalipi (7) Maṅgalyalipi (8) Aṅgulīyalipi (9) Sakārilipi (10) Brahmavalilipi (11) Pāruṣyalipi (12) Drāviḍalipi (13) Kirātalipi (14) Dākṣiṇyalipi (15) Ugralipi (16) Saṃkhyālipi (17) Anulomalipi (18) Avamūrdhalipi (19) Daradalipi (20) Khāṣyalipi (21) Cīnalipi (22) Lūnalipi (23) Hūnalipi (24) Madhyākṣaravistaralipi (25) Puṣpalipi (26) Devalipi (27) Nāgalipi (28) Yakṣalipi (29) Gandharvalipi (30) Kinnaralipi (31) Mahoragalipi (32) Asuralipi (33) Garuḍalipi (34) Mṛgacakralipi (35) Vāyasarutalipi (36) Bhaumadevalipi (37) Antarīkṣadevalipi (38) Uttarakurudvīpalipi (39) Aparagauḍānīlipi (40) Pūrvavidehalipi (41) Utkṣepalipi (42) Nikṣepalipi (43) Vikṣepalipi (44) Prakṣepalipi (45) Sāgaralipi (46) Vajralipi (47) Lekhapratilekhalipi (48) Anudrutalipi (49) Śāstrāvartā [*lipi] (50) Gaṇanāvartalipi (51) Utkṣepāvartalipi (52) Nikṣepāvartalipi (53) Pādalikhitalipi (54) Dviruttarapadasandhilipi (55) Yāvaddaśottarapadasandhilipi (56) Madhyāhāriṇīlipi (57) Sarvaruta-saṃgrahaṇīlipi (58) Vidyānulomāvimiśritalipi (59) Ṛṣitapastaptā rocamānā [*lipi] (60) Dharaṇīprekṣiṇīlipi (61) Gaganaprekṣiṇīlipi (62) Sarvauṣadhiniṣyandā [*lipi] (63) Sarvasārasaṃgrahaṇī [*lipi] (64) Sarvabhūtarutagrahaṇī [*lipi]. The names of the scripts vary considerably in different text editions; compare, e.g., the list as given in Rājendralāla Mitra's edition (Bibliotheca Indica no. 15 [Calcutta: The Asiatic Society, 1877], 143–4).

this list, however, is limited by several factors. Its date, first of all, is uncertain. While the *Lalitavistara* as such is known to be fairly old (a version of it had already been translated into Chinese in A.D. 308),[7] different versions of the text must have existed at various times, and certain indications in the extant script list (notably the inclusion of no. 23, Hūnalipi, "the script of the Huns") suggest a date for the list in its present form not earlier than the fourth century A.D. The several geographical names such as Aṅgalipi, Vaṅgalipi, and Pūrvavidehalipi (nos. 4, 5, 40) also suggest a relatively late period by which the Brāhmī script had become extensively differentiated into local varieties.

Second, the names of many of the scripts are difficult to evaluate. Only the first two, Brāhmī and Kharoṣṭī (i.e., Kharoṣṭhī; see 2.2.2 and 2.3.5), can be positively identified with known scripts. As for the rest, they consist mainly of geographical terms which can presumably be connected with the appropriate local derivatives of Brāhmī (though in view of the chronological questions they cannot be specifically identified),[8] and of terms which are apparently descriptive of graphic or calligraphic characteristics (e.g., no. 25 Puṣpalipi, "the flower script," no. 41 Utkṣepalipi, "the upward-flowing script," etc.). Some of the latter group might be identified with various calligraphic scripts preserved in inscriptions (see 2.5.3), but this is hardly more than a guess. Other names, such as nos. 26–8, Devalipi "script of the gods," Nāgalipi "script of the Nāgas," and Yakṣalipi "script of the Yakṣas," are presumably fanciful, and the total number of scripts (64) is a conventional one, which also must give rise to suspicions as to the historicity of the list as a whole.

Similar but much briefer lists of eighteen (again, a stereotypical number) scripts are also preserved in several Jaina canonical Prakrit texts. The oldest form of the list, which appears in the *Pannavaṇā-sutta* and the *Samavāyāṅga-sutta*, includes (like the Buddhist lists) Baṃbhī (= Brāhmī, no. 1) and Kharoṭṭhī (= Kharoṣṭhī, no. 4).[9] According to Bühler (OIBA 25–7), the Jaina list is probably independent from and "in all probability is considerably older than that of the Buddhists" (26). Particularly notable is the inclusion of the "Javaṇāliyā" (v. l. Javaṇāṇiyā) script (no. 2), presumably referring to the Greek alphabet (Sanskrit *yavanānī*). But otherwise, as in the Buddhist lists, most of the scripts mentioned cannot be clearly identified with forms of writing known from epigraphic remains. It is also interesting to note that the list

7. John Brough, BSOAS 40, 1977, 85.

8. The twelfth script, the Drāviḍalipi or "Dravidian" script, was identified by Bühler (BIP 2; OIBA 24) with the distinct southern variety of Brāhmī represented by the Bhaṭṭiprōḷu inscriptions (2.2.5.1), but in view of the probable late date of the list this specific identification is questionable (cf. the remarks in IC II.673).

9. The Jaina lists are cited and discussed by Albrecht Weber in *Indische Studien* 16, 1883, 280 and 399–401. The earliest version in *Pannavaṇā-sutta* as cited by Weber reads (with variant readings from the Jaina-Āgama-Series edition [no. 9, part 1; ed. Muni Puṇyavijaya, Dalsukh Mālvaṇiā, and Amritlāl Mohanlāl Bhojak (Bombay: Shri Mahāvīra Jaina Vidyālaya, 1969), 38, I.107]):

(1) Baṃbhī (= Brāhmī) (2) Javaṇāliyā ("Greek") (3) Dāsāpurīya [Dosāpuriyā] (4) Kharoṭṭhī (= Kharoṣṭhī) (5) Pukkharasāriyā (6) Bhogavaïyā (7) Pahārāiyāu [Paharāīyāo] (8) Aṃtarikariyā [Aṃtakkhariyā] (9) Akkharapuṭṭhiyā (10) Veṇaïyā (11) Niṇhaïyā (12) Aṃkalivī (13) Gaṇitalivī (14) Gaṃdhavvalivī (15) Āyāsalivī [Ayaṃsalivī] (16) Māhesarī (17) Dāmilī (18) Poliṃdā [Poliṃdī] (399). The list in *Samavāyāṅga-sutta* 18 is essentially similar but has several variants. Other, evidently later, Jaina script lists are cited by Weber, ibid., 400–1.

is presented with the introductory remark *bambhīe naṃ livīe aṭṭhārasaviha-likkhavihāṇe paṇṇatte*, "18 different forms of writing of the Brāhmī script are known." This evidently means that the term "Brāhmī" applies to writing as such (presumably referring to its legendary creation by Brahmā, as discussed earlier; cf. OIBA 25), as well as to a particular script, no. 1 in the list which follows, which may or may not actually refer to what modern scholars call "Brāhmī" script (2.2.2).

Other than these, very few references to script types and names have been located in Sanskrit and related literatures, so that the further study of the origin and development of the Indic scripts must be pursued from the evidence of the documents (almost exclusively epigraphic for the earlier phases) themselves.

2.1.2 *The antiquity of writing in India of the historical period*

O. von Hinüber, *Der Beginn der Schrift . . .* [BS]; H. Falk, *Schrift im alten Indien* [SAI].

After more than a century of study, the early history of writing in India remains problematic. It begins with the still undeciphered script found on the seals and other relics of the Indus Valley civilization, which flourished, according to recent estimates, around the second half of the third and first half of the second millennium B.C. But after the decline of the Indus Valley culture, the graphic record of India is virtually a total blank for well over a thousand years until the time of the Aśokan inscriptions, the earliest definitely datable written records of the historical period, around the middle of the third century B.C. From this time on, written records (epigraphic and, in later centuries, manuscript and other nonepigraphic sources) become increasingly common, so that the development of the Indian scripts and their many derivatives both in and outside of India can, for the most part, be traced in considerable detail from Aśoka's time to the present day.

But practically nothing is known of what might have happened in the long period between (very roughly) 1750 and 260 B.C. Certain bits of evidence have been proposed as missing links between the protohistoric and historical writings. For example, graffiti found on megalithic and chalcolithic pottery from southern and western India were discussed by B. B. Lal,[10] who noted (23–4) resemblances of some of the shapes found in these graffiti to both Indus Valley script characters and letters of the Brāhmī script. However, Lal concluded with the suitably cautious note that "to stress the point that the symbols do have a phonetic, syllabic or alphabetic value would indeed be presumptuous in the present state of our knowledge" (24). A few inscriptions, or pseudo-inscriptions, have been proposed as specimens of "prehistoric" writing or "missing links" between the Indus Valley script and Brāhmī, for instance, the Vikramkhol "inscription," but none of these examples of supposed prehistorical writing is convincing.[11] In short, the evidence currently available does not permit us to determine conclusively whether the art of writing simply died out in the second millennium B.C., to be replaced much later by unrelated systems, or whether (though this seems much less likely) some form of it, as yet undiscovered, somehow survived and reemerged in the form of the scripts of historical times.

10. "From the Megalithic to the Harappa: Tracing Back the Graffiti on the Pottery," *Ancient India* 16, 1960, 4–24.

11. Possible connections between the Indus Valley writing and Brāhmī are further discussed in section 2.2.3.1.

Because of the virtual absence of actual documentary evidence for writing in the blank period, many historians and epigraphists have addressed the question of the possibility of literacy in pre-Mauryan India through the examination of literary and other evidence. The literature on the subject is far too extensive to be presented in detail here. The discussions by Burnell (SIP 1–11), Bühler (OIBA 5–35 and BIP 3–6), Ojhā (BPLM 1–16), Pandey (PIP 1–22), and Sircar (IIEP 104–6) may be taken as more or less representative of earlier opinions, of which a complete survey and up-to-date analysis is provided in Falk's SAI. To begin with Vedic literature, certain authors (notably Ojhā in BPLM 9–13 and, mostly following him, Pandey and others) have claimed evidence for a literate culture in the later Vedic texts, and even in the *Ṛg Veda*, on the grounds of references therein to poetic meters, grammatical and phonetic terms, very large numbers, and relatively complex arithmetic calculations. But it is by no means certain that such cultural phenomena presuppose literacy, and it may be argued to the contrary that the absence of a single explicit and indisputable reference to writing anywhere in early Vedic literature suggests that the Vedic culture was a preliterate one.[12]

The testimony of Greek and Latin authors on writing in early India has been studied by many scholars[13] but remains somewhat inconclusive. For example, Nearchos, who visited northwestern India around 325 B.C., explicitly mentions that Indians wrote letters (ἐπιστολὰς) on cotton cloth. This observation is usually assumed to refer to the Kharoṣṭhī script, but it has recently been suggested[14] that Nearchos may actually have been referring to writing in Aramaic. Megasthenes, who lived in northeastern India some two decades after Nearchos, stated that the Indians "did not know written characters" (οὐδὲ γὰρ γράμματα εἰδέναι αὐτούς), but it is not entirely certain whether this is a blanket statement[15] or refers only to the immediate context of legal procedures in which the comment was made. The confusion on this issue among the classical historians seems to be reflected in Strabo's comment, with reference to Nearchos' report, that "others opine that they did not make use of written characters."

The Pāli Buddhist canon, especially the *Jātakas* and the *Vinaya-piṭaka*, contains numerous explicit references to writing and written documents, particularly to "private and official correspondence by means of letters" (OIBA 7). But it is uncertain whether any of these references can really be taken to represent the state of things in pre-Mauryan India, as Bühler and others have claimed, since all or most of them seem to belong to the later strata of the canon (BS 22–54; SAI 270–83). In Pāṇini's *Aṣṭādhyāyī* (3.2.21) we seem to have a clear reference to early writing in the term *lipi/libi* 'script'.[16] Pāṇini's date is a matter of complex controversy, but an authoritative recent opinion is that "the evidence available hardly allows one to date Pāṇini later than the early to mid fourth

12. See the classic presentation of this position in F. Max Müller's *History of Sanskrit Literature So Far as It Illustrates the Primitive Religion of the Brahmans* (London: Williams and Norgate, 1859), 455–80. See also BIP 5 and, more recently, BS 18 and SAI 240–56.

13. Most recently and authoritatively by von Hinüber (BS 19–21) and Falk (SAI 290–7).

14. By von Hinüber, BS 21; cf. SAI 290.

15. So von Hinüber, BS 20; cf. SAI 291–3.

16. Although even this has been questioned; see BS 57. The term *grantha* (*Aṣṭādhyāyī* 1.3.75, 4.3.87, 4.3.116), though normally rendered "book," need not necessarily refer to a written composition (SAI 261–2, 298–9).

century B.C.,"[17] which would seem to provide us a strong indication of writing before the Mauryan period. But here too (as in the case of Nearchos), it has recently been suggested[18] that the script known to Pāṇini might be Aramaic rather than any Indian script.

As to archaeological and epigraphic evidence for the antiquity of writing in the historical period, we have only a small handful of brief archaic inscriptions (see 4.3.1.2) which could conceivably be somewhat older than the Aśokan inscriptions. But the weight of scholarly opinion nowadays[19] is in favor of dating such early records as the Piprāwā, Sohgaurā, and Mahāsthān inscriptions as contemporary with or later than Aśoka.[20] Certain paleographic characteristics of the early inscriptions, such as the absence of distinction in some records (e.g., Mahāsthān) of vowel length—mostly for vowels other than *a* and *ā*—have sometimes been taken as an indication of their pre-Aśokan antiquity; yet the very same phenomena have been invoked by others in support of arguments for a recent origin and short period of development for the Brāhmī script. Equally inconclusive is the matter of alleged regional variations in early Brāhmī. Bühler (OIBA 40; cf. BIP 6–8) took this as evidence that "the letters of the [Aśokan] edicts had been used at least during four or five hundred years," but more recent studies by C. S. Upasak and A. H. Dani (see 2.2.4) have largely discredited the supposed regional variants of Aśokan Brāhmī, and some (e.g., S. R. Goyal in OBS 7–10) have taken the geographical unity of the Aśokan script as evidence that it must have been a recent invention or development.

However, a new body of material has recently come to light that seems to support the older theory that Brāhmī existed before Mauryan times, that is, in the fourth century B.C. or possibly even earlier. This is a small group of potsherds bearing short inscriptions, evidently proper names, which were found in the course of excavations at Anurādhapura, Sri Lanka in strata which are said to be securely assigned by radiocarbon dating to the pre-Mauryan period.[21] Various dates have been proposed for these graffiti, ranging from the sixth to the early fourth century B.C. The more recent publications on the subject have tended to favor the later date within this range, but in any case, these inscriptions still seem to show that Brāhmī did indeed predate the Mauryan period. Some doubts remain, however, as to the chronological significance of these inscriptions; it is possible, for example, that the inscribed potsherds were intrusive in the strata concerned, and actually date from a later period, although the excavators have argued against this scenario.

17. George Cardona, *Pāṇini: A Survey of Research* (Mouton: The Hague/Delhi: Motilal Banarsidass, 1976), 268.

18. BS 58; SAI 258.

19. Reviewed in SAI 177–88.

20. All attempts to attribute specific dates to certain of the early inscriptions have been decisively discredited. For example, Ojhā's (BPLM 2–3) dating of the Baṛlī inscription (SI 89–90) to the year 84 of a supposed Jaina era of 527 B.C., i.e., to 443 B.C., is out of the question; Sircar dates the inscription to the late second century B.C. on paleographic grounds. The alleged specimens of Kharoṣṭhī and Brāhmī letters on coins of the Achaemenian emperors of Iran are also doubtful (see 2.3.2 n. 132).

21. See S. U. Deraniyagala, *The Prehistory of Sri Lanka: An Ecological Perspective* (Archaeological Survey of Sri Lanka, 1992), 2.739–50; F. R. Allchin, *The Archaeology of Early Historic South Asia: The Emergence of Cities and States* (Cambridge: Cambridge University Press, 1995), 163–81 and 209–16; R. A. F. Coningham, F. R. Allchin, C. M. Batt, and D. Lucy, "Passage to India? Anuradhapura and the Early Use of the Brahmi Script," *Cambridge Archaeological Journal* 6, 1996, 73–97 (esp. 76–7); and further references provided in these sources.

In conclusion, both the literary and the epigraphic evidence for the antiquity of historical writing in India are disappointingly inconclusive, since virtually all of the testimony is in one way or another vague or ambiguous. Probably the most cogent single piece of literary evidence for writing before the Mauryan period is Pāṇini's reference to script (*lipi*), although the uncertainties as to his date partially vitiate the value of this testimony. Moreover, although it seems clear that this proves the existence of some form of writing in Pāṇini's home region of northwestern South Asia in or before the mid-fourth century B.C., there is no explicit indication as to what type of script[22] he is referring to. Although, as noted earlier, Falk and von Hinüber have recently suggested that may have been Aramaic, there is actually no cogent reason to rule out Kharoṣṭhī, which therefore may well date back to the mid-fourth century B.C. or quite possibly even earlier (see 2.3.2 and 2.3.6). But even if this is so, there is no direct evidence for the use of Brāhmī before the time of Aśoka. Thus, the trend of recent writings such as BS[23] and SAI has been to emphasize an empirical interpretation of the actual surviving data, which leads to the conclusion that at least Brāhmī, and probably Kharoṣṭhī as well, did not exist before the Mauryan period, and hence that (leaving aside the protohistoric Indus script) writing originated in India no earlier than the late fourth century B.C. However, the recent discovery, mentioned above, of apparently pre-Mauryan graffiti in Sri Lanka has cast some doubt upon this point of view.

Moreover, many other authorities have found it difficult to imagine that the evidently high level of political organization and cultural complexity that had been reached in the pre-Mauryan period could have existed without writing. Thus various estimates for a hypothetical prehistory of Indian writing have been proposed. Bühler's suggestion (OIBA 84; also BIP 16) of an early date of ca. 800 B.C., or possibly even earlier, for the "introduction of the prototypes of the Brāhma letters" into India is hardly plausible in light of modern knowledge, but more cautious estimates such as that of A. B. Keith that "the real development of writing belongs in all likelihood to the fifth century B.C." are not unreasonable.[24] This more traditional point of view has recently been maintained by, among others, K. R. Norman.[25] Like other proponents of pre-Mauryan writing, Norman (279) attributes the absence of any surviving written records before the time of Aśoka to the fact that early writing was primarily used for ephemeral documents. The practice of writing monumental inscriptions on stone was presumably an innovation of Aśoka himself, possibly under the inspiration of the Achaemenian empire of neighboring Iran. Before Aśoka, writing was probably

22. As has been noted in various sources, most recently SAI 259–61, the interpretation of Pāṇini's prescription (4.1.49) of the feminine adjective *yavanānī* as referring to *lipi*, i.e., the Greek script, is based on a *vārtikā* of Kātyāyana and hence does not prove anything about Pāṇini's own knowledge of Greek script.

23. E.g., BS 22: "Fremde Beobachtungen sprechen also in Übereinstimmung mit den Zeugnissen aus Epigraphik und Numismatik eindeutig dafür, daß es in Indien vor Aśoka keine Schrift gegeben hat, wenn man von den indischen Provinzen des Achämenidenreiches absieht." ("Thus, foreign observations clearly agree with the testimony of epigraphy and numismatics that there was no writing in India before Aśoka, with the exception of the Indian provinces of the Achaemenian empire.")

24. In E. J. Rapson, ed., *Cambridge History of India*. Vol. 1: *Ancient India* (Cambridge: Cambridge University Press, 1922), 126.

25. In his review of von Hinüber's BS in JRAS, ser. 3, vol. 3, 1993, 277–81. See also R. Salomon, "On the Origin of Early Indian Scripts" [review article on von Hinüber's BS, Falk's SAI, etc.], JAOS 115, 1995, 271–9, esp. 278–9.

used principally, if not exclusively, for economic and administrative, as opposed to literary and monumental, purposes; perishable materials such as palm leaves, tree bark, and (according to Nearchos) cloth, which have little chance of surviving the rigors of the Indian climate, were used. Thus, according to this view, we need not be surprised that no early specimens of Indian writing have survived, and their absence does not prove that they never existed.

Such hypothetical pre-Mauryan writing would presumably (though not necessarily; see Goyal, OBS 2, 30) have been some protoform of Brāhmī and/or Kharoṣṭhī script. The nondifferentiation of vowel length in Kharoṣṭhī generally, and also, as noted earlier, in some early specimens of Brāhmī, suggests that a pre-Aśokan Brāhmī would not yet have distinguished vowel quantity. Similarly, indications from the extant early specimens suggest that the notation of consonant groups would have been rudimentary or even totally absent in their presumptive prototypes. The protoscripts may also have had an incomplete array of phonemes vis-à-vis Sanskrit, since they were presumably developed for recording early MIA dialects rather than Sanskrit. The confusion between *s* and *ṣ* in some early Brāhmī inscriptions (see 2.2.4), for example, suggests that the earliest forms of the script did not have distinct characters for the three sibilants of Sanskrit. The script that we actually have in the Aśokan inscriptions thus could be a refined and standardized "national" script, developed under Aśoka for purposes of governing his vast pan-Indian empire, on the basis of an earlier form of Brāhmī or proto-Brāhmī script, of which the Anurādhapura graffiti may be a specimen.

In short, two schools of thought are dominant with regard to the problem of the antiquity of writing in historical India. One side sees no cogent archaeological or literary evidence for the existence of writing, and particularly of Brāhmī script, before the Mauryan period. The other camp finds this hard to accept on pragmatic grounds, and moreover now sees archaeological evidence of pre-Mauryan Brāhmī in the Anurādhapura graffiti, which are allegedly datable to the early fourth century B.C. at the latest. The issue remains unresolved, though it may be hoped that further discussions and examinations of the new evidence may ultimately lead to a consensus.

2.1.3 Characteristics of Indic writing

With only a few partial exceptions (see n. 37 and 2.2.5.1), all of the Indic scripts (that is, Brāhmī and its derivatives, and Kharoṣṭhī) follow the same basic principles of graphic representation. This system is, in historical terms, a modified consonant-syllabic script whose basic unit is the graphic syllable (which by definition ends with a vowel) typically consisting of a consonant with or without diacritic modification to indicate the following vowel, and/or other modifications such as nasalization indicated by the *anusvāra* sign. Various diacritic strokes are added to the top or bottom of the consonantal character to indicate the vowels *ā*, *i*, *ī*, *u*, *ū*, *ṛ*, and so on, but the vowel *a* is treated as inherent in the consonant. That is to say, an unmarked consonant is to be read with the vowel *a*; thus early Brāhmī 𑀓 = modern Devanāgarī क = *ka*; 𑀓𑀸 = का = *kā*; 𑀓𑀺 = कि = *ki*, and so on.

This system, and particularly the inherent vowel rule, leads to certain complications. First, to represent a syllable consisting of a vowel only, without a preceding consonant,[26] these scripts require a set of full vowel signs in addition to the more frequently used diacritic vowels; thus Brāhmī 𑀅 = Devanāgarī अ = *a*; 𑀆 = आ = *ā*, and so on. Second, the representation of consonants which are not immediately followed by vowels, that is, of consonant clusters and of word, line, or sentence final consonants, also requires special techniques. Consonant clusters are represented by various types of ligatures of the consonants concerned, joined together or abbreviated in such a way as to make it evident that the prior consonant(s) are to be pronounced together with the following one(s), without an intervening vowel. Thus in Brāhmī the syllable *tva* must be written as 𑀢𑁆𑀯 (= Devanāgarī त्व) in order to distinguish it from 𑀢𑀯 = *tava* (तव). Final consonants are indicated either by a reduced form of the normal consonant or by a special diacritic sign (called *virāma* or *halanta*) indicating cancellation of the inherent vowel (e.g., Devanāgarī क् = *k*, not *ka*).[27]

The Indic system of writing is difficult to classify in terms of the traditional typology of writing systems which recognizes three main script types, namely, logographic, syllabic, and alphabetic.[28] The Indian system is syllabic in the sense that its basic graphic unit is the syllable (*akṣara*), but it differs from a pure syllabary in that the individual phonetic components of the syllable are separately indicated within the syllabic unit. It thus resembles an alphabet insofar as the vowels have a separate and independent notation but cannot be called a true alphabet in that the vowels do not have a fully independent status equal to that of the consonants (this being the defining characteristic of an alphabet in the strict sense of the term). Although the Indic scripts do have alphabetic symbols for the vowels in the "full" or initial vowel characters, these were never extended beyond their restricted use for vowels not preceded by a consonant, and thus did not attain full alphabetic status.

Various terms have been suggested for this type of script, intermediate between syllabary and alphabet, such as "neosyllabary,"[29] "pseudoalphabet," or "alphabetic syllabary."[30] There is as yet no commonly accepted term in the relatively rudimentarily developed field of grammatology for scripts of this type. Thus, for the present it may be best to refer to it by general descriptive terms such as semisyllabary or semialphabet (since it partakes of significant features of both systems), or, more pre-

26. Such occurrences are relatively rare in Sanskrit, which in general disallows vowel hiatus within and between words, so that in Sanskrit texts the full or initial vowels mostly occur at the beginning of a sentence or line of verse. They are commoner in Prakrit and other languages which do permit vowel hiatus, but even here they are often avoided by writing a consonant such as *y* or *v* to represent an intervocalic glide.

27. The notation of final consonants is a relatively late development, first appearing in the earlier centuries of the Christian era (2.2.5.2). This is due to the fact that Prakrit, in which all of the early inscriptions are written, does not permit word final consonants, so that their notation only became necessary later when inscriptions began to be written in Sanskrit.

28. Ignatz Gelb (*A Study of Writing* [Chicago: University of Chicago Press, 1953], 188) admits to "disturbing problems" in connection with the typological classification of the Indic and similar script types, and does not reach a definite conclusion on the point.

29. James G. Février, *Histoire de l'écriture* (Paris: Payot, 1959), 333.

30. Fred W. Householder Jr., *Classical Journal* 54, 1958–59, 382. Recently Peter T. Daniels (JAOS 110, 1990, 730) has suggested the name "abugida," "from the Ethiopian word for the auxiliary order of consonants in the signary." This term, however, is more likely to appeal to Semitists than to Indologists, who might prefer a name like "*akṣara* script," this being the Indic term which would come closest to a designation of this type of writing.

cisely, as "diacritically (or alphabetically) modified consonant syllabary." Whichever terminology one might prefer to adopt, the Indic script family, comprising all of the derivatives and modifications of Brāhmī script in India and many other parts of Asia, is the principal representative of its type among the scripts of the world. The only other major example of this type is the Ethiopian script, which employs a similar system of vowel notation by diacritic signs attached to the preceding consonant, and which has, like the Indic scripts, an inherent or neutral vowel *a* but does not regularly form consonantal conjuncts.[31]

The process of development of the Indic system is for the most part not directly traceable in the extant materials, wherein the system appears almost fully developed[32] from the beginning. But parallels from the history of script developments elsewhere in the world make it a priori likely that such a modified consonantal syllabary developed from a pure consonantal syllabary, whose prototype presumably (and in the case of Kharoṣṭhī virtually certainly) would be a Semitic script of this type.[33] If this assumption is correct, the addition of diacritic vowel markers to the basic consonants would be a natural way to adapt the Semitic system to Indic languages, which, unlike Semitic languages, could not be conveniently and economically represented without vowels.[34]

The development of the inherent *a* and of consonantal conjuncts can be readily explained by reference to the phonetic characteristics of Sanskrit and related Indic languages. The vowel *a* is statistically strongly predominant in these languages, so that it is both natural and economical to assign it as inherent in all consonants.[35] Since the early Indic scripts seem to have been originally used exclusively or principally for MIA languages, which unlike Sanskrit have few clusters of nonhomorganic consonants, the inherent vowel system did not at first cause any significant complications. For such consonantal groups as do occur in MIA consist mainly of nasal plus homorganic stop, easily represented by the *anusvāra*, and geminates, which were simply represented by the single consonant. It was presumably only later, when these scripts began to be applied to formal literary uses and to the Sanskrit language, that the complications necessitated by the inherent vowel—mainly the frequently cumbersome consonantal conjuncts—arose. From a practical point of view, one could easily imagine a system wherein a simple vowel cancellation marker would be put to use to eliminate the need for all conjuncts. But, in fact, this was not done, whether because the conventions of the system had become so

31. These striking similarities have led some scholars to posit a historical connection between the two script groups, suggesting that the Ethiopic may have developed under the influence of an Indic model (e.g., Suniti Kumar Chatterji, *India and Ethiopia from the Seventh Century B.C.*, The Asiatic Society Monograph Series, vol. 15 [Calcutta: Asiatic Society, 1968], 49–56; see also Gelb, op. cit., 188). This is plausible on historical grounds, in view of well-attested trade contacts between India and East Africa in ancient times. Nevertheless, other authorities are inclined to attribute the similarity to parallel but separate developments, or to Greek influence on the Ethiopic script; see, e.g., David Diringer, *The Alphabet*, 231–2.

32. However, see section 2.2.4 for some important exceptions.

33. See further discussions in sections 2.2.3 and 2.3.6.

34. This process is in principle not different from various other secondary devices developed to indicate vowels in other Semitic and Semitic-derived scripts, such as the pointing systems used in Hebrew and Arabic, or even the fully alphabetized vowels of Greek. It is not possible to say for certain why this particular type of modification arose in India, but it may be that an already established linguistic concept of the *akṣara* or syllable as the essential unit of language favored a system which preserved the syllabic unit over other theoretically possible developments, such as full alphabetization.

35. O. von Hinüber, BS 16; but see also n. 170 for a different interpretation.

firmly entrenched that they were not subject to fundamental reform, or through the influence of the previously mentioned linguistic principle of the *akṣara*, or for other reasons; the vowel-cancelling marker alluded to earlier is, in general, used only when there is no other way to represent a vowelless consonant, such as at the end of a word, sentence, or line.[36] In any case, the result was that the Indic system, remarkable for precision if not for simplicity, has been preserved virtually unchanged in nearly all of the many scripts used for Sanskrit and other Indo-Aryan languages.[37]

2.2 The Brāhmī Script and Its Derivatives

2.2.1 Geographical and chronological range

Unlike Kharoṣṭhī, which was always geographically limited and died out at a relatively early period (see 2.3.1 and 2.3.2), the Brāhmī script (see table 2.1) appeared in the third century B.C. as a fully developed pan-Indian national script (sometimes used as a second script even within the proper territory of Kharoṣṭhī in the northwest) and continued to play this role throughout history, becoming the parent of all of the modern Indic scripts both within India and beyond. Thus, with the exceptions of the Indus script in the protohistoric period, of Kharoṣṭhī in the northwest in the ancient period, and of the Perso-Arabic and European scripts in the medieval and modern periods, respectively, the history of writing in India is virtually synonymous with the history of the Brāhmī script and its derivatives.

2.2.2 The name of the script

Until the late nineteenth century, the script of the Aśokan (non-Kharoṣṭhī) inscriptions and its immediate derivatives was referred to by various names such as "lath" or "Lāṭ,"[38] "Southern Aśokan," "Indian Pali," "Mauryan," and so on. The application to it of the name Brāhmī [sc. *lipi*], which stands at the head of the Buddhist and Jaina script lists (see 2.1.1), was first suggested by T[errien] de Lacouperie,[39] who noted that in the Chinese Buddhist encyclopedia *Fa yüan chu lin* the scripts whose names corresponded to the Brāhmī and Kharoṣṭhī of the *Lalitavistara* are described as written from left to right and from right to left, respectively. He therefore suggested that the name Brāhmī should refer to the left-to-right "Indo-Pali" script of the Aśokan pillar inscriptions, and Kharoṣṭhī to the right-to-left "Bactro-Pali" script of

36. This restriction has, however, been somewhat relaxed in modern usage due to the exigencies of printing, in which some consonantal ligatures are impractically cumbersome and are therefore sometimes split up by use of the *halanta* sign.

37. Note that some Indic scripts which have been adapted for non-Indo-Aryan languages have introduced simplifications that eliminate the need for consonantal conjuncts. Such is the case, e.g., in Tamil (see also 2.2.5.1), which regularly writes vowelless consonants in their full syllabic form and marks them with a dot (*puḷḷi*) to indicate that no vowel follows (e.g., கண்டம் *kaṇṭam*, 'piece').

38. This name arose from the occurrence of Aśokan inscriptions on pillars known colloquially in northern India as *lāṭh* (< Skt. *yaṣṭi*).

39. "Did Cyrus Introduce Writing into India?" *Babylonian and Oriental Record* 1, 1886–87, 58–64 (esp. 59–60). As noted by Falk (SAI 84, 106), Terrien de Lacouperie evidently got the references in question from the note of T. Choutzé (pseudonym of Gabriel Devéria) in the *Revue de l'Extrême-Orient* 1, 1882, 158–9, though he does not mention him.

TABLE 2.1. Early Brāhmī Script

VOWELS

Full or initial forms

a 𑀅	i 𑀇	u 𑀉	e 𑀏	o 𑀑	aṃ 𑀅𑀁
ā 𑀆	ī 𑀈	ū 𑀊	ai 𑀐		

Medial (postconsonantal) forms

ka 𑀓	ki 𑀓𑀺	ku 𑀓𑀼	ke 𑀓𑁂	ko 𑀓𑁄	kaṃ 𑀓𑀁
kā 𑀓𑀸	kī 𑀓𑀻	kū 𑀓𑀽	kai 𑀓𑁃	kau 𑀓𑁅	

CONSONANTS

	Unvoiced unaspi-rated	Voiced aspirated	Voiced unaspi-rated	Voiced aspirated	Nasal	Semi-vowel	Sibilant
Guttural	ka 𑀓	kha 𑀔	ga 𑀕	gha 𑀖	ṅa 𑀗		ha 𑀳
Palatal	ca 𑀘	cha 𑀙	ja 𑀚	jha 𑀛	ña 𑀜	ya 𑀬	śa 𑀰
Retroflex	ṭa 𑀝	ṭha 𑀞	ḍa 𑀟	ḍha 𑀠	ṇa 𑀡	ra 𑀭	ṣa 𑀱
Dental	ta 𑀢	tha 𑀣	da 𑀤	dha 𑀥	na 𑀦	la 𑀮	sa 𑀲
Labial	pa 𑀧	pha 𑀨	ba 𑀩	bha 𑀪	ma 𑀫	va 𑀯	

Conjunct consonants (representative examples)

khya 𑀔𑁆𑀬	tva 𑀢𑁆𑀯	pta 𑀧𑁆𑀢	pra 𑀧𑁆𑀭
mha 𑀫𑁆𑀳	rva 𑀭𑁆𑀯	sta 𑀲𑁆𑀢	sya 𑀲𑁆𑀬

Note: These are normalized forms, based on letters found in Aśokan inscriptions, where available; otherwise from other earliest citations elsewhere.

the rock inscriptions from the northwest. Lacouperie's suggestion was adopted by his contemporaries, most significantly by Bühler[40] in his influential works, and thereby became the accepted term.

While the name Brāhmī for the ancient Indian national script is no doubt in a general sense correct, it should be kept in mind that we do not really know precisely what form or derivative of the script the authors of the early script lists were referring to as

40. The expression "Brāhma alphabet" used by Bühler in OIBA has, however, been supplanted in modern usage by "Brāhmī" [*lipi*].

"Brāhmī," nor whether this term was actually applied to the script used in the time of Aśoka.[41] The name Brāhmī is thus used loosely, as a matter of convenience, by modern scholars to refer to the Aśokan script and to its varieties and earlier derivatives (distinguished by regional or dynastic terms such as "early southern Brāhmī" or "eastern Gupta Brāhmī") until about the end of the Gupta period in the sixth century A.D. After this time, the scripts have for the most part differentiated into distinct regional and local varieties, and are conceived as separate scripts denoted by descriptive or, more commonly, geographical terms (e.g., Siddhamātṛkā [post-Gupta northern script] or proto-Kannada). The terminology for the various premodern Brāhmī-derived scripts is, however, largely unstandardized and typically made up ad hoc, due mainly to the lack of attested indigenous terms for many of them (2.1.1). D. C. Sircar broadly categorizes the stages of development into "Early," "Middle," and "Late Brāhmī" periods, corresponding (in northern India) to the third through first centuries B.C., the first century B.C. through third century A.D., and the fourth through sixth centuries A.D., respectively (IIEP 113), though others refer to his "Late Brāhmī" as "Gupta script" (cf. Gai, IIE, 34). A. H. Dani, however (in DIP), considers such dynastic terminology misleading and prefers to use only regional and geographical categories (see 2.2.5.2).

2.2.3 The origin of Brāhmī

Bühler, OIBA; S. P. Gupta and K. S. Ramachandran, eds., OBS; Falk, SAI 109–67.

The origin of the Brāhmī script is one of the most problematic and controversial problems in Indian epigraphy. Most opinions on the question fall into one of two camps: the proponents of an indigenous Indian origin for Brāhmī, and those who see it as a borrowing or adaptation from some non-Indian (usually Semitic) prototype.[42] Within each camp there are also several versions of the two principal theories; in the following two subsections the major representatives of each theory will be briefly summarized.[43]

2.2.3.1 Theories of indigenous Indian origin

Some early scholars, most prominent among them Alexander Cunningham,[44] proposed theories of the origin of Brāhmī from a pictographic-acrophonic system based on the model of Egyptian hieroglyphic writing, wherein, for example, the Brāhmī letter *kha* would be derived from a pictorial representation of a hoe or mattock by association with the root *khan* 'to dig'. Such theories are purely speculative and imaginative, and do not merit further consideration; in the words of Isaac Taylor, "Such an elastic

41. On this point, see the warnings in IC II.667 and OBS 99.

42. It has been noted (e.g., S. R. Goyal in OBS 6–7) that nowadays most of the proponents of the theory of indigenous origin are Indians, while nearly all Western scholars subscribe to the theory of Semitic borrowing; and there is no doubt some truth in Goyal's comment that some of their views have been affected by "nationalist bias" and "imperialist bias," respectively.

43. The literature on the origin of Brāhmī is too vast to be presented in full detail here. Moreover, a great deal of what has been written on the subject is trivial, presenting no real new material or insights. An extensive though not complete bibliography of the subject is given in N. P. Rastogi's *Origin of Brāhmī Script*, 141–61. Almost all of the relevant materials are included in the more general bibliography in SAI (15–66).

44. *Inscriptions of Asoka* (CII 1), 49–63.

method [as Cunningham's] may establish anything, or—nothing."[45] Other early speculative theories attributed the origin of Brāhmī in the protohistoric period to various "races," such as the Dravidians[46] or the "enlightened Aryans."[47]

Somewhat more sophisticated than these superficial theories are the arguments of G. H. Ojhā in BPLM, who was highly critical of Bühler's Semitic derivation (see 2.2.3.2.4) and was inclined to doubt any foreign derivation, though he avoided denying the possibility altogether. Ojhā concluded (30) that an indigenous origin is most likely, although the precise source and development cannot be specified. R. B. Pandey (PIP 35–51) argued more categorically in favor of an indigenous origin, concluding that "the *Brāhmī* characters were invented by the genius of the Indian people who were far ahead of other peoples of ancient times in linguistics and who evolved vast Vedic literature involving a definite knowledge of alphabet" (51).

Since the discovery in the 1920s and subsequent decades of extensive written artifacts of the Indus Valley civilization dating back to the third and second millennia B.C., several scholars have proposed that the presumptive indigenous prototype of the Brāhmī script must have been the Indus Valley script or some unknown derivative thereof. This possibility was first proposed[48] by S. Langdon in 1931,[49] supported by G. R. Hunter,[50] and endorsed by several later authorities,[51] most significantly by D. C. Sircar.[52]

It has already been mentioned (2.1.2) that such a connection between the protohistoric Indus writing and the later Brāhmī script should not be taken for granted, that is, it should not be assumed a priori that two scripts of the same cultural area but different periods must be historically or genetically connected. It is all too easy, given the large number of characters in the Indus script (over four hundred), to find superficial connections between similar shapes of some characters in the two scripts, but these are of little value unless and until the Indus script itself is convincingly deciphered and the alleged graphic similarities can be correlated to phonetic values. Various claims to decipherment of the Indus script based on such superficial comparisons with Brāhmī, such as that of Langdon and many since him, are not at all convincing and have little if any scholarly value. Equally unconvincing are the various claims put forward for the Vikramkhol and other pseudoinscriptions (see 2.1.2) as constituting a link between the Indus Valley and Brāhmī scripts.[53]

45. *The Alphabet*, I.307 n. 1.

46. Edward Thomas, JRAS, n.s. 5, 1871, 421–2 n. 2. See also, more recently, T. N. Subramanian in SITI III.2, 1587–1608.

47. John Dowson, "The Invention of the Indian Alphabet," JRAS, n.s. 13, 1881, 102–20 (quoted 118).

48. It is, however, interesting to note that as early as 1877 Cunningham (*Inscriptions of Asoka*, 61) proposed as a possible ancestor of Aśokan Brāhmī a single inscribed seal from Harappa, which was then an isolated find whose significance had not yet become clear; Cunningham estimated its date as not later than 500 or 400 B.C.

49. "The Indus Script," ch. 23 of John Marshall, *Mohenjo-daro and the Indus Valley Civilization* (London: Arthur Probsthain, 1931), II.423–55.

50. *The Script of Harappa and Mohenjodaro and Its Connection with Other Scripts*, Studies in the History of Culture, no. 1 (London: Kegan Paul, Trench, Trubner & Co., 1934).

51. E.g., Pandey (PIP 51), who suggests a connection with the Indus Valley script ("The *Brāhmī* was derived from pictographs, ideographs and phonetic signs, the earliest specimens of which are to be found in the Indus Valley inscriptions"), but does not elaborate any further.

52. SI I.242 n. 1; IIEP 107–8, 111; EINES 85. See also OBS 70–1 and 84–5.

53. E.g., K. P. Jayaswal, "The Vikramkhol Inscriptions," IA 62, 1933, 58–60.

There is, however, at least one feature of the Indus script which could in fact indicate a systemic connection with the historical scripts of India. The former script has a large number of what appear to be compounded and/or diacritically modified forms of the basic characters, which are reminiscent of the characteristic patterns of the Indic scripts of the historical period (2.1.3). Hunter[54] hypothesized that this system functioned to indicate, among other things, vowel variations, exactly as in Brāhmī, and ventured (92–3, 102–3) to directly derive some of the Brāhmī vowel diacritics from Indus Valley signs. He also pointed out (54) a possible relationship with the Brāhmī system of conjunct consonant formation. These parallels, noted by Hunter and others since him (e.g., Dani, DIP 16–7), are certainly intriguing, and could actually reflect some historical connection, direct or indirect, between the scripts. Nevertheless, in view of the still undeciphered status of the Indus script and the huge chronological gap between it and the earliest attested scripts of the historical period, it would be premature to try to explain and evaluate the significance of the apparent typological similarities.

Recently several writers have put forth theories to the effect that Brāhmī was purposefully invented ex nihilo in or around the time of Aśoka. S. R. Goyal, for example,[55] argued that the phonetically logical structure, primary geometric forms, and geographical uniformity of early Brāhmī show that it was "an invention of the grammarians" (10) of the time of Aśoka. Similar arguments were presented by T. P. Verma, who proposed an origin in Buddhist circles.[56] N. P. Rastogi, in *Origin of Brāhmī Script*, offered a purely formal presentation of "the origin of the Brāhmī script from the geometric signs in the Vedic period" (139).

The strongest point in favor of the invention theory is the stiffly symmetrical, geometric appearance of Aśokan Brāhmī, which does indeed give the impression of an arbitrarily created script. But this superficial feature does not necessarily prove anything about the history of the script; Aśokan Brāhmī as we have it could be a formalized monumental version of a preexisting script of more cursive aspect. Moreover, despite its superficially regular and standardized appearance, closer analysis reveals variations in individual letter forms and systemic features (see 2.2.4) which are suggestive of a reformed version of a preexisting script. For other reasons as well, the invention theories are not persuasive.[57] The comparative study of the history of the evolution of writing systems worldwide shows that the invention ex nihilo of a highly sophisticated script would be unusual, if not completely unique. Arbitrarily created scripts are generally based, to a greater or lesser degree, on preexisting scripts which the creators of the new script know or at least have seen. Moreover, as will be seen later (2.2.3.2.4 and 2.2.3.2.5), there are clear indications that a Semitic script, presumably Aramaic, served, in part at least, as a model for Brāhmī. In any case, all of the invention theories are purely speculative, lacking any hard historical or documentary support.

54. Op. cit. (n. 50), 1 and 51–8.

55. "Brāhmī—An Invention of the Early Mauryan Period," in OBS 1–53.

56. *The Palaeography of Brāhmī Script in North India*, 8, and "Fresh Light on the Origin of Brāhmī Alphabet," JOI 13, 1964, 360–71 (esp. 367).

57. See also the generally critical discussions of Goyal's invention theory in OBS 67–125.

2.2.3.2 Theories of non-Indian (Semitic) origin

2.2.3.2.1 Greek. James Prinsep, the decipherer of Brāhmī (see 6.2.1), was the first to suggest a possible connection between Greek and the ancient Indian scripts, namely, that "the oldest Greek . . . was nothing more than Sanskrit [*sic*] turned topsy turvy!"[58] This relationship was reversed by K. Ottfried Müller,[59] who proposed that Brāhmī was derived from Greek after the invasion of Alexander the Great. A modified version of the Greek theory was proposed by J. Halévy,[60] who derived six of the Brāhmī characters (*a*, *ba*, *ga*, *dha*, *tha*, and *na*) from the corresponding Greek letters, and the rest of the characters from Kharoṣṭhī (see 2.3.7) and Aramaic. While composite alphabets are not in principle impossible, as in the example of the Coptic script which supplements the Greek alphabet with six characters from demotic Egyptian, Halévy's derivation from three separate prototypes is obviously forced.

Although the theory of Greek origin won some early followers,[61] it had fallen out of favor until recently, when it was revived by Falk in SAI (109–12 and 338–9). Falk, influenced by the arguments of Halévy, sees Brāhmī as an intentional creation of the time of Aśoka, created on the model of Kharoṣṭhī and Greek. According to him, the formation of Brāhmī was influenced by Greek, particularly in respect to its direction of writing (cf. 2.2.3.2.4), its monumental ductus, the differentiation (in contrast to Kharoṣṭhī) of short and long vowels, and the specific formation of some characters, especially ʘ *tha*, which he connects with Greek θ *theta* (SAI 111). Although the arguments for a Greek influence on the general ductus of Brāhmī (cf. n. 61) are plausible, it would seem that Greek had little influence on the specific formation of the Brāhmī characters. The example of *tha* and *theta*, stressed by Falk, is an isolated and exceptional case for which other possible explanations are available (see 2.2.3.3). The development in Brāhmī of a system for the differentiation of vowel quantity can more easily be seen as indigenous, in light of the long-standing Indian tradition of sophisticated phonetic analysis, than as an influence from Greek. Whereas the short/long vowel pairs in Brāhmī are indicated by a complete and regular system of variations of a basic form or diacritic for each vowel, in Greek script they were represented by an entirely different (and defective) system involving distinct and unrelated alphabetic signs (e.g., ε *epsilon*/ η *ēta*). In light of these very different approaches to the notation of vowel quantity, it is doubtful whether Brāhmī derived even the basic concept from a Greek prototype. Thus although it is possible that Brāhmī was influenced by Greek in the formation or development of its superficial aspect, the evidence for an underlying role in the formation of the script itself is not strong.

58. JASB 6, 1837, 390.

59. *Göttingische Gelehrte Anzeigen* 1838, 252.

60. JA, ser. 8, vol. 6, 1885, 290ff.; see also *Revue Sémitique* 3, 1895, 256ff. For full references, see n. 77 and section 2.3.6.

61. See, for example, SAI 109–11. Diringer's account in *The Alphabet,* 335, of the adherents of the derivation of Brāhmī from Greek is inaccurate and misconstrues the views of some of the persons cited, notably of Émile Senart, who really suggested (in his review of Cunningham's *Inscriptions of Asoka,* JA, ser. 7, vol. 13, 1879, 535) nothing more than an "influence grecque . . . extérieure et secondaire" on the monumental character of the script.

2.2.3.2.2 Kharoṣṭhī. As noted earlier, Falk (SAI 338–9), influenced by Halévy (see also 2.3.8), saw Brāhmī as essentially based on Kharoṣṭhī with a strong secondary influence from Greek; according to him, "haben wir es bei der Brāhmī mit einer Neuentwicklung auf der Basis zweier Schriften zu tun"[62] (338). If it is true, as now seems nearly certain (see 2.1.2), that Kharoṣṭhī was older than Brāhmī, it can certainly be accepted that the overall graphic system which characterizes both (2.1.3) was adapted from the former to the latter, and in this limited sense Brāhmī can be said to be "derived" from Kharoṣṭhī. But in terms of the actual forms of the characters, the differences between the two Indian scripts are much greater than the similarities (see 2.3.7), and many more of the forms of the Brāhmī characters can be explained by reference to Aramaic and/or other Semitic scripts (2.2.3.2.3–2.2.3.2.5) than to Kharoṣṭhī. Although some of the Brāhmī forms, such as 𑀕 *ga* and 𑀣 *tha*, are explained by Falk (SAI 111) by reference to the corresponding Greek letters (γ *gamma* and θ *theta*; see earlier), the great majority of them can be accounted for by neither Greek nor Kharoṣṭhī.

2.2.3.2.3 South Semitic. An apparent relationship between Brāhmī and the ancient South Semitic scripts was noted by several early scholars[63] who noted similarities between certain Brāhmī letters and the corresponding characters of the Himyaritic inscriptions of South Arabia. A South Semitic prototype for Brāhmī was first proposed by François Lenormant in 1875,[64] and at greater length by W. Deecke in 1877.[65] A more plausible argument for a South Semitic (Sabaean) derivation was presented by Isaac Taylor[66] with a comparative chart (320) of the alphabets concerned.

Among the points argued in favor of the South Semitic hypothesis is, first of all, the direction of writing. South Semitic inscriptions were written from right to left, like other Semitic scripts, but also sometimes in boustrophedon, or, like Brāhmī, from left to right. Second, and more important, a South Semitic prototype for Brāhmī, or a hypothetical common ancestor, would provide plausible prototypes for several of the Brāhmī letters which are most problematic in the North Semitic derivation (2.2.3.2.4). Thus Brāhmī 𑀩 *ba*, for which a North Semitic prototype is problematic, is very much like some Sabaean forms of *bet* such as □ , as given by Taylor in his comparative chart. Likewise Brāhmī 𑀤 *da*, which also presents serious problems in the North Semitic derivation, has a much closer resemblance to such Sabaean forms of *dalet* as 𐩵 ; Brāhmī 𑀫 *ma* looks like Sabaean 𐩣 *mem*; and so on. According to Tay-

62. "In Brāhmī we are dealing with a new development on the basis of two scripts."

63. References given by Albrecht Weber, "Ueber den semitischen Ursprung des indischen Alphabets," ZDMG 10, 1856, 389–406 (esp. 402–5) = *Indische Skizzen* (Berlin: F. Dümmler, 1857), 127–50 (esp. 145–8).

64. *Essai sur la propagation de l'alphabet phénicien dans l'ancien monde* (Paris: Maisonneuve, 1875), I.152.

65. "Ueber das indische Alphabet in seinem Zusammenhange mit den übrigen südsemitischen Alphabeten," ZDMG 31, 1877, 598–612. Deecke proposed to derive both Brāhmī ("Indisch") and Himyaritic from a hypothetical Ur-South Semitic script, which, in turn, was derived from Assyrian cuneiform. A similar idea was espoused by T. W. Rhys Davids in *Buddhist India* (London: T. Fisher Unwin, 1903), 114.

66. *The Alphabet*, II.314–23.

lor, the South Semitic derivation can also be justified on historical and geographical grounds: "[F]rom the 10th to the 3rd century B.C. Yemen was the great central mart in which Indian products were exchanged for the merchandize of the West" (314), so that "there was . . . ample opportunity for the transmission to India of the Sabean alphabet" (315).

Despite these advantages, the South Semitic hypothesis also has several important weaknesses. First, the argument based on the common direction of writing in Brāhmī and some South Semitic inscriptions does not carry great weight; for, as will be discussed shortly (2.2.3.2.4), the overall importance of the factor of direction of writing has been exaggerated in much of the discussion of this subject. Second, as for the derivation of individual characters, for every case in which South Semitic offers a better prototype, there is at least one other where a North Semitic model is preferable. Brāhmī 𑀧 *pa*, for instance, is certainly more readily derivable from North Semitic 𐤐 *pe* than from the South Semitic forms of the letter. Finally, the historical arguments are similarly inconclusive, in view of the lingering uncertainty as to the antiquity both of the South Semitic inscriptions[67] and of Brāhmī itself.

For these reasons, the South Semitic hypothesis, though not completely without merit, no longer enjoys much support,[68] and Bühler's criticisms (OIBA 53–5) of Taylor's South Semitic models and arguments in favor of North Semitic prototypes for the Brāhmī letters have been generally accepted. The undeniable similarities between some South Semitic letters and their Brāhmī correspondents are nowadays usually considered by the proponents of a Semitic origin to be due to parallel but independent developments from an ultimate common prototype, conditioned, in part at least, by their common monumental form which was conducive to the development of plain geometric forms such as the square *bet*/*ba*.[69]

2.2.3.2.4 Phoenician. The possibility of a connection of the Indic scripts with North Semitic writing (see table 2.2) was noted as early as 1821 by Ulrich Friedrich Kopp.[70] But Kopp's comparisons (which, to his credit, were presented with the greatest hesitancy and restraint) were based on modern forms of the Indic scripts and hence did not permit of anything like reliable conclusions. The first comprehensive and authoritative treatment of the Semitic hypothesis was Albrecht Weber's influential "Ueber den semitischen Ursprung des indischen Alphabets" (see n. 63), in which he presented the first detailed comparison of the Phoenician script with early Brāhmī. Although the results were inevitably imperfect,[71] on the whole the argument is reasonably

67. See, e.g., J. Naveh, *Early History of the Alphabet*, 2d ed. (Jerusalem: Hebrew University, 1987), 43–4.

68. R. N. Cust, e.g., at first favored this theory but later retracted his support for it ("On the Origin of the Indian Alphabet," JRAS, n.s. 16, 1884, 325–59; see especially 351–4 and 359). Although Cust's article does not contribute much in the way of original ideas on this subject, it does provide useful summaries and evaluations of previous discussions, as well as bibliographic information. (See also Cust's article "The Origin of the Phenician and Indian Alphabets," JRAS 1897, 49–80.)

69. Cf. 2.2.3.2.1, n. 61. According to Senart, cited there, the common factor would be the secondary influence of Greek on the outward monumental form of both Brāhmī and South Semitic.

70. *Bilder und Schriften der Vorzeit* (Mannheim: privately printed, 1819–21), II.367–75.

71. Some of the identifications, such as that of Phoenician *ṣade* with Brāhmī *jha*, were obviously wrong.

TABLE 2.2. Comparison of the North Semitic and Early Indian Scripts

Semitic			Indic		
Value	Phoenician	Aramaic	Value	Kharoṣṭhī	Brāhmī
ʾ	𐤀	𐡀	a	𐨀	𑀅
b	𐤁	𐡁	ba	𐨦	𑀩
g	𐤂	𐡂	ga	𐨒	𑀕
d	𐤃	𐡃	da	𐨡	𑀤
h	𐤄	𐡄	ha	𐨱	𑀳
w	𐤅	𐡅	va	𐨬	𑀯
z	𐤆	𐡆	ja	𐨗	𑀚
ḥ	𐤇	𐡇	gha		𑀖
ṭ	𐤈	𐡈	tha	𐨠	𑀣
y	𐤉	𐡉	ya	𐨩	𑀬
k	𐤊	𐡊	ka	𐨐	𑀓
l	𐤋	𐡋	la	𐨫	𑀮
m	𐤌	𐡌	ma	𐨨	𑀫
n	𐤍	𐡍	na	𐨣	𑀦
s	𐤎	𐡎	sa	𐨯	𑀲
ʿ	𐤏	𐡏	e		𑀏
p	𐤐	𐡐	pa	𐨤	𑀧
ṣ	𐤑	𐡑	ca	𐨕	𑀘
q	𐤒	𐡒	kha	𐨑	𑀔
r	𐤓	𐡓	ra	𐨪	𑀭
š	𐤔	𐡔	śa	𐨭	𑀰
t	𐤕	𐡕	ta	𐨟	𑀢

convincing, and Weber's conclusion is not unjustified: "Sollte im Einzelnen die paläographische Identification Widerspruch und Berichtigung erfahren, so wünsche ich dergl. selbst auf das dringendste herbei, das allgemeine Resultat aber wird schwerlich angefochten werden können"[72] (401).

Weber's pioneering efforts were refined in the definitive statement of the North Semitic hypothesis by Georg Bühler in 1895, namely, in his classic *On the Origin of the Indian Brāhma Alphabet* (OIBA).[73] Bühler compared the early forms of Brāhmī from the Aśokan and other early inscriptions, including the aberrant forms of the Bhaṭṭiprōḷu inscriptions, with the corresponding letters of the North Semitic alphabet of the tenth to eighth centuries B.C. (to which period he attributed the Indian borrowing; see 2.1.2) as found in the early Phoenician inscriptions and other contemporary documents which were then known. He was thereby able to formulate a derivation which improved in several respects upon that of Weber. For example, Bühler gave Brāhmī *ca* as the derivative of *ṣade*, which is obviously preferable to Weber's *jha*. Likewise Bühler's *gha* from *ḥet* is clearly better than Weber's *ca*, as is his *kha* instead of Weber's *ka* as the derivative of *qoph*.

By no means, however, were all of Bühler's derivations beyond question. In order to account for graphic differences between many of the Brāhmī characters and their supposed Semitic prototypes, Bühler had to invoke certain general derivational principles (OIBA 56–8). For example, the "appendages" which constitute the distinctive portion of the letters are generally attached at the bottom or middle, rather than at the top as in Semitic; therefore, "a number of the Semitic signs had to be turned topsy-turvy or to be laid on their sides, while the triangles or double angles, occurring at the tops of others had to be got rid of by some contrivance or other" (57–8). But even if these principles are accepted, fewer than half of the equations of the twenty-two original Semitic characters with their alleged Brāhmī derivatives can be considered beyond doubt. Among these, only seven—*a*, *ga*, *tha*, *pa*, *ca*, *kha*, and *śa*—can be derived from their proposed prototypes with a minimum of manipulation, for example, by simple inversion as in the case of 𑀧 *pa* < 𐤐 *pe* and 𑀔 *kha* < 𐤒 *qoph*. The remaining fourteen derivations range from likely but paleographically uncertain, for example 𑀬 *ya* < 𐤉 *yod*, to highly problematic, as in 𑀫 *ma* < 𐤌 *mem*, 𑀭 *ra* < 𐤓 *resh* and 𑀩 *ba* < 𐤁 *bet*. In his explanations of some of the more difficult derivations Bühler could well be charged with abusing his rather vague principle of "some contrivance or other" (58) in the adaptation of the Semitic forms to the Indian pattern.

Moreover, the direct derivations from the twenty-two consonantal characters of the supposed North Semitic prototype account for less than half of the full Indic alphabet, which comprises at least forty-six[74] distinct characters. Bühler thus derived the remaining Brāhmī characters by a process of secondary development from the primary, Semitic-based characters. Most of his secondary derivations, such as those

72. "Though the paleographic identification may be subject to refutations and correction in details, I would most insistently maintain that the overall result can hardly be challenged."

73. Here Bühler acknowledged his debt to his predecessor with the comment that "the identifications agree for the greater part with Professor Weber's, whose important essay . . . very nearly solved the problem of the origin of the Brāhma alphabet" (55).

74. On the probable number of characters in the primitive form of Brāhmī, see OIBA 27–35.

of the aspirates 𑀨 *pha* and 𑀙 *cha* from the corresponding nonaspirates 𑀧 *pa* and 𑀘 *ca* are obvious, but others, such as *bha* and *dha*, are less convincing.[75] The retroflex consonants, which have no direct prototypes in Semitic, are derived, according to Bühler, by a similar secondary process, whereby, for instance, 𑀞 *ṭha* is a reduction of 𑀣 *tha* and 𑀝 *ṭa* a further reduction of *ṭha*.

Thus although Bühler's North Semitic hypothesis has much merit, it is far from perfect, and has not surprisingly been subjected to extensive criticism on various methodological, procedural, and historical grounds. Ojhā, for example (BPLM 24–6), was strongly critical of Bühler's manipulations of the forms of the supposed Phoenician prototypes, alleging that by such methods one could "derive" virtually any script from any other.[76] J. Halévy[77] objected, with good reason, to Bühler's citation of the aberrant forms of several letters of the Bhaṭṭiprōḷu script as intermediate forms between those of the Semitic prototype and their Aśokan Brāhmī reflexes.[78] He argued that since the Bhaṭṭiprōḷu inscriptions are at least fifty years later than the Aśokan,[79] Bühler's use of them constitutes a violation of the first part of his own guiding principle that "the comparison must be based on the oldest forms of the Indian alphabet and actually occurring Semitic signs of one and the same period" (OIBA 55).[80] Although some of Halévy's other criticisms of Bühler are completely unjustified, and although his own conclusions (see 2.2.3.2.1) are highly questionable, Halévy's methodological criticisms, especially those from the point of view of Semitic epigraphy, do expose significant weaknesses in Bühler's arguments.

Finally, there is the much discussed matter of the direction of writing. In support of his argument for a Semitic derivation, Bühler cited an early coin from Eraṇ bearing a Brāhmī legend running from right to left instead of the normal direction as a remnant of "a period during which the Brāhma characters were written in both directions" (OIBA 45), that is, of a transitional phase in the reversal of the original direction of writing of the Semitic prototype. This particular piece of evidence has been rejected by several scholars[81] on the grounds that reversed coin legends are not at all uncommon from various periods and regions. However, some more recent discoveries, such as the Eṟṟaguḍi Aśokan rock edicts written in semiboustro-

75. On the derivation of the aspirates *kha*, *gha*, and *tha*, see section 2.2.3.3.

76. By way of illustration, Ojhā shows how by such arbitrary alterations of forms one could formulate a pseudoderivation of Brāhmī from modern Roman script (26). But while it is true that several of Bühler's derivations did involve seemingly arbitrary alterations of the originals, Ojhā's criticisms are exaggerated and hence only partially justified, since, as we have seen, at least half of Bühler's derivations are reasonably cogent. Thus when Ojhā emphasizes (21) that only one Brāhmī letter (*ga*) agrees exactly with Phoenician, he hardly does justice to Bühler's carefully argued, if not invariably satisfactory, formulation; insisting on exact identity between prototype and derivative is just as unreasonable as arbitrarily concocting resemblances between dissimilar characters.

77. "Nouvelles observations sur les écritures indiennes," *Revue Sémitique* 3, 1895, 223–86 (discussed 234).

78. E.g., Bühler gives the Bhaṭṭiprōḷu form of *ja*, ⊏, as a link between Phoenician 𐤆 *zain* and Aśokan Brāhmī 𑀚 *ja*.

79. Actually, as it now appears, they may even be considerably later than that; see section 2.2.5.1.

80. The second part of this rule is also violated, according to Halévy (242–3), by Bühler's choice of North Semitic prototype letters from various inscriptions of widely differing regions and periods.

81. E.g., by E. Hultzsch in his otherwise favorable review of BIP in IA 26, 1897, 336. See also J. F. Fleet in the introductory note (3–4) to his English translation of Bühler's *Indian Paleography* (IA 33).

phedon,[82] have again raised the possibility that Brāhmī might sometimes have been written from right to left in the early phase of its development. The several early Brāhmī cave inscriptions from Sri Lanka written from right to left[83] could also be cited as a survival of the old Semitic direction of writing, but since they are probably considerably later than the Aśokan inscriptions[84] they may be nothing more than an anomalous local development. The evidence on this point is thus inconclusive, but in any case its overall importance has perhaps been exaggerated in many of the discussions of the origin of Brāhmī. Instability in direction of writing is a common phenomenon in ancient scripts generally, and in any case a reversal is attested in various derivatives of Semitic scripts such as Greek and Ethiopic. Thus the left-to-right direction of (most) early Brāhmī is not in and of itself any strong evidence against a Semitic origin.

2.2.3.2.5 Aramaic. A derivation of Brāhmī from the later North Semitic Aramaic script (see table 2.2) rather than the earlier Phoenician was proposed as early as 1874 by A. C. Burnell in SIP 8–9, and has more recently been endorsed by Diringer,[85] who is inclined to consider Brāhmī to be an adaptation rather than a "simple derivative" of early Aramaic. Paleographically the Aramaic derivation is plausible, since many of the early Brāhmī letters can be formally derived as well, or even better, from Aramaic as from Phoenician prototypes. The paleographic ramifications of this theory, however, have not yet been fully worked out. Historically and chronologically too, the Aramaic theory is much preferable to the Phoenician derivation. The widespread use of the Aramaic language and script as a lingua franca throughout the Near East and the Iranian world and as a bureaucratic language of the Achaemenian empire provides a ready explanation for its influence in India, in contrast to Bühler's weak historical, geographical, and chronological justifications for a Phoenician prototype. Moreover, the discovery since Bühler's time of six Mauryan inscriptions in Aramaic (4.3.7.3) strongly supports the hypothesis of an Aramaic connection.

However, a possible objection to the derivation of Brāhmī from Aramaic[86] is that, since it has been established with virtual certainty that the Kharoṣṭhī script is derived from Aramaic (2.3.6), it is hard to see why another, very different, Indic script would have developed from the same prototype in a contiguous region. If the hypothesis of the invention of Brāhmī under Aśoka's sponsorship (2.2.3.1) is correct, this re-creation may be attributed to the emperor's desire to invent a distinct imperial script, perhaps under the inspiration of Old Persian cuneiform, which would be suited to the promulgation of edicts in written form.[87] But it must be admitted that there is no direct statement to this effect in the edicts themselves.

82. Though the reversed writing of some of the lines at Erraguḍi may be due to the incompetence or ignorance of the engraver; see the comments on this point in OBS 31.

83. Besides the well-known Dūvegala cave inscription (SI I.242), S. Paranavitana (*Inscriptions of Ceylon*, I.xxii) notes no less than thirty-nine such inscriptions.

84. Sircar (SI I.242) dates the Dūvegala (Duwé Gala) inscription to the first century B.C.

85. *The Alphabet*, 336.

86. As noted by Senart, JA, ser. 7, vol. 13, 1879, 534.

87. As proposed by, among others, Falk (SAI 338–9), although he sees Kharoṣṭhī itself, rather than Aramaic, as the principal prototype of Brāhmī (2.2.3.2.1 and 2.2.3.2.2).

2.2.3.3 Observations and conclusions on the probable origin of Brāhmī

The various theories of an indigenous Indian origin for Brāhmī are all more or less speculative, and hence impossible to either prove or disprove. Nonetheless, it would be imprudent to dismiss them entirely. In particular, the possibility that there is ultimately some historical connection between the Indus Valley script and Brāhmī cannot be decisively ruled out, but unless and until some significant progress toward the decipherment of the former is achieved, we can only treat the matter as an unproven hypothesis.

The theory of a Semitic origin for Brāhmī, on the other hand, does have a strong, if not entirely conclusive, body of concrete evidence in its favor. The derivation, along the lines worked out by Bühler, has (as noted earlier, 2.2.3, n. 42) been generally adopted by Western scholars; typical is the opinion of Hultzsch that the North Semitic theory "is so well supported with facts that it cannot fail to meet with general acceptance."[88] But in South Asia, as we have seen (see 2.2.3 and 2.2.3.2.4), the Semitic hypothesis is not widely accepted, though there too some scholars, notably A. H. Dani in his influential work on Indian paleography (DIP 23–30),[89] have cautiously supported some form of Semitic derivation.[90] Part of the problem is that, despite the defects in Bühler's methodology and data, no one since him has undertaken a comprehensive and careful paleographic reexamination of the Semitic hypothesis. Hence evaluations of the theory have essentially consisted of discussions, supportive or critical, of Bühler's work; but it should be kept in mind that the shortcomings of Bühler's presentation do not necessarily discredit the Semitic hypothesis itself.

Moreover, searching for formal prototypes for each of the characters of early Brāhmī in one or the other alleged Semitic prototypes is one way, and not necessarily the most effective way, to address the problem. For even many of the supporters of the Semitic hypothesis concede that, in Dani's words, "[T]he Brāhmī letters are not literally 'derived' from the Semitic letters as is commonly understood, but are only based on them" (DIP 29).[91] In other words, the relationship of Brāhmī to an alleged Semitic parent script may be more analogous to, say, that of the Arabic script and its presumptive Nabataean parent, which is widely accepted even though it cannot be traced in every detail,[92] than it is to better attested derivations such as that of the Greek alphabet from Phoenician (which seems to have served as the model, consciously or otherwise, for the studies of Bühler et al.).

Thus it may be more revealing to pay more attention to systemic features and patterns instead of concentrating on the formal derivation of individual characters. From this point of view, the Semitic hypothesis is more convincing. For instance, the system of postconsonantal diacritic vowel indicators looks like a natural adapta-

88. IA 26, 1897, 336.

89. In the preface to the recent second edition of this book (1986), however, Dani expresses some second thoughts on the matter, suggesting that "for the origin of Brāhmī we should look elsewhere [than Semitic]" (ix).

90. Cf. also K. G. Krishnan in OBS 68: "The Semitic affiliation of some of the forms, as explained by Bühler, cannot be ignored, though it is . . . partial in its coverage."

91. See also Diringer, *The Alphabet*, 336.

92. See ibid., 270–1, and Naveh, *Early History of the Alphabet*, 160–1 and 221.

tion of the Semitic consonant-syllabic script for use in Indian languages (2.1.2 and 2.3.6). Similarly, the evident development of the retroflex consonants as modified forms of the corresponding dentals suggests an adaptation of a non-Indic prototype, since in an originally Indian system one would have expected independent signs for the two classes from the very beginning. Particularly revealing is the pattern of formation of the aspirate consonants. For while these are typically formed as modifications of the corresponding nonaspirates (2.2.3.2.4), there are some striking exceptions to this pattern, notably, ʔ *kha*, ɺ *gha*, and ʘ *tha*,[93] none of which bear any graphic relationship to the corresponding nonaspirates (+ *ka*, ∧ *ga*, and ⅄ *ta*) but which can be derived directly from Semitic prototypes, namely, ⲣ *qoph*, ɦ *ḥet*, and 6 *ṭet*, respectively. This pattern can hardly be coincidental, and is perhaps the single strongest systemic indication of a Semitic background.

In conclusion, there are strong systemic and paleographic indications that the Brāhmī script derived from a Semitic prototype, which, mainly on historical grounds, is most likely to have been Aramaic. However, the details of this problem remain to be worked out, and in any case it is unlikely that a complete letter-by-letter derivation will ever be possible; for Brāhmī may have been more of an adaptation and remodeling, rather than a direct derivation, of the presumptive Semitic prototype, perhaps under the influence of a preexisting Indian tradition of phonetic analysis.[94] However, the Semitic hypothesis is not so strong as to rule out the remote possibility that further discoveries could drastically change the picture. In particular, a relationship of some kind, probably partial or indirect, with the protohistoric Indus Valley script should not be considered entirely out of the question.

2.2.4 *Characteristics of Brāhmī in the Mauryan period (third century* B.C.)

The Brāhmī script as it first appears in inscriptions of the Mauryan period (see table 2.1) is an almost fully developed writing of the characteristic Indian diacritically modified syllabic type described earlier (2.1.3). The repertoire of the script as represented in the Aśokan inscriptions consists of six full (initial) vowel signs (*a, ā, i, u, e, o*), thirty-two consonants, and eight medial vowel diacritic signs (*ā, i, ī, u, ū, e, o, ai*), plus the *anusvāra* sign. The absence of the initial vowel signs *ī* and *ū* is no doubt a statistical accident due to their rarity, but other vowels which are absent in both full and diacritic form, such as *ṛ, ṝ*, and possibly *au*, apparently did not yet exist in the script, as they were developed only later when Brāhmī began to be used for writing Sanskrit (see 2.2.5.2). Among the consonants only the sign for *ṅa* is lacking, as is the *visarga*, no doubt also because they are not needed for the Prakrits which Brāhmī was used to record at this time.

Aśokan Brāhmī displays on the whole a uniform aspect, and although it was formerly believed[95] to have significant regional varieties, more recent studies have shown that the script was in fact essentially uniform all over India.[96] There are, however,

93. The cases of two other anomalous aspirates, *dha* and *bha*, seem to involve different circumstances.

94. Cf. DIP 28–30, and Diringer, *The Alphabet*, 336.

95. See, e.g., BIP 33–4.

96. C. S. Upasak, *The History and Palaeography of Mauryan Brāhmī Script*, especially 29–32 and 193; DIP 35; and section 2.1.2.

variant forms for many of the characters, which, though evidently not geographically determined, are still significant for the development of the script; see, for example, the several varieties of initial *a* noted in BIP 6. Also of interest are a few letters such as *dha* (𑀥 or 𑀥) and diacritic *o* (e.g., in 𑀦𑁄 or 𑀦𑁄, *no*), whose directional orientation has not been fixed (DIP 48).

The orthography of Brāhmī of the Mauryan period is also not fully developed or standardized. The notation of the three sibilants in some of the Aśokan inscriptions is inconsistent and inaccurate (especially in Kālsī rock edicts XI–XIV where, for example, *ṣuṣuṣā* = Skt. *śuśrūṣā*, XI. 29). Vowel quantity, especially the distinctions between *i/ī* and *u/ū*, is not always consistently noted, again at Kālsī in particular.[97] Consonantal conjuncts are in general constructed as in the later scripts, that is, by the graphic combination of the component characters, sometimes with abbreviation of one component; but the relative positioning of the components is not always phonetically accurate. For example, combinations with *r* are always constructed with the *r* above, regardless of its actual phonetic position, so that the same character (𑀭𑁆𑀯) represents both *rva* and *vra*.[98]

The other (non-Aśokan) early Brāhmī inscriptions, such as Sohgaurā, Piprāwā, and Mahāsthān (2.1.2), have an even more primitive orthography. They have no conjuncts, and do not distinguish *i/ī* or *u/ū* at all; Piprāwā seems not to have long vowels at all, except for one doubtful *ā*. These inscriptions also have a few variant letter forms, such as the *ma* (𑀫) at Sohgaurā; but due to the paucity of the materials it is difficult to evaluate their chronological significance. Thus while some scholars have attributed an early, pre-Mauryan date to some or all of this group, others (e.g., Dani, DIP 56–7) have dated them to the post-Mauryan era. All in all, it seems most likely that they are roughly contemporaneous with the Aśokan inscriptions. Their primitive orthography does not prove an early date for the inscriptions themselves, only the use of a less formal style than that of the Aśokan inscriptions, which occasionally show early signs of the influence of Sanskritic orthography.

2.2.5 The historical development and derivatives of Brāhmī

2.2.5.1 The "Śuṅga" period (second through first centuries B.C.*)*

After the Mauryan period, Brāhmī script began to undergo its gradual process of evolution (see tables 2.3 and 2.4). But, with the exception of the Bhaṭṭiprōḷu and early Tamil scripts (to be discussed shortly), the changes are at first mostly minor, so that Brāhmī of the first century B.C. is still not markedly different in appearance from its Mauryan predecessor. Nonetheless, certain of the formal evolutions first noted in this period (especially in the latter half thereof), such as the development of rudimentary head marks and the equalization of the vertical portions of certain letters, are important in prefiguring more radical formal changes which are to appear in the following centuries.

The head marks which begin to appear in certain inscriptions of this period (e.g., in the Hāthīgumphā inscription) in the form of a small triangle at the top of the ver-

97. Hultzsch, *Inscriptions of Aśoka* (CII 1), lxxi.

98. Other instances of apparently reversed conjuncts, such as 𑀬𑁆𑀯 *yva* for *vya*, are also quotable (see section 3.1.2.2).

TABLE 2.3. The Development of Brāhmī Script

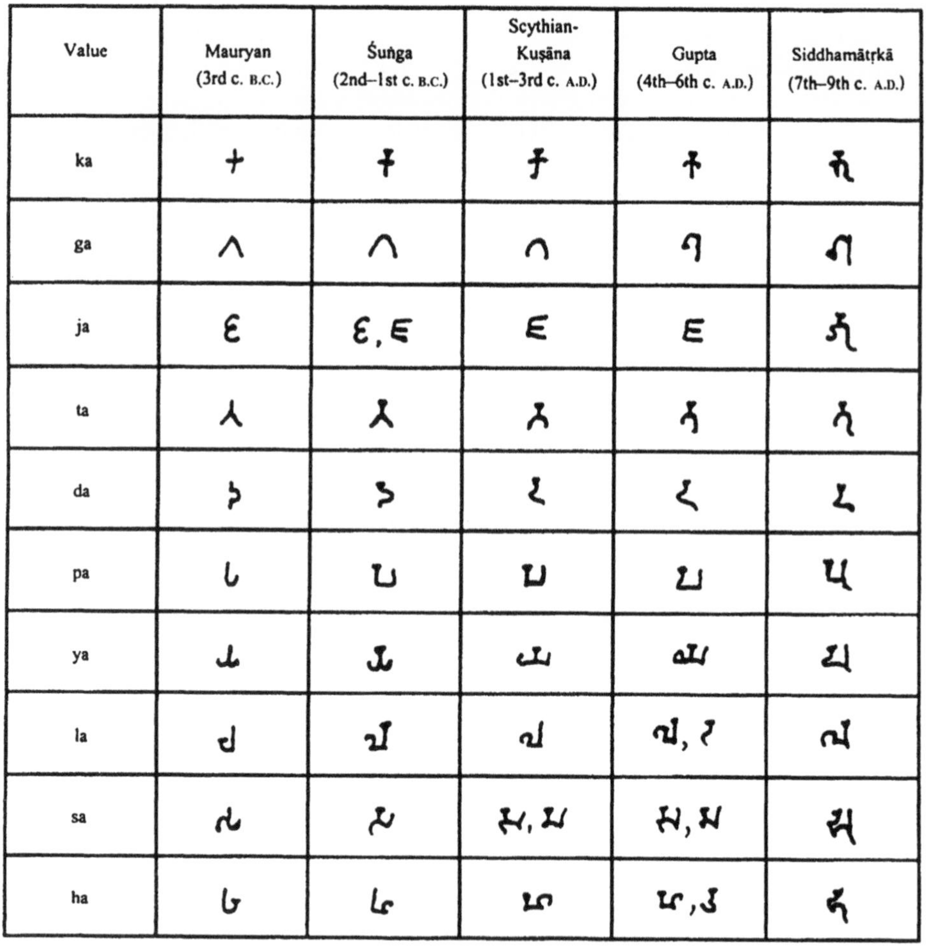
Value
Mauryan (3rd c. B.C.)
Śuṅga (2nd–1st c. B.C.)
Scythian-Kuṣāna (1st–3rd c. A.D.)
Gupta (4th–6th c. A.D.)
Siddhamātṛkā (7th–9th c. A.D.)
ka
ga
ja
ta
da
pa
ya
la
sa
ha

Note: These are selected representative North Indian characters in normalized forms.

TABLE 2.4. The Development of *ṆA* in Brāhmī and Its Derivative Scripts

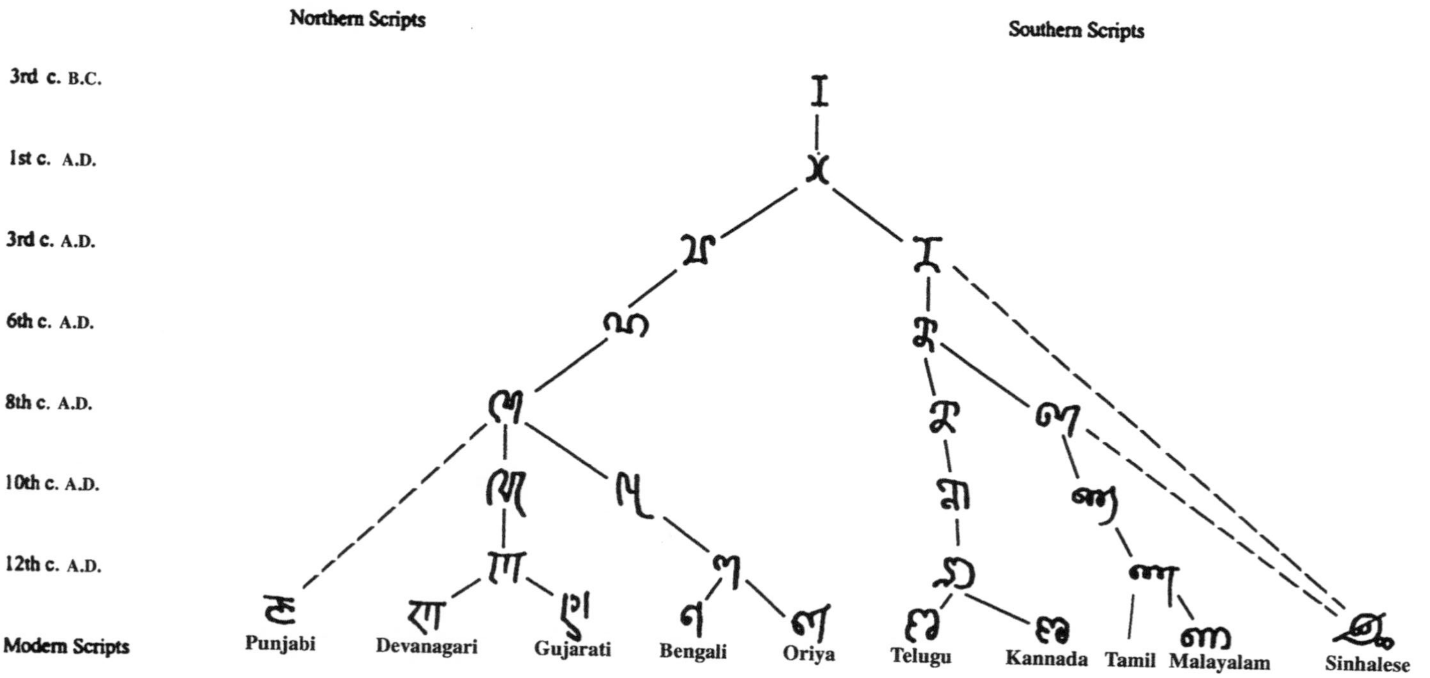

Note: This table presents in broad outline the development of a representative character, *ṇa*, from early Brāhmī to the major modern Indian scripts. Detailed charts for the development of each *akṣara* are provided in Sivaramamurti, IESIS 57–153

tical stroke are no doubt due to the influence of pen and ink writing,[99] in which such a mark naturally tends to appear at the point where the scribe begins the letter. This accidental formation eventually came to be perceived as a part of the letter form itself, so that it began to appear in epigraphic writing by way of imitation of pen and ink script. This head mark was to develop in the succeeding centuries into different shapes in different regions, eventually resulting in the formation of such characteristic features of medieval and modern Indian scripts as the square of the "box-headed" script, the continuous top line of Devanāgarī, the curved "umbrella" of Oriya, or the "check-mark" of Telugu.

The tendency toward equalization of the two verticals in such characters as 𑀧 *pa* and 𑀲 *sa*, which begins to make its appearance in some inscriptions of this period, also prefigures developments of later centuries wherein the letters tend to be remodeled into a square frame. This again is an influential development for the history of the derivative scripts, many of which (notably Devanāgarī) retain this pattern throughout their history.

Notable developments of individual characters in this period include the elongation of the vertical of the old cross-shaped *ka* of Mauryan Brāhmī leading to the "dagger-shaped" form of this letter (𑀓 > 𑀓); the rounding of the top of *ga* (𑀕 > 𑀕); the reversal in direction of *dha* (𑀥 > 𑀥); a tendency toward the development of angular forms in such letters as *ma* and *va* (𑀫 > 𑀫; 𑀯 > 𑀯); and the replacement of the old curved *ra* with a straight vertical shape (𑀭 > 𑀭). Among the few new characters which make their appearance in this period is the initial *ai* (𑀐), first seen in the Hāthīgumphā inscription (l. 1).

While the changes which Brāhmī underwent in this period in northern India are relatively minor and superficial, the Bhaṭṭiprōḷu inscriptions present a unique and radically different southern variety of the script. This script, found in nine inscriptions[100] on relic caskets from the *stūpa* at Bhaṭṭiprōḷu in Andhra Pradesh, differs from standard early Brāhmī in two important respects. First, the formation of five of the consonantal characters, namely *gha*, *ja*, *ma*, *la*, and *sa* (or *ṣa*)[101] is radically different. The character *ma*, for example, (𑀫) is upside-down compared with the standard form (𑀫) of the letter. Particularly interesting is the formation of *gha* (𑀖), which can be seen (EI 2, 323–4) as a secondary derivative of the sign for *ga*, unlike standard Brāhmī *gha*, which appears to be a distinct character probably derived directly from Semitic *ḥet*.[102]

99. See DIP 52–3.

100. A tenth inscription on a small piece of crystal is in a script which is much more like standard early Brāhmī, though it has a few features, such as *da* with the opening to the right, which agree with the aberrant local script rather than the standard.

101. The character in question (𑀱) was read by Bühler (EI 2, 324) as *ṣa* because of its paleographic similarity to standard *ṣa*, but Lüders (*Philologica Indica*, 213–29) provided cogent linguistic arguments (213–7) for reading it as *sa*. Although most modern scholars have followed Bühler, Lüders' reading seems to be preferable. (Note that the relation and distinction between *sa* and *ṣa* in early Brāhmī are often problematic; see 2.2.4 and 3.1.2.1 n. 5.)

It is worth noting that although Bühler's edition of the Bhaṭṭiprōḷu inscriptions is the one which is usually referred to and followed in subsequent publications, Lüders' readings and interpretations are very different from and much superior to Bühler's, and thus should be adopted as the standard.

102. OIBA 46; see section 2.2.4. Note, however, that Dani (DIP 70) sees the Bhaṭṭiprōḷu *gha* as a

The second peculiarity of the Bhaṭṭiprōḷu script is its system for notation of the postconsonantal vowels *a* and *ā*. Uniquely among all the early Indic scripts, at Bhaṭṭiprōḷu the inherent vowel system is discarded, and a consonant followed by *a* does have a vowel marker consisting of a short horizontal line at the upper right, similar to the sign for *ā* in standard Brāhmī; e.g., 𑀓 = *ka*. (*ā* in the Bhaṭṭiprōḷu script is marked with a further downward extension of the *a* diacritic, as in 𑀓𑀸 = *kā*.) Bühler (OIBA) explained that this device "seems to have been invented in order to avoid the necessity of forming the ligatures, which make the ordinary Brāhma alphabet cumbersome and difficult to read . . . , and in order to express final consonants more conveniently" (82). He evidently assumed that consonantal groups would have been written in this script by putting the prior member(s) in the bare form, without any diacritic, to indicate their vowelless state, thereby obviating the complication of conjunct consonants. But, as noted by Mahalingam (ESIP 120), no such vowelless characters or final consonants actually occur in the Bhaṭṭiprōḷu inscriptions, presumably because they were written in a vernacular Prakrit dialect. Bühler's explanation seems to presuppose that the script was also used for writing Sanskrit or more formal varieties of Prakrit in this period, but there is no evidence that this was the case. Rather, discoveries made subsequently to Bühler's writings, namely the Old Tamil Brāhmī inscriptions discussed later, suggest that this aberrant vowel notation system reflects innovations made in the environment of Dravidian rather than Indo-Aryan languages.

The significance of the anomalous consonant forms at Bhaṭṭiprōḷu is, however, still not entirely clear, especially in light of the prevailing uncertainty as to the date of the script; Bühler (EI 2, 325) tentatively dated the Bhaṭṭiprōḷu inscriptions at not later than 200 B.C., while Sircar (SI 224; cf. n. 5 there) places them at "about the end of the 2nd century B.C." These nonstandard consonant characters can hardly be dismissed as mere "mistakes" on the part of the engraver (so Dani, DIP 70), though Bühler (2.2.3.2.4) seems to have overemphasized their significance for the origin and history of Brāhmī. All in all, it seems more likely that the Bhaṭṭiprōḷu script represents a provincial offshoot of early Brāhmī in the south, rather than a separate line of development from a hypothetical Semitic prototype itself, as Bühler believed.

A second southern Indian variety of Brāhmī attributable to this period[103] is the script used in a series of brief dedicatory cave inscriptions from Tamil Nadu in an early form of the Tamil language. This alphabet has two notable peculiarities, which in some respects resemble those of the Bhaṭṭiprōḷu script. First, it has four entirely

---

reformed variant of the standard Brāhmī *gha*. See also section 2.2.3.2.4, on Bühler's treatment of the Bhaṭṭiprōḷu script in connection with his derivation of Brāhmī.

103. The dates of the Old Tamil inscriptions are uncertain and controversial. Iravatham Mahadevan, in "Tamil-Brahmi Inscriptions of the Sangam Age" (in R. E. Asher, ed., *Proceedings of the Second International Conference Seminar of Tamil Studies* [Madras: International Association of Tamil Research, 1971], 73–106), 83, stresses their overall close paleographic resemblance to Aśokan Brāhmī and hence dates the earliest specimens to the second and first centuries B.C. But Dani (DIP 72–4) places them in the first century A.D., citing the evidence of potsherds from Arikamēḍu bearing inscriptions in this script (AI 2, 1946, 109–14) which are stratigraphically datable to this period. However, Mahadevan points out that in some respects the Arikamēḍu inscriptions are paleographically more advanced than the early cave inscriptions, and thus his dating seems preferable.

new characters, interpreted as *ṉa*, *ṟa*, *ṛa*, and *ḷa*, which were evidently created in order to represent Dravidian phonemes not represented in standard (northern) Brāhmī. (It does not, however, share with Bhaṭṭiprōḷu the peculiar forms of the consonants *gha*, *ja*, etc.) Second, its system of vowel notation differs from that of standard Brāhmī and resembles that of Bhaṭṭiprōḷu. According to the authoritative interpretation of this system by Mahadevan,[104] in what appears to be the earlier form of this script a consonant written without a vowel diacritic is to be understood as representing the vowelless consonant itself, while the consonant written with the diacritic sign which denotes long *ā* in standard Brāhmī is to be read with either the vowel *a* or *ā*, depending on the context.[105] In other words, the script in question has essentially abandoned the "inherent vowel" principle.

Thus we find in the Tamil Brāhmī inscriptions a system of representation of pure (i.e., vowelless) consonants which seemed to be implied, but was not actually attested, in the Bhaṭṭiprōḷu inscriptions. Therefore, although the two scripts do not appear to be directly related paleographically, there evidently is a systemic relationship between them. The presence in Bhaṭṭiprōḷu of explicitly noted postconsonantal *a*, but without any examples of the expected "pure" or vowelless consonants, now looks, in light of the Tamil Brāhmī inscriptions, like the reapplication to Prakrit of a form of Brāhmī which had been previously modified for the representation of a Dravidian language. For, as explained by Mahadevan ("Tamil-Brahmi Inscriptions," 81–2), the systemic features of these early southern varieties of Brāhmī would seem to reflect phonetic features of Dravidian, such as the common occurrence of consonants in word final position, rather than of Prakrit, which has no word final consonants.

The subsequent historical development of the modified southern system, however, is not at all what one would have anticipated by comparison with the usual patterns of evolution of scripts. Surprisingly, the capability of the Bhaṭṭiprōḷu and Tamil Brāhmī scripts to write vowelless consonants in a simple manner and thus to obviate the need for consonantal conjuncts does not seem to have been continued in the later forms of the southern scripts. Indeed, as shown by Mahadevan (op. cit., 82–3), this innovative system actually is attenuated in some (perhaps later)[106] Tamil Brāhmī inscriptions, in which the unmarked consonant may represent either the pure consonant *or* the consonant plus *a*, and in still later inscriptions the system of vowelless consonants falls out of use entirely. Mahadevan attributes the failure of this tentative experiment toward alphabetization to the influence of the scripts of adjoining regions of India and Sri Lanka, which retained the standard Indic modified syllabic system;

104. In "Tamil-Brahmi Inscriptions of the Sangam Age"; see also his "Corpus of the Tamil-Brahmi Inscriptions," in R. Nagaswamy, ed., *Kalveṭṭik Karuttaraṅku/Seminar on Inscriptions, 1966* (Madras: Books [India] Private Ltd., 1968), 57–73; and T. V. Mahalingam, ESIP 120–2 and 140–1.

105. Mahadevan, "Tamil-Brāhmī Inscriptions," 79. Mahalingam (ESIP 120) thinks that the long vowel *ā* is sometimes noted by a doubled form of the diacritic, but no clear examples of this are actually visible in the reproductions of the inscriptions.

106. In "Some Aspects of the Tamil-Brahmi Script" (JESI 12, 1985, 121–8), Mahadevan expresses some doubts about his own earlier formulation of the chronological relation of the two forms of the script, considering it "more likely" that they were "more or less contemporaneous styles" (123). See also R. Nagaswamy, "The Tamil, Vatteluttu and Grantha Script," in *Proceedings of the Second International Conference Seminar of Tamil Studies* [see n. 103] II.410–5 (esp. 413).

in his words, the southern innovation was "too radical a departure from all the other systems of Indian writing" (83).[107]

2.2.5.2 *The first through third centuries* A.D.

In about the first three centuries of the Christian era, the gradual geographical differentiation of the Brāhmī script continued to the point that we begin to discern several distinct regional varieties. Although these local forms can still be considered essentially as varieties of the same script, they clearly foreshadow the development of separate local scripts which was to take place in the following centuries (cf. DIP 77–8). While it was formerly the standard practice to classify the scripts of this and the succeeding periods in dynastic terms ("Kuṣāṇa script," "Gupta script," etc.), Dani (DIP 78–9, 100–1; cf. 2.2.2) has argued that the traditional dynastic terminology is misleading and inaccurate, and has preferred to treat the paleographic development of Brāhmī in regional rather than dynastic terms. Thus, for the period in question, he discerns several local varieties, among which the Kauśāmbī, Mathurā, western Deccan, and eastern Deccan styles are of particular importance. Dani's geographical approach to historical paleography is undoubtedly a major improvement in this field, and will in general be followed here.

Among the new developments in this period, several characters such as *ṛ* (both initial and postconsonantal), *au*, *ṅa*, *ḥ* (*visarga*), and *halanta* (vowelless consonants)[108] first came into common use. These are, of course, the result of the growing popularity in this period of Sanskrit or "Epigraphical Hybrid Sanskrit" (EHS) (3.2) as inscriptional languages (see 3.3.1). For the same reason, we now see a further development of consonantal conjuncts, which become more frequent and more complex. Particularly noteworthy is the development of special modified or abbreviated forms of the semivowels *r* (in both preconsonantal and postconsonantal position, e.g.,  *rpa* and  *pra*) and *y* (postconsonantal), reflecting their statistical frequency in consonantal combinations in Sanskrit.[109]

The forms of the basic characters as well underwent significant modifications, such that for the first time in this period (especially in the latter half thereof) the script began to differ markedly in its overall appearance and ductus from the early forms of Brāhmī. Among the most important changes was the further development of the

107. Later scripts used for Tamil did, however, develop a vowel cancellation marker consisting of a dot above the consonant (*puḷḷi*; cf. n. 37) which has the same effect as the vowelless consonant system, i.e., eliminating the need for conjuncts, but which departs less radically from the standard Indic graphic principles. The *puḷḷi* is attested as early as the second century A.D. in Dravidian coin legends (D. C. Sircar, "Silver Coin of Vasishthi-putra Satakarni," EI 35, 1963–64, 247–52; see also R. Nagaswamy, "A Bilingual Coin of a Satavahana," in *Seminar on Inscriptions, 1966* [see n. 104], 200–2, and P. Panneerselvam, "Further Light on the Bilingual Coin of the Sātavāhanas," IIJ 11, 1968–69, 281–8), and is also referred to in the Tolkāppiyam (*Eṛuttadikāram*, *sūtra* 15). But it is difficult to know whether *puḷḷi* was a survival of the peculiar vowel notation system of the Tamil Brāhmī inscriptions, or evolved separately as a result of the internal phonetic characteristics of Tamil.

108. This is used only *in pausa* (sentence final or verse final position), not within or between words as in the Tamil systems discussed in the preceding section.

109. Note that a similar development takes place in Kharoṣṭhī; see section 2.3.4.

head mark, whose origins were first noticed in the preceding period. Now, the head mark becomes firmly entrenched as an intrinsic rather than incidental part of the letters, and is written as a distinct separate stroke. Moreover, we now begin to discern the different regional treatments of the head mark (DIP 79–81), which are to have such far-reaching consequences in later centuries (cf. 2.2.5.1).

Some of the consonantal characters were radically remodeled in this period. For instance, the old form of *da* with the bulge to the right (𑀤) was replaced by its mirror image (𑀤). The tendency toward the equalization of verticals in characters such as *pa* and *sa*, first noted in the preceding period, is now strengthened so that these and others tend to be molded into a square outline, which is reinforced by the angularized forms of some letters such as 𑀚 *ja*, 𑀫 *ma*, and 𑀱 *ṣa*. But in this period (especially in its later phases) we also see in other characters the contrary effects of cursivization (here, as elsewhere, reflecting the epigraphic imitation of pen-and-ink forms), which result in rounded and looped forms of such characters as 𑀢 *ta*, 𑀦 *na*, 𑀪 *bha*, and 𑀲 *sa*.

Also in this period there first emerged a tendency toward calligraphic elaboration. Thus characters such as *a*, *ka*, and *ra*, which end with verticals at the bottom, developed ornamental loops to the lower left (e.g., 𑀓 *ka*). The diacritic vowel signs were also often elaborated with extensions and flourishes. These more elaborate forms are characteristic of the Deccan style, especially in the eastern Deccan. Here, in inscriptions from such sites as Nāgārjunakoṇḍa, Amarāvatī, and Jaggayyapeṭa, we find extreme calligraphic developments with long vertical flourishes above and below many of the letters (cf. 2.5.3.1). In general, we can begin to perceive in this period a broad differentiation between the northern scripts, which are beginning to develop their characteristic squarish and angular forms, and the southern scripts with their typically rounded and flowing shapes.

2.2.5.3 *The fourth through sixth centuries* A.D.

During this period, conventionally referred to as the "Gupta era," the degree of regional differentiation continued to increase. The northern and southern groups were by now clearly differentiated, and other distinct regional scripts made their appearance, for instance, in central India. In the north, the inscriptions of the Guptas and their contemporaries were written in regional varieties of the northern script, which may be called, following Sircar's terminology (IIEP 113; cf. 2.2.2), "late Brāhmī." The varieties of the northern Gupta script have traditionally been classified as western and eastern, the latter being characterized mainly by cursivized forms of *la* (𑀮) and *ha* (𑀳) and the looped *sa* (𑀲). But Dani (DIP 102ff.) has shown that this division is oversimplified, and he classifies the northern script into regional subvarieties such as the Kauśāmbī (roughly equivalent to the old "eastern" style), Mathurā, and Malwa styles. In general, the northern scripts of the Gupta era are characterized by the continued extension of various forms of the head mark or, as it now can be called, the top line. The shapes of the individual characters also continued to develop; among the changes which prefigure important characteristics of later scripts are the prolongation of the right arm in 𑀕 *ga*, 𑀢 *ta*, 𑀪 *bha*, and 𑀰 *śa*; the looped form of 𑀦 *na*; and the development of the dot inside 𑀣 *tha* into a horizontal line.

In central India the peculiar "box-headed script" began to develop during this period. The principal characteristic of this script, namely, the square head mark, is noted in some northern Gupta inscriptions, but its full development, with the letters themselves molded into characteristically square, angular forms, first appeared in the inscriptions of the Vākāṭakas. This highly stylized script enjoyed a long period of popularity in central India, where it continued to be used into the seventh century,[110] and also spread to the south, where it appears in some Kadamba and Pallava inscriptions.

In the south, we now begin to see clearly, for instance, in the inscriptions of the Kadambas and early Cālukyas, the strong preference for rounded forms and wavy lines which is to characterize most of the southern scripts of subsequent centuries up to modern times.[111] In some inscriptions from the earlier part of this period we find peculiar aberrant forms, apparently cursive modifications, of certain letters such as *ta*, *na*, *ma*, and *sa* in the Mayidavōlu (SI I.457–61) and other early Pallava copper plates. But in general the southern scripts of this and subsequent periods tended to be more conservative as regards the basic shapes of the characters, which underwent less radical reformation than in the north.

2.2.5.4 The development of the regional scripts in the early medieval period (ca. seventh–tenth centuries A.D.*)*

Around the late sixth century, the so-called Gupta script of northern India evolved into a distinct new script for which the preferred name is Siddhamātṛkā,[112] which was to have a profound effect on the subsequent development of the northern scripts. Early specimens of this script include the Bodh-Gayā inscription of Mahānāman (A.D. 588/89; CII 3, 274–8) and the Lakkhā Maṇḍal *praśasti* (Appendix, no. 8). It continued to be used into the tenth century, undergoing a gradual transformation into Devanāgarī during the latter part of this period. Siddhamātṛkā was used as an epigraphic script not only in northern and eastern India but also in the west, where it replaced the southern-style scripts which until then had predominated there, and occasionally in the Deccan and even in the far south, for example, in the Paṭṭadakal biscript inscription (EI 3, 1–7; see 2.5.4). In this respect it prefigured the role of its daughter script, Devanāgarī, as a quasi-national script which was sometimes preferred to the local scripts for writing Sanskrit.

The Siddhamātṛkā script is principally characterized by a strongly angular aspect, with a sharp angle (whence the term "acute-angled script") at the lower right corner of each letter, reflecting the influence of pen-and-ink writing on the epigraphic script; by

110. So according to Sircar in IIEP 113; according to C. Sivaramamurti (IESIS 202) it remained in use into the eighth or ninth centuries.

111. This characteristic of the southern scripts is usually explained as a result of the exigencies of writing with a stylus on palm leaves. This explanation has, however, been challenged in IC II.680–1, where it is attributed to the influence of calligraphic tendencies.

112. The script has also been referred to by several other names, such as "acute-angled," "early Nāgarī," "Kuṭila," or "Vikaṭa." (The latter two result from apparent misinterpretations of descriptive terms found in various inscriptions; see Bühler, EI 1, 1892, 75–6; Fleet, CII 3, 201; and Sircar, EI 36, 1965–66, 50). The name Siddhamātṛkā is reported by Al-Bīrūnī, and appears to be corroborated by the term "Siddham" which is applied to it by Buddhist tradition in East Asia. This is thus one of the few cases wherein we know the traditional name for one of the premodern scripts (cf. 2.2.2).

the extension of the head mark into wedgelike or triangular forms (whence it is sometimes referred to as "nail-headed"); and by a strong tendency toward calligraphic elaboration, especially in the treatment of the vowel diacritics and subscript consonants (see 2.5.3.1). Some of the vowel signs are highly developed; in particular, the curves of diacritic *i* and *ī* are extended downward to the point that they are equal to or even greater in height than the consonant character to which they are attached, prefiguring the development of vertical lines as vowel markers in Devanāgarī. The shapes of certain letters underwent major alterations, particularly in the later stages of the script wherein the bipartite *ya* (य) and looped *ka* (क), which would become characteristic of Devanāgarī and other northern scripts, began to make their appearance.

In the far northwest, the Proto-Śāradā script first emerged around the beginning of the seventh century. This isolated variety is the ancestor of the later Śāradā and other scripts of the northwestern subgroup (see 2.2.5.5).

In the upper part of southern India, what may now be called the Telugu-Kannada script continued its separate development. Changes in the characters were largely determined by a strong tendency toward rounded and enclosed forms; thus క *ka* and ర *ra* have fully enclosed shapes, and the left member of య *ya* grew into an ovoid. The base of several letters such as *pa, da,* and *tha* (థ) developed a pronounced notch, which was to become characteristic of the later forms of the script.

In the far south, three scripts, namely, Grantha, Tamil, and Vaṭṭeṛuttu, made their appearance in the early medieval period; of these, the first was used for writing Sanskrit, the other two for Tamil. These scripts constitute a distinct subgroup, and while there is no question that all three are Brāhmī-derived, the precise details of their evolution are still somewhat unclear and controversial, due mainly to the paucity of inscriptional materials in the centuries immediately preceding their appearance. Although Bühler (BIP 75) thought that the Tamil script was derived from a northern alphabet, it is nowadays recognized that it, along with Grantha and Vaṭṭeṛuttu, developed from earlier southern scripts (cf. IIEP 124 and IESIS 222). Grantha and Tamil in their earlier stages resembled the forerunner of the Telugu-Kannada script, and are presumably derived from it. Vaṭṭeṛuttu, which Bühler (BIP 51–6) thought to be a cursive variety of Tamil, is nowadays generally considered to be a separately developed script; some scholars[113] have recently pointed out apparent affinities with the later stages of the Tamil Brāhmī script (2.2.5.1) and suggest that Vaṭṭeṛuttu is actually the descendant of it.

2.2.5.5 Developments in the later medieval period: Origins of the modern Indic scripts (*ca.* A.D. *1000 onward*)

In northern India, the late forms of Siddhamātṛkā gradually shaded into early versions of the modern northern scripts, the most important of which is the Nāgarī or Devanāgarī script.[114] Bühler (BIP 51) cited examples of inscriptions in Nāgarī, or showing Nāgarī characteristics, as early as the eighth or even seventh centuries, but V. S. Sukthankar[115] argued that there are actually no authentic specimens of this script

113. Mahalingam, ESIP 299–307; K. G. Krishnan, EI 40, 1973–74, 91–2.

114. On these terms, see IC II.678.

115. "Palaeographic Notes," in *Commemorative Essays Presented to Sir Ramkrishna Gopal Bhandarkar* (Poona: Bhandarkar Oriental Research Institute, 1917; reprint ed. as *R. G. Bhandarkar Commemoration Volume* [Delhi: Bharatiya Publishing House, 1977]), 309–22.

earlier than two Śilāhāra inscriptions from Kāṇheri dated A.D. 851 and 877/78 (CII 6, 3–8). By the beginning of the eleventh century, Devanāgarī has supplanted Siddhamātṛkā for epigraphic and literary purposes and has essentially attained its modern form, characterized by the horizontal top line across the entire character, rectangular corners and generally square frame, and fully extended vowel diacritics. The individual characters have by now undergone extensive, sometimes radical remodeling, as in the case of *ja*, *tha*, and *ha*. Thus, although numerous subvarieties of (Deva-) nāgarī are known from both epigraphic and literary sources from different times and regions, by about A.D. 1000 it can be said to have essentially achieved its standard form. As such, it became the closest thing to a national script of India for writing Sanskrit; although the regional scripts continued to be widely used for this purpose in medieval, and to a considerable extent still in modern, times, Nāgarī was not rarely used for Sanskrit inscriptions outside of northern India, including the Deccan and the far south (the so-called Nandi-nāgarī variety; for examples see IESIS 184–93).[116]

In the northeast, the local derivative of Siddhamātṛkā was the script known as Proto-Bengali or Gauḍī, which was current from the tenth to the fourteenth centuries.[117] This, in turn, gave rise to the modern eastern scripts, namely, Bengali-Assamese, Oriya,[118] and Maithili, which became clearly differentiated around the fourteenth and fifteenth centuries.

In the far northwest, Proto-Śāradā developed into the Śāradā script of Kashmir and neighboring hill regions, which was important both as an epigraphic and literary script in medieval times and as the forerunner of the Punjabi (Gurmukhī) and other scripts of the western Himalayas and adjoining areas.

In upper southern India, the Telugu-Kannada script began to approach the modern forms of Kannada and Telugu in the fourteenth and fifteenth centuries. These two scripts are only minimally differentiated, the main contrast being the shape of the head mark, which takes a form like a check mark in Telugu and a horizontal line with a hook at the upper right in Kannada.

In the far south, the Tamil and Grantha scripts continued to develop and approximated their modern forms by about the fourteenth and fifteenth centuries, as seen, for example, in the inscriptions of the Vijayanagara kings. At about the same period, the Malayalam script developed out of Grantha.

2.2.5.6 *Extra-Indian derivatives of Brāhmī*

In ancient times, Brāhmī and its derivatives were in use over a vast area of the Indian-influenced regions of Asia, and thus came to be the parent of several important scripts of these regions. The Tibetan script is evidently derived from a form of Siddhamātṛkā of about the seventh century, adapted to the phonetic structure of the Tibetan language. According to some authorities,[119] the Indian prototype came into Tibet through a central Asian intermediary.

116. Various other local scripts of northern and western India, such as Moḍi and Kāyethī, developed out of Nāgarī; of these, only the Gujarati script has attained any importance as an epigraphic script (see 3.4.3), the others being used mainly for ephemeral documents in the local languages.

117. See, for example, the Nālandā inscription of Vipulaśrīmitra, Appendix, no. 12.

118. The Oriya script actually appears to have had a composite origin, with secondary influences from the southern scripts and Nāgarī (IC II.680).

119. E.g., A. H. Francke, EI 11, 1911–12, 269.

The Sinhalese script is thought to be essentially a local development from an early form of Brāhmī, which is well attested in the early cave inscriptions of Sri Lanka (3.1.4.2.2 and 4.3.7.1). But the evolution of the Sinhalese script over the centuries has been strongly influenced by other Indian models, especially Grantha (see DIP 215–25, esp. 216).

In Southeast Asia, Indian scripts came into wide use from the early centuries of the Christian era on (4.3.7.5–4.3.7.11). Although northern scripts were occasionally found there, the predominant form was from the beginning a script which, according to most authorities, is derived from the southern script used by the early Pallava kings, often referred to as Pallava Grantha. Others, however (e.g., Sircar, IIEP 132–3), have noted paleographic similarities in the early Southeast Asian inscriptions to scripts of the western coastal region of India. In view of the close relationship between the early southern and western scripts, it is difficult to reach a definite conclusion as to the exact geographical origin of the early Southeast Asian form of Brāhmī (cf. DIP 232–3), but the predominant influence does seem to have been from the south.

Whatever may have been the precise origin of the Southeast Asian form of Brāhmī, it rapidly developed local characteristics of its own, which may be broadly characterized as a tendency toward curved and wavy lines (somewhat like those of the Telugu-Kannada script), calligraphic elaboration in the form of extended curves and curls, and a precise and artistic ductus.[120] Over the centuries this script gradually developed into local varieties, used both for Sanskrit and for the indigenous languages, and these in turn eventually evolved, through various processes of differentiation and phonetic adaptation, into the later and modern scripts used for Thai, Lao, Cambodian, and Burmese.[121]

2.3 The Kharoṣṭhī Script

S. Konow, *Kharoshṭhī Inscriptions . . .* (CII 2.1); A. M. Boyer, E. J. Rapson, and E. Senart, *Kharoṣṭhī Inscriptions Discovered by Sir Aurel Stein . . .* [KI]; C. C. Das Gupta, *The Development of the Kharoṣṭhī Script* [DKS]; S. J. Mangalam, *Kharoṣṭhī Script*; J. Brough, *The Gāndhārī Dharmapada* [GD]; G. Bühler, "The Origin of the Kharoṣṭhī Alphabet" [OKA]; SAI, 84–105.

2.3.1 Geographical range

The presumptive homeland and principal area of the use of Kharoṣṭhī script (see table 2.5) was the territory along and around the Indus, Swat, and Kabul River Valleys of

120. See, for example, the Văt Ph'u inscription, Appendix, no. 9.

121. On the origin and development of Cambodian and other Southeast Asian scripts, see the recent studies of J. G. de Casparis, "Palaeography as an Auxiliary Discipline in Research on Early South East Asia," in R. B. Smith and W. Watson, eds., *Early South East Asia: Essays in Archaeology, History and Historical Geography* (New York: Oxford University Press, 1979), 380–94, and H. B. Sarkar, "The Introduction of the Indian Art of Writing to Southeast Asia," chapter 7 of his *Cultural Relations Between India and Southeast Asian Countries* (New Delhi: Indian Council for Cultural Relations/Motilal Banarsidass, 1985), 168–79.

TABLE 2.5. Kharoṣṭhī Script

VOWELS

Full or initial forms

ǎ	ī	ǔ	e	o	aṃ

Medial (postconsonantal) forms

kǎ	kī	kǔ	ke	ko	kaṃ

CONSONANTS

	Unvoiced unaspirated	Voiced aspirated	Voiced unaspirated	Voiced aspirated	Nasal	Semi-vowel	Sibilant
Guttural	ka	kha	ga	gha			ha
Palatal	ca	cha	ja	jha	ña	ya	śa
Retroflex	ṭa	ṭha	ḍa	ḍha	ṇa	ra	ṣa
Dental	ta	tha	da	dha	na	la	sa
Labial	pa	pha	ba	bha	ma	va	

Conjunct consonants (representative examples)

kṣa	tra	tva	pra
rva	sta	spa	sya

Note: These are normalized forms based on inscriptions of ca. first century A.D.

the modern North-West Frontier Province of Pakistan; that is, the ancient Gandhāra and adjoining regions, with whose MIA language, nowadays usually called "Gāndhārī" (see 3.1.4.2.1), the script is almost invariably associated (see map 1). In Konow's words, "The Kharoshṭhī area proper may be defined as extending from about 69° to 73° 30' E. and from the Hindu Kush to about 33° N., and there can be little doubt that its place of origin was Gandhāra, perhaps more especially Taxila" (CII 2.1, xiv).[122]

But although Konow's general comments about the Kharoṣṭhī area "proper" still hold true, numerous discoveries since his time have provided many examples of inscriptions and other documents in Kharoṣṭhī script ranging over a much broader area.[123] To the far west and northwest, we can now add to the handful of inscriptions known to Konow several more specimens (for details see 4.3.7.3) from sites along the Kabul River in Afghanistan as far west as Wardak or Khawat,[124] some thirty miles west of Kabul. Recent archaeological excavations have also yielded numerous Kharoṣṭhī inscriptions from north of the Hindu Kush, in ancient Bactria, both in sites in northern Afghanistan such as Qunduz and in several places in the former Soviet republics of Uzbekistan and Tajikistan (see 4.3.7.3 and 4.3.7.4).

In the far north, graffiti in Kharoṣṭhī have recently been found in large numbers at various sites around Chilas and other places along the upper course of the Indus River (see 4.3.3.1). These new discoveries provide a connecting link between the central Kharoṣṭhī area and the previously isolated Kharoṣṭhī inscription from Khalatse[125] along the Indus in Ladakh.

To the south and southwest, sporadic examples of Kharoṣṭhī inscriptions were known to Konow (there are no major subsequent discoveries in this area) along the lower Indus as far as Mohenjo-Daro, and in Baluchistan;[126] and to the southeast, in Kāngrā[127] and in the region around Delhi and Mathurā.[128] Occasional stray finds of Kharoṣṭhī letters farther to the east and south are not indicative of significant use of the script in those regions. Thus a plaque with a Kharoṣṭhī inscription found at Kumrahār (Patna; CII 2.1, 177–8) is most likely an import from the northwest (CII 2.1, xiv), and the apparent occurrence of a few Kharoṣṭhī letters on the bases of pillars from Bhārhut (Satna Dist., MP) as reported by Cunningham[129] is of uncertain significance. Still farther afield, the well-known occurrence of the single word *lipikareṇa* in Kharoṣṭhī in three Aśokan inscriptions from Karnataka (see 4.3.1.1 n. 67) is evidently only a scribe's flourish.[130]

122. See also Konow's map of the findspots of Kharoṣṭhī inscriptions (CII 2.1, xiv), and the maps in G. Fussman, "Gāndhārī écrite, Gāndhārī parlée" (for reference see the bibliography), 434–5.

123. For a survey of these discoveries, see Fussman, "Gāndhārī écrite, Gāndhārī parlée," 444–51.

124. I.e., the Wardak vase inscription, CII 2.1, 165–70.

125. CII 2.1, 79–81.

126. Tor Ḍherai, CII 2.1, 173–6.

127. Both of the Kāngrā inscriptions, from Pāṭhyār (CII 2.1, 178) and Kanhiāra (ibid., 178–9), are biscripts, with the text given (with some variation) in both Kharoṣṭhī and Brāhmī.

128. Karnāl, CII 2.1, 179; Rāwal, ibid., 161–2; Mathurā, ibid., 30–49.

129. *The Stûpa of Bharhut*, 8 and pl. VIII.

130. Cf. Konow, CII 2.1, xiv. Reports by B. N. Mukherjee (e.g., *Quarterly Review of Historical Studies* 29.2, 1989–90, 6–14) of inscriptions in Kharoṣṭhī or a mixed Kharoṣṭhī-Brāhmī script from West Bengal and even farther to the east are of questionable validity; see SAI 91–2 for evaluation and further references.

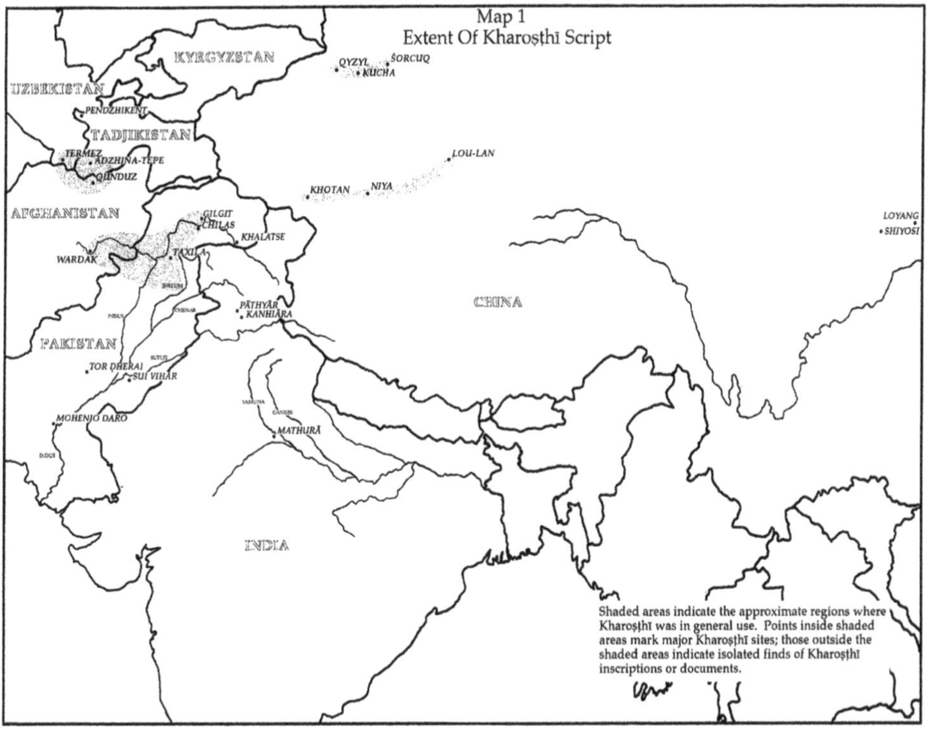

MAP 1
Extent of Kharoṣṭhī script

In the form of legends on the coins of the Indo-Greek and Scythian kings, Kharoṣṭhī script was also in use over a wide area of northern India and adjoining regions, including the western coastal region. Noteworthy in the latter region are the coins of the early Western Kṣatrapas Nahapāna and Caṣṭana, whose coins had legends in three scripts—Greek, Brāhmī, and Kharoṣṭhī.

Finally, in and around the third century A.D. Kharoṣṭhī was a major script for epigraphic and literary purposes in central Asia, as attested especially by the abundant finds of official documents of the Shan-shan (Kroraina) kingdom on the southern rim of the Tarim Basin written on leather and wood (see 4.3.7.12) as well as of other inscriptions, and by the birch-bark manuscript of the *Dharmapada* in Kharoṣṭhī script from the region of Khotan (Brough, GD). Some still unpublished Kharoṣṭhī documents, apparently of later date, have also been found at sites on the north of the Tarim Basin.[131] A few Kharoṣṭhī inscriptions have even been found in China proper, for instance, at Lo-yang (see 4.3.7.12).

Thus, while the Kharoṣṭhī script developed and remained concentrated in the Gāndhāra region, it also spread over a wide area within and far beyond the immediately adjoining portions of modern Pakistan and Afghanistan. The spread of Kharoṣṭhī was no doubt promoted by its use by the Indo-Scythian rulers, and especially by the

131. See n. 138.

Kuṣāṇa kings, who seem to have been responsible for its introduction into the north Indian heartland on the one hand and Bactria on the other. The expansion of Kharoṣṭhī was also intimately connected with the spread of Buddhism under the patronage of the aforementioned rulers, as is indicated by the content of the inscriptions from outlying regions such as Bactria and China; these inscriptions, mostly dedicatory and memorial in content, are often hardly distinguishable in form from similar inscriptions from India, and presumably reflect the presence of Gāndhārī-speaking Indian monks in the Buddhist monasteries of these places.

2.3.2 Chronological range

The Kharoṣṭhī script first appears in inscriptions in the Shāhbāzgaṛhi and Mānsehrā rock edicts of Aśoka, datable to the middle of the third century B.C. In these early records the script appears as a more or less fully developed system, which may be taken to indicate a significant prehistory. But it is difficult to estimate how long such a presumed developmental period might have taken, though it is likely on historical and paleographic grounds (see 2.3.6) that Kharoṣṭhī originated sometime during the Achaemenian era.[132] Bühler (OKA 50 = OIBA 98) was inclined on paleographic grounds to date the origin of Kharoṣṭhī to the earlier phase of this period, that is, around the beginning of the fifth century B.C., but in view of uncertainties about the details of his proposed Aramaic derivation (see 2.3.6), Bühler's early dating can be accepted only provisionally at best. On the other hand, late dates such as ca. 330 B.C. proposed by Halévy[133] or after 325 B.C. suggested by Falk[134] are problematic, especially if, as seems most likely, the *lipi* referred to by Pāṇini is Kharoṣṭhī (2.1.2). In short, there is no clear evidence to allow us to specify the date of the origin of Kharoṣṭhī with any more precision than sometime in the fourth, or possibly the fifth, century B.C.

Kharoṣṭhī continued to be the principal script of the northwest in the following centuries, flourishing during the so-called foreign period of the reigns of the Indo-Greek, Indo-Scythian, Indo-Parthian, and Kuṣāṇa kings from the first century B.C. to the second century A.D. But the script appears to have fallen out of general use in South Asia itself by sometime in the third century A.D. or shortly thereafter. The latest datable inscription in Kharoṣṭhī is probably Skārah Ḍherī (CII 2.1, 124–7), apparently dated in the year 399 of an unspecified era, usually presumed to be the "Old Śaka" era, which would put the date of the inscription around the middle of the third century A.D.[135] Two other Kharoṣṭhī inscriptions from Jamālgaṛhī and Hashtnagar (CII 2.1, 110–3 and 117–9) are dated in the years 359 and 384, presumably of the same era, confirming that the script was still in use around the period in question.

132. E. J. Rapson ("Counter-marks on early Persian and Indian Coins," JRAS 1895, 865–77) thought that some silver *sigloi* of the Achaemenian kings of Iran, dating from the fifth and fourth centuries B.C., bore countermarks consisting of *akṣaras* in Kharoṣṭhī (and Brāhmī; cf. 2.1.2 n. 20) scripts. However, Rapson's identification of these countermarks as syllables of the Indian alphabets was called into question by G. F. Hill ("Notes on the Imperial Persian Coinage," *Journal of Hellenic Studies* 39, 1919, 116–29) and is no longer generally accepted, so that they cannot be taken as specimens of pre-Mauryan Kharoṣṭhī.

133. JA, ser. 8, vol. 6, 1885, 267; *Revue Sémitique* 3, 1895, 378–80. (For full references see 2.3.6.)

134. SAI 104.

135. See section 5.5.1.2. Konow, following W. E. van Wijk, places the epoch of the era in question in 84 B.C., so that the date of the inscription would correspond to A.D. 315.

A series of Kharoṣṭhī image inscriptions from Jauliāñ (CII 2.1, 92–7) were attributed by John Marshall[136] on archaeological grounds to a date as late as the second half of the fifth century A.D., and taken as evidence that "Kharoshṭhī was still the ordinary script of the townspeople of Taxila" at this period. But Konow suspected that these inscriptions may have been copies of older ones, and thus do not constitute evidence that Kharoṣṭhī was still in active use at this late date. It is thus safest to conclude that Kharoṣṭhī probably fell out of general use in South Asia in or around the third century A.D., but it may have been used occasionally for another century or more.

This conclusion is supported by the material from central Asia, where the Kharoṣṭhī documents from Niya and other sites on the southern rim of the Tarim Basin (4.3.7.12) are also approximately datable to the third and early fourth centuries, mainly on the grounds of their co-occurrence with a Chinese document dated A.D. 269.[137] It is possible, however, that Kharoṣṭhī continued to be used in the cities of the northern rim of the Tarim Basin well after this time; documents in this script were reported to have been found there together with others in the Kuchean language datable to the seventh century.[138] But since these documents are still unpublished their significance remains uncertain, and there is still no firm evidence that Kharoṣṭhī survived much longer than the third century.

The decline of Kharoṣṭhī around the third century A.D. can presumably be attributed to historical developments of this time. With the decline and fall of the Kuṣāṇa empire, the center of political power in South Asia began to shift from the northwest toward northern and northeastern India. This development presumably reduced the importance of Kharoṣṭhī as the regional script of the former area, with the eventual result that it was supplanted entirely by the pan-Indian Brāhmī.

2.3.3 *Uses of Kharoṣṭhī*

In South Asia, the Kharoṣṭhī script is preserved principally in inscriptions, mostly on stone but also on metal and other materials, numbering in the hundreds. The vast majority of these are Buddhist records, mostly concerning pious donations and foundations. Kharoṣṭhī was also extensively used in the coin legends of the Indo-Greeks, Indo-Scythians, and other foreign rulers of India, as well as of some indigenous polities such as the so-called tribal republics of the Audumbaras, Kuṇindas, and Rājanyas. Kharoṣṭhī was rarely used by itself on coins; most specimens are biscriptual (or even triscriptual), in combination with legends in Greek and/or Brāhmī (2.3.1).

Kharoṣṭhī is also well attested, in relics from central Asia, in nonmonumental functions. In the Niya documents (2.3.1) it functions as an administrative script, while the manuscript of the *Dharmapada* attests to its literary usage.[139] Moreover, the fact

136. *Excavations at Taxila: The Stupas and Monasteries at Jauliāñ* (MASI 7, 1921), 10.

137. See John Brough, "Comments on Third-Century Shan-shan and the History of Buddhism," BSOAS 28, 1965, 582–612 (esp. 604).

138. IC II.672; H. W. Bailey in D. Winton Thomas, ed., *Essays and Studies Presented to Stanley Arthur Cook* (London: Taylor's Foreign Press, 1950), 121.

139. This latter function is also reflected in occasional quotations from canonical texts in inscriptions (see 7.3.2.2), and also by the use of Kharoṣṭhī for writing Sanskrit in a few of the central Asian documents (e.g., KI no. 511).

that some Chinese Buddhist texts reflect originals in the Gāndhārī language (see 3.1.4.2.1 n. 23), and hence, presumably, in Kharoṣṭhī script, confirms that Kharoṣṭhī was in its day a major vehicle of culture in the Buddhist circles of northwestern India. Thus the judgments of earlier scholars such as Bühler, which were based mainly on the somewhat misleading evidence of the bilingual coin legends and the then fairly sparse repertoire of inscriptions and other Kharoṣṭhī records, to the effect that "Kharoṣṭhī held always . . . only a secondary position by the side of the Brāhma alphabet even in Northwestern India"[140] are no longer valid in light of subsequent discoveries which have vastly enhanced our understanding of the important historical and cultural role of this script.

2.3.4 Paleographic features of Kharoṣṭhī

Unlike Brāhmī and the many scripts derived from it, Kharoṣṭhī, alone among Indic scripts,[141] is written from right to left. Unlike the highly symmetrical, "monumental" early Brāhmī script, Kharoṣṭhī has a cursive ductus which would seem to reflect an origin in a "clerk's" script, written with pen and ink.[142] The Kharoṣṭhī script also contrasts with Brāhmī in that it is top-oriented; that is, the distinctive features of each character tend to be at the top instead of at the bottom as in Brāhmī.

As noted earlier (2.1.3), Kharoṣṭhī employs essentially the same diacritically modified consonantal syllabic system of Brāhmī and its derivatives, despite some important differences in detail. The script comprises a basic set of consonantal symbols with inherent *a*, "full" vowel signs used for word initial and non-postconsonantal vowels, and diacritic signs attached to the consonants to indicate postconsonantal vowels. The main difference in graphic principle between Brāhmī and Kharoṣṭhī is that the latter for the most part[143] does not differentiate long and short vowels. That is to say, the vowel signs, both full and diacritic, designate vowel quality but not quantity. For example, the same sign represents either *i* or *ī*, and the inherent postconsonantal vowel can be read as either *a* or *ā* (to be understood by context); thus 𐨐 = *ka* or *kā*; 𐨐𐨁 = *ki* or *kī*, and so on. The full or initial vowel signs further differ from those of Brāhmī in that they are all constructed from the basic vowel sign for *a* to which are affixed the postconsonantal vowel diacritics to form initial *i*, *u*, and so on; thus 𐨀 = initial *a*/*ā*, while 𐨀𐨁 = initial *i*/*ī*.

As in Brāhmī, the inherent vowel system necessitates the formation of consonantal conjuncts or ligatures, though the methods and details of their formation in Kharoṣṭhī are somewhat different and sometimes problematic. The basic principle is the same as that of Brāhmī, with the two or more consonants of a phonetic cluster joined graphically from top to bottom, with or without abbreviation of one of them.

140. OKA 44 = OIBA 92; cf. also OIBA 51.

141. Except for occasional examples of early Brāhmī inscriptions written from right to left; see 2.2.3.2.4.

142. Cf. Bühler, OKA 49 = OIBA 97: "The Kharoṣṭhī alphabet is not a Pandit's, but a clerk's, alphabet."

143. For the development in the later period of a system for differentiating vowel quantity in Kharoṣṭhī, see section 2.3.8.

Some of the resulting conjuncts, for example, 𐨮𐨿𐨐 *ṣka* < 𐨮 *ṣa* + 𐨐 *ka*, are self-evident, but many others involve alterations of the constituent parts to the point that they may become unrecognizable. As in later forms of Brāhmī and its derivatives (see 2.2.5.2), *ra* (which is especially common in Kharoṣṭhī texts, since the Gāndhārī language tends to retain it in consonantal groups; see 3.1.2.3 and 3.1.4.2.1) develops special forms for both pre- and postconsonantal position: for example, 𐨪 *ra* + 𐨬 *va* > 𐨪𐨿𐨬 *rva*; 𐨬𐨿𐨪 = *vra*. Similarly (and again as in Brāhmī),[144] postconsonantal *ya* has a special form, as in 𐨯𐨿𐨩 *sya*.

Other consonantal combinations, particularly those involving stops and sibilants, are also prone to take special and often obscure forms in Kharoṣṭhī, for instance, 𐨯 *sa* + 𐨟 *ta* > 𐨯𐨿𐨟 *sta*. Some special consonantal signs are problematic in that both their graphic constituents and their phonetic value are uncertain, notably the common character 𐨲, which regularly corresponds to Sanskrit *kṣa*[145] but which can hardly be derived from a graphic combination of 𐨐 *ka* and 𐨮 *ṣa;* Dani (DIP 259) considers it a reduction of 𐨖 *cha,* while Rapson (KI III.320 n. 3) suggests a connection with 𐨮 *ṣa.* Thus it is not at all certain that Kharoṣṭhī characters of this type are really conjuncts in the standard sense of the term; they may have arisen from modifications of single consonants, or may have been created ad hoc to represent phonemes peculiar to the Gāndhārī language.

Such developments are characteristic of Kharoṣṭhī, which in general was more flexible and adaptable to linguistic change than Brāhmī, for instance, in creating diacritically or otherwise modified characters to indicate new sounds such as fricativized intervocalic consonants which developed in the Gāndhārī language (see 3.1.4.2.1). The virtual absence of such modified characters in Brāhmī and its premodern Indian derivatives does not indicate that the other MIA languages did not develop such new sounds, but rather that in the Sanskrit-dominated cultural milieu in which these scripts functioned the phonetic repertoire of Sanskrit and its immediate MIA derivatives was taken as definitive and unalterable. In the Kharoṣṭhī/Gāndhārī sphere, however, the influence of Sanskrit, while by no means totally absent,[146] was far less pervasive, so that the script was relatively free to grow and change in accordance with phonetic changes in Gāndhārī.

On the whole, Kharoṣṭhī orthography tends to be informal, approximative, and often inconsistent. Geminate consonants, for instance, are normally indicated by the single consonant, and unaspirate-aspirate clusters by the simple aspirate (e.g., *budha* for *buddha*).[147]

144. These similarities between the two scripts need not result from a direct influence of one on the other, but rather are presumably independent parallel developments conditioned by the statistical frequency in Gāndhārī and Sanskrit of conjuncts with semivowels, which naturally led to the creation of cursive ligatures.

145. On the phonetic value of this character, which is variously transliterated as *cha* (incorrectly), *ch'a*, or *kṣa*, see section 3.1.2.3.

146. A clear example of Sanskritization in Kharoṣṭhī/Gāndhārī is the Sui Vihār copper plate inscription (CII 2.1, 138–41), whose orthography is strongly Sanskritized, e.g., using *-sya* (rather than *-sa*) for the genitive singular ending.

147. These features are, however, not untypical of epigraphic Prakrits generally, especially in the earlier period; see 3.1.1.

2.3.5 The name of the script

The script which is nowadays generally known as Kharoṣṭhī (or Kharoṣṭī, Kharoṣṭrī, etc.) was until the end of the nineteenth century referred to by various names such as "Bactrian," "Indo-Bactrian," "Kabulian," "Bactro-Pali," "Ariano-Pali," and so on.[148] It was T[errien] de Lacouperie who proposed in 1886–87[149] that the name Kharoṣṭhī, the second in the list of sixty-four scripts in the *Lalitavistara* (2.1.1), should correspond to the northwestern script, on the grounds that the corresponding script in the *Fa yüan chu lin* is described as written from right to left. De Lacouperie's suggestion was adopted by Bühler and others, and has won nearly universal acceptance.[150]

The correct form of this name and its meaning, however, are still uncertain. Various spellings appear in different manuscripts of the various Buddhist and Jaina script lists: *kharoṣṭī*, *khaloṣṭī*, and *karottī* in the *Lalitavistara*; *kharostī* and *kharāstrī* in the *Mahāvastu*; and *kharoṭṭhī* and *kharoṭṭhiyā* in the Ardha-māgadhī dialect of the Jaina texts. In the *Fa yüan chu lin* the name of the script is given as *K'(i)a-lu-she-t'o* (in O. Franke's transliteration), which according to Franke[151] would correspond to Sanskrit *kharoṣṭha*. These testimonia are not sufficient to definitively reconstruct the original form of the name, and the now conventional spelling *kharoṣṭhī*, as adopted by Bühler in his authoritative works on paleography (BIP) and on the origin of the script (OKA), is by no means certain; some modern scholars prefer the forms *kharoṣṭī* or *kharostrī*.[152] Since the word was very likely not originally Sanskrit or even Indic, variations in spelling may have arisen partly from different Sanskritizations of the original name of the script.

As for the etymology of the name, in 1902 Sylvain Lévi[153] first proposed that the name was actually a geographical term, reconstructed as **kharoṣṭra* from the Chinese *K'ia-lu-shu-ta-le*, supposedly a toponym for Kashgar. R. Pischel,[154] however, doubted that a remote central Asian region could have given its name to the Indian script, and preferred the traditional attribution in the *Fa yüan chu lin* of the script (as first pointed out by de Lacouperie) to a sage *K'(i)a-lu-she-t'o*, which name, according to the accompanying gloss, means 'ass-lip', suggesting an Indic original *kharoṣṭha*. Lévi responded in 1904[155] with an expanded and modified statement of his views in which he reidentified the "Kharoṣṭra" country not specifically with Kashgar but rather

148. Cf. 6.2.2 n. 59. Alexander Cunningham (*Coins of Ancient India from the Earliest Times . . .* [London: B. Quaritch, 1891], 31) proposed the more appropriate term "Gandharian," but this suggestion did not win much acceptance (unlike H. W. Bailey's more successful suggestion many decades later of "Gāndhārī" for the language with which the script was linked; see 3.1.4.2.1).

149. *Babylonian and Oriental Record* 1, 59–60 (cf. 2.2.2 n. 39).

150. IC (II.670–2) still holds to the term "araméo-indien" for the earlier forms of the script in India on the grounds that the term "Kharoṣṭhī" properly applies to the central Asian form of the script; but this is probably not correct.

151. IA 34, 1905, 21 (see n. 154 for full reference).

152. See, e.g., B. N. Mukherjee, "A Note on the Name Kharoshṭhī," JAS 23, 1981, 13–15.

153. "L'écriture kharoṣṭrī et son berceau," BEFEO 2, 1902, 246–53 (esp. 248) = "The Kharoshtri Writing and Its Cradle," IA 33, 1904, 79–84 (esp. 81).

154. In O. Franke and R. Pischel, "Kaschgar und die Kharoṣṭhī," *Sitzungsberichte der königlich Preussichen Akademie der Wissenschaften zu Berlin* (*Phil.-hist. Klasse*) 1903, 184–96 and 735–45 = "Kashgar and the Kharoshthi," IA 34, 1905, 21–7 and 41–6.

155. "Notes chinoises sur l'Inde IV: Le pays de Kharoṣṭra et l'écriture kharoṣṭrī," BEFEO 4, 1904, 543–79 = "The Kharostra Country and the Kharostri Writing," IA 35, 1906, 1–30.

with the entire intermediate region between China and India, and endorsed the spelling *kharoṣṭrī* on the grounds that it could be connected with the "donkeys and camels" (Sanskrit *kharoṣṭra*) which are characteristic of the region in question.

None of these explanations being particularly convincing, several other suggestions of a non-Indic origin for the name Kharoṣṭ(h)ī have been offered. Albert Ludwig[156] proposed a derivation from an unattested Aramaic **ḥarūttā* predicted on the basis of the root *ḤRŠ* (Hebrew)/ *ḤRT* (Aramaic) 'engrave', and Bühler (OIBA 114 n. 1) seemed willing to accept this as an alternative to the traditional etymology. Others have looked for Iranian or semi-Iranian etymologies, most persuasive among which is Jean Przyluski's suggestion[157] connecting the name with that of *Kharaposta*, given in the *Mahāmāyūrī* as one of the *yakṣa*s of northwestern India and rendered into Chinese as 'hide of donkey' (<*khara* 'donkey' + Iranian *post* 'hide'). *Kharoṣṭha/ Kharoṣṭhī*, and so on, would evidently result from an incorrect Sanskritization of the Prakrit form of the word in question. According to Przyluski, the application of the name to the script can be attributed to the practice (actually attested in some of the central Asian Kharoṣṭhī documents) of writing on the hides of donkeys and other animals.[158] He also suggested a connection of the name Kharaposta with that of king Kharaosta, known from coins and from the Mathurā lion capital inscriptions. This suggestion was taken up by H. Humbach,[159] who proposed that the script was named directly after King Kharaosta, with whom its importation into India proper may have been associated. Humbach's explanation is endorsed by Falk (SAI 90). More recently, H. W. Bailey[160] has proposed several possible Iranian etymologies for *Kharoṣṭhī*, of which the most compelling is **xšaθra-pištra* 'royal writing'.

All in all, the question of the origin and meaning of the name Kharoṣṭhī remains problematic, but it appears that the connections noted by Przyluski et al. with the well-attested proper names Kharaposta and Kharaosta lie at the heart of the matter. In all probability *Kharoṣṭ(h)ī* is a Sanskritization of an original Iranian name whose etymology is uncertain. The connection with *khara* 'donkey' is probably nothing more than folk etymology, and the original term was most likely connected with Old Iranian **xšaθra* 'sovereignty', as noted by Bailey and others,[161] though the second part of the word remains unclear, as does the process by which the name in question became associated with the script.

2.3.6 The origin of Kharoṣṭhī

J. Halévy, "Essai sur l'origine des écritures indiennes," JA, ser. 8, vol. 6, 1885, 243–301; "Un dernier mot sur le kharoṣṭhi," *Revue Sémitique* 3, 1895, 372–89; G. Bühler, OKA; C. C. Das Gupta, DKS, ch. 17, "The Origin of the Script," 280–90; SAI 92–9.

156. "Über den Namen der alten linksläufigen Schrift der Inder," in *Gurupūjākaumudī: Festgabe zum fünfzigjährigen Doctorjubiläum Albrecht Weber* (Leipzig: Otto Harrassowitz, 1896), 68–71.

157. "Le nom de l'écriture kharosthi," JRAS 1930, 43–5 = "The Name of the Kharoṣṭhî Script," IA 60, 1931, 150–1.

158. Compare Skt. *pustaka* 'book' from the same Iranian *post*.

159. Review of DIP, *Orientalistische Literaturzeitung* 63, 1968, 489–91.

160. "Kharoštrī," in *Indo-Scythian Studies Being Khotanese Texts*. Vol.7 (Cambridge: Cambridge University Press, 1985), 46–9; see also JRAS 1978, 4.

161. For example, F. W. Thomas, EI 9, 1907–8, 139.

A connection between Kharoṣṭhī and the Semitic scripts (see table 2.2), particularly Aramaic, has been evident to scholars from an early period. The Semitic connection was first discussed in general terms by Edward Thomas[162] as early as 1858, and the particular connection with Aramaic was noted by Isaac Taylor.[163] The theory was further developed by J. Halévy ("Essai sur l'origine," 247–67), and was finally worked out in what has become the definitive statement by Bühler in OKA in 1895.

It was presumably the right-to-left direction of Kharoṣṭhī that first suggested a Semitic derivation.[164] This impression was reinforced by the generally Semitic appearance of the script, and especially by its obvious resemblance to Aramaic. This presumptive relationship has been successfully worked out in detail by the previously mentioned scholars to the point of virtual certainty. First of all, the historical circumstances of the development of Kharoṣṭhī from Aramaic are easily explained by reference to the Achaemenian conquests in the western borderlands of India; as noted by Bühler, "[T]he territory of the Kharoṣṭhī corresponds very closely with the extent of the portion of India, presumably held by the Persians" (OKA 47 = OIBA 95). Since Aramaic served as the lingua franca of the Persian empire, it is easy to imagine how the Aramaic alphabet could have been adapted to the local Indian language, namely, Gāndhārī, as "the result of the intercourse between the offices of the Satraps and of the native authorities" (OKA 49 = OIBA 97).[165] Moreover, the recent discoveries of Aśokan edicts in Aramaic, including passages with Prakrit words written in Aramaic script and provided with glosses in the Aramaic language (see 4.3.7.3), have confirmed the close connection of Aramaic with Indic languages and scripts in the Achaemenian period and following centuries.

Second, specific relationships between the individual characters of the two scripts have been clearly established. In refining the only partially satisfactory formulations of Taylor[166] and Halévy,[167] Bühler presented in OKA what has become the authoritative formulation of the derivation of Kharoṣṭhī from Aramaic. The derivations of most of the characters are self-evident and beyond reasonable doubt; for instance, Kharoṣṭhī 𐨦 *ba* < Aramaic 𐡁 *bet*, or 𐨣 *na* < 𐡍 *nun*. In several cases certain alterations of the Aramaic prototypes have to be posited, such as inversion,[168] as in Kharoṣṭhī 𐨫 *la* < 𐡋 *lamed*; cursivization and stroke reduction, as in 𐨒 *ga* < 𐡂 *gimel*; and other alterations such as the addition of an extra stroke to disambiguate characters of the new script, as in 𐨐 *ka* < 𐡊 *kaph*, with an extra stroke at the left to disambiguate the derived character from Kharoṣṭhī 𐨟 *ta*. Since most of these alterations follow regular patterns and are subject to logical explanation, they do not constitute a weakness in the proposed derivation. As in the case of the proposed Semitic derivation of Brāhmī (see 2.2.3.2.4), the Kharoṣṭhī characters for aspirate consonants are constructed either as secondary derivatives of the corresponding nonaspirates

162. In his editorial notes to James Prinsep's *Essays on Indian Antiquities*, II.143–70.

163. In *The Alphabet*, II.256–62.

164. But see the comments on direction of writing in section 2.2.3.2.4.

165. In this connection Bühler also referred to the use of the Iranian word *dipi* 'writing' and various derivatives thereof in the Kharoṣṭhī versions of the Aśokan edicts (OKA 46–7 = OIBA 95).

166. *The Alphabet*; in particular, see his chart of "The Iranian Alphabets," II.236.

167. "Essai sur l'origine"; see especially plate I, facing page 252.

168. This is in keeping with the top orientation of the derivative script; see section 2.3.4.

(e.g., *ga* > *gha*),[169] or by adaptation of a phonetically similar Aramaic character (e.g., *kha* < *qoph*). The derivation of the Kharoṣṭhī retroflexes is more problematic; Bühler takes them all as secondary derivatives within Kharoṣṭhī (e.g., *ṭha* < *ta* and *ḍa* < *da*), but the paleographic connections here are far from certain.

Third, as noted earlier (2.1.3), the diacritically modified syllabic system of Kharoṣṭhī can be best explained in historical terms as a refinement of the Semitic consonant-syllabic system.[170] The nondifferentiation of vowel length in Kharoṣṭhī can be seen as an intermediate stage of development between the consonant-syllabic Semitic prototype and the fully vocalized Indic system as found in Brāhmī.

Thus, the three main criteria—historical, paleographic, and systemic—for establishing genetic connections between scripts are satisfied in the derivation of Kharoṣṭhī from Aramaic. The theory has accordingly been accepted by nearly all authorities on the subject, including many of those (e.g., Ojhā, BPLM 31–7) who do not accept a Semitic origin for Brāhmī. R. B. Pandey (PIP 53–8) is virtually alone in completely rejecting a Semitic origin for Kharoṣṭhī in favor of the traditional view (as attested in Chinese sources; see 2.3.5) that "it was invented by an Indian genius whose nickname was *Kharoṣṭha*, as the letters resembled ass-lips" (58). But Pandey's arguments against the Semitic origin are not persuasive and do not present any significant challenge to it. More recently, C. D. Chatterjee[171] and following him V. S. Pathak[172] have expressed doubts about the Aramaic origin of Kharoṣṭhī, but their arguments are equally unconvincing.

This is not to say, however, that the Aramaic derivation as formulated by Bühler et al. is free of problems in all details. Bühler was severely criticized on methodological grounds by Halévy ("Un dernier mot," 380–1), who charged, not without cause, that Bühler used Aramaic forms from widely differing periods and places for his hypothetical prototypes of Kharoṣṭhī characters.[173] And among Bühler's specific formulations, Halévy (op. cit., 383) rejected the derivation of Kharoṣṭhī *śa* from Aramaic *ḥet* as an "idée bizarre"; while this, like many of Halévy's criticisms, seems unduly harsh, it does legitimately point out a weakness in Bühler's formulation. Also problematic on paleographic grounds is Bühler's derivation of *tha* as a secondary form from *ta*. Dani's suggestion (DIP 258–9) to derive Kharoṣṭhī *tha* directly from Aramaic *ṭet* (which, along with *'ain*, is one of the two Aramaic letters for which Bühler found no correspondent in Kharoṣṭhī) seems preferable, though the equation is paleographically uncertain.

Although such problems are not nearly weighty enough to cast serious doubts on the Aramaic derivation as a whole, they do show that the final word has yet to

169. According to Bühler (OKA 61 = OIBA 109), the extra stroke of *gha* and similarly derived aspirates represents a reduced form of the consonant *ha*.

170. According to Halévy ("Essai sur l'origine," 248–9), the Kharoṣṭhī vowel diacritics for *i* and *u* reflect the use of *yod* and *waw* as *matres lectionis* for these vowels in Aramaic, and the adoption of *a* as the inherent vowel in Kharoṣṭhī is due to the absence of any such graph for that vowel in the parent script.

171. "The Aramaic Language and Its Problems in the Early History of Iran and Afghanistan," in Samaresh Bandyopadhyay, ed., *Ācārya-vandanā: D. R. Bhandarkar Birth Centenary Volume* (Calcutta: University of Calcutta, 1984), 205–26 (esp. 210–4).

172. JESI 13, 1986, 7–8.

173. Cf. Halévy's similar criticism of Bühler's Brāhmī derivation, mentioned in section 2.2.3.2.4.

be said on the subject, which, after all, has not been comprehensively examined for nearly a hundred years.[174] The subject needs to be reevaluated in light of new data which was not available in Bühler's time, particularly the Mauryan Aramaic inscriptions.[175]

2.3.7 Connections between Kharoṣṭhī and Brāhmī

Certain common features of the Kharoṣṭhī and Brāhmī scripts, including both the overall similarity in their graphic principles and several specific paleographic features, suggest the possibility of some kind of historical connection between them. For example, Bühler (OKA 62–3 = OIBA 110) and others have noted parallels in the location of the postconsonantal vowel diacritics in the two scripts, with *i*, *e*, and *o* at the top of the consonantal character and *u* at the bottom. Among the formal resemblances between consonantal characters which could indicate some historical relationship, *kha*, *pa*, and *la* are, with due allowance for the normal processes of inversion and reversal, quite similar in the earliest forms of Brāhmī and Kharoṣṭhī; but these similarities could be attributed to a common Aramaic or other Semitic prototype. The apparent resemblance of the Kharoṣṭhī and Brāhmī signs for *bha* (𐨧, 𑀪) is intriguing, but the internal derivation of this letter in both scripts is problematic, so that it is difficult to draw any conclusion from it. Halévy ("Essai sur l'origine," 281–5), as a proponent of a direct derivation of Brāhmī from Kharoṣṭhī (2.2.3.2.2), made much of other apparent resemblances such as Brāhmī and Kharoṣṭhī *ña* (𑀜, 𐨙) and *ḍa* (𑀟, 𐨜), but their significance is doubtful as they appear to be separate secondary developments within the two systems.

Although many of the specific relationships of individual characters remain problematic, it can be generally assumed that the primary direction of influence would have been from Kharoṣṭhī to Brāhmī,[176] since it is now fairly certain (see 2.1.2) that the former is the older of the two scripts. Moreover, if the theory of an invention of Brāhmī under Aśoka, for which persuasive arguments have recently been proposed by von Hinüber and Falk, is correct, the common graphic system of both scripts (2.1.3) must have originally been developed in Kharoṣṭhī and later adapted and refined in Brāhmī.

Thus, while there are enough points of similarity to suggest at least a secondary relationship between Kharoṣṭhī and Brāhmī, the overall differences between the two render a direct linear development connection unlikely (cf. 2.2.3.2.2). The paleographic dissimilarity of the great majority of the basic characters of the two scripts suggests that Kharoṣṭhī and Brāhmī essentially developed separately from their presumptive Semitic prototype(s).

174. Das Gupta (DKS 284–90) criticizes several of Bühler's derivations on paleographic grounds (e.g., *ma* from *mem*, 287), but since he does not propose alternatives, his criticisms do not represent any significant advance.

175. Besides the example of *śa* mentioned earlier, other cases where these new inscriptions may clarify the derivation of Kharoṣṭhī characters include *da* and *ya* (as noted by Das Gupta, DKS 285–6).

176. On apparent influences of Brāhmī on Kharoṣṭhī in later times, see section 2.3.8.

2.3.8 The paleographic development of Kharoṣṭhī

Unlike Brāhmī and its derivatives, Kharoṣṭhī script did not undergo extensive paleographic changes in the course of its historical development. This is no doubt mainly due to the fact that its history (at least as known to us from extant documents) covers only some five centuries and takes place within a relatively limited geographical area, as opposed to Brāhmī, which developed over two millennia throughout India and in many other parts of Asia. Kharoṣṭhī can be treated essentially as one and the same script throughout its history, and, with the exception of the central Asian variety, does not have clearly differentiated local variants. The changes which the individual characters underwent were gradual and for the most part minor, so that it is difficult to establish reliable criteria for the paleographic dating of Kharoṣṭhī documents in anything other than broad terms such as "early," "middle," and "late." Even the central Asian form of the script is not essentially different from the Indian; many of its peculiar characteristics, such as its generally more cursive aspect, are attributable as much to the different physical character of the documents, which were written in pen and ink rather than carved into stone or metal, as to geographical variation.

Among the characters which do show clear chronological development, *sa* is often cited as the most reliable "test letter." In the early forms of Kharoṣṭhī of the Aśokan and Indo-Greek period, the head portion of *sa* is usually closed (𐨯). In the middle period of the Indo-Scythian and Indo-Parthian era, the head is typically open, but the vertical line still has a projection toward the top of the letter (𐨯). Finally, in the later phase of the script during the Kuṣāṇa period, the head is fully open (𐨯). This character, along with a few other test letters such as *ya* and *ca*, can be used to date Kharoṣṭhī documents in a broad fashion. But, as pointed out by Das Gupta (DKS, 102, 146), the three types of *sa* actually overlap considerably throughout the history of the script, so that to use it alone as a criterion for paleographic dating is an uncertain method at best (see 5.4.1).

Several other characters underwent similar developments involving cursivization and stroke reduction or reordering. The original form of 𐨐 *ka*, for example, developed into a secondary one in which the extra stroke at the right is combined with the top stroke (𐨐); this, in turn, led to a late form in which the right-hand portion curves around to the left to meet the vertical (𐨐). In certain cases paleographic changes resulted in the development of ambiguous letters, the most important case being *ya*, whose original angular form (𐨩) developed a horizontal line across the top (𐨩) which often makes it virtually identical with *śa* (𐨭). In some cursive hands, *ta* and *ra*, *ta* and *da*, *va* and initial *a*, and various other pairs of letters are so similar as to cause serious difficulties in interpretation.

The diacritic vowels were also subject to minor changes, notably postconsonantal *u*, which originally was written as a short horizontal line to the left of the foot of the consonant to which it is attached (e.g., 𐨐𐨂 *ku*) but later developed into a loop (𐨐𐨂). Similarly, the original mark for *anusvāra* (e.g., 𐨒𐨎 *gaṃ*), clearly recognizable as a miniature *ma*, later changed into a hook shape (𐨎) which disguises its origin. Certain combinations of consonants and vowel diacritics were subject to special cursive developments leading to ligatures in which the constituent parts are no longer readily apparent; for example, *mu* (with several other varieties) and *de*.

Several modified characters developed in Kharoṣṭhī of the middle and later periods. For instance, *s̱a* frequently appears in alternation with ordinary *sa* ( ), of which it is presumably a modification, perhaps derived from a reduction of the conjunct *sya*.[177] Several consonants, such as *ga*, *ḍa*, and *va*, were often written in intervocalic position with a diacritic mark consisting of a horizontal line added at the lower right, which is usually thought to represent a fricative pronunciation; for example, *g'a*. Such diacritically marked consonants are particularly common in the central Asian documents but also occur in some later Indian inscriptions, notably in the Wardak vase inscription (CII 2.1, 165–70). Another diacritic sign, again most common in central Asia but also found in India, is a horizontal line or dot above the character, which usually indicates an abridged conjunct consonant; thus *ṣ̄a* = *ṣṇa*, *c̄a* = *śca*, and so on.

Various further modifications arose in varieties of Kharoṣṭhī used to write texts or words of non-Gāndhārī origin. Most important, late Kharoṣṭhī records sometimes added a line or curve at the lower right of a consonant character to indicate a long vowel (e.g., = *kā*). A few sporadic and somewhat uncertain examples of this device are noted in inscriptions from India,[178] but it is much more common in the central Asian documents, especially those in Sanskrit (e.g., KI II nos. 511, 523). In the latter we also find signs for syllabic *ṛ*, the *vṛddhi* vowels *ai* and *au* (formed by combining the ordinary diacritics for *e* and *o* with the long vowel sign), vowelless consonants (see KI III.297), *ṅa*, and *visarga* (the last two being perhaps borrowings from Brāhmī). In the central Asian documents, non-Indic names and loan words were represented with the help of new conjuncts such as *pga*, *cma*, and *jhbo*. Many of the diacritically modified characters mentioned previously were also used for this purpose.

2.4 Numbers and Numerical Notation

BIP 76–87; IC II.683, 702–9; IIEP 125–8; BPLM 103–29; S. L. Gokhale, *Indian Numerals*; SAI 168–76.

2.4.1 Numerical notation in Brāhmī and the derived scripts

2.4.1.1 The old additive/multiplicative system

Numerical figures are found in Indic inscriptions from the earliest times, especially in the recording of dates but also in the details of financial or other transactions, the numbering of verses in metrical inscriptions (see 2.5.2.3), and in various other connections. Numbers in all periods have also been commonly expressed in words, either directly or (in later centuries) by means of chronograms and other indirect expressions (see 5.4.2.1.2).

177. See Brough, GD 67–70; see also GD 75–7, for the similar problem of the characters *ṭha* and *ṭ'ha*.

178. See Konow, CII 2.1, cxx, and Salomon, StII 7, 1981, 14.

The original Brāhmī numerical system (see table 2.6), as first found in the Aśokan and other early inscriptions, is essentially additive/multiplicative in principle. It had a full array of separate symbols, not only for the digits from 1 to 9 but also for the decades from 10 to 90, as well as separate signs for 100 and 1,000; the system thus comprised an array of twenty basic signs.[179] The figures for 100 and 1,000 were treated multiplicatively; for example, 400 would be represented as a ligature of 𑁕 4 and 𑁤 100, that is, 𑁤𑁕. But multiples of 2 and 3 were indicated by the addition of one or two horizontal ticks, respectively, at the right of the sign for 100 or 1,000; thus 𑁤- = 200 and 𑁤= = 300.

2.4.1.2 *Origin and history of the old Brāhmī numerical system*

Early specimens of Brāhmī numerals are found in the Aśokan inscriptions (only 4, 6, 50, and 200), in the cave inscriptions of the first century B.C. from Nānāghāṭ (SI I.192–7) and of the first century A.D. from Nāsik (EI 8, 59–96), and in the inscriptions of the Kuṣāṇas. A complete set of the figures is first found in the unique series of dated coins issued by the Western Kṣatrapas in the second to fourth centuries A.D., which provided important clues for the decipherment of the numbers. Besides the limited body of early materials, the analysis of the old numerical system is further complicated by the fact that the symbols were subject from the earliest times to considerable graphic variability, which increased over the centuries and eventually resulted in the notoriously diverse character of the numerical symbols in the different Brāhmī-derived scripts. Fortunately, in many inscriptions, for example at Nāsik, numbers are expressed in both words and numerical characters, and these instances, together with valuable hints furnished by the dates of the Kṣatrapa coins, were instrumental in the decipherment of the Brāhmī numerals.[180]

Although the system itself is nowadays fully understood, the historical origins of the numerical characters remain controversial. Several theories on this question are based on their apparent resemblance to certain letters of Brāhmī and related scripts. The first of these was Prinsep's hypothesis[181] that the number signs are derived from the characters for the initial letter of the Sanskrit word for each number. This theory, though accepted by F. Woepcke,[182] is obviously unsatisfactory. In 1877, Bhagvānlāl Indraji[183] declared that "all of [the numerals] . . . except the first three express letters or groups of letters"; thus the sign for 6 is interpreted as *phra* or *phrā*, 7 is *gra* or *grā*, and so on. In his postscript to Bhagvānlāl's article (47–8; see also BIP 77–81), Bühler accepted the theory, though he admitted that the actual "origin" of these numerals remained obscure, since no rationale could be discerned for the particular phonetic values attributed to the numeral signs.[184]

179. On the notation of fractions in the old system, see Dines Chandra Sircar, "Fractions in an Early Inscription," *Journal of the University of Gauhati* 1, 1950, 133–6.

180. See section 6.2.3 for details.

181. JASB 7, 1838, 352–3 = *Essays on Indian Antiquities* II.77.

182. "Mémoire sur la propagation des chiffres indiens," JA, ser. 6, vol. 1, 1863, 27–79, 234–90, and 442–529 (esp. 70–3).

183. "On the Ancient Nāgarī Numerals," IA 6, 42–8 (quoted 43).

184. As will shortly be shown, Bühler did not feel this theory to be incompatible with his belief in an ultimate Egyptian origin of the Brāhmī numerals, though he did not completely clarify his ideas as to the relationship between the two factors.

TABLE 2.6. Numerical Notation in Brāhmī and Kharoṣṭhī

Value	Brāhmī	Kharoṣṭhī
1	─	/
2	=	// , ⼞
3	≡	/// , ⼞
4	Ϝ	X
5	ʄ	/X
6	4	//X
7	)	///X
8	ʒ	XX
9	3	/XX
10	ⲁ	?·
20	θ	3
30	ʊ	?3
40	ʮ	33
50	ɿ	?33
60	ʃ	333
70	ʑ	?333
80	∞	3333
90	⊕	?3333
100	ᗰ	ʎ/ , ʓ
200	ᗱ	ʎ//
300	ᗱ	ʎ///
1,000	ʔ	ʮ─
2,000	ʔ	(not attested)
4,000	ʔʏ	(not attested)

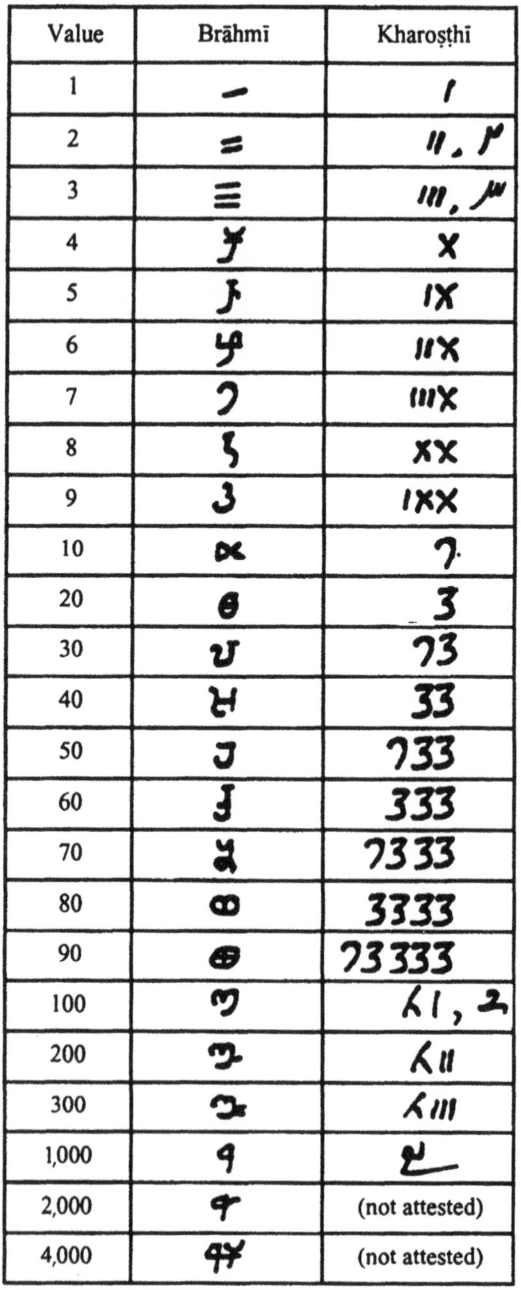

Representative Brāhmī forms are shown, mostly from Western Kṣatrapa coins; in practice, number signs in Brāhmī show much variation. The Kharoṣṭhī forms are from various inscriptions, with alternate forms from central Asian documents.

For this and other reasons[185] the idea that the numerical symbols are actually Brāhmī letters is not widely accepted.[186] While it is true that some of the numerical symbols in Brāhmī and several Brāhmī-derived scripts do bear a striking resemblance to phonetic characters, the correspondences are not regular enough to establish a convincing connection. It is more likely that we are dealing with an originally separate set of signs (whose origin remains to be determined) which tended to be adapted to graphically similar phonetic signs of the script by the scribes of various times and places. The relationship between the phonetic and numerical signs in Brāhmī thus seems to be essentially secondary and superficial.

Other scholars have therefore attempted to explain the Brāhmī numerals as borrowings from other scripts. Alexander Cunningham[187] claims to have been the first to note that the early Brāhmī figures for 5 through 9 resemble the "Ariano-Pali" (i.e., Kharoṣṭhī) letters for the initial syllables of the words for each number (e.g., Brāhmī 𑁖 5 resembles Kharoṣṭhī 𐨤 *pa* for *pañca*, etc.). This superficial resemblance was quite rightly rejected by Edward Thomas already in 1855,[188] as well as by J. Dowson[189] and Bühler (OIBA 52–3 n. 1). It nevertheless reappeared in modified form in E. Clive Bayley's essay "On the Genealogy of Modern Numerals,"[190] in which he assigns to the Brāhmī numerical system an "eclectic character" (346) arising from "a process of mixed borrowing and adaptation" (360) from various sources including Phoenician, "Bactrian" (i.e., Kharoṣṭhī), Egyptian, and possibly cuneiform. Although Bayley's hypothesis itself and the arguments used to support it are rather far-fetched, his references to the Egyptian hieratic numerals (356–8) are of interest.[191] For there are striking similarities in principle, and to some extent in the specific symbols, between the Egyptian and Indian numerals. The hieratic and demotic number system agrees with that of Brāhmī in having separate characters for the units, decades, 100, and 1,000, and its method of indicating multiples of the larger denominations is also similar, if not exactly identical, to the Indian method.

These factors induced Bühler (BIP 82) "to give up Bhagvānlāl's hypothesis" (i.e., the phonetic theory) and to accept the view that "the Brāhma numeral symbols are derived from the Egyptian hieratic figures," which position he expounded further in OIBA 115–9 (Appendix II: The Origin of the Ancient Brāhma Numerals). While many problems remain, it must be admitted that the similarities are quite striking. As was the case with Bühler's derivation of the Brāhmī alphabet from a North Semitic prototype (see 2.2.3.2.4), some of the resemblances between the corresponding Egyptian and Indic numeral signs are strong, but others much less so, so that establishing

185. Note, for example, such far-fetched identifications as that of 50 with "the *anunâsika* . . . as it occurs in the manuscripts of the *Mâdhyandina Śâkhâ* of the *White Yajurveda*," and 80 and 90 with the *upadhmānīya* and *jihvāmūlīya*, respectively (Bhagvānlāl, op. cit., 47).

186. See the critical comments by Ojhā (BPLM 106) and others (e.g., Gokhale, *Indian Numerals*, 48).

187. JASB 23, 1854, 703–4.

188. JASB 24, 558ff.

189. JRAS 20, 1863, 228–9 n. 1.

190. JRAS, n.s. 14, 1882, 335–76 (esp. 348–55).

191. A possible connection with Egyptian (demotic) numerals had already been briefly proposed by Burnell in 1874 (SIP 65), although Bayley does not refer to him.

connections between them involves considerable manipulation. In a few cases, notably the signs for 80 and 90, Bühler admits, "There is no actual resemblance between the Egyptian and Indian forms" (118). Another problem with the Egyptian derivation is historical, since, as Bühler admits (OIBA 119), the evidence for contact between India and Egypt in very early times is weak (Bayley's attempts [op. cit., 361–3] to establish such contacts notwithstanding), and in the absence of such corroboration the derivation can hardly be considered authoritative.

Recently, Falk (SAI 175–6) has proposed a possible influence from the early Chinese system of numerical notation, but the similarities are in fact less striking than those with Egyptian, and the historical and geographical arguments are even less cogent.

Thus some authors, unconvinced by the arguments for borrowing, hold out for an indigenous origin of the Brāhmī numbers. Ojhā, for example (BPLM 114), thinks that they are "independent creations of the Indo-Aryans" (*bhāratīya āryoṃ ke svatantra nirmāṇa*). Sircar, too (IIEP 126), says that they "appear to have developed out of certain signs of the pre-historic writing of India"; but neither author offers any direct proof for the presumed indigenous origin. A. H. Dani[192] has recently presented a scheme for an internal derivation of the Brāhmī numerical symbols from a (hypothetical) basic sign for 10, but this purely formal hypothesis is not compelling.

In conclusion, the problem of the origin of the Brāhmī numerals is roughly analogous to that of the Brāhmī script itself. We have, on the one hand, a proposal by Bühler et al. for a foreign origin, which is convincing to some extent but falls considerably short of real proof, on both formal and historical grounds;[193] and on the other hand, a camp which rejects Bühler's and other theories of borrowing and holds out for an indigenous origin, but without concrete evidence. However, it must be noted that the development of numerical notation figures does not necessarily follow the same principles as linguistic notation, nor is it necessarily linked to it. For whereas phonetic signs are normally completely arbitrary in form, numerical signs can often be derived as cursive reductions of collocations of counting strokes, as in the case of the figures for 1, 2, and 3, which resemble each other in many systems around the world, and, more significantly, in the hieratic Egyptian figures for the decades which are clearly derived from combinatory groups of the old hieroglyphic sign for 10. Thus, it is possible for independently derived systems of numerical notation to independently develop similar principles and even similar forms, so that it may well be that the old Indian numerical system was entirely indigenous in origin despite its apparent resemblance to the Egyptian system. This numerical system could also have been in origin entirely separate from, and perhaps older than, the Brāhmī script with which it came to be associated,[194] and this would explain the persistent failure of all attempts to interpret the numerical signs in terms of phonetic values derived from apparent resemblances to characters of Brāhmī or other scripts.

192. Preface to the second edition (1986) of DIP, ix–xvii.

193. It should be kept in mind that the formal derivation of numeral signs does not necessarily follow the same principles as those which apply to the derivation of phonetic characters. For while the latter are (effectively) purely arbitrary symbols, the former are often derivable, at least as far as the lower numbers are concerned, from combinations of simple counting strokes; so that the numbers from 1 to 3 or 4, and sometimes higher ones as well, may often resemble each other in widely separated and unrelated systems. For this reason, purely formal similarities between numerical symbols are less significant than those of phonetic signs.

194. Cf. G. R. Kaye, "The Old Indian Numerical Symbols," IA 40, 1911, 49–55 (esp. 50, 54).

2.4.1.3 The development of place-value notation

Despite outward changes in form, the old additive system of Brāhmī numerals remained stable until about the seventh century A.D., at which point the modern system of decimal place-value notation, which can represent any number of any size with only the nine digit symbols plus a sign for zero, began to come into use. There are, however, several problems involved in determining exactly what is the earliest epigraphic attestation of the new, or "place-value,"[195] system. First of all, there is the problem of spurious inscriptions; several inscriptions which were previously thought to provide early specimens of place-value numbers have proven to be spurious or at least of doubtful authenticity.[196] Most important among these is the Māṅkaṇī (formerly called Saṅkheḍā) copper plate inscription (CII 4.1, 161–5), bearing in place-value characters the date 346, which is presumably attributable to the Kalacuri era and hence equivalent to A.D. 594/95 (if a current year) or A.D. 595/96 (if expired). Although this inscription is widely cited both in specialized publications (e.g., BIP 83 and IIEP 127) and in general works on the history of mathematics[197] as providing the earliest specimen of a place-value date, cogent historical and contextual arguments have been presented by V. V. Mirashi[198] to show that this is very likely a spurious record, and hence does not prove the use of the new system in the sixth century A.D.

Second, there is the problem of the great variability and consequent difficulty in interpreting the numerical figures. A case in point here is the Sakrāī stone inscription, dated, according to B. Ch. Chhabra (EI 27, 27–33), in [Vikrama] 699 = A.D. 643, which would make it the earliest new-system date (disregarding the Māṅkaṇī/Saṅkheḍā plates). But the reading of the date is controversial, and the first figure might be 8 rather than 6 (op. cit., 30), so that this too cannot be definitely considered the earliest place-value date.

Actually, the earliest unquestionable inscriptional dates in the new system are not from India proper but from Southeast Asia. G. Coedès, in his important article "À propos de l'origine des chiffres arabes,"[199] pointed out several early place-value dates in the Śaka era on indubitably authentic Southeast Asian stone inscriptions, including two inscriptions from Indonesia and Cambodia dated in Śaka 605 = A.D. 683. Coedès thus

195. In many publications on the subject of Indian numerals, the old and new styles are routinely referred to as the "numerical" and "decimal" systems, respectively. But this terminology is inaccurate, since in fact *both* systems are both numerical and decimal. I therefore prefer the terms "additive" and "place-value," or simply "old" and "new."

196. This problem is not merely coincidental; for it would only be expected that forgers of copper plate grants in the centuries following the transition from the old to the new notation system would predate the forged documents in the new style to which they were accustomed, thus giving rise to a body of documents which purport to give dates in new-style numbers before they were actually in use (see also 5.3).

197. E.g., Georges Ifrah, *From One to Zero: A Universal History of Numbers*, tr. Lowell Bair (New York: Viking, 1985), 437–40. Ifrah, in accepting the evidence of the Saṅkheḍā (i.e., Māṅkaṇī) plates, states that "[t]o the best of my knowledge, no serious reason for questioning the authenticity of the Indian copperplate deeds has ever been stated" (440). But the objections raised by Mirashi, as cited shortly, are indeed "serious" reasons for doubt.

198. CII 4.1, 161–3; see also "A Note on the Māṅkaṇi Grant of Taralasvāmin," *Journal of the Ganganatha Jha Research Institute* 1, 1944, 389–94.

199. BSOAS 6, 1930–32, 323–8.

concludes that this system therefore must have been in use by the late seventh century, and probably earlier, in Southeast Asia and presumably also in India.[200]

Returning to India proper, the earliest definite specimen of pure place-value notation (as opposed to mixed or partial place-value notation, discussed later) now seems to be in the Siddhāntam plates of the Eastern Gaṅga king Devendravarman (EI 13, 212–6) dated (see Hultzsch, EI 18, 308) in the [Gaṅga] year 195, equivalent to approximately A.D. 693, or just ten years later than the Southeast Asian examples mentioned earlier. Another specimen from the same period is the Sudava plates (EI 26, 65–8) of Anantavarman, son of the aforementioned Devendravarman, dated [Gaṅga] 204 = A.D. 702. But undisputed cases of place-value notation continue to be somewhat scarce through the eighth century A.D.[201] Examples from the ninth century, such as the Tōrkhēḍē plates of [Śaka] 735 = A.D. 812 (EI 3, 53–8) and the Buckalā stone inscription of [Vikrama] 872 = A.D. 815 (EI 9, 198–200; see esp. 199 n. 1) are more secure.

After this time, that is, from about the middle of the ninth century onward, epigraphic notation of dates by the place-value system becomes standard. But the old system also continued to be used through the eighth century and sometimes even into the ninth, for instance, in the Barah copper plate of [Vikrama] 893 = A.D. 836 (EI 19, 15–19). An interesting illustration of the process of transition is provided by the Āhār stone inscription (EI 19, 52–62). This is a composite record of ten separate documents of different dates; the two earliest documents (nos. II and I), dated in [Harṣa] 258 and 259 = A.D. 864 and 865, respectively, use the old additive notation (cf. the editor's note, 58 n. 2), while all the later dates, from [Harṣa] 261 = A.D. 867 (no. IX) on, are in the new place-value system. This document thus allows us to precisely date the transition from old to new style in the area concerned (Bulandshahr Dist. in central northern India) to around A.D. 866.

We also find during the transitional period in and around the seventh century not a few cases of a curious hybrid system which combines features of the old and new systems. Several cases of this have been found, interestingly enough, among the copper plate inscriptions of the Eastern Gaṅga kings in whose later records, as mentioned previously, were found the earliest definite cases of the place-value system. Thus, as early as ca. A.D. 578 we find in the Urlām plates of Hastivarman (EI 17, 330–4; corrected reading of the date in EI 18, 308) the [Gaṅga] year 80 written with the old-style sign for 80 plus the new-style sign for 0, and in the Purlē plates of Indravarman (EI 14, 360–3; see also EI 18, 308) the Gaṅga year 137 = ca. A.D. 635 written as 100-3-7 and the day 20 as 20-0.[202] It thus appears that the transition from

200. Although both of the Southeast Asian inscriptions are in local languages, rather than Sanskrit, Coedès is no doubt correct in stating that the data do not justify the "étrange opinion" (324) of G. R. Kaye ("Notes on Indian Mathematics—Arithmetical Notation," JASB, n.s. 3, 1907, 475–508) that the symbolic number system originated in Southeast Asia and was imported thence into India, rather than vice versa. The early Sanskrit inscriptions of Southeast Asia generally give the dates in chronogram form, which presupposes the use of place-value numeration (see n. 203).

201. The Dhiniki inscription of Vikrama 794 = A.D. 738 (IA 12, 151–6) is now generally agreed to be spurious, but the Sāmangaḍ inscription (IA 11, 108–15) of the Rāṣṭrakūṭa king Dantidurga, dated Śaka 675 = A.D. 753/4, is a more likely instance, though its authenticity too has been called into question by V. S. Sukthankar in "Palaeographic Notes" (see n. 115), 313–7, mainly on paleographic grounds. The remarks of G. R. Kaye (op. cit., 484) on this point are misleading, as he quotes Fleet out of context.

202. For further references and examples see E. Hultzsch, EI 18, 1925–26, 307–8; IIEP 127; G. S. Gai, "Two Epigraphic Notes," *Journal of the Ganganatha Jha Research Institute* 6, 1949, 306–7;

the old additive system to the new place-value system, at least as far as epigraphic usage (which presumably mirrors popular usage) is concerned, was a gradual process. The displacement of the old style evidently took place slowly over a period of at least a century or so, and the new system itself underwent a process of gradual evolution in the seventh century, during which it was sometimes used in combination with features of the old style.[203] This matter has broader implications for the important question of the origin of the zero sign and the now universal decimal place-value system of numerical notation, which, according to some scholars (see, e.g., Ifrah, op. cit. [n. 197], 428ff.) is ultimately of Indian origin; but the literature on this question is vast and goes far beyond the scope of the present book.

2.4.1.4 Later developments of the numerical notation system

Once the new system came into universal use in or around the ninth century A.D., the subsequent history of numerical notation in the Brāhmī-derived scripts is essentially only a matter of the developments of outward forms of the symbols. These developments, however, are quite complex and not very well documented. Being a purely paleographic matter, they will not be presented here in detail; for further information the reader is referred to the standard works on paleography, especially BPLM, which presents this material in detail (103–27 and charts 71–76 and 84).[204] The later phases of development of the numerals in the regional scripts in particular have not yet been adequately studied.

2.4.2 Numerical notation in Kharoṣṭhī

The numerical notation of Kharoṣṭhī script (see table 2.6) follows an additive/multiplicative method essentially similar to that of the old Brāhmī system but considerably different from it in detail. Unlike the latter, which has separate signs for each of the units and decades, Kharoṣṭhī has symbols only for 1, 4 (a later development; see next paragraph), 10, 20, 100, and 1,000. All other numbers are indicated additively, somewhat as in Roman numerals; thus, for example, 76 would be written with the fig-

---

Subrata Kumar Acharya, "The Transition from the Numerical to the Decimal System in the Inscriptions of Orissa," JESI 19, 1993, 52–62; and B. N. Mukherjee, "The Early Use of Decimal Notation in Indian Epigraphs," JESI 19, 1993, 80–3.

203. Such is the picture to be derived from strictly epigraphic evidence; but if literary sources are taken into account, it would seem that the actual origins of the decimal place-value notation system must have been considerably earlier. Walter Eugene Clarke ("Hindu-Arabic Numerals," in *Indian Studies in Honor of Charles Rockwell Lanman* [Cambridge, Mass.: Harvard University Press, 1929], 217–36 [esp. 225–8]) noted indications from literary and scientific texts that place-value notation must have been in use well before the late seventh century; particularly noteworthy is the allusion to the *śūnyabindu*, or zero-sign, in Subandhu's *Vāsavadattā*, which must be earlier than the seventh century (Clarke, 225). Also significant is the attestation as early as Śaka 526 = A.D. 604 of the chronogram or numerical word system, which seems to presuppose the place-value system, in Sanskrit inscriptions from Southeast Asia (Clarke, 226; Coedès, op. cit. [n. 199], 325), though such chronograms are not attested until considerably later in India itself (Kaye, op. cit. [n. 200], 479–80; BIP 86).

204. Several of the standard paleographic studies treat numbers only briefly or not at all. Dani's DIP, e.g., did not cover the numerical symbols (cf. Gokhale, *Indian Numerals*, preface), although he has added some material on this subject in the preface to the second edition (see 2.4.1.2).

ures 20-20-20-10-4-1-1 (or in the earlier script, 20-20-20-10-1-1-1-1-1-1). The figures for 100 and 1,000 were subject to multiplicative treatment, as in Brāhmī; for example, 300 would be written as 3-100, and 2,000 as 2-1000.[205]

Like the Kharoṣṭhī script itself, its numerical system did not change greatly in the course of its history, though some significant developments did take place. The sign for 4, shaped like a Roman x, was apparently a secondary development, since in Aśokan Kharoṣṭhī 4 and 5 are written as 1-1-1-1(-1), while in all subsequent Kharoṣṭhī texts the special sign for 4 is used. The sign for 1,000 to date is known only from central Asian Kharoṣṭhī documents, though it probably existed in India as well. As shown by H. W. Bailey,[206] it is derived from an Aramaic ligature 'LP (i.e., *'alap*, 'thousand'). Also in the central Asian documents, we find cursively written combinations of the sign for 1 which have evidently developed into distinct characters for 2 (𐩁) and 3 (𐩂).

The origin of the Kharoṣṭhī numerical system presents no difficulties, as its derivation from Aramaic, like that of the script itself, is clear. Not only the system[207] but also all of the individual symbols[208] can be easily associated with the Aramaic, as represented, for instance, in the papyri from Elephantine (Egypt).[209]

2.5 Techniques of Epigraphic Writing

BIP 87–92; PIP 88–119; IIEP 128–31; SIE 83–97.

2.5.1 General comments

The technical features and visual qualities of Indic inscriptions vary widely, ranging from undecorated, strictly functional records to highly ornate and polished works of art. Especially in the earlier centuries, many inscriptions exhibit a rather casual attitude toward aesthetic quality and orthographic accuracy (see 3.3.8), which may be attributed in part to the marginal value traditionally accorded to the written as opposed to the spoken word in India (2.1.1). It is true that in some cases, for example, in Buddhist reliquary inscriptions that were meant to be permanently interred in *stūpa*s, legibility and visual aesthetic appeal may be considered inherently insignificant. Nevertheless, it is not uncommon to find extremes of carelessness in the plan-

205. On the decipherment of the Kharoṣṭhī numerical system, see section 6.3, p. 218.

206. "A Problem of the Kharoṣṭhī Script," in *Essays and Studies Presented to Stanley Arthur Cook . . .*, 121–3 (see n. 138).

207. The Aramaic system represented the digits up to 9 by simple combinations of the vertical stroke representing 1; this confirms that the later Kharoṣṭhī sign for 4 is a separate Indian development.

208. The Kharoṣṭhī symbol for 20 is often described (e.g., in IIEP 125) as a doubling of the Kharoṣṭhī 10, but comparison with the Aramaic prototype indicates that it is rather a direct borrowing of the Aramaic 20.

209. See Emil G. Kraeling, *The Brooklyn Museum Aramaic Papyri: New Documents of the Fifth Century B.C. from the Jewish Colony at Elephantine* (London: Yale University Press for the Brooklyn Museum, 1953). Papyrus 4 (168–9) has several numerical figures which are almost identical to the corresponding ones in Kharoṣṭhī.

ning and execution of inscriptions which were clearly meant to be seen and read; and while this is most common in minor private records, it can also be observed in royal inscriptions, as, for example, in the notorious case of the Erraguḍi rock edicts of Aśoka (see n. 82).[210] There are, of course, many exceptions to this pattern, especially in the late medieval period in which the arts of writing and engraving attained their highest development (see 2.5.3.1), but on the whole one must agree with Sircar (SIE 86) that "[t]he number of inscriptions carelessly written and engraved is . . . by far larger than those written and engraved carefully."

2.5.2 The technical execution of inscriptions

2.5.2.1 Preparation of surfaces

As with the general quality of the inscriptions, the degree of care in the preparation of the surfaces to be inscribed varies widely. In early records particularly, the inscriptions might be written directly on the intended surface with little or no preparation thereof; such is the case, for example, with many of the Aśokan rock inscriptions.[211] As time went on, however, more sophisticated techniques were developed, culminating in the very skillfully dressed and prepared polished stone slabs, often of large dimensions, used for many inscriptions of the medieval period (cf. SIE 70). Similarly, inscribed copper plates were frequently prepared with considerable skill and artistry, especially in later centuries, though cruder examples are also by no means rare.

2.5.2.2 Execution of the inscription

After the preparation of the intended surface, the letters of the inscription itself would usually be first written onto it in some temporary medium such as ink or chalk by a writer or scribe, known as *lipikāra, lekhaka, karaṇa/karaṇika, kāyastha,* and so on (see BIP 100–2 for further details). This preliminary step is discernible in occasional cases wherein the ink or paint is still visible in the inscription (e.g., at Bāndhogaṛh, EI 31, 168), or where the final step of carving the inscription was never carried out (e.g., the Giñjā hill inscription, ASIR 21, 1883–85, 119–20 [cf. EI 31, 168], and the Kasiā copper plate, ASIAR 1910–11, 73–7). The actual carving would then be carried out by an engraver (*sūtradhāra, śilākūṭa, rūpakāra,* etc.; cf. SIE 85). Sometimes, again mostly in the earlier period, the engravers seemed to be illiterate or minimally skilled, but in later times stone engraving became a legitimate art unto itself, and its expert practitioner came to be a person of some status (cf. IESIS 32–5) who would often (especially in later stone *praśastis*) be mentioned by name at the end of the inscription along with the composer and/or scribe.[212] The verbs typically used to

210. Note also J. Ph. Vogel's comments (EI 20, 1929–30), regarding the Nāgārjunakoṇḍa inscriptions, that "the careless manner in which they have been recorded is astonishing" (11).

211. The pillar edicts are written on exquisitely polished stone surfaces, but this preparation was evidently an aspect of the construction of the pillars themselves as monumental works of art, rather than as preparation for the inscriptions themselves.

212. For examples, see Appendix, no. 8, vv. 22–23, and no. 12, v. 13. For cases where all three persons involved in the preparation of the record, viz. the composer, scribe, and engraver, are mentioned, see EI I, 42, ll. 27–8; 48–9, ll. 21–2; and 80–1, ll. 25–6 (cf. BIP 101 n. 12).

denote the activities of composing, writing, and engraving are, respectively, √*kṛ* or (*vi-*) √*rac*; (*ul-* or *vi-*) √*likh*;[213] and *ut-*√*kṝ* or (*ni-*)√*khan*.

The normal method of writing was by incising or carving lines into the hard surface with a stylus, chisel, or other suitable implement. Some early inscriptions, mostly Kharoṣṭhī relic dedications on metal plates, are written with a series of dots (e.g., the Taxila silver scroll, CII 2.1, 70–7). In the later medieval period we sometimes find Indic-language inscriptions composed of raised letters (e.g., the Peshawar Museum inscription, EI 10, 79–81) in imitation of the standard practice in Islamic inscriptions.

2.5.2.3 Punctuation, numeration, and ornamentation

In general, punctuation is treated in Indic inscriptions (as in manuscripts) rather informally, and seems to have been considered more or less optional. In early inscriptions punctuation is often totally absent, or used very sporadically at best. A notable exception is the Kālsī version of the Aśokan rock edicts XI–XIII, where a single vertical line of punctuation is used frequently, albeit promiscuously and inconsistently.[214] Punctuation marks began to be employed with any regularity only in the Gupta era, when some metrical inscriptions have the ends of half verses and full verses marked regularly by a single short horizontal line and a double vertical line, respectively (e.g., the Mandasor pillar inscription of Yaśodharman, CII 3, 142–8). But even in this period these marks are used sporadically, and many inscriptions are still entirely unpunctuated.

In the inscriptions of the early medieval and succeeding periods, punctuation marks begin to be used somewhat more systematically, particularly in verse records. The system continues to consist principally of two marks, a half stop with a single line and a full stop consisting of two lines, but these marks take various forms at different times and places: straight or curved lines arranged vertically or horizontally, lines with various hooks and other appendages, and so on.[215] In general, the single mark is used to mark the half verse and the double mark or full stop the end of a verse, but usage in this respect is quite loose. Sometimes only the verse end is punctuated, sometimes each *pāda* is marked, and not infrequently the usage is inconsistent even within an inscription.[216]

The verses are often numbered consecutively, either in conjunction with or instead of the punctuation system mentioned previously. Verse numbering is first noted in the Allahābād inscription of Samudragupta (CII 3, 1–17), and is common in inscriptions of the medieval period and later; but here, too, usage is inconsistent.

As a rule, Indic inscriptions are written continuously to the end of the line without regard for grammatical or structural divisions. But in many early Sanskrit inscriptions before and during the Gupta era the lines are planned so as to correspond to metrical units, usually half verses (e.g., in the Mandasor pillar inscription, CII 3,

213. On the technical sense of this term, see Fleet, CII 3, 99 n. 3.

214. Note that these inscriptions are incompetently written in other respects as well; see section 2.2.4.

215. For details see BIP 88–9.

216. See, e.g., Appendix, no. 10.

142–8).[217] This system was largely abandoned in later centuries[218] (except in Southeast Asia, where it remained in use much longer),[219] and thereafter all inscriptions, verse and prose, are lineated at random without regard to content.

In general, especially in Sanskrit inscriptions, there is no separation or other explicit word division. In some earlier inscriptions in Prakrit and "Epigraphical Hybrid" dialect, however, words or phrases are occasionally separated by a space; such is the case, for example, in several of the Aśokan inscriptions (e.g., Rummindeī; Appendix, no. 1) and some of the Nāsik cave inscriptions (e.g., Nāsik no. 10, EI 8, 78–81), as well as in some Kharoṣṭhī inscriptions (e.g., Sui Vihār, CII 2.1, 139). Only rarely do we find a mark consisting of two short vertical lines one above the other, indicating a word divided between lines (equivalent to the modern hyphen; Nālandā ins., Appendix, no. 12, end of lines 2, 4, 5, etc.).

Abbreviations are commonly used in inscriptions of various periods, especially in connection with dating formulae. The word *saṃvatsara* 'year' in particular is subject to various abbreviations such as *saṃvat*, *saṃva*, *saṃ*, *sa*, and so on (BIP 91).[220] Other technical terms are frequently abbreviated, especially in copper plate inscriptions; for instance, *dū* for *dūtaka*, *brā* for *brāhmaṇa*, or *dra* for *dramma* (see IIEP 129).

It was customary from the earliest times to place various auspicious signs at the beginning of inscriptions, and sometimes also at the end or even in the middle (e.g., MI §44). Symbols such as the *svastika* and the triskele are used in some of the Aśokan inscriptions, for example, in separate rock edicts nos. 1 and 2 at Jaugaḍa (CII 1, 111–8). The Hāthīgumphā inscription of Khāravela (SI I.213–21) has *śrīvatsa* and *svastika* at the beginning in the left upper margin, and the "tree-in-railing" symbol at the end. Beginning in the early Christian era, it became customary to put the word *siddham* 'success(ful)' or its abbreviations and Prakrit equivalents (*sdha*, *sidhaṃ*, etc.) at the beginning of an inscription or in the left margin. In the Gupta era, a symbol, originally consisting of a curved stroke open to the left, was substituted for the word *siddham*, and this sign, in various developed forms, became the standard invocatory mark thereafter. It appears to have later been sometimes understood to represent *oṃ*, but, as shown by Nalinikanta Bhattasali,[221] it is probably more accurate to read it as equivalent to *siddham*. Other words and phrases, such as *siddhir astu* 'May there be success' or *svasti* 'well-being' (frequently used together with *siddham*) were also often put at the beginning or end of inscriptions. A sign consisting of a circle with a dot in the middle was sometimes written at the end of a record or section thereof; this was later confused with and written as the syllables *tha* or *cha*. Similar symbols

217. See the comments of Lüders, EI 24, 1937–38, 198, and n. 5; also Sircar, EI 35, 1963–64, 17.

218. This presumably happened as a result of the increasing use of different meters of varying length in ornate inscriptions, which makes it impossible to maintain lineation by verse, except by leaving blank spaces at the end of shorter verses; but this, with the characteristic Indian *horror vacuui*, was never done.

219. See, e.g., Appendix, no. 8.

220. For further examples of abbreviations in dating formulae, see section 5.4.2.2.

221. EI 17, 1923–24, 352; see also SIE 92–5. This interpretation has recently been further supported and refined by two studies published in G. Bhattacharya, ed., *Deyadharma*: Gustav Roth, "Mangala-Symbols in Buddhist Sanskrit Manuscripts and Inscriptions" (239–44), and Lore Sander, "Om or Siddham—Remarks on Openings of Buddhist Manuscripts and Inscriptions from Gilgit and Central Asia" (251–61).

and marks, sometimes developed into elaborate floral motifs, are used at the end of records, where they function as marks of both decoration and punctuation (see, e.g., EI 31, plate facing page 127, l. 212).

Many inscriptions, especially in medieval and later times, are accompanied by engraved illustrations of various sorts. These may take the form of auspicious symbols such as Śiva's bull Nandi, the Śiva-linga (e.g., CII 6, pl. XC), the conch shell (*śaṅkha*), lotus, and so on; or they may be representations of dynastic symbols, such as the Garuḍa on the copper plates of the Paramāras (CII 7.2, pl. I, IV, VI, etc.). Other illustrations refer specifically to the content of the record itself, such as the representation of the sun and moon (e.g., CII 6, pl. XC), alluding to the traditional blessing that a gift should last as long as the sun and moon; or of a donkey copulating with a woman or a pig, representing the mother of a violator of the gift according to the traditional "ass-curse" (e.g., IA 48, 1919, 47 and n. 33; EI 40, 1973–74, plate facing page 88), which is also sometimes explicitly spelled out in the text of the inscription.[222] *Satī* and other types of memorial stone inscriptions (see 4.1.4) are usually accompanied by representations, either visual or symbolic (typically in the form of a hand- or footprint), of the person memorialized.

Corrections and omissions are indicated by various means. Sometimes, as in Aśokan rock edict XII at Kālsī, l. 31 (CII 1, 42), an incorrectly written passage was simply crossed out and the correct reading entered above the line. In copper plates, however, the standard practice was to beat the incorrect passage flat and rewrite it, or simply to write over it without erasure (see, e.g., Appendix, no. 10, l. 36). Omitted letters or words could be inserted by simply writing them into, above, or below the appropriate place in the line. Longer omissions would typically be added in the margins; their intended location was usually indicated by placing the beginning of the added passage in the upper or lower margin at the appropriate vertical position, and denoting the line where it belonged by a number indicating the number of lines from the top or bottom. Numerous examples of corrections of these types are pointed out in the editor's notes to the Asankhali plates of Narasiṃha II, EI 31, 109–28. Alternatively, the placement of a marginal addition could be indicated in the text by the cross-shaped mark known as *kākapāda* or *haṃsapāda* (see, e.g., EI 3, 51 n. 9).

2.5.3 *Calligraphic writing*

IESIS 32–8; R. Salomon, "Calligraphy in Pre-Islamic India," in Asher and Gai, IEBHA, 3–6.

Unlike in China or the Islamic world, in traditional India calligraphy did not achieve the level of a major art, which is not surprising in view of what has been said earlier (2.1.1, 2.5.1) about the relatively low status of the written word in India. Nonetheless, many specimens of calligraphic writing from various periods do survive in Indic inscriptions, and some of them demonstrate a very high degree of skill and artistry, although this aspect of Indian epigraphy and paleography has received little attention in scholarly writing.

222. E.g., CII 7.2, 207, *yo na dadāti tasya mātā* [sic] *gardabho jabhāti* [sic], and pl. LVIII. See also EI 9, 1907–8, 164, *jo anyathā karoti tasya pitā gardabhaḥ śūkarī mātā.*

2.5.3.1 Calligraphic developments of the standard Brāhmī-derived scripts

Even in relatively early times we sometimes find Brāhmī[223] records which are engraved with considerable care and skill—for example, in the Nāsik cave inscriptions and in several of the Mathurā inscriptions (MI §18 and 118). But calligraphic writing proper, that is, writing with a systematically developed decorative component, first begins to appear around the second and third centuries A.D., for example, in the Bijayagaḍh Yaudheya inscription (CII 3, pl. xxxvi.B) in the north and in the inscriptions of the time of the Ikṣvāku kings at Nāgārjunakoṇḍa, Amarāvatī, Jaggayyapeṭa, and so on, in the south. These early calligraphic scripts are principally characterized by various forms and degrees of elongation and elaboration of the vowel diacritic signs, which is to remain the principal technique for calligraphic elaboration through the following centuries. The other major technique of decorative embellishment consists of various creative treatments of the principal consonantal characters themselves, as, for example, in the "box-headed" scripts of central India (see 2.2.5.3) in which all the letters are modeled into harmonious squared and angular forms. This type of embellishment by stylization was also employed in some later calligraphically developed scripts such as Siddhamātṛkā as well as in the "special calligraphic scripts" (see 2.5.3.2), often in conjunction with the technique of diacritic decoration.

The development of these techniques reached its climax in northern India in the seventh and eighth centuries, from which period several inscriptions in Siddhamātṛkā constitute masterpieces of calligraphic art; see, for example, the Lakkhā Maṇḍal *praśasti* (Appendix, no. 8; fig. 18), displaying the characteristic features of artistically angularized consonants and highly elaborated vowel signs. This type of ornamental script attains extreme forms in some cases, particularly in signatures such as those of the Emperor Harṣa on the Bānskheṛā plate (EI 4, 208–11; fig. 1) or of one Pūrṇṇāditya at the Rājīvalocana temple at Rājim (IEBHA, pl. 4). In the latter example the decorative portions of the vowel diacritics are elaborated into floral and animal-like motifs, a technique which is to be further developed in southern Indian calligraphy of succeeding centuries.

The golden age of calligraphic writing in the south occurred in the tenth to twelfth centuries. The calligraphic inscriptions of this period are characterized by extreme elaboration of the vowel diacritics and subscript consonants of the first and last lines, forming elaborate floral and zoological motifs as a decorative border at the top and bottom of the inscription; see, for example, the Śravaṇa-Beḷgoḷa inscription of Malliṣeṇa (EI 3, plates between pages 194 and 195).

2.5.3.2 The special calligraphic scripts

Besides the previously mentioned calligraphic varieties of the standard scripts, there also developed in the Gupta period and succeeding centuries calligraphic forms of writing which, though ultimately derived from standard Brāhmī, became so stylized and elaborate as to virtually constitute separate scripts. The first of these scripts, vari-

223. Kharoṣṭhī, for the most part, remained essentially a "clerk's script" and did not attain any significant degree of calligraphic development, though some specimens (e.g., the Mamāne Ḍherī pedestal inscription, CII 2.1, 171–2) show a skillful hand.

FIGURE 1. Signature of King Harṣa on the Bānskheṛā copper plate: *svahasto mama mahārājādhijrāja-śrīharṣasya* ("This is the signature of me, the Great King of Kings, Śrī-Harṣa"). From EI 4, plate facing page 210; copyright, Archaeological Survey of India.

ously referred to as "Ornamental Brāhmī" or (preferably) "Ornate Brāhmī," is characterized by squat, squarish, highly stylized characters. Short inscriptions in this script have been found in considerable numbers at various sites in northern, central, and upper southern India (see IEBHA, 5). They presumably record personal names or pilgrims' records (see 4.1.6), following the pattern, noted earlier, that the most elaborate calligraphic writings are primarily used for signatures. Because of the highly stylized forms of the letters of the Ornate Brāhmī inscriptions, they are extremely difficult to read, and few, if any, of them can be considered to have been satisfactorily deciphered.[224]

The second of the "special" scripts is Śaṅkhalipi or "shell characters" (fig. 2). Like Ornate Brāhmī, this highly ornate script, also evidently used principally for signatures, was in wide use over virtually all of India except the far south from approximately the fourth to the eighth centuries A.D.; over six hundred examples of this script are now known.[225] The characters are highly stylized, tending to conform to a general shape superficially resembling a conch shell or *śaṅkha*, whence the name applied to the script. Statistical and formal analysis of the characters indicates that they are derived from the characters of standard Brāhmī, but the changes are so extensive that it is still very difficult to authoritatively identify them.[226] Several claims of decipherment have been put forward, but they are not convincing.[227]

2.5.4 Biscript inscriptions

Biscript inscriptions, that is, those written in the same language repeated in different scripts, are found occasionally in various periods, though they are much less common than bilingual inscriptions (see 3.6). In the northwest, inscriptions were occasionally written in both Brāhmī and Kharoṣṭhī scripts, for instance, the Kanhiāra and Pāṭhyār inscriptions (CII 2.1, 178–9).[228] Another Brāhmī/Kharoṣṭhī biscript has recently been discovered in Mathurā (EI 40, 168–9). Inscribed seals often have leg-

224. See also R. Salomon, "Undeciphered Scripts of South Asia," in Jayanta Chakrabarty and D. C. Bhattacharyya, eds., *S. K. Saraswati Commemoration Volume: Aspects of Indian Art and Culture* (Calcutta: Ṛddhi-India, 1983), 201–12 (esp. 203–5).

225. See R. Salomon, "New Śaṅkhalipi (Shell Character) Inscriptions," *Studien zur Indologie und Iranistik* 11/12, 1986, 109–58, and references given there (esp. 109–10 n. 4).

226. Salomon, op. cit., 145–52.

227. See, for example, R. Salomon, "A Recent Claim to Decipherment of the 'Shell Script,'" JAOS 107, 1987, 313–5.

228. See also J. Ph. Vogel, "Two Brahmi and Kharoshthi Rock-Inscriptions in the Kangra Valley," EI 7, 1902–3, 116–9.

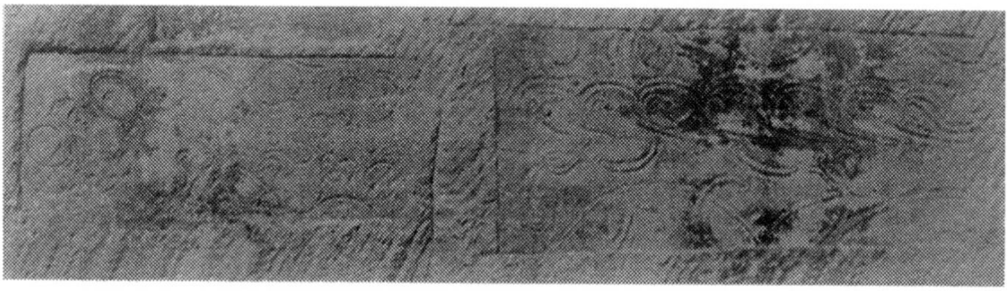

FIGURE 2. Shell character (Śaṅkhalipi) inscription from Siddha kī guphā, Deogaṛh (Lalitpur Dist., UP). Photograph courtesy of Michael D. Willis.

ends in both Brāhmī and Kharoṣṭhī (e.g., CII 2.1, 100, no. 2; 102, no. 11); one seal in the British Museum has the name of the owner in these two scripts and in Greek as well (JRAS 1905, 809–13).

Biscripts are also sometimes found among later inscriptions; these typically involve a combination of a local form or derivative of Brāhmī and a more widely used script such as Devanāgarī. A well-known example is the Paṭṭadakal pillar inscription of the time of the Cālukya king Kīrttivarman II (A.D. 754; EI 3, 1–7; see 2.2.5.4), with the full text given in both northern Indian Siddhamātṛkā and in the current local southern (proto-Telugu-Kannada) script. In other cases, such as the Kāngrā Jvālāmukhī *praśasti* (EI 1, 190–5), part of the inscription is written in the local script (Śāradā) and the rest in Devanāgarī.

2.6 Undeciphered Scripts

Besides the well-known problem of the Indus script (see 2.2.3.1), there remains a small residue of Indic scripts which are still substantially undeciphered.[229] These include the problematic extreme calligraphic "Ornate Brāhmī" and "shell characters" discussed earlier (2.5.3.2), and also some lesser-known scripts. Notable among these are a script found in Afghanistan which seems to resemble Kharoṣṭhī and which Fussman[230] suggests may have been used to record the Kambojī language, and another one, broadly resembling Brāhmī but of uncertain heritage, found on several terra-cotta seals from various sites (notably Chandraketugaṛh and Tamluk) in West Bengal and Bangladesh.[231]

229. See R. Salomon, "Undeciphered Scripts . . ." (see n. 224), 201–12.

230. BEFEO 61, 1974, 34.

231. See, e.g., D. K. Chakravorty, "Some Inscribed Terracotta Sealings from Chandraketugarh," JNSI 39, 1977, 128–34; and Salomon, "Undeciphered Scripts . . ." (see n. 224), 205–7, for further references.

3

The Languages of Indic Inscriptions

3.1 Middle Indo-Aryan ("Prakrit")

3.1.1 General remarks

In early Indian inscriptions the Prakrit, or, more precisely, the Middle Indo-Aryan (MIA) languages predominated. Indeed, from about the third to the first century B.C. these were the only languages in epigraphic use, and they continued to predominate for at least two centuries more, and longer in some regions. It was only in the early centuries of the Christian era that the "mixed dialect," or "Epigraphical Hybrid Sanskrit" (EHS), and Sanskrit began to appear, and for several centuries all three—MIA, EHS, and Sanskrit—were in use simultaneously. But the latter two gradually gained the upper hand over the Prakrits, and then Sanskrit gradually superseded both Prakrit and EHS (see 3.3.1–3.3.7). Thus the Prakrits practically ceased to be epigraphic languages by the early fourth century A.D. in northern India, and about a century later in the south.

The inscriptional Prakrits are diverse and largely unstandardized. Much more than is the case with the literary Prakrits of later times,[1] the morphology and especially the orthography of the inscriptional dialects is unstandardized and inconsistent, to the extent that it is not unusual to find the same word spelled several different ways within the same inscription. The orthography can be characterized as approximative, as contrasted to the precise orthography of Sanskrit inscriptions. Thus, for example, geminate consonants are almost always (except in some late specimens) represented by the single consonant, and the *anusvāra* is only sporadically used to indicate a homorganic nasal before a stop consonant, the nasal often being left unindicated. Among the Prakrit inscriptions in general, the earlier the inscription, the looser and more colloquial the language and orthography are likely to be (although the Aśokan inscriptions constitute in some respects an exception to this rule). Thus some of the earliest examples preserve a very informal, colloquial level of Prakrit, which may present serious problems in interpretation, while the later specimens often tend to approach Sanskritic usage in style, vocabulary, and orthography.

1. Literary Prakrits do appear occasionally in later inscriptions, but from a linguistic point of view this is a separate matter; see section 3.1.5.

3.1.2 The Prakrits of the Aśokan inscriptions

Grammatical descriptions: E. Hultzsch, *Inscriptions of Aśoka*, lvi–cxxxi; J. Bloch, *Les Inscriptions d'Asoka*, 43–88.

In general, the Prakrits of the Aśokan inscriptions (see 4.3.1.1) represent an early stage of development of MIA, in which, for example, the voicing and elision of intervocalic consonants are only occasional and sporadic, and some archaic features are preserved which are lost in later Prakrits, such as *ātmanepada* verb forms of the present tense (e.g., *karote*, Girnār IX.1–3) and the present participle (*vijinamane* [*sic*], Kālsī XIII.36). Moreover, the resolution of consonantal groups by assimilation or epenthesis (*svarabhakti*) is less advanced, especially in the western and northwestern dialects, than in later literary and inscriptional Prakrits. In these respects, then, the Aśokan Prakrits on the whole (and especially the western dialect of the Girnār and Bombay-Sopārā rock edicts) more closely resemble Pāli than any other of the literary forms of MIA.

Overall, the Aśokan inscriptions can be said to comprise three main dialects:[2] the eastern, the western, and the northwestern.

3.1.2.1 The eastern Aśokan dialect

Among the three Aśokan dialects the eastern dialect[3] clearly predominates, as it was the local language of the imperial capital at Pāṭaliputra (whence it is sometimes referred to as the "Chancellery Language"). The original versions of the edicts were drawn up in this dialect, to be translated later into the other dialects where deemed necessary. The majority of the Aśokan inscriptions, including all the pillar edicts and minor rock edicts (MRE),[4] as well as the rock edicts at Kālsī, Dhauli, Jaugaḍa, and Eṛṛaguḍi, are in this dialect, and in some of them it is obviously being used far beyond its original geographical range.

The distinctive features of the eastern dialect include:

1. The three sibilants of Sanskrit are represented by *s*.[5]
2. The dialect has only *l* for Sanskrit *r* and *l*; e.g., *lājā* = *rājā*.
3. The Sanskrit nasals *ñ*, *ṇ*, and *n* all become *n*.
4. Sanskrit *kṣ* becomes *kh*.
5. Consonantal groups are subject to resolution by *svarabhakti* more frequently than in the other dialects.

2. Some writers, e.g., Sukumar Sen (*A Comparative Grammar of Middle Indo-Aryan* [Poona: Linguistic Society of India, 1960], 10–11), posit a fourth dialect, the "Middle Eastern," for some of the rock edicts. But on the whole it is preferable to consider the languages of these texts, which show a mixture of eastern and western characteristics, as essentially the eastern dialect with sporadic admixture of westernisms, rather than as a distinct dialect.

3. For a specimen of this dialect see Appendix, no. 1 (Rummindeī minor pillar edict).

4. Though some of the MREs, especially those in the south, show an admixture of western forms, e.g., in preferring *r* to *l*; see n. 2.

5. Rock edicts X–XIII at Kālsī show all three sibilants used indiscriminately (e.g., X.27 has both *yaso* and *yaṣo* for Sanskrit *yaśas-*). Though this peculiarity has never been fully explained, it is evidently a matter of scribal confusion rather than a true dialect feature. The retroflex and palatal sibilants also occur occasionally in the minor rock edicts, sometimes with etymological justification (e.g., Maski l. 2, *vaṣāni* = Skt. *varṣāṇi*).

6. Final *-as* of Sanskrit (as in the nominative sing. masc. of noun stems in *a-*) becomes *-e*.
7. The locative sing. masc./neut. ends in *-si* (for *-ssi*).
8. The present participle *ātmanepada* often ends in *-mīna* (e.g., *pāyamīnā*, Delhi-Toprā V.8).

The main features of this dialect—the predominance of *l*, the nominative masculine in *-e*, the loss of *ñ* and *ṇ*, and the sibilant *s*[6]—accord on the whole with the later literary Prakrit known as Ardha-Māgadhī, whence it has been called by Lüders and others[7] "Old Ardha-Māgadhī."

3.1.2.2 The western Aśokan dialect

The western dialect appears only in the rock edicts of Girnār and the Bombay-Sopārā fragments. Its characteristics include:

1. The three Sanskrit sibilants become *s*.
2. Both *r* and *l* are retained as in Sanskrit.[8]
3. The Sanskrit nasals *ñ*, *ṇ*, and *n* are retained.
4. Sanskrit *kṣ* generally becomes *cch* (but occasionally also *kh*).
5. Many consonantal clusters are retained, especially those involving the semivowels (*kr*, *tr*, *pr*, *vy*, etc.).[9] Sanskrit *st* and *sth* are sometimes reflected by the anomalous combination *sṭ* (written *ṭs*; e.g., *sṭitā* = *sthitāḥ*, Girnār, VI.4).
6. Sanskrit *-as* becomes *-o*.
7. The locative sing. masc./neut. ends in *-e* or *-mhi*.
8. The gerund ends in *-tpā* (written *-ptā;* see 2.2.4) = Sanskrit *-tvā*.

In general, the western dialect is the one most similar to literary Pāli and the later inscriptional Prakrits. It contrasts with the other dialects (especially the eastern one) in its generally archaic aspect, in both phonetics and morphology (e.g., the *ātmanepada* verb *karote*, cited earlier). The Girnār edicts also frequently differ from the other dialect versions in vocabulary; for instance, Girnār has *pas(s)ati* (= *paśyati*, I.5) where the others have *dakhati/dekhati*, and *paṃthesū* instead of *mag(g)esu* (II.8; for other examples see Bloch, *Les Inscriptions d'Asoka*, 83–4).

3.1.2.3 The northwestern Aśokan dialect

The language of the rock edicts at Shāhbāzgaṛhī and Mānsehrā is essentially an early form of the MIA dialect which is nowadays known as Gāndhārī (see 3.1.4.2.1).[10] Like all records in Gāndhārī, these inscriptions are written in the Kharoṣṭhī script,

6. This is the principal feature which distinguishes the dialect from the "true" Māgadhī of later literature, which has only *ś*.

7. See Oskar von Hinüber, *Das ältere Mittelindisch im Überblick* (Österreichische Akademie der Wissenschaften, Phil.-hist. Klasse, Sitzungsberichte 467 = Veröffentlichungen der Kommission für Sprachen und Kulturen Südasiens 20; Wien: Akademie der Wissenschaften, 1986), 27–8.

8. The Bombay-Sopārā fragment of rock edict IX even has *r* in place of Sanskrit *l* (*phara*, *maṅgara* = *phala*, *maṅgala*). It is not certain whether this is a true dialectal feature or the result of hypercorrection.

9. In the script, however, many of the conjuncts are reversed. E.g., the conjunct *pr* is actually written as *rp*, with the sign for *r* above the *p* (𑀧𑀼). This is probably a graphic rather than a dialectal peculiarity; see section 2.2.4.

10. On dialectal differences between Aśokan and later "Gāndhārī," see Burrow, "The Dialectal Position of the Niya Prakrit," BSOS 8, 1935–37, 419–35 (esp. 419–22).

whose graphic peculiarities—particularly the absence of notation of vowel quantity—tend to obscure some of the features of the language. The principal distinctive features of the dialect include:

1. The three sibilants are maintained, generally as in Sanskrit (but see also item 5).
2. Both *r* and *l* are retained as in Sanskrit.
3. The Sanskrit nasals *ñ*, *ṇ*, and *n* are retained.
4. Sanskrit *kṣ* is apparently retained in the form of a special character (Y; see 2.3.4), variously transliterated as *kṣ*, *ch*, *ch'*, and so on, whose precise phonetic value is uncertain.[11]
5. Many consonantal clusters are retained, especially those with *r*; but the latter are frequently subject to metathesis, for example, in *dhrama* = *dharma* and *krama* = *karma*.[12] Special developments include *ṣy* > *ś* (e.g., *manuśa* = *manuṣya*, Shāhbāzgaṛhī II.4; cf. item 8) and *sv* and *sm* (in the locative sing. ending) > *sp* (e.g., *spagraṃ* = *svargam*, Shāhbāzgaṛhī VI.16).
6. Final *-as* in Sanskrit is represented by *-o* at Shāhbāzgaṛhī, but at Mānsehrā generally by *-e* (see later remarks).
7. The locative sing. ends in *-e* or *-spi* (<* *-smin*; cf. item 5).
8. The future tense affix is *-iśa-* (< *-iṣya-* [see item 5]; e.g., *vaḍhiśati* = *vardhiṣyati*, Shāhbāzgaṛhī IV.9).

The dialects of the two northwestern sets of rock edicts diverge in several respects, notably in the treatment of final *-as* noted earlier (item 6). Thus as the equivalent of Sanskrit *rājñaḥ* (genitive), Shāhbāzgaṛhī has *raño* but Mānsehrā *rajine*, reminiscent of the eastern form *lājine*. Some dialectal peculiarities of Mānsehrā have thus sometimes been dismissed as "Māgadhisms," but this may not be the case; later Gāndhārī/Kharoṣṭhī inscriptions also vary between *-o* and *-e* (CII 2.1, cxii–cxiii), and recent research into the historical grammar of Gāndhārī[13] has shown that the notation of final vowels is highly inconsistent in Gāndhārī generally.[14]

All in all, the Aśokan inscriptions give a broad view of the dialect spectrum of MIA vernaculars in the third century B.C. But it must also be understood that they do not provide anything like a real dialect map of the time. For the geographical distribution of the dialects—especially of the eastern dialect—can hardly correspond with linguistic reality; the eastern dialect was obviously not the mother tongue of residents of the far north and the central south, though it was used for inscriptions (Kālsī, Erragudi, etc.) in those regions. Moreover, the languages as they are presented in the inscriptions are surely not exact renditions of the contemporary vernaculars. It has been suggested,[15] for example, that such features as the retention of consonantal clus-

11. H. W. Bailey (BSOAS 11, 1946, 774) suggests the pronunciations /ṭṣ/ or /ṭṣ'/.

12. This metathesis was formerly thought by some (notably Senart; IA 21, 1892, 148–50) to represent merely an orthographic peculiarity of Aśokan Kharoṣṭhī, as seems to be the case with the reversed conjuncts noted in the Girnār Brāhmī inscriptions (see n. 9). But it has been pointed out by Grierson (JRAS 1913, 682–3) and others since him (see discussion and references in von Hinüber, *Das ältere Mittelindisch*, 28–9) that such metatheses are characteristic of the Dardic languages of the northwest to the present day, and that such forms in Aśokan (and in later Gāndhārī/Kharoṣṭhī) inscriptions therefore must reflect actual dialect features.

13. Notably G. Fussman, "Gāndhārī écrite, Gāndhārī parlée," 473 and 479–80.

14. See also the comments of Brough in GD 115.

15. See for example Senart, IA 21, 1892, 146–8.

ters reflect orthographic conservatism and the influence of Sanskrit, and that the actual stage of phonetic development of MIA in Aśoka's time could have been further advanced than it would seem from the inscriptions.

3.1.3 Other inscriptions of the Mauryan era

The scanty epigraphic remains of the Mauryan period other than the records of Aśoka (see 4.3.1.2) are all from the northeast, and most of them exhibit the typical Ardha-Māgadhī features of the "Chancellery Language" (*-e* for *-as*, *l* for *r*, *s* for all sibilants, etc.). Some of these inscriptions, notably Mahāsthān (SI I.79–80) and Sohgaurā (SI I.82–3), seem to reflect a more colloquial and/or archaic variety of this dialect.

The Jogimāṛā cave inscription (ASIAR 1903–4, 128–31) is the only one from any period preserving what seems to be pure Māgadhī, showing the sibilant *ś* instead of *s* (e.g., *śutanuka . . . devadāśikyi* = *sutanukā devadāsī*) besides the aforementioned characteristic features of Ardha-Māgadhī.[16]

3.1.4 Later inscriptional Prakrits

3.1.4.1 Inscriptions in the west-midland dialect

After the Mauryan period there is a major shift in the linguistic features of the inscriptional Prakrits. The predominance of the eastern dialect of the Aśokan and other inscriptions of the Mauryan period ends abruptly; in fact, not a single inscriptional record in eastern dialect has been found from the post-Mauryan era. The dominant role in all regions except the northwest and Sri Lanka falls hereafter to a variety of Prakrit which most resembles, among the Aśokan dialects, the western dialect of the Girnār rock edicts, and which among literary languages has the most in common with Pāli and archaic forms of Śaurasenī. In other words, this dialect partakes of the typical characteristics of the western and central MIA languages: nominative singular masculine in *-o*, retention of Sanskrit *r* and *l*, predominance of the sibilant *s*, and so on.[17] Like the Aśokan Prakrits, this central-western epigraphic Prakrit is still relatively archaic, with only occasional intervocalic voicing of unvoiced stops and elision of voiced stops. But unlike some of the Aśokan inscriptions, consonant groups from Sanskrit are nearly always assimilated.[18]

The causes of the abrupt dialectal shift from east to west undoubtedly lie in political and historical developments, that is, the decline of Magadha as the center of power in northern India after the collapse of the Mauryan empire and the movement

16. The Nāgārjunī hill inscriptions of Aśoka's grandson Daśaratha (SI I.77–8) have in some places the sibilant *ṣ*, e.g., in the king's name *daṣalatha*, and in others *s*. But this variation may not be dialectally significant; cf. the similar cases in Kālsī and some other Aśokan inscriptions noted previously (3.1.2.1. n. 5).

17. For a specimen of this common epigraphic Prakrit, see Appendix, no. 3 (Bhārhut label inscriptions).

18. An apparent exception is the Besnagar pillar inscription of Hēliodōros (Appendix, no. 2), which contains conjuncts such as *tr* (*putreṇa*, l. A–3) and *dr* (*bhāgabhadrasa*, l. A–6). But these examples would seem to fall into the category of early orthographic Sanskritisms (see 3.2.3.2) rather than of phonetic archaisms.

of the center of political power in the following centuries toward the west and northwest.[19] Like the eastern dialect under Aśoka, the central-western dialect of the post-Mauryan era was used far beyond what must have been its original homeland. Thus we find inscriptions in this standard epigraphic Prakrit as far afield as Orissa in the east, for instance, in the Hāthīgumphā inscription (SI I.213–21), while in the south it is abundantly attested in inscriptions from such sites as Nāgārjunakoṇḍa and Amarāvatī. This central-western MIA dialect was, in fact, virtually the sole language in epigraphic use in the period in question, and therefore seems, like Pāli, to have developed into something like a northern Indian lingua franca, at least for epigraphic purposes, in the last two centuries B.C.

This is not to say that the inscriptions in this dialect, which Senart called "Monumental Prakrit,"[20] are totally devoid of local variations. On the contrary, we do occasionally find, in the southern inscriptions, for example, instances of the influence of the local (Dravidian) language, as in *ayira-haghāna* = *ārya-saṅghānām* at Nāgārjunakoṇḍa (*Āyaka*-pillar ins. C–2; SI I, 232, l. 10). There are also considerable variations in orthography, with inscriptions from the later part of the period in question, that is, those of about the third and fourth centuries A.D., showing an increasing precision, most notably in indicating geminate consonants which had hitherto almost always been represented by the corresponding single consonant (see examples cited in SIE 43–4). Stylistically too, there is a considerable range of variation, from the brief and unadorned style of the donative inscriptions from Buddhist *stūpa* sites such as Sāñcī and Bhārhut to the quasi-literary compositions of the Hāthīgumphā inscription of King Khāravela or the Nāsik inscription of the time of Vāsiṣṭhīputra Puḷumāvi (SI I.203–7). But all in all, the standard epigraphic or "Monumental" Prakrit can be treated as essentially a single language whose use spread far beyond its place of origin, and which should not be taken to represent the local vernacular of every region and period where it appears.[21]

3.1.4.2 Inscriptions in other MIA dialects

3.1.4.2.1 Gāndhārī

Grammatical descriptions: S. Konow, CII 2.1, xcv–cxv; J. Brough, GD 55–118; G. Fussman, "Gāndhārī écrite, Gāndhārī parlée."

In the northwest and adjoining regions, inscriptions of the post-Mauryan era (see 4.3.2) continued to be written in essentially the same language as the Aśokan rock edicts from this area, that is, the MIA dialect which used to be referred to as "Northwestern

19. See the comments of Mehendale, HGIP, xxxvii.

20. IA 21, 1892, 258.

21. For this reason, the methods of analysis followed by Mehendale in HGIP are misleading. His classification of Prakrit inscriptions of the post-Mauryan epoch into geographical groups (western, southern, central, and eastern) is valid only with reference to their findspots; but to trace separate linguistic developments within and influences among the various groups, as Mehendale does, is based on the misconception that each of them constitutes a distinct linguistic entity. As Senart showed in *Les Inscriptions de Piyadassi*, this is not the case, and most of the conclusions drawn by Mehendale concerning the trends and directions of phonetic and morphological change cannot be accepted. A definitive historical linguistic treatment of the post-Aśokan epigraphic Prakrit, bearing in mind the compli-

Prakrit" but which is nowadays more commonly called "Gāndhārī," following H. W. Bailey's suggestion.[22] The inscriptions in this language are invariably written in Kharoṣṭhī script and are virtually all Buddhist in content. They range in date from approximately the second century B.C. to the third or possibly fourth century A.D. (see 2.3.2), and their findspots extend from Afghanistan in the northwest to Mathurā in the southeast, with stray finds farther to the east and north (2.3.1).[23]

Inscriptional Gāndhārī preserves most of the characteristic features already mentioned in connection with its early form seen in the northwestern Aśokan dialect (3.1.2.3), such as the retention of the three Sanskrit sibilants and the tendency to preserve certain consonant groups, especially those with *r*. It also exhibits several further developments, notably the following:

1. Fricative pronunciations of certain intervocalic consonants, sometimes marked by a diacritic sign (cf. 2.3.8) resembling the subscript *r*, as in the Wardak inscription (CII 2.1, 170, l. 1), *bhag(r)avada* = *bhagavataḥ*.
2. A voiced sibilant (/z/) derived from intervocalic *s*, *dha*, etc., indicated by various spellings such as *majhe* < *māse* (Māṇikiāla stone ins., CII 2.1, 149, l. 1) and *bosisatva* < *bodhisattva* (Taxila silver scroll, CII 2.1, 77, l. 3).
3. In general, a more advanced stage of development with respect to the voicing and elision of intervocalic consonants, as compared to the contemporary Brāhmī inscriptions (cf. 3.1.4.1); see examples cited by Fussman, "Gāndhārī écrite, Gāndhārī parlée," 457.
4. A weakening of the distinction between Sanskrit *ṇ* and *n*, reflected in orthographic inconsistency in the use of the two characters (CII 2.1, cii–civ).
5. A weakening of the distinction between aspirate and nonaspirate consonants, perhaps attributable to the influence of the neighboring non-Indic languages (CII 2.1, ci–cii).
6. Extreme inconsistency in the notation of final vowels, which according to Fussman (473) indicates that they were largely neutralized in pronunciation. This is especially notable in the nominative singular masculine, for which the endings *-o*, *-e*, and *-a* are attested in the same phrase (examples in Fussman, 459–60).[24]
7. The occasional use (not surprising in view of the geographical position of the dialect) of loanwords from non-Indic languages such as Greek (e.g.,

---

cations introduced by loose standardization on the one hand and the vagaries of scribal usage and local influences on the other, remains to be written.

22. BSOAS 11, 1943–46, 764. Although Bailey's suggested name has been accepted and come into general use, it should be remembered that it is a modern creation and has no attestation in traditional materials (see 2.2.2, on the traditional names of scripts).

23. Until recently, besides the many inscriptions and central Asian secular documents in Gāndhārī, only one literary specimen of the language, namely the *Dharmapada* ms. from Khotan, definitively published by Brough (GD), was known. But a large collection of fragmentary Gāndhārī mss. on birch bark scrolls has recently been discovered, confirming, as had already been suspected on the basis of traces of Gāndhārī words in Buddhist texts translated into Chinese (see Fussman, "Gāndhārī écrite, Gāndhārī parlée," 442 n. 20), that Gāndhārī was a major Buddhist literary language. See R. Salomon, "A Preliminary Survey of Some Early Buddhist Manuscripts Recently Acquired by the British Library," JAOS 117, 1997, 353–8, and *Ancient Buddhist Scrolls from Gandhāra* (London/Seattle: British Library and University of Washington Press, forthcoming).

24. Cf. the earlier comments (3.1.2.3) concerning *-o* and *-e* in northwest Aśokan. Konow (cxiii) divided the post-Aśokan inscriptions into "an eastern *o*-dialect and a western *e*-dialect," but the recent study of Fussman, based on a much larger corpus, has shown that this distinction does not hold. The

meridarkha = μεριδάρχης; Swāt ins., CII 2.1, 4) and Saka (*erjhuṇa* = *alysānai/e'ysānai*; Takht-i-bāhī ins., l. 5, CII 2.1, 62 and xcvii).

The Kharoṣṭhī documents from central Asia (see 4.3.7.12) provide specimens of a separate dialect of Gāndhārī used far beyond its native region. These documents show that Gāndhārī became the official language of the Indianized kingdom of Shan-shan or Kroraina in the southeastern Tarim basin in about the third century A.D. (cf. 2.3.1 and 2.3.2). This "Niya Prakrit" or "Kroraina Prakrit," which was analyzed in detail by T. Burrow in *The Language of the Kharoṣṭhi Documents from Chinese Turkestan*, agrees on the whole fairly closely with the language of the post-Aśokan Gāndhārī inscriptions from India,[25] but also differs from Indian Gāndhārī in several significant particulars, such as the following:

1. Certain phonetic tendencies, such as a confusion between voiced and unvoiced consonants (more pronounced than in Indian Gāndhārī), and particularly a tendency to deaspirate Indic aspirates, apparently reflecting the phonetic structure of the (unattested) local dialect (Burrow, *Language*, 5 and 9).
2. The loss of distinction between endings for the nominative and accusative endings. The ending is generally *-a*, in both the singular (<*-e* according to Burrow, "The Dialectal Position," 421 and 424) and the plural (presumably for *-ā*).
3. The use of an ending *-tu* for the second person singular of all tenses of the verb; for example, *labhiśatu* 'you will get'. According to Burrow (*Language*, 43), this is "probably taken from the 2nd person of the pronoun."
4. The development of a periphrastic construction for the preterite active, consisting of the past participle plus the personal endings of the present, except for the third-person singular where the ending is omitted; for example, *triṭhemi* = **dṛṣṭaḥ* + *-mi* 'I saw'; *taḍita* = **tāḍitaḥ* 'he beat' (*Language*, 50–3).
5. The frequent use of the infinitive in *-aṃnae* (also occasionally found in Indian Gāndhārī; Burrow, *Language*, 49); for example, *karaṃnae* 'to do'.
6. The frequent use of postpositions not found in other MIA dialects, such as *prace* 'concerning' (<**pratyayam*) and *vaṃti* 'to, with' (<*upānte*; *Language*, 42).
7. The extensive use of loanwords from various non-Indic languages, especially from Iranian languages (*Language*, vii–viii), from the local "Krorainic" language which apparently was closely related to Tocharian (*Language*, viii–ix), and occasionally from Greek (e.g., *milima* = μέδιμνος; *Language*, 111).

3.1.4.2.2 Sinhalese Prakrit

Grammatical descriptions: S. Paranavitana, *Inscriptions of Ceylon*, I.xxvii–xlv; Wilhelm Geiger and D. B. Jayatilaka in Jayatilaka et al., eds., *A Dictionary of the Sinhalese Language* (Colombo: The Royal Asiatic Society, Ceylon Branch, 1935), I.1, xxiv–xxvii; Saddhamangala Karunaratne, EZ 7, 39–44.

The language of the Old Sinhalese or Sinhalese Prakrit inscriptions of about the third century B.C. to the third or fourth century A.D. (see 4.3.7.1) is characterized by several

---

entire question of the subdialects of Gandhari remains unanswered, due at least in part to the problems of the casual orthography which is characteristic of the Kharosthi/Gandhari inscriptions.

25. See also Burrow, "The Dialectal Position of the Niya Prakrit" (see n. 10), 419–35 (esp. 423–5); and recently, Colette Caillat, "Connections Between Asokan (Shahbazgarhi) and Niya Prakrit?" IIJ 35, 1992, 109–19.

unusual phonological features. Palatal *ś* generally predominates over the other sibilants, but Sanskrit sibilants also are frequently reflected by *h*. Sanskrit aspirates are generally represented by the corresponding nonaspirates (e.g., *dama* = *dharma*), but *jh* regularly replaces *j* (e.g., *rajha* = *rājā*; Paranavitana, xxxi; Karunaratne, 9). Otherwise, consonants in intervocalic position are generally preserved as in Sanskrit, though they are often subjected to voicing. Long vowels are commonly shortened, though according to some authorities this is merely a graphic device (Geiger and Jayatilaka, xxv–xxvi; contra, Paranavitana, xxviii).

The morphology of Sinhalese Prakrit is on the whole not much different from that of the other old inscriptional Prakrits. The nominative singular ends in *-e* and the genitive in *-sa*, *-śa*, or *-ha*.[26] In these respects, as in others such as the predominance of the palatal sibilants, the dialect appears to have been influenced by the Māgādhī of the Buddhist missionaries sent to Sri Lanka from northeastern India in the Mauryan period (Geiger and Jayatilaka, op. cit., xx).

3.1.5 Literary Middle Indo-Aryan in inscriptions

3.1.5.1 The literary Prakrits

The standardized literary Prakrits (mainly Māhārāṣṭrī, sometimes also Śaurasenī and Māgadhī) were occasionally employed in inscriptions of the medieval era,[27] either in independent Prakrit inscriptions or within Sanskrit inscriptions. The outstanding example of an independent literary Prakrit inscription is an inscription of the eleventh century A.D. at Dhār consisting of two "centuries" (actually 109 verses each) of Māhārāṣṭrī verses in praise of the tortoise *avatāra* (*avanikūrmmaśatam*) (EI 8, 241–60; cf. 4.1.8). Not surprisingly, Prakrit was also sometimes used for Jaina inscriptions, most notably the Ghaṭayāla inscription (JRAS 1895, 513–21), which is composed almost entirely of Āryā verses in Māhārāṣṭrī.

The literary Prakrits also occur in the inscriptional dramas (see 4.1.8 and 7.2.2.2.2), where they play their usual role as the language spoken by the lesser characters; thus we find specimens of Māhārāṣṭrī and Śaurasenī in the *Pārijātamañjarī-nāṭikā* at Dhār and the *Harakeli-nāṭaka* at Ajmer, and of these dialects plus Māgadhī in the *Lalitavigraharāja-nāṭaka*, also from Ajmer. Occasionally a Prakrit verse is also included in an ordinary Sanskrit inscription, for instance, verse 12 (in Māhārāṣṭrī) of the Vārāṇasī copper plate inscription of Karṇa (SI II.340).[28]

3.1.5.2 Pāli

Inscriptions in canonical Pāli[29] from India proper are relatively rare. Those examples which do occur are usually Buddhist inscriptions of cultic content (cf. 4.1.7), such as

26. Due to the brevity and formulaic character of the Sinhalese Prakrit inscriptions, there is almost no material for the study of finite verb morphology; such few verb forms as do appear are nearly all participial.

27. This is of course a purely literary phenomenon, historically unrelated to the use of the MIA vernaculars in early inscriptions.

28. For other examples of literary Prakrit together with other languages, see section 3.6.

29. It should be noted that in some early (and even some more recent) epigraphic publications the term "Pāli" has been inaccurately used to refer to various other MIA dialects.

the two Sārnāth stone inscriptions (EI 9, 291–3) recording the "Four Noble Truths" and the "Buddhist creed." Other Indian inscriptions in Pāli or closely related dialects include the *Pratītya-samutpāda* formulae on the Devnīmorī casket and in a Ratnagiri inscription.[30]

Unlike in India, Pāli inscriptions are found in large numbers in some Buddhist countries of Southeast Asia, especially Burma and Thailand, and also in smaller numbers in Sri Lanka and Cambodia (see 4.3.7.1 and 4.3.7.5–4.3.7.7).

3.2 Mixed or "Hybrid" Dialects

3.2.1 The character of "Epigraphical Hybrid Sanskrit" (EHS)

From about the first to the fourth century of the Christian era, a large number of inscriptions from northern, central, and occasionally also southern India were written in a peculiar language which is neither fully Sanskrit nor fully Prakrit but partakes of the characteristics of both. This language has accordingly been referred to by such terms as "mixed dialect," "Sanskrit influenced by Prakrit," or "Prakrit influenced by Sanskrit." In 1978, Th. Damsteegt coined the term "Epigraphical Hybrid Sanskrit" (EHS) in his book of the same name, on the analogy of Franklin Edgerton's "Buddhist Hybrid Sanskrit"; and although, like its prototype, the term is potentially misleading in some cases, it deserves to be, and largely has been, adopted for general use.

EHS texts are typically more or less Sanskritic in orthography but Prakritic in morphology and syntax. Thus a typical EHS word occurring frequently in the inscriptions is *bhiksuṣya* 'of (the) monk', corresponding to Sanskrit *bhikṣoḥ* and MIA *bhikkhus(s)a*. Here the stem is spelled as in Sanskrit, while the inflection is a pseudo-Sanskrit rendition of the Middle Indic *-ssa*. Similarly, the standard EHS dating formula is *etāye pūrvāye* or variants thereof, equivalent to Sanskrit *etasyāṃ pūrvāyām* 'on the aforementioned [date (*tithau*)]'.

An example of a typical EHS text,[31] in both content and form, is the Kaṅkālī Ṭīlā (Mathurā) *toraṇa* inscription (Lüders, MI §20 [Lüders' tr.]):

> *bhadata-jayasenasya āṃtevāsinīye dhāmaghoṣāye dān[o] pāsādo*
>
> "The temple (is) the gift of Dhāmaghoṣā (Dharmaghoṣā), the female disciple of the venerable Jayasena."

Notable here, among other characteristic features, is the juxtaposition of the Sanskrit genitive masculine ending *-sya* with the Prakrit feminines in *-āye* and *-īye*; the semi-Sanskritized stem of the proper name *dharmaghoṣā-* (according to Lüders' interpretation) contrasting with the un-Sanskritized stem of *pāsādo* (Skt. *prāsāda-*); and the spellings, influenced by MIA orthography, of *bhadata-* (for *bhadanta*) and *āṃtevasinīye* (for *aṃte-*).

It must be emphasized that EHS, like the epigraphic Prakrits, is by no means a standardized or a unified language. The orthography and morphology of EHS in-

30. See O. von Hinüber, "Epigraphical Varieties of Continental Pāli from Devnimori and Ratnagiri," in *Buddhism and Its Relation to Other Religions* [for full reference see Index of Inscriptions Cited s.v. Devnīmorī], 185–200 for these and for references to other Pāli inscriptions.

31. For a longer specimen of EHS, see Appendix, no. 5 (Sārnāth umbrella shaft ins.).

scriptions vary widely and unpredictably, and they display various grades or degrees of hybridism. In general, one may think in terms of more Prakritic varieties ("Prakrit influenced by Sanskrit," in the terminology used by Sircar in SI I) versus more highly Sanskritized varieties ("Sanskrit influenced by Prakrit").[32] But it must be understood that these divisions, like any categorization of EHS, are inevitably somewhat arbitrary. In actual practice, the boundaries between the two main types of EHS, and indeed between EHS as a whole and MIA on the one side and Sanskrit on the other, are far from clear.[33] It is probably impossible to establish fully objective criteria for EHS, particularly for the more Sanskritized varieties where there is no clear dividing line between Sanskritic EHS and informal epigraphic varieties of standard Sanskrit.[34] It may therefore be more appropriate to think of EHS in terms of a broad spectrum of partial Sanskritization, verging into pure MIA at one end and standard Sanskrit at the other.

3.2.2 Geographical and chronological distribution of EHS

The city of Mathurā and its environs are the source of the earliest and largest number of EHS inscriptions. Lüders' *Mathurā Inscriptions* (MI) thus constitutes the largest and most convenient corpus for the study of these documents. But from around the late first century A.D., many other inscriptions in EHS have been discovered over a wide range of India, particularly from the west, at sites such as Andhau in Gujarat and Nāsik in Maharashtra; from north central and northeastern India, at Sārnāth, Kosam, and so on; from central India, at Sāñcī; and even from the south, at Nāgārjunakoṇḍa.[35] Throughout the period in question, EHS coexisted as an epigraphic language with Prakrit and/or Sanskrit, but it was definitely the predominant language overall for the first three centuries of the Christian era in northern and central India. Although individual records of similar date may vary widely in their degree of hybridism, EHS does follow an overall pattern of development toward greater Sanskritization over the first four centuries of the Christian era. Thus from about the third century A.D. on, the standard epigraphic dialect ranges from moderately to highly Sanskritized EHS, with some specimens in completely or nearly standard Sanskrit. This variety is characteristic, for instance, of the later inscriptions of the Western Kṣatrapas and related dynasties of the third century.

Overall, the pattern of distribution of EHS inscriptions gives the impression that they radiate out from Mathurā toward the northeast and southwest. Thus the origins and development of EHS seem to parallel the foundation and spread of the kingdoms of the Scythian and Kuṣāṇa rulers in the heartland of India (see 3.2.3.2).

32. Damsteegt (EHS 143) similarly divides EHS inscriptions into "a) those basically in MIA, but with Sanskrit features; [and] b) those basically in Sanskrit, but with MIA features."

33. Note that Damsteegt devotes an entire section of his study (2.1, "Criteria") to a consideration of marginal cases of EHS.

34. See, e.g., MI §67; and for a highly Prakritic specimen, §137.

35. Damsteegt (156) also includes certain southern Indian copper plate inscriptions such as Penugoṇḍa, Maṭṭepāḍ, and Bāsim as examples of EHS; I would not agree with this classification, and treat them (3.3.4) as bilingual (Prakrit and Sanskrit) records.

3.2.3 The linguistic nature of EHS

3.2.3.1 Relation to Buddhist Hybrid Sanskrit

The epigraphic mixed dialects bear a clear and close linguistic relation to the idiosyncratic Sanskrit of Buddhist texts generally and particularly to the true "Buddhist Hybrid Sanskrit" (BHS) of texts such as the *Mahāvastu*. Although the epigraphic and literary hybrids do differ in particulars, this is at least in part due to the different character and content of the documents preserved in them. In any case, the variability of both of these unstandardized languages presents major obstacles to a detailed comparison. But despite these complications, there can be no doubt that the two represent different manifestations of the same basic linguistic phenomenon, namely, the gradual Sanskritization of MIA vernaculars. It is also certain that the hybrid language used in the first three centuries of the Christian era was neither an exclusively Buddhist nor an exclusively literary construction, as seems to be assumed by certain scholars (notably Edgerton) who did not sufficiently consider the epigraphic evidence. For among the hybrid inscriptions of this period, we have documents of not only Buddhist but also Brahmanical and Jaina content which are original compositions in the hybrid dialect.

Thus the epigraphic evidence contradicts the notion espoused by Edgerton and others that the specimens of hybrid dialects that we have are merely incomplete or imperfect translations into Sanskrit of texts originally written in MIA dialects; in other words, that the hybrid language is merely a literary artifact and not a real language. The inscriptions prove that hybrid Sanskrit was, or at least eventually became, a living linguistic entity, and thus support the position of Lamotte (HBI 638) and others that some Buddhist texts were actually composed in BHS.

3.2.3.2 The origins of EHS

This still leaves unanswered the question of the historical origins of the epigraphic (and Buddhist) hybrid dialect. In general, opinions on the controversial question of the motivations and mechanics of the semi-Sanskritization of MIA fall into two camps. The first is the school which holds that the hybrid is little more than a bad imitation of Sanskrit, that is, that its incomplete and imperfect Sanskritization reflects incompetence and ignorance on the part of the composers of the documents. Thus T. Burrow says that "such a mongrel language was actually employed by those who wished to employ the superior Sanskrit language but were not able to master its grammar."[36] K. R. Norman elaborates this view: "They [the donors] would presumably dictate in Pkt, and once it had become fashionable to write inscriptions in Skt, the scribes would 'translate', to the best of their ability, into that language. The correctness of the Skt depended, therefore, on the scribes' competence."[37]

36. *The Sanskrit Language*, The Great Languages (London: Faber and Faber, 1955), 61.

37. Review of Damsteegt, EHS, in *Lingua* 48, 1979, 293. A similar position was maintained by Senart in his important but by now largely outdated discussion in *Les Inscriptions de Piyadassi* of "Mixed Sanskrit," which he saw as essentially an orthographic phenomenon with no real linguistic basis: "Mixed Sanskrit is only a manner of writing Prâkrit, consisting in going as near as possible to the orthography and the etymological forms known to the religious language [i.e., Sanskrit]" (IA 21, 1892, 275).

The other school of thought tends to view the degree of hybridism in a given document as a matter not so much of knowledge or ability as of taste; thus Lamotte describes hybrid Sanskrit as "une langue littéraire où le dosage du prākrit et du sanskrit était laissé à leur appréciation personelle" (HBI 642; see also 638 and 645). The epigraphic evidence in particular tends to support the views of this second school. Especially worthy of note are cases such as the Morā well inscription (MI §113; see 3.3.2) where a single inscription comprises portions both in hybrid and in more or less standard Sanskrit, distributed according to function; here, as is usually the case, the prose portion is in hybrid language while the verse—which is composed for the occasion, not quoted from another source—is in good Sanskrit. Such cases indicate that Lamotte was correct in supposing that the use and degree of hybridism were essentially controlled by the taste and judgment of the composers of the texts, and that at least some of them could write in standard Sanskrit when they saw fit.

Certain grammatical features of the epigraphic language also support this view. Particularly interesting in this regard is the sporadic application of Sanskrit sandhi rules. The "wrong" application of sandhi is one of the most characteristic features of the epigraphic hybrid, and is often what most clearly distinguishes inscriptions in highly Sanskritized hybrid from fully standard Sanskrit; a characteristic example is the label inscription on the Kaniṣka portrait statue from Māṭ (Mathurā; MI §97), which reads *mahārājā rājātirājā devaputro kaniṣko*. Here the MIA nominative masculine ending *-o* is used instead of Sanskrit *visarga*, not only *in pausa* (*kaniṣko*) but also before *k* (*devaputro k-*). This usage is very common in EHS, and of course actually reflects not "wrong sandhi" but the retention of the old MIA ending in the otherwise (i.e., orthographically) Sanskritized word. Contrast with this the peculiar sandhi forms found in later Mathurā inscriptions of the posthybrid era, such as *śākyabhikṣuṇyār jayabhaṭṭāyār yad*. . . in the Kaṭrā pedestal inscription (MI §8) and *vīṣṇusyaḥ gomindrapūttrasyaḥ ha[ku]datta-p[au]ttrasyaḥ* (Mathurā Nāga statue ins., MI §161). Both of these inscriptions date from the Gupta period, when Sanskrit had become the standard epigraphic language, and in them we clearly do have incompetent attempts to write Sanskrit; the incorrect sandhi does not reflect underlying MIA forms, but simply the misapplication of Sanskrit rules improperly learned or understood by the composer.

Thus the combined evidence of grammar and usage speaks against the assumption that the hybrid language simply represented failed attempts to write Sanskrit and supports the notion that hybrid was a coherent (though not rigidly standardized) language in and of itself, and that those who wrote it did so intentionally. This is not to say, however, that the hybrids were consciously formulated and developed. Rather, the available evidence suggests that hybrid Sanskrit arose in the course of a gradual Sanskritizing movement which had its origins in the late centuries B.C., expanded in the early centuries of the Christian era, and culminated in the final triumph of classical Sanskrit in the Gupta era. Early tendencies toward Sanskritization, in the form of sporadic semi-Sanskritized orthography, appear in some Prakrit inscriptions of the pre-Christian era. Such "Prakrit influenced by Sanskrit" is seen, for example, in the Besnagar pillar inscription (Appendix, no. 2) in such spellings as *bhāgabhadrasa trātārasa* (l. A-6; cf. n. 18), and in the Pabhosā cave inscription (SI I.96), *rājño gopālīputrasa* (l. 1). The hybrids would seem to reflect the extension and regularization of these early tendencies toward Sanskritization. In other words, it seems that the semi-Sanskritized Prakrits of the early Christian era gradually attained a de facto status of their own as semiliterary languages; in Jean Filliozat's words, it was not merely a matter of "seulement sanskritisation de textes, mais encore sanskritisation de dialectes."[38]

Thus it is more likely that scribes and authors wrote in such a dialect not because they were unable to write in "pure" Sanskrit (or "pure" Prakrit) but simply because this had become the prevalent and preferred style of their time and place. The linguistic borders, in other words, between "Sanskrit" and "Prakrit" were probably not as strictly fixed in practical usage as they appear to be when the matter is viewed (as it usually is) from the point of view of formal literature. From the less formal Buddhist texts, and especially from the epigraphic remains of the period in question, we instead get the impression that a variety of dialects, or perhaps rather of dialectal styles, covering a broad spectrum from pure MIA to pure standard Sanskrit were available for varying purposes and contexts. The choice of a given dialect by a given writer was, to be sure, governed to some extent by his knowledge and level of education; but to an equal, and perhaps greater, extent, it was the content and nature of the document he was writing which would determine the appropriate level of Sanskritization.

Due to the limitations of the materials, it is not possible to specify with any precision the MIA dialect or dialects underlying the hybrid language. But both the geographical concentrations of the inscriptions in the Mathurā area and its predominant grammatical features such as the nominative masculine in *-o* indicate that the epigraphic dialect, like the Buddhist literary hybrid, reflects an underlying midland dialect (HBI 645).

Attempts to explain the motivations and linguistic forces shaping the development of the hybrids tend to focus on two main concepts. First, there is the idea, promoted by Joseph Mansion[39] and Filliozat,[40] that they essentially arose as a lingua franca enabling Buddhist monks from various regions of India to converse easily at a period in history when their local MIA dialects were beginning to diverge to the point where they were no longer easily mutually intelligible. This assumes, first of all, that the hybrid remains reflect an actual spoken language,[41] which would be difficult to prove. Other elements of the theory too are less than totally convincing. For one thing, it is questionable whether the MIA dialects of the time were really so different; from the available literary and inscriptional data, it would appear that they were not yet so widely divergent as to present major difficulties of communication. Moreover, while it is true that the literary remains of the hybrid language are virtually all Buddhist, the inscriptional data, as we have seen, include hybrid documents of all three major religious traditions, that is, Buddhist, Brahmanical, and Jaina; the statistical predominance of Buddhist records may simply reflect the predominance of Buddhism itself at the time in question. The development of hybrid Sanskrit may well have been influenced and promoted by the Buddhists, but the epigraphic evidence shows that hybridization was actually part of an overall lin-

38. Review of F. Edgerton, *Buddhist Hybrid Sanskrit Grammar/Dictionary*, *T'oung Pao* 43, 1954, 147–71 (quoted 168).

39. *Esquisse d'une histoire de la langue sanscrite* (Paris: Paul Geuthner, 1931), 109.

40. Op. cit., 164–6.

41. Cf. Filliozat, op. cit., 166, describing the hybrid language as "un langage réellement parlé."

guistic trend which transcended sectarian divisions. In the words of Lamotte, "le sanskrit mixte n'est pas un phénomène strictement bouddhique, mais s'insère dans l'évolution générale de la langue indienne" (HBI 638).

The second theory of hybridization places more emphasis on the status value of Sanskrit as the traditional language of the learned elite. According to this view, the early adoption of Sanskritic spellings and the ever-increasing Sanskritization of the epigraphic language, and eventually the adoption of classical Sanskrit itself, all reflect the irresistible influence of Sanskrit as the language of learning par excellence. In this connection it has been pointed out by several authors, from Sylvain Lévi[42] to Damsteegt (EHS 207–9), that the Sanskritizing trend was accelerated by the influence of the Scythian and Kuṣāṇa rulers of northern and western India in the period concerned. As foreigners, they were evidently inclined to patronize the elite language in an effort to legitimize their rule and emphasize their own Indianization. Thus it is no accident that the Sanskritized hybrid came into extensive use at precisely the time and place that the Kuṣāṇas and Śaka Kṣatrapas were ruling; just as it is no coincidence that the first major literary Sanskrit inscription, Rudradāman's Junāgaḍh rock inscription (see 3.3.3), was written on behalf of a Śaka king who, like his predecessors in Mathurā, was trying to appear "more Indian than the Indians."

All in all, the theories based on the status of Sanskrit seem to provide the strongest explanation for the gradual hybridization of the inscriptional Prakrits, and for the ultimate Sanskritization of Indian epigraphy. The status of Sanskrit was so deeply ingrained in traditional India that it slowly but surely eroded the precedent established by Aśoka (presumably for Buddhistic motivations) of using Prakrit for epigraphic purposes.

3.3 Sanskrit

3.3.1 The earliest Sanskrit inscriptions

It is, in the words of Louis Renou, "le grand paradoxe linguistique de l'Inde"[43] that Sanskrit, the linguistic parent of MIA, first appeared in inscriptions much later than its own descendants. For Sanskrit began to come into epigraphic use only in the first century B.C., according to the now generally accepted dating (mainly on paleographic grounds) for the oldest Sanskrit inscriptions, namely, the Ayodhyā (SI I.94–5) and the Ghosuṇḍī (SI I.90–1) and Hāthībāḍā (EI 22, 198–205) stone inscriptions.

The Ayodhyā inscription records in two lines of essentially standard Sanskrit the foundation by the "righteous king" (*dharmarājñā*) Dhana[*deva?] of a structure (*ketanam*) in memory of his father Phalgudeva.[44] The formation of the compound *dharmarājñā* instead of the theoretically correct *dharmarājena* is of no great conse-

42. "Sur quelques termes employés dans les inscriptions des Kṣatrapas," JA, ser. 9, vol. 19, 1902, 95–125 (esp. 117–9).

43. *Histoire de la langue sanskrite*, Les Langues du Monde 10 (Lyon: IAC, 1956), 84.

44. The paleographic estimate of a date in the first century B.C. is corroborated by the statement that the donor is the "sixth [in descent] of [i.e., from; cf. SI I.95 n. 3] General Puṣyamitra" (*senāpateḥ puṣyamitrasya ṣaṣṭhena*), since the Puṣyamitra referred to is presumably the founder of the Śuṅga dynasty in ca. 187 B.C.

quence, since compounds of this type are found frequently in less formal registers of Sanskrit. Also worthy of note is the apparent use of the genitive instead of the ablative in *puṣyamitrasya ṣaṣṭhena*, assuming that the usual interpretation[45] as "sixth [in descent] of [i.e., 'from'] . . ." is correct. But here, too, the intrusion of the stronger genitive case into the domain of the weaker ablative is not uncommon in informal Sanskrit usage.

The three inscriptions from Hāthībāḍā and one from Ghosuṇḍī are all separate renderings of the same text, recording the construction of a structure[46] for the worship of the deities Saṃkarṣaṇa and Vāsudeva. The text, which except for the beginning of the first line can be reconstructed from the four extant fragmentary versions, is again in essentially "correct" Sanskrit with a few possible exceptions. For instance, the word accompanying the names *saṃkarṣaṇa-vāsudevābhyāṃ* is spelled *bhagavabhyāṃ* instead of the expected *bhagavadbhyāṃ* in both versions (Hāthībāḍā A and Ghosuṇḍī) in which it is preserved; but this may be no more than a scribal error (cf. EI 22, 201). Also, it has been suggested (SI I.91 n. 1) that the donor's personal name, given as *sarvatāta*, "may be actually Sarvatrāta." But this is uncertain, as the king in question is otherwise unknown, and even if the inscription did record a Prakritic form of the ruler's name this would be of no great linguistic import, since personal names are frequently recorded in Prakritic forms in Sanskrit inscriptions.

In conclusion, then, the language of the Hāṭhībāḍā-Ghosuṇḍī inscriptions, like that of Ayodhyā, is essentially standard Sanskrit, though with some marginal indications of informal usage and style.

3.3.2 Early Sanskrit inscriptions from Mathurā

Except for these very few examples from the last century before the Christian era, the earliest Sanskrit inscriptions are found in Mathurā, which has yielded several records of the first and second centuries A.D., that is, the time of the Śaka Kṣatrapas and the early Kuṣāṇas, which are written in Sanskrit or a dialect very closely approaching it.[47] The earliest of the Sanskrit inscriptions from Mathurā are probably those of the time of the Kṣatrapa Śoḍāsa, who is dated with reasonable certainty to the early years of the first century A.D. The most important of these is the Morā well inscription discussed earlier (3.2.3.2; MI §113), which seems to record the dedication of a shrine to five epic heroes. The opening portion of this fragmentary inscription, recording its date, was written in the hybrid dialect (*mahakṣatrapasa rājūvulasa putrasa svāmi* . . .), while the remaining three lines are in Sanskrit, evidently including a verse in the *Bhujaṅgavijṛmbhita* meter (EI 24, 198). But for minor orthographic liberties of a type often seen in Sanskrit inscriptions (cf. 3.3.8.1), such as *ārcādeśāṃ śailāṃ* instead of *arcādeśān śāilān* (accusative plural), the latter part of the inscription is virtually standard Sanskrit.

A similar linguistic situation is observed in another fragmentary Mathurā stone slab inscription of Śoḍāsa's time (MI §178) whose first two lines appear to be in hybrid

45. Cf. SI I.95 n. 3.

46. *pūjāśilāprākāro nārāyaṇavāṭakā*; the exact sense of the phrase is uncertain.

47. Here, as in the case of the hybrid dialects discussed earlier, it is not always absolutely clear whether or not a given text should be labeled "Sanskrit."

dialect ("not quite correct Sanskrit," in Lüders' words) as indicated by the nonstandard sandhi in *pārvato prāsādo*, l. 2, but whose third and fourth lines seem to contain an *upajāti* verse in standard Sanskrit. A third inscription of Śoḍāsa's time (MI §115) on a doorjamb from Morā is in standard Sanskrit except for the typical hybrid form *svāmi(sya)* (l. 10). Other undated Sanskrit inscriptions attributable to the same general period include a fragment of a stone inscription from Kaṅkālī Ṭīlā (possibly a Jaina inscription) with text in *śārdūlavikriḍita* meter (MI §21) and a fragmentary Mathurā coping-stone inscription in "pre-Kuṣān characters and composed in pure Sanskrit" (MI §162), which is probably a Brahmanical dedication.

The Sanskrit inscriptions from the earliest phase at Mathurā show certain interesting patterns. First, they are mostly Brahmanical in affiliation. While the Kaṅkālī Ṭīlā inscription may be Jaina (it is too fragmentary to be identified), in any case there are no Buddhist inscriptions among them. Second, some of them comprise two dialects, with the practical portion (containing the date, etc.) in the hybrid language and a eulogistic portion in standard Sanskrit verse. Others, such as the Morā doorjamb inscription, are in standard Sanskrit but show occasional hybrid tinges in morphology or orthography.

Moving on to the period of the Great Kuṣāṇas (i.e., Kaniṣka and his successors, provisionally assumed here for purposes of discussion to have begun ruling in A.D. 78; cf. 5.5.1.4), we now find more Mathurā inscriptions in reasonably standard Sanskrit, including for the first time some of Buddhistic content. For instance, several of the pillar base donations from the Jamālpur mound (e.g., MI §47–9 and 53) are in standard Sanskrit or very close to it; for instance, §48, *aya[ṃ kum]bh[ako dā]naṃ saṅghaprakṛtān[ā]ṃ Bh[ad]raghoṣa-pramukhā(nāṃ)*. A longer inscription is the Īsāpur *yūpa* (MI §94) of the year 24 (= ca. A.D. 102?) of Vāsiṣka, commemorating the performance of a *dvādaśarātra* sacrifice in proper Sanskrit but for some minor orthographic variations (*gṛṣma-* for *grīṣma-* [l. 3]; hiatus in *-cchandogena iṣṭvā* [l. 6]). A few decades younger is a pedestal inscription from Tokri Ṭīlā (MI §99) recording donations, apparently Brahmanical, during the reign of Huviṣka (the date is lost) in more or less correct Sanskrit but with some peculiarities such as the apparent gerund *dṛśya* (l. 3) and the unclear word *nanayat* (l. 1).

Overall, a fair number (but still only a fraction of the total corpus) of the inscriptions of Mathurā from the early first to about the middle of the second century A.D. are written in fairly standard Sanskrit. Most of the Sanskrit inscriptions are Brahmanical in affiliation, and the Sanskrit of Buddhist inscriptions is more prone to hybridisms, though these are also not totally absent from the Brahmanical ones. In conclusion, although the hybrid dialect is still predominant, Sanskrit is beginning to establish itself as an epigraphic language in this era, especially in Brahmanical circles, continuing the trend which began in the first century B.C.

3.3.3 Sanskrit inscriptions from western India in the Kṣatrapa period

The inscriptions of the earlier house of Western Kṣatrapa kings, namely, the Kṣaharāta line of Nahapāna (middle of the first century A.D.?), are mostly in Prakrit or in hybridized Prakrit, with the important exception of Nāsik inscription no. 10 of Nahapāna's son-in-law Uṣavadāta (SI I.167–70). The opening portion of this inscription (ll. 1–3), eulogizing Uṣavadāta, is written in a fair approximation of standard Sanskrit with some hybrid features such as frequent sandhi hiatus (e.g., *dharmātmanā idaṃ*, l. 3) and hybrid morphology such as *bhojāpayitrā* (l. 1). The remainder of the inscription, recording the actual donations, is in a somewhat more hybridized style. Senart (EI 8, 79) pointed out that about the first half of the eulogistic portion is virtually a Sanskrit rendition (or, as Senart puts it, a "reproduction in Sanskṛit orthography") of the description of Uṣavadāta in the Prakrit Kārle cave inscription of the time of Nahapāna (SI I.171–2). The linguistic innovation in this inscription presumably reflects contemporary developments in Mathurā and adjoining regions, though it is not clear why Sanskrit was used for this inscription only; apparently, this is an instance of the orthographic options alluded to previously (3.2.3.2).

The Junāgaḍh rock inscription of Rudradāman (SI I.175–80), the greatest king of the second Western Kṣatrapa line of Caṣṭana, was written shortly after A.D. 150 and represents a turning point in the history of epigraphic Sanskrit. This is the first long inscription recorded entirely in more or less standard Sanskrit, as well as the first extensive record in the poetic style. Although further specimens of such poetic *praśastis* in Sanskrit are not found until the Gupta era, from a stylistic point of view Rudradāman's inscription is clearly their prototype. But as noted by Kielhorn[48] and others,[49] the language of the Junāgaḍh inscription is not pure classical Sanskrit in the strictest sense of the term. The orthography is inconsistent in the use of *anusvāra* and *visarga* and in the notation of double consonants, and the nonclassical retroflex *ḷ* occurs several times (e.g.,*pāḷī*, l. 1). Local dialect features are probably reflected in the lengthened vowels in *nīrvyājam avajītyāvajītya* (l. 12). *Vīśad-* instead of standard *viṃśati-* (l. 7) also reflects local dialect pronunciation of the epic variant *viṃśat-* (cf. *sīha* for *siṃha* in the Gundā ins., discussed in the next paragraph). *Patinā* instead of *patyā* (l. 11) in the sense of 'lord' is likewise a common epicism, though technically incorrect. Other questionable uses from the classical point of view include *anyatra saṃgrāmeṣu* instead of . . . *saṃgrāmebhyaḥ* (l. 10; cf. Kielhorn, EI 8, 40 n. 2) and the redundant *ā garbhāt prabhṛti* (l. 9). The language of the Junāgaḍh inscription is thus a close approach to high classical Sanskrit, but, like early literary Sanskrit generally, it shows the influence of the less formal epic-vernacular style in which some of the grammatical niceties of Pāṇinian/classical Sanskrit were not observed. But the nonstandard features in question are in general not of the same order as those which characterize the hybrid and hybrid-influenced inscriptions of Mathurā. Thus although we can suspect that the inspiration for using Sanskrit for epigraphic purposes emanated from Mathurā (there are clear historical connections between the Western Kṣatrapas and the Scythian dynasties of Mathurā), the source of the Sanskrit of the Junāgaḍh inscription was evidently the preclassical literary style current among the literati of the day rather than the Sanskritized hybrid of Mathurā and adjoining regions.

This literary style of Sanskrit was not, however, employed in the inscriptions of the time of the Western Kṣatrapa rulers who succeeded Rudradāman. These inscrip-

48. EI 8, 39–40.

49. E.g., Renou, *Histoire de la langue sanskrite*, 96, refers to "des épismes linguistiques."

tions, which are unofficial records, reflect a less formal style which retains some characteristics of the hybrid language. A typical example is the Gundā inscription (SI I.181–2) of the time of Rudrasiṃha I (Śaka 103 = A.D. 181), which contains such nonstandard forms as *(tri)yuttaraśate* for *tryuttara-* and *rudrasīhasya* for *rudrasiṃhasya* (cf. *vīśad-* for *viṃśat-* in the Junāgaḍh inscription), as well as the hybrid sandhi *rājño kṣatrapasya*. Inscriptions of contemporary dynasties in western India show similar linguistic characteristics. A Sātavāhana inscription of the time of Vāsiṣṭhīputra Śrī-Sātakarni (second century A.D.) from Kaṇherī (Bühler, IA 12, 1883, 272) is in hybridized Sanskrit (e.g., *śrī-sāta[karṇ]ī[s]ya*, l. 1). From a slightly later period, the Kānākheṛā inscription (SI I.186–7) of A.D. 279 is in mostly standard Sanskrit but still shows some features reminiscent of hybrid, such as the causative participle *khānāpito* (l. 6).

Also from the third century A.D., we have several Sanskrit inscriptions on *yūpa*s from Baḍvā (SI I.91–2) and Barnāla (EI 26, 118–23) in Rajasthan. Their language still shows significant hybrid characteristics, most strikingly in the dating formula *kṛtehi* or *kritehi* for Sanskrit *kṛtaiḥ*, i.e., "in [lit. 'by'] Kṛta [= Vikrama] years." This follows the familiar pattern of inscriptions from the early centuries of the Christian era (e.g., the Morā well inscription discussed earlier), with the portions concerning the date and other mundane information in more Prakritic language. This suggests that everyday documents were still being written in MIA or mixed dialects at this time, so that people would habitually employ set phrases like *kṛtehi* in recording dates, even at the head of documents which were to be composed in Sanskrit.[50]

3.3.4 Early Sanskrit inscriptions from the Deccan and southern India

In general, Sanskrit began to appear in southern Indian inscriptions somewhat later than in the north, and also lagged behind in its gradual adoption there as the primary epigraphic language. The first significant body[51] of southern Sanskrit inscriptions is from Nāgārjunakoṇḍa, where, in addition to many Prakrit inscriptions, a few in Sanskrit have also been found. Most of these date from the reign of the later Ikṣvāku king Ehavala Cāntamūla, who probably reigned in the late third and/or early fourth centuries A.D. The earliest dated Sanskrit inscription from Nāgārjunakoṇḍa, of the year 11 of king Ehavalaśrī (= Ehavala Cāntamūla; EI 33, 147–9), records a Brah-

50. The Devnīmorī stone casket inscription (SI I.519), dated in the year 127 of the "Kathika kings" (*kathikanṛpāṇām*), is written entirely in correct classical style. The date of the inscription, however, is controversial; Sircar (ibid.) interprets it as a year of the Śaka era, equivalent to A.D. 205. Others, however, such as P. Srinivasan (EI 37, 67–8), judge the inscription to be considerably later on paleographic grounds and think that the otherwise unknown "Kathika" era may be equivalent to the Kalacuri-Cedi era, in which case the date of the inscription would be ca. A.D. 376. The latter opinion is preferable on linguistic grounds, as the classical style would be quite typical of the early Gupta era but unusual for the early third century (see also 5.5.1.16).

51. An anomalously early inscription in what appears to be hybrid Sanskrit (cf. EHS 144) is the fragmentary Amarāvatī slab inscription of the Sātavāhana ruler Gautamīputra Śrī-Yajña Sātakarṇi, of about the late second century A.D. (JAIH 4, 7–8). But here (as also in the case of the Kaṇherī Sātavāhana inscription discussed earlier) the unusually early Sanskritization is probably due to Sātavāhana contacts with the Western Kṣatrapas.

manical (Śaiva) donation in good classical verse (*anuṣṭubh* and *sragdharā* meters). A pillar inscription of the sixteenth regnal year of the same king (EI 34, 17–20), also of Śaiva content, is in Sanskrit prose but with numerous hybrid characteristics such as the frequent absence of sandhi (e.g., *naptryāḥ mahātalavarasya*, l. 6) and the suppression of the dative in the introductory invocation (*namo bhagavate mahādevasya puppabhaddrasvāminaḥ*, l. 1). A Buddhist inscription of Ehavala's year 24 in Sanskrit prose (EI 35, 11–13) shows similar linguistic features, including hybrid inflections such as *bharyyāya śreṣṭhinīya*. A fragmentary fourth Sanskrit inscription on a pillar from the same site (EI 35, 17–18), probably of the same period, records a Buddhist donation in good classical verse.

Thus we have at Nāgārjunakoṇḍa examples of both standard and hybridized Sanskrit in both Buddhist and Brahmanical records, and all from a period when Prakrit inscriptions were also still being written. The determining factor in the linguistic choice seems to be neither sectarian nor chronological but verse versus prose: standard or near-standard Sanskrit is used in versified inscriptions, while hybridized Sanskrit appears in the prose texts. This distinction is reminiscent of similar patterns in earlier inscriptions from the north, notably the Morā well inscription.

Several of the early specimens of epigraphic Sanskrit from other southern Indian sites occur in bilingual Sanskrit and Prakrit records. A typical example is the Bāsim copper plates of the Vākāṭaka ruler Vindhyaśakti II (SI I.430–5), who ruled around the middle to late fourth century A.D. In this inscription the introductory genealogical portion (ll. 1–5) is in Sanskrit, while the remainder, that is, the functional portion of the grant, is in Prakrit.[52] Here once again the situation is comparable to that of some northern inscriptions of an earlier period, such as Nāsik no. 10 (see 3.3.3).

Similar patterns emerge in this period in the far south. For example, the older copper plate inscriptions of the early Pallavas (Mayidavolu and Hīrahaḍagalli, SI I.457–61 and 461–6), datable to about the fourth century A.D., are in Prakrit, but on some of them the king's name on the seal is given in Sanskrit. Some slightly later records, such as the Guṇapadeya copper plate of the time of Skandavarman (SI I.467–9) have imprecatory verses (*bahubhir vasudhā dattā . . .* , etc.) at the end in Sanskrit. A further step toward the adoption of Sanskrit is illustrated by the Maṭṭepāḍ copper plates of King Dāmodaravarman (EI 17, 327–30). These come from approximately the same region and period (late fourth century A.D.) as the Guṇapadeya plates but are written primarily in Sanskrit, with only the portion enumerating the donees and their shares in Prakrit; and even the Prakrit shows the influence of Sanskritic orthography, for example, in *kāśyapanandijjasya aṃśo 1* (l. 13).

This shift from Prakrit to Sanskrit around the latter part of the fourth century A.D. in southern India is also attested in the inscriptions of several other dynasties (see SIE 44–5 for further references). A particularly clear case appears in two copper plate inscriptions of the Śālaṅkāyanas from Kānukollu (EI 31, 1–10). The earlier set, dated in the year 14 of Nandivarman, is Prakrit except for the imprecatory verses at the end (as in the Guṇapadeya inscription mentioned previously), while the later set, issued in the first year of Nandivarman's grandson Skandavarman, is in Sanskrit. According to Sircar (SIE 44), these inscriptions are datable to the fourth and fifth centuries, respectively.

52. See Sircar's comments in SI I.430 n. 2.

Finally, after this transitional period in the fourth and early fifth centuries A.D., Prakrit fell out of use completely in southern Indian inscriptions. For the next few centuries Sanskrit was the sole epigraphic language, until the regional Dravidian languages began to come into use around the seventh century (see 3.5.1).

3.3.5 Early Sanskrit inscriptions from other regions

With the exception of the very early Ayodhyā inscription discussed earlier (3.3.1), there are few early Sanskrit inscriptions from eastern and northeastern India. Some brief records of the "Magha" kings of Kauśāmbī of the second century A.D. are in Sanskrit or in a highly Sanskritized hybrid: for example, the Bāndhogaṛh inscriptions nos. 18 and 19 of Vaiśravaṇa (and apparently also the fragmentary no. 14 of Śivamagha; EI 31, 184–6) and the Kosam pillar inscription (EI 24, 146–8) of Vaiśravaṇa. Apart from such scattered and marginal examples, the earliest true Sanskrit inscription from the northeast (besides Ayodhyā) is probably the Susuniyā (West Bengal) rock inscription (SI I.351–2), datable to about the middle of the fourth century.

From the far north, a notable set of relatively early Sanskrit inscriptions in more or less correct classical style are the Jagatpur (Dehradun Dist., UP) *aśvamedha* brick inscriptions of King Śīlavarman (SI I.98–9), dated paleographically to about the third century A.D.

Outside of India proper, the oldest Sanskrit inscription is probably the Võ-cạnh (Vietnam) stele inscription, composed in standard Sanskrit prose and verse (*vasanta-tilakā* and *śārdūlavikrīḍita*).[53] Its date is highly controversial, but some time in the third century A.D. is the most likely (see 4.3.7.8); if this date is correct, this record would be at least as advanced linguistically and stylistically as the contemporary epigraphs within India.[54] From about the fifth century A.D., Sanskrit inscriptions become common in various countries outside of India, particularly Cambodia, Vietnam, and Nepal.

3.3.6 The emergence of Sanskrit in the Gupta period

It was during the reign of the early Gupta emperors in the fourth century A.D. that Sanskrit was finally established as the epigraphic language par excellence of the Indian world. The turning point appears in the inscriptions of Samudragupta (middle to late fourth century), especially the Allahabad pillar inscription (SI I.262–8), which, despite a few trivial orthographic irregularities, is often held up as a model of high classical literary style of the mixed prose and verse (*campū*) class. From this point on, all the inscriptions of the Guptas and their neighbors and feudatories in northern India were written in correct classical Sanskrit; and, as we have already seen (3.3.4), similar developments followed soon after in southern India and elsewhere.

53. See Claude Jacques, BEFEO 55, 1969, 117–24.

54. It is interesting to note that, somewhat surprisingly, Prakrit was not used as an epigraphic language in Southeast Asia; see Jean Filliozat, BEFEO 55, 1969, 112.

Thus by about the end of the fourth and beginning of the fifth centuries A.D., Sanskrit had at last established itself as virtually the sole language for epigraphic use throughout India. Prakrit, from this time onward, virtually fell out of epigraphic use, with occasional exceptions for literary effect or sectarian considerations (see 3.1.5). Sanskrit continued to enjoy its privileged position in the north for many centuries, until regional NIA and "Islamic" languages (3.4 and 3.5.2) began to appear in inscriptions of the medieval period; even then Sanskrit was never completely supplanted, and has continued to be used sporadically up to modern times. In the south, the regional (i.e., Dravidian) languages made their appearance earlier and more prominently (3.5.1), but there too not entirely at the cost of Sanskrit, which continued to be used as an alternative to or in bilingual combination with the Dravidian languages throughout the ancient and medieval periods.

3.3.7 Summary: Historical and cultural factors in the development of Sanskrit as an epigraphic language

Near the end of the pre-Christian era, we find a smattering of inscriptions of Brahmanical content recording religious donations and foundations in standard or nearly standard Sanskrit, and we may assume that these are isolated survivals of what must have been an increasingly common practice in this period. About the beginning of the Christian era, we begin to find more examples of epigraphic Sanskrit among the abundant inscriptions from Mathurā and surrounding regions, and it appears to be more than coincidence that this development appeared at precisely the time when this area of northern India came under the domination of the Scythian "Kṣatrapa" rulers (see 3.2.3.2). This suspicion is confirmed by the appearance, in the next century, of Sanskrit inscriptions in the domains of the early Western Kṣatrapas in Maharashtra and Gujarat, culminating in Rudradāman's Junāgaḍh rock inscription, the first long epigraphic text in virtually classical language and style.

Thus it appears that the use of Sanskrit for inscriptions was promoted, though not originated, by the Scythian rulers of northern and western India in the first two centuries of the Christian era. Their motivation in promoting Sanskrit was presumably a desire to establish themselves as legitimate Indian or at least Indianized rulers and to curry the favor of the educated Brahmanical elite. In other words, the forces and motivations behind epigraphic Sanskritization were evidently the same as those which promoted the development and spread of the hybrid language at the cost of MIA, and indeed these two developments must have taken place more or less simultaneously. As discussed earlier, for several centuries there was available to the composers and scribes of inscriptions a range of linguistic choices comprising MIA, hybrid, and Sanskrit, from which the appropriate dialect could be chosen according to such factors as the purpose and contents of the record, its sectarian affiliations, or simply personal preferences and abilities. But the direction of movement along this spectrum was consistently toward Sanskrit, promoted by the previously mentioned legitimizing motivations of the non-Indian rulers, as well as by the inherent status of this elite language. Thus eventually, and inevitably, Sanskrit completely supplanted Prakrit and the mixed dialects.

The spread of epigraphic Sanskrit to the south in subsequent centuries can also be attributed to the influence, direct or indirect, of the Western Kṣatrapas. In this connection it is significant that the earliest southern Indian Sanskrit inscriptions come from Nāgārjunakoṇḍa (see 3.3.4), since other inscriptions from the same site attest to the connections of the Kṣatrapas and other western Indian rulers with it; for instance, a Nāgārjunakoṇḍa memorial pillar inscription of the time of King Rudrapuruṣadatta (EI 34, 20–2) attests to a marital alliance between the Western Kṣatrapas and the Ikṣvāku rulers of Nāgārjunakoṇḍa.

The movement toward Sanskrit was thus already well entrenched by the early years of the Gupta empire, when Sanskrit was adopted as the sole administrative language for epigraphic and (presumably) other purposes, and when the high classical style became the standard mode. The Guptas thus merely brought to its logical conclusion a gradual process which had been going on for the previous four centuries or so. The adoption of Sanskrit by the Guptas is sometimes thought to represent a Brahmanical revival under their auspices; and while there may be something to this, it would be a serious oversimplification to picture the triumph of Sanskrit merely as a victory of the Brahmanical language over the MIA and hybrid dialects associated with the Buddhists and Jains. It is certainly true that, on the whole, Sanskrit was first and most frequently employed epigraphically in Brahmanical circles (as in Ayodhyā, Hāṭhibāḍā/Ghosuṇḍī, etc.), and that many of the earliest and best specimens of Sanskrit from subsequent sites such as Mathurā and Nāgārjunakoṇḍa are in Brahmanical records. But several other early Sanskrit inscriptions from these sites are Buddhist, and possibly also Jaina (Kaṅkālī Ṭīlā). Particularly interesting is the situation at Nāgārjunakoṇḍa, where the Sanskrit inscriptions seem to be distributed equally, in terms of number and style, between Buddhist and Brahmanical records. Thus while the Brahmans and their clients may have led the way in the Sanskritization of epigraphic language, the Buddhists did not lag far behind and were no doubt also influential in the process.

These patterns should not, however, be uncritically extrapolated to nonepigraphic contexts. It should be kept in mind that, in the words of Burrow, "[T]he inscriptional evidence gives a very one-sided picture of the contemporary linguistic conditions. . . . Sanskrit was always, even when the use of Prakrit was most flourishing, the primary literary language of India."[55] In other words, the limited and sporadic use of Sanskrit in inscriptions prior to the Gupta era does not mean that Sanskrit as a language of literature, culture, and ritual was in abeyance but simply that inscriptions were not yet felt to be literary documents worthy of its use. The gradual Sanskritization of inscriptions reflects, on the one hand, the formalization of inscriptions into a mode of literary expression, and on the other, the spread of Sanskrit into the administrative realm, which was fully accomplished under the Guptas and their contemporaries.

3.3.8 Linguistic characteristics of inscriptional Sanskrit

The style and quality of inscriptional Sanskrit varies over a wide range from the finest classical to the near-illiterate. In broad terms, one may discern three levels.

The first level comprises more or less standard classical Sanskrit, found most frequently in inscriptions from the Gupta era down to the early medieval period, particu-

55. *The Sanskrit Language* (see n. 36 for reference), 59.

larly in records of the *praśasti* class. Examples of the high classical style are very numerous; among the outstanding ones, in terms of both grammatical correctness and literary polish, may be mentioned the Allahabad inscription, the Aihoḷe inscription of the time of Pulakeśin II (SI II.443–50), and the Deopāṛā inscription of Vijayasena (SI II.115–22).[56] But even in inscriptions of this class, it is not uncommon to find occasional lapses from the strictest standards of classical grammar and orthography (cf. 3.3.8.1). Thus in the Allahabad inscription we find *ḷ* for *ḍ* in *-vyāluḷitena* (l. 8) and *prithivyām* for *pṛthivyām* (l. 24), and in Deopāṛā *mānsa* for *māṃsa* (l. 8). Some inscriptions written in what may broadly be called classical Sanskrit show stronger tendencies toward a colloquial style, as in the Junāgaḍh inscription, whose epicisms and other nonclassical features have been discussed earlier (3.3.3).

The second level comprises a looser, more vernacular style, characteristic of what might be termed "functional Sanskrit,"[57] frequently found in Sanskrit inscriptions, particularly of the medieval era. Such documents partake in substantial but varying degrees of vernacularisms in orthography, vocabulary, syntax, and so on (see 3.3.8.1–3.3.8.4 for details). The first part of the Sīyadoṇī inscription (EI I, 162–79) is a good example of this variety of epigraphic Sanskrit, whose author(s), in Kielhorn's words, "were evidently influenced by, and have freely employed words, phrases, and constructions of, their vernacular" (163). A typical example of this style is the following version of a formulaic malediction (l. 6): *yo kopi puruṣaḥ paripanthanākhaśrā karoti utpādayati sa pañcamahāpātakai lipyati* ("Any person who causes or instigates obstruction [or] damage[58] is guilty of the five great sins").

The third level comprises semiliterate Sanskrit, found in some inscriptions, typically later copper plate charters, often from eastern India. An example is the Madras Museum plates (originally from an unknown site in Orissa) of the time of Narendradhavala (EI 28, 44–50), whose language, in the words of the editor, "is only seemingly Sanskrit and is greatly influenced by the local dialect" (45). Here, for example, the malediction is rendered (ll. 21–2) as *sadatāṃ vā paradatām vā / yo hareti vasundharā / viṣṭhāyāṃ kṛmi bhuta pitṛbhi śaha pacyate*.[59] A comparison of this with the example cited in the preceding paragraph (the inscriptions are roughly contemporary, both dating from around the tenth century) shows that we are indeed dealing with a different level of linguistic competence; while the author of the Sīyadoṇī inscription evidently had a somewhat limited command of Sanskrit, the text of the Madras plates is, as Sircar states, merely a poor imitation of Sanskrit.

The following summary of the typical peculiarities of inscriptional Sanskrit therefore does not take the third class of inscriptions into account, since from the linguistic point of view they are of more interest for the study of the underlying vernacular

56. See also section 7.2.2.3.

57. Similar types of Sanskrit used for practical functions are also attested in some relatively late nonepigraphic sources, including manuals for letter writing such as the *Lekhapaddhati* or for instruction in spoken Sanskrit such as the *Uktivyaktiprakaraṇa*.

58. For *khaśrā* Kielhorn suggests "compare the Hindī *khasar* 'damages, loss, injury, fraud'" (165).

59. The intended verse is the familiar *svadattāṃ paradattāṃ vā yo hareta vasundharām / saviṣṭāyāṃ kṛmir bhūtvā pitṛbhis saha pacyate* ("He who would steal land given by himself or by someone else becomes a worm in his own excrement and rots along with his ancestors"). Cf. section 4.1.2.3(i), and see SIE 196 for references and variants.

than of Sanskrit. The features described are characteristic mainly of the second class of inscriptions, that is, those in informal or "practical" Sanskrit, although, as already noted, many of them are also to be found in the generally more formal and correct inscriptions of the first group. This fact is linguistically significant because it indicates an overall consistency within epigraphic Sanskrit; the features enumerated here are not a mere random accumulation of "errors," but rather establish consistent patterns of usage of nonformal Sanskrit which not rarely slip over into the more formal register. In other words, epigraphic usage in Sanskrit has a grammar of its own,[60] a sketchy outline of which is given in the following sections; a more detailed study of the subject remains to be done.

3.3.8.1 Orthography and sandhi

Ṛ is often written as *ri*, and sometimes also vice versa. See the example of *ri* for *ṛ* in the Allahabad inscription, noted earlier, and examples of the converse in the Rāmṭek stone inscription of the time of Rāmacandra (EI 25, 7–20), *pṛyatamā* for *priyatamā* (l. 19) and *tṛbhuvana-* for *tribhuvana-* (l. 31).

Ḷ is sometimes written for *ḍ*, mainly in early Sanskrit inscriptions. See the example noted earlier (Allahabad).[61]

Notation of *anusvāra* and nasals is often in violation of strict orthographic rules. *Anusvāra* is commonly used *in pausa* in place of *m*. *Ṅ* or *n* is often written for *ṃ* before sibilants and *h*, for example, *vaṅśa-* for *vaṃśa-* (Bhitarī ins., SI I.323, l. 13); *mānsa* (Deopāṛā ins., cited in 3.3.8). Final *-n* before consonants is sometimes written as *ṃ*, for example, *pañcedrāṃ sthāpayitvā* (Kahāuṃ pillar ins., Appendix, no. 7, l. 11).[62]

Notation of doubled consonants is often inconsistent. Words such as *sattva*, *ujjvala*, and *sattra* are very commonly written *satva*, *ujvala*, *satra*, and so on. The doubling of intervocalic *ch* is not always observed. The optional doubling of consonants in conjunction with *r* or *y* (e.g., *karttā* or *kartā*) is frequently but by no means regularly applied, even within the same inscription.

In many later Sanskrit inscriptions, especially from northern and eastern India, the distinction between *v* and *b* is not consistently maintained, and often the two are represented by the same character and not distinguished at all. Similarly, in many such inscriptions *s* and *ṣ*, and sometimes also *ś*, are frequently interchanged. The distinction between *n* and *ṇ* is not always correctly maintained.

Besides these common orthographic irregularities, Sanskrit inscriptions also occasionally display spellings which reveal nonstandard or vernacularized pronunciations, such as *āśvoja* for *āśvayuja* in the Mandasor stone inscription of the time of Naravarman (SI I.397–8, l. 3).

60. This form of Sanskrit is by no means exclusive to the inscriptional language. Most of its characteristics can also be found in, or at least resemble, those of the less formal literary varieties of the language, particularly those of the epic and of some strata of Buddhist literature; see R. Salomon, "Linguistic Variability in Post-Vedic Sanskrit," in C. Caillat, ed., *Dialectes dans les littératures indo-aryennes*, 275–94 (esp. 282–4, "Epigraphical Sanskrit").

61. Further examples given in H. Lüders, "Zur Geschichte des *l* im Altindischen" in *Antidōron: Festschrift Jacob Wackernagel* (Göttingen: Vandenhoeck & Ruprecht, 1923), 294–308 = *Philologica Indica*, 546–61.

62. See also examples in the Morā well ins., cited earlier (3.3.2).

Sandhi is left unapplied not only in prose (see 3.3.2) but also, not infrequently, in verse, especially at the juncture between *pādas*.

3.3.8.2 Morphology

The formation of causative verbs and their derivatives with the *-p-* affix where not called for by Pāṇinian rules is particularly characteristic of epigraphic Sanskrit. This occurs in both early Sanskrit inscriptions, as in *bandhāpitaś* in the Gundā stone ins. (A.D. 181; SI I.181–2, l. 5), and later, for example, *karṣāpayato* (= *karṣayato*) in the Dhulev plate (EI 30, 4, 1.3). The late (A.D. 1264) Verāval inscription (SI II.402–8), which presents a good example of the second class of "functional" epigraphic Sanskrit described earlier, contains numerous forms of this type, including several derivatives of √*vṛt* (*varttāpanārthaṃ*, *varttāpanīyaṃ*, *varttāpayatāṃ*, ll. 21, 34, 35), and *lopāpayati* (l. 42).

Also typical of epigraphic Sanskrit, particularly of the second class mentioned previously, are nonstandard gerunds formed contrary to the rule of distribution of the suffixes *-tvā* and *-(t)ya* to simple and prefixed roots, respectively. A notable case is the Jodhpur stone inscription of Bāüka (SI II.236–41) with three gerunds of this type: *prahatvā*, *tyajya*, and *stambhya* (ll. 15, 17).

A pleonastic *-ka* suffix is frequently applied to nominal and participial forms, for example, in *-[u]tpannakotpadyamānaka-* and *kāritaka-* in the Khoh copper plate of Śarvanātha (CII 3, 135–9, ll. 9,11).[63]

Other miscellaneous morphological peculiarities are far too numerous to list here. One example is the frequent formation of compounds of *mahant-* with *mahat-* or other stem forms, rather than *mahā-*, as the prior member; for example, *mahaddyuti* in the Sakrāī inscription (EI 27, 27–33, l. 6) and *mahaddharmma-* (also *mahāntadharmma-*!) in the Sīyadoṇī inscription (EI 1, 162–79, ll. 8, 20, 29, etc.).

3.3.8.3 Syntax

A notable peculiarity of epigraphic syntax is the mixing of active and passive constructions, as in *prapittrācāryeṇa . . . kṛtavān* in the Paraśurāmeśvara temple inscription (EI 26, 126–7, ll. 1–2) and *sa ca sa ca . . . tālī dātavyā* in Sīyadoṇī (EI 1, 174, l. 9). Like many of the features enumerated in this section, this peculiarity has parallels in inscriptional Prakrit, for instance, in MI §150, *kūṭubiniye . . . pratiṭhāpeti*, and in some of the Nāgārjunakoṇḍa inscriptions, for example, B 5 *mahādevi rudradharabhaṭarikā imaṃ selakhaṃbaṃ . . . patiṭhapitaṃ* (SI I.231, l. 4).

3.3.8.4 Vocabulary

Sanskrit inscriptions (like those in other languages) contain a large number of words which are rarely or, quite often, never attested in nonepigraphic Sanskrit. The majority of this vocabulary consists of technical terms, typically connected with such matters as agriculture, weights and measures, coinage and currency, revenues and taxation, local and territorial administration, and various other official terms and

63. See also the comments of Fleet in CII 3, 69, and of Bühler in EI 1, 74 n. 28.

titles.[64] Also included in this category are abbreviations of technical and other terms (see 2.5.2.3). The definitive collection of epigraphic terminology, particularly of technical vocabulary but also including some of the other types mentioned subsequently, is D. C. Sircar's *Indian Epigraphical Glossary* (IEG).

There is also a stock of semitechnical words which are exclusive to or characteristic of epigraphic Sanskrit. This class includes terms such as *pūrvā* in the special sense of 'the preceding [date]' (cf. 3.2.1) or 'the preceding [*praśasti*]', and *satka* 'belonging to' (EI 1, 164).[65]

Inscriptions not infrequently also provide examples of rare or otherwise unattested words of a poetic or literary rather than technical character; see, for example, the "rare Sanskrit words" (*aśvīya* 'a number of horses', *ānandathu* 'joy', etc.) cited by Hultzsch from the Mōṭupalli inscription (EI 12, 188). Inscriptions thus also constitute an important source for the lexical study of classical Sanskrit, for which see S. P. Tewari's *Contributions of Sanskrit Inscriptions to Lexicography*.[66]

It has traditionally been the practice in epigraphic studies to regard orthographic and grammatical peculiarities of the type noted previously as mere errors, and to correct them either in the text itself (usually by adding the "correct" form in parentheses) or in the notes. This often leads to a situation where inscriptional texts, particularly those written in the less formal modes, are burdened with an inconvenient number of notes correcting often trivial variants. Moreover, as pointed out by Ramesh in his essay "Indian Epigraphy and the Language Medium" (RIE 44–8), it is not only impractical but also misleading to indulge in such overcorrection of informal epigraphic Sanskrit; in his words, such "departures from Pāṇinian rules of grammar, which are dubbed as inaccuracies by the epigraphists, need not necessarily have appeared ungrammatical to the composers and contemporaneous readers of those inscriptions and, on the other hand, may have been accepted as legitimate usages" (45). This position is supported by the fact that many inscriptions contain what Ramesh (44) calls a "formal" portion, containing genealogical and eulogistic passages written in the high literary style, as well as an "operative" or technical portion presenting the legal details of the document formulated in the less formal vernacularized epigraphic Sanskrit described earlier (3.3.8). Thus Ramesh is no doubt correct in his claim that inscriptions prove that "there was, in the early and medieval periods, a Sanskrit for the common man, a living Sanskrit as against the literary or classical or Pāṇinian Sanskrit" (46). The peculiar features of epigraphic Sanskrit, whether one prefers to look upon them as errors or as legitimate linguistic or stylistic variants, are an important source of linguistic data which throws light both on the history of the Sanskrit language[67] as a means of functional and official communication (as opposed to a purely literary vehicle) and on its relations with the various vernaculars with which it coexisted.

64. Not surprisingly, such vocabulary includes many loanwords, borrowed directly or in a pseudo-Sanskrit form, from the local languages, including MIA, NIA, Dravidian, and others; see, e.g., the case mentioned in n. 58.

65. See Renou's *Histoire de la langue sanskrite* (ref. in n. 43), 100 n. 1, for a brief sampling of such typical epigraphic vocabulary.

66. See also K. Bhattacharya, "Recherches sur le vocabulaire des inscriptions sanskrites du Cambodge."

67. E.g., the frequent orthographic interchange of *ṛ* and *ri* alluded to earlier (3.3.8.1) establishes that the modern northern Indian pronunciation of syllabic *ṛ* as *ri* goes back at least as far as Gupta times.

3.4 The New Indo-Aryan (NIA) Languages

D. B. Diskalkar, "Inscriptions in Sanskritic Provincial Languages," JOI 6, 1956–57, 129–39; SIE 53–60.

The study of inscriptions in the New Indo-Aryan languages could well be described as the stepchild of Indian epigraphy. Compared with the attention which has been paid to Old and Middle Indo-Aryan inscriptions on the one hand, and to Dravidian on the other, NIA epigraphy is virtually an untouched field. Reliable collections and studies are lacking for most of the NIA languages (Tuḷpuḷe's *Prācīna Marāṭhī Korīva Lekha* is one of the few important exceptions), and many of the collections and editions of individual inscriptions are in local publications and/or in the various regional languages concerned, rendering them difficult of access to the scholarly community as a whole. Although editions of NIA inscriptions are occasionally published in EI and other major journals, the majority have been merely reported in ARIE, often with only the vague designation of "local dialect," and never properly published elsewhere. Because of these problems, it is difficult to provide a comprehensive and reliable survey of the subject; what is presented here is based on the available published materials but can hardly be considered complete or authoritative.

The neglect of the NIA inscriptions is attributable to various factors (see Diskalkar, 129). For one thing, none of them can claim any great antiquity. Moreover, they have on the whole less historical importance than those in the other Indic and Islamic languages (i.e., Arabic and Persian; see 3.5.2), the majority of them being private records of a rather humble character. Nevertheless, they are worthy of much more attention than has until now been accorded to them, as they are potentially excellent sources of data for such subjects as social history, religion, and historical linguistics.

The earliest clear-cut specimens of NIA languages (notably Marathi and Oriya; see 3.4.1 and 3.4.2) appear in inscriptions of about the eleventh century. It is often difficult, however, to specify a precise date for the earliest epigraphic attestation of a given NIA language, as their emergence is gradual (not unlike the situation with Sanskrit at a much earlier time). Occasional traces of NIA have been observed within Sanskrit records somewhat before the eleventh century, and the earliest definite specimens are typically mixed in varying degrees with Sanskrit. Even in later centuries, it is very common for NIA inscriptions to be bi- or multilingual with Sanskrit, Dravidian, other NIA languages, or Islamic languages.

The dates of earliest epigraphic attestation for the various NIA languages vary widely, as do the degrees to which they are developed as epigraphic languages. These discrepancies are due to various historical and geographical factors, most importantly the date and extent to which Islamic governments were established in the different regions (see SIE 53). In those portions of northern and central India in which Islamic rule was firmly entrenched at an early date, the Islamic languages directly supplanted Sanskrit as the principal epigraphic medium, whereas the NIA languages developed in this function in areas where Islamic rule was established only later in the medieval period. This accounts, for example, for the discrepancy between Oriya, which became one of the most important NIA epigraphic languages, and neighboring Bengali, which was almost negligible in this respect; for Bengal was one of the first parts of India to come under Islamic rule, while Orissa was among the last.

In some regions—again, most notably in Maharashtra and Orissa—the regional NIA vernaculars were even elevated to the rank of imperial languages. In such cases one may suspect the influence of neighboring Dravidian-speaking regions, in which epigraphic use of the local vernacular, instead of or in addition to Sanskrit, was a long-established tradition.[68] In these regions we find the vernaculars regularly used for official records of the usual sorts. Elsewhere, NIA inscriptions are predominantly private in character; especially common are memorial records of various types.

3.4.1 Marathi

Śaṃ. Go. Tuḷpuḷe, *Prācīna Marāṭhī Korīva Lekha* ["Old Marathi Inscriptions"]; A. Master, "Some Marathi Inscriptions, A.D. 1060–1300," BSOAS 20, 1957, 417–35; A. V. Naik, "Inscriptions of the Deccan," 55–8, etc.; V. V. Mirashi, *Inscriptions of the Śilāhāras* (CII 6); D. B. Diskalkar, JOI 6, 132–7; SIE 53–5.

The epigraphic material in Marathi is the most abundant and best-documented among the NIA languages. The principal reference sources are Master's brief anthology of sixteen inscriptions and Tuḷpuḷe's larger though by no means exhaustive compilation of seventy-six texts. Diskalkar (132) estimates a total of some three hundred inscriptions in Marathi, of which about two hundred are from Maharashtra proper and the rest from neighboring territories, mainly Karnataka and Andhra Pradesh. Marathi first began to appear in inscriptions around the eleventh century A.D.,[69] and Marathi inscriptions became especially common in the twelfth and thirteenth centuries when the language was widely used by the Yādavas of Devagiri and the Śilāhāras of northern Konkan (see CII 6) for their inscriptions. Marathi continued to be used epigraphically in the later medieval period, for instance in the records of the Ādil Shāhis, and even into the European period; an interesting late (A.D. 1803) Marathi inscription is the long history of the Tanjore Marathas inscribed on the wall of the Bṛhadīśvara temple in Tañjāvur (V. Srinivasachari and S. Gopalan, *Bhoṃsle Vaṃśa Caritra*).

Most Marathi inscriptions are of the usual types of the period concerned, that is, donative or memorial records on stone, and copper plate charters; according to Diskalkar (132), the former type constitutes about three-quarters of the total. The majority are written in Devanāgarī, but some are in the Moḍī and Kannada scripts. As with other NIA language inscriptions, many of the Marathi inscriptions are bilingual. Very common are bilinguals of various types with Sanskrit, for example, Sanskrit copper plate charters with some of the "functional" portions written in Marathi and exhibiting varying degrees of linguistic admixture between Sanskrit and Marathi (see Master, 417–8). Many later Marathi inscriptions are bilingual with other languages such as Kannada, Telugu, or Persian. There are, of course, also monolingual Marathi inscriptions; the Dīve Āgar plate, for example (Tuḷpuḷe, 10–14; Master, 422–3; EI 28, 121–4), is an early copper plate grant composed entirely (except for the date in Sanskrit) in Old Marathi.

68. Cf. the comments of Kunjabihari Tripathi in *The Evolution of Oriya Language and Script*, v.

69. Occasional Marathi words and usages have also been noted in some inscriptions of the tenth century, e.g., the Marmuri copper plates (*Journal of the Bombay Historical Society* 2, 213–4).

3.4.2 *Oriya*

K. Tripathi, *The Evolution of Oriya Language and Script*; idem, *Prācīna Oṛiā Abhilekha*; R. Subrahmanyam, *Inscriptions of the Sūryavaṃśi Gajapatis of Orissa.*

After Marathi, Oriya is the most abundantly attested and important among the inscriptional NIA languages; Diskalkar (JOI 6, 129) estimates the number of Oriya inscriptions at 150, and Tripathi presents a selection of 71 Oriya inscriptions from A.D. 1051 to 1568 in *The Evolution of Oriya Language and Script* (222ff.).[70] These records are found in various districts of Orissa as well as in neighboring districts of Andhra Pradesh, Madhya Pradesh, and West Bengal. The early manifestations of Oriya in inscriptions follow a pattern similar to that of Marathi. Characteristics of the Oriya language can first be discerned in inscriptional Sanskrit of the tenth century A.D., for instance, in the Madras Museum Plates (EI 28, 44–50).[71] Oriya proper began to appear sporadically in inscriptions of the eleventh and twelfth centuries, the earliest specimen being dated A.D. 1051 (Tripathi, *The Evolution*, 222–4), and became common in the thirteenth and following centuries. Oriya was used frequently in the records of the Eastern Gaṅga kings and of their successors, the Sūryavaṃśī Gajapatis. Many later inscriptions of local dynasties as well as private records continued to be written in Oriya into the eighteenth, nineteenth, and even the early twentieth centuries (e.g., ARIE 1951–2, no. A.20).

Most Oriya inscriptions are the usual donative stone records and copper plate charters. The early ones were written in "Gauḍī" or "Proto-Bengali" script, which gradually developed into a distinct Oriya script from the fourteenth century onward. Oriya inscriptions were also sometimes written in the Devanāgarī (e.g., Tripathi, *Evolution*, 248–9) or Telugu (ibid., 229–31) scripts. Like the Marathi inscriptions, many of them are bilingual (or trilingual), but the proportion of inscriptions in Oriya alone is larger than for Marathi. The multilingual records include inscriptions in Oriya together with Sanskrit and/or Telugu, Tamil (e.g., Bhubaneswar stone ins., EI 32, 229–38), and Hindi (e.g., Baripāḍā Museum stone ins., OHRJ 2, 94–8).

3.4.3 *Gujarati*

D. B. Diskalkar, *Inscriptions of Kathiawad.*

Inscriptions in Gujarati from various parts of the modern state of Gujarat, especially the Kathiawar and Kacch regions, number well in the hundreds; for examples see Diskalkar, nos. 79, 82–3, 85, 87–8, 90, and so on, and ARIE 1969–70, nos. B.22–138. Gujarati linguistic features appear in some Sanskrit inscriptions of the fourteenth century (e.g., Diskalkar nos. 36–7, etc.; *New Indian Antiquary* 1, 587–8), and inscriptions written entirely or nearly entirely in Gujarati date from the second half of the fifteenth century on. The latest Gujarati inscription cited by Diskalkar (no. 193) is dated Vikrama Saṃvat 1935 = A.D. 1879.

70. Several Oriya inscriptions are also transcribed (in Devanāgarī) in SII 5 (nos. 1006, 1119, 1121, 1132–3, 1152, 1161) and 6 (nos. 654, 697, 700–3, 748–9, 778, 895, 903, 908–9, 927, 1089, 1145–65).
71. See 3.3.8.3 and SIE 58.

The majority of Gujarati inscriptions are private dedicatory or memorial records. The former typically record land grants, the foundation or repair of temples or mosques, or the digging of wells. Memorial inscriptions are very frequently seen on memorial pillars or *pāliyās*, typically recording deaths in battle ("hero-stones") or by *sahagamana* ("*satī*-stones"). Pilgrims' records are also common (e.g., ARIE 1969–70, no. B.24, etc.). Many of the Gujarati inscriptions are informally or incompetently written.

Gujarati inscriptions are generally written in Devanāgarī script or its local variant, called Boṛiyā, but some are inscribed in script forms similar to modern Gujarati (NIA 1, 588). Bilingual (and sometimes trilingual) inscriptions, usually with Sanskrit or Persian, are found in some numbers, but the majority of Gujarati inscriptions are monolingual.

3.4.4 Hindi and related languages and dialects

Due to the linguistic complexities involved and the generally poor documentation of the materials, the study of inscriptions in Hindi and related languages is particularly problematic. As a matter of convenience the term "Hindi" is used here in a very loose sense, as in the other literature on the subject. The documents concerned actually cover a wide geographical and dialectal range, but since no comprehensive linguistic study of them has been attempted it is in most cases not possible to specify the dialects concerned, and it is regrettably necessary to resort to vague terms such as "Hindi" or "Rājasthānī."

Inscriptions in various dialects of Hindi in the relatively strict sense of the term are found mainly in central and eastern Madhya Pradesh.[72] (NIA inscriptions from Uttar Pradesh are rare, presumably because of the early establishment of Islamic dynasties there; see Diskalkar, JOI 6, 138, and section 3.4.) There seems to be a particular concentration of Hindi inscriptions in the territory of the former Gwalior State and adjoining regions; these inscriptions are catalogued and briefly described in H. N. Dvivedī's *Gvāliyara Rājya ke Abhilekha*.[73] They consist largely of *satī*- and other memorial stones, image inscriptions, and other private records from the thirteenth century on.[74]

Hindi inscriptions from the eastern regions come mainly from relatively remote districts such as Damoh and Bastar. Here we find official stone inscriptions and copper plate charters of various local dynasties dating from the sixteenth and following centuries, for example, the Dantewāṛā bilingual[75] (Sanskrit and Hindi) inscription (EI 12, 242–50).

From Rajasthan and adjoining areas of western Madhya Pradesh we have numerous inscriptions of the fourteenth and following centuries in the local NIA dialects,

72. For inscriptions in Hindi (and Punjabi) from Azerbaijan, see section 4.3.7.4.

73. The concentration of Hindi inscriptions in this region of central India may, however, be only apparent, as a result of their being relatively well documented in this book.

74. A Jaina image inscription from Radeb tentatively dated Vikrama (10)78 (= A.D. 1022) and described as being in Hindi was noted in the Annual Report of the Archaeological Department of Gwalior State for Vikrama 1992 (35, ins. no. 39), but this has apparently never been published in detail and hence cannot be taken as firm evidence of the epigraphic use of Hindi in the eleventh century (see SIE 55 and n. 3).

75. Like several of the NIA bilingual inscriptions, this is a "true" bilingual (see 3.6), with (approximately) the same text repeated in Sanskrit and Hindi.

which, however (for reasons stated earlier), cannot be specified with any linguistic precision on the basis of currently available published materials. Most of the material concerned is published only in the form of brief summaries in the various numbers of ARIE (e.g., 1962–63, nos. B.849–954, passim), wherein the language is usually cited only as "local dialect" or occasionally as "Rājasthānī."[76] The vernacular inscriptions of Rajasthan are mainly memorial and *satī*-stones[77] and other stone records concerning the usual matters, that is, grants and donations, temple foundations and renovations, construction of wells, pilgrims' records, and so on. A few of these records have been published in detail in various journals; see, for example, several inscriptions in Sanskrit and "Rājasthānī Bhāṣā" published by L. P. Tessitori in JPASB, n.s. 12, 1916, 92–116.

Of an entirely different character is a unique inscription from Dhār containing a poetic composition entitled *Rāüla-vela* by a poet named Roḍa (*Bhāratīya Vidyā* 17, 130–46; 19, 116–28), which is datable on paleographic grounds to approximately the eleventh century. The precise identification of the language of this composition is problematic, as it appears to imitate characteristics of various contemporary dialects by way of a pastiche. But the underlying dialect seems to be a transitional stage between late Apabhraṃśa and early western NIA,[78] and hence this curious inscription can be considered as an early epigraphic specimen of Hindi in the broad sense of the term.

Vernacular languages were also used epigraphically in some of the hill-states of the Himalayan foothills in medieval times. Among these languages (again, loosely classed here under "Hindi"), Cambyālī is the most important as an inscriptional medium. This language, which shows affiliations with eastern dialects of Punjabi,[79] was used in combination with Sanskrit in the copper plate charters of the local kings of Chamba from the fourteenth to the nineteenth centuries. These inscriptions were published in a scholarly edition in B. Ch. Chhabra's *Antiquities of Chamba State, Part II*, which is thus one of the few authoritative collections of NIA inscriptions. Unlike most of the "Hindi" inscriptions described in this section, which are written in the several varieties of Devanāgarī script, the Chamba records are in Devāśeṣa, a local script intermediate between Śāradā and Ṭākarī (Chhabra, 2–3). Some late (nineteenth-century) inscriptions from Gaṛhwāl in the "local dialect" have also been reported (ARIE 1948–49, nos. A.7–10; SIE 55 n. 8).

As is generally the case with NIA, the inscriptions in Hindi and affiliated languages are frequently bilingual, especially with Sanskrit as already noted, but also occasionally with other languages such as Oriya (3.4.2). Also common are inscriptions from central India written in Hindi or Rājasthānī together with Persian or Urdu.[80]

76. For further references see Māṅgīlāl Vyās' *Rājasthāna ke Abhilekha* and *Mārvāṛa ke Abhilekha*.

77. On these see B. D. Chattopadhyay, "Early Memorial Stones of Rajasthan: A Preliminary Analysis of Their Inscriptions," in S. Settar and G. D. Sontheimer, eds., *Memorial Stones*, 139–49.

78. See R. S. McGregor, *Hindi Literature from Its Beginnings to the Nineteenth Century*, A History of Indian Literature, vol. 8, fasc. 6 (Wiesbaden: Otto Harrassowitz, 1984), 7–8; cf. Bhayani in *Bhāratīya Vidyā* 17, 132.

79. See B. Ch. Chhabra, *Antiquities of Chamba State, Part II*, 13.

80. Urdu, though strictly speaking an Indo-Aryan language, is traditionally treated in epigraphic contexts along with Persian and Arabic as a part of Islamic epigraphy, and hence will be discussed in that connection in section 3.5.2.

3.4.5 *Bengali and other eastern NIA languages*

As noted earlier (3.4), the eastern NIA languages, except for Oriya, on the whole have not been widely used for epigraphic purposes. In Bengali we have several dedicatory temple inscriptions,[81] mostly from the eighteenth and nineteenth centuries but dating back in one case to the fifteenth.[82] Some of these are bilingual with or mixed with Sanskrit. There are also a few other stone inscriptions in Bengali (e.g., ARIE 1975–76, no. B.45/D.272, bilingual with Arabic), and some late copper plate records of the kings of Tripura in the seventeenth and eighteenth centuries (ARIE 1951–52, nos. A.13–19) are written in Bengali and Sanskrit.

Assamese inscriptions are similarly late and few in number, at least as far as they are reported in published sources. Some copper plates of the Ahom kings of the eighteenth century in Sanskrit and Assamese have been noted (ARIE 1957–58, nos. A.3–5), as well as a few stone inscriptions (ibid., nos. B.65, 74–5).

A seventeenth-century inscription in Maithili has been published in R. K. Choudhary's *Select Inscriptions of Bihar*, 138 (cf. SIE 60).

3.4.6 *Nepali*

Nepali did not become an important inscriptional language until relatively recently, the principal epigraphic languages of Nepal in earlier times being Sanskrit and Newari (see 3.5.3.3 and 4.3.7.2). It is only during the time of the Shāh kings in the eighteenth and nineteenth centuries that donative and dedicatory stone inscriptions in Nepali (often together with Sanskrit) were written in good numbers.[83]

3.4.7 *Sinhalese*

Due no doubt to its special geographical and cultural setting, the pattern of the development of Sinhalese as an epigraphic language is entirely different from that of the NIA languages of India proper. Unlike other NIA languages, Sinhalese and its direct linguistic predecessors were the main languages of inscriptions from early times in Sri Lanka. According to Geiger and Jayatilaka's formulation,[84] the period of the Sinhalese Prakrit or Old Sinhalese inscriptions (see 3.1.4.2.2) ended about the third or fourth century A.D. and was followed by a "Proto-Sinhalese" period from the fourth to the eighth century, represented by the relatively sparse (see 4.3.7.1) epigraphic remains of that period. The more abundant inscriptions of the medieval period, especially of the ninth to the thirteenth century, represent the "Medieval Sinhalese" phase, at which stage. in Geiger's words, "the language has now become a modern Indian idiom and . . . the principal and most characteristic features of the modern language are recognisable" (op. cit., xxix).

81. See A. K. Bhattacharyya, *A Corpus of Dedicatory Inscriptions from Temples of West Bengal*, nos. 56, 58, 62, 74, 96, 106, 115, 116, etc.

82. Bhattacharyya, op. cit., no. S-1, A.D. 1490.

83. See section 4.3.7.2 for references.

84. In *A Dictionary of the Sinhalese Language* (see 3.1.4.2.2), xxiv–xxxi.

Most of the medieval and later Sinhalese inscriptions, some of which are of great length, are on stone. They generally record foundations, grants, regulations, and other matters pertaining to Buddhist monastic establishments.[85]

3.5 Other (Non-Indo-Aryan) Languages in Indian Inscriptions

Although the primary subject matter of this book (see the preface) is restricted to epigraphic material in the Indo-Aryan languages, it may be useful to briefly summarize the other inscriptional material found in India. Needless to say, the following is meant only as a very general introduction and has no pretensions to completeness.

3.5.1 Dravidian languages

The epigraphy of the Dravidian languages constitutes an enormous field of study in itself, which can be presented here only in the broadest outlines, although ideally Dravidian epigraphy cannot be completely separated from Indo-Aryan epigraphy, there being a great deal of geographical, historical, linguistic, and stylistic overlapping between the two fields. Although for the most part Dravidian inscriptions are less ancient than the Indo-Aryan ones, their numbers overall, and especially in the medieval period and in the Tamil and Kannada languages, are very great, perhaps greater than those of the Indo-Aryan languages.

Major publication and reference sources for Dravidian inscriptions are mentioned in section 8.1.2 (esp. *South Indian Inscriptions* and *Epigraphia Carnatica*). The complete literature of the field is vast, but there is unfortunately still no single authoritative study of the subject as a whole.[86]

3.5.1.1 Tamil

Inscriptions in what is now generally agreed to be an early form of Tamil date from approximately the last centuries before and/or the first centuries after the beginning of the Christian era (see 2.2.5.1). There are also a few Tamil inscriptions datable on paleographic grounds to the second through sixth centuries A.D.,[87] but Tamil's emergence as a full-fledged epigraphic language actually began during the reign of the Pallavas, some of whose copper plate inscriptions from the seventh century onward were bilingual in Tamil and Sanskrit. This practice was continued by succeeding dynasties of the Tamil country such as the Coḷas and Pāṇḍyas, but some of their copper plates (especially in the later centuries) were in Tamil only. The majority by far of Tamil inscriptions are donative and other stone records, especially on temple walls, mostly dating from the Coḷa era and later; these number in the many thousands. As

85. See also section 4.3.7.1 for further information.

86. Brief surveys of Dravidian inscriptions are given by D. C. Sircar in SIE 46–52 and by D. B. Diskalkar in JAHRS 21, 1950–52, 163–8.

87. See I. Mahadevan, "Tamil-Brāhmī Inscriptions of the Sangam Age" (ref. in 2.2.5.1 n. 103), 84–5.

with other Dravidian languages, Tamil generally predominates in stone inscriptions and private records, while Sanskrit tends to be retained for imperial grants on copper plates.

3.5.1.2 Kannada

Next to Tamil, Kannada is the earliest and most important of the Dravidian epigraphic languages. The earliest Kannada epigraphs, such as the Halmiḍi (S. Śrīkaṇṭha Śāstri, *Sources of Karṇāṭaka History* [for reference see Index of Inscriptions Cited], 20) and Bādāmi Vaiṣṇava cave (IA 10, 59–60) inscriptions, date from around the late sixth or early seventh century A.D. From this time onward, inscriptions in Kannada, mainly private donative records on stone but also some royal copper plate charters, are extremely common.[88] Many of these are bilingual with Sanskrit or occasionally other languages.

3.5.1.3 Telugu

Like Kannada, Telugu first appeared in inscriptions at about the end of the sixth century A.D.; the earliest Telugu inscriptions are usually considered to be the Kalamaḷḷa and Eṟraguḍipāḍu inscriptions of the early Telugu Coḷa dynasty (EI 27, 220–8). The subsequent development of Telugu as an epigraphic language also follows similar lines to those of Kannada, with private dedicatory stone records predominating. Though numerous, Telugu records are not as abundant as those in Kannada.

3.5.1.4 Malayalam

Compared with the other three major Dravidian literary languages, Malayalam is of much less epigraphic significance, coming into use only around the fifteenth century. The number of stone and copper plate inscriptions in Malayalam is thus far smaller than in the other Dravidian languages.

Among other Dravidian languages, a few late inscriptions in Tulu have also been reported; for references see SIE 52.

3.5.2 Islamic languages (Arabic, Persian, Urdu)

Z. A. Desai, "Arabic and Persian Inscriptions," AI 9, 1953, 224–32; SIE, 31–8; V. S. Bendrey, *A Study of Muslim Inscriptions*.

Inscriptions in the Islamic languages[89] first appeared in India in the last decade of the twelfth century A.D. (Desai 226) and gradually became more numerous, especially in the sixteenth and seventeenth centuries, and continued into the nineteenth. In the earlier centuries Arabic was the preferred language, but from the fourteenth century on Persian became more prevalent, while Urdu came into use only from the mid-

88. Diskalkar (JAHRS 21, 167) estimates that there are twenty-six thousand Kannada inscriptions.

89. "Islamic" is used here as a term of historical and cultural convenience, rather than as a linguistic category; cf. n. 80.

eighteenth century on. Bilinguals among these languages, especially Arabic and Persian, are common, as are bilinguals with Indic languages (e.g., Persian and Sanskrit or Kannada). In general, Islamic inscriptions are most numerous in northern India, but they are found in virtually all parts of the subcontinent.

The majority of the inscriptions in Islamic languages are dedicatory in nature, recording the construction of mosques or other religious buildings, or of secular works such as wells, gates, forts, and so on. Other common types are endowments, administrative records, and memorials (tombstones, etc.).

Unlike Indo-Aryan and Dravidian inscriptions, the Islamic inscriptions do not constitute a major primary source of historical information, not only because they are of no great antiquity but, more importantly, because (unlike earlier times) extensive historical chronicles are available for the period concerned. Nonetheless, Indo-Muslim epigraphy is important as a source of corroborative and supplementary historical and cultural data.[90]

3.5.3 Other non-Indic languages

D. B. Diskalkar, "Inscriptions of Foreign Settlers in India," JIH 34, 1956, 39–52.

3.5.3.1 (Non-Islamic) Semitic, Iranian, and other Near Eastern languages

Aramaic and a mixed "Aramaeo-Iranian" are represented in six inscriptions of the Mauryan era from Pakistan (Taxila) and Afghanistan (see 4.3.7.3). Several hundred brief inscriptions in Sogdian have been found in the Shatial region on the upper Indus,[91] as well as a few others from Ladakh.[92] Some inscriptions in Parthian and Bactrian were also found on the upper Indus.[93] Inscriptions in Pahlavi have been found in western and southern India; the most important examples are the Pahlavi pilgrims' records in the Kāṇheri caves (IA 9, 265–8 = ICTWI 62–6) dating from the early eleventh century, and the Christian inscriptions in the churches at Madras and Koṭṭayam (IA 3, 308–16; West, EI 4, 1896–97, 174–6), some of which may be as early as the seventh or eighth century. A few Christian inscriptions in Syriac have also been found at Koṭṭayam and other places in South India (e.g., IA 3, 314).

Some medieval inscriptions in Hebrew have been found in southern India, for example, a tombstone of A.D. 1269 from Chennamangalam (IA 59, 134–5).[94] A similar Hebrew inscription of A.D. 1251, together with two others in Himyaritic, were found in Bhuj (EI 19, 300–2), but these are thought to have been brought to India from South Arabia (301). There are also a few Hebrew graffiti from near Chilas among

90. For examples see Desai, 229–32.

91. Helmut Humbach, "The Sogdian Inscriptions of Thor-Shatial," *Journal of Central Asia* 8, 1985, 51–7; Nicholas Sims-Williams, "The Sogdian Inscriptions of the Upper Indus: A Preliminary Report," in K. Jettmar, ed., *Antiquities of Northern Pakistan*, I.131–7; Sims-Williams, *Sogdian and Other Iranian Inscriptions of the Upper Indus*.

92. N. Sims-Williams, "The Sogdian Inscriptions of Ladakh," in K. Jettmar, *Antiquities of Northern Pakistan*, II.151–63.

93. Humbach, op. cit., 57. Some other inscriptions of the Kuṣāṇa period in Bactrian, notably the Surkh-Kotal (Afghanistan) inscription of Kaniṣka (JA 246, 345–440), are found outside of India proper.

94. For other examples and references, see Diskalkar, 43–4.

the newly discovered inscriptions on the upper Indus (K. Jettmar, *Orientalia Iosephi Tucci Memoriae Dicata* [for reference see Index of Inscriptions Cited], II.667–70). Armenian tombstone inscriptions, mostly of the seventeenth and eighteenth centuries, are found in fair numbers in various parts of India, especially in Bengal, Madras, and the west coast, for example, the epitaph at the Little Mount, Madras (EI 6, 89).[95]

3.5.3.2 European languages

Although Greek was extensively used in coin legends in northern India in the "foreign period," and although from the neighboring region of Afghanistan we have Aśokan and other Greek inscriptions (see 4.3.7.3), in India proper only a very few minor epigraphic specimens of it have been discovered in the form of inscribed potsherds from the Swat region (e.g., Birkoṭ-Ghundai; *Journal of Central Asia* 7, 49–53). There are also a few tombstone inscriptions from the colonial period in modern Greek (ARSIE 1912, 86).

Several other European languages are represented in inscriptions of the modern period, that is, from the sixteenth century onward. The earliest of these are the numerous Portuguese inscriptions from Goa, Daman and Diu, Bassein, and other Portuguese settlements.[96] Some of the inscriptions of the Portuguese and other European settlers are composed in Latin. Tombstones and other inscriptions in Dutch dating from the seventeenth and eighteenth centuries are found in the Dutch settlements in western and southern India (e.g., Chingleput; EI 24, 123–6).[97] There are similar though less numerous records in French, mostly from the eighteenth and nineteenth centuries. Finally, inscriptions in English are very common all over India from the seventeenth century on; these include inscriptions on tombs and other memorial records, administrative orders, foundations, and the like.

3.5.3.3 Sino-Tibetan languages and Chinese

Only a few late inscriptions in Sino-Tibetan languages of the border regions of India have been published. Inscriptions in Manipuri have been compiled by M. Bahadur and P. G. Singh in *Epigraphical Records of Manipur*. A few late copper plate inscriptions in Ahom are noted in SIE 60. Stone and copper plate inscriptions in Newari of the Malla period, usually bilingual with Sanskrit, are regularly found in Nepal from the late fourteenth century A.D. and become very common in the sixteenth to eighteenth centuries (see 4.3.7.2 for references). Also quite common are ritual and historical inscriptions in Tibetan found in many parts of the Himalayan regions of India; see, for example, IA 35, 1906, 237–41, 325–33 (A. H. Francke).

Inscriptions in Sino-Tibetan languages of East and Southeast Asia are also occasionally found in India, generally in the form of pilgrims' records or Buddhist dona-

95. For other examples, see Diskalkar, 45–6, and ARIE 1962–63, nos. D.98–9, and 1966–67, no. B.192.

96. See J. H. da Cunha Rivara, *Inscripções Lapidares da India Portugeuza* (Lisboa: Imprensa Nacional, 1894). For other references see Diskalkar, 48–9.

97. See also ARSIE 1909, 121–4; 1911, 90–1; and 1912, 85–6.

tions. At Bodh-Gayā, for example, inscriptions have been found in Burmese (EI 11, 118–20) and Chinese (JRAS, n.s. 13, 552–72). Some Chinese inscriptions have also been discovered in other parts of India, for example, several recently found at Chilas, Hunza-Haldeikish, and other sites in northern Pakistan.[98]

3.6. Bilingual and Multilingual Inscriptions

As will be clear from the several examples already noted in this chapter (and as would have been expected in any case in such a linguistically complex cultural area as India), inscriptions in two or more languages are common. The majority of these involve Sanskrit and one or more other languages; for example, Sanskrit and Prakrit (examples cited in 3.3.4) in inscriptions of the transitional period of the fourth and fifth centuries A.D. Beginning around the sixth century, inscriptions in Sanskrit and one of the Dravidian languages become common. In the medieval period, Sanskrit is often combined with one of the Islamic languages, especially Persian, or with one of the NIA languages.

These Sanskrit bilinguals are for the most part not "true" bilinguals, that is, the same text repeated in full in two languages, but rather contain a single text divided on functional grounds between the languages concerned. Typically, the invocatory, genealogical, and concluding portions will be in Sanskrit, while the "functional" portions recording the specific details of the gift, transaction, and the like, will be in the other language (3.3.4). In the medieval period we also find non-Sanskrit bilinguals, involving two NIA languages or an NIA and a Dravidian language (e.g., the Bhubaneswar Oriya-Tamil inscription, cited in 3.4.2). Among this group we do find some true bilinguals, for example, the Baripāṛā Museum Oriya-Hindi inscription (3.4.2).

Trilingual inscriptions are also not rare. Examples include the Kurgoḍ inscription (EI 14, 265–78) in Sanskrit, Prakrit, and Kannada, and the Ciṛuvroli copper plates (EI 34, 177–88) in Sanskrit, Telugu, and Oriya.

98. Ma Yong in Jettmar, *Antiquities of Northern Pakistan*, I.139–57; Thomas O. Höllman in ibid., II.61–75.

4

Survey of Inscriptions in the Indo-Aryan Languages

4.1 Typological Survey

SIE 2–5; IIEP 73–5; IGI II.49–62; PIP 123–48; IC I.158–9; A. V. Naik, "Inscriptions of the Deccan," 17–23; SITI III.2, 181–209.

In terms of their purpose and contents, the majority of the epigraphic materials in the Indo-Aryan languages fall into the two broad categories of "donative" and "panegyric" records (4.1.1–4.1.3). However, the full range of their contents is very broad, comprising not only the several other categories described below but also combinations of the various types. Strictly speaking, few, if any, of the categories listed here are completely distinct and exclusive, and many of them overlap; for example, purely eulogistic inscriptions are rare, and most of the records placed in this group also partake of the character of donative and/or memorial records. Not only are the categories not mutually exclusive, they are also to some extent arbitrary; thus different writers on the subject have presented different arrangements, and no one formulation can be considered definitive. The divisions offered here should therefore be understood as convenient, rather than authoritative and mutually exclusive categories; various other classifications are given in the sources cited.

4.1.1 Royal donative and panegyric inscriptions (praśasti)

Donative proclamations and panegyrics issued by or on behalf of ruling kings, called *praśasti*s, are typically engraved on stone slabs or pillars.[1] Despite their largely panegyric content and tone, they are rarely purely eulogistic in content; nearly all of them record some donation or memorial which serves as the ostensible occasion for the record.[2]

1. See the following specimens in the Appendix: Kahāuṃ pillar ins. (no. 7), Lakkhā Maṇḍal *praśasti* (no. 8), Burhānpūr ins. (no. 14).

2. As a matter of convenience and convention, royal inscriptions on stone are generally classed under the heading of panegyrics, as opposed to donative inscriptions on copper plates. But in actual

Royal inscriptions of a purely exhortatory character are rare, and in fact are virtually limited to the inscriptions of Aśoka (4.3.1.1). Purely administrative records are equally unusual, again being practically restricted to the earliest period, as in the Sohgaurā (SI I.82–3) and Mahāsthān (SI I.79–80) inscriptions which record official proclamations concerning measures for the prevention of famine. The Hāthīgumphā inscription of Khāravela (SI I.213–21), describing the king's achievements year by year, approximates the character of a pure panegyric, which is rare elsewhere.

More typical are the inscriptions of later centuries which sing the ruler's praises on the occasion of a particular foundation or donation. Pillar inscriptions may record the erection of the pillar itself in memory of a king's victories (*jayastambha* or *kīrtistambha*), for instance, the Allahabad pillar of Samudragupta (SI I.262–8) or the Mandasor pillar of Yaśodharman (SI I.418–20). Other pillar inscriptions are primarily religious in intent, being dedicated to deities such as Garuḍa (*garuḍadhvaja;* e.g., Besnagar pillar ins., Appendix, no. 2), Viṣṇu (*viṣṇor dhvajaḥ;* Meharaulī pillar ins., SI I.283–5; fig. 3), or Śiva (Bhitarī ins., SI I.321–4).[3]

Most frequently, however, royal inscriptions on stone slabs and, less commonly, on pillars record donations, foundations, or endowments of temples, images, and public works of various kinds. The Aihoḷe stone inscription of Pulakeśin II (SI II.443–50), for example, records the erection of a Jaina temple, and the Deopāṛā stone inscription of Vijayasena (SI II.115–22) a temple and image of Pradyumneśvara (Harihara). Dedications of waterworks and wells are common, for instance, the Junāgaḍh inscription of Rudradāman (SI I.175–80) and the Tāḷagunda inscription of the time of Śāntivarman (SI I.474–9). Especially in the earlier period, inscriptions on cave walls record their construction and dedication to monastic or ascetic orders (4.2.1.3). Other types of endowments to monastic and Brahmanical orders or to individuals are also common, such as gifts of villages (similar to those recorded in copper plate inscriptions), for example, in the Mahākūṭa inscription of Maṅgaleśa (IA 19, 7–20). Inscriptions of this latter type, recording royal donations to temples and engraved on the temple walls themselves, became extremely common in southern India in the medieval period.

Stylistically, such royal donative/panegyric records tend toward lofty poetic modes, whether composed entirely in prose (Hāthīgumphā, Junāgaḍh, Mahākūṭa), in mixed prose and verse (Allahabad), or in verse only (Aihoḷe, Deopāṛā, etc.). Verse compositions are generally preferred, especially in later centuries. Ornate poetic compositions of this sort are often signed by the composer, who was usually a court poet of the eulogized ruler; such figures as Hariṣeṇa, author of the Allahabad inscription, or Ravikīrti, composer of the Aihoḷe *praśasti*, are otherwise unknown, but others, such as Umāpatidhara, poet of the Deopāṛā inscription, are known from other compositions or at least from quotations in poetic anthologies (see 7.2.1.3).

---

practice, stone inscriptions sometimes closely resemble copper plate charters in style and content (see the earlier introductory comments).

3. Pillar inscriptions in the form of *yūpas* may also memorialize Vedic sacrifices; see section 4.2.1.2.

FIGURE 3. Meharaulī (Delhi Union Territory) pillar inscription with the inscription of Candra. Photograph courtesy of Timothy Lenz.

A typical inscription of this class would begin with an auspicious sign or invocation such as *svasti* followed by one or more *maṅgala* (invocatory) verses, and then an account of the ruling king's lineage, full of lavish praises of his own and his ancestors' physical power and beauty, moral qualities and reputation, just rule, conquests, learning and artistic skills, and so on. The actual purpose of the inscription, namely, the dedication or memorial, is typically mentioned only at or near the end of the text. This is often followed by concluding, benedictory, and/or signature verses giving the composer's name (e.g., Appendix, no. 8, vv. 21–23).

FIGURE 4. Sātalur (Krishna Dist., AP) copper plate grant of Eastern Cālukya king Vijayāditya III. From Sivaramamurti, IESIS, pl. IV.

This format is, of course, most typical of the classical and postclassical era, when both form and style became highly stylized and stereotyped. Panegyrics of the pre- and early classical periods tend to be more varied and original in their literary qualities, as in the vivid description of the destruction and rebuilding of Lake Sudarśana in the Junāgaḍh inscription.

4.1.2 Land grant (copper plate) charters

B. Ch. Chhabra, "Diplomatic of Sanskrit Copper-Plate Grants"; A. Gaur, *Indian Charters on Copper Plates*, vii–xiii; SIE 103–60; PIP 145–6.

Inscriptions on copper plates recording land grants[4] are exceedingly common almost everywhere in India,[5] numbering well into the thousands, and their study is an important subfield within Indian epigraphy. Such inscriptions are engraved on one or more plates of copper which vary widely in size but generally reproduce the shape of traditional nonepigraphic writing materials such as palm leaves and bark strips, or sometimes stone stelae. Smaller examples, usual in the earlier centuries, are typically about two to three inches high and five to six inches long; later specimens are often large, in the range of fifteen to twenty inches. The plates are usually prepared with

4. See specimens in fig. 4 and Appendix: Baroda copper plate inscription of Karkkarāja (no. 10).
5. Despite their abundance in India proper, copper plate inscriptions are generally not common outside of India, though they are sometimes found in Nepal (see 4.3.7.2) and Burma (see 4.3.7.5). In Indonesia, copper plate inscriptions in Javanese, but not in Sanskrit, are quite numerous.

some care in order to protect the writing from damage and wear; often the edges are raised to prevent the plates from rubbing together, and sometimes the outer plates or faces are left blank. The writing usually goes along the longer direction of the plates, though inscriptions written across the shorter dimension are not uncommon, especially in eastern India and in the plates of the Vijayanagara kings in southern India. Charters on multiple plates are joined together with a ring (occasionally two rings, one at each end) of copper or bronze which is inserted through holes in the plates. The ends of the ring are soldered together onto a seal, usually of bronze, which is intended to certify the authenticity of the document and to prevent tampering by the addition or removal of plates. The number of plates varies widely; in general, later specimens are larger and longer, and examples with several dozen plates and weighing as much as two hundred pounds total are known (Chhabra 4; SIE 124).

The usual purpose of copper plate inscriptions is to record donations, usually by kings or their functionaries, of villages or (somewhat less commonly) of cultivated fields to Brahmans who are felt to be especially deserving by virtue of their learning or holiness. They may also record endowments to temples or other religious institutions, and copies in stone of inscriptions of this type are frequently found engraved on the walls of the temples in question. Occasionally, the grantees may be *kṣatriya*s or other non-Brahmans, as in the grant of a field to a general (*senāpati*) in a Kadamba inscription from Halsi (IA 6, 23–4). Similar grants to Buddhist and Jaina venerables and institutions are also not uncommon, particularly in western, eastern, and southern India (e.g., SI I.531). The grantees were normally entitled to all rights and revenues accruing from the granted lands in perpetuity, the details of the grant and benefits thereof being spelled out, often in great detail.

The earliest specimens of copper plate charters come from southern India, issued by the early Pallava and Śālaṅkāyana dynasties and datable, according to Sircar (SIE 107), to about the middle of the fourth century A.D.[6] Although these early examples are in Prakrit, in form and style they are essentially the same as the more elaborate Sanskrit copper plate inscriptions which became so abundant in succeeding centuries. Probably the oldest extant copper plate grant from northern India is the Kalāchalā grant of Īśvararāta, in Sanskrit, dated on paleographic grounds by Sircar (EI 33, 303–6) to the later part of the fourth century A.D.

There is clear evidence, however, that the origins of the copper plate charters or their prototypes go back farther than the fourth century, for some of the donative cave inscriptions of the Western Kṣatrapa and Sātavāhana kings from Nāsik, datable to the first or second century, are evidently copies on stone of original documents written on portable materials, possibly copper (SIE 108). The antiquity of the practice of recording land grants on copper plates is also attested by their description in early *dharmaśāstra* texts such as the *Viṣṇu-* and *Yājñavalkya-smṛti*s and the commentaries thereon (SIE 104–5). Here and elsewhere (including in the inscriptions themselves), the copper plate charters are referred to by such terms as *tāmraśāsana*, *tāmrapaṭṭa*, *tāmraphalī*, *dānaśāsana*, and so on.

6. The Tañjāvur grant of the Western Gaṅga king Arivarman dated Śaka 169 = A.D. 248 has been cited as possibly the earliest copper plate inscription (Gaur, *Indian Charters*, x and 8), but is in fact clearly a late forgery (Fleet, IA 8, 212).

Copper plate inscriptions in Sanskrit began to be more common in the Gupta period, and in the following centuries became abundant and more lavish in size and style. The genealogical, laudatory, and benedictory portions are often elaborated at great length and typically constitute the bulk of a record, as is the case in the Baroda copper plate grant of Karkkarāja (Appendix, no. 10), in which forty of the seventy-three lines of the inscription are taken up by the genealogy and eulogy of the donor. In this respect, the more elaborate copper plate inscriptions have come to resemble in content and style the panegyric stone inscriptions described previously (4.1.1).

The tradition of recording land grants on copper plates continued throughout the medieval era and even into the European period,[7] and in certain cases such documents have been adjudged to be still legally valid in modern times.[8]

In general, the donative or "functional" parts of the inscriptions are in prose, while the formal portions of the genealogy and so on are often versified, especially in the longer and more ornate specimens. But there are occasional examples of copper plate inscriptions written entirely in verse, such as the Rajamundry plates of Raghudeva (SI II.195–209).

Since the use of copper instead of ordinary perishable writing materials reflects a desire to establish the document as a permanent record, in effect a deed to the granted lands, it is not surprising that copper plates are most often found underground where they had been buried for safekeeping by the grantees or their descendants according to the traditional Indian practice.[9] Such finds are usually made accidentally by villagers in the course of plowing their fields or digging a foundation for a house. A copper plate inscription of the more ornate type would typically contain all or most of the following sections.[10]

4.1.2.1 Preamble

(a) Invocation. The invocation or *maṅgala* typically consists of an auspicious word, most commonly *siddham* (expressed by word or symbol), often followed by one or more verses in praise of various deities. [Appendix, no. 10, line 1][11]

(b) Place of issue. The place of issue, normally the capital city of the issuing king or a military camp (*jayaskandhāvāra*), is usually mentioned after the invocation, typically in the ablative case. Most often this is just a single word or phrase, but

7. For examples of copper plate inscriptions in Sanskrit and/or vernacular languages as late as the eighteenth and nineteenth centuries, see ARIE 1957–58, nos. A.3–5; OHRJ 2, 1953, 47–56; and Gaur, *Indian Charters*, 23–4.

8. See P. V. Kane, *History of Dharmaśāstra*, vol. II, pt.2, 865.

9. In several cases copper plates have been found inside buried urns in which they had been placed for further protection; see, e.g. EI 28, 1949–50, 175–6.

10. The terminology and formulation here are based largely on that of Chhabra and Sircar (who mostly follows Chhabra). This scheme is intended merely as a typical pattern; in actual practice, copper plate charters vary widely in their ordering and inclusion or exclusion of the standard elements and in the degree of detail and elaboration accorded to them. For the historical background of the development of the stylistic conventions of copper plate and other formal records, see O. Stein, "Formal Elements in Indian Inscriptions," IHQ 9, 1933, 215–26.

11. For purposes of illustration, reference is given for each section to the appropriate lines in the copper plate inscription of Karkkarāja given in the Appendix.

in some ornate inscriptions this part is expanded into an elaborate poetic description of the place. In many inscriptions, however, the place of issue is not specified at all. [line 43]

(c) Grantor's name and genealogy. The name of the grantor, normally a king, is supplied along with his titles and epithets and often (especially in later inscriptions) detailed genealogical and other information. In ornate inscriptions this portion may be developed at great length, giving long and detailed, if bombastic and exaggerated, accounts of the dynastic history of the issuing authority. This portion is thus often the most important one from the historian's point of view (cf. 7.1.1). [lines 1–41]

(d) Address. After the grantor is introduced, the text specifies the officers and other authorities who are to be officially informed of the transaction. These are given in the accusative case as object of a verb such as *ājñāpayati* or *ādiśati* 'commands' or *bodhayati* 'informs', followed by a formulaic phrase such as *viditam astu vo yad* . . . ("Be it known to you that . . ."). The sometimes very extensive lists of officials provided here constitute an important source for the study of administrative structures (7.1.2). [lines 41–3]

4.1.2.2 Notification

(e) Specification of the gift. The grant usually next specifies the name and location of the granted land. This may be one or more villages or fields, specified in terms of the administrative subdivisions (*viṣaya, maṇḍala, bhukti*, etc.) in which they fall. The territory in question is often further delimited by specifying its borders (*sīman, āghāṭana*) with reference to neighboring villages and natural or artificial features such as rivers, forests, marking stones, and so on. This is usually followed by a list, often extensive, of *parihāra*s 'exemptions' or 'privileges' to be enjoyed by the grantees, such as *acātabhaṭaprāveśya* 'not to be entered by royal agents and police', *sodraṅga* 'together with the *udraṅga* revenues', and so forth.[12] [lines 46–51]

(f) Names of the grantees. The names of the grantees, almost always Brahmans, are given with appropriate identification as to their descent, place of birth or residence, *śākhā* and *gotra* affiliation, and so on. Sometimes verses eulogizing the virtues of the grantees are inserted here. The number of grantees may be anywhere from one to over a hundred; the Karandai plates of Rājendra Coḷa (K. G. Krishnan, *Karandai Tamil Sangam Plates*, 55; cf. SIE 135) list 1,083 grantees. In the case of multiple recipients, the shares to be enjoyed by each grantee are usually separately specified. [lines 44–5]

(g) Occasion. Land grants were typically announced on astrologically auspicious occasions for gift giving such as eclipses or *saṃkrānti*s (solar passages). Such a special occasion is mentioned where applicable, though this section is often omitted. [not in Baroda plates]

(h) Intention and/or function. The grantor usually specifies the particular benefit which he hopes to obtain from his pious gift, such as long life, glory, or spiritual

12. A complete list of *parihāra*s is given in IEG 388–408.

merit for the donor himself and his parents in this life and the next.[13] This section is sometimes omitted. The function of the grant is also sometimes mentioned; this typically involves such pious activities as funding a Brahman's daily worship, feeding Brahmans, or maintaining a temple. [lines 43–4]

4.1.2.3 Conclusion

(i) Exhortation. This portion typically comprises the issuing king's command to respect the grant in perpetuity, often specifying the benefits of doing so and the evil consequences of violating a gift. This statement is usually supported by the quotation of well-known exhortatory verses attributed to Vyāsa, Manu, Rāma, and others about land gifts and their sanctity. Sometimes as many as twenty such verses are cited. Among the most commonly quoted verses, usually attributed to Vyāsa, is *bahubhir vasudhā bhuktā rājabhiḥ sagarādibhiḥ / yasya yasya yadā bhūmis tasya tadā phalam* // ("The Earth has been enjoyed by many kings from Sagara onward. Its fruits belong to whomever possesses it at any time").[14] [lines 54–68]

(j) Date. The inscriptions are usually dated, sometimes only by year (regnal or of an era), but often, especially in later records, with full details of month, fortnight, *tithi*, weekday, and sometimes also *nakṣatra* and other astronomical information (see 5.4.2.2). The location of the date within the inscription varies considerably; in some records it appears at the very beginning, or together with the "occasion" (item g). [line 52]

(k) Names of officers and functionaries. The inscription usually gives at the conclusion the name(s) of one or more functionaries involved in the ordering and execution of the grant. Most commonly mentioned is the conveyer of the royal order, usually referred to as *dūta(ka)* or *ājñā/ājñapti*. The writer and scribe is also often named, and sometimes the composer and engraver as well (see 2.5.2.2). [lines 68–70]

(l) Authentication. The inscription is often authenticated at the end by the purported[15] signature of the issuing king, usually with the formula *svahasto 'yaṃ mama*. . . ("This is my signature . . .)." The signature is sometimes engraved in larger or more ornate characters (cf. 2.5.3.1), as if to demonstrate the king's authority or skill in writing. The document is further authenticated and guaranteed by the royal seal on the ring attached to the plate(s), which is often inscribed with a dynastic motto and/or the royal insignia. [lines 68–9]

Special types of copper plate charters include "blanks" such as the Chittagong plate of Kāntideva (EI 26, 313–8), containing only the formulaic portions and omitting the functional section for details and specifications, which were presumably supposed

13. The donor's intention is also sometimes alluded to at the beginning of the notification, with a reference to the transitory nature of earthly life and property as contrasted to the permanence of a gift. [ll. 40–1]

14. For a comprehensive list of such verses, see SIE 170–201.

15. The signatures were presumably not actually engraved on the plate by the kings themselves but rather copied from an archetype.

to have been filled in at a later date. There are also several examples of reissues or palimpsests, wherein an old and presumably invalid or inoperative copper plate was reinscribed after the old inscription had been obliterated, as in the Veligalani grant (EI 33, 275–92). In some cases the original text is still partially legible, for example, the Nūtimaḍagu plates (EI 25, 186–94; cf. SIE 91, 124–5).

Forged and altered copper plate inscriptions are also well documented. These include both copies or imitations made at a later date which were apparently meant to be passed off as the original documents, such as the Nālandā and Gayā spurious plates of Samudragupta (SI I.270–4), and altered plates wherein, for instance, the names of the donees or the granted village have been changed. Such "spurious" documents are usually crudely executed and more or less readily identifiable by their linguistic, stylistic, chronological, and paleographic inconsistencies.[16]

4.1.3 Private donations

Inscriptions recording private donations,[17] usually of a religious character, are very numerous, ranging from simple brief records in Middle Indo-Aryan, Sanskrit, or regional languages, to highly elaborate *praśasti*-style Sanskrit inscriptions. The majority are on stone, though some, mostly image dedications, are on metal. A typical inscription of this type might mention the date (regnal or era); the donor's name, title(s), occupation, and place of residence or origin; the nature of the donation or endowment; its intention or purpose; and the names of the relatives and associates of the donor who are to partake of its benefits.

Beyond these typical features, however, private donative records are highly diverse in content, character, and style. Ornate donative records such as the Mandasor stone inscription of the time of Kumāragupta and Bandhuvarman, recording the construction and subsequent renovation of a Sun temple by the silk weavers' guild (SI I.299–307), may be stylistically almost indistinguishable from royal *praśasti*s; in fact, these classes sometimes overlap in that many of the "private" donations involve the relatives, officials, and other associates of kings. Less formal donative records, however, may contain only the basic information of the type outlined previously, or even just the donor's name in the genitive case on a donated object; numerous examples of this class are found among the inscriptions at Buddhist *stūpa* sites such as Sāñcī and Bhārhut.[18]

The objects of private donations are in general similar to those of royal donations: tanks, wells, and drinking places; temples or endowments to temples for repairs, maintenance, or daily ritual activities; caves for monastic residences; images of deities; villages or agricultural lands; and so forth. Buddhist donative inscriptions typically record the dedication of *stūpa* structures or reliquaries (fig. 5) and other portable objects (cf. 4.2.1.5). Jaina donative inscriptions on temple walls and images are common, especially in western and southern India in the later centuries.

16. For examples and details, see section 5.3.

17. See the following specimens in the Appendix: Besnagar pillar ins. (no. 2); Kalawān copper plate ins. (no. 4); Sārnāth umbrella shaft ins. (no. 5); Tiruveṅkāḍu temple ins. (no. 11); Nālandā ins. (no. 12); Pabhosā Jaina ins. (no. 15).

18. For example, *Isidatasa dānaṃ* 'Gift of Isidata [Ṛṣidatta]' (Bhārhut A 86, CII 2.2, 47). See also section 4.2.1.3.

FIGURE 5. Silver Buddhist reliquary of Prince Indravarman. Photograph courtesy of the Shumei Culture Foundation.

4.1.4 Memorial inscriptions

Inscriptions in memory or honor of deceased persons, usually relatives of the sponsor of the inscription, are fairly common from an early period. Early examples, mostly in Prakrit, include records which refer to themselves by such terms as *laṭhi* or *yaṭhi* (Skt. *yaṣṭi*) '(memorial) pillar',[19] or *chāyākhaṃbha/chāyāthaṃbha* (*chāyāstambha*) 'image pillars',[20] found at Nāgārjunakoṇḍa and other Buddhist sites. Memorial pillars often commemorate persons killed in battle, as in some of the Nāgārjunakoṇḍa inscriptions (e.g., EI 35, 14–6) and in the Gaṅgaperuru inscription (EI 36, 207–8) memorializing one Gona who was killed in a cattle raid (*gogahana*). A well-known early (A.D. 510) Sanskrit inscription of the same class is the Eraṇ inscription of the time of Bhānugupta (SI I.345–6), recording the death in battle of Goparāja and his

19. For example, the Andhau inscriptions of the time of Caṣṭana and Rudradāman (SI I.173–5).
20. On the meaning of this term, see D. C. Sircar and K. G. Krishnan, EI 34, 1961–62, 20–1.

wife's *satī*. A Jaina inscription of about the seventh century from Śravaṇa-Beḷgoḷa (EI 4, 22–8) commemorates the suicide by starvation of an *ācārya* Prabhācandra.

Other Sanskrit memorial inscriptions commemorate a dead wife, as in the Sāngsi inscription (EI 28, 129–33), or daughter, as in the recently discovered twelfth-century memorial stele from Candrāvatī (JOI 32, 76–81). Far more common from medieval and later times, however, are *satī*-stones recording the suicides of widows and hero-stones memorializing warriors killed in battle. These types, which are particularly common in southern and western India (especially Karnataka and Rajasthan), are usually engraved on a stone slab together with visual or symbolic representations of the deceased (cf. SIE 89). Though they are most commonly written in the local Dravidian or NIA vernacular, Sanskrit inscriptions in these classes are by no means rare, for example, the Bassi inscription commemorating the *satī* of the three wives of the Cāhamāna king Ajayapaladeva in A.D. 1132 (EI 37, 163–4).[21]

Buddhist inscriptions recording the dedication of *stūpa*s containing the relics of deceased monks have been found at various sites from an early period.[22] A relatively large selection of such inscriptions from Kāṇherī has been published recently (JESI 5, 110–12; IEBHA 55–9).

4.1.5 Label inscriptions

Sculptures and other works of art are sometimes furnished with inscriptional labels identifying the figure or scene depicted.[23] Some early examples of label inscriptions are found in the royal portrait galleries of the early Sātavāhana rulers at Nānāghāṭ (ca. first century A.D.; SI I.190–2) and of the Kuṣāṇa kings at Māṭ (first or second century A.D.; MI §97–8, 100; fig. 6; cf. 4.2.1.4), with the name of the royal figure portrayed given in the genitive (Nānāghāṭ) or nominative (Māṭ) case.

Label inscriptions also served to identify narrative sculptures, most notably in the remains of the Bhārhut *stūpa*, which include several dozen inscriptions labeling divine figures, scenes from the Buddha's life, *jātaka* and *avadāna* stories, and so on (CII 2.2, part B). Eight label inscriptions also accompany scenes from the legends of the Buddha on a stele from Amarāvatī (*Ancient India* 20–1, 1964–65, 168–77). In later centuries, label inscriptions were often affixed to statues of deities, for instance, on the sixty-four *yoginī*s of the Causāṭh-yoginī temple of Bheṛāghāṭ (ca. tenth century A.D.; R. K. Sharma, *The Temple of Chaunsathyogini at Bheraghat*).

Label inscriptions were also used in painting, though surviving examples are rare. Fragments of a painted inscription in cave 17 at Ajaṇṭā which served as a label to the accompanying fresco were identified by Lüders as verses from Āryaśūra's *Jātakamālā*.[24] Painted inscriptions in Sanskrit and hybrid dialect consisting of labels or signatures have been found in the Buddhist remains of Chinese central Asia (see 4.3.7.12).

21. On memorial stones in general, see S. Settar and Gunther D. Sontheimer, eds., *Memorial Stones*, especially B. D. Chattopadhyaya, "Early Memorial Stones of Rajasthan" (139–49) and H. Sarkar, "The Cāyā[*sic*]-stambhas from Nāgārjunakoṇḍa" (199–207).

22. See Gregory Schopen, "An Old Inscription from Amarāvatī and the Cult of the Local Monastic Dead in Indian Buddhist Monasteries," JIABS 14, 1991, 281–329.

23. See the following specimen in the Appendix: Bhārhut label ins. (no. 3).

24. *Nachrichten von der Königlichen Gesellschaft der Wissenschaften zu Göttingen*, Phil.-hist. Klasse, 1902, 758–62 = *Philologica Indica*, 73–7.

FIGURE 6. Māṭ (Mathurā) portrait statue of King Kaniṣka: the inscription reads *mahārājā rājātirājā devaputro kaniṣka* ("The Great King, King over Kings, Son of the Gods, Kaniṣka"). From John M. Rosenfield, *The Dynastic Arts of the Kushans* (Berkeley and Los Angeles: University of California Press, 1967), fig. 2; reprinted by permission of the University of California Press.

4.1.6 Pilgrims' and travelers' records

Brief inscriptions recording the visits of pilgrims are often found at various sites,[25] especially on the walls or pathways of temples and other sacred sites of Buddhist, Brahmanical, and Jaina affiliation. Most commonly such inscriptions consist simply of the pilgrim's name in the nominative or bare stem form, or occasionally in the

25. See the following specimen in the Appendix: inscription on the Kosam pillar (no. 13).

genitive. Large numbers of inscriptions of this type are often grouped together, for instance, at such sites as Bhuilī (ARIE 1961–62, nos. B.909–66) and Devaprayāg (ARIE 1948–49, nos. B.56–88). More elaborate examples also include the title(s) of the pilgrim and a verbal formulation such as *praṇamati* '[So-and-so] bows' (or *praṇamati nityaṃ nityam* '. . . bows over and over'), *likhitam* 'written [by so-and-so]', or *ihāgataḥ/iha prāptaḥ* '[So-and-so] came here'. Occasionally pilgrims' records may be several lines long with more elaborate formulations, as in some of the inscriptions from Jāgeśvar (EI 34, 250–1). Inscriptions of this class are frequently written in ornate scripts of various kinds (see, e.g., the inscriptions from Sondhia, EI 34, 248 and facing plate), including the highly calligraphic "Ornate Brāhmī" and "Shell Characters" (e.g., Muṇḍeśvarī, JBRS 62, 104–8; cf. 2.5.3.2).

Recent expeditions in the valley of the upper Indus and adjoining areas of northern Pakistan have revealed several hundred new inscriptions recording the names of travelers at sites in and around Chilas, Gilgit, and Hunza (see 4.3.3.1 for references).

4.1.7 Cultic inscriptions

Cultic inscriptions are those records whose content or purpose is purely religious or devotional, as opposed to donative or memorial. In the Brahmanical or "Hindu" sphere, such inscriptions usually take the form of devotional texts or *stotra*s written on temple walls or pillars.[26] The deities addressed in inscriptions of this type (some of which are of considerable literary merit; cf. 7.2.2.2.3) include Śiva (the *Halāyudha-stotra* from Māndhātā, EI 25, 173–82), Sūrya (Cittapa's *stotra* at Vidiśā, EI 30, 215–9; Udaipur eulogy, JESI 8, 97–100), and Vyāsa Dvaipāyana (Satyanārāyaṇa pillar ins.; Gnoli, *Nepalese Inscriptions in Gupta Characters*, no. XI).[27] Some of the texts recorded in inscriptions of this type, for instance, the *Halāyudha-stotra*, are also known from manuscript sources (see 7.2.2.2.3).

An example of a Jaina inscription evidently belonging to this category is the Bijoliā rock inscription, recording an otherwise unknown *Uttamaśikhara-purāṇa*.[28]

Cultic inscriptions are particularly common in the Buddhist sphere, presumably because written texts were generally accorded greater sanctity by Buddhists than by followers of the Brahmanical tradition.[29] Buddhist canonical and quasi-canonical texts inscribed on such materials as stone, brick, terra-cotta, or metal (bronze, gold, etc.) are common both in and outside of India. A text which was particularly favored for epigraphic treatment is the *Pratītya-samutpāda-* or *Nidāna-sūtra*, which is inscribed on several bricks from Nālandā dating from the sixth century A.D. (EI 21, 193–204; EI 24, 20–2), on stone slabs from Ratnagiri (D. Mitra, *Ratnagiri*, II.411–22), and on various other materials from other sites (see EI 21,

26. This practice is still widely current; the marble slabs inscribed with verses from texts such as the *Bhagavadgītā* on the walls of the Viśvanātha temple at Varanasi and many other modern temples would also, strictly speaking, fall into this class.

27. See also the two centuries of verses in Māhārāṣṭrī Prakrit eulogizing the tortoise incarnation of Viṣṇu at Dhār (EI 8, 241–60; see also 3.1.5.1).

28. See SIE 71 and Kielhorn, JRAS 1906, 700–1. The full text of this inscription has apparently never been published.

29. Cf. N. P. Chakravarti, EI 21, 1931–32, 196–7; S. Paranavitana, EZ 4, 1934–41, 236–7; cf. 2.1.1.

195) including gold leaves[30] from Burma[31] and Indonesia.[32] A similar gold leaf manuscript of the *Pañcaviṃśati-sāhasrikā Prajñāpāramitā* has recently been discovered at Jetavanārāma (Anurādhapura), Sri Lanka.[33]

Most common of all are the copies on bricks, metal images, terra-cotta plaques, and other materials of the so-called Buddhist creed, that is, the ubiquitous verse *ye dharmā hetuprabhavā*. . . or its equivalents in hybrid Sanskrit or Pāli, which are found in great numbers both in India[34] and in other Buddhist countries (see, e.g., 4.3.7.3, 4.3.7.5, and 4.3.7.6). Inscriptions on stone and other materials of *dhāraṇī*s are also common in India (e.g., Cuttack Museum, EI 26, 171–4) and elsewhere, for example, Sri Lanka (Abhayagiri, JIABS 5, 100–8) and China (see 4.3.7.12). Also in this class are the ubiquitous Tibetan "prayer-stones" inscribed with *oṃ maṇi padme hūṃ* and other Sanskrit *mantra*s (see 4.3.7.12, n. 134).

4.1.8 Literary inscriptions

Under this heading comes a small but important set of inscriptions whose content is primarily literary. Some well-known examples present the texts of otherwise unknown dramas inscribed on stone slabs: the *Lalitavigraharāja-nāṭaka* and *Harakeli-nāṭaka* from Ajmer (IA 20, 201–12) and the *Pārijātamañjarī-nāṭikā* or *Vijayaśrī-nāṭikā* from Dhār (EI 8, 96–122). Although these dramas also partake of the character of *praśasti*s in that they are intended to glorify the kings in whose courts they were composed and inscribed (the *Pārijātamañjarī* is explicitly described as a *praśasti*; EI 8, 98), they can nevertheless be considered essentially literary pieces (see also 7.2.2.2.2).

The occasional examples of inscriptional *khaṇḍa-* and *mahā-kāvya*s, such as the huge *Rājapraśasti-mahākāvya* of Raṇachoḍa in twenty-four *sarga*s inscribed at Udaypur (EI 29–30, Appendix; see 7.2.2.2.1), are of a similar character; though in form the Udaypur inscription is a *mahākāvya,* in content it is primarily eulogistic and dedicatory.

4.1.9 Seal inscriptions

Inscriptions on seals and sealings,[35] which were used to authenticate and protect letters, legal and administrative documents, and the like, form an important field of study which, though closely allied to numismatics, is traditionally treated within the sphere of epigraphy. Thousands of inscriptions in this class are known, often found in large

30. Documents of this type are formally and functionally speaking equivalent to manuscripts, but since they are inscribed on a hard material they are conventionally treated as inscriptions in the scholarly literature.

31. In Pāli; see section 4.3.7.5.

32. See J. G. de Casparis, *Prasasti Indonesia* II.47–167; see also section 4.3.7.11.

33. *Nachrichten der Akademie der Wissenschaften in Göttingen,* 1983, 189–207. See also section 4.3.7.1 for another inscribed version of this text from Sri Lanka.

34. E.g., Guṇṭupalli (I. K. Sarma, JESI 5, 59) and Ratnagiri (D. Mitra, *Ratnagiri*, II.284, 290. See also Daniel Boucher, "The *Pratītyasamutpādagāthā* and Its Role in the Medieval Cult of the Relics," JIABS 14, 1991, 1–27.

35. Technically, a seal is a mold made of a hard material such as fired clay, stone, or copper used to form an impression or sealing on a soft material, usually clay. Thus a seal inscription in the strict

numbers at a single archaeological site; for instance, 710 individual pieces with 1,100 separate seal impressions, mostly inscribed, were found at Basāṛh, the ancient Vaiśālī (ASIAR 1903–4, 101–22). Other important sites which have yielded large numbers of seal inscriptions include Bhīṭā, Nālandā, Besnagar, and Rājghāṭ. Seals and seal inscriptions are most frequently published in the various reports of the ASI and in the *Journal of the Numismatic Society of India* and other numismatic publications. Kiran Kumar Thaplyal's *Studies in Ancient Indian Seals* provides a detailed survey of the subject.

Inscribed seal(ing)s typically comprise a graphic or symbolic device accompanied by a legend below or around it. The simplest legends consist of the owner's name given in the nominative, genitive, or bare stem form. More elaborate formulae may add the individual's title(s), father's name, and other genealogical information. The most extended formulae are found on royal seals such as those of the Gupta and other kings, providing a full dynastic genealogy; see, for instance, the Nālandā clay seals of Narasiṃhagupta, Kumāragupta [III], and Viṣṇugupta (CII 3, rev. ed., 354–8, 364).[36]

Besides royalty and private individuals, many seal inscriptions belong to various governmental officials, guilds and other economic organizations, or temples, monasteries, and other religious institutions. Others are devotional in character, recording the name of a deity or pious formulae such as *jitaṃ bhagavatā* ("The Lord has triumphed") or *dharmo rakṣati rakṣitaḥ* ("Dharma protects when protected").[37] Among Buddhists, seal(ing)s with the *ye dharmā hetuprabhavā* formula are common (see 4.1.7).

4.1.10 Miscellaneous inscriptions

Inevitably, there is a residue of miscellaneous inscriptions which do not fit into any of the usual categories just described.[38] Among these are examples of inscriptional types which, though common in other ancient cultures, are rare in India. These include inscriptions of purely administrative content (other than the ubiquitous donative land grant and temple endowment records), which, except for the very early Mahāsthān and Sohgaurā inscriptions, are very rare in India proper. Many of the Kharoṣṭhī documents from central Asia, however (see 4.3.7.12), do fall into this class. Records of purely secular foundations, as opposed to the ubiquitous religious donations, are also rare; an example is the Bādāmi inscription of Vallabheśvara (EI 27, 4–9) commemorating the fortification of the hill of Vātāpi. Secular economic records and documents from ancient and medieval India are also extremely rare, presum-

---

sense appears in reverse or mirror image, while a sealing inscription appears in the normal direction. In practice, however, the term "seal" is often loosely used to apply to sealing inscriptions (which are much more common) as well as to seals in the proper sense.

36. Similar seal inscriptions on metal (usually bronze or copper) were usually originally parts of copper plate grants from which they have been detached (e.g., the Aśīrgaḍh copper seal ins. of Śarvavarman, CII 3, 219–21; fig. 7). In such cases the inscriptions are often described and treated as separate "seal inscriptions." But there are also copper and bronze seals which were originally separate items (see 4.2.2.1 and 4.2.2.2).

37. See Thaplyal, *Studies in Ancient Indian Seals*, 163–4, 328.

38. See the following specimen in the Appendix: Niya (central Asian) Kharoṣṭhī document (no. 6).

FIGURE 7. Aśīrgaṛh (Nimar Dist., MP) copper seal of Śarvavarman. From Fleet, CII 3, pl. XXX; copyright, Archaeological Survey of India.

ably because they were recorded only on perishable materials, but are well represented among the central Asian Kharoṣṭhī documents.

What might be called "personal" or "lyrical" inscriptions are also rare, though a few interesting exceptions are known, notably the very early Jogimāṛā and Sitābeṅgā inscriptions (see 4.3.1.2). An example from later times is the newly discovered Gwalior stone inscription recording the hunting exploits[39] of King Naravarman (thirteenth century A.D.; EI 38, 310).

There are also some special inscriptional genres which are characteristic of and peculiar to India. Notable among these are the grammatical inscriptions from Ujjain, Dhār, and Ūn (CII 7.2, 83–9), which summarize the traditional scheme of Sanskrit grammar in elaborate serpentine designs (*sarpabandha*), one of which (Ujjain) is described in the accompanying verse as a *varṇanāgakṛpāṇikā* or 'alphabetical snake-

39. Memorial inscriptions recording hunting exploits are common in Kannada inscriptions; see C. V. Rangaswami, "Memorials for Pets, Animals and Heroes," in S. Settar and G. D. Sontheimer, eds., *Memorial Stones*, 235–41.

scimitar' (fig. 8). Also characteristically Indian are the "footprint" inscriptions, consisting of a descriptive or eulogistic text accompanying a pair of engraved footprints of a deity, saint, or king, as in the Nāgārjunakoṇḍa footprint slab ins. (EI 33, 247–50). Several outstanding early examples of this genre have also been found in Java.[40]

4.2 Survey by Form and Material

D. B. Diskalkar, *Materials Used for Indian Epigraphical Records*; SIE 61–82; IGI II.24–49; BIP 92–8; PIP 67–87; BPLM 142–58; IC I.157; A. V. Naik, "Inscriptions of the Deccan," 1–13; SITI III.2, 213–29; SAI 308–13.

4.2.1 Stone

By far the commonest materials used for Indic inscriptions are stone surfaces of various types. In general, softer varieties of fine-grained stones are preferred; frequently used types include sandstone, basalt, slate, trap, and steatite. Inscribed stone objects comprise a wide variety of forms, which may be summarized as follows.

4.2.1.1 Slabs

Some inscriptions, particularly from the earlier periods, are inscribed directly onto rough stones with little or no preparation of the surface. Such is the case, for instance, with the Aśokan rock inscriptions. More commonly, however, the rock surface is subjected to varying degrees of preparation involving smoothing and polishing of the area to be inscribed. Later and more elaborate stone inscriptions, especially those of the *praśasti* class (see 4.1.1), are typically inscribed on rectangular stone slabs, sometimes very large, which were previously cut to size and carefully polished. Such slabs would usually be built in the walls or other parts of temples, palaces, and other structures. Long inscriptions, especially those of literary content (4.1.8), could be inscribed on a series of slabs (as many as twenty-five in the case of the *Rājapraśasti* at Udaypur). Stone slab inscriptions may also serve devotional purposes, as in the inscribed and sculpted slabs (*āyāgapaṭa*s) of the Buddhists and Jains, or the inscribed footprint slabs of gods or revered personages (see 4.1.10).

4.2.1.2 Freestanding pillars and steles

Early examples of inscribed columns include the Aśokan pillars and the Besnagar pillar of Hēliodōros (see Appendix, no. 2). Later pillar inscriptions may be panegyric, donative, devotional, or memorial in function (4.1.1 and 4.1.4). *Yūpa*s or sacri-

40. See J. Ph. Vogel, "The Earliest Sanskrit Inscriptions of Java"; see also sections 4.2.1.1 and 4.3.7.11.

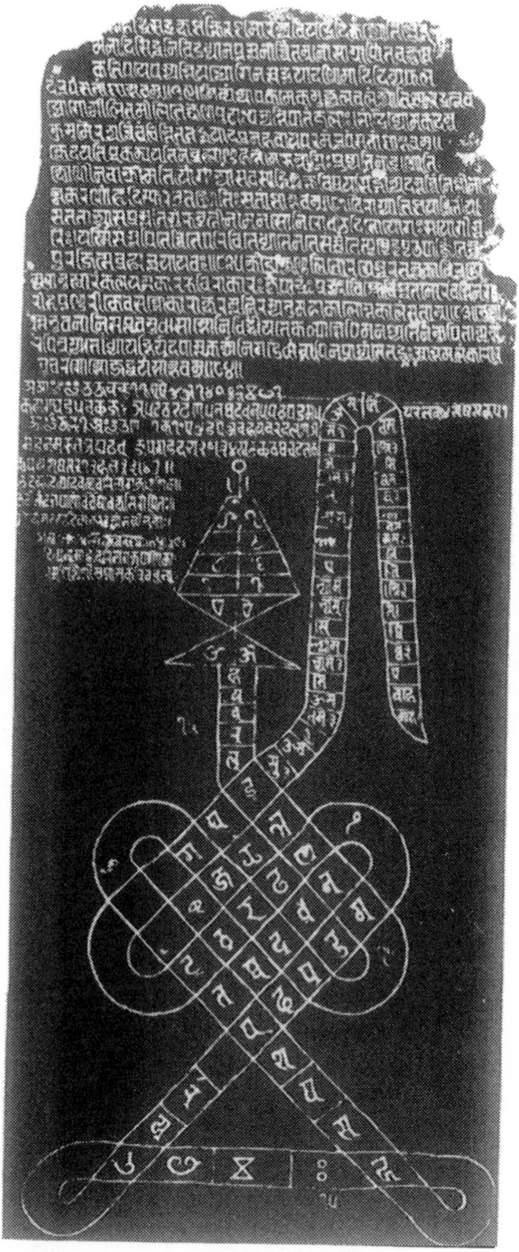

FIGURE 8. Dhār (Mahākāleśvara Temple) *sarpabandha* inscription. From CII 7.2, pl. XXVII; copyright, Archaeological Survey of India.

ficial pillars commemorating the performance of Vedic sacrifices are common in the early centuries of the Christian era.[41]

Inscribed steles or freestanding upright stones are most commonly seen in India proper in the form of hero- or *satī*-stones from western and southern India (4.1.4). Stele inscriptions in general are much more prevalent in Cambodia (4.3.7.7) and other parts of Southeast Asia, where they are the usual material for stone inscriptions.

4.2.1.3 *Structural elements*

From the earliest times inscriptions, usually of a dedicatory character, were commonly engraved on the walls, facades, columns, pillars, pilasters, railings, gates, doorways, and other parts (including even floors and ceilings) of stone structures such as excavated caves, *stūpas*, temples, palaces, and wells.[42] The cave temples of western India and the *stūpas* of central India such as Sāñcī and Bhārhut, for example, bear hundreds of dedicatory and explicatory inscriptions (4.1.3 and 4.1.5). In later centuries many temples, especially Jaina temples in western India and Hindu temples in the south, were heavily inscribed on their walls and pillars with inscriptions recording dedications and endowments.

4.2.1.4 *Images and statuary*

Stone sculptures, most commonly images of deities and other religious figures but also sometimes portraits of royal and other secular personages, are often inscribed, usually by way of recording the donor of the images and/or identifying the portrait (4.1.5). In some early examples the inscription is written on the object itself, as in the case of the Patna *yakṣa* inscription (SI I.93–4), carved on the shoulder of the statue. In the case of Buddhist images, the inscription may be written on the halo around the deity's head, as in the "Aśo-raya" inscription (JRAS 1982, 142–3 and 149–50). In later examples, however, the usual practice was to record the donation on the pedestal of the statue; such pedestal inscriptions are common in the Brahmanical, Buddhist, and especially the Jaina traditions.

4.2.1.5 *Portable objects*

Inscriptions on smaller, portable stone objects are also common, particularly among the Buddhists. Inscribed stone reliquaries for bodily relics of the Buddha and other venerables are common in the earlier centuries. Stone bowls are also occasionally inscribed (e.g., Kailwan, EI 31, 229–31; Termez, *Vestnik Drevnei Istorii* 1974.1, 117–22), as are other miscellaneous items such as lamps (e.g., Utmanzai, EI 23, 289) and weights.[43]

41. See B. Ch. Chhabra, "Yūpa Inscriptions," in *India Antiqua: A Volume of Oriental Studies Presented by His Friends and Pupils to Jean Philippe Vogel, C.I.E.* (Leyden: E. J. Brill, 1947), 77–82; see also section 7.3.1.1.

42. Cf. Naik, "Inscriptions of the Deccan," 4.

43. Diskalkar, *Materials*, 28. See also Stanislaw J. Czuma, *Kushan Sculpture: Images from Early India* (Cleveland: Cleveland Museum of Art, 1985), 163–4.

4.2.2 Metals

4.2.2.1 Copper

Copper, by far the most common metal used for inscriptions in India, is second only to stone in overall frequency. The great majority of inscriptions on copper are copper plate land grant charters, which number in the thousands (4.1.2). Though far less common, other types of inscriptions on copper are also known, especially Buddhist records on such copper objects as dedicatory tablets,[44] relic caskets,[45] ladles,[46] seals,[47] and bells.[48]

4.2.2.2 Bronze

Inscriptions on bronze are also fairly common, though much less so than on copper. The most common types of bronze inscriptions are those on religious images, recording dedicatory and/or devotional messages on the pedestals (e.g., the Ākoṭa Jaina bronzes, ARIE 1952–53, nos. B.16–48), and on seals. The latter are most commonly found attached to copper plate charters (see 4.1.2), although separate bronze seals are also known.[49] The Sohgaurā plaque, though often referred to as "copper," is actually of bronze (SIE 79) and is hence the earliest specimen of an inscription in that metal. Other inscribed objects, notably Buddhist relic caskets, are also sometimes of bronze (e.g., Wardak, CII 2.1, 165–70).

4.2.2.3 Brass

Inscriptions on brass and similar alloys are found most commonly on sculptured images (especially Jaina ones, according to Diskalkar).[50] A few inscribed Brahmanical brass images of about the eighth century have been published.[51] Occasionally inscriptions are found on other brass objects, such as a seal (Kosambi, ASIR 10, 4) or trident (Uttarkāśī, *New Indian Antiquary* 3, 34–6). Inscribed masks of royal or divine figures made of brass or similar alloys are sometimes found in the Himalayan regions, for instance, the *aṣṭadhātu* mask from Nirmaṇḍ (*Acta Orientalia* 1, 230–4) and the "Court Mask" (JA 279, 137–74).

4.2.2.4 Iron

Inscriptions on iron are rare, the only important specimen being the inscription of King Candra (= Candragupta II?) on the iron pillar at Meharauli (CII 3, 139–42). An iron object, believed to be a branding iron, with the Brāhmī letters *jaya* in reverse

44. E.g., Sui Vihār, CII 2.1, 138–41, and Kara, EI 22, 37–9.
45. E.g., Kurram, CII 2.1, 152–5.
46. E.g., Taxila and Bedadi, CII 2.1, 87–9.
47. Taxila, CII 2.1, 100–1, nos. 4–9 and 11; see also Thaplyal, *Studies in Ancient Indian Seals*, 3 and n. 3.
48. Cambā; B. Ch. Chhabra, *Antiquities of Chamba State* II.175–6.
49. See Thaplyal, *Studies in Ancient Indian Seals*, 3 and n. 4.
50. *Materials*, 33; cf. Ojhā, BPLM 154.
51. See J. Ph. Vogel, ASIAR 1902–3 ("Inscriptions of Chamba State"), 240–4.

was found at Nālandā (JBORS 23, 128–9). In later times, iron weapons such as cannons were sometimes inscribed, most commonly in NIA or Islamic languages but sometimes also in Sanskrit (e.g., Ajaygaṛh, ARIE 1969–70, no. B.203).

4.2.2.5 Gold

Inscriptions, usually Buddhist dedicatory, votive, or ritual records, are sometimes found on gold. Among these are Kharoṣṭhī inscriptions on a gold plate and on two rings from Taxila (CII 2.1, 83–6, 100, nos. 1 and 2), as well as the recently discovered Senavarma gold plaque inscription (IIJ 29, 261–93). Another newly found Kharoṣṭhī reliquary has letters inset with gold on a schist reliquary box (Utarā ins., IIJ 31, 169–77). Buddhist canonical texts were written on gold leaves in several Buddhist countries, including Burma (4.3.7.5), Sri Lanka (4.1.7), and Indonesia (4.1.7; 4.3.7.11). Gold bars with Kharoṣṭhī inscriptions have been found in Uzbekistan (4.3.7.4).

4.2.2.6 Silver

As with gold, most inscriptions on silver are Buddhist Kharoṣṭhī records. Inscriptions of this class published in CII 2.1 include a scroll (70–7), vase (81–2), cups (97–8), plates (98–9), and a sieve (99), all from Taxila, and a disk (151) from Māṇikiāla. An inscribed silver scroll was also found at Bhaṭṭiprōḷu (Lüders, *Philologica Indica*, 223). According to Ojhā (BPLM 152 and n. 4), inscribed silver plates and other objects can also be found in Jaina temples.

4.2.2.7 Other metals

Examples of inscriptions on other metals such as tin or lead have occasionally been reported,[52] for instance, a Pāli manuscript on "tinplate" from Burma (*Journal of the Pali Text Society* 1883, 140).

4.2.3 Earthen materials

4.2.3.1 Terra-cotta and clay

The most common inscribed earthen objects are seals and sealings of terra-cotta or unbaked clay. These are found in large numbers, especially in northern India, from virtually all periods (4.1.9). Buddhist votive inscriptions on clay bearing the "Buddhist creed" *ye dharmā hetuprabhavā* . . . and other formulae are common from many sites in India and elsewhere (4.1.7). Other, less common types of inscribed terra-cottas include donative records (e.g., the terra-cotta plaque ins., EI 30, 85–7),[53] labels,[54] and spheres of uncertain purpose.[55]

52. See, e.g., Diskalkar, *Materials*, 44–5, and SIE 79 n. 7.
53. Numerous late examples are given in A. K. Bhattacharyya, *A Corpus of Dedicatory Inscriptions from Temples of West Bengal.*
54. See, e.g., Yoganand Shastri in IVMD, 71–6.
55. Sarjug Prasad Singh, JAIH 3, 1969–70, 17–22.

4.2.3.2 *Bricks*

Bricks with passages from canonical texts or *dhāraṇīs* have been found at several Buddhist sites (e.g., Nālandā; 4.1.7). Brahmanical inscriptions recording Vedic sacrifices such as the *aśvamedha* are sometimes found on bricks which were presumed to have been part of the sacrificial complex (e.g., Jagatpur, SI I.98–9).[56] Other inscribed bricks contain names only, presumably those of their donors (e.g., MI §116 and 120). An unusual example of a legal document inscribed on a brick was found at Jaunpur (JUPHS 18, 196–201).

4.2.3.3 *Pottery*

Donative Buddhist inscriptions on pots or (more often) potsherds are common in India[57] and in other formerly Buddhist lands such as Afghanistan and Uzbekistan (4.3.7.3 and 4.3.7.4). Inscriptions of this class are frequently painted rather than incised, and most of them are in Kharoṣṭhī script. Inscribed pots and vases from some non-Buddhist sites are also known.[58]

4.2.4 *Wood*

Despite clear evidence from literature, art, and archaeology that wooden boards were commonly used as writing materials for practical documents in ancient India,[59] such documents have not survived in India proper, no doubt due to climatic factors. However, hundreds of Kharoṣṭhī documents written in ink on tablets and other wooden objects have been discovered in central Asia (4.3.7.12).[60] A few inscribed wooden objects which happened to be preserved in favorable environments have survived in India proper, notably a wooden pillar from Kirārī (EI 18, 152–7) and a beam in the *caitya*-cave at Bhājā (IAAR 1955–56, 29).

4.2.5 *Miscellaneous materials*

4.2.5.1 *Crystal*

A few inscriptions have been found on seals and other objects of crystal. These include the British Museum seal of Avarighsa (or Avariysa; EI 36, 275–84) and two Buddhist monastery seals (*Numismatic Chronicle*, 6th ser., vol. 10, 230–1). An early inscription was found on a hexagonal piece of crystal from the Bhaṭṭiprōḷu *stūpa* (EI 2, 329).

4.2.5.2 *Glass*

Some inscribed glass seals have been found, for instance, at Patna (JBORS 10, 189–201).

56. For further references see SIE 73 n. 4, and section 7.3.1.1.
57. E.g., Tor Ḍherai, CII 2.1, 173–6; Peshawar, EI 28, 125–9; and Sālihuṇḍam, EI 28, 135–7.
58. E.g., Walā, IA 14, 1885, 75, and Naṇḍūru, JAHRS 19, 203–7.
59. See Diskalkar, *Materials*, 63, and Thaplyal, *Studies in Ancient Indian Seals*, 13 and n. 6.
60. Similar documents on leather were found together with the wooden documents in central Asia, but it is doubtful whether leather was ever used for writing in India proper, due to religious taboos.

4.2.5.3 Carnelian

A few inscribed carnelian seals are known, for example, the Paris carnelian (CII 2.1, 7) and the Perak (Malaysia) seal of Viṣṇuvarman (Chhabra, *Expansion of Indo-Aryan Culture*, 35–6).[61]

4.2.5.4 Ivory and bone

Ivory and bone seals with Brāhmī inscriptions have been found at several sites, such as Bhīṭā (ASIAR 1911–12, 48), Rupar (IAAR 1953, 123), Kauśāmbī (IAAR 1958, 76), Besnagar (ASIAR 1913, 217, no. 64), and Tripurī (JNSI 16, 73–4).[62]

4.2.5.5 Shell

Two conch shells with Prakrit inscriptions were found at Sālihuṇḍam (IAAR 1958–59, 8), and an inscribed seal of shell was excavated at Taxila (Marshall, *Taxila*, II.682). Two Buddhist inscriptions on tortoise shell were discovered in Basupāṛā, Bangladesh (JAS, 3d ser., vol. 15, 101–8).

4.2.5.6 Cloth

References in literature (see 2.1.2) and inscriptions attest that cotton and silk cloth[63] were commonly used as writing materials in ancient India,[64] but due to climatic factors no such documents of an early date survive (cf. 4.2.4). Several Jaina documents and manuscripts on cloth from the medieval period have however been reported.[65] Also, several Brāhmī and Kharoṣṭhī inscriptions on silk have been discovered at Lou-lan (KI no. 697) and Mīrān in central Asia (M. A. Stein, *Serindia* I.495).

4.3 General Survey of Inscriptions

The following survey is intended to give a broad overview of important types and groups of inscriptions in the Indo-Aryan languages. Specific inscriptions are cited as important or typical specimens of a common type, especially for the later periods where materials are more abundant; no attempt at an exhaustive listing is made. Special emphasis is placed on important new inscriptions discovered within the past twenty years or so, as many of these inscriptions are not mentioned in the standard reference works.

There is no other detailed survey of Indic inscriptions along geochronological or dynastic lines. Brief summaries are to be found in IC I.159–72 and in Fleet's

61. Further examples are given by E. J. Rapson in JRAS 1905, 813–4.

62. Further examples and references in IA, 3d ser., vol. 5, 1971, 128 n. 3.

63. Strictly speaking, cloth is not an epigraphic material, but since it is generally treated as such in Indological research it is included here.

64. Diskalkar, *Materials*, 72–4; SIE 66–7.

65. Diskalkar, *Materials*, 74; SIE 66–7.

"Survey of the Inscriptions" in the *Encyclopaedia Britannica*, 11th ed. (1910–11), vol. 14, 623–5 (through the sixth century A.D. only).

4.3.1 *Inscriptions of the Mauryan period (third century B.C.)*

4.3.1.1 *Inscriptions of Aśoka*

E. Hultzsch's edition of the Aśokan inscriptions in CII 1 is still the standard reference source, though out of date in several respects, especially in that it does not include inscriptions discovered since its publication in 1925 (Eṟraguḍi, Bombay-Sopārā, Amarāvatī, Sannati, ten versions of the minor rock edicts, and the Greek and Aramaic inscriptions). J. Bloch's *Les Inscriptions d'Asoka* (1950) is a convenient and reliable shorter text and translation edition, but it is also seriously outdated. Older editions such as those of É. Senart (*Les Inscriptions de Piyadassi*, 1881) and A. C. Woolner (*Aśoka Text and Glossary*, 1924) are superseded by the more recent ones. The new discoveries up to 1979 are presented in D. C. Sircar's *Aśokan Studies*. A new complete edition of the Aśokan inscriptions is an urgent desideratum (cf. 6.6).

There are many other general editions and translations of the Aśokan edicts, too numerous to mention here. Among the abundant translations into English and many other languages, D. C. Sircar's *Inscriptions of Aśoka* (1967) is worthy of note as a reliable semipopular edition.

Bibliographical information is provided in M. A. Mehendale's *Aśokan Inscriptions in India* (1948), 60–99; in F. R. Allchin and K. R. Norman's "Guide to the Aśokan Inscriptions" (*South Asian Studies* 1, 1985, 43–50); and in the bibliographic supplement (732–5) to the English edition of É. Lamotte's *History of Indian Buddhism from the Origins to the Śaka Era* (1988). The last two provide references to many of the new discoveries, except for the most recent ones (see 4.3.1.1.1).

Several more recent books and monographs have concentrated on detailed critical editions of particular subgroups, by type or by location, within the Aśokan corpus. These include L. Alsdorf's *Aśokas Separatedikte von Dhauli and Jaugaḍa* (1962), U. Schneider's *Die Grossen Felsen-Edikte Aśokas* (1978), P. K. Andersen's *Studies in the Minor Rock Edicts of Aśoka*. Vol.1: *Critical Edition* (1990), and U. Niklas' *Die Editionen der Aśoka-Inschriften von Eṟraguḍi* (1990).

Articles on particular inscriptions or linguistic, textual, and historical aspects of the Aśokan records are far too numerous to list here comprehensively. Worthy of note among the more recent works are those of Ludwig Alsdorf, Collette Caillat, Klaus Janert, K. R. Norman, Ulrich Schneider, and D. C. Sircar; partial listings can be found in the bibliographic sources noted here, although no complete and up-to-date bibliography exists. The articles of some of these authors are conveniently available in collections of their articles such as Sircar's *Aśokan Studies*, Alsdorf's *Kleine Schriften*, and, especially, Norman's *Collected Papers*.

The inscriptions of Aśoka, the great Mauryan emperor and patron of Buddhism who ruled ca. 272–232 B.C., are the best-known and most widely studied Indian inscriptions. But they are also highly untypical in several respects, first of all in their pattern of distribution, with the same or similar texts duplicated in widely scattered parts

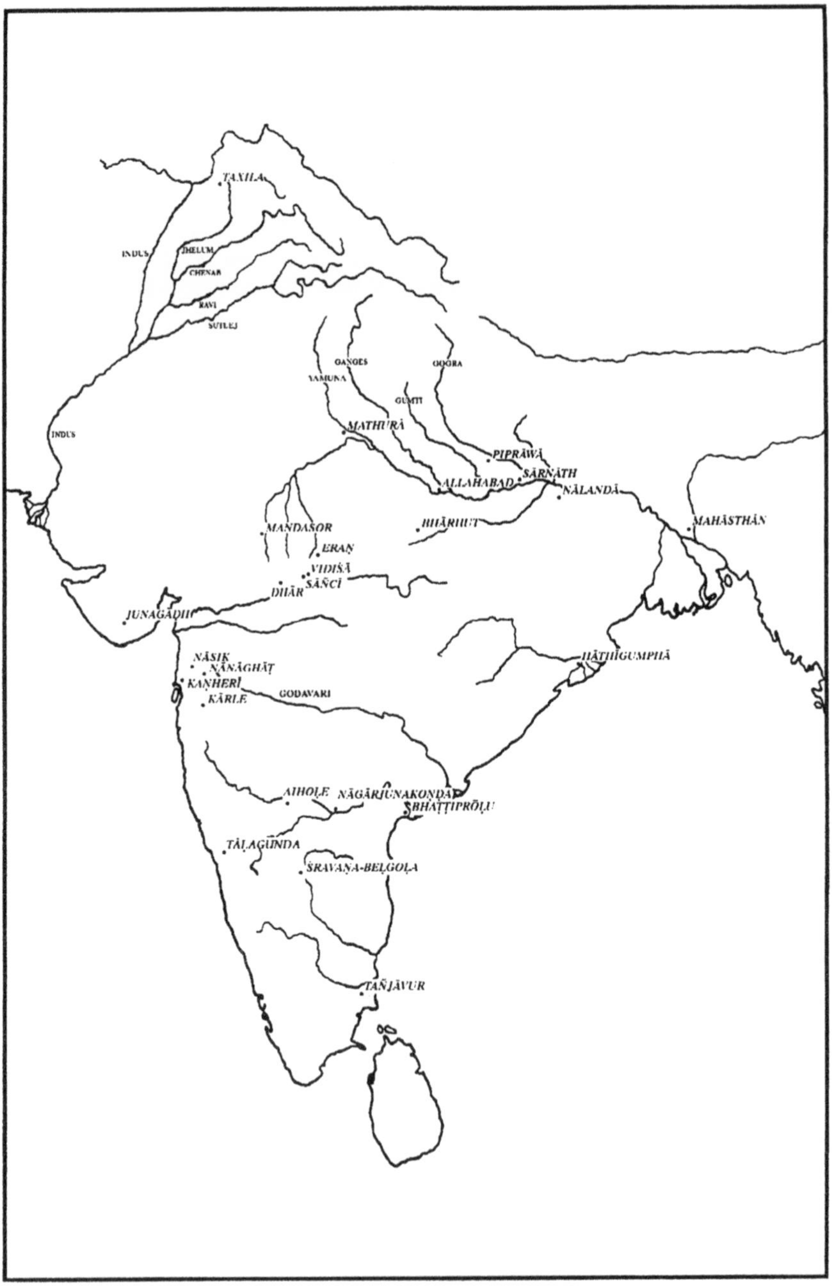

MAP 2
Some Major Epigraphic Sites

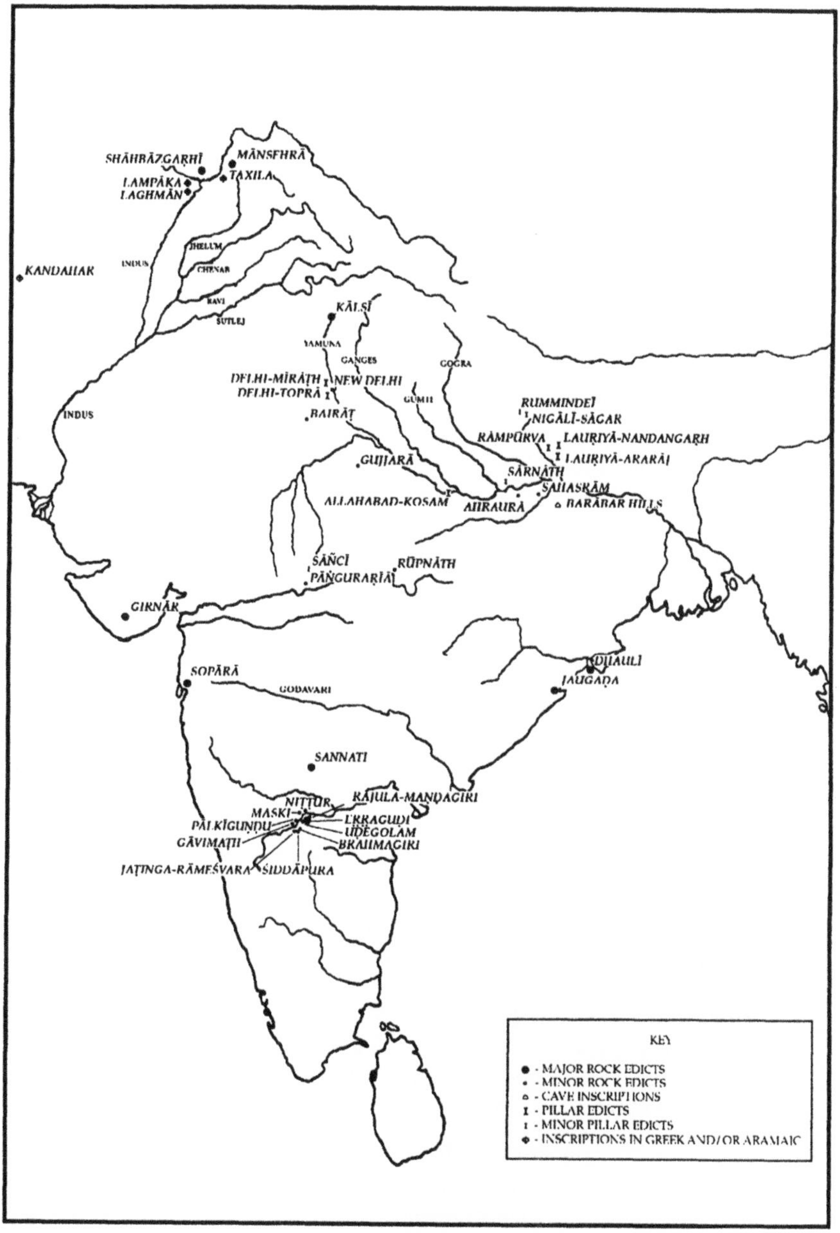

Map 3
Location of Aśokan Inscriptions

of the country. Their style and content are also unusual, for the most part involving proclamations of the emperor's moral and religious sentiments as expressed personally by him in the first person. Despite having been intensively studied for over a century and a half, the Aśokan inscriptions remain problematic in several respects, and many points of interpretation are still controversial.

The Aśokan inscriptions are written in various MIA dialects which are referred to collectively as the "Aśokan Prakrits." The principal dialect is the eastern, which evidently represents the imperial language of the Mauryan dynasty and its capital at Pāṭaliputra (modern Patna, Bihar). All of the pillar edicts and several of the rock edicts are in this language. Other rock inscriptions, however, are written in the western (notably Girnār) and northwestern ("Gāndhārī"; Shāhbāzgaṛhī and Mānsehrā) dialects.[66]

With the exception of the northwestern rock edicts (and those in non-Indian languages, i.e., Greek and Aramaic; see 4.3.7.3), all of the Aśokan inscriptions are written in the earliest attested form of the Brāhmī script. Only the Shāhbāzgaṛhī and Mānsehrā rock inscriptions are in Kharoṣṭhī.[67]

The Aśokan inscriptions are the earliest Indian epigraphs which can be dated with any certainty, if not the absolutely earliest ones.[68] The inscriptions are dated in the regnal years of Aśoka, ranging from the eighth (rock edict XIII) to the twenty-seventh (pillar edict VII, Delhi-Toprā). These regnal dates can be correlated to absolute years, that is, approximately 264–245 B.C., from various external sources, mainly by the references by name to five contemporaneous Greek kings (*yonarāja*) in rock edict XIII.

The inscriptions of Aśoka are divided into two main groups, rock edicts and pillar edicts. The former group is further subclassified into (major) rock edicts (including the separate rock edicts), minor rock edicts, and cave inscriptions; the latter into (major) pillar edicts and minor pillar edicts. The minor rock edicts were apparently the earliest group, followed by the (major) rock edicts, while the pillar edicts were the last to be promulgated.

4.3.1.1.1 Major rock edicts. The major rock edicts consist of a set of fourteen proclamations inscribed on rocks at the following sites (arranged from north to south):

1. Shāhbāzgaṛhī (Peshawar Dist., NWFP, Pakistan)
2. Mānsehrā (Hazara Dist., NWFP, Pakistan)
3. Kālsī (Dehra Dun Dist., UP)
4. Girnār (Junagadh Dist., Gujarat) (fig. 9)
5. Bombay-Sopārā (Thana Dist., Maharashtra; now in Prince of Wales Museum, Bombay. Only two fragments of edicts VIII and IX.)
6. Eṟṟaguḍi (Kurnool Dist., AP)

The rock edicts are concerned with such matters as the protection of animal life by decreasing the number of creatures killed in the royal kitchen (I); the provision by the king of public works such as medical clinics and tree planting (II); the pro-

66. For details see section 3.1.2.

67. There is, however, one word, *lipikareṇa*, 'by the scribe', written in Kharoṣṭhī in the scribe's signature appended to the minor rock edicts (otherwise in Brāhmī) at Brahmagiri, Śiddāpura, and Jaṭiṅga-Rāmeśvara.

68. See also sections 2.1.2 and 4.3.1.2.

FIGURE 9. Girnār (Junāgaḍh) rock with the Aśokan rock edicts and the inscriptions of Rudradāman and Skandagupta. From E. J. Rapson, *Ancient India from the Earliest Times to the First Century A.D.* (Cambridge: Cambridge University Press, 1916), pl. I; reprinted with permission of Cambridge University Press.

motion of public morality (III, IV, VII, XI, etc.); and respect for rival sects (*pāṣaṇḍa*, XII). Of special interest is edict XIII, by far the longest of the group, in which Aśoka expresses his regrets for the enormous loss of life and other suffering inflicted in the course of his conquest of Kaliṅga.

Two further sets of rock edicts from the Kaliṅga territory contain edicts I–X and XIV, but in place of XI–XIII have two "separate rock edicts":

7. Jaugaḍa (Ganjam Dist., Orissa)
8. Dhauli (Puri Dist., Orissa)

The two separate edicts at Jaugaḍa and Dhauli contain exhortations to the royal officers (*mahāmātra*) at Samāpā and Tosalī, respectively, to respect and enforce the king's wishes. Finally, a recently discovered stone slab containing fragments of the so-called Kaliṅga edicts XII and XIV and of separate edicts I and II has been found outside of the Kaliṅga region:

9. Sannati (Gulbarga Dist., Karnataka)

4.3.1.1.2 Minor rock edicts. The minor rock edicts are now known from seventeen sites (arranged from north to south):

1. New Delhi (also referred to as Amar Colony or Bahapur; Delhi Union Territory)
2. Bairāṭ (Jaipur Dist., Rajasthan)
3. Gujjarā (Datia Dist., MP)
4. Sahasrām (Rohtas [formerly Shahabad] Dist., Bihar)
5. Ahraurā (Mirzapur Dist., UP)
6. Rūpnāth (Jabalpur Dist., MP)
7. Pāṅguṛāriā (Sehore Dist., MP)
8. Maski (Raichur Dist., Karnataka)
9. Gavīmaṭh (Raichur Dist., Karnataka)
10. Pālkīguṇḍu (Raichur Dist., Karnataka)
11. Niṭṭūr (Bellary Dist., Karnataka)
12. Uḍegoḷam (Bellary Dist., Karnataka)
13. Rājula-Maṇḍagiri (Kurnool Dist., AP)
14. Eṟṟaguḍi (Kurnool Dist., AP)
15. Brahmagiri (Chitradurga Dist., Karnataka)
16. Śiddāpura (Chitradurga Dist., Karnataka)
17. Jaṭiṅga-Rāmeśvara (Chitradurga Dist., Karnataka)

The first ten of these sites contain the text of minor rock edict I only, which describes Aśoka's increased religious zeal and exhorts his subjects to pursue similar goals. Numbers 11–17 also include minor rock edict II (in varying forms), recommending respectful behavior toward parents, elders, and teachers. Several of the minor rock edicts are recent discoveries, the newest among them being Ahraurā (1961), New Delhi (1966), Pāṅguṛāriā (1976), and Niṭṭūr and Uḍegoḷam (1977).

An individual rock edict, known only in one copy, was also found at Bairāṭ and is now in the Asiatic Society, Calcutta.[69] It is addressed directly to the Buddhist community (*saṃgha*) and recommends seven texts for their study (see 7.3.2.2).

Three cave inscriptions in the Barābar hills (Gaya Dist., Bihar) record the gift of the caves to the Ājīvikas by a King Piyadasī, who is presumably Aśoka.

4.3.1.1.3 Pillar edicts. The pillar edicts comprise a basic set of six edicts preserved on Mauryan sandstone pillars in six places:[70]

1. Delhi-Toprā[71]
2. Delhi-Mīraṭh[72]
3. Lauṛiyā-Ararāj (East Champaran Dist., Bihar)
4. Lauṛiyā-Nandangaṛh (West Champaran Dist., Bihar) (fig. 10)
5. Rāmpurvā (West Champaran Dist., Bihar)
6. Allahabad-Kosam.[73]

69. This inscription is sometimes referred to by other names such as Calcutta-Bairāṭ, Bhābṛā, Bhairāṭ-Bhābṛā, minor rock edict III, etc.

70. In addition, there has recently come to light a small fragment from somewhere in northern Pakistan of what seems to be Aśokan pillar edict VI; see K. R. Norman, *South Asian Studies* 4, 1988, 100–2. There is, however, considerable doubt as to its authenticity (op. cit., 101 n. 6).

71. The pillar was originally in Toprā, Ambala Dist., Haryana, but was brought to Delhi by Fīrūz Shāh Tughluq in or around A.D. 1368 and installed in his fort there.

72. The pillar was originally in Mīraṭh (Meerut), Mirath Dist., UP, but was also transported to Delhi by Fīrūz Shāh and erected there on The Ridge.

73. The pillar is now in the fort at Allahabad but is generally believed to have been brought there from Kosam (Kauśāmbī), Allahabad Dist., UP.

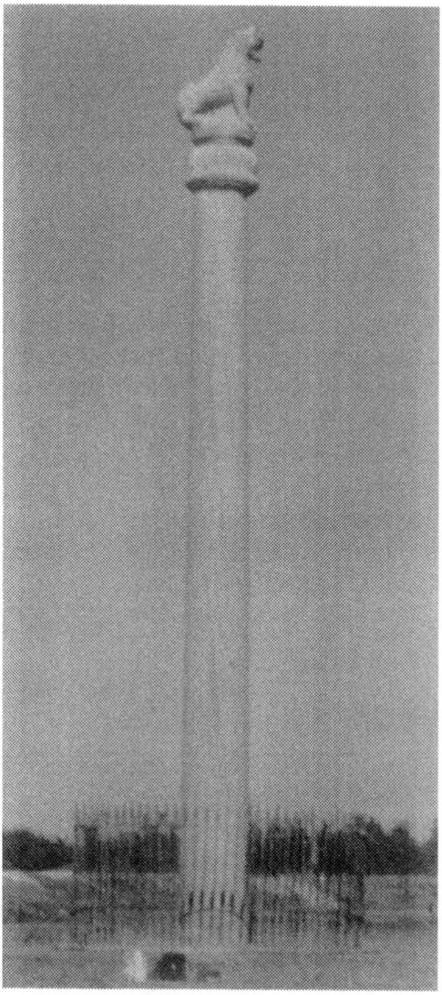

FIGURE 10. Lauṛiyā-Nandangaṛh Aśokan pillar. Photograph courtesy of Frederick Asher.

The six basic pillar edicts, which unlike the rock edicts show only minor textual and dialectal variations in the different versions, are mainly concerned with the propagation of Aśoka's moral principles, his *dhamma*, including gentleness, tolerance, and personal concern for his subjects' well-being.

The Delhi-Toprā pillar only has in addition a seventh text, which is the longest of all the Aśokan edicts. For the most part, it summarizes and restates the contents of the other pillar edicts, and to some extent those of the major rock edicts as well.

The Allahabad-Kosam pillar contains, in addition to the six principal edicts, two brief additional inscriptions. The first of these is usually referred to as the "Queen's Edict" since it mentions the gifts of the king's "second queen" (*dutīyāye deviye*). The second additional record is the so-called Schism Edict, addressed to the *mahāmātra*s at Kosambī (Kauśāmbī), which refers to the punishment to be inflicted on monks or nuns who cause schisms within the Buddhist *saṃgha*.

4.3.1.1.4 Minor pillar edicts. Two of the minor pillar edicts, at

1. Sāñcī
2. Sārnāth

contain similar but more extensive texts on the banishment of schismatics. The latter adds a note on the king's orders for the preservation and propagation of the order itself.

The two other minor pillar edicts at

3. Nigālī Sāgar
4. Rummindeī

are both located in the Bhairwa District, Nepal. The Nigālī Sāgar inscription records the king's visit to the site and his expansion of the *stūpa* of the Buddha Konākamana there. The Rummindeī inscription celebrates the site as the birthplace of the Buddha and commemorates the king's visit there. These two inscriptions are different in content and character from Aśoka's other edicts, representing, in effect, his personal "pilgrim's records." In this respect, unlike his other records, they prefigure types of inscriptions which were to become common in later times (cf. 4.1.6).

Finally, a fragment of a pillar inscription which has been reliably, though not definitely, ascribed to Aśoka has been discovered recently at the *stūpa* of

5. Amarāvatī (Guntur Dist., AP).

4.3.1.2 Other inscriptions of the Mauryan period

Besides the Aśokan inscriptions, there are a very few brief inscriptions from northern and eastern India in Prakrit language and Brāhmī script which can be attributed on paleographic and historical grounds to the Mauryan era, that is, the third century B.C. or thereabouts. These include the three Nāgārjunī Hill cave inscriptions of Aśoka's grandson Daśaratha (SI I.77–8), which, like the nearby Barābar cave inscriptions of Aśoka, record the donation to Ājīvika monks of caves for residence during the rainy season.

Two other official or semiofficial epigraphs from northeastern India attributable on paleographic grounds to the Mauryan period are the Mahāsthān stone plaque (SI I.79–80) and the Sohgaurā bronze plaque (SI I.82–3). Both of these records are usually understood to contain instructions for the storage of surplus grain and other products as a precaution against famine, but due to their archaic dialect and orthography the details of their interpretation are difficult and controversial.

The inscription on the Buddhist relic vase from Piprāwā (SI I.81) records the deposit of bodily relics, probably of the Buddha (though this interpretation has been disputed). Some scholars, for instance, J. F. Fleet, have attributed this inscription on paleographic and orthographic grounds to a pre-Aśokan or even pre-Mauryan date, making it the earliest Indian inscription of the historical era; but this is no longer generally accepted, mainly on archaeological grounds.[74]

74. See SI I.81 n. 7, and K. M. Srivastava, JESI 2, 1976, 100–10. Most recently, Herbert Härtel, in Heinz Bechert, ed., *The Dating of the Historical Buddha*, Abhandlungen der Akademie der Wissenschaften in Göttingen, Philologisch-Historische Klasse, dritte Folge, 189 (Göttingen: Vandenhoeck & Ruprecht, 1991), 75, expresses the opinion that the Piprāwā vase could not be earlier than the second century B.C.

Two short inscriptions from the Sītābeṅgā and Jogimāṛā caves on the Rāmgaṛh hill (ASIAR 1903–4, 123–31) are estimated on paleographic grounds to belong to about the third century B.C. The Jogimāṛā inscription is particularly interesting both for its language, being the only pure epigraphic specimen of Māgadhī (see 3.1.3) and for its unusual content (4.1.10), recording the love of one Devadina for Śutanukā, a temple prostitute (*devadaśikyi*).[75]

4.3.2 Inscriptions of the Śuṅga period (ca. second to first centuries B.C.)

During the so-called Śuṅga period[76] inscriptions become somewhat more common, though the overall number of sites is still relatively small. Most records of this time are short Brāhmī inscriptions in Prakrit from northern and central India, though there are also a few from the east and south.

One of the most important of the early Śuṅga inscriptions is the Besnagar pillar inscription (Appendix, no. 2), recording the erection of a *garuḍa-dhvaja* by one *Heliodora* (i.e., Hēliodōros), who was the Greek ambassador (*yonadūta*) from King Aṃtalikita (i.e., Antialkidas) to King Kāśīputra Bhāgabhadra, presumably a Śuṅga ruler.

The Buddhist *stūpa* site of Bhārhut has yielded some 225 inscriptions,[77] of which 141 are donative in nature while the remaining 84 are labels describing the accompanying sculptural representations of *jātaka*s, *avadāna*s, and so on (cf. 4.1.5). A Bhārhut pillar inscription (CII 2.2, 11–12) recording the donation of a gateway (*toraṇa*) "during the reign of the Śuṅgas" (*suganaṃ raje*) provides the only epigraphic attestation of the dynastic name *Śuṅga*.

A similar corpus from approximately the same period consisting of 842 mostly donative inscriptions is found at the *stūpa* site of Sāñcī.

Among the several other records of this period from northern and central India are the earliest known inscriptions in Sanskrit (see 3.3.1). These are the Ghosuṇḍī (SI I.90–1) and Hāthībāḍā (EI 22, 198–205) stone inscriptions of about the first century B.C. and the Ayodhyā stone inscription (SI I.94–5), which is probably slightly later.

Among the recent discoveries in northern India from this period is the Reh stone *liṅga* inscription, attributed by G. R. Sharma (*The Reh Inscription of Menander*) to the Indo-Greek king Menander, though as shown by B. N. Mukherjee (JAIH 12, 1978–79, 150–5) this attribution is unjustified. Also worthy of note is the Pratāpgaṛh

75. Several other early Brāhmī inscriptions, such as Deoṭek (V. V. Mirashi, *Studies in Indology* I.109–17) and Baṛlī (K. P. Jayaswal, JBORS 16, 1930, 67–8) have been attributed by some scholars to the Mauryan, or even the pre-Mauryan period. But more cautious scholars are generally inclined to attribute these records to the Śuṅga period on the grounds of paleographic features which are slightly more advanced than Aśokan Brāhmī.

76. This name (like some others in this chapter) is merely a term of convenience, referring to the best-known but by no means the only dynasty ruling in this period.

77. Lüders published 218 Bhārhut inscriptions in CII 2.2, and 7 additional records now in the Allahabad Museum were added by Sircar in EI 33, 57–60. The original site of Bhārhut has been dismantled, and the relics and inscriptions found there are scattered in various collections, the largest number being in the Indian Museum, Calcutta.

stone pillar inscription (EI 39, 79–80) recording the erection of the pillar by a *bhāgavata* Utararakhita (Uttararakṣita). Excavations at Pauni have yielded a few dozen Buddhist donative and label inscriptions similar to those from Sāñcī and Bhārhut (S. B. Deo and J. P. Joshi, *Pauni Excavation*). Other recent finds include an umbrella shaft inscription from Pāṅguṛāriā (EI 40, 119–20) and the Sūryamitra stone inscription in the National Museum, Delhi (EI 40, 165–7).

From eastern India, the most important inscription of the Śuṅga period is the Hāthīgumphā inscription of Khāravela (SI I.213–21), which records the dedication of residential caves to Jaina monks and contains a detailed, year-by-year account of Khāravela's exploits. The Hāthīgumphā inscription is poorly preserved, so that its readings, translation, and historical interpretation by different scholars vary widely, and it is not possible to establish a single standard version (cf. 5.2). Some further light has been shed on the history of Khāravela's little-known Mahāmeghavāhana dynasty by a new inscription duplicated on four different pillars from Guṇṭupalli (JESI 5, 49–51), mentioning a King Siri Sada (= Śrī-śāta?) who may have been a successor of Khāravela.[78]

An important epigraphic site of the Śuṅga period in southern India is the *stūpa* at Bhaṭṭiprōḷu (Krishna Dist., AP), which yielded ten short Buddhist relic dedications (SI I.224–8). These inscriptions are of particular interest for their dialectal and especially their paleographic peculiarities, including the use of a diacritic mark to indicate postconsonantal *a* (see 2.2.5.1). Several early dedicatory *stūpa* inscriptions resembling those from northern India (Bhārhut and Sāñcī) in form, content, and paleography have also been found at Amarāvatī (*Ancient Ceylon* 3, 97–103).

4.3.3 Inscriptions of the Indo-Greek and Indo-Scythian era (ca. second century B.C. *to third century* A.D.*)*

4.3.3.1 Kharoṣṭhī inscriptions from the northwest

During the period of the domination by a series of foreign rulers including the Indo-Greeks, Scythians, Parthians, and Kuṣāṇas, a large number of inscriptions in Kharoṣṭhī script and Gāndhārī or northwestern Prakrit language were recorded in northwestern India and adjoining areas of modern Pakistan, Afghanistan, Uzbekistan, and Tajikistan (see 2.3.1). The basic source for this material is still Konow's *Kharoshṭhī Inscriptions* (CII 2.1), which contains ninety-six inscriptions, but this is badly outdated, since many more Kharoṣṭhī inscriptions have been discovered since its publication in 1929, especially in recent years (as discussed later). An up-to-date list and bibliography of Kharoṣṭhī inscriptions are given by G. Fussman in "Gāndhārī écrite, Gāndhārī parlée," 444–51 and 488–98.

The majority of Kharoṣṭhī inscriptions record Buddhist relic deposits, donations to monasteries, image dedications, and so on. Most are written on stone, though inscriptions on metals (copper, bronze, silver, and gold) and on earthen materials are also known. The Kharoṣṭhī inscriptions are conventionally divided into those of the

78. Several other significant inscriptions of later centuries were also found at Guṇṭupalli; see JESI 5, 51–9, and I. K. Sarma, *Studies in Early Buddhist Monuments and Brāhmī Inscriptions of Āndhradēśa*, ch. 3.

Indo-Greek and Scytho-Parthian phase (second century B.C. to first century A.D.) and those of the Kuṣāṇa period (first to third centuries A.D.).

Among the most important and representative Kharoṣṭhī inscriptions of this period are the Mathurā lion capital inscriptions (CII 2.1, 30–49), recording various donations by the family of the Mahākṣatrapa Rajula to the Sarvāstivādin monks; the Takht-i-Bāhī stone inscription of the time of Gondophernes (CII 2.1, 57–62), which furnishes an important fixed point in the chronology of the Scytho-Parthian period; and the Kurram relic casket inscription (CII 2.1, 152–5), recording the *pratītya-samutpāda* formula in Gāndhārī.

A large number of Kharoṣṭhī inscriptions have been discovered and published in recent decades, including several of considerable historical and cultural importance. Among these are the Brussels Buddha image inscription (BEFEO 61, 54–8), which provided a rare instance of a dated Gāndhāran sculpture; the Mathurā pedestal inscription (EI 40, 168–9), one of the few biscript (Kharoṣṭhī and Brāhmī) records (see 2.5.4); the Indravarman relic casket inscription (JAOS 102, 59–68), which proved the existence of an era dating from the ascension of the Scythian king Azes I which can be identified with the "Vikrama" era (see 5.5.1.3); and the Senavarma relic deposit inscription on a gold leaf (IIJ 29, 261–93), which is the longest Kharoṣṭhī record known to date.[79]

Recent explorations in the valleys of the Indus River and its tributaries in northern Pakistan have brought to light nearly two hundred short Kharoṣṭhī inscriptions of about the first to third centuries from the Chilas, Alam Bridge, and Hunza-Haldeikish sites.[80] These and other sites in the Chilas-Gilgit region have also yielded many thousands of inscriptions of various periods, mostly somewhat later, in Brāhmī and other scripts and languages (see 3.5.3.1 and 3.5.3.3).[81] Most of these inscriptions are brief graffiti or travelers' records but are nonetheless of considerable historical, cultural, and linguistic importance. The abundant epigraphic material from this region is being published in the volumes of *Antiquities of Northern Pakistan* (see the bibliography, s.v. Karl Jettmar) and in the *Materialen zur Archäologie der Nordgebiete Pakistans* series.[82]

4.3.3.2 Brāhmī inscriptions from northern and central India

From the early centuries of the Christian era we have a large number of dedicatory stone inscriptions in Brāhmī script, many of them Buddhist but some also Jaina and Brahmanical, associated with the reigns of the Indo-Scythian Kṣatrapas of Mathurā and the great Kuṣāṇa kings (Kaniṣka and his successors). The language of most of

79. Many other Kharoṣṭhī inscriptions, including numerous Buddhist reliquaries from undisclosed sites in Pakistan, have been published in recent years and are continuing to be published by, among others, H. W. Bailey, G. Fussman, B. N. Mukherjee, and R. Salomon in JRAS, BEFEO, JAS, JESI, IIJ, JAOS, and other journals.

80. See G. Fussman, "Inscriptions de Gilgit," BEFEO 65, 1978, 1–64, and "Les Inscriptions kharoṣṭhī de la plaine de Chilas," in K. Jettmar, ed., *Antiquities of Northern Pakistan*, I.1–40.

81. See O. von Hinüber in Jettmar, *Antiquities of Northern Pakistan*, I.41–106. On the north Pakistan inss. in general, see also Ahmad Hasan Dani, "The Sacred Rock of Hunza," *Journal of Central Asia* 8, 1985, 5–124, and *Chilas: The City of Nanga Parvat (Dyamar)*.

82. Vol. 1, M. Bemmann and Ditte König, *Die Felsbildstation Oshibat*; vol. 2, G. Fussman and D. König, *Die Felsbildstation Shatial*. For recent discoveries of Kharoṣṭhī inscriptions outside India, see sections 4.3.7.3 and 4.3.7.4.

these inscriptions is Epigraphical Hybrid Sanskrit, but some, especially the later ones, are in more or less standard Sanskrit. The majority of the inscriptions of this group are from Mathurā and are collected in H. Lüders' *Mathurā Inscriptions*. Other specimens have been found farther to the south and east, mainly at Buddhist sites such as Set-Mahet, Sāñcī, and Sārnāth. A typical example of the inscriptions of this group is the Sārnāth umbrella shaft inscription of the time of Kaniṣka (Appendix, no. 5).

Several important new Kuṣāṇa inscriptions have been found in recent years. Among these are the Govindnagar (Mathurā) inscription of Kaniṣka's year 12 (EI 40, 197–8); the Agra inscription of Kaniṣka's year 16 (JESI 4, 76–7); the Govindnagar inscription of Huviṣka's year 25 (EI 40, 198–200); the Mathurā inscription of Huviṣka's year 50 (JESI 10, 71–2); and a Śaivite inscription from Mathurā (EI 39, 9–10).

4.3.3.3 Inscriptions from western India

4.3.3.3.1 Inscriptions from the cave temples. A large number of dedicatory inscriptions, mostly Buddhist, in Brāhmī script and Prakrit or hybrid language are found in the rock-cut cave temples of Maharashtra, particularly at Kārle, Junnār, Nāsik, Nānāghāṭ, Bhājā, Beḍsā, and Kāṇherī. Of special historical importance are the inscriptions of the Sātavāhana and early Western Kṣatrapa kings from the first four of these sites. The inscriptions of this group are conveniently collected in J. Burgess and Bhagwanlal Indraji's *Inscriptions from the Cave-Temples of Western India* (ICTWI), although this is not the most up-to-date source for readings.[83]

Particularly important inscriptions of this class for both political and literary history are the Nāsik inscription of Uṣavadāta (SI I.167–70), describing his exploits and donations on behalf of his father-in-law, Nahapāna, and the Nāsik inscription of the reign of Vāsiṣṭhīputra Puḷumāvi (SI I.203–7), eulogizing the late King Gautamīputra Sātakarṇi (see 7.2.1.1).

4.3.3.3.2 Inscriptions of the later Western Kṣatrapas. Several dedicatory stone inscriptions in Sanskrit or hybrid language belonging to the reigns of the later Western Kṣatrapa line of Caṣṭana (the so-called Kārdamaka line) have been found in the Kathiawar and Kacch regions of Gujarat. The Western Kṣatrapa inscriptions are collected in V. V. Mirashi's *History and Inscriptions of the Sātavāhanas and the Western Kṣatrapas*. By far the longest and most important of these is the Junāgaḍh rock inscription of Rudradāman (SI I.175–80), which is the earliest (ca. A.D. 150) long Sanskrit inscription and is of great historical and literary significance. An important recent discovery in this class is the Andhau inscription of the year 11 of the reign of Caṣṭana (JAIH 2, 104–11), whose earliest previously known date was 52.[84]

4.3.3.4 Inscriptions of southern India

In the period corresponding to the Scytho-Parthian era in northern India, a large number of stone inscriptions, mostly Buddhist dedications, were being recorded in south-

83. For further references, see SI I.164–73 and 189–212.
84. See also section 5.5.1.4.

ern India at major *stūpa* sites such as Nāgārjunakoṇḍa, Amarāvatī, and Jaggayyapeṭa (all in Andhra Pradesh). These inscriptions are generally written in Brāhmī of the early southern variety and in Prakrit language. From Nāgārjunakoṇḍa we have several dozen inscriptions on columns and other stone surfaces, mostly recording the donations of the Ikṣvāku royal family who ruled around the second and third centuries A.D. (EI 20, 1–37; 21, 61–71; 35, 1–36, etc.).[85] Other inscriptions at Nāgārjunakoṇḍa as well as Amarāvatī and Jaggayyapeṭa record donations associated with the Sātavāhana and other dynasties (see Jas. Burgess, *The Buddhist Stupas of Amaravati and Jaggayyapeta*).

In recent years more inscriptions of this type have been discovered at several other sites in Andhra Pradesh and elsewhere in southern India, notably Sālihuṇḍam,[86] Kesanapalli,[87] and Sannati.[88] Recent epigraphic discoveries at Amarāvatī have included new inscriptions of this and other periods.[89]

4.3.4 Inscriptions of the Gupta era (fourth to mid-sixth centuries A.D.)

4.3.4.1 Inscriptions of the imperial Guptas

The inscriptions of the Gupta emperors of northern India, nearly all in Sanskrit language and late Brāhmī script, are compiled in J. F. Fleet's *Inscriptions of the Early Gupta Kings* (CII 3, 1888) and in D. R. Bhandarkar's revised edition of CII 3 (1981).[90] The majority of the Gupta inscriptions are stone records on rocks, pillars, and cave walls, but there are also several copper plate, clay seal, and miscellaneous inscriptions. Many of the Gupta inscriptions, especially those on rocks and pillars, are of the *praśasti* class (see 2.1.1), while others are purely dedicatory, recording Brahmanical, Buddhist, or Jaina donations and mentioning the ruler only in connection with the date. Several royal seal inscriptions provide detailed dynastic genealogies and are of great value for historical reconstruction.

The outstanding historical and literary record of the Gupta period is the Allahabad pillar inscription of Samudragupta (SI I.262–8), recording the king's exploits and conquests in elaborate mixed verse and prose. Another important record of the *praśasti* type is the Junāgaḍh rock inscription of Skandagupta (SI I.307–16), inscribed on the same stone as Aśoka's Girnār rock edicts and the Rudradāman inscription, documenting the reconstruction of Lake Sudarśana.

Among recent discoveries of Gupta inscriptions, the Vidiśā image inscriptions of the time of Rāmagupta (CII 3, rev. ed., 231–4) are extremely important in supporting the historicity of Rāmagupta, previously known only from literary sources as the elder brother of Candragupta II. Other recent finds include new inscriptions from the reign of the late Gupta king Budhagupta from Mathurā (JESI 9, 6–11) and Śaṅkarpur (JESI 4, 62–66).

85. For summaries of the inss. at Nāgārjunakoṇḍa and related sites, see P. R. Srinivasan and S. Sankaranarayanan, *Inscriptions of the Ikshvāku Period.*

86. Srikakulam Dist., AP; R. Subrahmanyam, *Salihundam*, 119–23.

87. Guntur Dist., AP; A. W. Khan, *A Monograph on an Early Buddhist Stupa at Kesanapalli*, 2–5.

88. Gulbarga Dist., Karnataka; M. S. Nagaraja Rao in IEBHA 41–5.

89. I. Karthikeya Sarma, JESI I, 1974, 60–74; 7, 1980, 18–21.

90. For details, see section 8.1.2.

4.3.4.2 *Inscriptions of the contemporaries and successors of the Guptas in northern and central India*

Sanskrit inscriptions, mostly copper plate land grants, of the feudatory and allied dynasties of the Guptas were collected by Fleet in CII 3, nos. 17–81. These include the records of the Vākāṭakas of Vidarbha and the Parivrājakas and Uccakalpas of Bundelkhand. Twenty-seven Vākāṭaka inscriptions were subsequently published by V. V. Mirashi in CII 4. Inscriptions from the time of the decline of the Guptas in the early to mid-sixth century include those of the early Maukharis, Yaśodharman of Mandasor, and the Hun (*Hūṇa*) kings Toramāṇa and Mihirakula. The Mandasor inscriptions of Yaśodharman (Fleet, CII 3, nos. 33–5) are of particular interest for their outstanding literary, calligraphic, and historical value.

Among the several significant new records of this period which have come to light in recent years, the Hisse-Borālā inscription of Devasena (EI 37, 1–8) provides important chronological data on the early Vākāṭaka kingdom.[91] Two recent discoveries have an important bearing on the history of the Huns in India: the Sanjeli copper plates (EI 40, 175–86) showed that they ruled as far south as Gujarat, while the Rīsthal stone inscription of the Aulikara ruler Prakāśadharman (IIJ 32, 1–36) refers to that previously unknown king's triumphs over Toramāṇa.

4.3.4.3 *Inscriptions of southern India*

In the years corresponding to the early Gupta period in the north, the most important southern Indian inscriptions are the copper plates of the early Pallava kings found in Andhra Pradesh and Karnataka (SI I.457–72), datable on paleographic grounds to about the fourth century A.D. Though written in Prakrit, they prefigure in style and content the Sanskrit copper plate charters which are to become so abundant all over India in later centuries.

From the fifth and sixth centuries we have a good number of stone and copper plate inscriptions in Sanskrit (and occasionally Prakrit) of various southern dynasties such as the Cālukyas, Nalas, Traikūṭakas, Eastern Gaṅgas, Viṣṇukundins, Śarabhapurīyas, Śālaṅkāyanas, Kadambas, and Western Gaṅgas. An outstanding document of this class is the Tāḷagunda inscription of the time of the Kadamba king Śāntivarman (SI I.474–9), with thirty-four verses of ornate Sanskrit recording the construction of a tank.

4.3.5 *Inscriptions of the post-Gupta or "Medieval" era (mid-seventh to tenth centuries A.D.)*

In the centuries following the Gupta dynasty, and especially from the eighth century onward, the epigraphic remains of South Asia become increasingly abundant, to the point that it is no longer possible to describe them in detail but only in terms of gen-

91. Several new sets of Vākāṭaka copper plates have also been found recently in Maharashtra, at Māṇḍhal (EI 41, 68–76 and 159–80), Masoda (JESI 10, 108–16), Pauni (EI 38, 53–6), and Yavatmal (*Vishveshvaranand Indological Journal* 21, 78–84).

eral dynastic and geographical groupings. Lists of the inscriptions of many of the dynasties are available in various sources; for the period in question here, see the lists of inscriptions at the end of individual chapters and in the general bibliography (470–90) of R. C. Majumdar, ed., *The Age of Imperial Kanauj*. For detailed (though not up-to-date) references see the lists by Kielhorn and Bhandarkar in EI 5 and 7 and 19–23, respectively.[92] Complete lists of inscriptions are often to be found in various books on the history of individual dynasties, and in the regional anthologies (see 8.1.3.2). Important anthologies of specific corpora will be cited in the following sections. Sircar's *Select Inscriptions II* provides the only representative general sampling of inscriptions of this period.

In this period the epigraphic materials in Indo-Aryan languages consist, with few exceptions, of Sanskrit inscriptions in the various local derivatives of Brāhmī script, verging at the later part of the period into their modern forms (Devanāgarī, Telugu-Kannada, etc.). The bulk of the texts are still copper plate land grants, ever increasing in number and length, and dedicatory and/or panegyric stone inscriptions on slabs, pillars, or image pedestals. The style in general tends to be increasingly formal and ornate, including many specimens of *kāvya* in the high classical style. A typical stone inscription of this period is the Lakkhā Maṇḍal *praśasti* (Appendix, no. 8). The Aihoḷe inscription of Pulakeśin II (SI II.443–50) is an especially important document for literary as well as political history (see 7.2.1.2). A typical copper plate charter is the Baroda grant of Rāṣṭrakūṭa Karkkarāja II (Appendix, no. 10).

4.3.5.1 Northern India

In the earlier phase of this era, that is, the seventh and eighth centuries, important northern Indian inscriptions belong to such powers as the Maukharis, the Later Guptas, the rulers of Kanauj such as Harṣa and Yaśovarman, and other associated dynasties (see K. K. Thaplyal, *Inscriptions of the Maukharīs, Later Guptas, Puṣpabhūtis and Yaśovarman of Kanauj*). The dominant northern Indian dynasty in succeeding centuries (eighth to tenth) is the Gurjara-Pratīhāras, of whom a few dozen inscriptions of the usual type are known. Important recent discoveries in this group include a stone inscription now in New Delhi from the reign of the early Gurjara-Pratīhāra king Vatsarāja (EI 41, 49–57), which is the earliest known record (A.D. 795) of this dynasty.

4.3.5.2 Western India

From western India in the earlier part of this era we have inscriptions, mostly copper plates, of local dynasties such as the Maitrakas of Valabhī and Cālukyas of Gujarat. Many of the inscriptions of these and other kingdoms of western and central India are collected by V. V. Mirashi in CII 4, *Inscriptions of the Kalachuri-Chedi Era*. In later centuries, inscriptions of early Rajput dynasties such as the Chandellas, Paramāras, and Cāhamānas (Chauhāns) begin to appear in this region.

92. For bibliographical details, see section 8.2.2.

4.3.5.3 Eastern India

The inscriptions of the Pāla kings of Bihar and Bengal, comprising a few dozen copper plates and stone inscriptions (including several image dedications), are the principal epigraphic documents from eastern India in this period. An important new discovery in this class is the Jagjībanpur copper plate of Mahendrapāla (*South Asian Studies* 4, 71–3) which proved that that king was in fact a Pāla ruler and not, as had previously been believed, a Gurjara-Pratīhāra interloper.

In Orissa there are numerous inscriptions of the Karas, Bhañjas, and other minor dynasties.

4.3.5.4 The Deccan

Among the dynasties of the Deccan, we have from the earlier phase of the period in question the inscriptions of the Cālukyas of Bādāmi, which include, besides Kannada and bilingual (Kannada and Sanskrit; cf. 3.6) records, several important Sanskrit inscriptions including the Aihoḷe inscription noted previously. There are also several dozen inscriptions, mostly copper plate grants, of the Rāṣṭrakūṭas, including several important recent discoveries such as the Bhindhon plates of Ka(r)kkarāja (JESI 10, 30–5), an important document for the early history of the dynasty; the Tarasādī plates of the time of Amoghavarṣa, giving the earliest date for that king (JOI 20, 155–62); and the Barsi plates (JESI 11, 106–13), which provide new information on Kṛṣṇa I's invasion of central India. In the eastern Deccan, the most important records of this period belong to the Eastern Cālukyas and Eastern Gaṅgas.

4.3.5.5 Southern India

In the far south, inscriptions of such dynasties as the Pallavas, Coḷas, Pāṇḍyas, and (Western) Gaṅgas are now found in increasingly large numbers. Dravidian languages, mainly Tamil, come into wide use for inscriptional purposes and largely, though by no means completely, supplant Sanskrit, which is still often used in bilingual documents. Two important recently discovered copper plate grants from Velañjeri (R. Nagaswamy, *Thiruttani and Velanjeri Copper Plates*) are representative of the bilingual (Sanskrit and Tamil) copper plate grants of the later Pallavas and the Coḷas. The Pallavas issued stone inscriptions in Sanskrit (examples in SII 1), while most of the very abundant stone records of the Coḷas (SII 2, 13, 19, etc.) and other dynasties of the far south were in Tamil.

4.3.6 Inscriptions of the "Islamic period" (eleventh to eighteenth centuries A.D.)

In the earlier centuries of this era, while Hindu kingdoms were still ruling most of India, the proliferation of Sanskrit inscriptions continued. In general the inscriptions are of the same types as the preceding period, but even more abundant. This proliferation is not only one of sheer numbers but also of issuing authorities, reflecting the increasing political fragmentation of the times. Thus, as in the preceding section, the inscriptions can be discussed only in broad terms; for bibliographical information and lists of inscriptions see the general bibliography (795–822) in R. C. Majumdar, ed., *The Struggle for Empire*, and the sources mentioned in the preceding section.

The Indo-Aryan inscriptions of this period are generally in Sanskrit, but the NIA languages were coming into use gradually at different times and places (see 3.4). During the early and middle phases of this period, the various local scripts (used for both Sanskrit and vernacular inscriptions) took on fully developed and independent forms which in most cases are similar to those of the modern Indic scripts.

With the consolidation of Islamic rule over much of India from the late twelfth century onward, Sanskritic inscriptions became gradually less common, though they continued to be recorded in good numbers well into the fourteenth century, especially in central and southern India. From the fifteenth century on, Sanskrit inscriptions became still rarer, being largely supplanted by those in Persian, Arabic, Dravidian, and NIA languages (see 3.5.2). Bilingual inscriptions are quite common in this period, especially in the south (Sanskrit plus Tamil, Kannada, or Telugu) but sometimes in the north as well (Sanskrit plus NIA languages such as Marathi, Hindi, etc., or Islamic languages such as Persian or Arabic).

Sanskrit inscriptions nevertheless did continue to be written into the eighteenth and occasionally the nineteenth centuries,[93] and while many of the later examples are inferior in both quality and historical significance, there are still some significant records, for example, the Udaipur *Rājapraśasti* (cf. 4.1.8 and 7.2.2.2.1). In general inscriptions of the Islamic era, and especially the later examples, are less extensively studied and documented than those of earlier times, but they are nonetheless of considerable interest and importance as literary, historical, and social documents.

Typical stone *praśasti*s of this period are the Deopāṛā stone inscription of Vijayasena (SI II.115–22) and the Nāgpur Museum stone inscription of Naravarman (SI II.391–401). A good specimen of the elaborate southern Indian copper plates of this era are the bilingual (Sanskrit and Tamil) Leiden plates (twenty-one in number) of Rājendra I Coḷa (EI 22, 213–66).

The principal dynasties under whose rule Sanskrit inscriptions were issued during the Islamic era include:

Western India: Cālukyas of Gujarat, Cāhamānas (Chauhans), Guhilas, Paramāras,[94] Rathoḍas, Śilāhāras[95]
Northern India: Gāhaḍavālas, Kacchapaghātas, Tomaras
Central India: Candellas, Kalacuris
Eastern India: Bhañjas, Candras, Khaḍgas, Pālas, Senas, Varmas, (Bengal); Bhauma-Karas, Eastern Gaṅgas, Gaṅgas, Śailodbhavas, Somavaṃśīs, Sūryavaṃśīs (Orissa); Bhaumas (Assam)
The Deccan: Cālukyas of Kalyāṇa, Eastern Cālukyas of Veṅgi, Eastern Gaṅgas, Kākatīyas, the kingdoms of Vijayanagara, Yādavas of Devagiri
The far south: Coḷas, Hoysaḷas, Pāṇḍyas

93. See, e.g., D. R. Bhandarkar's *List of the Inscriptions of Northern India*, nos. 1061–76.
94. Collected in CII 7.2 (H. V. Trivedi, *Inscriptions of the Paramāras*) and A. C. Mittal, *The Inscriptions of Imperial Paramāras*.
95. Collected in CII 6 (V. V. Mirashi, *Inscriptions of the Śilāhāras*).

Inscriptions in Sanskrit issued by or under Muslim rulers are also found in some numbers, for instance, the Burhānpūr inscription of Ādil Shāh (Appendix, no. 14), recording the dedication of a mosque. Often these are bilingual (Sanskrit and Arabic or Persian).[96] Nondynastic Sanskrit inscriptions of various sorts, mostly private donative records, are also found in good numbers throughout this period; especially common are Jaina temple dedications and image inscriptions.

Significant new discoveries from this era include the Siyan stone inscription of Nayapāla (EI 39, 39–56) and the Udaipur stone slab with a eulogy of the sun god (JESI 8, 97–100). From southern India, the Karandai Tamil Sangam plates (discovered in 1950 but not published until 1984; K. G. Krishnan, MASI 79) provide another specimen of the huge and elaborate (fifty-seven plates weighing a total of 111.73 kilograms) bilingual (Tamil and Sanskrit) Coḷa land charters.

4.3.7 Extra-Indian inscriptions

Inscriptions in Indo-Aryan languages from outside of the geographical boundaries of traditional India as defined for this study (i.e., the modern nations of India, Pakistan, and Bangladesh) number in the thousands and constitute a major branch of the field of Indian epigraphy. Such extra-Indian inscriptions are found from Egypt to Vietnam, and from Azerbaijan to Indonesia.[97] Their form and content are equally diverse, sometimes very similar to corresponding material from India, as in the case of many of the specimens from Afghanistan and Southeast Asia, sometimes radically different, as in most of the material from Chinese central Asia. Almost without exception,[98] the epigraphs are written in Indic scripts, either in their original Indian form or in local variants or derivatives thereof (especially in Southeast Asia). Many of the extra-Indian inscriptions, particularly in Southeast Asia, are bilinguals.[99]

Sources for the study of extra-Indian inscriptions are scattered in a very wide variety of publications in many languages, not always easily accessible; an attempt is made here to provide references to the major sources for each country. No comprehensive survey of this subject has been previously available, though brief accounts of some of the material can be found in SIE 202–18 (Chapter VI, "Indian Epigraphy Abroad") and IC I.171–2 (Southeast Asia only).

4.3.7.1 Sri Lanka (Ceylon)

Sri Lankan inscriptions in Indian and Ceylonese languages are published in *Epigraphia Zeylanica* [EZ]. Important anthologies are E. Müller, *Ancient Inscriptions in Ceylon,* and S. Paranavitana, *Inscriptions of Ceylon.* For general

96. Several inss. of this type have been published in *Epigraphia Indo-Moslemica* and *Epigraphia Indica: Arabic and Persian Supplement* (see 8.1.1), e.g., the Bīdar inscription (EI, *Arabic and Persian Supplement,* 1962, 81–4) in Sanskrit and Persian.

97. In this book the inscriptions are grouped geographically by reference to modern nations rather than (as has generally been the practice) by obsolete designations (Champa, Annam, Turkestan, etc.) or broad regional categories (Indo-China, Southeast Asia, central Asia, etc.).

98. The only significant exception is the (partially) Indic texts in Aramaic script from Afghanistan (see 4.3.7.3).

99. "Bilinguals" in the broader sense of the term; see section 3.6. For a rare true bilingual from Cambodia, see Kamaleswar Bhattacharya, BEFEO 52, 1964, 2.

bibliography, see H. A. I. Goonetileke, "Writings on Ceylon Epigraphy: A Bibliographical Guide," in *Ceylon Historical Journal* 10, 1960–61, 171–207.

Several thousand inscriptions in Sanskrit, Pāli, Tamil, and especially in various stages of Sinhalese have been discovered in Sri Lanka. The scripts employed include early regional varieties of Brāhmī, the Sinhalese script at various stages of development, and occasionally other northern and southern Indian scripts. Most of the Sri Lankan inscriptions are on stone, especially cave walls; a few are on copper and other metals. The great majority of Sri Lankan inscriptions are concerned with dedications of various kinds to the Buddhist monastic community and regulations concerning its affairs.

The oldest Sri Lankan inscriptions consist mostly of dedications of caves to the Buddhist *saṃgha*, usually written in a local variety of old Brāhmī script above the entrance to the caves. These and other similar early inscriptions, numbering well over a thousand, are dated on historical and paleographic grounds from about the third century B.C. to the third or fourth century A.D. Their language is referred to as "Old Sinhalese" or "Sinhalese Prakrit" (see 3.1.4.2.2). Several of the earlier inscriptions of this group (39 out of 1,234 in Paranavitana, *Inscriptions of Ceylon* I) are written from right to left instead of the usual left to right; a few (e.g., no. 1099) are inscribed in boustrophedon (cf. 2.2.3.2.4).

Most of the later Sri Lankan inscriptions are written in more advanced forms of the Sinhalese variety of Brāhmī script and of the Sinhalese language which developed out of Sinhalese Prakrit. Such inscriptions are relatively rare between the fourth to eighth centuries, but stone inscriptions, mostly recording royal proclamations and grants to Buddhist establishments, become very common in the ninth to twelfth centuries (see 3.4.7). A particularly interesting and important body of materials is the literary graffiti from Sīgiri, published by S. Paranavitana in *Sigiri Graffiti*.

Sanskrit inscriptions written in either Sri Lankan or northern Indian scripts are considerably less common than those in Sinhalese; only seventeen are listed in Malini Dias, "Sanskrit and Pali Inscriptions of Ceylon" (*Ancient Ceylon* 1, 1971, 105–9). Among the most important specimens are the Tiriyāy rock inscription (seventh century; EZ 4, 151–60 and 312–19), eulogizing the *Girikaṇḍi-caitya;* the Jetavanārāma stone inscription (ninth century; EZ 1, 1–9), recording detailed regulations for the conduct of Buddhist monks; and the Indikaṭusäya copper plaques (EZ 3, 199–212; 4, 238–42), recording fragments of the *Pañcaviṃśati-sāhasrikā Prajñā-pāramitā* and the *Kāśyapa-parivarta.*[100]

Pāli inscriptions are, somewhat surprisingly, very rare; Dias (op. cit.) lists only three. An interesting example of a Pāli inscription (originally misread as "mixed Sanskrit") is the Abhayagiri copper plate (EZ 3, 169–71), containing a verse from the *Vaṭṭaka Jātaka*.

4.3.7.2 Nepal

Anthologies of inscriptions from Nepal in Sanskrit and other languages (mainly Newari) include Bhagvânlâl Indraji and G. Bühler, "Inscriptions from Nepal," IA 9, 1880, 163–94; S. Lévi, *Le Nepal* III; R. Gnoli, *Nepalese Inscriptions in Gupta Characters;*

100. See section 4.1.7 for other related inscriptions.

D. R. Regmi, *Medieval Nepal, Part IV*; D. R. Regmi, *Inscriptions of Ancient Nepal*; H. Jośī, *Nepāla ko Prācīna Abhilekha;* Dh. Vajrācārya, *Licchavikālakā Abhilekha;* and Dh. Vajrācārya and Ṭ. Śreṣṭha, *Śāhakālakā Abhilekha* [*Pahilo Bhāga*]. See also the *Abhilekha-saṃgraha*, and various articles in Nepali journals such as *Pūrṇimā*, *Kailash*, and *Journal of the Nepal Research Centre*.

Sanskrit inscriptions in Brāhmī script and its local derivatives are found in Nepal in large numbers from the fifth century[101] until recent times. The inscriptions of the Licchavi period (fifth–ninth centuries), numbering about two hundred, mostly on stone, have tended to attract the attention of epigraphists and historians; most of the anthologies cited here consist exclusively or mainly of inscriptions of this period.[102] This material includes some outstanding specimens of the *praśasti* style, such as the Cāṅgu-Nārāyaṇa pillar inscription of Mānadeva (SI I.378–82), which is the oldest dated inscription of Nepal ([Śaka?] 386 = A.D. 464/65).

Inscriptions of the post-Licchavi period, though numerous, are in general less well documented, though they have begun to attract more attention in recent years in such publications as Regmi's *Medieval Nepal, Part IV*, *Abhilekha-saṃgraha*, Vajrācārya and Śreṣṭha's *Śāhakālakā Abhilekha*, and in several articles published in the journals cited earlier. Many of the later inscriptions are bilingual in Sanskrit and Newari.[103] Stone inscriptions continue to predominate, but copper plates are also not rare (cf. 4.1.2 n. 5).[104]

Some late inscriptions of Nepal, mostly from the seventeenth and eighteenth centuries, are written in Nepali[105] or Nepali and Sanskrit; for examples see Vajrācārya and Śreṣṭha's *Śāhakālakā Abhilekha* and *Abhilekha-saṃgraha* 12.

The inscriptions of Nepal generally record royal grants of land or privileges (*prasāda*) of various kinds, temple endowments or reconstructions, dedications of images or *liṅga*s, and so forth. In style and formula they generally resemble the corresponding types of records from India. On the whole, inscriptions of Brahmanical affiliation predominate, especially in the earlier period, but Buddhist records are also common throughout.

4.3.7.3 Afghanistan

Six inscriptions of the time of Aśoka in Aramaic and/or Greek have been found, some of them in recent years, in Afghanistan.[106] Another fragmentary Aramaic inscription, probably of Aśoka, was found in Taxila (Pakistan); see SI I.78–9. While these records do not, strictly speaking, fall within the linguistic range of this book, they are worthy of mention here, first of all because most of them are translations or at

101. The Aśokan (third-century B.C.) minor pillar inscriptions from Rummindeī and Nigālī Sāgar are from the Terai region of Nepal but are here treated together with the other Aśokan inscriptions (4.3.1.1.4).

102. A useful inventory of Licchavi inscriptions is given in M. Slusser, *Nepal Mandala*, I.403–19.

103. Cf. section 3.5.3.3; see also Slusser, op. cit., 393.

104. See, e.g., M. R. Pant and A. D. Sharma, *The Two Earliest Copper-plate Inscriptions from Nepal*, and Regmi's *Medieval Nepal IV*, nos. 14, 17, etc.

105. Cf. section 3.4.6; see also Slusser, op. cit., 394.

106. For references see Allchin and Norman's *Guide to the Aśokan Inscriptions* (*South Asian Studies* I, 1985), 46; F. R. Allchin and Norman Hammond, *The Archaeology of Afghanistan from Earliest*

least free adaptations of Indic (Prakrit) originals; thus, for example, the Kandahār [II] Greek inscription is a rendering of portions of Aśokan rock edicts XII and XIII (JA 252, 137–57). Moreover, two of the Aramaic inscriptions, namely Pul-i-Darunta (BSOAS 13, 80–88) and Kandahār [III] (JA 254, 437–70) consist of phrase-by-phrase renderings of the original Prakrit texts transliterated into Aramaic script and accompanied by glosses in the Aramaic language; these inscriptions thus constitute, in effect, bilingual Prakrit and Aramaic documents.

During the Kuṣāṇa period (i.e., the early centuries of the Christian era), Kharoṣṭhī/Gāndhārī inscriptions, typically on reliquaries or potsherds, similar in form and content to the contemporary records from India (see 4.2.3.3), are common in Afghanistan. These are concentrated in the eastern part of the country, on the fringe of the Indian cultural region, but some also come from farther afield to the southwest (e.g., Dasht-e Nāwur) and north (e.g., Qunduz). Important examples include the Wardak relic bowl inscription (CII 2.1, 165–70), the Bīmarān vase inscription (CII 2.1, 50–2), the Begrām bas-relief inscription (EI 22, 11–14), and the Jalālābād stone inscription (*Acta Orientalia* 16, 234–40). Excavations in recent decades have revealed many more inscriptions of this type; among the more important specimens are those from Haḍḍa (BEFEO 66, 5–9), Dasht-e Nāwur (BEFEO 61, 19–22), and Qunduz (BEFEO 61, 58–61).[107]

Some later Sanskrit inscriptions in late Brāhmī of about around the fifth to eighth centuries have also been found in Afghanistan in recent decades. Worthy of note are the Dilberjin fresco inscription (*Drevniaia Baktriia* [for reference see Index of Inscriptions Cited], 170–1); the Gardez inscription on an image of Gaṇeśa (EI 35, 44–7); and the Umā-Maheśvara image inscription from Tapa Skandar (JESI 1, 1–6). Several Buddhist inscriptions of this period with the "Buddhist creed" (cf. 4.1.7) on votive clay tablets have also been discovered at Ghaznī (*East and West*, n.s. 20, 74–7). An unusual and enigmatic Brāhmī inscription on a mud-plaster floor was found at Tapa Sardār (*East and West*, n.s. 29, 265–9).

Several Sanskrit inscriptions in Śāradā script from the Śāhī period (eighth–ninth centuries) have also been found in Afghanistan.[108] Two such inscriptions from Laghmān have recently been published (JESI 12, 63–8), but the readings are uncertain due to their poor condition.

4.3.7.4 Uzbekistan and neighboring central Asian republics

Archaeological excavations in recent decades in southern Uzbekistan (formerly USSR) have yielded several dozen specimens of Indic inscriptions from various sites in the region of ancient Bactria, mainly Kara Tepe and Faiaz Tepe near Termez in Uzbekistan. (A few have also been found at Pendzhikent, Adzhina Tepe, and other

---

Times to the Timurid Period (London: Academic Press, 1978), 192–8; G. Djelani Davary, "A List of the Inscriptions of the Pre-Islamic Period from Afghanistan," StII 3, 1977, 11–22 (esp. 11–12); and B. N. Mukherjee, *Studies in the Aramaic Inscriptions of Aśoka*, 23–42.

107. For further references see Davary, "A List of the Inscriptions," 12.

108. For references see Allchin and Hammond, *The Archaeology of Afghanistan*, 245, and Davary, *Studia Iranica* 10, 1981, 57–8.

sites in neighboring Tajikistan.) Most of these date from the Kuṣāṇa period. The majority of the relics (like the contemporary ones from nearby Afghanistan) are potsherds with dedicatory inscriptions in Kharoṣṭhī script and Gāndhārī language; these are collected by M. I. Vorob'eva-Desiatovskaia in "Pamiatniki pis'mom kxaroshtxi i braxmi iz sovetskoi Srednei Azii" (see the bibliography), and by V. V. Vertogradova in *Indiiskaia Epigrafika iz Kara-tepe v Starom Termeze*. This collection also includes some dedicatory and imprecatory[109] inscriptions in Brāhmī script and Buddhist Sanskrit.

The newest discoveries in this region have included dedicatory Kharoṣṭhī inscriptions on stone and clay from Termez (*Vestnik Drevnei Istorii* 1974.1, 116–26) and on gold ingots from Dal'verzin-Tepe (*Vestnik Drevnei Istorii* 1976.1, 72–9).

Some late (eighteenth–nineteenth centuries) inscriptions in Hindi and Punjabi have been found in the fire temple of the former Indian community in Suruhani in Azerbaijan (*Epigrafika Vostoka* 9, 83–7). Sporadic finds of Indian inscriptions have also been reported in other republics of the former Soviet Central Asia such as Kirgizstan (ARIE 1960–61, no. B.632).

4.3.7.5 Burma (Myan Mar)

The main sources for inscriptions of Burma[110] are *Epigraphia Birmanica* (I–IV, 1919–28); G. H. Luce and Pe Maung Tin, eds., *Inscriptions of Burma*; and Chas. Duroiselle, *A List of Inscriptions Found in Burma*.

Inscriptions in Sanskrit and Pāli, generally of Buddhist content, are found in fair numbers in Burma from about the sixth century on. Three Sanskrit inscriptions on stone from the reign of the Candra kings of Arakan dating from about the sixth to eighth centuries were published by E. H. Johnston in "Some Sanskrit Inscriptions of Arakan," BSOAS 11, 1943–46, 357–85. The most important of these is the pillar inscription of Ānandacandra at Mrohaung, containing a lengthy *praśasti* (Johnston, 373–82). Three further Arakan inscriptions from Vesālī, including a copper plate, have been published by D. C. Sircar (EI 32, 103–9; EI 37, 61–6). Like many of the other Burmese Sanskrit inscriptions, the script of the Candra inscriptions is derived from the contemporary styles of northeastern India, as opposed to the Pāli inscriptions which are typically in Burmese script.

Numerous inscriptions in Sanskrit and Pāli, mostly from about the sixth to eighth centuries, have been found at sites in Hmawza (Old Prome, the ancient Śrīkṣetra; ASIAR 1926–27, 171–80; 1927–28, 128, 145; 1928–29, 105–9). Most of these inscriptions consist of dedicatory or ritual formulae such as the "Buddhist creed" or passages from Buddhist canonical texts on clay votive tablets, inscribed images, and gold plates (see also the Maunggun gold plates, EI 5, 101–2). Several are bilingual, in Sanskrit and Pyu or Pāli and Pyu.

109. Cf. O. von Hinüber, "A Brāhmī-inscription from Kara-Tepe," *Studies in Indo-Asian Art and Culture* 6, 1980, 123–5.

110. The sources listed here are mostly concerned with materials in Burmese, Mon, and other non-Indic languages but also contain some Sanskrit and Pāli inscriptions. Specific references to Indic-language materials are given in this section.

Similar inscriptions in Pāli and Sanskrit on votive clay tablets of the eleventh century were also found at Pagàn (ASIAR 1926–27, 161–71). A bilingual Sanskrit and Tamil inscription from Pagàn in Grantha and Tamil characters of the thirteenth century records a dedication to a Vaiṣṇava temple by a native of southern India (EI 7, 197–8).

Pāli inscriptions, usually bilingual with Burmese or other local languages, are common in later times, even up to the modern era (see Duroiselle's *List of Inscriptions*, passim). An exceptionally important late (A.D. 1476) bilingual (Pāli and Talain [Mon]) document is the Kalyāṇasīmā (Pegu) inscription of King Dhammaceti (Taw Sein Ko, *The Kalyāṇī Inscriptions*). This lengthy document on ten slabs, recording the consecration of and establishing regulations for the meeting place (*sīmā*) of monks, contains a vast body of information on the history and practice of Buddhism in Burma.

4.3.7.6 Thailand

Inscriptions in Indic languages are found, along with those in Thai and other non-Indian languages, in the following anthologies: G. Coedès, *Recueil des inscriptions du Siam* (note especially the "Liste des inscriptions du Siam" in vol. 1, 13–36); *Prachum Silā Čhārųk* [reprint and continuation of Coedès' *Recueil*]; *Čhārųk nai Prathēt Thai; Čhārųk Samai Sukhōthai.*

Several dozen Sanskrit and Pāli inscriptions dating from about the fifth to sixteenth centuries A.D. have been found in Thailand. Probably the earliest Sanskrit inscription of Thailand is the Srideb inscription (B. Ch. Chhabra, *Expansion of Indo-Aryan Culture*, 70–2), dated paleographically to around the fifth century. In the seventh to twelfth centuries, Sanskrit inscriptions become quite common; see, for example, the Khăn Thevăda and Ban Bųng Kē stele inscriptions (BEFEO 22, 57–60 and 62–4).

Several of the major Sanskrit inscriptions of eastern Thailand belong to the Khmer kings of neighboring Cambodia (cf. 4.3.7.7 and 4.3.7.9). A particularly important record of this class is the bilingual (Sanskrit and Khmer) Sdok Kak Thoṃ inscription of Udayādityavarman (A. Chakravarti, *The Sdok Kak Thoṃ Inscription*), which relates in detail the history of a prominent priestly family and their relations with contemporary kings over two and a half centuries. There are also a few Sanskrit inscriptions from southern (peninsular) Thailand, such as the Ligor inscription of King Viṣṇu of Śrīvijaya (Coedès, *Recueil*, II.20–4) recording the dedication of several Buddhist *stūpas* and *caityas*.

In later centuries, Pāli inscriptions (often bilingual with Thai) are more common, while Sanskrit becomes rarer, for example, the Văt Don bilingual stele inscription of the early thirteenth century (BEFEO 25, 189–92). Votive tablets bearing the familiar Buddhist creed are often found in Thailand, in both Sanskrit and Pāli.[111]

4.3.7.7 Cambodia

The main collections of Cambodian inscriptions in Indian languages (some together with inscriptions in Khmer) are A. Barth and A. Bergaigne, *Inscriptions sanscrites du*

111. See G. Coedès, "Tablettes votives bouddhiques du Siam," in *Études Asiatiques* 1, Publications de l'École Française d'Extrême-Orient 19 (Paris, 1925), 145–67.

Cambodge; G. Coedès, *Inscriptions du Cambodge*; R. C. Majumdar, *Inscriptions of Kambuja*; and C. Jacques, *Corpus des inscriptions du pays khmer*. Facsimiles of the inscriptions were published by L. Finot in *Inscriptions du Cambodge*. There are numerous studies of the Cambodian inscriptions from various standpoints; noteworthy are K. Bhattacharya, "Recherches sur le vocabulaire des inscriptions sanskrites du Cambodge"; Bhattacharya, *Les Religions brahmaniques dans l'ancien Cambodge d'après l'épigraphie et l'iconographie*; M. K. Sharan, *Studies in Sanskrit Inscriptions of Ancient Cambodia*; and S. Sahai, *Les Institutions politiques et l'organisation administrative du Cambodge ancien* (*VIe-XIIIe siècles*).

The Indic inscriptions of Cambodia constitute the largest and most important corpus among the extra-Indian inscriptions in Sanskrit. They number in the hundreds, including several of great length, and range in date from about the fifth or sixth to the thirteenth or fourteenth centuries. The great majority are in Sanskrit, including many Sanskrit and Khmer bilinguals, besides the numerous inscriptions in Khmer alone; a few late inscriptions are in Pāli (e.g., K 501, 754).[112]

The Cambodian inscriptions are generally written on stone, especially on stelae found at the great temple sites of Angkor Vat, Angkor Thom, and others. Like most of the Indic inscriptions of Southeast Asia, they are usually written in scripts related to southern and western Indian styles of late Brāhmī and in the local script derived therefrom,[113] but several inscriptions from the time of Yaśovarman (ninth–tenth centuries) are recorded as biscripts in the local script and in northern Indian Siddhamātṛkā. The inscriptions are usually dated in the Śaka era.

The primary purpose of virtually all of the Cambodian inscriptions is to record pious donations or foundations of various types by kings and other royal figures, government officials, and private individuals. The recipients include both religious institutions and learned or venerated individuals. In general, Śaiva institutions predominate, although Vaiṣṇava and Buddhist establishments are by no means neglected, and references to syncretistic cults, especially of Śiva and Viṣṇu, are characteristic. The gifts themselves are often lavish, as in the Práḥ Khan inscription of Jayavarman VII (K 908) recording the donation of 20,400 images, 13,500 villages, 306,372 slaves, and so on (v. 177). The provisions of the grants are often spelled out in great detail, usually in the Khmer portions of bilingual inscriptions but sometimes also in Sanskrit.

The Sanskrit inscriptions of Cambodia have won praise for their literary and scholarly qualities and the skill of their composition and execution. They are composed, almost without exception, in classical verse, and many are quite long, consisting of as many as 218 (Mébon inscription of Rājendravarman, K 528) or even 298 verses (Prè Rup inscription of Rājendravarman, K 806).[114] Ornate meters such as *Śārdū-*

112. Following the standard practice, Cambodian inscriptions are cited here according to the numbers in Coedès' *Liste générale des inscriptions du Cambodge* = *Inscriptions du Cambodge*, vol. 8, 73–255, which is a revised version of the Cambodian portion of Coedès' *Liste générale des inscriptions du Champa et du Cambodge*. In Coedès' system, K = Khmer, i.e., Cambodia, as opposed to C = Champa, i.e., Vietnam.

113. See section 2.2.5.6 n. 121 for references.

114. These inss. have been translated into English by M. K. Sharan in *Select Cambodian Inscriptions* (*The Mebon and Pre Rup Inscriptions of Rajendra Varman II*).

lavikrīḍita or *Sragdharā* are frequently used, as is learned vocabulary (see K. Bhattacharya, "Recherches sur le vocabulaire"). The style is typically highly ornate, especially in the eulogistic portions of royal grants, which often carry the *praśasti* style to extremes. Also characteristic of the Cambodian Sanskrit inscriptions are learned references to literary and technical texts, some of which are useful for historical studies of Sanskrit literature.[115] Pāṇinian grammatical allusions, as in vv. 48, 124, 214, and 219 of Prè Rup, are also typical.

As sources for political and cultural history the Cambodian inscriptions are of incomparable value not only for their volume but also for their relative precision as to dates and historical details. The Práḥ Nok inscription (K 289), for instance, describes the military campaigns of a General Saṃgrāma in far more detail than is usually to be found in Indian inscriptions.

4.3.7.8 Vietnam

Sanskrit inscriptions from Vietnam are compiled in A. Bergaigne, *Inscriptions sanscrites de Campā*, and R. C. Majumdar, *Champa.*

The kingdom of Campā in modern Vietnam has yielded several dozen Sanskrit or bilingual Sanskrit and Cham inscriptions dating from approximately the third (Võ-cạnh; see next paragraph) to the early fourteenth century. Most of these inscriptions are on stelae, but some are on stone or metal (e.g., C 145[116] = Majumdar no. 130, on a silver jug). Most are dated in the Śaka era. They are generally in verse or mixed verse and poetic prose (Bergaigne, 183), though some early records are primarily or exclusively in prose. The great majority record royal dedications or donations to temples and monasteries, especially Śaivite but also sometimes Vaiṣṇava (e.g., C 1 and 136 = Majumdar nos. 121 and 11) and Buddhist (C 66 and 138 = Majumdar nos. 31 and 37).

The Võ-cạnh inscription (C 40 = Majumdar 1) is considered the earliest Sanskrit inscription of Southeast Asia, although its precise dating is a matter of controversy.[117] It is usually placed in the third century.[118]

In style, the Campā inscriptions generally follow the *praśasti* mode, though they are not as impressive as the Cambodian inscriptions. Some characteristic peculiarities of usage have been noted in them, such as *hi* and *sma* in initial position and the optative with preterite sense (Bergaigne, 189 and 220–1). Typical examples of elaborate Campā inscriptions are the two inscriptions on the faces of a stele from Glai Lamau (C 24 = Majumdar 24 a and b), recording in ornate (but not always classically correct) prose and verse King Indravarman I's dedication of an image of Śiva (ins. a) and donations to Śaṅkara-Nārāyaṇa (b).

115. See, e.g., IC I.171, on the date of Suśruta.

116. Inscriptions from Vietnam are conventionally referred to by their number (C = Champa, i.e., Vietnam) in Coedès' *Liste générale des inscriptions du Champa et du Cambodge*; cf. n. 112).

117. See de Casparis, "Palaeography as an Auxiliary Discipline" (ref. in 2.2.5.6 n. 121), 382, and references given there and on 392 n. 13; see also section 5.4.1.

118. The inscribed seals found at Oc-eo (Vietnam) are evidently older, but they were probably made in India and imported to Southeast Asia; see de Casparis, op. cit., 381.

4.3.7.9 Laos

There are a few inscriptions in Indian languages from Laos,[119] mostly Sanskrit records of the Khmer empire from the seventh to the twelfth century A.D. (e.g., K 363, 367). An interesting early record (ca. fifth century) is the Văt Luong Kău inscription of King Devānīka, recording the foundation of a new Kurukṣetra *tīrtha* (K 365). The Sai Fong inscription (K 368) of Jayavarman VII provides a detailed account of the dedication and regulations of a hospital.

Buddhist inscriptions in Pāli occur in the later centuries; see, for example, BEFEO 3, 1903, 660–3 (L. Finot), for inscriptions of about the sixteenth century on votive steles and gold leaves.

4.3.7.10 Malaysia

Indic inscriptions from Malaysia are listed by R. C. Majumdar in "Early Inscriptions in the Malay Peninsula (up to the Fifth Century A.D.)" (Appendix to ch. I.V of *Suvarnadvipa*, 88–90). Some of these inscriptions were published by B. Ch. Chhabra in *Expansion of Indo-Aryan Culture*, 18–26 and 35–6. Reproductions of several of the inscriptions are provided in S. Durai Raja Singam, *India and Malaya Through the Ages (A Pictorial Survey)*, 3d ed. (Kuantan, Malaya, 1954).

Most of the relatively few Indic inscriptions from Malaysia are short Sanskrit records of Buddhistic content on stone, dating from about the fourth to the eighth century, found in the northwestern corner of the country. The most notable among them is the Buddhagupta inscription of about the fifth century (Chhabra 20–6), recording a dedication by a sea captain (*mahānāvika*) from Raktamṛttikā, probably in Bengal (SI I.497 n. 3). Several Buddhist inscriptions have also been found at Kedah.[120]

4.3.7.11 Indonesia

For general reference (but not a complete list) see L.-C. Damais' "Liste des principales inscriptions datées de l'Indonésie" (BEFEO 46, 1952, 1–105). Anthologies of Indonesian inscriptions in general are found in J. G. de Casparis, *Prasasti Indonesia* and B. R. Chatterjee, *India and Java*. Part II: *Inscriptions* [including inscriptions of the Malay Peninsula, Borneo, Java, and Sumatra]. See also the various articles by H. Kern collected in vols. 6 and 7 of his *Verspreide Geschriften*. For Java, see H. B. Sarkar, *Corpus of the Inscriptions of Java*; for Bali, W. F. Stutterheim, *Oudheden van Bali I*.[121]

Sanskrit inscriptions on stone slabs, pillars, images, and other materials are found in good numbers in Indonesia, especially on the island of Java but also on Sumatra, Borneo, and Bali. These inscriptions are mostly written in varieties of late Brāhmī resembling the Pallava script of southern India and in the local scripts (Old Javanese, etc.) derived therefrom; but a few are also in a northeastern Indian script conven-

119. The inscriptions from Laos are generally treated together with those of Cambodia; for sources and references see section 4.3.7.7.

120. See Chhabra, *Expansion of Indo-Aryan Culture*, 18–20, and H. G. Quaritch Wales, *Journal of the Malayan Branch of the Royal Asiatic Society* 18, 1940, 7–10 and 23–4.

121. The Sanskrit inscriptions in Roelof Goris, *Prasasti Bali*. Vol. 1: *Inscripties voor Anak Wungçu*, 108–15, are taken directly from Stutterheim.

tionally referred to as "Pre-Nāgarī"[122] or "Early Nāgarī."[123] A few of the Indonesian inscriptions are bilinguals, consisting of texts in Sanskrit and local languages such as Old Malay and Old Javanese.

Possibly the earliest Indonesian inscriptions are the Kutei (Borneo) Yūpa stone inscriptions of King Mūlavarman (SI I.498–500) of about the early fifth century, though later inscriptions from Borneo are rare.[124]

Of a similar antiquity are the inscriptions of King Pūrṇavarman from western Java.[125] There are several more Sanskrit inscriptions in Java in the middle period, around the eighth and ninth centuries, and a few later ones, mostly Buddhist, from the eleventh to fourteenth centuries.

Sanskrit inscriptions from Sumatra range in date from the seventh or eighth[126] to the fourteenth century. As in Java, most of the later inscriptions are Buddhistic.

A few Sanskrit inscriptions, mostly dating to about the ninth and tenth centuries, have been found on Bali.[127]

4.3.7.12 China

The Kharoṣṭhī documents from Xinjiang were published by A. M. Boyer, E. J. Rapson, and E. Senart in *Kharoṣṭhī Inscriptions Discovered by Sir Aurel Stei* [KI] and translated by T. Burrow in *A Translation of the Kharoṣṭhi Documents from Chinese Turkestan;* see also Burrow's *Language of the Kharoṣṭhi Documents from Chinese Turkestan.*

Archaeological expeditions in Chinese Central Asia (i.e., the region of the Takla Makan Desert in the Xinjiang-Uighur Autonomous Region of the People's Republic of China, formerly referred to as Chinese Turkestan) have yielded, besides a wealth of ancient literary documents in Sanskrit, hundreds of epigraphic and quasi-epigraphic texts in Indic scripts and languages. These materials for the most part are radically different in form and content from epigraphs found in India and elsewhere.

The largest body of material in this category consists of the documents written in Kharoṣṭhī script and in a local variety, sometimes called Niya or Kroraina Prakrit, of northwestern or Gāndhārī Prakrit (3.1.4.2.1). Boyer, Rapson, and Senart published 764 documents from the Niya River, Endere, and Lou-lan sites in KI, and 18 additional texts were subsequently published by J. Brough (BSOS 9, 1937–39, 111–23); in recent years several more documents of this type have come to light.[128] These documents are usually written with ink on wooden or leather tablets.[129] They are mostly official and economic records of about the third century of the local

122. E.g., de Casparis, *Prasasti Indonesia*, II.176.

123. See de Casparis, *Indonesian Palaeography*, 35–7.

124. See Chhabra, *Expansion of Indo-Aryan Culture*, 48–57.

125. See J. Ph. Vogel, "The Earliest Sanskrit Inscriptions of Java."

126. De Casparis, *Prasasti Indonesia*, II.6–10.

127. Stutterheim, *Oudheden van Bali.* See also Stutterheim, "A Newly Discovered Pre-Nāgarī Inscription on Bali," *Acta Orientalia* 12, 1933, 126–32 (but note corrections by L.-C. Damais in BEFEO 44, 1951, 121–8).

128. See R. Salomon, *Bulletin d'Études Indiennes* 4, 1986, 341–51, and *Central Asiatic Journal* 32, 1988, 98–108; Lin Meicun, BSOAS 53, 1990, 283–91.

129. They are thus not "inscriptions" in the strictest sense of the term but are conventionally treated as such; see preface.

kingdom known as Kroraina or Shan-Shan, and provide detailed information about the everyday bureaucratic workings of this kingdom. They thus constitute a body of practical data of a type which is very rare in India itself for the corresponding period.

Other sites in central Asia have yielded various specimens of Indic epigraphic and quasi-epigraphic records in both Kharoṣṭhī and Brāhmī. At Mīrān, for example, there are several short Kharoṣṭhī inscriptions among the wall paintings.[130] Paintings at other cave temple sites such as Qyzyl and Bezeklik are sometimes labeled with Sanskrit inscriptions in central Asian Brāhmī; outstanding examples were found in Bezeklik temple no. 9.[131]

A rare example of an Indian inscription from China proper is the Kharoṣṭhī stone record from the neighborhood of Lo-yang (BSOAS 24, 517–30). Recently, a bronze Buddha with a pedestal inscription in Kharoṣṭhī has also been found at Shifosi in Chang'an county, Shaanxi Province.[132] Inscriptions recording Sanskrit Buddhist *dhāraṇī*s in Siddhamātṛkā and other Indic scripts are found in some numbers in China; an outstanding example is the polyglot inscriptions from Chü Yung Kuan with the *Uṣṇīṣavijaya-* and *Tathāgatahṛdaya-dhāraṇī*s in Lanstsha (Nepali) as well as in Tibetan and four other non-Indic scripts.[133] Several other *dhāraṇī* inscriptions in Siddhamātṛkā on stone, brick, and other materials have been found in Yünnan Province.[134]

4.3.7.13 Egypt

A few records in Indic languages and scripts of about the first or second century A.D., evidently written by Indian traders, have been found in Egypt, including a Prakrit inscription in southern Brāhmī on a potsherd from Quseir (JAOS 111, 731–6). There are also a few fragments of Old Tamil inscriptions from the same site (ibid.).

130. M. A. Stein, *Serindia*, I.529–32. For inscriptions on silk from Mīrān and Lou-lan, see section 4.2.5.6.

131. H. Lüders, *Sitzungsberichte der königlich Preussichen Akademie der Wissenschaften* [Berlin], 1913, 864–84 = *Philologica Indica*, 255–74.

132. Lin Meicun, "A Kharoṣṭhī Inscription from Chang'an," in Li Zheng et al., eds., *Papers in Honour of Prof. Dr. Ji Xianlin*, 119–31.

133. See Jiro Murata, ed., *Chü-Yung-Kuan: The Buddhist Arch of the Fourteenth Century A.D. at the Pass of the Great Wall Northwest of Peking*, 2 vols. (Kyoto: Faculty of Engineering, Kyoto University, 1957).

134. See Walter Liebenthal, *Monumenta Serica* 12, 1947, 1–40; D. C. Sircar, JAIH 3, 1969–70, 36–41; and Oskar von Hinüber, *Journal of the Siam Society* 77, 1989, 55–59. Similar Buddhist ritual inscriptions of Sanskrit *mantra*s or *dhāraṇī*s in Siddhamātṛkā are also found in Japan and other Buddhist countries of East Asia. Ritual inscriptions of Sanskrit *mantra*s in Tibetan script, especially the *oṃ maṇi padme hūṃ* prayer stones, are ubiquitous in Tibet (cf. 4.1.7).

5

Methods of Epigraphic Study

5.1 The Presentation of Inscriptional Texts

5.1.1 Reproduction of the original inscription

Ideally, an epigraphist should study and edit an inscription from the original stone, copper plate, or other surface on which it is written. In practice, however, this is often not practically feasible, so that the editor must rely on some means of reproduction of the original. Of course, even if one does have access to the original, a reproduction should be made for future use and for publication, since a published edition of an inscription should include a good illustration of the original along with the edited transcript, to enable the readers to check the editor's readings.

Such reproductions of inscriptions may be in the form of eye copies, mechanical reproductions, or photographic copies. Of the three methods, the eye copy is obviously the least reliable, in that "the eye-witness is recording not so much what is there as what he thought he saw there."[1] Although eye copies were widely employed in early epigraphic publications[2] such as the early volumes of JASB and the Old Series of ASIR, they are nowadays rarely used for publication purposes except where physical circumstances prevent the preparation of copies by other methods. Eye copies do, however, still have practical value in that they may be prepared in the field to serve as a check or backup for mechanical or photographic reproductions.

Mechanical reproductions usually take the form of "rubbings" of various kinds. (Simple tracings are usually not reliable.) The standard technique in India is to prepare estampages (or "squeezes," as they are known in other fields)[3] by affixing wet paper of a suitable thickness (preferably a high-quality paper especially made for the purpose) to the inscribed object after thorough cleaning and beating it firmly with a brush, thereby preparing a cast of the inscription itself. This is then inked in order to bring out contrast (the field appearing dark, the characters white), and the finished

1. A. G. Woodhead, *The Study of Greek Inscriptions*, 77.

2. See EI 1, 1892, 1.

3. Casts in latex and other substances, sometimes used for the reproduction of inscriptions in other areas of the world (see, e.g., Woodhead, *The Study of Greek Inscriptions*, 80–2), are not generally used in India.

product is photographically reproduced for publication.[4] The advantage of estampages is that they are objective and, if carefully and skillfully prepared, the least subject to distortion of all methods of reproduction. Their chief disadvantage is that it requires considerable skill, time, and material to prepare a good estampage, especially in the case of large inscriptions (such as are common among stone inscriptions in India); this can involve considerable difficulties when, as is often the case, the inscriptions are in situ in remote locations. Rubbings are also not entirely immune to distortion; for instance, it is often difficult to distinguish in an estampage between holes or cracks in the stone and intentionally inscribed marks such as *anusvāra*.

Photographic reproductions are nowadays somewhat more widely used in Indian epigraphic studies than in past decades, often as a supplement to, rather than a substitute for, mechanical reproduction. Producing a high-quality photograph of an inscription requires considerable skill and professional equipment; once again, these are sometimes difficult to bring to bear in the field, where it is also often difficult or impossible to obtain ideal lighting conditions, natural or artificial. Moreover, photographs of inscriptions, even when expertly prepared, are prone to introduce distortions or optical illusions; for example, it may be easier to distinguish a crack in a stone from an engraved line in an estampage than in a photograph. For these reasons, and also because professional photographic equipment may be difficult to obtain, transport, and use in India, photography remains a secondary method. Ideally, though, an epigraphist would want to prepare both mechanical and photographic reproductions of an inscription, as well as an eye copy, each acting as a check on the other.

5.1.2 Presentation of the edited text

Indic inscriptions are normally published with a transcribed or transliterated text, either in Roman characters or in one of the modern Indian scripts. Of the latter, Devanāgarī is the standard (except for publications in various regional languages) for Sanskrit and Sanskritic inscriptions, while Dravidian inscriptions are usually published in Roman transliteration or in the modern form of the script used for the language of the inscription (or sometimes in both, as in *Epigraphia Carnatica*).

The system of Roman transliteration generally used for archaeological and epigraphic publications in India[5] (e.g., in *Epigraphia Indica* and *Corpus Inscriptionum Indicarum*) is essentially the Indian variety (with *ṛi* and *ṛī* instead of *ṛ* and *ṝ*, *ch* and *chh* for *c* and *ch*, and *sh* for *ṣ*) of the standard modern system for Sanskrit and related languages. Special features of this epigraphic transliteration system are that the Sanskrit vowels *e* and *o* are normally noted as long (*ē, ō*),[6] and that special symbols for

4. IC I.156–7; [Jas. Burgess], "On Copying Inscriptions," IA 2, 1873, 183–7.

5. In this book, as in epigraphic studies published in the West generally, the standard modern European transliteration system for general Indology has been followed, rather than the epigraphically modified Indian system.

6. This is done because the system is intended to serve not only for Indo-Aryan but also for Dravidian inscriptions, in which *e* and *o* are sometimes graphically distinguished for length. The distinction is, however, superfluous for Sanskritic inscriptions; thus, e.g., Sircar disregards it in SI (I.xvi).

the *jihvāmūlīya* and *upadhmānīya* varieties of *visarga* (*ẖ*, *ẖ*) are used when represented as such in Sanskrit inscriptions.[7]

Punctuation marks, insofar as they are present in the original inscription (see 2.5.2.3), should be reproduced in the transcript. But punctuation is often minimal or even wholly absent, so that editors commonly add appropriate punctuation marks of their own to facilitate reading. This is done especially in versified texts where caesurae and verse endings are unmarked; in such cases appropriate punctuation is added with some indication, normally square brackets plus asterisk, that they are absent in the original. Verse numbers, when not present in the original, may be added in the same way.

It is also common practice to introduce certain other forms of punctuation not in the original to facilitate reading; thus a single hyphen (-) is often used to separate members of a compound word, while a double horizontal line (=) denotes characters which belong to different words but which are joined in one *akṣara* according to orthographic and/or sandhi rules in the original inscription (e.g., *dharmma-setur=nṛpāṇām*). The latter device is peculiar to epigraphic publications, where a faithful reproduction of the original orthography is desirable for paleographic studies.[8]

In addition to the introduction of punctuation, editors often see fit to regularize and correct the text to a greater or lesser extent. Inscriptions often contain more or less obvious scribal errors, and these are corrected, in the standard transliteration scheme of the EI and CII, by adding the correct *akṣara* in parentheses after the wrong one (e.g., *anumattā(ntā)*). A less obvious emendation may be indicated in parentheses with a question mark. *Akṣaras* which are damaged or worn but can be read with reasonable certainty are indicated in square brackets; if the reading is doubtful, a question mark is added. Letters which are wholly lost or which were omitted by the scribe, but which can be conjecturally supplied, are inserted in square brackets with an asterisk.[9]

In addition to such more or less mandatory corrections, many editors also choose to correct or regularize minor orthographic variations which are common in inscriptions (see 3.3.8.1), such as the writing of double consonants for single or vice versa (e.g., *patra(ttra)*), *ṅ* for *anusvāra* before sibilants (e.g., *vaṅśa(ṃśa)*), *anusvāra* for final *m* in pausa, confusions between *ś* and *s*, nonapplication of external sandhi, and so on. In such cases, however, a degree of caution is advisable, as the editor runs the risk of engaging in hypercorrection by applying to old inscriptions strict orthographic standards which have actually developed only in relatively recent times in connection with the printing of Sanskrit texts. In addition, the extensive correction of minor variants tends to burden the text with dozens or even hundreds of trivial corrections or footnotes. More importantly, hypercorrection when carried to extremes can actually distort linguistic and paleographic data.[10] All things considered, the editor of an in-

7. For Dravidian inscriptions, the following additional symbols are also used: *r̤* and *n̤* for the alveolars (= ṟ and ṉ in nonepigraphic standard transcription); *l̤* for the retroflex frictionless continuant (ழ; *r̤* or *ḻ* in nonepigraphic transcription); and *ḷ* for "retroflex" *l*. (The latter is also used occasionally in Sanskritic inscriptions, where it appears as a dialectal variant for *l*; see 3.3.8.1.)

8. Cf. the comments by Fleet in CII 3, intro., 194.

9. Sircar, in SI I.xv, proposes to distinguish the two cases by indicating lost syllables with [*] and scribally omitted ones with (*).

10. See RIE 44–8, and section 3.3.8.4.

scription must give careful thought to the degree of correction and standardization to be imposed on an inscriptional text, and when in doubt should leave the text as it stands.

5.2 Translation and Interpretation of Inscriptions

Ideally, the published edition of an inscription should include a translation into an appropriate modern language, though this is by no means always done. In the case of long and highly formulaic or repetitive texts, it may be appropriate to compile a summary or abstract of the contents rather than a complete translation.

For several reasons, inscriptions present special problems and difficulties of interpretation over and above those usually encountered in Indic texts. Their language, first of all, is frequently nonstandard in various respects. The earlier inscriptions are in MIA dialects which diverge in varying degrees from the Prakrits known from literary and grammatical sources, and they exhibit all of the troublesome peculiarities of orthography and morphology characteristic of archaic and nonstandardized languages. Not untypical in this respect are the Aśokan inscriptions, in which several problematic passages still remain to be satisfactorily explained. Later inscriptions, mostly in Sanskrit, present problems of their own. Many of them are composed in ornate *kāvya* style, which has to be read in archaic scripts and without benefit of commentaries; the interpretation of such texts, too, is not always free from doubt, and requires a high level of expertise in Sanskrit literature as well as in epigraphy.

An even more serious difficulty, which applies in varying degrees to most inscriptions, is the peculiar vocabulary, comprising an extensive body of special technical terminology peculiar to inscriptions (especially to land grants and other quasi-legal documents) which is largely unattested elsewhere in Sanskrit literature. However, thanks to the labors of many scholars over the years, and especially to the compilations by Sircar in IEG and in SIE (327–434), such technical terms are now largely though by no means completely understood.[11] Words from archaic vernacular languages, not always easily understood, are also commonly inserted in Sanskrit inscriptions (cf. RIE 49). Abbreviations of various technical terms, sometimes obscure, are also common (see 2.5.2.3).

Besides the linguistic, orthographic, and stylistic problems, the translator of an inscription is often faced with the difficulties of interpreting worn or fragmentary inscriptions. A great many Indic inscriptions, including several of particular historical importance, are poorly preserved, often to the degree that readings and interpretations become a matter of uncertainty and controversy. A notable case is the Hāthīgumphā inscription of Khāravela, whose linguistic obscurities and badly worn condition have produced widely differing interpretations entailing significant historical consequences.[12]

In addition to the requisite persistence and intuition, the interpretation of incomplete or otherwise problematic texts can be facilitated by a comparative approach.

11. See also sections 3.3.8.4 and 7.5.

12. For example, an earlier interpretation (now discredited) of this inscription led some historians to believe in a nonexistent "Mauryan era"; see section 5.5.1.17.

Because inscriptional texts tend, to a greater or lesser degree, to be formulaic and stereotyped, missing or uncertain sections of one inscription can often be clarified or reconstructed by comparisons with related inscriptions of similar content. Although this method is time-consuming and difficult, especially in view of the overall inadequacy of reference sources available for epigraphic work, it is almost always rewarding and worth the effort. Indeed, it can be said that as a rule no one inscription can be adequately studied without reference to several, or often many, others (though by no means have all editors been sufficiently diligent in following this rule).

Some recent preliminary studies have indicated that the reconstruction of damaged inscriptions can be significantly aided by the use of computerized techniques of image enhancement such as thresholding, averaging, line detecting, and so forth.[13] (For preliminary reports on the use of computers for the compilation of statistical data from inscriptions, see S. K. Havanur, "Analysis of Inscriptional Data Through Computer," JESI 14, 1987, 50–5; and Riccardo Garbini, "Software Development in Epigraphy: Some Preliminary Remarks," JESI 19, 1993, 63–79. Though potentially promising, such techniques have not yet been widely put into practice.)

5.3 Authentication of Inscriptions

J. F. Fleet, "Spurious Indian Records," IA 30, 1901, 201–23; D. C. Sircar, "Spurious Epigraphs," SIE 435–9 (Appendix I).

In examining a new inscription, an editor should always consider the possibility that it may be spurious; for forgeries and other spurious texts,[14] both ancient and modern, are not at all rare among Indian inscriptions, especially copper plate charters. References to forged inscriptions occur both in inscriptions themselves (as discussed later in this section) and in Sanskrit literature. Various law books, such as the *Manusmṛti* (9.232) and *Viṣṇu-smṛti* (5.9) prescribe the death penalty for "forgers of royal orders" (*kūṭaśāsanakartṝṃś ca rājā hanyād,* Viṣṇu); here *śāsana* refers to copper plates as well as to ordinary documents.[15]

Modern forgeries are occasionally produced for motives of financial profit; Sircar (SIE 436–9) notes some recent cases of forged Aśokan and Kharoṣṭhī inscriptions in India, and other forgeries of Kharoṣṭhī inscriptions have been produced in Pakistan. In the nineteenth century, too, several forgeries were exposed, intended either as historical hoaxes (Fleet, 203 and 208) or, like most of the ancient forgeries, to support fraudulent claims to ownership of land.[16]

Much more common are the ancient forgeries, of which the great majority are copper plates. This is hardly surprising in view of their function as land deeds and of

13. See Gift Siromoney, "Computer Techniques of Image Enhancement in the Study of a Pallava Grantha Inscription," *Studies in Indian Epigraphy* [= JESI] 2, 1976, 55–8; and Gift Siromoney, R. Chandrasekaran, and M. Chandrasekaran, "Machine Recognition of an Ancient Tamil Script of the Chola Period," JESI 6, 1979, 18–9.

14. The term "spurious" refers both to inscriptions which were copied or reproduced for more or less innocent motives and to outright forgeries.

15. Nandapaṇḍita on *Viṣṇu* 5.9; P. V. Kane, *History of Dharmaśāstra* vol. 2, pt. 2, 867.

16. E.g., EI 6, 1900–1, 58; EI 9, 1907–8, 294–5.

the relative ease with which they could be forged (Fleet, 211–2). Dozens of cases of forged, spurious, or altered copper plate inscriptions have been authoritatively identified; Fleet's list (214–23) contains fifty-nine instances, and many more could now be added. Such spurious documents are most common in southern India, especially in southern Karnataka (Fleet 212; Sircar 435). Copper plates of certain southern dynasties, particularly the Cālukyas, Western Gaṅgas, and the Vijayanagara kings were particularly subject to forgery. Although most of the spurious inscriptions come from the medieval period, earlier examples are also known. The Rāwal Kharoṣṭhī inscription is, according to Konow's interpretation (CII 2.2, 162), a well-intentioned if incompetent copy of an authentic inscription from Shakardarra (CII 2.1, 159–60). Two copper plate inscriptions from Nālandā and Gayā (SI I.270–4), purporting to belong to the reign of Samudragupta (fourth century A.D.), are generally regarded as forgeries made in later centuries to replace the lost authentic originals.

The claims to proprietorship of land which motivated most forgeries may have been in some cases entirely fraudulent, but more often the spurious documents were probably drawn up in order to replace originals that had been lost, destroyed, or stolen. Of the former type we have interesting testimony in the Tārācaṇḍī rock inscription of A.D. 1169 (EI 34, 23–7), whose purpose is to declare null and void a spurious copper plate charter (*kutāmvram* [*sic*]) issued by a servant of the Gāhaḍavāla king Vijayacandra, who had been bribed by the ever-greedy Brahmans (*sarvvathā lampaṭā amī dvijāḥ*) of Suvarṇṇahala.[17] Interestingly enough, the original forged charter referred to in the Tārācaṇḍī inscription was subsequently discovered and published (Sūnahar grant, EI 35, 153–8; see also SIE 435). Like many of its kind, it proved to be a rather crude forgery whose blatant grammatical and graphic incompetence make it no surprise that it was exposed within three years of its production.

The practice of manufacturing new grants as substitutes for lost originals is attested by authorized reissues of original copper plate charters which had been lost (usually by fire). One example is the Nidhanpur plates (EI 12, 65–79), which conclude with a verse certifying the new document as an officially authorized replacement.[18] Similarly, the Kurud plates (EI 31, 263–8) were duly issued to replace an original written on palm leaves (*tāla-patra-śāsana-*, l. 6) which was destroyed in a house fire. More commonly, however, the replacement grants are more or less amateurish imitations by the owners themselves attempting, often with little success, to duplicate the language and script of the original. There are also a fair number of instances in which genuine documents have been altered, often in a shockingly clumsy manner, in order to change the terms of the grant. In the Paiṭhān plates, for example (EI 3, 103–13), the names of the donees have been altered and their number reduced from seven to four (ll. 47–54). In the Sāmangaḍ plates (IA 11, 108–15), the names of the granted village and the neighboring villages have been similarly altered (see 112 n. 14).

17. Note also the case of the Madhuban copper plate of Harṣa (EI I, 67–75), which was issued to supersede a spurious grant (l. 10, *kūṭaśāsanena bhuktaka iti vicārya yatas tacchāsanaṃ bhaṅktvā* . . .).

18. *Śāsanadāhād arvāg abhinavalikhitāni bhinnarūpāṇi / tebhyo a*[*sic*]*kṣarāṇi yasmāt tasmān naitāni kūṭāni //* ("Because after the burning of the plates, these newly written letters are of different form [from those of the previous inscription], they are not forged" [Bhattacharya's translation]).

Spurious grants can usually be detected by the presence of various kinds of anomalies and anachronisms: paleographic and orthographic, linguistic and stylistic, historical, or calendrical (Fleet, 202–3 and 209–11). The most obvious mark of a spurious record is paleographic characteristics which are incompatible with the ostensible date of the record. Although paleographic dating is far from a precise technique (see 5.4.1), in many cases the script is so obviously inappropriate as to raise serious doubts, as in the case of a Western Gaṅga charter from Tañjāvur (Tanjore) dated Śaka 169 = A.D. 248, whose script according to Fleet (EI 3, 161) belongs to the tenth century. In some cases the forger may attempt to imitate archaic script forms, but such efforts are usually fairly transparent. Gross incompetence in orthography (though it sometimes appears in legitimate records) may also be an indication of spuriousness, as in the case of the forged Sūnahar grant of Vijayacandra discussed previously, whose orthography is so poor as to render it nearly incomprehensible in places (EI 35, 153–4).

Anachronistic linguistic usages or a gross lack of control of the language of the document, as in the aforementioned Sūnahar grant, may also be grounds for suspicion (Fleet, 203), as are peculiarities or inconsistencies of style, such as the use of titles which are inappropriate or unfamiliar for a given ruler, for example, the title *paramabhāgavata* applied to Samudragupta in the Nālandā plate (SI I.270 n. 4). Syntactic inconsistencies which may indicate the copying of passages from other texts are likewise suspicious; for instance, in the same record, the titles of Samudragupta are given in the genitive while his name is in the nominative (SI I.270 n. 3), suggesting that the epithets had been copied onto the spurious grant from a record of one of Samudragupta's successors.

Historical anomalies may be so blatant as to prove an inscription to be a forgery, as in the case of four grants purporting to be issued by the legendary king Janamejaya (Fleet, 206 and 219–21). Historical fabrications were, of course, not always so clumsy, but more subtle efforts may also be exposed when, for instance, they provide incorrect or impossible dates for known historical figures.

Details of the dating often provide the most reliable grounds for doubting the authenticity of an inscription. Besides historically inadmissible dates of the types already mentioned, weekdays or astronomical data such as eclipses which prove incorrect when checked by calculation are the commonest reason for such suspicions. The incorrect or anachronistic use of particular eras or dating systems similarly provides a clue to a spurious document (see 5.4.3.2).

It should be stressed, however, that no one of these defects necessarily proves in and of itself that an inscription is spurious. A date which cannot be verified by calculation is not necessarily unauthentic, as the many varieties and complexities of Indian calendrical reckoning frequently cause unaccountable irregularities; or the irregularity may be simply due to innocent errors in calculation by the original framers of the document (see SIE 226–8, and section 5.4.3.2).[19] It is only when a combination of these suspicious characteristics is present, or when one or more of them are

19. Conversely, a verifiable date does not necessarily prove that an inscription is genuine, since a correct date from an authentic document may be copied into a forgery; or even, conceivably, the forgers might have gone to the trouble of calculating the correct date. For examples of spurious inscriptions with regular dates, see Kielhorn, IA 24, 1895, 9–10 (= KS II.687–8).

found in blatant form, that an editor can confidently dismiss an inscription as spurious. Thus, while many cases of spurious inscriptions are definite or at least can be established beyond reasonable doubt, there are quite a few records whose authenticity remains a matter of controversy. This tends to be the case particularly among inscriptions of those dynasties for which several definite cases of forgery have been established, thus casting suspicion on other records of the same dynasty. The copper plates of the Western Gaṅgas provide a striking example. They were in years past the subject of a heated controversy between Fleet, who considered many of them forgeries, and Lewis Rice, who maintained their authenticity; and while it is now beyond question that Fleet was correct that at least some of them were spurious, K. V. Ramesh warns in his recent edition of the Western Gaṅga inscriptions that Fleet "was too drastic in condemning outright most of them as forgeries or spurious," and opines that the final decision in some cases may have to be a matter of "intuitive feeling."[20]

It should be kept in mind, finally, that spurious inscriptions are not necessarily devoid of historical value or interest. Since most of them are genuinely ancient (if not as ancient as they claim to be), they may well contain at least partially valid historical information especially when, as is often the case, they are more or less faithful (if incompetent) attempts at reproducing a valid original. For example, the dates 5 and 9 given in the spurious copper plates of Samudragupta are taken by some historians as indicating that he, and not Candragupta I, was the founder of the Gupta era (SI 270–1 n. 4; cf. 5.5.1.6). Moreover, even if the dates of the inscriptions themselves cannot be trusted, the historical material presented in them by way of genealogical and eulogistic preamble is usually unaltered from the original; in Fleet's words, "[T]here are . . . no general grounds for assuming any deliberate falsification of such items of real history" (206). For these reasons, then, spurious ancient inscriptions—as opposed to modern forgeries—are normally felt to be legitimate objects of scholarly study and worthy of publication in the usual channels (with, of course, due attention being called to their spuriousness).

5.4 Dating of Inscriptions

5.4.1 Undated or inadequately dated inscriptions; paleographic dating and problems thereof

K. V. Ramesh, "The [F*]utility and (F)utility of Palaeography in Dating Undated Inscriptions," *Studies in Indian Epigraphy* [=JESI] 3, 156–62; RIE 51–62 (ch. V: "Scriptal Ramifications and Palaeographical Dating of Undated Inscriptions," a revised and expanded version of the preceding).

In the cases—all too frequent, especially among earlier inscriptions—where a record has no explicit date, or only a date whose absolute value cannot be definitely ascertained, epigraphists must resort to estimating the date on the basis of paleographic analysis by comparing the script of the undated record with specimens of similar scripts from other dated or datable inscriptions. Because this method is inherently

20. *Inscriptions of the Western Gangas*, xix n. 1.

imprecise, paleographic dating should in general be treated as a last resort. Other dating techniques, such as historical analysis based on references to persons or events of known date, or chronological analysis based on linguistic or archaeological data, may supersede or be used in conjunction with paleographic estimates. But the fact remains that, since so many inscriptions are undated or inadequately dated, paleographic dating, imperfect as it may be, must be employed in a great many cases.

The inherent imprecision of this method alluded to earlier is due mainly to the variability in writing styles and forms at any given place and time in history. Though it is true that in the long run scripts, like languages, follow more or less consistent courses of development, this does not mean that at any given time and place one and only one form of a script is in use. On the contrary, there will always be a variety of script forms for different contexts and purposes in simultaneous use in any particular place; and the stage and pace of development will by no means always be the same in different, even adjoining regions. Individual and idiosyncratic variations must also be kept in mind; for example, in the past, as in modern times, an older person tended to write in a more old-fashioned style than a younger contemporary.[21] But despite these and other limiting factors, it has often been the practice to assign relatively precise dates to undated inscriptions on the basis of simple paleographic comparisons, which are sometimes chosen arbitrarily and evaluated in a superficial manner.

Given the relatively undeveloped state of comparative paleography in India, as well as the inherent limitations of the method, it will not be surprising that the results obtained are often unsatisfactory. Any number of instances could be cited where widely varying dates have been proposed by reputable scholars for the same inscription. For instance, the undated Võ-cạnh inscription, the earliest Sanskrit inscription from Southeast Asia (see 4.3.7.8), has been dated on paleographic grounds to anywhere from the third to the fifth century A.D.[22] The situation is hardly any better in the case of inscriptions with dates in regnal years of unknown rulers or in unspecified eras. The year 30 of an unspecified era in the Muṇḍeśvarī inscription of the time of Udayasena, for example, was attributed by R. D. Banerji (EI 9, 285 and 290) to the Harṣa era, equivalent to A.D. 635, while N. G. Majumdar (IA 49, 25) assigned it to the Gupta era and dated the inscription to A.D. 348–49.[23] Ramesh (RIE 55–7) cites several other cases where dates for a given inscription arrived at by paleographic estimate vary by two centuries or more. The problem is particularly acute in connection with the dating of the earliest inscriptions (other than those of Aśoka), where, due to the paucity and brevity of the materials, all undated, it is all but impossible to establish a convincing relative, let alone absolute, sequence for paleographic dating. Moreover, given the inherent flexibility of paleographic dating, there is often a temptation (not always resisted) to manipulate it in order to

21. Cf. Woodhead, *The Study of Greek Inscriptions*, 29 and 62–3. The limitations of paleographic dating are by no means peculiar to India but rather constitute a general principle of paleographic studies.

22. See 4.3.7.8 and references given there in n. 117; see esp. Kamaleshwar Bhattacharya, *Artibus Asiae* 24, 1961, 219–24.

23. See also more recently G. S. Gai in IEBHA 129–31, who would place the inscription in the early to middle sixth century.

confirm a preconceived notion of an inscription's date or to prove some historical argument (cf. RIE 55).

The dating of inscriptions by paleographic estimate alone is thus an approximate method at best, even as carried out by reputed experts in the field. In recent years a few scholars, notably Ramesh and A. H. Dani in his *Indian Palaeography*, have attempted to refine our knowledge of the regional, local, and stylistic subvarieties of the various Indian scripts. Ramesh has emphasized the importance of distinguishing "settled and stylized 'urban' writing" from "'rural' or rustic paleography" (RIE 58–9; cf. JESI 3, 157–61). Inscriptions in the latter style, according to Ramesh, tend to appear to be later in date than contemporary records in more formal writing.[24] He therefore concludes (RIE 62; cf. JESI 3, 161–2) that in estimating the date of an inscription on paleographic grounds one must take into consideration first of all the nature of the writing, whether "urban" or "rural," and make suitable adjustments; and second, one must also keep in mind considerations of "dynastic, regional or religious influence" on the relative speed or conservatism in paleographic developments. Finally, he declares, "Where palaeography is the lone consideration in suggesting a date for an early inscription which contains no other sort of supplementary internal evidence, the suggested date must always be taken to represent the date so suggested + or –100 years" (ibid.) The examples cited above of widely differing dates for particular inscriptions would seem to confirm this rule, since the estimates tend to vary over a range of roughly two hundred years.

Dani, too, has emphasized the limitations of paleographic dating, warning against the common practice of relying on one or a few "test letters" for paleographic dating, since "we must allow a margin for the transition period in which the new and old forms were used simultaneously" (DIP, 132). Paleographic dating "can never supply infallible dates" (ix); "this is too much to expect from palaeography" (11).

Thus while it is true that in certain cases, where a relatively large and cohesive body of securely dated material is available for comparison, a somewhat higher level of precision may be attainable, as a general rule of thumb it would be wise to adopt Ramesh's principle of plus or minus one hundred years for the range of accuracy of paleographic dating. In the past many epigraphists have paleographically dated inscriptions to a range as short as a quarter of a century, but such precise claims should not be uncritically accepted.

5.4.2 Dated inscriptions

Inscriptions may be dated in any number of ways, ranging from a simple year date (regnal or era) to detailed specifications of the year, month, *tithi* (lunar day), weekday, and/or other calendrical and astronomical data. From the point of view of epigraphic methodology, it is convenient to discuss the systems of year dating and those of more specific dates separately.

24. Chronological illusions created by differences between formal and informal styles are also by no means peculiar to India; see Woodhead, *The Study of Greek Inscriptions*, 64.

5.4.2.1 Year dates

5.4.2.1.1 Regnal years The practice of dating records in the regnal years[25] of a king, as opposed to years of a continuous era, was widespread in early centuries throughout India, beginning with the inscriptions of Aśoka. In the early centuries of the Christian era several dynasties such as the Sātavāhanas, Ikṣvākus, and Vākāṭakas continued to record only regnal years in their inscriptions, and in the medieval period the Pālas and some other eastern dynasties and the Pallavas, Coḷas, and Pāṇḍyas in the south still used regnal years exclusively or primarily.

A typical simple formulation of a regnal year date would contain the ruler's name and titles in the genitive case with a word for 'year' in the locative, such as *saṃvatsare* (often abbreviated *saṃvat* or *saṃ*) or less commonly *varṣe* (or their Prakrit equivalents), plus the date in words, numerical figures, or both; for example, *ūdākasa dasama-savachare*, "in the tenth year of Ūdāka," in the Pabhosā cave inscription (SI I.95–7).[26] More elaborate formulae, particularly in Sanskrit verse inscriptions, may involve other constructions such as the locative absolute, as in the Eraṇ boar inscription of Toramāṇa (SI I.420–2): *varṣe prathame pṛthivīm pṛthukīrttau pṛthudyutau / mahārājādhirāja-śrī-Toramāṇe praśāsati* . . . ("While the Great King of Kings, the Illustrious Toramāṇa of vast fame and glory was ruling the Earth, in (his) first year . . ."). Further details of the date such as month, *tithi*, weekday, and so on, may or may not be included with the regnal year (see 5.4.2.2).[27]

Unless, as is occasionally the case, such regnal dates are accompanied by a second date in an established era, they do not by themselves provide an absolute date for the record. Such regnally dated inscriptions must therefore be subjected to the same techniques of dating by paleographic or other methods as are applied to undated inscriptions. It is often possible, however, to establish approximate or occasionally even exact values for such dates by means of historical synchronizations for the rulers concerned. Thus in the case of the regnally dated Aśokan inscriptions, rea-

25. The precise calendrical significance of a "regnal year" is not always completely clear. That is to say, we do not always know on exactly what date or occasion (accession to the throne, formal coronation, etc.) the regnal year began, and how this regnal year was correlated with the current calendrical year. In some cases, this seems to have produced calendrical complications; see, e.g., the cases noted in "Regnal Years" (IA 39, 1910, 217–24), and below in connection with the Cālukya-Vikrama era (5.5.1.13).

26. Unusual types of early regnal dates include the Bhārhut pillar inscription (CII 2.2, 11–12) dated only "during the reign of the Śuṅgas" (*suganaṃ raje*) without a specific year, and the Hāthīgumphā inscription (SI I.213–21) which chronicles the king's reign year by year (*padhame vase . . . dutiye ca vase . . . tatiye puna vase . . .*, etc.).

27. Some medieval and later records from Orissa recorded regnal years counted according to the *aṅka* system in which the first year and all years whose unit figure is 6 or 0, except for 10, are skipped over (i.e., the years 1, 6, 16, 20, 26, etc.); see IA 19, 1890, 255–6, and Monmohan Chakravarti, JASB 72, part 1, 1903, 100. Thus, e.g., a period enumerated as twenty-five regnal years according to the *aṅka* system corresponds to only twenty-one normal years (EI 28, 1949–50, 242). There were evidently several variations of this system, which is sometimes said to be based on a sixty-year cycle; see further G. Ramadas, JBORS 17, 1931, 179–80; R. Subrahmanyam, *Inscriptions of the Sūryavaṃśi Gajapatis of Orissa*, xxxi–ii; and A. K. Bhattacharyya, *A Corpus of Dedicatory Inscriptions from Temples of West Bengal*, Appendix B, 190–1.

sonably accurate absolute dates have been established by the synchronization of Aśoka's regnal years with the contemporary Greek kings to whom he refers in his rock edict XIII (see 4.3.1.1 and 7.1.1.1). Among the regnally dated inscriptions of various dynasties of the early Christian era and later, we often have a fair number of records of successive rulers on the basis of which a dynastic succession list can be drawn up. The relative chronology of the dynasty can then often be correlated with known absolute dates; thus the regnal dates of the Vākāṭakas can be established with fair precision on the basis of their relations with the Guptas, and the Pālas can be approximately dated by their interactions with the Gurjara-Pratīhāras and Rāṣṭrakūṭas. (In each of these cases, of course, the latter-mentioned dynasty dated its records in known historical eras.) Even where such historical synchronizations are not available, paleographic dating may be applied as a supplementary technique, and when we have a sequence of regnally dated records of a particular dynasty this method is considerably more reliable than when applied to a single record or a few isolated records.

In this way, regnally dated inscriptions can often be ascribed absolute dates with relative precision, at least as compared to undated inscriptions. The chronological reconstruction of a dynasty from regnally dated records is of course still only approximative, as the period of reign for each king can be given only as a minimum, based on the highest regnal date preserved for him in known inscriptions; the actual time of his rule, assumed to be as great as, or more likely greater than, this figure, can only be estimated (cf. 7.1.1.1).

5.4.2.1.2 Years of an era. Beginning in the first century B.C. some inscriptions were dated in continuous eras.[28] This system gradually became more prevalent and was the standard practice in most regions by the early centuries of the medieval era. These continuous or historical eras evidently arose as continuations or extensions of a regnal reckoning of a given king by his successors, who instead of beginning a new reckoning commencing from their own accessions continued counting years from the previous king's dates (SIE 242–3). This development is explicitly indicated in the Mathurā pillar inscription (SI I.277–9) dated in the fifth regnal year of Candragupta II (. . . *śrīcandraguptasya vija(*ya)-rājya-saṃvatsa(*re) paṃcame 5*) and in the sixty-first year of the "continued reckoning" (*kālānuvarttamāna-saṃvatsare ekaṣaṣṭhe* [*sic*] *60 1*), that is, of the Gupta era (5.5.1.6).[29] Such an extended regnal-year system would then become a dynastic reckoning, and this in turn would often continue in use, sometimes with a change of name, long after the founding dynasty had fallen.[30]

28. Systems of continuous historical reckoning seem not to have been an indigenous Indian notion, as the earliest genuine historical eras were founded by foreign rulers. But once established, such systems were initiated by many later dynasties of Indian origin (SIE 235–50).

29. Cf. also a similar dating formula in a newly discovered inscription of [Gupta] year 121 from Mathurā (Govindnagar): *saṃvatsaraśate ekaviṃśottaraśate* [*sic*] *100 20 1 kālānuvarttamānasaṃvatsare* . . . (EI 40, 1973–74, 20–2).

30. See the various examples discussed in section 5.5, particularly the Vikrama and Śaka eras (5.5.1.3 and 5.5.1.4).

The name of the era is often but by no means always explicitly noted. In the early dates of a given era, the name was often omitted, it being understood that the date referred to the currently ruling king or dynasty. In later centuries, too, the name of the era was frequently left out, presumably since the prevalent era at a given time or place was a matter of common knowledge. But as noted earlier (5.4.1), unspecified eras can present serious problems for the modern interpreter.

The date of an era may be given in numerical figures, words, or both. In verse inscriptions, especially from later centuries, it was a common practice to give the date in the form of a chronogram (*bhūtasaṃkhyā*), with the digits expressed by words for items associated with particular numbers. The suggested numbers are to be read in reverse order[31] (according to the principle *aṅkānāṃ vāmato gatiḥ*, "numerals run leftward") with an understood place value notation; that is to say, the first word in the chronogram gives the units digit, the second the tens, and so forth. For example, in an inscription from Kalna, the date is given by the chronogram *vāṇa-vyoma-dharādhar-endu-gaṇite śāke*, "In the Śaka year enumerated by the arrows [5], the sky [0], mountains [7], and the moon [1]," that is, in Śaka 1705 = A.D. 1783. Lists of the words used with numerical significance are to be found in SIE 230–3, Kane, *History of Dharmaśāstra* vol. 5 pt.1, 701–3, and BIP 84–6.[32]

Combinations of regnal and era years are not uncommon. An important early instance is the Takht-i-bāhī inscription of the time of Gondophernes (SI I.125–6), dated in his regnal year (*vaṣa*) 26 and the year 103 of an unspecified era (*saṃbatsarae*), presumably the Azes/Vikrama. Such combined dates can be of great historical value in establishing absolute chronologies.

Inscriptions dated in two or more different eras are also common, especially among later inscriptions. Such dates include combinations of historical eras such as the Vikrama and Śaka;[33] of historical and astronomical eras, as in the Aihoḷe inscription (SI II.443–50) dated in Kaliyuga era 3735 and Śaka 556 = A.D. 634/35; or of historical and cyclical years, as in the inscriptions of the Parivrājaka kings (CII 3, 93–116) dated in the Gupta era and in the twelve-year cycle of Jupiter (5.5.2.2). The sixty-year cycle of Jupiter (5.5.2.3) is very frequently combined with the Śaka era dates in inscriptions of southern dynasties; see Kielhorn, IA 25, 1896, 268–70 = KS II.729–31. An exceptional case of multiple dating is the Verāval stone inscription (SI II.402–8) dated in four eras, the Hijrī (Islamic era), Vikrama, Valabhī, and Siṃha.

For information on these and other eras used in Indic inscriptions, see section 5.5.

31. Occasionally, however, chronograms are intended to be read in normal order; see, e.g., EI 34, 1960–61, 178.

32. In some later southern Indian inscriptions, chronograms were composed according to the *katapayādi* system, in which the consonants *ka* to *ña* had the numerical values 1 to 0 (*ka* = 1, *kha* = 2, . . . *jh* = 9, *ña* = 0), *ṭa* through *na* again 1 to 0, *pa* through *ma* 1 to 5, and *ya* through *ha* 1 to 8 (sometimes also *ḷa* = 9); see BIP 86–7, SIE 222 and 234, and BPLM 123). Such *katapayādi* chronograms follow the usual right-to-left principle; vowels have no value, and only the last consonant in a conjunct is counted. Thus, e.g., *Śālivāhaśake* . . . *dāsavandya-mite* in the Honnehaḷḷi inscription (EI 34, 205–6) represents Śaka 1478 (*ya* = 1, *va* = 4, *sa* = 7, and *da* = 8. For other examples, see EI 3, 1894–95, 38, ll. 40–41; EI 4, 1896–97, 203–4, etc.

33. For examples, see Kielhorn, IA 20, 1891, 410 = KS II.608.

5.4.2.2 Specific dates

Beginning in the last two centuries B.C., the practice of recording dates by the day as well as year gradually came into use. The earliest examples, mostly in inscriptions of Indo-Greek and Indo-Scythian kings, usually give a (regnal) year, month, and day of the month.[34] The Shinkoṭ reliquary inscriptions of the time of Menander and Vijayamitra (SI I.105, l. 2), for example, contain the date *vaṣaye paṃcamaye 4 1 veśrakhasa masasa divasa paṃcaviśraye*, "In the fifth (5) [regnal] year [of Vijayamitra], twenty-fifth day of the month Vaiśākha." Several inscriptions from this period use Macedonian rather than Indian months; the Sui Vihār inscription of the eleventh year of Kaniṣka, for example (SI I.139, l. 1), is dated on the twenty-eighth day of *daïsiṃka masa*, that is, of Daisios.[35]

Some inscriptions of the first to fifth centuries A.D., mostly Śaka and Kuṣāṇa inscriptions in Brāhmī from the Mathurā region, are dated in year (regnal or era), season (*grīṣma*, *varṣā*, or *hemanta*), number of the month in the season, and day of the month. For instance, the Mathurā Jaina image inscription of the time of Huviṣka (SI I.155–6) is dated *savasare 40 4 . . . gṛṣyamasa* [= *grīṣmamāsa*] *3 divasa 2*, "In the year 44, month 3 of summer, day 2." Pingree describes this system as "an amalgamation of the Indian tradition of three seasons (*ṛtus*) . . . with the northwestern tradition of counting twenty-nine or thirty days in each month" (op. cit., 357).[36]

Inscriptions of approximately the same period from the Deccan, the south, and the northeast are usually dated by year, season, number of the lunar fortnight (*pakṣa*) [rather than month] within the season, and day of the fortnight. For example, the Kārle cave inscription of the Sātavāhana king Vāsiṣṭhīputra Puḷumāvi (SI I.210) is dated *savachare catuvise 20 4 hemaṃtāna pakhe tatiye 3 divase bitiye 2*, "In the twenty-fourth (24) [regnal] year, the third (3) fortnight of winter, the second (2) day." Dates of this type are common among inscriptions of the Sātavāhanas and Ikṣvākus in the Deccan as well as among northern kingdoms such as Maghas of Kauśāmbī and the kings of Bāndhogaṛh (Pingree, op. cit., 358).

The classical dating system, with the year, month, fortnight of the lunar[37] month (*pakṣa*), and lunar day (*tithi*)[38] of the fortnight,[39] first appears sporadically in inscriptions of the early centuries A.D., mainly those of the Western Kṣatrapas. For example, the Gundā inscription (SI I.181–2) is dated *varṣe triyuttaraśate* [*sic*] *100 3 vaiśākhaśuddhe paṃcama . . . tithau*, "in the year one hundred and three (103), in the bright (fortnight) of Vaiśākha, on the fifth *tithi*." This system gradually spread,

34. Occasional examples of this dating system are found as late as the Gupta period; see David Pingree, "A Note on the Calendars Used in Early Indian Inscriptions," JAOS 102, 1982, 355–9 (esp. 357).

35. See Pingree, op. cit., 355–6, for further details and examples.

36. Cf. Sircar, SI I.121 n. 3, characterizing this system as "a compromise between the Greek . . . and Indian . . . systems of dating," and SIE 246.

37. In later centuries in certain parts of India, mainly Bengal and the far south, the solar months (Meṣa, Vṛṣabha, Mithuna, etc.) were sometimes cited instead of lunar months; see SIE 223 and A. Venkatasubbiah, *Some Śaka Dates in Inscriptions*, 66–9.

38. On the precise definition of *tithi*, see the "Technical note on *tithis*" (5.4.3.3).

39. Occasionally the day of the full month, undivided into fortnights, is given, either in place of or in addition to the *tithi* of the fortnight; see EI 8, 1905–6, 289.

first through the Deccan and central India, and eventually throughout the subcontinent; by the Gupta period it appears to have become more or less standard.[40] The Udayagiri inscription of the time of Candragupta II (SI I.279), for instance, is dated *saṃvatsare 80 2 āṣāḍhamāsaśukle*[read *-ai*]*kadaśyām*, "In the [Gupta] year 82, on the eleventh [*tithi*] of the bright [fortnight] of the month of Āṣāḍha."

To this basic information additional data of varying types and amounts may be added. The *nakṣatra* occupied by the moon is often noted in later inscriptions but also occurs as early as the second century in the Gundā inscription noted previously (*rohiṇi*[sic]*-nakṣatra-muhūrtte*). The weekday (*vāra* or *vāsara*) is first clearly noted[41] in the Eraṇ inscription of the time of Budhagupta, [Gupta] 165 = A.D. 484 (SI I.335, l. 3) in the phrase *suraguror ddivase*, "on Thursday." In subsequent centuries the citation of the weekday becomes more or less standard. (This practice is important in that it permits the verification of dates in later inscriptions; see 5.4.3.2.)

Other types of calendrical and astronomical details sometimes added to dates of inscriptions of the Gupta period and later, especially in connection with dates in the Śaka era,[42] include the *yoga* (period in which the combined longitudinal motion of the sun and moon equals one *nakṣatra* or 13° 20'), *karaṇa* (half-*tithi*), and *lagna* (zodiacal sign rising).[43] Sometimes still further data such as the season (*ṛtu*), *rāśi* (sun's zodiacal sign), half-year (*ayana*, i.e., *dakṣiṇāyana* or *uttarāyaṇa* /*udagayana*), and time of day in *ghaṭikā*s ("hours" of forty-eight minutes) are provided. Special astronomical circumstances such as the sun's entry into zodiacal signs (*saṃkrānti*/*saṃkramaṇa*), especially the *viṣuva(t)-saṃkrānti* or entries into the equinoctial signs and the *dakṣiṇāyana-* and *uttarāyaṇa-saṃkrānti* or entries into the solstitial signs, may also be mentioned. Particularly common are references to solar or lunar eclipses (*grahaṇa, uparāga*), since these were considered especially auspicious times for the granting of gifts.[44] Citations of eclipses are useful for verifying dates, since their occurrences can be readily checked in various standard reference sources such as Th. Ritter von Oppolzer's *Canon der Finsternisse*.[45]

A typical example of a complex date from a late inscription is that of the Ajmer slab inscription containing the *Harakeli-nāṭaka* (IA 20, 212), reading *saṃvat 1210 mārga-sudi 5 āditya-dine śravaṇa-nakṣatre makarasthe candre harṣaṇa-yoge bālava-karaṇe*, "In the [Vikrama] year 1210, the bright [fortnight of] Mārga[śīrsa], [*tithi*] 5, Sunday, in the *nakṣatra* Śravaṇa, with the moon in Makara, the *yoga* Harṣaṇa, and *karaṇa* Bālava."[46]

40. Details in Pingree, op. cit., 359.

41. But see also SIE 219 n. 2.

42. Kielhorn, IA 20, 1891, 412 = KS I.610.

43. See Fleet, IA 18, 1889, 162 n. 1.

44. F. Kielhorn, "Die Sonnen- und Mondfinsternisse in den Daten Indischer Inschriften," *Nachrichten von der Königlichen Gesellschaft der Wissenschaften zu Göttingen*, Phil.-Hist. Klasse, 1896, 59–75 = KS II.826–42. See also Venkatasubbiah, *Some Śaka Dates*, 19–27.

45. Wien: Kaiserliche Akademie der Wissenschaften, 1887. English translation, *Canon of Eclipses*, by Owen Gingerich (New York: Dover, 1962).

46. For an even more elaborate date, including specific times of day, see the Burhānpūr mosque inscription (Appendix, no. 14), ll. 5–6. In the case of such precise dates, the day and time cited in the inscription is presumably that of the ceremonial performance of the gift, foundation, etc., commemorated in the inscription, rather than that of the actual incision of the inscription itself.

Various abbreviations were often employed in the notation of dates. The seasons (in the older dating systems) were often abbreviated as *he* or *hema*, *va* or *vā*, and *gri* or *gī* for *hemanta*, *varṣā*, and *grīṣma* (or their Prakrit equivalents), respectively. The days of the bright (*śukla*/*śuddha*/*sita*) and dark (*kṛṣṇa*/*bahula*/*asita*) fortnights are commonly abbreviated as *śudi* or *sudi* (= *śukla-divase* etc.) and *badi*/*vadi* (= *bahula-divase* etc.) or *vadya*,[47] respectively. (For further examples of abbreviations, see BPLM 160 n. 5 and SIE 220.)

In many inscriptions a formulaic phrase such as *etasyāṃ pūrvāyām*, "At this aforementioned [time (*velāyām*), or lunar day (*tithau*)]," *asyāṃ saṃvatsara-māsa-divasa-purvāyām*, "On this aforementioned year, month, and day," or the like, would be added after the date by way of introducing the body of the document.[48]

5.4.3 Conversion and verification of inscriptional dates

H. Jacobi, "The Computation of Hindu Dates in Inscriptions, &c.," EI 1, 1892, 403–60; Jacobi, "Tables for Calculating Hindu Dates in True Local Time," EI 2, 1894, 487–98; R. Sewell and Ś. B. Dîkshit, *The Indian Calendar*; Sewell, *Indian Chronography*; Sewell, *The Siddhāntas and the Indian Calendar*; L. D. Swamikannu Pillai, *Indian Chronology*; Swamikannu Pillai, *An Indian Ephemeris, A.D. 700 to A.D. 1799*; V. B. Ketkar, *Indian and Foreign Chronology*.

5.4.3.1 Conversion of years of Indian eras into dates of the Christian era

Years in Indian eras can be roughly converted to the corresponding years of the European calendar by adding or subtracting an appropriate conversion factor based on the epoch of the particular Indian era in question.[49] But this must be done with caution, as there are at least three possible equivalents for any one year of an Indian era, depending on (1) the month of the date (since the Indian years do not begin at the same time as European years) and (2) whether the Indian year is reckoned as expired (*atīta*, *gata*) or current (*vartamāna*).[50] For example, a date with the year Śaka 780 may correspond to a date in A.D. 857 or 858, depending on the month, if it is a current year, or in A.D. 858 or 859 if it is expired. In each case, the earlier A.D. date will correspond to dates in approximately the first nine and a half months of the Indian year (assuming that the year in question begins with Caitra = March/April),[51] and the latter to the last two and a half months. Thus the precise B.C./A.D. equivalent

47. The precise meaning of this latter abbreviation is uncertain; see Kane, *History of Dharmaśāstra* vol. 5, pt. 1, 670.

48. For further details, see SIE 219 n. 3.

49. A convenient table for rough conversion of years is given in A. L. Basham's *The Wonder That Was India* (New York: Grove Press, 1959), 495. For more detailed information, see Ketkar, *Indian and Foreign Chronology*, 18–19 and 211 (table 38).

50. In general, expired years (i.e., those counted by the last complete year) are more common in Indian dates than current years (those counted by the year in progress, as in modern A.D. years), so that when there is no means of checking it is usually assumed that an unspecified year is expired. But usage in this regard is by no means consistent, even in the same era, and an effort should always be made to establish which type of year is being cited.

51. On this point see section 5.4.3.2.

of an Indian year can be determined only if the nature of the year (current or expired) is known and the month is provided. Further complications arise in certain cases, for instance, in connection with eras such as the Kalacuri-Cedi or Lakṣmaṇasena (5.5.1.5 and 5.5.1.15), whose precise epochs are uncertain or variable.

5.4.3.2 *Conversion and verification of specific dates*

The determination of correspondences for specific dates involves complex calculations for which several methods are available, for example, those given by Jacobi in EI I, 406–8 and by S. B. Dikshit in CII 3, intro., Appendix II, 145–59.[52] But as a matter of convenience, the usual practice is to consult the tables provided in Swamikannu Pillai's *Indian Ephemeris*, providing equivalents in the European calendar for dates in the more common Indian eras which are adequate for general or preliminary purposes. But due to the complexities of Indian calendrical reckoning, they should not be treated as conclusive.[53]

It is therefore always desirable to verify an inscriptional date whenever sufficient data (at a minimum, year, month, *tithi*, and weekday) are provided; that is to say, the data should be checked and if necessary calculated to confirm (or deny) that the given weekday (or eclipse, *saṃkrānti*, etc.) did in fact fall on the specified date, thereby confirming (or denying) the tentative European equivalent for the date in question. The verification of a weekday and/or of other astronomical and calendrical specifications such as eclipses, *saṃkrānti*, *nakṣatra*, *yoga*, cyclical year of Jupiter (see 5.5.2.2 and 5.5.2.3), and so on involves complex calculations requiring specialized knowledge of astronomical systems, which are facilitated by the systems and tables provided by Jacobi (EI 1, 408–37) and the other sources listed at the beginning of section 5.4.3.[54] Such calculations, however, involve several variables and complicating factors which must be taken into consideration, and which are not always explicitly stated in the document itself. These include the era, which is often not specified; the nature of the years, whether expired or current, also frequently unspecified;[55] whether the year began in Caitra (*caitrādi*, the "northern" year) or Kārttika (*kārttikādi*, the "southern" year), or occasionally in some other month such as Āṣāḍha or Śrāvaṇa; and whether the months are counted as ending with the full moon (*pūrṇimānta*, the "northern" system) or the new moon (*amānta*, the "southern" system),[56] or whether they are solar rather than lunar months.[57] When any or all of this information is un-

52. These systems yield the corresponding "English" or "old-style" date, i.e., the date according to the Julian calendar which was current in England until September 2, 1752.

53. Mainly because Pillai's dates are based on mean beginnings of *tithis*, whereas the dates recorded in inscriptions were based on the real local beginnings of *tithis* (see the "Technical note on *tithis*," 5.4.3.3).

54. For examples of the full procedure for calculation of the Western equivalents of Indian dates, see Jacobi, 408–12.

55. Or sometimes incorrectly specified; see Kielhorn, IA 25, 1896, 266 = KS II.727.

56. See Jacobi, EI 1, 406.

57. See n. 37. According to Venkatasubbiah (*Some Śaka Dates in Inscriptions*, 66–7), the names of the lunar months are sometimes applied to what are really solar months, and vice versa; such deviations can be determined only by calculation.

known or uncertain, multiple calculations must be made for each possibility before a final verdict is passed (Jacobi, 406).

When, as is not infrequently the case, a date cannot be verified even when all such variables are taken into account, it may be labeled as irregular (Venkatasubbiah, x), and the precise European equivalent cannot be definitely determined. Such irregular dates are taken in some cases as an indication that the inscription bearing it is a spurious record or later forgery (see 5.3) in which the forger did not bother, or was unable, to correctly calculate the alleged date. However, it is important to keep in mind that an irregular date is not *necessarily* a spurious date.[58] It is a priori equally likely that an unverifiable date results from honest errors or inaccuracies at various points in the calculation and recording of the date (cf. SIE 227–8).

5.4.3.3 Technical note on tithi*s*

The dates in Indian inscriptions and other documents are given according to the "civil day," that is, the normal solar day running from local sunrise to sunrise; but the number within the fortnight of the month which is assigned to the civil day on which the recorded transaction or dedication took place is actually the number of the true lunar *tithi* which was current at sunrise on that civil day. The *tithi* is strictly speaking an astronomically calculated "lunar day," that is, the period, equal to one-thirtieth of a lunar month, in which the moon attains 12° of longitude of elongation from the sun. Such lunar days may begin at any time during the solar or civil day, and moreover do not correspond exactly in length to a solar day, being on the average slightly shorter. (One lunar month of 30 *tithi*s equals slightly less than 29½ civil or solar days.) This system, which is intended to correlate as precisely as possible the solar and lunar cycles, necessitates various adjustments to accommodate the natural imbalances between these cycles. Thus, for instance, when it happens that a *tithi* begins shortly after sunrise on one day and ends before the next sunrise (i.e., before the beginning of the next civil day), the number of that *tithi* will be skipped, that is, not be attached to any civil day, and becomes an expunged lunar day or *kṣaya-tithi*. Conversely, it can also happen that the same *tithi* is current at two successive sunrises, in which case the civil day beginning with the second sunrise will be numbered by the same *tithi*, as an intercalary day or *adhika-tithi*. (The system is analogous to that of intercalary and expunged months (*adhika-māsa* or *mala-māsa* and *kṣaya-māsa*), which are determined by passage[s] of the sun into a new zodiacal mansion during a lunar month.) These special features are occasionally alluded to in inscriptional dates, and must be taken into account in the calculations.[59]

This combined luni-solar calendrical system may give rise to several uncertainties and variations. For when a true *tithi* begins at or very near sunrise on a given civil day, the date assigned to that civil day will depend on the precise calculation of the moment of the *tithi*'s commencement. This calculation may vary significantly depending on which of the five traditional astronomical systems or *pakṣa*s (*Brahma-*

58. See, e.g., Fleet's remarks on the numerous irregular dates in Cālukya inscriptions: "the records are not necessarily to be rejected as not genuine" (*Gazetteer of the Bombay Presidency* I.2, 446 n. 6).

59. See, e.g., Kielhorn, IA 20, 1891, 411 = KS I.609.

siddhānta, *Ārya-siddhānta*, etc.) was used to calculate the *tithi*, due to their differing solar models and parameters for the movements of the heavenly bodies; the moment of the expiry of a *tithi*, which is critical to calculations of dates, may vary by as much as an hour or even more according to different *pakṣas* (Jacobi, EI I, 403). It is therefore necessary to check results by the different systems in any case where the result is in doubt, for example, where the weekday calculated by the general system falls one day before or after the one specified in the document, or where the end of the astronomical *tithi* falls within three hours of sunrise.[60] Moreover, in calculating the date for a given inscription adjustments must always be made for the conversion of mean Laṅkā time as given in the tables to true local time according to the latitude and longitude of the place of issue, insofar as this is known (Jacobi, 412; cf. n. 53). Here, too, the variations between mean time and local time may affect the moment of the end of the *tithi* and thus produce a different civil date.

By way of example of these and the other complications involved in the verification of inscriptional dates, we may cite the Cāndpur boar inscription (ASIR 10, 97; Kielhorn, IA 19, 354 = KS I.556), which is dated *sa[ṃ*]vat 1207 jyeṣṭha-vadi 11 ravau*, that is, Sunday, the eleventh day of the dark fortnight of Jyeṣṭha, [Vikrama] 1207. On the basis of the *Sūrya-siddhānta*,[61] Kielhorn calculated the following possible equivalents of this date:

1. If the [Vikrama] year 1207 is taken as a northern (*caitrādi*) current year and the month as *pūrṇimānta*:	Thursday, May 5, 1149 A.D.
2. Northern current year, *amānta* month:	Friday, June 3, 1149
3. Northern expired year, *pūrṇimānta*:	Tuesday, April 25, 1150
4. Northern expired year, *amānta*:	Wednesday, May 24, 1150
5. Southern (*kārttikādi*) expired year, *pūrṇimānta*:	Monday, May 14, 1151
6. Southern expired year, *amānta*:	Tuesday, June 12, 1151

None of these dates gives a satisfactory equivalent for the weekday of the inscription's date, namely, Sunday. However, when the fifth alternative (southern expired year, *pūrṇimānta*) is recalculated according to the *Brahma-siddhānta*, the civil day numbered by the eleventh *tithi* of the dark fortnight of Jyeṣṭha is the day *before* that arrived at by the *Sūrya-siddhānta*, namely, Sunday, May 13, 1151, and this is presumably the correct equivalent of the date of the inscription.

Even when a date cannot be verified by the usual methods, further circumstances must be taken into consideration before dismissing it as "irregular." Kielhorn, for example,[62] notes numerous instances in which the date of an inscription cannot be verified for the year given, but does work out for the preceding or following year, or sometimes for the preceding or following year but one. Such cases are so common

60. Kielhorn, IA 19, 1890, 21 (= KS I.514) n. 1. Kielhorn (ibid., 354–7 = I.556–9) lists several cases in which recalculation according to different astronomical systems enabled him to verify a date which might otherwise have appeared incorrect, and thus to authenticate a record which might otherwise have wrongly been suspected to be spurious.

61. From Jacobi's tables in IA 17, 1888, 145–81. These were superseded by his tables in EI 1, which were based on European systems rather than on any one Indian *pakṣa* (441).

62. IA 19, 1890, 364–9; 24, 1895, 4–5 = KS I.566–71; II.682–3.

that they probably do not indicate forged or erroneous dates but rather some kind of consistent calendrical irregularity or dislocation, perhaps resulting from confusion between expired and current reckonings (cf. Sewell, *Indian Calendar*, 40 n. 2). Such cases, and related problems of seemingly irregular dates, have been treated at length by Venkatasubbiah in *Some Śaka Dates in Inscriptions* (esp. 31–48 and 95–6), who suspects that they are connected with various complications involving the calculation by different systems of the year of the sixty-year cycle of Jupiter (2–19; 96). Venkatasubbiah shows that a given Indian date may theoretically have as many as twenty-eight possible Western equivalents (72), all of which must be duly considered and tested before a date is condemned as "irregular," and he is highly critical of arbitrary emendations by scholars of dates which "seem to them to be irregular" (viii), warning that "one has to be very circumspect in pronouncing any given date to be irregular" (93).

5.5 Appendix: Eras Used in Indo-Aryan Inscriptions

General references: A. Cunningham, *Book of Indian Eras*; IC II, 736–8; L. D. Swamikannu Pillai, *Indian Chronology*, 43–5; BPLM, 159–96; J. F. Fleet, "Hindu Chronology," in *Encyclopaedia Britannica*, 11th ed. (1910–11), vol. 13, 491–501; R. Sewell and Ś. B. Dîkshit, *The Indian Calendar*, 39–47; SIE, 251–326; V. V. Mirashi, "Epigraphical Research" (see 8.2.1 n. 15 for ref.), 515–22.

5.5.1 Continuous (historical or pseudohistorical) eras

5.5.1.1 Kaliyuga era of 3102 B.C.

J. F. Fleet, "The Kaliyuga Era of B.C. 3102," JRAS 1911, 479–96 and 675–98.

The Kaliyuga era is a pseudohistorical era, supposed to originate from the beginning of the Kali aeon. Traditional associations with events of epic history (Fleet, 676–9) notwithstanding, in reality the Kaliyuga is an artificial creation of astronomers, fabricated at a much later date to provide a convenient chronological base for astronomical and calendrical calculations. The initial date corresponds to Friday, February 18, 3102 B.C. (Fleet, 479), at the time of an approximate mean conjunction of the sun, moon, and planets at the first point of the *nakṣatra* Meṣa (Fleet, 489–95). The first current Kaliyuga era year thus corresponds to 3202–3201 B.C., and the first expired year to 3101–3100 B.C. Since Kaliyuga years are normally counted as expired, they can be converted to A.D. years by subtracting 3101 or 3100 (depending on the month).

In use as in origin, the Kaliyuga is primarily an astronomer's era; it is used only occasionally for civil and epigraphic functions. The earliest epigraphic attestation is in the Aihoḷe inscription (SI II.443–50), dated in Kaliyuga 3735 and Śaka 556, corresponding to A.D. 634/35. Some later inscriptions are dated in the Kaliyuga era, especially those of the Kādambas of Goa.[63] Inscriptional dates in the Kaliyuga era are usually given together with years of other eras, either historical (most commonly

63. Fleet 689–94; Kielhorn's *List of Inscriptions of Southern India*, EI 7, nos. 249, 254, 262, and 269.

Śaka; occasionally others such as Vikrama) or cyclical (usually years of Jupiter, as in the Kādamba inscriptions).

5.5.1.2 "Old Śaka" era (epoch uncertain)

It is generally agreed that the dates in an unspecified era of several early Kharoṣṭhī (and perhaps a few Brāhmī) inscriptions of the Scythian period cannot, on geographical and historical grounds, be attributed to known historical reckonings such as the Vikrama and Śaka eras. Such inscriptions are ascribed to a hypothetical reckoning generally referred to as the "Old Śaka" era, to distinguish it from the Śaka era of A.D. 78 (5.5.1.4). Among the earlier inscriptions usually attributed to this Old Śaka era are the Taxila copper plate of the year 78 (CII 2.1, 23–9) and the Taxila silver vase of 191 (CII 2.1, 81–2). Several later Kharoṣṭhī inscriptions with dates in the three hundreds of an unspecified era, for example, Skārah Ḍherī (399; CII 2.1, 124–7) are also usually attributed to this era, as is a Brāhmī Jaina inscription from Mathurā dated 299 (IA 37, 33–4).[64] In several cases, scholars disagree as to which inscriptions are to be attributed to the Old Śaka era.

Even more controversial is the exact epoch and historical origin of this presumed era. Suggestions as to its epoch range from ca. 248–247 B.C. (H. Lüders' "Parthian era")[65] to 84–83 B.C. (S. Konow in CII 2.1, xci).[66] Some scholars have proposed even earlier epochs in connection with some of the inscriptions of this class, for instance, P. H. L. Eggermont's Sarvāstivādin era of 383 B.C.[67] and J. Ph. Vogel's Seleukid era of 312 B.C.[68] Many other epochs have been proposed between these extremes, including 170 B.C.,[69] 158 B.C. ("Menander era"),[70] 155 B.C.,[71] 129 B.C.,[72] and so on. Some scholars, such as Narain[73] and Konow,[74] posit *two* early eras, one in the third or second century B.C. and another "Pahlava" era beginning around 90 B.C.

Most, if not all, of these theories involve complicated manipulations of inadequate and uncertain data, and can be characterized as speculative at best. The epoch of the Old Śaka era remains very much an open question, which probably cannot be conclusively answered on the basis of the documents currently available.

64. Some scholars also attribute the dates of Bactrian inscriptions from Surkh Kotal, Kara Tepe, and other central Asian sites to this era; see B. N. Mukherjee, *Central and South Asian Documents on the Old Saka Era*, 46–81.

65. "The Era of the Mahārāja and the Mahārāja Rājātirāja," in Bimala Churn Law, ed., *D. R. Bhandarkar Volume* (Calcutta: Indian Research Institute, 1940), 281–9 (esp. 288); supported by Konow, *Acta Orientalia* 20, 1948, 115, and Sircar, SIE 244.

66. This date was later retracted by Konow, who also proposed several others at various times; see the critique of his position by J. E. van Lohuizen–de Leeuw in *The "Scythian" Period*, 6–20.

67. In A. L. Basham, ed., *Papers on the Date of Kaniṣka*, 91.

68. ASIAR 1903–4, 259.

69. B. N. Mukherjee, *Central and South Asian Documents on the Old Śaka Era*, passim; K. W. Dobbins, *Śaka-Pahlava Coinage*, 139 ("Era of Eukratides").

70. A. D. H. Bivar in Basham, *Papers on the Date of Kaniṣka*, 418.

71. W. W. Tarn, *The Greeks in Bactria and India*, 500–1, and A. K. Narain in Basham, *Papers on the Date of Kaniṣka*, 237 ("Yavana era").

72. Van Lohuizen–de Leeuw, *The "Scythian" Period*, 33.

73. Basham, *Papers on the Date of Kaniṣka*, 237.

74. *Acta Orientalia* 20, 115.

5.5.1.3 Vikrama era of 58 B.C.

F. Kielhorn, "Examination of Questions Connected with the Vikrama Era," IA 19, 1890, 20–40, 166–87, 354–74; 20, 1891, 124–42, 397–414 = KS I.513–612.

The Vikrama era, or *Vikrama-saṃvat* as it is commonly called, is, along with the Śaka era (5.5.1.4), the most important epigraphic era, appearing (under various names) in the dates of many hundreds of inscriptions down to modern times. In general, the Vikrama era has been predominant in western and northern India (except Bengal), while the Śaka is widely current in the south.

In inscriptions of the earlier centuries of the Christian era, the "Vikrama" era is known by various other names such as *Kṛta* (e.g., Baḍvā *yūpa* inscriptions, SI I.91–2) and *Mālava* (e.g., Mandasor inscription of Kumāragupta and Bandhuvarman, SI I.299–307; "*mālavānāṃ gaṇasthityā*"). It is only from the ninth century[75] onward that the current name "Vikrama" was used in connection with this era.[76]

This latter fact indicates that the traditional explanation of the Vikrama era as commemorating the expulsion of the Śakas from Ujjain by the legendary King Vikramāditya has no historical basis. The actual historical origins of the Vikrama era have in the past been much debated, and until recently were highly controversial. But the recent discovery of inscriptions (particularly the Indravarman relic casket, JAOS 102, 59–68) dated in the years of the "Late King Azes" (*maharayasa ayasa atidasa*), that is, in the era of the late Azes I as distinguished from the then-ruling Azes II, has established that the former was the founder of an era, and this era can be associated with reasonable certainty with the one that later came to be known as Vikrama (cf. 4.3.3.1), on chronological and archaeological (BEFEO 67, 31) grounds.

The years cited in the Vikrama era are generally counted as expired, and only exceptionally as current (Kielhorn, IA 20, 398). Two calendrical systems are followed, the so-called northern Vikrama year beginning in the month of Caitra (*caitrādi*) and the "southern" year beginning in Kārttika (*kārttikādi*).[77] The months may be either 'northern' *pūrṇimānta* or 'southern'[78] *amānta*. An expired Vikrama year is converted to an A.D. date by subtracting 57 or 56, depending on the month; for a current year, 58 or 57 is subtracted.

5.5.1.4 Śaka era of A.D. 78

F. Kielhorn, "On the Dates of the Śaka Era in Inscriptions," IA 23, 1894, 113–34; 24, 1895, 1–17, 181–211; 25, 1896, 266–72, 289–94; 26, 1897, 146–53 = KS II.657–747.

Dates in the Śaka era are extremely common, numbering in the thousands, in inscriptions from southern India where the era is the standard system from the early Cālukya

75. The Dhiniki inscription (IA 12, 151–6) is dated in Vikrama 794 = A.D. 738, but the date is irregular and the inscription is probably spurious.

76. Sircar (SIE 254–5, and *Ancient Malwa and the Vikramāditya Tradition* [Delhi: Munshiram Manoharlal, 1969], 165–6) suggests that the name Vikrama arose from a later association with Candragupta II Vikramāditya.

77. Kielhorn (IA 20, 399–400) shows that these regional designations, based on prevalent modern practice, do not actually reflect historical reality as both systems were in wide use in many parts of northern India until a relatively late date.

78. Here too Kielhorn (IA 20, 401) shows that these geographical designations are not historically accurate.

times (sixth century) onward. Śaka dates are also not uncommon in western India (Gujarat and Saurashtra), eastern India (Bengal, Assam, etc.), and in parts of central India adjoining the south; they also appear sporadically in inscriptions from various parts of northern India. The Śaka era is also the standard dating system in Sanskrit inscriptions in Southeast Asia (especially Cambodia and Java). Like the Vikrama era, it is still current in India today, mainly in the south and the west.

Dates in the Śaka era are labeled by various expressions such as *śaka-(nṛpa-)kāle*, *śaka-varṣeṣv atīteṣu*, *śaka-varṣe*, *śālivāhana-śake*,[79] *śāke*, and so on.[80] Unlike the dates of some other eras such as Vikrama and Kalacuri-Cedi, Śaka era dates, except for those of the early centuries, are almost always explicitly labeled as such.[81] The earliest authentic[82] epigraphic reference to this era by the name "Śaka" is now the Vāḷa inscription of Suketuvarman, dated in Śaka 322 = A.D. 400 (EI 40, 54, ll. 8–9).[83] The dates of some still earlier inscriptions, notably those of the Western Kṣatrapa rulers of the line of Caṣṭana, are referable to the Śaka era, though they are not explicitly designated as such.[84]

The historical origin of the Śaka era is highly controversial. The reigns of various kings have been suggested as its starting point, but nowadays the majority (though by no means unanimous) point of view is that Kaniṣka I was the founder of the Śaka era, and that therefore the (unspecified) dates of the inscriptions of the "Great Kuṣāṇas" (i.e., Kaniṣka himself and his successors) are actually the earliest Śaka dates.[85] But the Kuṣāṇa chronology remains very problematic, and the Kaniṣka theory is by no means proven. While the early Western Kṣatrapa ruler Nahapāna can no longer be considered a possible founder of the Śaka era,[86] the discovery of an Andhau inscription dated in the year 11 of the reign of Caṣṭana (JAIH 2, 104–11) may be invoked in support of the theory that he and not Kaniṣka was the founder of the Śaka era.[87] In any case, the name of the era clearly points toward an origin with one of the

79. The name "Śālivāhana," first occurring in the twelfth century, reflects an effort to establish an indigenous origin for the era by associating it with a legendary Hindu king (whose historical prototype is probably the Sātavāhana king Gautamīputra; SIE 262); cf. the case of the "Vikrama" era (see n. 76).

80. See Kielhorn, IA 26, 148–53, for details.

81. Kielhorn, IA 26, 148–9.

82. Several earlier Śaka dates are all in spurious inscriptions; Kielhorn, IA 24, 181–2; Fleet, JRAS 1910, 818.

83. The significance of this date in this context was not pointed out in the published edition of the Vāḷa inscription. In most recent publications, the Hisse-Borālā ins. of Śaka 380 (EI 37, 1–4) is cited as the earliest explicit Śaka era date.

An inscription of the Ābhīra ruler Īśvaradeva (IAAR 1967–68, 52) is said to be dated in the year 254 (or 154; B. N. Mukherjee, JESI 7, 1980, 5 n. 12) of the Śaka era, referred to as such; but this record has apparently not been fully published, so this remains unconfirmed.

84. The dates of the inscriptions of the time of the early Western Kṣatrapa ruler Nahapāna, ranging from 41 to 45, are believed by many scholars to be Śaka years, but they are more likely to be regnal.

85. For detailed discussions and various points of view on the Kaniṣka question, see Basham, ed., *Papers on the Date of Kaniṣka*.

86. As was argued by Fleet, JRAS 1910, 820.

87. See V. V. Mirashi, *The History and Inscriptions of the Sātavāhanas and the Western Kṣatrapas*, 110–2. If the founder of the Śaka era is, in fact, someone other than Kaniṣka, then the dates of the inscriptions of the time of Kaniṣka and his successors must be regarded as a separate era. The epoch of such an era, according to most scholars who do not accept Kaniṣka as founder of the Śaka era, would

nonindigenous dynasties of the first century A.D. The legend recorded by Brahmagupta, Al-Bīrūnī, and others that it was founded to mark the second expulsion of the Śakas by Vikramāditya, while an obvious fabrication, thus reflects a distorted memory of original historical fact.

Śaka dates in inscriptions are normally counted as expired, but current years are also found, especially in the eleventh and twelfth centuries (Kielhorn, IA 25, 267). The years are *caitrādi* and the months *amānta* (but occasionally *pūrṇimānta* in the north).[88] Śaka era dates are sometimes combined with dates in other eras, such as Vikrama; and in southern Indian inscriptions of the medieval and later times the year of the sixty-year Jupiter cycle (5.5.2.3) is usually specified along with the Śaka year.

The Śaka era theoretically began on the first day of Caitra in A.D. 78. Expired Śaka years are converted to A.D. dates by adding 78 or (for the dark half of Pauṣa and for Māgha and Phālguṇa) 79. For current years, add 77 or 78.

5.5.1.5 Kalacuri-Cedi era of ca. A.D. *248*

V. V. Mirashi, *Inscriptions of the Kalachuri-Chedi Era* (CII 4), Int., i–xxx; Mirashi, "The Kalacuri-Cedi Era," *Annals of the Bhandarkar Oriental Research Institute* 27, 1946, 1–55.

The Kalacuri or Cedi era is used in more than 100 inscriptions from western and central India from the fifth to the thirteenth century. The records so dated can be divided into an earlier group (fifth through eighth centuries) from western India, consisting of inscriptions of the Traikūṭakas, early Kalacuris, Gurjara-Pratīhāras, Cālukyas of Gujarat and other minor dynasties, and a later group (ninth to early thirteenth centuries) in central India, mostly belonging to the later houses of the Kalacuri line. The earliest unquestionable Kalacuri-Cedi era date is 207 = A.D. 457 in a Traikūṭaka inscription (CII 4.1, 22–5); the latest is 969 = A.D. 1218 in an inscription of the Kalacuris of Ratanpur (CII 4.2, 549–54).

The inscriptions of the early group are all dated with only the word *saṃvatsara* or an abbreviation thereof, without specification of the era. It is therefore not always certain whether or not a particular date is to be attributed to the Kalacuri or to another era. For instance, the inscriptions of the kings of Uccakalpa were formerly assigned to this era, but are now usually considered to be dated in Gupta years (SIE 283). In the later group, the era is sometimes specified as *kalacuri-saṃvat*, *cedi-*

---

fall sometime in the first half of the second century A.D. (although some would argue for a later date, even as late as the third century). The inscriptional dates of the later Kuṣāṇas range only up to 99, but according to some authorities (notably van Lohuizen-de Leeuw, *The "Scythian" Period*, 235–6; also "The Second Century of the Kaniṣka Era," *South Asian Studies* 2, 1986, 1–9), several of these dates actually belong to the second century of the era, with the hundreds figure omitted. This theory has, however, been strongly criticized, e.g., by G. Fussman in "Numismatic and Epigraphic Evidence for the Chronology of Early Gandharan Art," in Marianne Yaldiz and Wibke Lobo, eds., *Investigating Indian Art: Proceedings of a Symposium on the Development of Early Buddhist and Hindu Iconography*, Veröffentlichung des Museums für Indische Kunst, vol. 8 (Berlin: Museum für Indische Kunst, 1987), 67–88 (esp. 72).

88. Kielhorn, IA 25, 271–2. Some Śaka era inscriptions are dated in solar rather than lunar months (ibid., 270–1).

saṃvat, *cedi-diṣṭa-saṃvat*, or the like (CII 4.1, xxii–iii); these are the source of the modern scholarly term "Kalacuri-Cedi" for the era, which, however, does not occur as such in any inscription.

The historical origin of the Kalacuri-Cedi era is problematic, in part because we have no records of it earlier than its third century. It is thus not known what historical event in or around A.D. 248 the commencement of the era in question commemorates. The accession of the Ābhīra kings Īśvaradatta or Īśvarasena has been suggested, but the former now seems to be disqualified by the recent discovery of a coin of his dated [Śaka] 154 = A.D. 232/33.[89] Īśvarasena, who is known only from a Nāsik inscription dated in his regnal year 9, is believed by many scholars (including Mirashi, xxiv–xxv) to have been the true founder of the era, which would then be an extension of his regnal reckoning. But, as noted by Sircar (SIE 283), this theory is conjectural at best, and the question remains open.

The approximate epoch of the Kalacuri-Cedi era was determined long ago by historical correlations between inscriptions dated in it and related inscriptions dated in the Vikrama era (Mirashi, i–iv), but the calculation of its precise starting point and the details of its calendrical system are still problematic. Kielhorn[90] originally proposed July 28, A.D. 249 (= Bhādrapada *sudi* 1, Vikrama 307 current) as the first day of the era but later changed this to September 5, A.D. 248 (= Āśvina *sudi* 1).[91] Mirashi has since reanalyzed the question with the benefit of some new dates which were not available to Kielhorn, and has come to the conclusion (xxii) that there were in effect two separate epochs of the era, the early dates corresponding to an initial date of Kārttika[92] *sudi* 1 = September 25, A.D. 249 and the later group to October 6, A.D. 248. According to Mirashi, the years of this era are generally expired, but occasionally current, and he explains the second epoch as having originally arisen from a misunderstanding of a current year as an expired one (ibid.). Mirashi also cites further evidence (xi; cf. IHQ 25, 1949, 81–6) that the inscriptions of the early Kalacuri kings dated in this era were based on a third epoch year of A.D. 250–51. The peculiar situation as to the epoch(s) of the Kalacuri-Cedi era seems to be connected with a repeated confusion between expired and current eras, which over the centuries could lead to dislocations of two or even more years;[93] but the entire situation still remains to be definitively clarified.[94]

As a matter of convenience, expired Kalacuri years are conventionally converted to A.D. years by adding 248/49, but a precise equivalent must be separately calculated for each date. In cases where sufficient information such as a weekday or other calendrical details (eclipses, etc.) are not provided, it may not be possible to definitively specify the corresponding A.D. year.[95]

89. B. N. Mukherjee, JAIH 9, 1975–76, 237–40; Shobhana Gokhale, JNSI 40, 1978, 34–6.

90. "The Epoch of the Kalachuri or Chedi Era," IA 17, 1888, 215–21 = KS I.449–55.

91. "Die Epoche der Cedi-Aera," in *Festgruss an Rudolf von Roth* (Stuttgart: W. Kohlhammer, 1893), 53–6 = KS II.653–6.

92. Mirashi concluded that the Kalacuri years follow the standard *kārttikādi* southern year, rather than an *āśvinādi* or *bhādrapadādi* scheme as proposed by Kielhorn.

93. Cf. the apparently similar cases of dislocation of one or more years in connection with other eras such as Vikrama and Śaka, discussed earlier (5.4.3.2).

94. See SIE 284 n. 2.

95. For example, CII 4.1, 40 n. 3; 48 n. 1.

The months of Kalacuri-Cedi era dates, according to Mirashi, were originally *amānta* in western India but were adapted to the northern *pūrṇimānta* system in the central Indian inscriptions. Kalacuri dates are not usually combined with any other eras. A few examples do, however, give years of the twelve- or sixty-year cycles of Jupiter (CII 4.1, xxix).

5.5.1.6 Gupta-Valabhī era of A.D. *319*

J. F. Fleet, CII 3, Introduction, 16–136; "The Gupta-Valabhi Era," IA 20, 1891, 376–89.

The Gupta era was current in northern, western, and parts of eastern India during the Gupta period (third to sixth centuries A.D.), and continued in use in the following centuries in western India under the name Valabhī by association with the Maitrakas of Valabhī, the erstwhile feudatories of the Guptas who continued to use the era after the demise of their imperial overlords. The latest (Gupta-)Valabhī date is in the Verāval inscription (SII II.402–8), Valabhī 945 = A.D. 1264. The era is mentioned under both names by Al-Bīrūnī (CII 3, 23–33).

The earlier dates in this era are denoted by the neutral term *saṃvatsara* or its abbreviations. The earliest genuine Gupta date[96] is in the Mathurā pillar inscription (SI I.277–9) dated in the regnal year 5 of Candragupta [II] as well as in the "continuous year" (*kālānuvarttamāna-saṃvatsare*), that is, Gupta era 61 (cf. 5.4.2.1.2). Many later inscriptions explicitly attribute the dates to the Guptas in such phrases as *gupta-prakāle gaṇanāṃ vidhāya*, "reckoning in the Gupta era" (Junāgaḍh inscription of Skandagupta, SI I.307–16, l. 15). The earliest occurrence of the name Valabhī is in the year 574 (EI 9, 1907–8, 4).

Due to the absence of authentic early dates, the precise historical origin of the Gupta era is uncertain.[97] Most historians are inclined to attribute it to the accession of Candragupta I, though it might also have been founded by one of his lesser-known predecessors Śrīgupta or Ghaṭotkaca, or by his son Samudragupta.[98]

The precise epoch of the Gupta era according to Fleet's calculations[99] would be the first day of the bright fortnight of Caitra, A.D. 319. According to him, the early inscriptions of this era followed the northern *caitrādi* and *pūrṇimānta* calendar, and most of the years were recorded as current.[100] Current Gupta years are thus converted to A.D. years by adding 320 or 321; expired years, 319 or 320. The dates of the "Valabhī" years from western India follow the southern *kārttikādi/amānta* scheme,

96. Excluding the probably spurious Nālandā and Gayā grants of Samudragupta (SI I.270–4), dated in the [Gupta] years 5 and 9.

97. Fleet's theory (CII 3, intro., 130–6) of a Nepali (Licchavi) origin for the era is no longer plausible; see D. R. Bhandarkar's revised edition of CII 3, 180–1.

98. See section 5.3 (on the Nālandā and Gayā spurious copper plates), and SIE 285.

99. CII 3, intro., 79 and 127.

100. The question of whether Gupta years are to be interpreted as current or expired is, however, not entirely settled. R. G. Bhandarkar ("The Epoch of the Gupta Era," JBBRAS 17.2, 1887–89, 80–98) argued that Gupta years are generally expired, and that the epoch year of the original (northern) Gupta era is thus A.D. 318/19 rather than 319/20 (91–92). See also K. B. Pathak, "New Light on Gupta Era and Mihirakula," in *Commemorative Essays Presented to Sir Ramkrishna Gopal Bhandarkar* (see 2.2.5.5 n. 115 for full reference), 195–222.

so that the dates are set back five months and the conversion figures for A.D. are 319/20 and 318/19 for current and expired years, respectively.

5.5.1.7 *Gāṅga (Gāṅgeya) era of ca.* A.D. *498 (?)*

Some two dozen inscriptions, mainly from the districts of Ganjam (Orissa) and Vizagapatnam (AP), of the early Eastern Gaṅga kings of Kaliṅga are dated in an era which is usually labeled by a neutral expression such as *pravarddhamāna-vijaya-rājya-saṃvatsaraḥ* in the earlier records but which later on is explicitly called *gāṅga-* or *gāṅgeya-*. The year was also employed by some of the feudatories of the Eastern Gaṅgas such as the Eastern Kadambas, in whose records it is referred to as the Gāṅga-Kadamba era. Dates in this era range from the year 39 (Jirjingi plates, SI I.485–8) to 526 (Chicacole plates, JBORS 18, 272–95).

The epoch of the Gāṅga era has been a long-standing point of controversy, but it is now generally agreed that it must have begun at some time around the end of the fifth century. The principal evidence in favor of this date is the correlation[101] of the dates of two copper plate inscriptions of the Kadamba feudatory Dharmakheḍi, namely, Gāṅga 520 (Sānta Bommāli, JAHRS 3, 171–80) and Śaka 917[102] = A.D. 995 (Mandāsā; JBORS 17, 175–88). Since the Sānta Bommāli inscription is dated in the reign of the Gaṅga sovereign Devendravarman, who is the son of Anantavarman of the Mandāsā inscription, the date of the former, namely, Gāṅga 520, must be some years later than the latter; thus Gāṅga 520 must be slightly later than Śaka 917 = A.D. 995, and the epoch of the Gāṅga era must be some time not long after A.D. 475 (cf. SIE 290).

Several specific dates in or around the last decade of the fifth century have accordingly been proposed on the basis of astronomical and historical data, the most convincing arguments being those of Mirashi[103] for an epoch in A.D. 498/99. But others have proposed slightly different dates, for example, 495/96 (Jogendra Chandra Ghosh)[104] or 497/98 (B. V. Krishna Rao),[105] and even the fifth-century epoch has not gone unchallenged. Most notably, R. C. Majumdar has argued strenuously for an epoch around the middle of the sixth century on the basis of his reading of the date of the Mandāsā plates as Śaka 967 or 976 rather than 917.[106] The historical questions are complicated by the ambiguous and repetitive nomenclature of the Gaṅga rulers involved and the consequent uncertainties about their identities.[107] All in all, the epoch in the late fifth century can be considered the most likely, but the question is not yet entirely closed.

101. First noted by R. Subba Rao in JAHRS 5, 1930–31, 261–76.

102. According to Mirashi's interpretation of the date (EI 26, 334–5), which, however, is not certain; see the next paragraph.

103. "Epoch of the Ganga Era," EI 26, 1941–42, 326–36; "A Further Note on the Epoch of the Ganga Era," EI 27, 1947–48, 192; "A Note on the Ponnuturu Plates of Ganga Samantavarman," EI 28, 1949–50, 171–4.

104. "The Initial Date of the Gāṅgeya Era," IA 61, 1932, 237–8.

105. "The Commencement of the Victorious Ganga Era," JAHRS 11, 1937, 19–32.

106. "The Epoch of the Gāṅga Era," *Indian Culture* 4, 1937–38, 171–9.

107. For further details see Majumdar's edition of the Māḍagrāma grant (EI 31, 45–52), which he reads as confirming a later epoch, and the criticisms in Sircar's note on the same record (ibid., 53–6), supporting the earlier epoch.

Whatever may have been its precise epoch, the era can be presumed to have originated, according to the usual pattern, from the extension of the regnal years of an early ruler. This was presumably Indravarman, the issuer of the Jirjingi plates of the year 39, or perhaps his immediate predecessor (SIE 290).

The years of the Gāṅga era could evidently be counted either as current or expired,[108] and were probably *caitrādi*.[109] The months were *pūrṇimānta* in earlier records but later on *amānta*.[110]

5.5.1.8 *Harṣa era of* A.D. *606*

It is generally, though not quite unanimously, agreed that a few dozen inscriptions of the early medieval period which are dated in years of an unspecified era should be attributed to an era derived from a continuation of the regnal years of the great Emperor Harṣa of Kanauj. Harṣa's accession is generally believed to have taken place in A.D. 606, which is thus taken as the epoch of this "Harṣa" era. Epigraphic dates which have been attributed to the era in question range from 22 and 25, which are regnal years of Harṣa's own inscriptions (Bānskheṛā, SI II.221–3, and Madhuban, EI 1, 67–75), to 563 (Pañjaur, IA 26, 31–2). But, except for the latter date, all other recorded Harṣa dates are under 300, the latest being 298 in the Āhār inscription (EI 19, 52–62).[111]

Because the dates in question are usually given only with neutral terms such as *saṃvat*, the attribution of particular dates to the Harṣa era is often uncertain and controversial. Thus of forty inscriptions attributed in Bhandarkar's *List of the Inscriptions of Northern India* (nos. 1385–421, 2042–4) to the Harṣa era, fully half are listed as questionable.[112] The inscriptions whose dates are attributed with relative certainty to this era are generally from northern and central India, including the Punjab and Bihar. Several inscriptions from outlying regions such as Rajasthan, Orissa, and Nepal have also been ascribed by some authorities to the Harṣa era, but at least some of these attributions are doubtful.[113]

Indeed, the very existence of the Harṣa era has not gone unchallenged, mainly because none of the inscriptions explicitly refer the era to him. The principal evidence for the existence of such an era is the Al-Bīrūnī's reference to it among the five historical Indian eras (Śrī-Harṣa, Vikramāditya, Śaka, Valabha, and Gupta) which he cites.[114] But because of Al-Bīrūnī's evident uncertainty about the era,[115] the am-

108. Mirashi, EI 26, 333; 27, 192.

109. EI 26, 330.

110. EI 28, 171–4.

111. The last date (l. 22) in the Kāman inscription, which is a composite record containing seven dates probably of the Harṣa era, was read by Mirashi (EI 24, 329–36) as 299, but Sircar (EI 36, 52–3) corrects the reading to 279.

112. For a supplementary list of inscriptions dated in the Harṣa era, see SIE 296.

113. See the discussions under the Bhāṭika, Bhauma-Kara, and Nepali eras (5.5.1.9, 5.5.1.11, and 5.5.1.12).

114. E. Sachau, *Alberuni's India*, II.5.

115. He apparently refers to two eras of Harṣa, one (perhaps fictitious) dating four hundred years earlier than the Vikramāditya (Vikrama) era, the other 664 years after Vikramāditya, i.e., beginning in A.D. 606.

biguity of the epigraphic evidence, and the chronological uncertainties about Harṣa's dates as attested in Chinese sources, some scholars, notably R. C. Majumdar,[116] have questioned, if not actually denied, the historical reality of the era. Others, however, notably Sircar,[117] have argued vigorously in favor of it, and it is generally accepted as a legitimate epigraphic era.

5.5.1.9 Bhāṭika era of A.D. *624*

Several dozen inscriptions[118] (many of them unpublished) from Jaisalmer (Rajasthan) and the surrounding area are dated in years of a *bhāṭika-saṃvat*. The inscriptional dates in this era range from 534 (= A.D. 1157) to 993 (= A.D. 1617).[119] Several of the inscriptions with dates in Bhāṭika years are also dated in the Vikrama era (and occasionally in Śaka as well),[120] and some have detailed dates with weekdays and other information. This information has made it possible to ascertain the epoch year of the Bhāṭika era as A.D. 624/25, or possibly 623/24; the discrepancy apparently arises from confusion between expired and current years (SIE 314–5).

The historical origin of the Bhāṭika era is disputed. Sircar (SIE 314–5), noting its close synchronization with the Islamic Hijrī era of A.D. 622, its use in western India near the region of the early Arab incursions into India, and the absence of early dates in the era, thinks that it is a solar modification of the Muslim era (cf. 5.5.1.16). Sharma (233), however, thinks that it represents the genuine era of the Rajput Bhāṭi clan. Mirashi[121] attributes the Bhāṭika era to the Mahārāja Bhetti of the Dhulev copper plate (EI 30, 1–4), but this is refuted by Sircar.[122] Mirashi also suggests (EI 30, 3) that some of the dates of inscriptions from Rajasthan and other regions, previously taken as Harṣa years, should be attributed to the Bhāṭika era; but this too is disputed by Sircar (ibid.).

5.5.1.10 Kollam era of A.D. *824*

F. Kielhorn, "Dates of the Kollam or Kolamba Era," IA 25, 1896, 53–6 and 174.

This era, known in Tamil as *Kollam-āṇḍu* and in Sanskrit as *Kolamba-varṣa* (or *-vatsara*, etc.),[123] was widely used in inscriptions from Kerala and adjoining regions of Tamil Nadu, mostly in Dravidian (Tamil and Malayalam) inscriptions but occasionally also in Sanskrit records.[124] The earliest date in the Kollam era is 149 = A.D.

116. "The Harṣa Era," IHQ 27, 1951, 183–90; 28, 1952, 280–5.

117. "Harṣa's Accession and the Harṣa Era," IHQ 27, 1951, 321–7; "Harṣa's Accession and Era," IHQ 29, 1953, 72–9; SIE 291–7.

118. The most complete list of Bhāṭika era inss. is in Dasharatha Sharma, "Some Dates in the Bhāṭika Era and Its Connected Problems," IHQ 35, 1959, 227–39. See also G. S. Gai, "A Note on the Bhāṭika Era," IHQ 35, 1959, 65–8, and SIE 314–6.

119. The Bhāṭika dates 1012 and 1078 are given by Sharma (op. cit., 232–3) as doubtful.

120. Gai, op. cit., 65–7; Sharma, op. cit., 234–5.

121. "The Harṣa and Bhāṭika Eras," IHQ 29, 1953, 191–5.

122. "Note on the Dhulev Plate of Maharaja Bhetti," EI 30, 1953–54, 5–7.

123. In modern works it is sometimes referred to as the "Malayāḷam year," e.g., IA 25, 1896, 192.

124. E.g., IA 2, 1873, 360–1; EI 4, 1896–97, 204.

973,[125] and the system has continued in use up to modern times. The epoch of the era is fixed at A.D. 824 by a Tamil inscription from Trivandrum[126] dated in Kollam 776 and the current Kali year 4702 = A.D. 1601. Dates in this era are thus converted to A.D. by the addition of 824/25. The Kollam era follows a solar calendar, the year beginning with the solar month Siṃha (= Bhādrapada) or Kanyā (= Āśvina) (Kielhorn, 53). The years are usually cited as current.

The Kollam era is traditionally associated with the foundation of the city of Kollam (Quilon), and the dates are often given as years "after Kollam appeared" (*kollandōṉṟi*).[127] But since Kollam is known to have existed well before the epoch of this era,[128] this tradition does not appear to be historically accurate. It is interesting to note that the years within each century of the Kollam era correspond to those of the semicyclical Saptarṣi era (5.5.2.1); that is to say, for example, the Kollam year 428 would correspond to the Saptarṣi year [43]28 (Kielhorn, 54 n. 4). This parallel led P. Sundaram Pillai[129] to suggest (118) that the Kollam era is actually an adaptation of the Saptarṣi era, and this hypothesis is supported by the fact that the earliest epigraphic occurrence of the latter, A.D. 804 (the Baijnāth *praśasti;* see 5.5.2.1), comes before the commencement of the Kollam era. But there is a serious problem in that the Saptarṣi era was prevalent in the far north of India, while the Kollam belongs to its southernmost regions. Because of this geographical discrepancy, Pillai's hypothesis can be accepted only provisionally; but no better explanation has been offered.

5.5.1.11 Bhauma-Kara era of A.D. *831* (?)

D. C. Sircar, "The Era of the Bhauma-Karas of Orissa," IHQ 29, 1953, 148–55; SIE 297–302.

The inscriptions of the Bhauma-Kara kings of Orissa and some of their feudatories are dated in years of an unspecified era, denoted *saṃvat*, ranging from 20[130] to 198 (Daspalla plates, EI 29, 189–94).[131] While these dates were formerly attributed by some scholars[132] to the Harṣa era (5.5.1.8), it is now generally agreed that they belong to a separate era of the Bhauma-Karas, presumably originating from a continuation of the regnal dates of an early ruler, probably Kṣemaṅkaradeva.

Sircar was able to establish on the basis of historical synchronizations with known dates of the Bhañja and Somavaṃśī kings that the Bhauma-Kara era must have begun around the middle of the first half of the ninth century, and astronomical data in the aforementioned Daspalla inscription enabled him to specify its probable epoch

125. EI 9, 1907–8, 234–9.

126. *Travancore Archaeological Survey* 2, 1910–13, 28.

127. E.g., EI 9, 236, l. 1.

128. BPLM 179 n. 3.

129. "Miscellaneous Travancore Inscriptions," IA 26, 1897, 113–8.

130. See R. C. Majumdar, *The Age of Imperial Kanauj*, 80 n. 30.

131. In several of the later dates of this era the first digit has been read as 200, but as shown by Sircar (IHQ 29, 150) it is actually 100.

132. E.g., Binayak Mishra, *Orissa Under the Bhauma-Karas* (Calcutta: Vishwamitra Press, 1934), 77–9.

as A.D. 831.[133] Though not absolutely conclusive, this is certainly the most precise and convincing suggestion to date.

5.5.1.12 Nepali or Newari era of A.D. 879, and other eras of Nepal

F. Kielhorn, "The Epoch of the Newar Era," IA 17, 1883, 246–53.

The later inscriptions of Nepal in Sanskrit and/or local languages (see 4.3.7.2) are dated in an era labeled *nepāla-varṣa-*, *nepālābda-*, and so on, which has continued in use into modern times. The era was determined by Kielhorn to begin on October 20, A.D. 879, so that its expired years are converted to A.D. by the addition of 879/80. The years are *kārttikādi,* and usually cited as expired; the months are *amānta*. According to the Nepali *vaṃśāvalīs*, the era was founded by King Jayadevamalla,[134] but R. C. Majumdar suspects that it was "really the Śaka era with eight hundreds omitted."[135]

This last point is connected with the question of the two earlier eras used in the inscriptions of Nepal. The earliest group of Nepal inscriptions includes dates from 386 to 535 of an unspecified era (*saṃvat*). Though in the past these dates were thought to belong to the Vikrama, Gupta, or a separate "Licchavi era,"[136] they are nowadays generally attributed to the Śaka era. The second group of inscriptions, which begins during the reign of King Aṃśuvarman, comprises dates ranging from 30 to 194 in another unspecified era. These were formerly attributed by several scholars to the Harṣa era, but Luciano Petech[137] has established from Tibetan evidence that the era dates from A.D. 576 and probably represents a continuation of the regnal years of Aṃśuvarman. R. C. Majumdar, however,[138] notes again a coincidence with the Śaka era and suggests that the second Nepali era was also based on the Śaka, restarted after its five hundredth year in or about A.D. 578.

5.5.1.13 Cālukya-Vikrama era of A.D. 1076

The Cālukya-Vikrama era was founded by the Kalyāṇi Cālukya King Vikramāditya VI (Tribhuvanamalla) upon his accession to the throne in A.D. 1076. The era is found in several dozen inscriptions from Karnataka and adjoining regions,[139] mostly in Kannada or Kannada and Sanskrit, of the reign of Vikramāditya VI and his immediate successors, under such terms as *śrīmac-cāḷukya-vikrama-kāla-* (or *-varṣa-*),

133. "The Era of the Bhauma-Karas," 155; EI 29, 1951–52, 191; SIE 302.

134. Bhagavanlal Indraji, IA 13, 1884, 414.

135. "The Eras in Nepal," JAS, ser. 4, vol. 1, 1959, 48.

136. Beginning in A.D. 110 according to Lévi (*Le Népal*, III.9).

137. "The Chronology of the Early Inscriptions of Nepal," *East and West*, n.s. 12, 1961, 227–32.

138. Op. cit. (n. 135), and "The Chronology of the Early Kings of Nepal," in D. R. Bhandarkar et al., eds., *B. C. Law Volume* (Calcutta: Indian Research Institute, 1945), I.626–41; supported by Sircar, SIE 271 n. 2 and 297.

139. For examples of Cālukya-Vikrama dates, see Kielhorn's *List of Inscriptions of Southern India* (EI 7), nos. 185–90, 193–219, 247. Numerous further examples are in SII XI.2 (*Bombay-Karnatak Inscriptions*, ed. N. Lakshminarayan Rao, 1952).

śrī-vikrama-kāla-, *vīra-vikrama-kāla-*, and so on.[140] A few of the inscriptions explicitly refer to Vikramāditya's act of superseding the current eras (i.e., Vikrama and Śaka) and instituting his own,[141] which is the first clear attestation we have of the foundation of an era as an intentional act (though this may well have been the case with some earlier eras).

Dates in Cālukya-Vikrama years range from 1 to at least 94 (Kielhorn's *List*, no. 247), and perhaps as high as 137.[142] There are several inscriptions of the first year of the era, and these, plus the fact that the Cālukya years are regularly mentioned along with the years of the sixty-year cycle of Jupiter (5.5.2.3), have made it possible to fix the epoch of the era with reasonable certainty at A.D. 1076, and specifically on Caitra *sudi* 1, Śaka 998 = March 8, A.D. 1076.[143]

However, there are several complications in connection with the epoch of the Cālukya-Vikrama era, especially in that the Jupiter years cited in various inscriptions do not agree with the epoch of Śaka 998,[144] and Kielhorn[145] notes that a remarkably large proportion of dates of the Cālukya-Vikrama era appear to be irregular in terms of weekdays and other data. The apparent dislocations in the Cālukya-Vikrama dates may be attributable to a combination of unsettled political conditions[146] and calendrical problems such as confusion between current and expired years. But despite these complications the epoch of A.D. 1076, as originally proposed by Fleet[147] and endorsed by Sircar, appears to be correct.[148]

5.5.1.14 Siṃha era of A.D. 1113

A few medieval Sanskrit inscriptions (see Bhandarkar's *List of the Inscriptions of Northern India*, nos. 1460–6) from the Kathiawar region have dates in or attributable to the Siṃha era (*śrī-siṃha-saṃvat*), whose epoch year corresponds to A.D. 1113/14. This figure is deduced from records with multiple dates in the Siṃha and other eras, usually Vikrama, such as the Bombay Royal Asiatic Society plates (IA 18, 108–16) of Siṃha 96 and Vikrama 1266 [expired] = A.D. 1209. Some of the inscrip-

140. BPLM 181; Fleet, "The Chālukya Vikrama-varsha, or Era of the Western Chālukya King Vikramāditya VI," IA 11, 1879, 187–93.

141. Fleet, op. cit., 187–8; "The Dynasties of the Kanarese Districts of the Bombay Presidency," *Gazetteer of the Bombay Presidency* I.2, 447.

142. See Venkatasubbiah, *Some Śaka Dates in Inscriptions*, 54.

143. Fleet, "The Dynasties," 446–7; Sircar, "Note on Wadageri Inscription of Chalukya V.S. 1," EI 34, 1960–61, 193–6.

144. See P. B. Desai, "The Chālukya Vikrama Era," *Quarterly Journal of the Mythic Society* 48 (Karnataka Number), 1957–58, 6–15, and Venkatasubbiah, op. cit., 91. See also the new data and comments provided by C. T. M. Kotraiah in JESI 10, 1983, 64, which, however, seem to gloss over the complexity of the problem.

145. IA 22, 1893, 111 = KS II.638.

146. Sircar, EI 34, 196.

147. "The Dynasties," I. 2, 447.

148. Some of Vikramāditya's Cālukya successors, as well as several kings of succeeding dynasties such as the Kaḷacuryas, Hoysaḷas, and Kadambas, imitated Vikramāditya's practice by dating their records in regnal years phrased in such a way as to suggest pretensions to founding a continuous era; for example, *śrīmac-cāḷukya-vikrama-nūrmmaḍi-Tailapadeva-varṣada 4 neya* (Venkatasubbiah, op. cit., 57). On such pseudoeras, see Venkatasubbiah, 2; Fleet, IA 11, 192; and "The Dynasties," I.2, 503.

tions concerned are dated only with the word *saṃvat* (e.g., Bhandarkar's nos. 1460, 1462, 1464), so that their attribution to the era in question is not certain.[149] The latest date in the Siṃha era is 151 of the Verāval inscription (SI II.402–8), indicating that the era was never more than a relatively short-lived local system. The calendar of the Siṃha era seems to have followed an *āṣāḍhādi*, or perhaps *caitrādi*, year, with *amānta* months.[150]

The historical origin of the Siṃha era is uncertain. Bhagavānlāl Indraji[151] held that it was founded to commemorate the conquest of Kathiawar by the Gujarat Cālukya ruler Siddharāja Jayasiṃha; but this theory, as well as some others, was criticized by Ojhā (BPLM 182–3), who suggested that the era may have been initiated by some petty king, perhaps otherwise unknown, of Kathiawar.

5.5.1.15 Lakṣmaṇasena era of A.D. *1178 (?)*

R. C. Majumdar, *History of Ancient Bengal* (Calcutta: G. Bharadwaj & Co., 1971), 241–8.

A few inscriptions of about the thirteenth century from the Gayā region of central Bihar (Bhandarkar's *List of the Inscriptions of Northern India*, nos. 1467–70) are dated in years of "the expired reign of Lakṣmaṇasena" (*lakṣmaṇasenasyātītarājye saṃ*, etc.), with dates ranging from 51 to 83.[152] Now an era known as Lakṣmaṇa-saṃvat (often abbreviated *la saṃ*) is well known from the colophons of dated manuscripts, and was still in use in relatively modern times in north Bihar, but its epoch is problematic. According to Kielhorn's calculations,[153] its epoch year should be A.D. 1118/19; but some Lakṣmaṇasena dates in old and modern documents reflect various epochs ranging from 1107 to 1119 (Majumdar, 247). However, literary evidence[154] which was not available at Kielhorn's time has shown that the Sena King Lakṣmaṇasena's accession actually took place in A.D. 1178/79, and the Lakṣmaṇasena-saṃvat inscriptions are in all probability to be attributed to an era commencing with this date, rather than to the "Lakṣmaṇa-saṃvat" of ca. 1119, as had previously been maintained by N. G. Majumdar, R. D. Banerjee, and others.[155] This dating of the inscriptions also yields consistent calendrical and historical results.[156]

But the relationship between this epigraphic era of 1178/79 and the literary Lakṣmaṇasena era with an epoch some sixty years earlier remains problematic. Vari-

149. BPLM 183 n. 6.

150. Kielhorn, IA 22, 1893, 108–9 = KS II.635–6; SIE 305.

151. *Gazetteer of the Bombay Presidency* I.1, 176.

152. The Bisapī plate (IA 14, 190–1) dated in Lakṣmaṇasena year 293 and *sana* 807 is probably spurious; see G. A. Grierson, "On the Genuineness of the Grant of Çiva-siṃha to Vidyāpati-ṭhakkura," JASB 68, 1899, 96.

153. "The Epoch of the Lakshmanasena Era," IA 19, 1890, 1–7 (= KS I.506–12).

154. The colophon of Śrīdharadāsa's poetic anthology *Saduktikarṇāmṛta* is dated in Śaka 1127 and (apparently) in regnal year 27 of Lakṣmaṇasena (Chintaharan Chakravarti, "Date of Accession of King Lakṣmaṇasena," IHQ 3, 1927, 186–9), a date which is supported by other literary references (C. Chakravarti, "Date of Ballālasena," IHQ 5, 1929, 133–5).

155. For references to the abundant literature on this controversy, see the notes in Majumdar, op. cit.

156. Sircar, "Lakṣmaṇasena's Samvat," IHQ 34, 1958, 21–8, and SIE 276–7.

ous explanations have been proposed, for example, that the latter era was reformulated at some later date from the birth instead of the accession of Lakṣmaṇasena,[157] or that the two systems derive from the reigns of two different kings of the same name. This much-discussed problem still awaits full clarification (cf. SIE 277–8).

5.5.1.16 Other historical and pseudohistorical eras

Various other eras are occasionally used in Indic inscriptions.[158] An inscription from Gayā (IA 10, 341–7) is dated in the year 1813 of the era of the Buddha's Nirvāṇa (*bhagavati parinirvṛte saṃvat 1813*). According to Indraji, this reflects an era commencing in 638 B.C., but Sircar (SIE 277) puts its epoch at 544 B.C.[159]

The Jaina or Vīra-nirvāṇa era, known from Jaina texts, is occasionally also found in inscriptions (BPLM 163). The era dates from 527 B.C. according to Śvetāmbara tradition, or 662 B.C. according to the Digambaras (BPLM 163; SIE 321). A late epigraphic example of the Jaina era from Śravaṇa-Beḷgoḷa, dated Jaina era 2493 / Vikrama 1888 / Śaka 1752 = A.D. 1830 (IA 25, 346, no. 6), follows the Digambara system.

The Gokāk inscription (EI 21, 289–92) is dated in the 845th year of the otherwise unknown "Āguptāyika kings" (*āguptāyikānāṃ rājñām . . . varṣa-*). Paleographically the inscription seems to belong to the sixth or seventh century A.D., which would put the putative origin of the era around the third or second century B.C., but it is impossible to say anything about its origin (though the editor of the inscription very tentatively suggests a possible connection with Candragupta Maurya). Sircar (SIE 326) suspects that it may be a fabricated system.

The Devnīmorī stone casket inscription (SI I.519) presents a similar enigma with its date in the 127th year of the "Kathika kings" (*kathikanṛpāṇāṃ*). Most scholars

157. See, e.g., Pramode Lal Paul, "The Origin of the Lakṣmaṇasena Era," *Indian Culture* 2, 1936, 579–84; A. S. Altekar, "New Light on the History of Bihar and the Origin of Lakshmana Samvat," *J. N. Banerjea Volume* (Calcutta: Department of Ancient Indian History and Culture, University of Calcutta, 1960), 110–5.

158. Certain minor local eras which are not generally used for inscriptions in Indo-Aryan languages are not treated here. Information on these and other nonepigraphic eras such as the Cochbihar, Faslī, and Magī eras is provided in SIE (305–17) and BPLM (186–95).

159. The discrepancy results from differing interpretations of the value of the dates of the Lakṣmaṇasena era (5.5.1.15) in other inscriptions of the King Aśokacalla mentioned in the Gayā inscription. In any case, this isolated late instance obviously does not indicate a genuine continued tradition of dating according to years of the Buddha in India. See also Cornelia Mallebrein, "Inschriftliche Quellen zur Datierung des historischen Buddha in Indien. Die Inschrift aus Bodh-Gaya, datiert in das Jahr 1813 n.N.," in Heinz Bechert, ed., *The Dating of the Historical Buddha/Die Datierung des historischen Buddha*, Symposien zur Buddhismusforschung, IV, 1/Abhandlungen der Akademie der Wissenschaften in Göttingen, Philologisch-historische Klasse, Dritte Folge, no. 189 (Göttingen: Vandenhoeck & Ruprecht, 1991), 344–57.

It was formerly thought that the numeral 256 at the end of some versions of Aśoka's minor rock edict I marked a year of an era dating from the Buddha's nirvāṇa. But it is now generally believed that the numeral 256 refers to a number of nights rather than years, either the nights spent by Aśoka on pilgrimage tour (see Jarl Charpentier, IA 43, 1914, 132; Sircar, *Aśokan Studies*, 78–9) or, according to a recent reinterpretation (Harry Falk, ZDMG 140, 1990, 96–122), the total number of fast days he passed in Buddhist monastic establishments.

are inclined to understand this as an alternate term for a known era (presumably either Śaka or Kalacuri-Cedi), but the significance of the term remains obscure.[160]

The Hijrī (Muslim) era of A.D. 622 is occasionally used in late inscriptions in Sanskrit and other Indic languages, usually in combination with dates in an indigenous Indian era such as Vikrama; for instance, the Verāval inscription (SI II.402–8) is dated in the "year 662 of the Prophet Muhammad" (*bodhaka-rasūla-mahaṃmada-saṃvat 662*) as well as in the Siṃha, Valabhī, and Vikrama eras (cf. 5.4.2.1.2). Some of the several Indian variations and adaptations of the Hijrī era are also occasionally found in Indic inscriptions; for instance, some late inscriptions of Bengal[161] are dated in the Malla era of A.D. 694/95 or in the Bengali era (*sāna* or *sāla*) of A.D. 593/94,[162] both of which are ultimately derived from the Hijrī (SIE 312–4). In some Orissan inscriptions the term *sana* refers to the Amlī era, another local derivative of Hijrī (e.g., Baripāṛā Museum inscription, OHRJ 2, 94–8).[163]

A single inscription on a Jaina bronze image from Satruñjaya is dated in the year 4 of a Siddha-hema-kumāra era, apparently a short-lived system initiated, according to Umakant P. Shah,[164] between A.D. 1142/43 and 1150/51. Shah speculates that the era was named after the Gujarat Cālukya kings Siddharāja Jayasiṃha and Kumārapāla and the Jaina scholar Hemacandra.

The Ilāhī era (Tārīkh-i Ilāhī) instituted by the Mughal emperor Akbar in A.D. 1556 is recorded in a Jaina inscription from Pattan (EI I, 319–24) of the *allāï* year 41 and [Vikrama] 1652 = A.D. 1596.

Some late inscriptions are dated in *Iṃgrejī san* or *Isvī* years, that is, the Christian era, for example, the Tañjāvur Bṛhadīśvara Temple inscription (V. Srinivasachari and S. Gopalan, *Bhoṃsle Vaṃśa Charitra*, 101), dated *iṃgrejī san 1803 isvī ḍisaṃbar 13* (December 13, 1803).

5.5.1.17 Phantom eras

Among the eras previously postulated on epigraphic grounds but subsequently discredited is the Mauryan era (e.g., BPLM 164–5), formerly thought to occur in the Hāthīgumphā inscription (l. 16), on the basis of the wrong reading *rāja-muriya-kāle*.[165] The existence of a Nanda era proposed by R. C. Majumdar[166] on the basis of literary and epigraphic evidence is also highly dubious (SIE 324–5).

160. See also section 3.3.3, n. 50.

161. See A. K. Bhattacharyya, *A Corpus of Dedicatory Inscriptions from Temples of West Bengal*, 16ff.

162. See also Amitabha Bhattacharyya, "The Bengali Era in the Inscriptions of Late Mediaeval Bengal," *Indian Museum Bulletin* 21, 1986, 38–43.

163. Note that Sircar (SIE 314–5) thinks that the Bhāṭika era is also an adaptation of Hijrī; see section 5.5.1.9.

164. "A Jaina Bronze Dated in Siddha-Hema-Kumara Samvat from Satrunjaya (Saurashtra)," in M. S. Nagaraja Rao, ed., *Madhu: Recent Researches in Indian Archaeology and Art History. Shri M. N. Deshpande Festschrift* (Delhi: Agam Kala Prakashan, 1981), 237–8.

165. Sircar, SI I.218, reads . . . *mu[khi]ya-kala-* . . . ; see SIE 324, and section 5.2.

166. "A Passage in Alberuni's India—A Nanda Era?" JBORS 9, 1923, 417–8.

5.5.2 *Cyclical (astronomical) eras*

5.5.2.1 *Saptarṣi era*

F. Kielhorn, "A Note on the Saptarshi Era," IA 20, 1891, 149–54 = KS II.617–22.

The *saptarṣi-samvat* (or, as it is more commonly called in inscriptions, *śāstra-saṃvatsara* or *laukika-saṃvatsara,* etc.) is a cycle of twenty-seven hundred years based on a fancied movement of the constellation of the Seven Sages (*saptarṣi*, Ursa Major) through the twenty-seven *nakṣatra*s, spending one hundred years in each. A cycle of this era is said to have begun twenty-six years after the beginning of the Kali era (3102 B.C.), that is, in 3076 B.C. Another cycle should then have begun in 376 B.C., but in practice complete dates in the era are given continuously from 3076 B.C. (e.g., Saptarṣi 4951 = A.D. 1875; Kielhorn 151, no. 2) when used for literary purposes such as the dating of manuscripts. But in inscriptions, the dates of this era are given with omitted hundreds; that is to say, only the year of the current hundred-year phase is noted.[167] For example, in the Baijnāth *praśasti* (EI 1, 107, l. 32), which is the earliest clear[168] epigraphic instance of this era, the date is given simply as "the eightieth year" (*saṃvatsare* ['*]*śītitame*), probably = A.D. 804. The corresponding year of an A.D. century can be derived by adding 24 or 25 to the Saptarṣi year.

Despite this incomplete notation, it is possible in many though not all cases to determine precise A.D. equivalents for dates in this era, either because the Saptarṣi date is given together with years of standard eras such as Śaka and/or Vikrama,[169] or by deduction from historical names or events mentioned in the inscription. This latter method is particularly productive because most of the inscriptions dated in the Saptarṣi era come from Kashmir and adjoining regions for which we have relatively abundant historical information from literature. For instance, the Ārigom stone inscription (EI 9, 300–2) is dated only in the Laukika (i.e., Saptarṣi) year 73, but it mentions an earlier King Siṃha who can be identified with Jayasiṃha, a king of Kashmir in the twelfth century known from Kalhaṇa's *Rājataraṅgiṇī*, so that the inscription can be dated to A.D. 1197. Even when there is no accompanying historical or chronological information, the correct century of an inscription dated in the Saptarṣi era can usually be estimated paleographically with some confidence (see 5.4.1).

Inscriptions dated in the Saptarṣi era are found with some frequency, but only in the mountain regions of northern India, mainly in Kashmir, Kangra, and Chamba.[170] Most examples date from the medieval or later periods.

167. The Saptarṣi era is thus strictly speaking neither a continuous nor cyclical reckoning but a combination of, or rather compromise between, the two types; see the comments of J. Mitchiner in JAIH 10, 1976–77, 55–6 and 92.

168. In the Hisse-Borālā inscription the Śaka date 380 is accompanied by what seems to be a year (the reading of which is uncertain) in a system evidently related to the Saptarṣi era, as it is accompanied by a phrase which has been read (EI 37, 6) as *saptarṣaya uttarāsu phā[lgunī*]ṣu*, "[while] the Seven Sages were in Uttara-Phālguṇa." However, the exact significance of this date is uncertain; see the references given in the Index of Inscriptions.

169. E.g., Kielhorn 152, no. 6; B. Ch. Chhabra, *Antiquities of Chamba State* II.161 and 163.

170. Many examples in J. Ph. Vogel and B. Ch. Chhabra, *Antiquities of Chamba State*, parts I and II. See also Bhandarkar's *List of the Inscriptions of Northern India*, nos. 1438–45, 1447–58.

Years of the Saptarṣi cycle are usually denoted as current and *caitrādi;* the months are *pūrṇimānta* (Kielhorn 153–4).

5.5.2.2 Twelve-year cycle of Bṛhaspati (Jupiter)

S. B. Dikshit, "The Twelve-Year Cycle of Jupiter," Appendix III to introduction to CII 3, 161–76; see also ibid., 101–24.

The twelve-year cycle of Bṛhaspati is based on the period of the sidereal revolution of Jupiter in approximately twelve solar years. The twelve years of the cycle are given names corresponding to those of the ordinary lunar months, assigned according to the longitude of Jupiter's heliacal rising; for example, if Jupiter rises in Kṛttikā or Rohiṇī, its year is named Kārttika (see Dikshit, 163, table VIII, for a complete list). The years of the twelve-year Jupiter cycle are sometimes denoted by the simple names (e.g., *vaiśākhe saṃvatsare*) and sometimes (mostly in the inscriptions of the Parivrājakas) with the prefix *mahā-* (e.g., *mahā-viśākhe saṃvatsare*).

The twelve-year cycle of Jupiter is found occasionally in Sanskrit inscriptions from various regions, including northern, southern, and eastern India,[171] beginning in the late fifth century. Only about a dozen such dates are known in all, of which six belong to the Parivrājaka feudatories of the Guptas.[172] A few others occur in the inscriptions of the early Rāṣṭrakūṭas,[173] the Kadamba king Mṛgeśavarman,[174] and Anantavarman of Kaliṅga.[175] The Dhulev plate of Mahārāja Bhetti (EI 30, 1–7) dated in the *aśvayuja-saṃvatsara* of Bṛhaspati, is probably the latest occurrence (late seventh century?; cf. 5.5.1.9) of the twelve-year cycle of Jupiter in Sanskrit inscriptions.

Dates in the twelve-year cycle are usually given in combination with other eras such as Gupta years in the case of the Parivrājaka inscriptions or regnal years in the inscriptions of Mṛgeśavarman. Only the Siripuram plates are dated in Jupiter years alone.

5.5.2.3 Sixty-year Cycle of Bṛhaspati (Jupiter)

The sixty-year cycle of Bṛhaspati was originally calculated on the basis of Jupiter's passage from one *rāśi* (zodiacal sign) to the next in a period approximating a solar year (actually 361+ days). Due to the discrepancy of about four days, when strictly reckoned the cycle requires the suppression of one Jupiter year every eighty-five solar years. The sixty years are noted by name (Prabhava, Vibhava, Śukla, etc., in the southern system)[176] rather than number. There are slightly variant systems in northern and southern India,[177] the latter being the principal one in epigraphic usage. In earlier

171. There is also one doubtful instance from Nepal; see D. R. Regmi, *Inscriptions of Ancient Nepal* III.31–2 (Chabihil inscription).

172. CII 3, nos. 21–5, plus the Betul plates (EI 8, 284–90).

173. Pāṇḍaraṅgapallī plates, *Annals of the Bhandarkar Oriental Research Institute* 25, 40–2, and Nagardhan plates, CII 4.2, 611–7.

174. See J. F. Fleet, "Sanskrit and Old Canarese Inscriptions," IA 6, 1877, 24–5; 7, 1878, 35–7.

175. Siripuram plates, EI 24, 47–52.

176. For a full list of the names, see SIE 267–8.

177. E.g., the northern cycle begins with Vijaya, which is the twenty-seventh year of the southern cycle.

inscriptional examples the Jupiter year was calculated by the actual position of the planet,[178] but from about the ninth century on this system was discarded and the Jupiter years came to be, in effect, merely a set of names applied to the normal solar or luni-solar years in a cycle of sixty years;[179] this latter system is the one which is followed in the vast majority of epigraphic dates.

The sixty-year cycle of Jupiter is very widely used in inscriptions, especially in medieval and later inscriptions from the south. The earliest definite[180] inscriptional attestation is in the Mahākūṭa inscription (IA 19, 7–20), dated in the Siddhārtha year (no. 53 of the cycle), probably = A.D. 602. In this and in some later inscriptions the Jupiter year is given by itself or with a regnal year, but much more commonly the Jupiter year is accompanied by a date in an era, usually Śaka, rarely Vikrama. In general, the sixty-year cycle is far more common in southern Indian inscriptions, in both Sanskrit and Dravidian languages; from about the ninth century on, nominal Jupiter years (see the preceding paragraph) are regularly noted there, usually together with the Śaka year.

178. Kielhorn, IA 25, 1896, 269 = KS II.730.

179. Kielhorn, IA 25, 268 = KS II.729.

180. Sircar thought that the word *vijaya* in the dates of two Ikṣvāku inscriptions from Nāgārjunakoṇḍa (EI 35, 1–7) referred to the initial year of the northern (see n. 177) sixty-year Jupiter cycle, equivalent to A.D. 273 and 333, but this interpretation is doubtful.

6

The History of Indian Epigraphic Studies

A. Cunningham, ASIR 1 (1862–65), Introduction, i–xliii; A. F. R. Hoernle, *Centenary Review of the Asiatic Society of Bengal from 1784 to 1883*. Part 2: *Archaeology, History, Literature, &c.* (Calcutta: The Asiatic Society of Bengal, 1885; reprint, The Asiatic Society, 1986); J. F. Fleet in *Gazetteer of the Bombay Presidency* I.2, Article III ("The Dynasties of the Kanarese Districts of the Bombay Presidency"), i–v; E. Windisch, *Geschichte der Sanskrit-Philologie und Indischen Altertumskunde*, 33–34 and 97–123; Windisch, *Philologie und Altertumskunde in Indien*; S. Roy, *The Story of Indian Archaeology 1784–1947* (cf. also *Ancient India* 9, 1953, 4–52); EINES 81–94 ("Study of Indian Epigraphy and Palaeography"); RIE 29–40 ("History of Indian Epigraphical Studies"); O. P. Kejariwal, *The Asiatic Society of Bengal and the Discovery of India's Past 1784–1838* (Delhi: Oxford University Press, 1988).

6.1 The Pioneering Era: Early Readings of Indian Inscriptions (1781–1834)

The study of inscriptions was totally absent from the traditional curriculum of Sanskrit learning, so that the field of Indian epigraphy was born only with the beginning of European Indology in the late eighteenth century. While there is definite evidence that old inscriptions, particularly copper plate charters, were in ancient times sometimes studied for practical purposes,[1] it is equally clear that really ancient inscriptions written in archaic characters that were no longer legible through direct comparison with current scripts were as mysterious to traditional scholars as they were to the Europeans who first encountered them in the modern era. This is witnessed by the well-known incident reported by the historian Shams-i Sirāj 'Afīf in which Fīrūz Shāh Tughluq (1351–88) attempted unsuccessfully to have the inscriptions on the Aśokan pillars which he brought to Delhi (see 4.3.1.1.3 nn. 71 and 72) read by Brahmans.[2]

1. As evidenced by Kalhaṇa's reference in his *Rājataraṅgiṇī* (I.15) to the consultation of old epigraphic records (*pūrvabhūbhartṛ-pratiṣṭhā-vastu-śāsanaiḥ*) for the purpose of historical research. See also RIE 29.

2. H. M. Elliot (ed. John Dowson), *The History of India as Told by Its Own Historians: The Muhammadan Period* (London: Trübner & Co., 1867–77), III.352. The old Brāhmī inscriptions must

The first publication of an old Indian inscription was by the "Sanscrit-mad"[3] (Sir) Charles Wilkins (1749–1836),[4] one of the greatest of the pioneer Indologists, in his article "A Royal Grant of Land, Engraved on a Copper Plate, Bearing Date Twenty-three Years Before Christ; and Discovered Among the Ruins at Mongueer. Translated from the Original Sanscrit, by Charles Wilkins, Esq. in the Year 1781,"[5] in *Asiatick Researches* (AR) 1 (1788), 123–30.[6] This was followed by "An Inscription on a Pillar near Buddal" in AR 1, 131–41.[7] These articles, like most of the earliest epigraphic papers published in AR, consist only of translations, without the text of the inscription and with little or no introductory matter. Both of Wilkins' inscriptions date from the Pāla period, about the ninth century A.D.; although decidedly archaic, the script of these two epigraphs could be read by comparisons to the modern and archaic forms of Devanāgarī and Bengali scripts known in Wilkins' time,[8] and he was thus able to produce interpretations of the inscriptions which were substantially accurate, though by no means correct in all points. His estimate of the age of these inscriptions, however, was off by nearly a millennium, because he interpreted the date *samvat 33* of the Muṅgir inscription as a year of the Vikrama era equivalent to 23 B.C., whereas in fact it is a regnal year of Devapāladeva, who ruled in the first half of the ninth century.

An even more remarkable achievement by Wilkins was his translation, published as a letter in AR 1, 279–83, of the record now known as the Nāgārjunī hill cave inscription of the early Maukhari king Anantavarman.[9] While his comment that the script is "very materially different from that we find in inscriptions of eighteen hundred years ago" is due to his incorrect dating of the Muṅgir plate alluded to earlier,

---

have remained comprehensible for some centuries after they were written, but there is little clear evidence as to how long. The reference in l. 8 of Rudradāman's Junāgaḍh rock inscription (SI I.175–80) of about A.D. 150 to Candragupta Maurya and Aśoka Maurya might imply that the Aśokan edicts carved on the same rock were still legible in the second century A.D. But the later inscription does not specifically refer to the Aśokan edicts, and provides the names of local administrators of the region in Mauryan times who are not mentioned in the older inscriptions, indicating that the historical information was derived from some other source. It thus remains doubtful whether the Aśokan inscriptions were still comprehensible some four hundred years after they were inscribed (see also Falk, SAI, 328).

3. So called by H. Colebrooke; see Windisch, *Geschichte der Sanskrit-Philologie*, 23 n. 1.

4. On Wilkins, see E. H. Johnston, "Charles Wilkins," in Mohammad Shafi, ed., *Woolner Commemoration Volume*, Mehar Chand Lachhman Das Sanskrit and Prakrit Series, vol. 8 (Lahore: Mehar Chand Lachhman Das, 1940), 124–32; and Mary Lloyd, "Sir Charles Wilkins, 1749–1836," in *Indian Office Library and Records: Report for the Year 1978* (London: Foreign and Commonwealth Office, 1979), 8–39. The dates for Wilkins' life given by Windisch (*Geschichte der Sanskrit-Philologie*, 23), 1750–1833, are evidently incorrect.

5. According to Lloyd, op. cit., this article "had been first published in Calcutta in 1781, printed by Wilkins" (21 n. 27). The paper was presented to the Asiatic Society on July 7, 1785; see Sibadas Chaudhuri, ed., *Proceedings of the Asiatic Society*. Vol. 1: *1784–1800* (Calcutta: The Asiatic Society, 1980), 57.

6. The inscription in question is the Muṅgir (Monghyr) copper plate of Devapāladeva (IA 21, 253–58).

7. The Bādāl pillar inscription of the time of Nārāyaṇapāla (SI II, 87–91). The paper was presented to the society on July 14, 1785 (Chaudhuri, *Proceedings*, 58).

8. Sircar refers to "the application of his knowledge of the late medieval Bengali and Nāgarī scripts gradually acquired from a study of manuscripts" (EINES 81).

9. Presented March 17, 1785 (Chaudhuri, *Proceedings*, 47).

he was nonetheless correct that "the character is undoubtedly the most ancient of any that have hitherto come under my inspection." (Anantavarman is now known to have ruled sometime in the sixth century A.D.) It is truly remarkable that Wilkins was somehow able to read the late Brāhmī of this period, which, unlike the scripts of three centuries later, is very different from modern scripts both in its general form and in many of its specific characters. It is thus not entirely clear how, beyond pure perseverance and genius, Wilkins managed to read this inscription, but presumably he did this by working back from the script of the Pāla period which he had already mastered.[10] In any case, his translation, while once again not always correct, proves beyond question that he could read the late Brāhmī, or early Siddhamātṛkā, script of the sixth century. We may compare, for example, his translation of the first verse:

> When the foot of the Goddess was, with its tinkling ornaments, planted upon the head of *Maheeshasoor*, all the bloom of the new-blown flower of the fountain was dispersed, with disgrace, by its superior beauty. May that foot, radiant with a fringe of refulgent beams issuing from its pure bright nails, endue you with a steady and an unexampled devotion, offered up with fruits, and shew you the way to dignity and wealth! (282)

with the standard rendition by J. F. Fleet in CII 3, 227:

> May the foot of (the goddess) Dēvī, fringed with the rays of (*its*) pure nails point out the way to fortune, endowing with a (*suitable*) reward your state of supplication which is such as befits the expression of firm devotion;—(that foot) which, surpassing in radiance all the beauty of a full-blown waterlily, was disdainfully placed, with its tinkling anklet, on the head of the demon Mahishāsura![11]

Here Wilkins has clearly read and construed the verse correctly. Elsewhere in this and other articles his translations are less accurate, and not infrequently he errs in dividing words and compounds, in construing the syntax of complex verses, or in rendering idiomatic expressions.[12] But despite such inevitable imperfections, Wilkins' treatment of these difficult documents is nothing short of remarkable, given the almost nonexistent resources available at the time.[13]

Another renowned pioneering Indologist who made important early contributions to epigraphy was Sir William Jones (1746–94). Though less of a specialist in this field than Wilkins before and Colebrooke after him, Jones amply demonstrated his

10. The precise order in which Wilkins translated his first three inss. is not certain, but it is clear that he worked on the Muṅgir ins. first, in 1781, and that the Nāgārjunī and Bādāl inss. followed in the period between 1781 and his presentation of all three inss. to the society in 1785 (see Kejariwal, *The Asiatic Society*, 43–4).

11. The text, in Fleet's reading (227), is *unnidrasya saroruhasya sakalām ākṣipya śobhāṃ rucā sāvajñaṃ Mahiṣāsurasya śirasi nyastaḥ kvaṇannūpuraḥ / devyā vaḥ sthirabhaktivādasadṛśīṃ yuñjan phalenārthitāṃ diśyād acchanakhāṅśujālajaṭilaḥ pādaḥ padaṃ saṃpadāṃ //.*

12. E.g., Wilkins translates the beginning of the third verse of the Nāgārjunī inscription as "honor was achieved from the deed of death near the uprising ocean," evidently reading *udīrṇa-mahārṇav-opa-maraṇa-vyāpāra-labdhaṃ yaśaḥ*; the correct reading and translation (by Fleet) are *udīrṇa-mahārṇav-opama-raṇa-vyāpāra-labdhaṃ yaśaḥ*, "the renown that he had acquired in the occupation of war resembling . . . the great swollen ocean."

13. The same may be said of Wilkins' subsequent translation (AR 2, 1790, 167–9) of two further Maukhari inss. from the Barābar and Nāgārjunī caves (= CII 3, 221–6).

acumen in his comments (142–4) on Wilkins' first two papers in AR 1, published as "Remarks on the Two Preceding Papers. By the President" (i.e., Jones). Here, with the assistance of the *paṇḍita* "Rádhácánta" (i.e., Rādhākānta [Śarman] Tarkavāgīśa),[14] he offered several constructive criticisms of Wilkins' readings and renderings.[15]

The first six volumes of AR (1788–99) contained, besides the papers already noted, a few more articles translating, describing, and/or illustrating old inscriptions, by Wilkins,[16] Rādhākānta,[17] Jones,[18] and several others. These early contributions included the first publication of a copper plate grant by "Rámalóchan Pandit,"[19] who was also one of Jones' *paṇḍitas*. But the next momentous contributions were those of the great early Indologist Henry T. Colebrooke (1765–1837). His first epigraphic paper was the "Translation of One of the Inscriptions on the Pillar at Dehlee, Called the Lāt of Feerōz Shah" (AR 7, 1801, 175–82), in which he retranslated the inscription of the Cāhamāna king Vigrahapāla (on the Delhi-Toprā Aśokan pillar) which had previously been translated "as explained by Rádhácánta Sarman" in AR 1 (see n. 17). This article made three major contributions to the study of epigraphy. First, Colebrooke correctly interpreted the date (Vikrama 1220 = A.D. 1164), which had been wrongly read by Rādhākānta as 123. Second, he provided an accurate transliterated text of the inscription, together with a facsimile reproduction; this constituted a major methodological advance and set the pattern for epigraphic publications ever since. Third, he also included complete and reliable facsimiles of the Aśokan inscriptions on the same pillar; and although he made no progress toward interpreting these, he thereby brought them to the attention of and made them available to the scholarly public, laying the groundwork for their decipherment some thirty-five years later.

Colebrooke's second major epigraphic contribution was his paper "On Ancient Monuments, Containing Sanscrit Inscriptions" in AR 9 (1807), 398–444. Here he published nine Sanskrit inscriptions, mostly copper plate grants, with texts in Devanāgarī and English translations. But the most important contribution of this paper is found in Colebrooke's introductory remarks concerning the importance of inscriptions in general:

> In the scarcity of authentic materials for the ancient, and even for the modern, history of the *Hindu* race, importance is justly attached to all genuine monuments, and especially inscriptions on stone and metal, which are occasionally discovered through various accidents. If these be carefully preserved and diligently examined; and the facts, ascertained from them, be judiciously employed towards elucidating the scattered information, which can be yet collected from

14. On Rādhākānta, see Rosane Rocher, "The Career of Rādhākānta Tarkavāgīśa, an Eighteenth-Century Pandit in British Employ," JAOS 109, 1989, 627–33. In the early decades of Indology it was the standard and approved practice to enlist the assistance of *paṇḍitas* in interpreting Sanskrit inscriptions and other documents. These *paṇḍitas* were often, but by no means always, given due credit for their efforts in the publications of English authors, so that it is not always easy to fully evaluate the nominal authors' real contributions. It appears, however, that Wilkins deciphered his inscriptions without the aid of *paṇḍitas* (see Kejariwal, *The Asiatic Society*, 43).

15. For further information on Jones' contribution to epigraphic studies, see Garland Cannon, "Early Indian Epigraphy and Sir William Jones," JAS 19, 1977, 1–13 (esp. 4).

16. AR 1, 284–7; 2, 167–9 (see also n. 13).

17. AR 1, 379–82.

18. AR 3, 1792, 38–53.

19. AR 1, 357–67. See also the comments by Kejariwal, *The Asiatic Society*, 50–1.

> the remains of Indian literature, a satisfactory progress may be finally made in investigating the history of the *Hindus*. That the dynasties of princes, who have reigned paramount in *India*, or the lines of chieftains, who have ruled over particular tracts, will be verified; or that the events of war or the effects of policy, during a series of ages, will be developed; is an expectation, which I neither entertain, nor wish to excite. But the state of manners, and the prevalence of particular doctrines, at different periods, may be deduced from a diligent perusal of the writings of authors, whose age is ascertained: and the contrast of different results, for various and distant periods, may furnish a distinct outline of the progress of opinions. A brief history of the nation itself, rather than of its government, will be thus sketched. (398)

Here Colebrooke is the first to clearly recognize the special importance of inscriptions as a source for the political and cultural history of India. And although he somewhat pessimistically underestimated their value for the former, it must nonetheless be recognized that in this oft-quoted passage Colebrooke set the agenda for future Indian epigraphic studies down to the present day, just as his first article had established the standard methodological format for them.[20]

In the following three decades the study of Indian inscriptions continued at a slow but steady pace, without any major breakthroughs. We find in the pages of volumes 12 through 20 (1816–30) of AR sporadic publications of Sanskrit inscriptions, mostly of the medieval period, by such scholars as W. Price, A. Stirling, E. Fell, R. Jenkins, E. C. Ravenshaw, and especially H. H. Wilson.[21] Although the earliest Indian scripts remained undeciphered in this period, the knowledge of the many varieties of Brāhmī-derived local scripts was gradually being filled in; Wilson, for example, first published and translated a copper plate inscription in the central Indian box-headed script (see 2.2.5.3) in AR 15 (1825), 499–515, with the assistance of a Jain scholar named Sri Verma Suri, who had evidently mastered various early scripts in the course of his service under Colin Mackenzie. The latter's collection of several thousand[22] stone and copper plate inscriptions in Sanskrit and Dravidian languages in southern India was among the important epigraphic activities in this period, along with those of James Tod, who collected many medieval Sanskrit inscriptions from Rajasthan and published translations of some of them (by the Jain Yati Jñānacandra) in his *Annals and Antiquities of Rajasthan*.

6.2 The Era of Decipherment (1835–1860)

After the slow but steady progress of the first three decades of the nineteenth century, the study of Indian inscriptions erupted in a blaze of glory in the middle of the 1830s. The "Glanzjahre"[23] of 1834 to 1838 were largely, though by no means exclusively, due to the remarkable efforts and insights of James Prinsep (1799–1840), who

20. Colebrooke also published several other medieval copper plate and stone inss. in the *Transactions of the Royal Asiatic Society* 1, 1823–27, 201–6, 230-9, 462–6, and 520–3.

21. For a comprehensive bibliography of early epigraphic articles in AR and JASB, see Hoernle's "Classified Index to the Scientific Papers in the Society's Publications from 1788 to 1883" in the *Centenary Review*, i–xxxiv.

22. 8,076 according to Cunningham in ASIR 1, xxix.

23. Thus appropriately called by Windisch, *Geschichte der Sanskrit-Philologie*, 98.

came to India in 1819 as assistant to the assay master of the Calcutta Mint and remained until 1838, when he returned to England for reasons of health. During this period Prinsep made a long series of discoveries in the fields of epigraphy and numismatics[24] as well as in the natural sciences and technical fields. But he is best known for his breakthroughs in the decipherment of the Brāhmī and Kharoṣṭhī scripts.

6.2.1 Decipherment of the early Brāhmī script

Although many Sanskrit inscriptions had been published since the time of the pioneers Wilkins and Colebrooke, and although some of the later scripts derived from Brāhmī had been successfully read, inscriptions of the Gupta period and earlier remained incomprehensible when Prinsep began his epigraphic researches in the early 1830s; this, despite Wilkins' having already read, four decades earlier, inscriptions of the sixth century. Renewed progress in the decipherment of early Brāhmī[25] began in 1834 with T. S. Burt's procurement of reliable facsimiles of the inscriptions on the Allahabad pillar,[26] including the Aśokan pillar edicts and the "Queen's Edict" as well as the inscription of Samudragupta. Prinsep's "Notes on Inscription No. 1 [the Aśokan inscriptions] of the Allahabad Column"[27] broke the first ground in the reading of Mauryan Brāhmī script. In this brief paper Prinsep displayed a combination of intuition and methodical thought which would do any modern decipherer proud. He expressed, first of all, doubts as to "whether the language this character . . . expresses is Sanscrit" (116), noting especially the "rare occurrence of double letters" (i.e., conjunct consonants). Although in subsequent articles between this one and his final breakthrough three years later Prinsep seems to have changed his mind and considered that the unknown language was Sanskrit,[28] in the end his first intuition that the inscriptions were not in Sanskrit proved to be correct. Given what little was known at the time of the history of the Indic languages, this was a remarkable insight, since it would have seemed almost automatic to assume that the language of such clearly ancient inscriptions would be Sanskrit.

Equally impressive was Prinsep's arrangement, presented in plate V of JASB 3, of the unknown alphabet, wherein he gave each of the consonantal characters, whose phonetic values were still entirely unknown, with its "five principal inflections" (117), that is, the vowel diacritics. Not only is this table almost perfectly correct in its arrangement, but the phonetic value of the vowels is correctly identified in four out of five cases (plus *anusvāra*); only the vowel sign for *i* was incorrectly interpreted as *o*. Moreover, Prinsep also provided statistical counts for each principal consonantal character and its vocalic "inflections" and noted "other forms occurring." All in all, this table is a model of sophisticated decipherment technique, comparable, mutatis

24. For a collection of his essays on these subjects, together with extensive supplementary notes by Edward Thomas, see *Essays on Indian Antiquities, Historic, Numismatic, and Palaeographic, of the Late James Prinsep.*

25. Referred to in early works by various names, most commonly "lath [i.e., *lāṭ*] character" and "Indian Pali" (see 2.2.2).

26. See JASB 3, 105–13.

27. JASB 3, 1834, 114–8.

28. See, e.g., JASB 3, 487.

mutandis, to the famous grids developed by Michael Ventris for the decipherment of the Cretan Linear B syllabary[29] more than a hundred years later. Prinsep also provided a statistical count of the letters appearing on a page of a Sanskrit text (the *Bhaṭṭikāvya*) for purposes of "aiding the investigation of the powers of the unknown alphabet" (118). Although Prinsep's final decipherment was ultimately to rely on paleographic and contextual rather than statistical methods (cf. Hoernle, *Centenary Review*, 60), it is still no less a tribute to Prinsep's genius that he should have thought to apply such modern techniques to his problem.[30]

Burt's facsimiles of the Allahabad inscriptions were in the meantime also serving as a stimulus to the study of the later Brāhmī script of the Gupta era; in his "Remarks upon the Second Inscription of the Allahabad Pillar,"[31] A. Troyer published in March 1834 a translation of the inscription of Samudragupta based on a transcription into Devanāgarī by Madhava Rao, head librarian of the Sanscrit College.[32] While the transliteration and translation were very incomplete and inaccurate, Troyer did succeed in identifying the names of the kings Candragupta [I] and Samudragupta, though he was inclined to identify them as rulers of the Mauryan, rather than the then virtually unknown Gupta, dynasty.[33] In June of the same year,[34] W. H. Mill published an improved, though still far from accurate, version[35] of the same inscription.

Then, in October 1834, B. H. Hodgson presented his discovery of "Ancient Inscriptions in the Characters of the Allahabad Column"[36] (i.e., in Mauryan Brāhmī) on columns at Mathiah and Radiah, that is, the Aśokan pillars nowadays known as Lauṛiyā-Nandangaṛh and Lauṛiyā-Ararāj.[37] In his "Note on the Mathiah Láth Inscription,"[38] Prinsep made several important steps toward the decipherment of Mauryan Brāhmī. First, he noted that "*all three inscriptions* [i.e., the Delhi, Allahabad, and Mathiah/Lauṛiyā-Nandangaṛh Aśokan pillar inscriptions] *are identically the same*" (484), and he identified a recurrent series of fifteen syllables "which may be supposed to be some formula of invocation" (483); this, in fact, eventually turned out to be the introductory formula *devānaṃpiye piyadasi lāja hevaṃ āha*, "The Beloved

29. See John Chadwick, *The Decipherment of Linear B*, 2nd ed. (Cambridge: Cambridge University Press, 1970). On modern decipherment techniques in general, see E. J. W. Barber, *Archaeological Decipherment: A Handbook* (Princeton: Princeton University Press, 1974).

30. In his conclusion to this important article, Prinsep voices the opinion, again correct, that the decipherment of the ancient Indian script should be much simpler than that of the cuneiform and Egyptian hieroglyphic writings, and urges on his countrymen to turn "fresh attention to the subject, lest the indefatigable students of Bonn or Berlin should run away with the honor of first making it known to the learned world" (118).

31. JASB 3, 118–23.

32. According to Troyer, "It was principally the alphabet of the Mahámalaipur inscriptions [published by Benjamin Guy Babington in *Transactions of the Royal Asiatic Society* 2, 1828, 258–69] that enabled Madhava Rao to transcribe . . . the remains of the inscription" (119); the contributions of Wilkins' decipherment of the "Gya" (i.e., Nāgārjunī) inscriptions is also acknowledged.

33. See also Prinsep, JASB 3, 115–6.

34. JASB 3, 257–70.

35. Cf. the comments of Fleet in CII 3, 1.

36. JASB 3, 481–3.

37. On the equivalents of the early and modern geographical designations of the Aśokan inscriptions, see Windisch, *Geschichte der Sanskrit-Philologie*, 106 and 108 n. 4.

38. JASB 3, 483–7.

of the Gods, King Priyadarśin, speaks thus." Even more importantly, he correctly identified (485) the consonants 𑀬 and 𑀯 as *ya* and *va* on the basis of their resemblance to the corresponding letters in the "Gya alphabet" (see n. 32) and of their frequent occurrence as the lower, that is, latter, members of consonantal conjuncts; and he also seems to have tentatively identified the all-important character for *sa*. These discoveries did, however, lead Prinsep temporarily to the incorrect conclusion that there was "little doubt that . . . the language [is] Sanscrit" (487; see p. 204).

Finally, with regard to the contents of the inscriptions Prinsep commented: "Whether they mark the conquests of some victorious rájá;—whether they are as it were the boundary pillars of his dominions;—or whether they are of a religious nature, bearing some important text from the sacred volumes of the Bauddhists or Brahmins, can only be satisfactorily solved by the discovery of the language, and consequently the import these curious monuments are intended to convey" (487). How typical, once more, of Prinsep's powers of intuition that each of the three alternatives he proposed turned out to be at least partially correct!

The third volume of the JASB also contained one other significant contribution to the decipherment of Brāhmī, this one by J. Stevenson, entitled "Restoration and Translation of Some Inscriptions at the Caves of Carlí" (i.e., Karle).[39] In this paper Stevenson was able to correctly identify, by comparison with the text of the Allahabad Gupta inscription published in March of the same year, twelve consonants (*ka*, *ga*, *ja*, *ta*, *tha*, *da*, *pa*, *ba*, *ya*, *ra*, *va*, and *sa*) in at least some of their occurrences in the dedicatory inscriptions at these caves, which date to about the first century A.D.[40] Stevenson thus succeeded in providing some phonetic values for the oldest form of Brāhmī to date; though how very far he was from a true decipherment can be demonstrated by a comparison of his translation (498) of his inscription A as "To the Triad. I, Arodhana, lord of Jambudwípa (India), the obtainer of victories, of a truly victorious disposition, the commander of the world, the chastiser of the earth, and exalted above paradise, slaughter every foe that rises against me" with the correct translation by Burgess and Indraji:[41] "Sēṭh Bhūtapāla, from Vejayanti, has established a rock-mansion, the most excellent in Jambudvīpa."[42]

The next major step toward decipherment was made by Christian Lassen in a letter to Prinsep published by the latter in JASB 5.[43] Here Lassen correctly read, by reference to Tibetan and "Pali" (i.e., Brāhmī) letter forms, the Brāhmī legend on the reverse of a coin of the Indo-Greek king Agathocles as *agathukla rája*.[44] With this discovery, the partial knowledge of Brāhmī was pushed back into the pre-Christian era.

After the important contributions of Stevenson and Lassen, the initiative passed back into the capable hands of Prinsep. His next step was presented in "The Legends

39. JASB 3, Oct. 1834, 495–9.

40. See 498, "Alphabet as far as decyphered."

41. ICTWI, 28, ins. no. 1.

42. The text, as read by Burgess and Indraji, is *vejayaṃtitā seṭhiṇā bhūtapālenā selagharaṃ pariniṭhapitaṃ jabudipamhi uttama*. See also Prinsep's comments (JASB 3, 487 n. 6) on Stevenson's readings, which he partly accepts, although his alphabet "does not convert the context into intelligible Sanscrit."

43. Nov. 1836, 723–4.

44. On the basis of this important discovery, Lassen could be credited with the first correct reading of an inscription in early Brāhmī, though he cannot be said to have deciphered the script as a whole.

of the Saurashtra Group of Coins Deciphered" in JASB 6.[45] Here Prinsep offered partially correct readings of the hybrid Sanskrit legends on the coins of Western Kṣatrapa rulers of the third and fourth centuries, though he erred in reading *kṛtrima* 'elected [king]' instead of *kṣatrapa* and in reading the name elements *-sena* and *-siṃha* both as *Sáh*. He did, however, correctly identify several conjunct consonants such as *jña*, *mna*, and *śva*, as well as the hybrid Sanskrit genitive ending *-sa*; and this latter discovery provided the clue that set the stage for his greatest breakthrough.

This came in the modestly titled "Note on the Facsimiles of Inscriptions from Sanchí near Bhilsa, Taken for the Society by Captain Ed. Smith, Engineers," published in June 1837,[46] in which Prinsep presented the definitive decipherment of the oldest forms of the Brāhmī script. The final key turned out to be hidden in some two dozen brief inscriptions, dating to the second or first century B.C., which had been copied by Edward Smith from the Buddhist *stūpas* at Sāñcī; concerning these, Prinsep made the following oft-quoted remarks:

> I was struck at their all terminating with the same two letters, 𑀤𑀸𑀦𑀁. Coupling this circumstance with their extreme brevity and insulated position, which proved that they could not be fragments of a continuous text, it immediately occurred that they must record either obituary notices, or more probably the offerings and presents of votaries, as is known to be the present custom in the Buddhist temples of *Ava*; where numerous *dwajas* or flag-staffs, images, and small *chaityas* are crowded within the enclosure, surrounding the chief cupola, each bearing the name of the donor. The next point noted was the frequent occurrence of the letter 𑀲, already set down incontestably as *s*, before the final word:—now this I had learnt from the *Saurashtra* coins, deciphered only a day or two before, to be one sign of the genitive case singular, being the *ssa* of the Páli, or *sya* of the Sanscrit. "Of so and so the gift," must then be the form of each brief sentence; and the vowel *á* and *anuswara* led to the speedy recognition of the word *dánam*, (gift,) teaching me the very two letters, *d* and *n*, most different from known forms, and which had foiled me most in my former attempts. Since 1834 also my acquaintance with ancient alphabets had become so familiar that most of the remaining letters in the present examples could be named at once on re-inspection. In the course of a few minutes I thus became possessed of the whole alphabet, which I tested by applying it to the inscription on the *Delhi* column. (460–1)[47]

The alphabet presented by Prinsep at the end of this article (475) proves that he did indeed substantially decipher the early Brāhmī script; his identifications of the characters are all correct except for the one that he identified as *ṛ*, which is actually *jha*, and the five others (*gha*, *ṅa*, *jha*, *ña*, and *o*) that he was not able to find. He also correctly concluded that the script is the earliest form and parent of all other Indic scripts (474).

Prinsep's readings and translations of the Sāñcī donative inscriptions themselves are, however, only partially correct; his no. 25, for instance (462), is read as *Vajágato*

45. Mar. 1837, 377–92.

46. JASB 6, 451–77.

47. A more vivid and personal view of Prinsep's breakthroughs is provided in the extracts of his letters "in his own spirited language" to Alexander Cunningham quoted by the latter in ASIR 1, ix–xvi. Typical of Prinsep's "ardent enthusiasm" (xvii) are his cheers "'Chulao bhai, juldee puhonchoge'" ("Go on brother, we shall soon get there," in Cunningham's note, x) and "Hurrah for inscriptions!" (xv).

dánam "The gift of VRIJÁGÁN," whereas the correct reading[48] is *vajigutasa dānaṃ* "The gift of Vajiguta." The inaccuracies in Prinsep's interpretations of the Sāñcī inscriptions (and of the other inscriptions he subsequently published) can be attributed only in part to the imperfect copies of the originals he had available to him; more significant was his inadequate knowledge—which he frequently and candidly confessed[49]—of Sanskrit and other Indian languages. But although none of Prinsep's editions of early inscriptions can be considered anything like standard, this does not in any way diminish his great achievements, which were primarily those of a paleographer and decipherer rather than of a linguist and epigraphist.

Prinsep next turned his efforts to the interpretation of the Aśokan and other early inscriptions. In the same article (469) he presented a substantially correct reading of the introductory Aśokan formula *devānaṃpiye piyadasi lāja hevaṃ āha* (see p. 205) and some other recurrent passages. He also recognized (confirming his initial intuition; see p. 204) that "the language is . . . not Sanskrit, but the vernacular modification of it," that is, Prakrit. But he did not yet realize the significance of the dialectal variations in the inscriptions from different regions, referring to them as "grammatical errors." Nor did he correctly recognize the author of these records, identifying the king called "Beloved of the Gods" with Devānaṃpiyatissa of Ceylon (473).[50]

In the subsequent parts of JASB 6 and in the next volume (7, 1838), Prinsep published a series of articles giving complete readings and translations of various early Brāhmī inscriptions, including the Aśokan pillar inscriptions,[51] the Nāgārjunī inscriptions of Aśoka's grandson Daśaratha,[52] the inscriptions at Udayagiri and Khaṇḍagiri (including the Hāthīgumphā inscription),[53] the Aśokan rock inscriptions,[54] the Girnār (Junāgaḍh) inscription of Rudradāman,[55] and further inscriptions from Sāñcī.[56] In these articles (as also in his continuing series of articles on later inscriptions, mostly under the title "Facsimiles of Ancient Inscriptions," which had begun in JASB 5) the interpretations and translations continue to be uneven. In some passages, for example, in his translation of the Aśokan rock edict I,[57] Prinsep produced a reasonably accurate rendering, but elsewhere he strayed far from the mark. But here again it is his paleographic contributions which are lasting, as in JASB 7, 271–6, where he presented his "Completion of the Alphabet," a virtually perfect interpretation of Aśokan Brāhmī.

While Prinsep's success as a decipherer looms large in Indian studies, his decipherment of Brāhmī usually gets little if any attention in general studies of decipherment of ancient scripts worldwide. This is at least in part because, as Prinsep himself

48. By N. G. Majumdar in Marshall and Foucher, *The Monuments of Sanchi*, I.302.

49. For example, JASB 3, 487; 6, 452 and 567.

50. The correct identification of "Piyadasi" with Aśoka was made shortly afterward by George Turnour (JASB 6, 791), from his acquaintance with the Pāli historical texts of Ceylon.

51. JASB 6, 566–609.

52. JASB 6, 676–9.

53. JASB 6, 1072–91.

54. JASB 7, 156–67, 219–82.

55. JASB 7, 334–56.

56. JASB 7, 562–7.

57. JASB 7, 249.

realized from the outset (see n. 30), the decipherment of Brāhmī was relatively simple when "compared with the difficulties of the Persepolitan [i.e., Old Persian], or cuneiform character . . . or the more abstruse hieroglyphics of Egypt."[58] Prinsep's methodology was also less spectacular than that of the decipherers of cuneiform and Egyptian, mainly in that the decipherment of early Brāhmī was largely achieved by a gradual reading back of progressively more ancient forms of Indian scripts from the modern forms which were their direct descendants. Analytic methods such as statistical, positional, and contextual analysis did provide Prinsep with the keys to his major breakthrough, but they were ultimately supplementary to the paleographic method. This is why, after the crucial discovery in the Sāñcī inscriptions, virtually the entire picture of Brāhmī fell into place almost instantly (p. 207). Prinsep does not tell us exactly what he knew, or suspected, about Brāhmī up to this point, but it is clear from his own earlier articles as well as those of other contributors such as Stevenson and Lassen that the key to early Brāhmī was very nearly at hand, and the Sāñcī breakthrough was but the final stage in what was essentially a gradual process of paleographic reconstruction. The importance of the Sāñcī discovery, great as it was, should thus not be overestimated, as it sometimes is. In the perspective of the history of the study of the Brāhmī script in its various forms and derivatives, it was merely the last step on a long road.

None of this, however, should be taken as minimizing Prinsep's contributions as a whole. Despite his weaknesses on the linguistic side and the important assistance provided to him by others, he still stands as the unquestioned master of the early phase of Indian epigraphic and paleographic studies. His stature may be measured by what happened after he left India in 1838 and died in 1840; the flood of epigraphic articles in JASB immediately diminished to a trickle from volume 8 (1839) on, and the leadership in epigraphic research was only gradually taken up by other institutions and journals (see 6.2.3).

6.2.2 Decipherment of the Kharoṣṭhī script

Unlike Brāhmī, which was known since the late eighteenth century, nothing whatsoever was known about the script nowadays called Kharoṣṭhī[59] before the third decade of the nineteenth century. At that time, the discovery by General Chevalier Ventura, Charles Masson, and others of huge numbers of bilingual coins of the Indo-Greek and Indo-Scythian kings, with Greek legends on the obverse and Kharoṣṭhī on the reverse, and their publication by Masson, Prinsep, and Lassen first brought this hitherto unknown script to the attention of scholars.[60] The first attempts at decipherment were published by Prinsep in 1835 in his "Further Notes and Drawings of

58. JASB 3, 118.

59. In the early publications discussed here, the script is referred to by various names, such as "Bactrian," "Indo-Bactrian," and "Ariano-Pali"; see section 2.3.5.

60. At this time very few Kharoṣṭhī inscriptions were yet known, presumably because most of them come from territories in the northwest which were not yet under British control. Only the Māṇikiāla *stūpa* inscriptions and the Shāhbāzgaṛhī Aśokan rock edicts were available during the years when Kharoṣṭhī was first studied, so that the early decipherments were achieved almost exclusively from numismatic materials.

Bactrian and Indo-Scythic Coins"[61] and by C. L. Grotefend (son of G. F. Grotefend, the famous decipherer of the Old Persian cuneiform script) in 1836 in "Die unbekannte Schrift der Baktrischen Münzen."[62] At this time the legends on the reverse of the Indo-Greek coins were generally thought to be in "Bactrian" or "Pehlevi,"[63] and both of these initial attempts were partially led astray by the assumption that the inscriptions were written in, and followed the graphic patterns of, Semitic or Iranian languages. Thus Prinsep was led to read *malakao malako* instead of the correct *maharajasa mahatasa* (= Greek ΒΑΣΙΛΕΩΣ ΜΕΓΑΛΟΥ; Skt. *mahārājasya mahataḥ*). He did note, however, that "if the language of our coins be Zend [i.e., Pehlevi], the word *melek*, for king, should not be expected in it. . . . It was this circumstance that led me to imagine the reading might be *maharáo:* but the combination *maharáo-maharó* is inadmissible, and overthrows the conjecture."[64] It is typical of Prinsep's intuitive powers that, even when he was wrong, he suspected the truth, and was soon to fully realize it.

Despite their misconceptions, the early efforts of Prinsep and Grotefend were by no means wasted. Both of them succeeded in correctly identifying the phonetic values of several characters of the unknown script by comparing recurring sequences in it with the corresponding titles in the Greek legends on the obverse of the bilingual coins. Thus Prinsep was able to correctly isolate the "Pehlevi" sequences corresponding to the names of the Greek kings Apollodotus, Eukratides, Menander, Antialkidas, and others,[65] and because he was dealing with proper names transliterated into an unknown script he was able to correctly identify several characters of the unknown script even without knowing what language he was dealing with; in his own words:

> It immediately struck me that if the genuine Greek names were faithfully expressed in the unknown character, a clue would through them be formed to unravel the value of a portion of the Alphabet, which might in its turn be applied to the translated epithets and titles, and thus lead to a knowledge of the language employed. Incompetent as I felt myself to this investigation, it was too seductive not to lead me to an humble attempt at its solution. (329)[66]

Noting, for example, that the same character, 𐨀, occurred at the beginning of the names of Apollodotus, Antimachus, Antialkidas, and Azes, Prinsep correctly identified it as *a* (329). He was similarly able to correctly isolate the characters for the initial vowel

61. JASB 4, 1835, 327–48.

62. *Blätter für Münzkunde 2* (no. 26), 1836, 309–14 + pl. XXIV.

63. See, e.g., Masson, JASB 3, 1834, 164, etc. Prinsep refers to "the Bactrian form (if we may so call it) of the Pehlevi character" (JRAS 4, 327).

64. JASB 4, 335.

65. JASB 4, pl. XX, nos. 21–33. Here Prinsep acknowledged the assistance of Masson, who "first pointed out in a note addressed to myself . . . the Pehleví signs, which he had found to stand for the words *Menandrou*, *Apollodotou*, *Ermaiou*, *Basileos*, and *Soteros*" (ibid., 329).

66. The use of transliterated proper names as a key to breaking into an unknown writing system is a technique which has been successfully exploited in other decipherments, e,g, in Jean-François Champollion's decipherment of Egyptian hieroglyphic writing beginning from the names of Ptolemy and Cleopatra and in the elder Grotefend's identification of the names of the Achaemenian kings Darius and Xerxes in the Old Persian inscriptions.

e and for the consonants *ma*, *ya*, *pa*, and *na* (330) and also came close to identifying a few others such as ϛ *kha*, corresponding to Greek X in the name of Antimachus (332). Although his immediate progress by this method was limited, it was ultimately to prove more fruitful.

Meanwhile Grotefend, working along similar lines as Prinsep (though evidently not aware of the latter's article), made similar progress, correctly identifying eight characters (initial *a* and the consonants *ta*, *da*, *pa*, *ma*, *ra*,[67] *la*, and *ha*) from the correspondences between the kings' names in the Greek and Kharoṣṭhī legends. He also correctly identified some syllabic combinations such as *me* (in the name of Menander) and *li* (in Lysias).

Beyond this, however, both Prinsep's and Grotefend's efforts were largely blocked by their failure to realize that the language of the unknown script was an Indian one, and specifically a dialect of Prakrit. It was not yet clear at this time that the regions of the far northwest where these coins were found, corresponding to modern eastern Afghanistan and northern Pakistan, had been part of the Indian world in ancient times, and it was thus only natural that scholars of the time should have thought at first in terms of Iranian languages. As a result, Grotefend and Prinsep only vaguely and partially realized that the graphic system was of the Indic variety, with vowels attached diacritically to the consonants they followed, rather than left unindicated as in Semitic scripts or represented alphabetically as in Greek.[68] This led both of them into the crucial error of identifying the character Ϸ, which appeared as the final of every word in the Kharoṣṭhī coin legends, as *o*, which Grotefend (310) compared with the nominative ending in *-o* in the legends in Greek script on the Kuṣāṇa coins, and which Prinsep thought to represent a termination of either Semitic, Greek, or "Zend" (op. cit., 329–30); but both failed to recognize it as the Prakrit genitive suffix *-sa* (i.e., *-ssa*).

But in July 1838 Prinsep published his crucial article "Additions to Bactrian Numismatics, and Discovery of the Bactrian Alphabet,"[69] in which he announced his discovery of the true Indic character of the Kharoṣṭhī legends: "I threw off the fetters of an interpretation through the Semitic languages, and at once found an easy solution of all the names and the epithets through the pliant, the wonder-working *Páli*" (643).[70] He thus realized that the word-ending character ϷP was not *o* but the Prakrit genitive *sa* ("[coin] of . . ."),[71] and this enabled him to read the first word of

67. Grotefend's reading of ra (op. cit., 311) was a pure stroke of luck. He identified it from the third consonant in the word which he read as *maha-rāo* (correctly *maharajasa*) by a comparison with the word he read as *rao* in the Bactrian Greek legend on the coins of the Kuṣāṇa kings. This latter word, we now know, is not *rao* but the Iranian *shao*, with the Bactrian Greek character Ϸ representing *sh*. Thus Grotefend was lucky enough to correctly identify Kharoṣṭhī *ra* by comparing it with an incorrectly read Greek letter in an Iranian word for 'king'!

68. Cf. the comments by Lassen in *Zur Geschichte der griechischen und indoskythischen Könige in Baktrien*, 16.

69. JASB 7, 636–55.

70. Here as elsewhere, Prinsep, like others of his time, uses "Pāli" to refer to middle Indic vernaculars, i.e., the Prakrits, in general; see section 3.1.5.2 n. 29.

71. Prinsep mentions that he came to this realization by noticing "the same letter (affected with the vowel *i*) in two Greek names" (op. cit., 642) in nonfinal position. The names in question are presumably *lisiasa* (Lysias) and *pilasinasa* (Philoxenos).

the legends correctly as *maharajasa* (instead of *malakáo*), and thence to correctly identify at least seventeen characters.[72]

Besides identifying almost half of the basic consonants of Kharoṣṭhī, Prinsep at this point began to understand the graphic principles governing the script. He correctly noted that (unlike Brāhmī) the initial vowel signs were "formed by modifications of the alif as in the Arabic,"[73] while the postconsonantal vowels were indicated diacritically as in Brāhmī, and he correctly identified the diacritic forms for *i*, *e*, and *u* (but not *o*; 640). He did not clearly realize that there are no special signs for long vowels in the script but seemed to have some suspicions to this effect (640, 643). He also attempted, though with little success, to identify some consonantal conjuncts (643).

Although Prinsep is clearly the foremost figure in the decipherment of Kharoṣṭhī, a good deal of credit must also be given again[74] to Christian Lassen, who almost simultaneously[75] made major breakthroughs in his *Zur Geschichte der griechischen und indoskythischen Könige in Baktrien*. Working along the same general lines and from the same published materials as Prinsep, Lassen correctly identified eleven characters (*a*, *kha*, *ja*, *ta*,[76] *na*, *pa*, *ma*, *ya*, *ra*, *la*, and *ha*). He failed, however, to make the all-important discovery of *sa*, which he continued to read as a final *o*, for example, in *mahārājo* (33).[77] Lassen also made some important general observations about the script and language of the coin legends. He realized that the vowel *a* was inherent in all consonants, and that there was no *virāma* sign (18). He had a partial understanding of the vowel diacritics (21ff.), though less clearly stated than Prinsep's; and like Prinsep, he also suspected the absence of long vowels (22). Moreover, he more accurately designated the language of the legends as "Prakrit" (as opposed to Prinsep's "Páli"), noting similarities to the Prakrits of the classical dramas (55), though he arrived at this, ironically enough, for the wrong reason; since he still read *sa* as *o*, he read the epithet *mahatasa*, 'great' (Gk. ΜΕΓΑΛΟΥ), as *mahato* (43), which he took as a Prakrit nominative (rather than genitive).

Despite the simultaneous discoveries by Prinsep and Lassen, the Kharoṣṭhī script did not fall into place at once as happened in the case of Brāhmī, where the breakthrough with the Sāñcī inscriptions almost immediately enabled Prinsep to compile

72. The initial vowels *a*, *e*, *i*, and *aṃ*, and the consonants *ka*, *kha*, *ja*, *ta*, *da*, *pa*, *ba*, *ma*, *ya*, *ra*, *la*, *ha*, and *sa* (op. cit., 639-43). Here, as elsewhere in connection with the decipherment of Kharoṣṭhī, it is difficult to give precise figures for numbers of characters identified, due to such complications as the high degree of graphic variability and ambiguity of several of the *akṣaras*.

73. Op. cit., 639; see section 2.3.4.

74. Cf. section 6.2.1 n. 44.

75. As noted by Windisch (*Geschichte der Sanskrit-Philologie*, 110), the foreword to Lassen's book is dated August 1838, while Prinsep's article appeared in July of the same year and had not yet been seen by Lassen.

76. Lassen (26-9) was unable to clearly differentiate *ta* and *da*, which are very similar in numismatic and some inscriptional varieties of Kharoṣṭhī. But as he was aware of the problem, it seems fair to credit him with at least one of the characters.

77. Lassen, however, did accept Prinsep's correct identification of *sa* when it became known to him; see the notes in Roer's English translation of *Zur Geschichte der griechischen und indoskythischen Könige in Baktrien*, JASB 9, 263 and 357 (= 13 and 44 of the separate reprint edition; see the bibliography for details).

a virtually complete alphabet of early Brāhmī. The discoveries from the Indo-Greek coins yielded less than half of the characters of the Kharoṣṭhī script, and the task of completing the inventory took far longer than with Brāhmī. Prinsep was not to make any further contributions to the subject in the short time left to him, although, as Cunningham remarked in 1840, "had James Prinsep lived, he would long before this have perfected what he had so successfully begun."[78] The next major advance was thus left to Edwin Norris (1795–1872), who published in 1846[79] the first reliable transcription of a stone inscription in Kharoṣṭhī, namely Aśokan rock edict VII at Shāhbāzgaṛhī,[80] which had been discovered by A. Court in 1836. The text, presented synoptically with the corresponding Brāhmī versions at Girnār and Dhauli (306–7), is not perfect but is on the whole remarkably accurate given its early date and the imperfect reproductions then available. It is presumably on the basis of this text that Norris was able to compile his chart of "The Alphabet" (before 303), which is a remarkable tribute to his paleographic skill; it contains 35 simple characters, plus a few variants and conjuncts, nearly all correctly identified, and is thus the first reasonably accurate presentation of the script as a whole. Only the sign given for *tha*, 𐨠, is incorrect, this character being really an alternative form for *ṭha*.[81] Norris also included a brief but accurate account of the system of vowel notation and of the formation of conjuncts with following *r*. Thus although Norris' edition of the complete Shāhbāzgaṛhī edicts, promised for the next number of the JRAS, did not appear,[82] his brief article nonetheless constituted a major step toward the complete decipherment of the Kharoṣṭhī script.

In the meantime, Alexander Cunningham had been pursuing in a series of articles in the JASB the study of the bilingual coins and their legends, to the point that he was able to claim in 1845 (before Norris' alphabet!) that he had "found the Ariano-Pali equivalent for every letter of the Sanskrit alphabet."[83] In 1854 he claimed for himself "the discovery of the true values of eleven letters, or of just one-third of the Ariano-Pali alphabet,"[84] as well as of the value of several consonantal conjuncts. To Prinsep he credited the discovery of seventeen of the consonants, and to Norris only six. Much later in his life Cunningham voiced similar claims, adding, with a hint of pique, "It is perhaps curious to note, that though all these readings have now been generally adopted, scarcely one of them has been acknowledged as mine."[85] Cunningham's claims for a prominent role in the decipherment of Kharoṣṭhī are, however, difficult to evaluate. The "discoveries" he claims for various characters are scattered through his various numismatic studies (to which he often gives only vague

78. JASB 9, 887.

79. "On the Kapur-di-Giri Rock Inscription," JRAS 8, 303–14.

80. Then known as Kapur-di-Giri; see n. 37.

81. The precise phonetic value of this character has still not been definitely determined (see Brough, GD, 75–7, for the problems involved with this and related Kharoṣṭhī characters), so that Norris can surely be forgiven his error.

82. This was finally accomplished by H. H. Wilson in JRAS 12, 1850; see section 6.2.3.

83. JASB 14, 430.

84. JASB 23, 714.

85. "Coins of the Indo-Scythians," *Numismatic Chronicle*, 3d ser., vol. 8, 1888, 201–48 (quoted 204; reprinted in *Coins of the Indo-Scythians, Sakas, and Kushans* [Varanasi: Indological Book House, 1971]). Cunningham also expressed similar sentiments in ASIR 1, xxxvii and xl–xli.

references) and are usually presented there in readings of coin legends without any paleographic explanation. They are nowhere collected or discussed in any detail, and some of them are clearly wrong, for instance, *ng* (i.e., *ṅa*) based on a misreading of *ṇa* in the Māṇikiāla silver disk inscription (JASB 14, 431); in fact, Kharoṣṭhī has no character for *ṅa*. His claim of having discovered the characters for *ca* and *cha*[86] is typically misleading. In the original article to which he is presumably referring[87] the two characters are transliterated identically (*Chatrapasa apratihatachakrasa . . .*), without accompanying commentary or explanation.[88] In any case, it is now known that the character Y identified by Cunningham as *chh* (i.e., *cha*) actually represents, or at least corresponds to, Sanskrit *kṣa* rather than *cha* (see 2.3.4).

Thus while it is undoubtedly true that Cunningham did discover several of the letters which he claimed (e.g., *ga*, correctly read on the coins of Gondophernes and in the Māṇikiāla bronze casket inscription), his sketchy presentations and questionable interpretations make it difficult to confirm many of his claims. One therefore cannot help but suspect that his repeated claims to a major role in the decipherment of Kharoṣṭhī are somewhat inflated. Surely he played a significant part, for which he has been accorded due credit in subsequent publications (e.g., BIP, 18), but he cannot be said to have equaled the brilliant insights and fundamental contributions of Prinsep and his other predecessors. In balance it may be fairest to say that the decipherment of Kharoṣṭhī was a combined effort in which Prinsep again takes the place of honor, with Lassen and Norris making important contributions and Cunningham, Grotefend, and Masson playing significant secondary roles.

By the sixth decade of the nineteenth century, the Kharoṣṭhī script had been substantially deciphered, although much remained to be done by way of refining the understanding of the script and applying it to the interpretation of the inscriptions, of which a good number had by then been discovered. This was a gradual process which continued at a slow pace, not only through the rest of the nineteenth but on into the twentieth century, and indeed up to the present day; for by no means have all of the intricate problems of Kharoṣṭhī paleography and orthography yet been solved (see n. 81). It will thus be clear that the decipherments of Brāhmī and Kharoṣṭhī took very different courses, and that the latter was ultimately a far more difficult problem. Although the first steps might have seemed relatively simple, given the presence of not one but thousands of little Rosetta stones in the form of the bilingual Indo-Greek coins, there were also some serious obstacles. First of all, the script has no modern descendants, such as were so helpful to the decipherers of Brāhmī; and though its roots in Semitic scripts were more or less clear from the beginning, the connections were not so paleographically transparent as to be of much help for the initial decipherment. Second, the decipherers were hampered by the linguistic situation; for even after the early incorrect assumptions about Pehlevi, Bactrian, and so on were discarded and it became clear that the language of the inscriptions was an Indian Prakrit, only very gradually did it become clear that the dialect in question, namely, what is

86. "Coins of the Indo-Scythians," 203; ASIR 1, xl.

87. JASB 23, 1854, 690.

88. In ASIR 1, xl, he apparently tries to clarify the matter after the fact by noting that "*Ch* is found in *aprati-chakra* [*sic*], 'invincible with the discus', *chh* in *chhatrapa* or Satrap."

nowadays known as Gāndhārī (3.1.4.2.1), was significantly different in grammatical and, especially, phonetic structure from the Prakrits known from literary sources. Still further obstacles were presented by the aberrant orthographic characteristics of Kharoṣṭhī, such as the lack of vowel quantity notation and the peculiarities and ambiguities in its formation of consonantal conjuncts (2.3.4). Moreover, reflecting its origins as a "clerk's script," Kharoṣṭhī has a high degree of graphic ambiguity, such that several common characters like *ta*, *da*, and *ra* may be difficult to distinguish even for those who are familiar with the script (see n. 76); such problems were noticed but not solved by early decipherers such as Prinsep.[89] The problem of graphic ambiguity was further aggravated for these pioneer scholars by their necessary reliance on numismatic texts, which are often imperfectly written, incomplete, or otherwise unclear; and while the repetitiousness of coin legends was helpful at the initial stages, the amount of data provided by a series of personal names and a small repertoire of titles and epithets ultimately proved to be limited. It is thus no coincidence that a tolerably complete picture of the alphabet began to emerge only when scholars turned to the study of recently discovered Kharoṣṭhī inscriptions (6.2.3 and 6.3).

6.2.3 Other developments during the era of decipherment

After the pioneering works of Prinsep and Norris, further progress in the study of the Aśokan inscriptions continued at a slow but steady pace in the fifth and sixth decades of the nineteenth century. The Bairāṭ (or Bhābṛā, Calcutta-Bairāṭ, etc.; see 4.3.1.1.2 n. 69) rock inscription, discovered by T. S. Burt in 1840 and published by M. Kittoe in the same year,[90] was the first known example of the separate or minor rock edicts. In 1850[91] H. H. Wilson published a detailed study with synoptic texts of the fourteen rock edicts in the three versions then known, namely, Girnār, Dhauli, and Kapur-di-Giri (i.e., Shāhbāzgaṛhī). Though far from authoritative, Wilson's edition represents a major step in the reading and understanding of the Aśokan inscriptions.[92] Several of the Aśokan edicts known at the time were also published by Eugène Burnouf in Appendix 10 of *Le Lotus de la bonne loi*.[93]

During the same period progress also continued to be made in the study of the Kharoṣṭhī script and the inscriptions written therein. An important discovery was the biscript Brāhmī and Kharoṣṭhī inscription from Kanhiāra, first published by E. C. Bayley in 1854[94] and reedited by Edward Thomas in 1858 in his edition of Prinsep's *Essays on Indian Antiquities* (I.159–61). Among his extensive additions to Prinsep's articles in the same work, Thomas provided facsimiles and transcriptions of a few other Kharoṣṭhī inscriptions, including the Māṇikiāla stone inscription (I.143–6),

89. JASB 7, 641.
90. JASB 9, 616–9.
91. JRAS 12, 153–251.
92. Despite his superior understanding of the text, however, Wilson (op. cit., 234–51) still refused to accept Turnour's identification of King Piyadassi of the inscriptions with Aśoka of the Ceylonese Pāli tradition. But he did at least retract his arguments against the Buddhist character of the inscriptions in his revised edition of the Bairāṭ inscription in JRAS 16, 1856, 357–67.
93. Paris: Imprimerie Nationale, 1852.
94. JASB 23, 57–9.

the Bīmarān reliquary (I.105–9), and the Wardak vase (I.161–5), as well as a "Review of the Bactrian Alphabet" (II.144–67); the accompanying plate XI (facing page 166) summarizes the Kharoṣṭhī script as then known, with minor improvements in detail on what had been presented by Norris in 1846.

In the meantime, the study of Indian inscriptions of the later centuries was by no means being neglected. Sanskrit inscriptions continued to be published sporadically in the pages of the JASB, especially by Rājendralāla Mitra and by Fitz-Edward Hall, who was the first American to pursue the study of Indian epigraphy.[95] More importantly, the Asiatic Society's practical monopoly on epigraphic studies was broken in the 1840s as inscriptions began to be regularly published in other journals, notably the *Journal of the Royal Asiatic Society* and the *Journal of the Bombay Branch of the Asiatic Society*. Besides the already mentioned articles published by Wilson and others in the JRAS, W. H. Wathen published several copper plate and stone inscriptions from western India in JRAS[96] as well as in JASB;[97] and Walter Elliot published in the former journal[98] a paper on "Hindu Inscriptions," announcing the presentation to the Royal Asiatic Society of a collection of 595 medieval southern Indian inscriptions in Sanskrit and Kannada and summarizing the historical information provided by them. It was the JBBRAS, however, that from the commencement of its publication in 1842 became the most prolific source of epigraphic studies. A large number of articles on inscriptions from western India, especially the early cave temple inscriptions from Kāṇherī, Kārle, Nāsik, and so on, and on copper plate inscriptions were published in the first five volumes of the journal (1842–54) by such scholars as John Wilson, LeGrand Jacob, Ball Gungadhur Shastree, and J. Stevenson.[99]

The most important independent epigraphic publication in this period was Alexander Cunningham's book *The Bhilsa Topes; or, Buddhist Monuments of Central India*, which included transcriptions and translations of over two hundred of the Sāñcī inscriptions. While these are still by no means definitive, they do represent considerable advances over the readings given by Prinsep in his famous article in JASB 7; for example, the inscription which Prinsep read as *Vajāgato dānam* (6.2.1) was read by Cunningham (150, no. 3) as *Vaja-Gutasa dānam* ("Gift of Vajra-Gupta"), considerably closer to the correct reading *Vajigutasa dānaṃ*.

During this period, good progress was also made toward a full understanding of the numerical signs and system used in Brāhmī inscriptions (cf. 2.4.1.2). The study of the number signs began with Prinsep's article "On the Ancient Sanskrit Numerals,"[100] discussing the characters on the obverse of coins of the "Sáh Kings" (i.e., the Western Kṣatrapas), which Prinsep correctly determined to be numerals, and the figures in some copper plate inscriptions from Gujarat which were dated in both numbers and words. Prinsep's grasp of the specifics of the system was, however, defec-

95. See also his several publications of inscriptions in JAOS 6, 1860, and 7, 1862.

96. JRAS 2, 1835, 378–99; 3, 1836, 94–105 and 258–71; 4, 1837, 109–14 and 281–6.

97. JASB 4, 1835, 477–87.

98. JRAS 4, 1837, 1–41; reprinted "with the corrections and emendations of the Author" in *Madras Journal of Literature and Science* 7, 1838, 193–232.

99. On the history of the Bombay Branch of the Royal Asiatic Society and the JBBRAS, see Windisch, *Philologie und Altertumskunde in Indien*, passim.

100. JASB 7, 1838, 348–54.

tive, mainly because he did not realize that the system involved was additive, rather than place-value as in later numerical notation (2.4.1.3); he therefore arrived at several wrong readings, interpreting, for example, the symbol for 300 as 3. Edward Thomas in 1850[101] was the first to correctly recognize the additive nature of the system, that is, that "the figures employed were incapable of . . . attaining any accession of power from relative position" (33), and he further explicated it in 1855 in his article on "Ancient Indian Numerals."[102] Important supplementary information on this subject was gathered from the Nāsik inscriptions, which contain many dates and other numbers written in numerical symbols; this enabled J. Stevenson in 1853[103] to correctly identify the hitherto unknown figures for 10 and 20 and to recognize the basic character for 1,000, although he did not correctly interpret its various combinations. From this material, Thomas was able to publish an essentially accurate table of the early Brāhmī numbers in his edition of Prinsep's *Essays on Indian Antiquities*, plate XLa (facing page 84). Further advances were added in 1862[104] by Bhau Daji,[105] who gave a nearly complete chart of the system (231), and in 1877 by Bhagvānlāl Indraji,[106] who clarified the values of the remaining problematic signs.

The first edition of Christian Lassen's *Indische Alterthumskunde* (1847–62) marked the first comprehensive effort at incorporating epigraphic evidence into a study of ancient Indian political and cultural history. In II.44 Lassen discussed the function and significance of inscriptions in a study of this type, following the famous remarks of Colebrooke quoted earlier (p. 202). Lassen's work set the pattern for future studies of early Indian history, with its heavy reliance on epigraphic and numismatic sources.

6.3 The Period of Maturity (1861–1900)

The state of epigraphic studies at the beginning of the 1860s is reflected in such papers as Bhau Daji's edition of the Junāgaḍh inscription of Rudradāman published in the JBBRAS in 1863.[107] Although this important record had already been published several times before,[108] Bhau Daji's edition and translation show definite improvements and can be said to be the first version which comes close to an authoritative edition. While not quite correct in all respects, it provides a substantially accurate text and translation that were to be improved upon in later editions such as that of Kielhorn in EI 8 (1905–6) for the most part only in matters of detail.[109]

101. "On the Dynasty of the Sáh Kings of Suráshtra," JRAS 12, 27–47.
102. JASB 24, 551–71. See also his editorial notes in Prinsep's *Essays on Indian Antiquities*, II.80–4.
103. "On the Násik Cave-Inscriptions," JBBRAS 5, 35–57; see esp. fig. 18.
104. "The Ancient Sanskrit Numerals in the Cave Inscriptions, and on the Sah-Coins, Correctly Made Out," JBBRAS 8, 1863–66, 225–33.
105. But according to Bühler, "the results of [this] article belong chiefly to Bhagvānlāl Indrājī, though his name is not mentioned" (BIP 77 n. 5).
106. "On the Ancient Nāgarī Numerals," IA 6, 42–8.
107. JBBRAS 7, 113–21.
108. See the bibliography in Lüders' *List of Brāhmī Inscriptions* (EI 10), no. 965.
109. Cf. Windisch, *Philologie und Altertumskunde in Indien*, 6–7.

The state of Kharoṣṭhī studies at the same period is attested by Rājendralāla Mitra's new edition, published in 1861,[110] of the important Wardak inscription. While still far from completely correct, this was the most mature treatment of a non-Aśokan Kharoṣṭhī inscription to date. Further progress was demonstrated soon afterward by J. Dowson's important article "On a Newly Discovered Bactrian Pali Inscription; and on Other Inscriptions in the Bactrian Pali Character" in 1863.[111] Here Dowson reviewed all the Kharoṣṭhī inscriptions known at the time; and although his versions are less close to definitive than was Bhau Daji's edition of the Junāgaḍh inscription, this reflects the overall lagging of Kharoṣṭhī studies behind Brāhmī rather than any shortcoming in Dowson's scholarship. Dowson's article represents a major advance in the study of Kharoṣṭhī inscriptions, attributable to the greater number of inscriptions that had become available as well as to his scholarly and cautious approach to them. It also contained (228–47) the first good explanation of the numerical system of Kharoṣṭhī (see 2.4.2), correcting the errors of Cunningham, who had incorrectly assumed that the numbers followed a decimal/place-value system. Hence the principal credit for determining the values of Kharoṣṭhī numerals goes to Dowson.

Thus by the early 1860s the study of Indian inscriptions was poised at the edge of maturity. And although the rest of that decade did not see any major breakthroughs, a steady flow of papers continued to appear, for the most part in the same journals as mentioned in connection with the previous period. The JBBRAS in particular continued to be the predominant vehicle for inscriptional studies, publishing, among others, a large number of articles by Bhau Daji; others who made important contributions through the Bombay Society include J. F. Fleet, Bhagvānlāl Indraji,[112] and R. G. Bhandarkar. But the most important development in this decade, which was to have far-reaching consequences for epigraphic studies even to the present day, was the establishment by the British government of the Archaeological Survey of India (ASI) under Alexander Cunningham as archaeological surveyor to the government of India and, after 1870, as Director General of the Survey. Between 1861 and 1885 Cunningham and his assistants (J. D. Beglar, A. C. Carlleyle, and H. R. W. Garrick) undertook a series of archaeological surveys of northern and central India which were published in the form of twenty-three Reports (Old Series) (ASIR) between 1871 and 1887.[113] These reports included a very large number of inscriptions, some previously known but subjected to new examination, and many entirely new. The inscriptions were illustrated in facsimile form and described, in varying degrees of detail and accuracy, in the text. While the accounts of the inscriptions in the volumes of the ASIR do not constitute anything like authoritative editions, they did make available to epigraphists a vast body of material which was to occupy their attention for many years to come.[114] Moreover, the foundation of the ASI marked a commitment

110. JASB 30, 337–47.

111. JRAS 20, 221–68.

112. On Bhagvānlāl, see Javerilal Umiashankar Yajnik's "Memoir" in JBBRAS 17.2, 1887–89, 18–46.

113. The first three reports were initially published as supplements to JASB 32–4 (1863–65).

114. Some of the materials concerned were later separately published by Cunningham himself in his monographs, notably *The Stûpa of Bharhut* and *Mahâbodhi, or the Great Buddhist Temple Under the Bodhi Tree at Buddha-Gaya.*

(albeit a grudging and sporadic one, in the early years) by the government of India to pursue and support archaeological and epigraphic research, which were thereby established as permanent and recognized fields. From this time onward, most Indian epigraphic studies have been carried out, directly or indirectly, under the auspices of the ASI.

Another turning point in the history of epigraphic studies was reached in 1872 with the issue of the first volume of *The Indian Antiquary* (IA), subtitled *A Journal of Oriental Research in Archaeology, History, Literature, Languages, Folklore, &c, &c*, under the editorship of James Burgess. This was the first Indological journal to be explicitly dedicated to, among other subjects, archaeological research; and this field, by the standards of the era, implied a prominent role for epigraphy. IA thus immediately became the leading vehicle for the publication of inscriptions (although others, notably JBBRAS, continued to play an important role), and in the volumes published in the remainder of the nineteenth century the most frequent contributors of epigraphic articles include such great names as G. Bühler, J. F. Fleet, E. Hultzsch, Bhagvānlāl Indraji, F. Kielhorn, and B. Lewis Rice.[115] The editions and translations of inscriptions in IA were consistently of high quality from the very beginning, so that many of the articles published in the early volumes remain definitive today.

The next landmark was the publication in 1877 of the first volume of the Corpus Inscriptionum Indicarum (CII),[116] Cunningham's *Inscriptions of Asoka*. The need for such a series, along the lines of the Corpus Inscriptionum Graecarum, had long been felt, and as early as 1837[117] Prinsep referred to "the long-expected '*Corpus inscriptionum Indicarum.*'" According to Cunningham's preface, the series was originally planned for three volumes, containing the inscriptions of Aśoka, of the Indo-Scythians and Satraps, and of the Guptas and contemporary dynasties, in order "to bring together, in a few handy and accessible volumes, all the ancient inscriptions of India which now lie scattered about in the journals of our different Asiatic Societies" (i). Although the actual subsequent publication of the CII differed considerably from this original scheme, and although Cunningham's edition of the Aśokan edicts was soon to be superseded by Émile Senart's *Les Inscriptions de Piyadassi* (1881), and eventually by E. Hultzsch's revised edition of CII 1 in 1925, the publication of this volume was nonetheless a major development in setting the precedent for the continued publication of the CII up to the present day. The volume also illustrates the continuing discovery of Aśokan inscriptions, including new versions of the rock edicts from Kālsī and Jaugaḍa and minor rock edicts from Sahasrām, Rūpnāth, and Bairāṭ.

The progress of the CII was further promoted by the appointment in January 1883 of John Faithfull Fleet as epigraphist to the government of India for a term of three years, "with the primary duty of preparing the volume [of CII] that was to contain the Inscriptions of the Early Gupta Kings" (CII 3, preface, 1). This goal was reached

115. For references to these and other papers in IA up to 1921, see Lavinia Mary Anstey's *Index to Volumes I–L (1872–1921): Indian Antiquary*. The journal continued to be published until 1933 (vol. 62), when it was superseded by the *New Indian Antiquary*, published in nine volumes from 1938 to 1947. A "Third Series" of the *Indian Antiquary* was published in five volumes from 1964 to 1971.

116. See also section 8.1.2.

117. JASB 6, 663; see also EI 1, v–vi.

with Fleet's publication in 1888 of the volume in question. His success can be measured by the fact that, although his volume was superseded by the revised edition by D. R. Bhandarkar published in 1981, it remains an indispensable research tool and in some respects at least is still more reliable than the volume which superseded it.[118] When Fleet's appointment as government epigraphist expired in June 1886, Eugen Hultzsch was appointed to succeed him in August of the same year and continued to occupy this office until 1903.

The year 1888 also marked the publication (in October) of the first fascicle of the *Epigraphia Indica* (EI). The EI was initially conceived as a sort of supplement to CII; James Burgess, the editor, states in his preface, "This volume is thus to be regarded as properly one of the series of the *Corpus Inscriptionum Indicarum*, and practically may stand as the fourth volume of that publication" (vi). The purpose of the EI was to facilitate the prompt publication of newly discovered inscriptions, since the compilation of the volumes of the CII was already proving to be a far more complex and time-consuming project than originally foreseen. But here, too, as in the case of the CII itself, the original plan for the EI proved to be overly modest; and it soon became clear that, rather than being a sort of ancillary to the CII, the EI was to take on an independent and continuing life of its own. Publication of the journal, originally conceived as a quarterly, was at first somewhat sporadic, so that the first volume was not completed until 1892; but from the third volume on, the EI was regularly issued as a biennial in eight quarterly parts.[119] The remaining years of the nineteenth century saw the publication of the first five volumes of EI under the editorship of Burgess (vols. 1 and 2) and Hultzsch (vols. 3–5), containing articles by many scholars, most prolific among whom were Fleet, Hultzsch, G. Bühler, and F. Kielhorn. The high standards maintained in these early volumes made EI the premier epigraphic journal, although IA, JBBRAS, and other journals continued to print important articles in this field. With these developments, the last two decades of the nineteenth century constituted a sort of classical age in the study of Indian epigraphy, in which publications were characterized by both great quantity and excellent scholarship.

While the publications discussed here tended to concentrate mainly on northern Indian and Sanskritic materials (although southern and Dravidian materials were also included in EI from the beginning, and were to become more prominent in years to come), equally momentous developments were taking place in the same period in the field of southern Indian epigraphy. In 1879 [B.] Lewis Rice published *Mysore Inscriptions*, containing translations of 175 inscriptions, and in 1886 the first volume of *Epigraphia Carnatica* (EC), while in 1890 vol. 1 of South Indian Inscriptions (SII) appeared under Hultzsch's editorship. The two latter publications were to constitute, in effect, southern Indian counterparts to the northern-oriented CII and would ultimately far outstrip the latter in the amount of material published.

118. See JAOS 105, 1985, 788.

119. See also section 8.1.1.1. For further details of the history and publication of EI, see Sircar's foreword to Lahiri's index in EI 34, part 6, 1962, Appendix, i–vi (reprinted, with minor additions, in EINES 153–9).

Besides the continued issues of these serial publications, the last decade of the nineteenth century also saw for the first time the publication of authoritative epigraphic research guides and anthologies. Although the earliest work on Indian paleography, A. C. Burnell's *Elements of South-Indian Palaeography*, had originally appeared as early as 1874, the first attempt at an overall study of Indian paleography was Gaurīśaṃkara Hīrācaṃda Ojhā's *Bhāratīya Prācīna Lipimālā*, published in 1894. This important and original publication was largely but not completely superseded in 1896 by Georg Bühler's *Indische Palaeographie*, a work of such stature that, although inevitably outdated, it continues (like Fleet's *Inscriptions of the Early Gupta Kings* in the CII) to be a useful and important reference work even to the present day. Bühler's essays *On the Origin of the Indian Brāhma Alphabet* and "The Origin of the Kharoṣṭhī Alphabet," first published in 1895,[120] also marked a major step in the development of epigraphic studies, providing cogent theories on the origin of the Indian scripts which, if not universally accepted, have also never been completely refuted. Another important achievement of the last years of the nineteenth century was Kielhorn's *List of the Inscriptions of Northern India from About A.D. 400*, which was published as an appendix to EI 5 (1898–99) and was both an important research tool in itself and also a model for other inscription lists to be published subsequently (see 8.2.2).

All in all, the last three decades of the nineteenth century may be said to constitute, along with the time of the great decipherments of the 1830s, the greatest years in the study of Indian inscriptions. Several of the works published in this period have remained standard through the years, and many of the editions of individual inscriptions published in EI, IA, and other journals are still authoritative. Some of the greatest names in Indian epigraphy—Bühler, Kielhorn, Hultzsch, and Fleet may be singled out for special honor—were most active in these years, and it is also worthy of note that during this period continental scholars, especially Germans (many of whom, like the three just mentioned, served under the auspices of the British government of India) and Frenchmen, first became involved in good numbers in this field, which had previously been largely the preserve of Englishmen and Indians. The expanding interest in the field is also reflected by the appearance of numerous epigraphic articles in continental journals such as the *Zeitschrift der Deutschen Morgenländischen Gesellschaft* and *Journal Asiatique*. Among French scholars, besides Émile Senart and others working in the field of India proper, A. Barth and Abel Bergaigne deserve special mention for having initiated research in the vast field of extra-Indian epigraphy with their pioneering work in the inscriptions of Indo-China (see 4.3.7.7 and 4.3.7.8).

6.4 The Modern Period (1901–1947)

As a result of the great strides made at the end of the preceding century, epigraphy was by the beginning of the twentieth century a well-established field of study and

120. See sections 2.2.3.2.4 and 2.3.6 for details.

research. Publication of the standard epigraphic journals and serials such as EI, CII, IA, SII, and EC continued at a steady pace through the first half of the century, promoted in part by continuing discoveries of new inscriptions. But in this period many of the new materials were found not so much by chance or in the course of superficial surveys as in earlier days but as a product of planned and systematic archaeological excavations. Inscriptions could thus be studied not only in and of themselves but also in a chronological and archaeological context. In this sense, the turn of the century may be said to mark the beginning of the era of archaeological epigraphy in India. This development reflects the influence of Sir John Marshall, who served as director general of the Archaeological Survey of India from 1902 to 1934 and transformed the survey from an agency essentially involved in antiquarian collection to one sponsoring orderly excavations carried out according to the scientific standards prevailing at the time.

Among the excavations undertaken under Marshall's auspices that yielded major epigraphic finds were those at Sārnāth, Nālandā, Bhīṭā, and Basāṛh. The results of such excavations were reported in detail in the New Series of Annual Reports (ASIAR), which commenced in 1902 and continued until 1937. The commitment of the new regime to epigraphic studies was further demonstrated by the creation in 1906 of the post of "Government Epigraphist for India," in the person of Sten Konow, and by the support obtained for the central Asian expeditions of Marc Aurel Stein in the first two decades of the twentieth century, which resulted in epigraphic discoveries of vast significance (see 4.3.7.12).

The two new volumes of the CII published during this period marked major milestones. The first was Hultzsch's revised edition of volume 1, *Inscriptions of Aśoka*, published in 1925. This volume not only replaced Cunningham's original edition of CII 1, which had already been superseded long ago (see p. 219), but also incorporated and improved upon the editions of various Aśokan inscriptions published in the meantime by É. Senart, H. Kern, Bühler, and others. Hultzsch's volume also included several inscriptions which had not yet been discovered at the time of the earlier edition, including the rock edicts at Mānsehrā, the Rāmpurvā pillar edicts, the minor pillar edicts from Nepal (Rummindeī and Nigālī Sāgar) and Sārnāth, and the minor rock edicts from Mysore (modern Karnataka), indicating continuing progress in the discovery as well as the study of Aśokan inscriptions. The second new volume was Sten Konow's *Kharoshṭhī Inscriptions with the Exception of Those of Aśoka*, issued in 1929 as CII volume 2, part 1.[121] The publication of this volume marked at long last a stage of maturity and development in Kharoṣṭhī studies such as had already been attained for Brāhmī several decades earlier.

In the period in question, and in its latter half in particular, Indian scholars began to be increasingly active and influential in the field of epigraphy. Whereas at the turn

121. As noted earlier (p. 219), the second volume of the CII had originally been planned to cover inscriptions of the "Indo-Scythians and Satraps." In the preface to his volume (v), Konow mentions a subsequent plan to publish a volume of Kharoṣṭhī and Brāhmī inscriptions to be edited by Lüders and Rapson, but this too was not carried out. Part 2 of vol. 2 by Lüders was finally published posthumously in 1963 and was limited to the inscriptions of Bhārhut, so that the original plans for the second volume were never completed.

of the century the subject had been dominated by Europeans, by the middle of the twentieth century it had become largely the preserve of Indians. Volume 17 (1923–24) of EI, for instance, was the first to be edited exclusively by an Indian scholar (H. Krishna Sastri), and since then all of the editors of the journal have been Indians. Among the many scholars who became active and prominent in the field during this period were R. D. Banerji, D. R. Bhandarkar, N. P. Chakravarti, B. Ch. Chhabra, N. P. Majumdar, V. V. Mirashi, N. Lakshminarayanan Rao, and D. C. Sircar.

Another important new trend in this period was the increasing number of collections and anthologies of inscriptions. This reflected a need for assembling and arranging the body of published Indian inscriptions—by now very vast—in some sort of systematic and accessible format. Thus we find in this period, for the first time, numerous publications of collections of inscriptions arranged by province or region, religious affiliation, and so on.[122] By far the most important anthology was the first edition, published in 1942, of vol. 1 of D. C. Sircar's general collection, *Select Inscriptions Bearing on Indian History and Civilization*. This was the first comprehensive anthology of Sanskrit and Sanskritic inscriptions arranged on geohistorical principles, and its publication marked a major step in the maturing of the field, definitively distilling and summarizing the researches of the preceding 150 years.

6.5 Indian Epigraphy Since Independence (1947 to the Present)

Interest in Indian epigraphy has continued to flourish since independence, with the steady support of the central government and several of the states, though this has unfortunately coincided with a serious decline (which had already begun in the preceding period) in the study of this subject in the West. Several prominent figures such as Chhabra, Mirashi, and G. S. Gai stand out in the postindependence era, but the definitive publications of D. C. Sircar—most importantly *Indian Epigraphy* (1965), *Indian Epigraphical Glossary* (1966), and *Select Inscriptions* (revised ed. of vol. 1, 1965; vol. 2, 1983)—establish his undisputed place as the master of Indian epigraphy in the modern era; his death in 1984 was an irreparable loss to the field.

The other major development in epigraphic publications in this period is the continuation of the CII. Since independence, volumes 2.2 and 4 through 7, as well as a revised edition of volume 3, have been published.[123] The publication of H. Lüders' *Bhārhut Inscriptions* as CII 2.2 finally marked the completion of the second volume, which had been planned since Cunningham's time (see n. 121). Although finally published posthumously only in 1963, the volume actually represents work undertaken by Lüders many years earlier, as is also the case with his *Mathurā Inscriptions* (1961), which was originally planned to be part of CII 2 (see E. Waldschmidt's introductory note, 5). More recently, the commencement of the publication of the *Journal of the Epigraphical Society of India* (JESI) in 1975 brought into being an important new vehicle for epigraphic research.

122. For details and examples, see section 8.1.3.
123. For details, see section 8.1.2.

The publication of anthologies and secondary works has also burgeoned in recent decades. Collections of inscriptions by state and region, works on general and specific paleographic topics, and historical and cultural studies of various corpora are being published in far greater numbers than ever before.[124] Among recent works of this class which uphold the best traditional standards of epigraphic research may be mentioned A. K. Bhattacharyya's *Corpus of Dedicatory Inscriptions from Temples of West Bengal* and Mukunda Madhava Sharma's *Inscriptions of Ancient Assam*. Nor has the modern period witnessed any slowing in the rate of discoveries of inscriptions; new items, including several of major importance (see various examples noted in section 4.3), continue to be found at a steady pace, as a result both of chance finds and of systematic surveys and planned expeditions. In the latter category, several of the excavations undertaken by the central and local archaeological departments have yielded abundant epigraphic results, for instance, those at Sālihuṇḍam, Sannati, and Nāgārjunakoṇḍa.

At present, the study of Indian inscriptions is carried on principally under the auspices of the Office of the Director of Epigraphy (formerly Government Epigraphist) at Mysore (formerly Ootacamund), who also serves as the editor of EI; this office is currently held by Madhav N. Katti. The foundation of the Epigraphical Society of India in 1975 was an important development, and this society now holds a prominent position in the field. Epigraphy is pursued at most major universities in India, many of which have established separate departments for epigraphy and ancient Indian history, and at some institutions in neighboring South Asian countries such as Pakistan and Sri Lanka.

6.6 Future Prospects and Desiderata

Despite the continued support by governmental and educational institutions in South Asia, it cannot be said that all is well with the study of epigraphy in India nowadays. The general decline in standards and interest in Sanskrit and Sanskritic studies in India is having a deleterious effect on the quality, if not the quantity, of some epigraphic work (see EINES 92), though it is encouraging that, as noted previously, some excellent publications are still appearing. Outside South Asia there have been some signs of a revival of interest in epigraphy in Europe and North America, where the work of such scholars as Harry Falk, Gérard Fussman, Oskar von Hinüber, and Gregory Schopen has stimulated new interest in this field.

Although well-trained epigraphists will continue to be needed in the foreseeable future to publish the new inscriptions that will undoubtedly continue to be found and to reedit previously known ones, there are many other tasks that await them. Most urgent is the need for comprehensive computer databases of the now unmanageably vast published epigraphic material; very little has been done in this direction, and the need for it is growing constantly. The compilation of more regional, dynastic, and thematic corpora of inscriptions is still an urgent desideratum. Although much

124. See sections 8.1.3–8.2.3.

progress has been made in this area (see 8.1.3), collections of such important materials as the inscriptions of the Kuṣāṇas, revised corpora of the Aśokan and Kharoṣṭhī inscriptions, and a definitive anthology of Buddhist inscriptions are still lacking. Finally, the integration of the study of inscriptions into academic disciplines such as history, art, and religion remains inadequate in many respects, and both epigraphists and specialists in the several disciplines must continue to strive for better communication and cooperation.[125]

125. See ch. 7 for details and examples.

7

Epigraphy as a Source for the Study of Indian Culture

7.1 Epigraphy and History

7.1.1 Political and dynastic history

SIE 13–30; David P. Henige, "Some Phantom Dynasties of Early and Medieval India: Epigraphic Evidence and the Abhorrence of a Vacuum," BSOAS 38, 1975, 525–49; J. F. Fleet, "The Present Position of Indian Historical Research," IA 30, 1901, 1–27 (≈"Epigraphy," in IGI II, 1–88; cf. 8.2.1); L. B. Alayev, "Methods of Studying Epigraphy as a Historical Source," in IVMD, 33–40.

It has already been explained (ch. 1) that inscriptions constitute the principal source for the history of pre-Islamic India, providing a large majority of the total information available; and that, were it not for inscriptions, we would not know even the most basic rudiments of the dynastic chronology of India before A.D. 1000. But the reconstruction of history from primarily epigraphic and other archaeological sources, as opposed to literary ones, involves many special problems and requires the development and application of appropriate analytic techniques. The main problem is that most inscriptions are not essentially historical documents (cf. Fleet, "The Present Position," 22, and SIE 23) but rather donative or panegyric records which may incidentally record some amount of historical information. Thus the standards of objectivity, precision, and comprehensiveness that guide modern historical thought are completely absent in these sources, and the modern scholar must exercise cautious critical judgment in evaluating them.

7.1.1.1 Chronology and genealogy

Inevitably, the picture of the dynastic history of ancient and medieval India to be drawn from epigraphic and other sources is not only incomplete but also replete with uncertainties. For several of the earlier dynasties, such as the Śuṅgas, we have only the most meager epigraphic fragments, which must be combined with whatever supplementary evidence may be gleaned from literary sources to reconstruct a rough chronological and historical sequence. But for many later dynasties, especially in the medieval period, the picture is much brighter; in the case of such dynasties as the Rāṣṭrakūṭas, for instance, where epigraphic remains are relatively abundant, we can reconstruct a reasonably detailed account of their history, chronology, and geography. The difference between the earlier and later periods lies not only in the amounts of epigraphic material available but also in their contents. Thus in the early period we find such extraordinarily vague formulations as a dating merely "during the reign of the Śuṅgas" (*suganaṃ raje = śuṅgānāṃ rājye*; Bhārhut pillar ins., l. 1; SI I.87–8), whereas in medieval inscriptions the dating formulae and historical situation are often detailed and explicit. As an ideal example, in the inscriptions of the Eastern Cālukyas the genealogical introduction not only includes the usual eulogistic description of the forefathers of the current king but also states the number of years of their rule (SIE 19–20), enabling historians to reconstruct that dynasty's chronology with particular precision.[1]

In most cases, of course, the situation lies somewhere between these two extremes. More typically, for dynasties for which we have a reasonable number of records dated in a continuous era, we can reconstruct a dynastic chronology with reasonable accuracy. The main problem is usually that for determining the earliest and latest dates of any particular ruler we are at the mercy of chance finds of dated inscriptions, and the precise date of transition of rule can be known only in such cases as we are fortunate enough to have records of two kings dated in the same or at least in successive years. Otherwise, we can only estimate these dates based on the range of attested dates for each king. The result of this situation is that for many of the better-represented dynasties of the medieval period, for example, the Rāṣṭrakūṭas or the Gurjara-Pratīhāras, we can usually date each king at least within a range of a few years, and frequently to the year.[2]

But we are less well informed with regard to earlier, less abundantly attested dynasties or to those which dated their records in regnal years only. The chronology of the Pālas, for example, is considerably less certain than that of the contemporary Rāṣṭrakūṭas, not because of any scarcity of materials but because their records are dated only in regnal years. Regnally dated records require some type of historical synchronization which can provide absolute chronological "anchor points." These are typically provided (if at all) by reference to historical personages or events known from other sources, the classic case being the absolute dating of Aśoka's regnally dated inscriptions provided by chronological correlation with the known dates of the five Hellenistic kings (Turamāyo = Ptolemy II Philadelphus of Egypt, etc.) referred to in his rock edict XIII, which enabled historians to definitively fix Aśoka's reign at around the middle of the third century B.C.

With regard to the genealogy of the various dynasties too, the state of our understanding varies considerably. In general, the succession of rulers can be determined from genealogical accounts in the inscriptions themselves, especially from the early medieval period onward, when it became customary to provide a quasi-historical preface to inscriptions (cf. SIE 14–15, and sections 4.1.1 and 4.1.2.1c). But the record

1. For other examples of precise dating, see Fleet, "The Present Position," 9–10.

2. For examples of the types of chronological difficulties which can arise with era-dated inscriptions, see R. K. Dikshit's *Candellas of Jejākabhukti*, 17–9.

is often less clear, especially in earlier inscriptions which lack full genealogical accounts. In such cases, the recurrence of the same name in different generations can be troublesome, as in the case, for example, of the Kuṣāṇas or the Guptas, where the repetitions of the names Kaniṣka and Kumāragupta,[3] respectively, have caused no end of frustration to modern historians.[4] Equally troublesome is the practice, especially in later inscriptions, of referring to the same king by two or even more different names in different records, which sometimes produces serious or even insoluble genealogical problems; see, for example, the problems of Gurjara-Pratīhāra genealogy discussed in R. C. Majumdar, ed., *The Age of Imperial Kanauj*, 37.

Finally, there is the problem of inconsistencies between the genealogies of a particular dynasty as given in different inscriptions, or between genealogies as preserved in inscriptions and in noninscriptional sources such as literature. To choose a well-known example, Skandagupta, an important late ruler of the imperial Guptas, is well known from several inscriptions from the time of his own rule but is not mentioned in the genealogies of the Gupta kings who succeeded him. The explanation here, as in most such cases, is that he was not succeeded by his own descendants but by his brother and/or the latter's son(s).[5] As emphasized by Henige (op. cit., 538 and 546; cf. also Goyal, op. cit., 306), the lineages given in inscriptions are typically genealogies, not king-lists. The result is that when, as is very commonly the case in ancient India (and elsewhere; Henige 539–40), the throne did not pass directly from father to son in every generation but rather from brother to brother or nephew to uncle, the strictly genealogical lists of the later kings would pass over one or more of their predecessors on the throne. This phenomenon of "collateral suppression" creates many problems in the reconstruction of royal genealogies, especially when the inscriptional material is scanty, and it has led, as convincingly demonstrated by Henige, to many cases of inaccurate or downright imaginary dynastic reconstructions by insufficiently critical historians.

In this respect and in others as well, the strong cautions urged by Henige against "latter-day 'dynasty building'" (526), "a maximum of inference based on a minimum of satisfactory data" (525), and "epigraphic legerdemain" (528) should be heeded by epigraphists and historians. Given the usual shortage of data, there is always a temptation to indulge in the construction of more detailed dynastic genealogies than is justified by the materials. But scholars must avoid such temptation and understand and work within the limits imposed by epigraphic information; they must, in Henige's words, "recognize the inherent limitations of their materials" (539).

7.1.1.2 Geographical and historical data

Such cautions are equally applicable to descriptions of the geographical extent of the Indian dynasties. The central territories and extent of the various kingdoms

3. Needless to say, the conventional designation of such kings as Kumāragupta I, Kumāragupta II, etc., is a modern practice which was not followed in the original records.

4. On this matter, see also Henige, "Some Phantom Dynasties," 530–3.

5. The details of the later Gupta succession are highly uncertain and controversial; see, e.g., S. R. Goyal, *A History of the Imperial Guptas* (Allahabad: Central Book Depot, 1967), 304–34. The situation is typical of the problems of reconstructing the later and declining phases of dynasties from skimpy and inconsistent epigraphic data.

attested in inscriptions are generally deduced on the grounds of (1) the findspots of the inscriptions themselves and (2) claims of territories and conquests made in the inscriptions. The first method has two main limitations. First, the geographical record preserved by inscriptions, like their chronological record, is necessarily incomplete, providing merely random spots in a larger field; and also as in the case of chronological reconstruction, it is only in such cases (which are the minority) where we have a reasonably large number of records for a particular ruler that we can determine anything like a clear picture of the extent of his realm. Second, it cannot always be assumed that the findspots of inscriptions are their original location, particularly in the case of copper plates, which were sometimes removed from their original location by grantees who migrated to a different region.[6] Thus a single instance of a portable inscription found outside the known limits of a ruler's realm should not be automatically accepted as evidence of his vast conquests, but a consistent pattern of this may be historically.[7]

The territorial and military claims put forth in the inscriptions themselves are even more problematic. That many rulers (or rather their court poets), especially in medieval times, shamelessly exaggerated the territorial extent of their empires or spheres of influence is well established. The question is how to distinguish fact, or at least a core of fact, from the conventional bombast and rhetorical exaggeration of the *praśasti* style. A classic contrast is provided by the claims of *digvijaya* or conquest of the whole world (i.e., of India) made on behalf of Samudragupta in the Allahabad pillar inscription and of the Aulikara ruler Yaśodharman in the Mandasor pillar inscription. In the case of the former, the extensive and detailed list of kings and territories in the south, west, and north of India whose conquest or submission Samudragupta claimed lends a semblance of credence, so that historians generally accept that he did in fact rule over or at least raid the places in question, despite the absence of any corroborative evidence. In Yaśodharman's *praśasti*, on the other hand, the claims of sovereignty from the Lauhitya (Brahmaputra) River in the east to the ocean in the west and from the Mahendra Mountain in the south to the Himālayas in the north are obviously formulaic, and no historian would be willing to credit Yaśodharman with anything like a pan-Indian empire.[8] Thus the rule of thumb followed by most historians with regard to such claims is that the more specific and nonformulaic they are, the more likely they are to be historically justified; in Sircar's words, "Vague claims are generally less reliable than definite statements involving the mention of the personal names of adversaries" (SIE 27).

Especially in later inscriptions, such grandiose and obviously spurious claims to vast territories become almost routine, even to the extent that poetic considerations overrule historical plausibility; thus in the Khajurāho inscription (EI 1, 126, v. 23) the Candella king Yaśovarman is described as *kośalaḥ kośalānāṃ naśyatkaśmīravīraḥ śithilitamithilaḥ kālavan mālavānāṃ*, "who seized the treasuries of Kośala, who destroyed the heroes of Kashmir, who weakened Mithila, and was like Death to

6. For examples, see Fleet, "Epigraphy," IGI II.28.

7. But such cases must be treated with caution. Thus the apparent conquest of Bihar and Bengal by the Gurjara-Pratīhāra king Mahendrapāla has recently been shown to be an illusion (G. Bhattacharya, *South Asian Studies* 4, 1988, 71–3).

8. For other examples, see SIE 25–7.

Malwa." Here, in Sircar's words, "It seems that the lure of alliteration . . . carried the poet far away from historical accuracy" (SIE 27).[9] Moreover, even those boasts of victory which are based on historical fact are almost invariably couched in highly rhetorical style in which mundane details of time, place, and military strategy are rarely specified.

Given this situation, historians will naturally wish to evaluate the claims put forth in the inscriptions in the light of corroborative evidence, whether in the form of material from other inscriptions or from literary or other alternative sources. For instance, Pulakeśin II's claims in the Aihoḷe inscription (SI II.443–50, v. 23) of a victory over Harṣa finds explicit corroboration in the testimony of the Chinese pilgrim Hsüan Tsang, and hence can be considered reliable. Corroboration from other inscriptions is often harder to establish, due not only to the general problems of the historical evaluation already alluded to but also to the tendency of the poets to gloss over, distort, or simply ignore their patrons' military defeats (SIE 27–8). In some cases, however, such corroboration can be established, for example, in the case of Gurjara-Pratīhāra Nāgabhaṭa's victory over his Pāla enemy referred to in the Gwalior *praśasti* (SII II.242–6) which is confirmed by similar statements in the separate records of three of Nāgabhaṭa's subordinate allies: "[T]he combined testimony of the four different records, coming from four different sources, . . . leave no doubt that Nāgabhaṭa scored a great victory over his Pāla rival Dharmapāla."[10] "The Pāla records," on the other hand, not untypically "make no reference to this struggle."[11]

Occasionally we do find cases where a conflict is reported from both sides, and here we are faced with special problems of analysis. For instance, the same Gurjara-Pratīhāra King Nāgabhaṭa's war with Indra, the Rāṣṭrakūṭa king of Gujarat, seems to be alluded to in inscriptions in which victory is claimed by both sides; in such a case, if no further determination is possible, "It may be concluded . . . that no party gained a decisive victory."[12] A similar problem has been raised by the recent discovery of the earliest inscription of the imperial Gurjara-Pratīhāras (New Delhi ins.; EI 41, 49–57), in which King Vatsarāja's forces are said to have conquered all of Karnataka (*avajitāśeṣa-Karṇṇāṭa-*, ll. 5–6), while his contemporary in that region, the Rāṣṭrakūṭa king Dhruva, explicitly claims in his inscriptions to have defeated Vatsarāja. Here the editors comment, "These claims and counterclaims of victory are, more or less, a conventional part of epigraphic poetry and may indicate either the uncertain nature of the outcome of the battles . . . or may pertain to different battles in which the results were successively reversed and for which we do not have tangible evidence" (52). Such conflicting claims, in other words, can be settled or reconciled, if at all, only when other evidence, for example, the locations of subsequent inscriptions of the rulers concerned, provide clear corroboration of the claims of one or the other of them.

Such, in short, are some of the typical problems which confront the historian in attempting to evaluate the highly rhetorical, subjective, and often intentionally vague statements of eulogistic inscriptions. The results, not surprisingly, are more often than

9. For other examples, see D. K. Ganguly, *History and Historians in Ancient India* (New Delhi: Abhinav Publications, 1984), 51–2.

10. Majumdar, *The Age of Imperial Kanauj*, 26.

11. Ibid., 48.

12. Ibid., 25.

not less than entirely satisfactory. For the earlier periods of Indian history we often have little more than the vaguest outlines of events and chronologies. In the classical and medieval periods we are somewhat better off, but even here we have, with rare exceptions, only the bare outlines of chronology and events and relatively little in the way of details to flesh out the skeleton of history. There will always be many uncertainties, and any historical study based on epigraphic sources will inevitably be filled with qualifications like "probably," "possibly," and "it would appear that." Indeed, any such study that is *not* provided with such stipulations should be viewed with suspicion.

7.1.2 Administrative, economic, and social history

In recent decades, several scholars have begun to undertake more detailed and sophisticated analyses of various aspects of political science, economics, and social history on the basis of inscriptional evidence. Such studies are primarily based on the copious documentation provided by later southern Indian inscriptions, especially those of the Coḷa and Vijayanagara kingdoms, which are sufficiently numerous and detailed to permit significant statistical analysis, as is generally not the case with the sparser data available from the north. The inscriptions in question include very large numbers (in the thousands) of stone temple inscriptions in Sanskrit and/or Tamil (or other Dravidian languages) recording various transactions, typically endowments or donations to the temples, which provide a wealth of information on virtually all aspects of social and economic life. These inscriptions have given rise to a sizable body of scholarly literature on medieval southern India which combines the study of inscriptions with modern methods of historical and social scientific research. In view of the ever-increasing volume and diversity of the literature in question, it can be introduced here only in outline; the studies cited are meant only to provide representative or outstanding examples of the genre, especially of more recent studies and of those which concentrate particularly on information derived from epigraphic sources.

Among the several topics which have recently been addressed via the study of inscriptions, one of the most important and controversial is the nature of the state and of kingship among the traditional Indian kingdoms, with the Coḷa empire serving as the focus for most studies. The central figure in these studies is Burton Stein, whose works, most notably *Peasant State and Society in Medieval South India*, have stimulated extensive discussion and further research. Although Stein's characterization of the Coḷa empire (and by extension of other traditional Indian kingdoms) as a "pyramidal segmentary state" with a king whose principal function is more ritual than executive has not been universally accepted,[13] it has come to constitute the central focus of subsequent discussion of the subject.

Numerous studies of administrative and bureaucratic systems in southern India and elsewhere have also been undertaken on the basis of epigraphic data. Noteworthy recent efforts along these lines include the studies of Noboru Karashima and his collaborators, which are conveniently compiled in his *South Indian History and Society: Studies from Inscriptions* A.D. *850–1800* (esp. 55–68). Studies of these sub-

13. See, e.g., the reservations expressed by Noboru Karashima in *South Indian History and Society: Studies from Inscriptions* A.D. *850–1800*, xxv–xxviii.

jects are typically based on official terms and titles culled from the inscriptions. Such titles, however, are often unknown from other sources and are not always etymologically transparent, so that their significance must be inferred, with varying degrees of success, from the contexts in which they appear in the inscriptions.

Systems of land tenure and modes of agricultural production have also been the subject of numerous studies based on or making extensive use of epigraphic data. Much of the argument has focused on the persistent controversy as to whether or not the term "feudalism" can be properly applied to the medieval states; see, for example, D. C. Sircar, ed., *Land System and Feudalism in Ancient India.* Some recent studies, such as those of Stein and Karashima (see esp. *South Indian History and Society*, 3–35), have succeeded in raising the discussion of land tenure to a higher level by avoiding ideological preconceptions and concentrating on analysis of the actual data provided by the inscriptions.

Revenue systems are another important aspect of historical and economic studies for which inscriptions constitute a principal source of information, especially, once again, for South India. Among recent works, those of Karashima (compiled in *South Indian History and Society*, 69–158) are again noteworthy for their scrupulous attention to epigraphic details; although here too (as in the case of the official titles) many of the technical terms for types of taxes remain to be satisfactorily elucidated.

Patterns of trade, both external and internal, can also sometimes be traced with some precision from the epigraphic records. Here, too, the Coḷa empire has been the focus of attention, as, for example, in Kenneth R. Hall's *Trade and Statecraft in the Age of Cōlas.*

Studies of traditional Indian society also look primarily to inscriptions for clues about the actual social situation at various times and places, as a check to the highly normative and theoretical formulations of social ideals provided in the Dharmaśāstras and other literary works. For the earlier periods, and in general for northern India, the information is, as usual, sparse, consisting for the most part of odd scraps of data from which it is difficult to draw anything like a comprehensive overall scheme.[14] Once again, it is in the medieval south, and particularly in the Coḷa period, that epigraphic data attain a critical mass that allows for detailed studies of social structures and caste relationships and their historical developments. Here too the studies of such scholars as Stein (e.g., *Peasant State and Society*, 173–215) and Karashima (*South Indian History and Society*, 36–68) are representative of the application of sophisticated modern methods to the study of Indian society on the basis of epigraphic data. Also worthy of note is K. Sundaram's *Studies in Economic and Social Conditions of Medieval Andhra* (A.D. *1000–1600*).

7.2 Epigraphy and the Study of Indian Literature

G. Bühler, *Die indische Inschriften und das Alter der indischen Kunstpoesie*; C. Sivaramamurti, IESIS, 38–48; V. Raghavan, "Sanskrit and Epigraphy," in *Sanskrit: Essays on the Value of the Language and the Literature* (Madras: Sanskrit Education Society,

14. Though this is not to deny that a good deal of interesting information is available; see, e.g., D. C. Sircar's *Studies in the Society and Administration of Ancient and Medieval India.* See also the general comments by Aloka Parasher in "Epigraphy as a Tool for Writing Social History," JESI 18, 1992, 62–73.

1972), 67–76; D. B. Diskalkar, "Indian Epigraphical Literature," JIH 37, 1959, 319–39, and "The Influence of Classical Poets on the Inscriptional Poets," JIH 38, 1960, 285–302. [For anthologies of literary inscriptions, see 8.1.3.1.]

7.2.1 Inscriptions as a source for the history of Indian literature

7.2.1.1 Inscriptions and the chronology of Indian literature

Inscriptions constitute an important source for the study of the history of Sanskrit and Prakrit literature in several respects, first of all by providing a general chronological framework. As was first clearly shown by Bühler in his classic work *Die indische Inschriften und das Alter der indischen Kunstpoesie*, early specimens of *kāvya* style preserved in inscriptions such as the Nāsik cave inscription of the time of Vāsiṣṭhīputra Śrī-Puḷumāvi, Rudradāman's Junāgaḍh inscription, and the Allahabad Pillar *praśasti* of Samudragupta establish that *kāvya* in Sanskrit and Prakrit was an established art already by the second century A.D. and that it had become fully standardized and widespread by the Gupta era. This suggests that the origins of the *kāvya* style must be even earlier (Bühler, 243), and in fact we now know that inscriptional specimens of *kāvya* are now available as early as the beginning of the first century.[15] This conclusion is consistent with the evidence of the literary sources themselves, notably the works of Aśvaghoṣa which point toward a flourishing *kāvya* in the first century A.D., and the poetic citations in Patañjali's *Mahābhāṣya* which seem to push the origins of *kāvya* back to the second century B.C.

7.2.1.2 Inscriptions as a source for the dating and identification of authors and literary works

Inscriptions not infrequently assist in providing precise or approximate dates for prominent literary figures. The classic case is the Aihoḷe inscription (EI 6, 1–12), which provides a definite *terminus ante quem* of A.D. 634/35 for both Kālidāsa and Bhāravi in the form of a boast by its composer Ravikīrti of having equaled in his verses the renown of those two great poets (ll. 17–18, *ravikīrttiḥ kavitāśrita-kālidāsa-bhāravi-kīrttiḥ*). Other inscriptional testimonia in earlier inscriptions, in the form of what seem to be imitations or adaptations of Kālidāsa's verses, enable us to push his *terminus ante quem* further back; the Mahākūṭa inscription of A.D. 602 (IA 19, ll. 1–2), for example, contains a phrase in prose (*yathāvidhihutāgnīnāṃ yathākāmārccitārtthināṃ*) which is evidently borrowed from *Raghuvaṃśa* I.6.[16]

Other poets can be dated indirectly from inscriptional information. The date of Rājaśekhara, for example, can be fixed with relative precision to around A.D. 900 on the basis of inscriptional dates for his patron, Mahendrapāla of the Gurjara-Pratīhāra

15. As noted by D. C. Sircar in his editor's note (83) to the 1970 reprint edition of Bühler's essay. On the development of *kāvya* style in southern inscriptions, see Sircar's "Kāvya Style in Inscriptions of the Successors of the Sātavāhanas," Appendix (ch. IX, 379–89) to *Successors of the Sātavāhanas in Lower Deccan* (Calcutta: University of Calcutta, 1939). See also section 3.3.2.

16. Kielhorn, EI 6, 3–4. It is also alleged (Bühler, *Indian Inscriptions*, 142–3; Kielhorn, *Nachrichten von der königlichen Gesellschaft der Wissenschaften zu Göttingen*, Philologisch-historische Klasse 1890, 251–3 = KS I.392–4) that verses in the Mandasor inscription of Kumāragupta and Bandhuvarman (A.D. 492) are imitations of ones in the *Meghadūta* and *Ṛtusaṃhāra*, but these cases are less certain.

dynasty. The generally accepted dating for Māgha, author of the *Śiśupālavadha*, around the late seventh century is based mainly on the identification of the king Varmalākhya or Varmalāta mentioned in the poem's colophon with Varmalāta of the Vasantgaḍh inscription of A.D. 625 (EI 9, 187–92).

7.2.1.3 Specimens of the compositions of known literary figures preserved in inscriptions

In a fair number of cases, inscriptions provide us with references to and/or specimens of the works of poets who are otherwise known from their own works, or from separate verses preserved in anthologies, or by laudatory references in the works of other poets. The outstanding case here is that of Umāpatidhara, who is known from the reference in Jayadeva's *Gītagovinda* (I.3a, *vācaḥ pallavayaty umāpatidharaḥ*) and from many quotations in poetic anthologies;[17] but the only extant continuous composition by him is the Deopāṛā inscription (SI II.115–22). The compositions of several other poets otherwise known only from anthologies are preserved in inscriptions.[18] For example, the Rāghavacaitanya whose *stotra* to Jvālāmukhī-Bhavānī is quoted in the Kāngrā Jvālāmukhī *praśasti* (EI I, 190–5) is probably to be identified with the poet of the same name who is cited in the *Śārṅgadhara-paddhati* and other anthologies. And six poets mentioned in the Govindpur stone inscription (EI 2, 330–42), including Gaṅgādhara, the composer of the record itself as well as five of his kinsmen, are identifiable with authors quoted in Śrīdharadāsa's *Saduktikarṇāmṛta*.

Several poets known from extant literary compositions are also the authors of inscriptional panegyrics. For example, Trivikramabhaṭṭa, the composer of the two Bagumrā copper plates of the Rāṣṭrakūṭa king Indrarāja III (EI 9, 24–41), is identified with the Trivikramabhaṭṭa who wrote the *Nalacampū*; and Someśvaradeva, author of the *Kīrtikaumudī*, composed a *praśasti* inscribed at Mount Abu (EI 8, 208–19).

Instances in inscriptions of quotations, adaptions, or imitations of verses by well-known classical poets are very numerous; examples are compiled in IESIS 39–41, JIH 38, 286–9, and RIE 107–8.[19] The most commonly cited poet in inscriptions is, not surprisingly, Kālidāsa. The famous *maṅgala-śloka* of his *Abhijñāna-śākuntala*, *yā sṛṣṭiḥ sraṣṭur ādyā . . .* , for example, is quoted in the Sāncor inscription of Pratāpasiṃha (EI 11, 64–7), and the initial verse of the *Raghuvaṃśa* (*vāgarthāv iva saṃpṛktau . . .*) is cited in a Hūli inscription of Cālukya Vikramāditya VI (EI 18, 196–9 [ins. F]), as is that of the *Vikramorvaśīya* in an inscription from Jhānsi (EI 40, 87–90).

Besides Kālidāsa, other famous poets who are emulated in inscriptions include Māgha (Pathārī pillar ins., EI 9, 250) and Bhāravi (Aihoḷe). In such cases the inscriptional poet sometimes seems to try to outdo his famous predecessor; in Aihoḷe, for example, Ravikīrti goes one up on Bhāravi's *pṛthu-kadamba-kadambaka*

17. On these see Ludwik Sternbach, *Poésie sanskrite conservée dans les anthologies et les inscriptions*, I.xxx–xxxi and 85–93.

18. For this and other cases, see ibid., passim (also II.xxxvii–xxxix).

19. See also C. Sivaramamurti, *Sanskrit Literature and Art—Mirrors of Indian Culture*, Memoirs of the ASI, no. 73 (New Delhi: ASI, 1970), 99–102.

(*Kirātārjunīya* 5.9) with his *pṛthu-kadamba-kadamba-kadambakam* (v. 10; cf. EI 6, 8 n. 6).

Another *kavi* who is frequently cited in inscriptions is Bāṇa. The *maṅgala-śloka* of his *Harṣa-carita, namas tuṅgaśiraścumbicandracāmara-cārave* . . . is quoted in many Western Cālukya and Vijayanagara inscriptions, while his prose (along with that of Subandhu, author of the *Vāsavadattā*) serves as the model for the style of many inscriptions, for example, the Rādhanpur plates (EI 6, 239–51, esp. 240; see also JIH 38, 288–9).

Verses from literary texts are also sometimes quoted in label inscriptions (4.1.5), serving to explain the theme of an accompanying painting or sculpture. Such is the case, for example, with the verses from Āryaśūra's *Jātakamālā* accompanying paintings in cave 2 at Ajaṇṭā,[20] and a verse from Hāla's Sattasaï (I.20) on the pedestal of a sculpture from Tewar (IHQ 28, 379–85).

Such inscriptional quotations and paraphrases may be of importance in tracing not only the original dates of composition of literary works but also the process of their propagation around India. The classic case is the Anāwāḍā (Gujarat) inscription (IA 41, 20–1) of A.D. 1291 which quotes a verse (I.16) of Jayadeva's *Gītagovinda*, showing that this text had become known in the West within a century of its composition in eastern India.

7.2.2 Inscriptional texts as literature

7.2.2.1 The genre of praśasti

The literary genre peculiar to inscriptions is the *praśasti* or panegyric. As discussed previously (4.1.1), inscriptional *praśasti*s are usually presented in an ostensible context of a record of donation, but the bulk of the text is typically taken up by the eulogistic description of the donor, typically a king or royal minister but sometimes also a religious leader or sect. The compositions of this class are often explicitly labeled in the colophon as *praśasti*; in fact, this usage was so common that sometimes the text is simply referred to as *pūrvā* 'the preceding [sc. *praśasti*]'. Sometimes more general terms such as *kāvya* are applied to this class of composition, for example, in the Allahabad pillar and Tālaguṇḍa inscriptions.

In general, the style of the inscriptional poems tends to mirror prevailing literary tastes. Early examples such as the Junāgaḍh and Tālaguṇḍa inscriptions exhibit a more epic-like flavor in both language and style (Bühler, *Indian Inscriptions*, 191; EI 8, 28), reflecting similar tendencies in the literary *kāvya*s of the preclassical period, such as those of Aśvaghoṣa. Inscriptions of the classical era, especially those of the Guptas and their contemporaries in the north, reflect the creative vigor and ornate classical style of the period and are among the best of their genre. Later *praśasti*s, on the other hand, often reflect the stiff and pedantic character of postclassical poetry.

Strictly speaking, the inscriptional *praśasti*s do not constitute a completely distinct poetic genre; rather, they are for the most part adaptations of standard genres to special purposes. On the whole (as noted by Bühler, *Indian Inscriptions*, 138; also

20. Lüders, *Philologica Indica*, 73–77 = *Nachrichten der Akademie der Wissenschaften zu Göttingen*, Phil.-Hist. Klasse 1902, 758–62.

Diskalkar, JIH 37, 326), the *praśasti*s are closely modeled on the *mahākāvya* style. But some earlier specimens partake of other genres as well; thus the Allahabad pillar inscription in mixed verse and prose reflects the *campū* style, and this and other prose inscriptions such as Mahākūṭa also show the characteristics of the prose *kāvya* style of the *ākhyāyikā*s (*Indian Inscriptions*, 173).

But despite their adherence to prevailing literary modes, the inscriptional compositions do not seem to have attained much acceptance in the literary tradition. Of the many notable poets such as Hariṣeṇa (Allahabad), Vatsabhaṭṭi (Mandasor), and Kubja (Tālaguṇḍa) whose names are preserved in inscriptional colophons,[21] very few are known in the standard literary tradition.[22] Cases such as that of Umāpatidhara (discussed in 7.2.1.3) are very much the exception rather than the rule, and are restricted to the medieval period. The genre of *praśasti* does, however, receive some explicit recognition in the later literary tradition, especially in the anthologies. The *Subhāṣitaratnakośa*, for example, has a brief separate section on this genre (the *praśasti-vrajyā*, section 46, containing 14 verses), though none of these have yet been correlated with actual inscriptions.[23] Other anthologies contain a few verses from known inscriptions; for instance, verses from Umāpatidhara's Deopāṛā *praśasti* are cited in Śrīdharadāsa's *Saduktikarṇāmṛta* (vv. 7, 23, 24, and 30 = *Saduktikarṇāmṛta*[24] 1614, 1455, 1395, and 1454).[25]

Nonetheless, direct correlations between the literary and the inscriptional texts are on the whole disappointingly few.[26] It would appear that, for one thing, *praśasti*s were essentially ephemeral compositions; in Diskalkar's words, "[T]he praśastis were rarely copied down and circulated among the literary world. They had their importance for the time being and though remembered by the court poets were forgotten by the general scholarly world" (JIH 38, 298). Second, it seems that, in many cases, "the inscriptional poets were not always real poets of inspiration but poets of accomplishment" (ibid., 298) who were "really practical men" and "more pandits than poets" (ibid., 299); that is to say, becoming a favored court poet may often have had more to do with political than literary skills. Moreover, poets of true talent who did attain to such positions may have expended their best efforts on other compositions (though unfortunately very few of such have been preserved; cf. Diskalkar 301), while the composition of panegyrics was perhaps more a labor of daily bread than of love.

7.2.2.2 Standard literary genres preserved in inscriptions

7.2.2.2.1 Kāvya (poetry). There is a fair number of inscriptions which do partake of the character of *praśasti* insofar as their intention is to glorify the poet's patron portrayed in them as the hero, but which are essentially compositions of the standard

21. For an extensive (though admittedly not complete) list of signed authors of poetic inscriptions, see D. B. Diskalkar, "Sanskrit and Prākrit Poets Known from Inscriptions," JOI 7, 1957–58, 78–85.

22. See Diskalkar, JIH 38, 297, for further examples.

23. Cf. the comments of Daniel H. H. Ingalls in his introduction to the *praśasti-vrajyā* in his translation of the *Subhāṣitaratnakośa* (*An Anthology of Sanskrit Court Poetry*, Harvard Oriental Series, vol. 44 [Cambridge, Mass.: Harvard University Press, 1965], 409).

24. Ed. Sures Chandra Banerjee (Calcutta: K. L. Mukhopadhyay, 1965).

25. Further examples in Diskalkar, JIH 38, 292 and 298.

26. Cf. Diskalkar, JIH 38, 297–8.

literary genres.[27] These include *kāvyas* of various types, including a few late specimens of full *mahākāvyas*, notably the *Rājapraśasti-mahākāvya* at Udaypur.

Briefer poems which can be classed as *khaṇḍa-kāvyas* are also known, notably the several poems of the poet Narasiṃha inscribed near Warangal in Andhra Pradesh. His creations include a charming romantic adventure in sixty-two verses at Urusukoṇḍa (EI 41, 219–44) and an incomplete *niroṣṭhya-kāvya* (poem using no labial sounds) at Hanumakoṇḍa (EI 36, 209–18).

7.2.2.2.2 Nāṭaka (drama). Complete or partial texts of some otherwise unknown dramas of the medieval period are preserved on inscribed stone slabs which were originally fixed on palace walls. These are the *Lalitavigraharaja-nāṭaka* of Somadeva and the *Harakeli-nāṭaka* attributed to the Cāhamāna king Vigraharājadeva, both of which were inscribed at Ajmer, and the *Pārijātamañjarī-nāṭikā* or *Vijayaśrī-nāṭikā* from Dhār (see 4.1.8 for references).

7.2.2.2.3 Stotra (devotional songs). More common among literary inscriptions are poems of the *stotra* or devotional hymn genre,[28] which were often placed on the walls of temples. Here, contrary to the general pattern discussed previously, we find several cases where the inscriptional text matches a known literary composition. For example, the *Halāyudha-stotra* to Śiva, preserved in an inscription from the Amareśvara temple at Māndhātā, is also preserved in several manuscripts (EI 25, 174). The fragmentary hymn to the sun from Vidiśā (EI 30, 215–9) by Cittapa provides us with a composition by a poet otherwise known only from numerous quotations in the anthologies.

Sometimes *stotras* are imbedded within larger inscriptions of the *praśasti* class. Such is the case with the *Gaurīśvara-stotra* in the first Baijnāth *praśasti* (EI 1, 97–112) and the hymn to Jvālāmukhī-Bhavānī in the Kāngrā Jvālāmukhī *praśasti* (EI 1, 190–5).[29]

7.2.2.3 Evaluation of inscriptional texts as literature

As mentioned before (7.2.2.1), the position of epigraphic compositions within the Sanskritic literary tradition is more or less marginal. Much of the *praśasti* literature, it must be conceded, is not much better than hackwork. Nevertheless, there are not a few cases where inscriptional *kāvya* rises above the ordinary level. Besides the well-known *praśastis* which are often cited as outstanding specimens of inscriptional poetry (Allahabad, Tālaguṇḍa, Mandasor, Aihoḷe, etc.), many other inscriptions could be mentioned as examples of good poetry; for example, the Cāṅgu-Nārāyaṇa pillar inscription (SI I.378–82), with such fine turns of phrase as *pramṛṣṭakanaka-ślakṣṇāvadātacchaviḥ*, "whose skin was bright and smooth as burnished gold" (l. 52).[30] Among prose inscriptions, the Mahākūṭa inscription, among others, has been

27. Cf. section 4.1.8.

28. Cf. section 4.1.7.

29. For other examples of inscriptional stotras, not preserved in literature, see section 4.1.7.

30. Also often cited in this connection are the Sanskrit inscriptions of Cambodia, several of which display all the standard features of the elaborate *kāvya* style (see 4.3.7.7).

singled out for praise (cf. Naik, "Inscriptions of the Deccan," 30). Some of the inscriptional *stotras* are of high quality, for example, the Māndhātā Halāyudha-stotra which expresses deep and sincere feelings of devotion in eloquent poetic style, as in the following verse (v. 63, ll. 47–48):

> *avyaktākṣarajalpitair api śiśoḥ prītir ggurūṇāṃ bhavet*
> *tenāsmadvacanaṃ malīmasam api syāt tuṣṭihetus tava /*
> *śrāntas tvadguṇakīrttanāt kimapi yat puṇyaṃ mayopārjitaṃ*
> *tena syāj jananāntare pi mahatī tvayy eva bhaktir mama //*

> A baby might please his parents even with babbling nonsensical sounds; so too may my words, faulty though they may be, bring you some satisfaction. And whatever merit I may have earned by exhausting myself in singing your praises, by that may I be born again with deep devotion to you alone.

Altogether, the inscriptional records embody both the best and worst of Sanskrit poetry: its richness and variety of style and imagination, and its stiffness and pedantry. All of the standard features of the classical tradition—the various regional styles, the many *alaṃkāras* of sound and sense, the elaborate wordplay and manipulations of multiple meanings, even the *citra-kāvya* or visually configured verses[31]—are abundantly attested. In short, the inscriptional corpus constitutes an important branch of Indian literature as a whole which is not only significant as a historical tool but also worthy of study as a literary corpus in its own right.

7.3 Epigraphy and the Study of Religion

D. C. Sircar, *Studies in the Religious Life of Ancient and Medieval India*; V. Upādhyāya, *Prācīna Bhāratīya Abhilekha*, I.100–30.

As is the case with many other branches of Indology, epigraphy provides a solid geographical and chronological groundwork for the historical study of the religious traditions of ancient India. Among the many aspects of the history of religions which can be elucidated by inscriptions are the growth and relative popularity at different times and places of various devotional cults (see, e.g., 7.3.1.2), for which subject Sircar's *Studies in the Religious Life of Ancient and Medieval India* constitutes a fundamental source of information. Inscriptions also reveal patterns of royal patronage to different religions and sects, providing a framework for their historical developments. The typical pattern is one of multiple patronage, wherein the same ruler may sponsor, for instance, both Brahmanical and Buddhist institutions. It is also common to find different rulers of the same line lending their support to different establishments, according to their personal preferences; the emperor Harṣa, for example, is described in his inscriptions (e.g., Bānskheṛā, EI 4, 208–11) as the descendant of devotees of the Sun (*paramādityabhakta*) but was himself a Śaivite (*paramamāheśvara*) and is known from other sources (mainly the Chinese pilgrim Hsüan Tsang) to have also patronized Buddhism. Similarly, the earlier kings of the Candra

31. See, e.g., the *padma-bandha* and *cakra-bandha* in two inscriptions from Bōthpur (nos. 51 and 52), in P. Sreenivasachar, *A Corpus of Inscriptions in the Telingana Districts*, part II, 148–9, 157–61, 197.

dynasty of East Bengal were Buddhists, while their successors Lahaḍacandra and Govindacandra adopted Vaiṣṇava and Śaiva faiths, respectively.[32]

7.3.1 The Brahmanical/Hindu tradition

7.3.1.1 The Vedic tradition

While epigraphy obviously has little to offer for the historical study of the Vedic era itself, it nonetheless does provide useful information about the preservation and continuation of the Vedic tradition in the classical and postclassical periods. Inscriptions, especially copper plate grants with their often extensive lists of Brahmans and their Veda and *śākhā* affiliations, provide an important source for the history and especially for the geographical affiliations of the various Vedic schools; this material has been extensively utilized by, among others, Louis Renou[33] and, more recently, Michael Witzel.[34]

Numerous historical records of the performance of Vedic sacrifices, especially the *aśvamedha* (horse sacrifice), are preserved in inscriptions from about the second century B.C. onward, for example, in the Hāṭhibāḍā/Ghosuṇḍī inscriptions and the Ayodhyā inscription of Dhanadeva.[35] Sometimes the king is said to have performed the *aśvamedha* several times, and/or to have done several other *yajñas*, as in the case of Pravarasena and the Bhāraśiva kings mentioned in the records of the Vākāṭakas (e.g., CII 5, 12, ll. 1–6). An interesting early record of the performance of multiple sacrifices together with details of the *dakṣiṇā* paid is provided by a Sātavāhana inscription from Nānāghāṭ (SI I.192–7).

A second class of records of this type comprises those which directly commemorate the performance of Vedic sacrifices with inscriptions on the bricks of the sacrificial altar itself, for instance, the Jagatpur inscriptions from the fourth *aśvamedha* of King Śīlavarman (*caturthasyāśvamedhasya caityo yaṃ śīlavarmaṇaḥ;* cf. 4.2.3.2); or on stone *yūpas* which reproduce the wooden ones actually used in the sacrifice (4.2.1.2).

7.3.1.2 The Vaiṣṇava tradition

Several inscriptions provide important information on the history of the various Vaiṣṇava sects, especially for the earlier period of their development.[36] An outstanding

32. D. C. Sircar, *Epigraphic Discoveries in East Pakistan*, 51–2.

33. *Les Écoles védiques et la formation du Veda*, Cahiers de la Société Asiatique 9 (Paris: Imprimerie Nationale, 1947), pars. 47, 73, 117, 197–9; *Le Destin du Véda dans l'Inde*, Études Védiques et Pāṇinéennes 6; Publications de l'Institut de Civilisation Indienne 10 (Paris: Éditions E. de Boccard, 1960), 29; and "The Vedic Schools and the Epigraphy," in *Siddha-Bhāratī or the Rosary of Indology* [Siddheshwar Varma Festschrift], ed. Vishva Bandhu, Vishveshvaranand Indological Series 2 (Hoshiarpur: Vishveshvaranand Vedic Research Institute, 1950), II.214–21.

34. "Materialien zu den vedischen Schulen I. Über die Caraka-Śākhā," StII 7, 1981, 109–32 (esp. 128–31); "Regionale und überregionale Faktoren in der Entwicklung vedischer Brahmanengruppen im Mitteralter (Materialien zu den vedischen Schulen, 5)," in Hermann Kulke and Dietmar Rothermund, eds., *Regionale Tradition in Südasien*, Beiträge zur Südasienforschungen 104 (Stuttgart: F. Steiner Verlag Wiesbaden, 1985), 37–75 (esp. 40).

35. For a detailed compilation of inscriptional records of the *aśvamedha*, see Sircar, "Hiraṇyagarbha and Aśvamedha," *Studies in the Religious Life*, 164–82.

36. This material has been extensively compiled and utilized by Suvira Jaiswal in *The Origin and Development of Vaiṣṇavism: Vaiṣṇavism from 200 BC to AD 500*, 2d ed. (New Delhi: Munshiram Manoharlal, 1981); see esp. 27–9.

example is the Hēliodōros pillar at Besnagar (Appendix, no. 2), which not only provides evidence for the Bhāgavata cult at an early time (second century B.C.) but also indicates that non-Indians, that is, Greeks, were included among its adherents (Jaiswal, op. cit., 189). The recently discovered Pratāpgaṛh inscription (EI 39, 79–80) recording the erection of a pillar by a donor characterized as *sacā-bhāgavatena* or "true Bhāgavata" provides further testimony for the same cult in Rajasthan at about the same period.

Several other inscriptions from the late B.C. to the early A.D. period provide further information about the Bhāgavata and related cults, notably that of Saṃkarṣaṇa and Vāsudeva, attested in the Hāṭhibāḍā/Ghosuṇḍī inscriptions and in a Nānāghāṭ inscription (SII I.192–7, l. 1). The prominent cultic position of Saṃkarṣaṇa (Baladeva) at this time is indicated by the fact that his name is given first in the *dvandva* compound of the names of the paired deities in these inscriptions (e.g., *namo saṃkasana-vāsudevānaṃ* in Nānāghāṭ; Jaiswal, 58). Later cultic developments are illustrated by, for example, the Basupāṛā tortoise shell inscriptions from East Bengal (JASB 15, 101–8; cf. 4.2.5.5), which attest to a mixed cult incorporating Vaiṣṇava and Buddhist worship with that of the local tortoise deity Dharma.

Among the other aspects of the historical development of Vaiṣṇava tradition which can be elucidated by the study of inscriptions is the *avatāra* doctrine. Thus a Pallava inscription from Mahābalipuram, datable to the late seventh or early eighth century (MASI 26, 4–7), provides a list of ten *avatāras* including the Buddha which is an important bit of evidence in tracing the historical development of this concept.[37]

7.3.1.3 The Śaiva tradition

Epigraphic testimony is particularly useful for the history of some of the Śaiva traditions; the relevant information is compiled by V. S. Pathak in his *History of Śaiva Cults in Northern India from Inscriptions*.[38] Several medieval inscriptions provide detailed genealogies of lineages of Śaiva sages; most notably, the inscriptions of the Tripurī Kalacuri kings provide abundant information on the Mattamayūra Śaivācāryas whom they patronized, enabling scholars to reconstruct the lineages of the various branches of their institutions, as well as giving information on their monastic structures and rules, literary activities, and the like.[39] The high degree of political influence attained by Śaivite *ācāryas* in some other dynasties is attested by inscriptions in which the ruling king appears to have actually ceded his authority to the *rājaguru* (Sircar, *Studies in the Religious Life*, 152–55).

Other Śaiva sects for which inscriptions provide important data include the Kāpālikas and Kālāmukhas; this material has been treated in detail by David N. Lorenzen in *The Kāpālikas and Kālāmukhas: Two Lost Śaivite Sects*,[40] esp. 24–31 and 98ff. Important information on the early history of the Vīraśaivas is provided by Ablūr inscription E (EI 5, 237–60; cf. also SITI III.2, 200).

37. Cf. Ludo Rocher, *The Purāṇas*, A History of Indian Literature, vol. 2, fasc. 3 (Wiesbaden: Otto Harrassowitz, 1986), 107 and 111. For a later epigraphic account of the ten *avatāras*, see the Ajmer stone inscription (EI 29, 178–82, vv. 12–21).

38. See also his "Some Obscure Śaiva Cults as Known from Inscriptions," IHQ 35, 1959, 120–31.

39. Pathak, op. cit., 32–7, 46–50; Mirashi, CII 4.1, cl–clix; see also EI 37, 120–1.

40. Berkeley: University of California, 1972.

7.3.1.4 Śākta and other traditions

In similar ways, inscriptional records provide firm geographical and chronological anchors for the historical study of the Śākta and other of the less orthodox streams within the Brahmanical/Hindu tradition; examples are provided in Sircar, *Studies in the Religious Life*, 94–7. Other "popular" cults such as those of the worship of *yakṣas* and *nāgas* are documented from an early period in the form of inscribed statues from Mathurā, Bhārhut, Patna, and other sites (cf. 7.4.1.3).

7.3.2 Buddhism

A. M. Shastri, *An Outline of Early Buddhism*; É. Lamotte, *Histoire du bouddhisme indien* [HBI]; M. Shizutani, *Indo Bukkyō Himei Mokuroku*.

7.3.2.1 Sectarian and monastic organization

Although the origins of Buddhism predate the period from which inscriptions are available, inscriptions still constitute a critically important source for the history of Buddhism in India from early times, since many of the oldest extant inscriptions, such as those of Aśoka and the Piprāwā inscription, are of Buddhist content. Among the aspects of Buddhist history for which inscriptions are particularly useful is the development of the various schools and sects; Buddhist donative inscriptions, which usually specify the sectarian affiliation of the recipients, have enabled historians to construct a much more precise geographical and chronological framework for the sects than would have been possible from the historically vague literary and canonical sources.[41] This information has enabled Buddhologists to reconstruct at least a broad picture of the relative dominance of various sects at various points in history. Further details on sectarian and monastic organization are also sporadically available; in some (exceptional) cases, the data are sufficient to give a reasonably detailed view of the situation prevailing at a particular time and place, as, for example, in Mathurā during the Kuṣāṇa period, for which the names of over a dozen Buddhist *vihāras* are attested in inscriptions (Shastri, *An Outline of Early Buddhism*, 120–21).

The abundant private donative inscriptions (4.1.3) are also very useful for the analysis of patterns of patronage of the various Buddhist establishments, revealing such information as the sex, social standing, and ethnic affiliations of the donors. Examples of studies utilizing such materials are Bimala Churn Law, "Bhikshunis in Indian Inscriptions" (EI 25, 1939–40, 31–4), and Gregory Schopen, "On Monks, Nuns, and 'Vulgar' Practices: The Introduction of the Image Cult into Indian Buddhism" (*Artibus Asiae* 49, 1988–89, 153–68).

7.3.2.2 Formation of the canon

Inscriptions also shed some light on the complex problems of the formation and history of the various Buddhist canons. An important early instance is Aśoka's Bairāṭ (Bhābhṛā) rock edict (cf. 4.3.1.1.2), in which the emperor recommends seven spe-

41. For lists and discussions of inscriptionally attested sects, see Lamotte, HBI 578–84; Shastri, *An Outline of Early Buddhism*, 68–111; and Shizutani, *Indo Bukkyō Himei Mokuroku*, 153.

cific texts for the special study and attention of Buddhist monks and lay followers. Although there are serious problems in identifying these texts with those in the extant canon (HBI 256–9; bibliography, 258 n. 74) and in evaluating their significance in connection with the establishment of a fixed canon, the Bairāṭ inscription nonetheless provides an important clue for the canonical formulations of the early Buddhist church.

Among later Buddhist inscriptions we find occasional quotations from canonical works, such as the citation of the *pratītya-samutpāda* in the Kurram casket inscription (CII 2.1, 152–5) and other records (see 4.1.7), which provide clues as to the prevalent authoritative texts and their language. For example, a passage in the Indravarman Casket inscription appears to be a quotation or adaptation from the *Ekottarāgama*, implying that this collection was extant in some form in northwestern India in the early first century A.D.[42] Also, Sanskrit versions of well-known verses from the *Dhammapada* and other texts prevalent in the early A.D. period are attested by three inscriptions from Swat (EI 4, 133–5), and a Pāli terra-cotta inscription from Hmawza provides the earliest evidence of the Pāli canon in Burma (JA, ser. 11, vol. 2, 193–5).

7.3.2.3 Doctrinal developments and cultic practices

Inscriptional evidence can provide a balance to the literary/canonical accounts of doctrinal developments within Buddhism, and not infrequently presents a picture which casts doubt on prevailing views derived from the latter sources. The development of the Mahāyāna as an independent sect, for example, appears on the basis of epigraphic sources to have been considerably later than received opinion would have it.[43] Conversely, concepts such as the transfer of merit which are traditionally associated with the Mahāyāna are found to be prevalent in pre-Mahāyāna or "Hīnayāna" inscriptions.[44] The resolution of such apparent conflicts of evidence is no simple matter, but there can be no question that in Buddhological studies as a whole the testimony of the inscriptions has not generally been given the weight it merits, and that the entire field of the history of Buddhism, which has traditionally been dominated by a strongly text-oriented approach, must be reexamined in its light. The studies of É. Lamotte and more recently of G. Schopen have opened the door to this more pragmatic approach, but much more remains to be done; in the words of the latter scholar, "This perfunctory preference for formal literary sources—which is quite common in historical works on Indian Buddhism—can only result in 'histories of Buddhism' which have little relationship to what practicing Buddhists actually did."[45]

In the field of popular practice, too, the inscriptions yield a wealth of information which may be absent or disguised in the more commonly consulted canonical

42. R. Salomon and G. Schopen, "The Indravarman (Avaca) Casket Reconsidered: Further Evidence for Canonical Passages in Buddhist Inscriptions," JIABS 7, 1984, 107–23 (esp. 120–1).

43. See Gregory Schopen, "Mahāyāna in Indian Inscriptions," IIJ 21, 1979, 1–19.

44. G. Schopen, "Two Problems in the History of Indian Buddhism: The Layman/Monk Distinction and the Doctrines of the Transference of Merit," StII 10, 1985, 9–47 (esp. 36).

45. JAOS 108, 1988, 536. See also Schopen's "Archaeology and Protestant Presuppositions in the Study of Indian Buddhism," *History of Religions* 31, 1991, 1–23.

texts. Our knowledge and understanding of the beliefs and practices of the relic cult, for example, have recently been vastly enhanced by the discovery of new inscriptions and the reanalysis of older ones bearing on this important aspect of popular Buddhism.[46]

7.3.3 Jainism and other sects

The very abundant and relatively well-documented inscriptions of the Jainas (8.1.3.4), especially in western India of the medieval period, offer a rich fund of information for the study of Jaina religion, ethics, and especially monastic organization. These sources have been extensively utilized in such general historical studies as Asim Kumar Chatterjee's *Comprehensive History of Jainism* and P. B. Desai's *Jainism in South India and Some Jaina Epigraphs*. Jai Prakash Singh's *Aspects of Early Jainism [As Known from the Epigraphs]* attempts a general survey of Jainism from epigraphic sources, but the results are less satisfactory. Paul Dundas' general study of Jaina religion and practice, *The Jains*, also extensively utilizes epigraphic data for chronological and historical corroboration.

Inscriptions provide abundant details on the history of Jaina sectarian and monastic history and organization, in the form of the names, lineages, and positions of many Jaina clerics (cf. IC I.170). This data may be profitably used as a corroborative and supplementary source to information provided in the canonical literature. Works addressing Jaina sectarian history that make extensive use of inscriptional information include Shantaram Bhalchandra Deo's *History of Jaina Monachism from Inscriptions and Literature* (especially Part IV, "Jaina Monachism from Epigraphs") and Muni Uttam Kamal Jain's *Jaina Sects and Schools*. As examples of particular epigraphic documents with significant bearing on sectarian history, we may cite an inscription from Pattana (EI 1, 1892, 319–24) which provides a list of twenty-four heads of the Kharatara-gaccha and describes the patronage of that community by the Mughal emperor Akbar, and an old manuscript copy of a lost inscription from Śatruñjaya recording the resolutions of a council of Śvetāmbara monks in A.D. 1242.[47]

Studies of other aspects of Jaina history and practice may also benefit from epigraphic evidence, as, for example, in S. Settar's *Inviting Death*, a study of ritual death among Jains at Śravaṇa-Beḷgoḷa based largely on over one hundred commemorative records.

Inscriptions are also sometimes useful in the historical study of minor sects. A. L. Basham, for example, in his classic study of the Ājīvikas,[48] cites inscriptions attesting to the continued presence of members of this sect in the Tamil country as

46. E.g., Schopen, "On the Buddha and His Bones: The Conception of a Relic in the Inscriptions of Nāgārjunakoṇḍa," JAOS 108, 1988, 527–37; see also Schopen, "Burial '*ad Sanctos*' and the Physical Presence of the Buddha in Early Indian Buddhism: A Study in the Archaeology of Religions," *Religion* 17, 1987, 193–225 (esp. 204–5).

47. See Umakant Premanand Shah, "A Forgotten Chapter in the History of Śvetāmbara Jaina Church *or* A Documentary Epigraph from the Mount Śatruñjaya," *Journal of the Asiatic Society of Bombay* 30, 1953, 100–13.

48. *History and Doctrines of the Ājīvikas: A Vanished Indian Religion* (London: Luzac, 1951; reprint, Delhi: Motilal Banarsidass, 1981), 187–96.

late as the fourteenth century. Even the heterodox skeptics of the Lokāyata tradition are attested in inscriptions, as noted by B. A. Saletore,[49] who has traced several references to them in Karnataka inscriptions of the tenth to fifteenth centuries.

7.4 Epigraphy and the Study of the Arts

F. M. Asher and G. S. Gai, eds., *Indian Epigraphy: Its Bearing on the History of Art* [IEBHA]; RIE 122–41 ("Epigraphy and Indian Art and Architecture").

7.4.1 The visual arts

7.4.1.1 Epigraphy as a chronological guide to the study of the visual arts

Given the paucity of information on the subject from literary records, inscriptions constitute a crucial source of information on the chronology and history of the visual arts—sculpture, architecture, and painting—in traditional India. The chronology, both relative and absolute, of these arts is to a great extent reconstructed from accompanying inscriptions, dated explicitly or by paleographic estimate. Typically, the developmental history of a given school or phase of Indian art is constructed around a basic chronological framework derived from those specimens which are accompanied by dated or datable inscriptions. Thus, for example, Joanna Williams introduces her study of the development of Mathurā sculpture of the fifth century with the remark "First we must establish a scaffolding of dated pieces, upon which other works can be placed."[50] Williams thus takes sculptures inscriptionally dated to the Gupta years 97, 113, 115, and 125 as the fixed points for her discussion (op. cit., 67–73) and estimates the dates of other, undated pieces by comparisons with these dated ones.[51]

In cases such as these, where we have a sufficiently large and geographically and stylistically coherent body of materials, including several securely dated pieces, this method of chronological reconstruction can be highly productive. Needless to say, however, this is by no means always the case. At least as often as not, especially in earlier periods, the picture is much less clear. Among the problems which may arise, we may not always have enough, or even any, dated inscriptions to establish a secure chronological framework, so that we must resort to other techniques, mainly dating by paleographic estimate. However, paleographic dating is in itself a notoriously imprecise chronological tool (see 5.4.1), and when it is employed in conjunction with estimated dating on stylistic grounds, which is an equally imprecise method, the problems are multiplied. Thus it frequently happens that paleographic analysis

49. "Historical Notices of the Lokāyatas," *Annals of the Bhandarkar Oriental Research Institute* 23, 1942, 386–97.

50. Joanna Gottfried Williams, *The Art of Gupta India: Empire and Province* (Princeton: Princeton University Press, 1982), 67.

51. For another example of the application of this technique, see Pramod Chandra's reconstruction of the chronology of northern Indian sculpture of the sixth to twelfth centuries in *Stone Sculptures in the Allahabad Museum: A Descriptive Catalogue* (Poona: American Institute of Indian Studies, [1970]), 23–32.

may suggest one conclusion about the relative or absolute chronological place of an inscribed work of art, while stylistic analysis of the work itself may suggest a different conclusion. For instance, the Kārle cave temple of the time of Nahapāna is attributed by most historians to the first century A.D. on paleographic grounds, while some art historians would prefer to date it on stylistic criteria to the first century B.C.[52]

In such a case, where two approximative dating methods suggest conflicting results, the scholar (whether art historian or epigraphist) faces the question of which method is more precise or reliable. Not surprisingly, art historians are often inclined to consider stylistic analysis as a more precise standard. For example, Karl Khandalavala says, "Where stylistic features conflict with the paleographical evidence, the former are much to be preferred in arriving at conclusions as to the period of a particular sculpture" (IEBHA 68); similarly J. E. van Lohuizen-de Leeuw claims that "we receive far more support from the development which the style in these hundred years passed through, than from the changes in the form of the characters during the same period, because characters are more conservative than art, which is more liable to be affected by fashion and taste" (*The "Scythian" Period*, 264). Particularly important on this point are the comments of Pramod Chandra: "[T]he conclusions drawn are being deduced not from the work of art itself but from something that happens to be written on it. Used cautiously, paleography can certainly help us as we try to reconstruct chronology, but it cannot determine it. . . . The paleography of an inscription on a sculpture may help in determining its date, but the date of a sculpture, on the basis of its style, has an equal claim to modify our understanding of the paleography."[53]

But the epigraphists naturally (and, as noted by Chandra, sometimes uncritically) tend to place a greater weight on the paleographic evidence; thus, for example, D. C. Sircar refers to the "less specific evidence such as that of architectural and sculptural style" (EI 33, 1959–60, 261). Ultimately, of course, one cannot make categorical judgments as to the relative weight of stylistic versus paleographic dating; in Chandra's words, "There is nothing to distinguish one technique as being inherently superior to the other" (op. cit., 68); apparent conflicts between the two must be judged on a case-by-case basis. The real problem may be that there are very few scholars, especially in this modern age of specialization, who are expert both in art history and in epigraphy and paleography, and one naturally tends to give the most weight to that body of evidence with which one is most conversant and comfortable. All that can be done in such a situation is to remind scholars in both fields of the benefits of communication and cooperation.[54] There is room for criticism on both sides. Art historians have often placed too much trust in secondary sources which provide convenient but questionable interpretations of the paleographic data, and have failed to closely examine the original sources, while epigraphists often tend to focus too closely on the inscriptions

52. Pramod Chandra, *On the Study of Indian Art* (Cambridge, Mass.: Harvard University Press, 1983), 68–9.

53. *On the Study of Indian Art*, 67–8; see also 21–2.

54. The publication of IEBHA represents a concerted attempt, albeit not entirely successful, to establish such communication. See also the supplementary comments by Gautam Sengupta in "Epigraphy and Art-History: On Some Inscribed Sculptures of Eastern India," JESI 16, 1990, 112–8.

themselves without paying due attention to the works of art on which they are written and the chronological or other evidence which may be provided thereby.[55]

Epigraphists should therefore always keep in mind that the art object can sometimes elucidate the accompanying inscription. An interesting application of this principle is Lohuizen-de Leeuw's use of stylistic as well as paleographic and contextual criteria in support of her theory that certain sculptures with two-figure dates are to be attributed to the second century of the Kaniṣka era, with the figure for 100 omitted (*The "Scythian" Period*, 235ff.). Although her "theory of omitted hundreds" has by no means been universally accepted (see 5.5.1.4 n. 87), her arguments are methodologically powerful in that they combine a sophisticated understanding of both epigraphic and art historical questions, constituting an important and all too rare exception to the specializing tendencies remarked upon previously.

Other types of problems arise in situations—again all too common—in which a few epigraphic and/or paleographic dates are available, but not enough of them to provide a solid chronological bedrock for the analysis of the evolution of art styles. Classic cases of this syndrome are the chronology of Gandhāran sculpture, or the dating of the later (the so-called Mahāyāna) caves at Ajaṇṭā. In the case of Ajaṇṭā, the principal sources are two undated inscriptions of the late Vākāṭaka period in caves 17 and 26, plus a few other inscriptions from other sites in the region. On the basis of these sources, combined with equally meager literary references, several chronological reconstructions, differing considerably from one another, have been proposed for this crucial phase of Indian sculpture and painting. Recent discussions[56] have tended to focus on the "short chronology" proposed by Walter Spink in numerous articles,[57] according to which the caves in question were constructed in a brief period of about two decades ca. A.D. 460–80. On the basis of the meager evidence, Spink provides (e.g., in *Ars Orientalis* 10) an extremely detailed and precise chronology, almost down to the year, of historical events and sequences of construction. This scheme is appealing in its seeming detail and precision, but it cannot escape the suspicions of the epigraphist and historian, since it is argued on the basis of tenuous and uncertain data from undated, fragmentary inscriptions and of literary citations (mainly from the *Daśakumāra-carita*) of doubtful relevance.[58] The lesson here is that we must resist the temptation to make the epigraphic data do more than it honestly can; at Ajaṇṭā, as is usually the case, the inscriptional material is simply insufficient to allow any more than a very broad and approximative chronological scheme.

7.4.1.2 Names of artists and schools provided by inscriptions

Although traditional Indian art tends to be anonymous, there are nonetheless a good number of sculptures and other works of art whose creators are mentioned by name

55. Cf. the comments of Pramod Chandra, op. cit., 22 and 44.

56. For a concise summary of the controversy, see Williams, *The Art of Gupta India* (for reference see n. 50), 181–7.

57. See, e.g., "Ajanta's Chronology: The Crucial Cave," *Ars Orientalis* 10, 1975, 143–69, and "Ajanta's Chronology: Politics and Patronage," in Joanna Williams, ed., *Kalādarśana: American Studies in the Art of India* (New Delhi: Oxford University Press and IBH/American Institute of Indian Studies, 1981), 109–26; further references given in Williams, *The Art of Gupta India*, 181–7.

58. See also the criticisms expressed by Williams, *The Art of Gupta India*, 181–7.

in accompanying inscriptions.[59] The artists in question are referred to by various titles such as *rūpakāra*, *śilpin*, *sūtradhāra*, or *citrakāra*. Such inscriptions are much commoner in the medieval period, especially in the monuments of certain dynasties such as the Hoysaḷas, but some earlier specimens are also known. An important case is that of the renowned sculptor Dinna of Mathurā, whose name is recorded (e.g., *pratimā ceyaṃ ghaṭitā dinnena māthureṇa*, "And this image was created by Dinna of Mathurā")[60] in four image inscriptions from Mathurā and Kasiā, and who seems to have been one of the master artists of his time.[61] One of these inscriptions (the Mathurā [Govindnagar] pedestal ins., EI 40, 20–2) is dated in the [Gupta] year 115, enabling us to date Dinna to the first half of the fifth century A.D. An evidently prominent sculptor of the Pāla-Sena school, Amṛta, is also now known from two inscribed pieces bearing his name (*amṛtena suśilpinā*).[62]

From the much more abundant material in later centuries, we learn the names not only of individual artists but also of familial or other lineages of artisans. For example, various followers of the artistic lineage of the Kokāsas (*śrīkokāsavaṃśa*; CII 4, 329, l. 43) are mentioned in several Kalacuri inscriptions of the twelfth to fifteenth centuries, and the eponymous Kokāsa is also mentioned in several Jaina texts.[63] These references to artisans and schools are potentially of great value for art history, for example, in helping to date pieces by known artists (Narasimha Murthy, IEBHA 215) or for refining our understanding of the development of local traditions (Misra, op. cit., 68).

7.4.1.3 Technical and iconographic information derived from inscriptions

Certain inscriptions—especially temple inscriptions from medieval southern India—provide information, sometimes in considerable detail, about architectural construction. The sequence and circumstances of the construction of the Tribhuvanacūḍāmaṇi-caityālaya at Mūḍabidure (South Kanara Dist., Karnataka), for example, are recorded in detail in a series of inscriptions of the fifteenth century (RIE 128–31). Details of the construction technique of the Īśvara temple of Tadalbāgi (Bijapur Dist., Karnataka) are recorded in an inscription of A.D. 1269 (SII 20, xxiv and 268).

Also useful are the occasional citations in dedicatory inscriptions of technical architectural terms. Such references may be of use in identifying and analyzing the characteristics of the styles and features in question (e.g., RIE 125ff.).[64]

59. Lists and discussions of names of artisans recorded in inscriptions can be found in R. N. Misra, *Ancient Artists and Art-Activity* (Simla: Indian Institute of Advanced Study, 1975), and C. Sivaramamurti, *Indian Sculpture* (New Delhi: Indian Council for Cultural Relations/Allied Publishers, 1961), 1–14. The subject is also discussed in several of the articles in IEBHA, notably R. N. Misra's "Artists of Ḍāhala and Dakṣiṇa Kosala: A Study Based on Epigraphs" (185–90) and A. V. Narasimha Murthy's "Study of the Label Inscriptions of the Hoysaḷa Sculptors" (215–20).

60. See D. C. Sircar, EI 35, 1963–64, 200.

61. Sircar, EI 39, 1971–72, 120; Williams, *The Art of Gupta India*, 68.

62. See G. Bhattacharya, "Susilpin Amrita," JESI 9, 1982, 20–2.

63. Misra, *Ancient Artists and Art-Activity*, 70; "Artists of Ḍāhala and Dakṣiṇa Kosala," IEBHA 187 and 189 n. 31.

64. An outstanding example of a study based on this approach is M. A. Dhaky's *Indian Temple Forms in Karṇāṭa Inscriptions and Architecture* (New Delhi: Abhinav Publications, 1977).

Inscriptions may also be helpful for the study of iconography by providing both descriptions of the attributes of various deities,[65] and labels (4.1.5) for sculpted or painted figures who might otherwise be difficult to identify, such as the numerous labeled *yakṣa* and *nāga* figures from Bhārhut, Patna, and other sites.[66] Since extant iconographic literature is generally late, such inscriptional labels often provide the earliest iconographic testimony for various deities. This type of information is also useful in connection with little-known, archaic, or local deities whose iconographic features may not be provided in the standard literary manuals of the subject, as, for example, the inscriptions labeling the *yoginīs* in the Caūsaṭh-yoginī temple at Bheraghāṭ.[67]

7.4.2 The performing arts

A few inscriptions, once again mostly from the south, provide extremely useful information on the performing arts, particularly music and dance.[68] Among the few inscriptions concerning music, the best known and most important is the Kuḍumiyāmalai inscription (EI 12, 226–37), which lists sets of notes arranged in groups of four (*catuṣprahārasvarāgāmāḥ*) for each of the seven *rāgas*. The inscription, which has been attributed by some authors to the Pallava king Mahendravarman I, is described by R. Sathyanarayana as "certainly the only primary evidence of contemporary musical practice in ancient India."[69]

Several inscriptions from Tamil Nadu recording the performance of various types of dances are collected by A. N. Perumal in "Art of Dance in the Temples of Tamil Nadu—Epigraphical Evidence" (JESI 5, 1978, 15–9). A remarkable epigraphic document referring to the classical dance is the label inscriptions, quoting the relevant verses from the fourth book (the *Tāṇḍava-lakṣaṇa*) of the *Bharata-nāṭyaśāstra*, which accompany the 108 sculptured figures depicting the corresponding dance poses (*karaṇas*) on the pillars in the eastern and western *gopurams* of the Naṭarāja temple in Cidambaram (ARSIE 1914, 40, 74–81).

7.5 Epigraphy and Linguistics

Although its relation to epigraphy is of prime importance, linguistics will not be discussed in detail here since the relevant material has already been covered in chapter 3. Suffice it to say that inscriptions provide a vast body of linguistic data which not only supplements but to some degree even supersedes information on the history and dialectology of the Indo-Aryan languages (as well as of the Dravidian and other South Asian language families) derived from noninscriptional, that is, literary, sources. The

65. Numerous examples provided in C. Sivaramamurti, "Iconographic Gleanings from Epigraphy," *Arts Asiatiques* 4, 1957, 35–70.

66. Ibid., 35–6.

67. See R. K. Sharma, *The Temple of Chaunsathyogini at Bheraghat.*

68. See IESIS 14 and SITI III.2, 183–4, for general comments on these inscriptions.

69. *The Kuḍimiyāmalai Inscription on Music*, vii.

principal justification for this statement is that inscriptions provide relatively uncontaminated linguistic data, as opposed to literary texts which are often altered and tampered with in various ways in the course of multiple copyings over the centuries. Moreover, inscriptions often provide specimens of otherwise unattested or poorly attested dialects. This is particularly true in connection with the Middle Indo-Aryan languages, as in the case of the Aśokan inscriptions which provide unique specimens of early MIA vernaculars (3.1.2), and of the Kharoṣṭhī inscriptions which give us extensive documentation for the distinctive "Gāndhārī" language, which until recently was known from only one literary text.[70] Also, as noted previously (3.2.3), inscriptions in the mixed or hybrid dialects constitute an important body of evidence that helps to clarify the linguistic status of the similar hybrid dialects of Buddhist Sanskrit literature.

Inscriptions are also an important source for the study of the history of the Sanskrit language, especially in that, once again, they provide us with numerous specimens of nonliterary usage, thereby revealing a type, or rather several types, of Sanskrit which were used for functional and legal purposes, and about which we would have known little from literary sources alone (see 3.3.8). Inscriptional Sanskrit also constitutes a major source of lexicographical data (3.3.8.4), including both special technical and legal terminology, as collected in Sircar's *Indian Epigraphical Glossary*, and literary usages not attested in texts, for which S. P. Tewari's *Contributions of Sanskrit Inscriptions to Lexicography* is the principal source. These resources, however, to date have not been adequately utilized in general dictionaries of Sanskrit; the *Encyclopaedic Dictionary of Sanskrit on Historical Principles* (Poona: Deccan College, 1976–) represents only a partial advance in this respect.[71]

Inscriptions in NIA languages too are often of considerable linguistic interest, especially in that many of them are among the earliest available specimens of the various languages; such is the case, for example, for Marathi, Oriya, and Sinhalese (see 3.4.1, 3.4.2, and 3.4.7) as well as for several of the Dravidian languages (3.5.1). Moreover, the inscriptions often provide more authentic and linguistically useful specimens of early NIA vernaculars than are available from the frequently artificial and highly Sanskritized literary sources.[72]

7.6 Epigraphy and Geography

D. C. Sircar, *Studies in the Geography of Ancient and Medieval India*; P. Gupta, *Geography in Ancient Indian Inscriptions (Up to 650 A.D.)*; Gupta, *Geographical Names in Ancient Indian Inscriptions*; T. R. Sharma, *Personal and Geographical Names in the Gupta Inscriptions*; RIE 141–50; V. Upādhyāya, *Prācīna Bhāratīya Abhilekha*, I.3–18; R. Stroobandt, *Epigraphical Find-spots*.

Inscriptions constitute the principal source for the study of the historical geography of pre-Islamic India, especially for the identification of toponyms; in the words of

70. That is, the Gāndhārī *Dharmapada*; see section 3.1.4.2.1 n. 23.
71. Cf. the comments of Tiwari, op. cit., 5–6.
72. See K. Tripathi, *The Evolution of Oriya Language and Script*, 9–10.

V. S. Agrawal, inscriptions are "[p]erhaps the richest and most authoritative source of Indian geography."[73] Although a complete compilation of the relevant data remains to be achieved, a large amount of material has already been collected in the sources just cited.

Among the most important uses of geographical data from inscriptions is the geographical identification of places known from literary or other nonarchaeological sources. Many important places have been successfully identified from inscriptions found at their sites; for example, Lumbinī, the traditional birthplace of the Buddha, is identified with Rummindeī in the Nepal Terai on the basis of the Aśokan pillar inscription found there which refers to the village Luṃmini as the Buddha's birthplace (cf. 4.3.1.1.4). More recently, the nearby site of Piprāwā has been definitively identified by K. M. Srivastava[74] with the Kapilavastu of Buddhist tradition on the grounds of numerous inscriptions found there on seals and on a pot which contain the name Kapilavastu.[75]

Inscriptions also provide us in a great many cases with the ancient names of places which are not known from other (i.e., literary) sources. For example, the original Sanskrit name of the modern village of Eraṇ in Sagar District, MP, which was a major city in the Gupta period, is given as Airikiṇa in inscriptions.[76] In many though by no means all cases, the small towns and villages mentioned in inscriptions (especially in copper plate charters) can be geographically identified with modern places bearing similar names. In such cases, however, particularly in connection with later inscriptions, it should not necessarily be assumed that the Sanskrit name given is actually the original toponym, as such names are sometimes ad hoc Sanskritizations of vernacular names.

The geographical data derivable from inscriptions is often sufficiently copious to permit a reasonably detailed reconstruction of the geographical and administrative structure of a given region at a given period. For a summary of such projects undertaken in connection with medieval central and western India, see H. D. Sankalia's "Historical Geography from Inscriptions."[77]

7.7 Other Fields

The subjects discussed so far do not begin to exhaust the contributions of inscriptions to Indological studies as a whole, and the list could be expanded almost ad infinitum; in this section only a few more examples may be given. For one, epigraphy constitutes a prime source of information for the field of *onomastics*. The prin-

73. IHQ 28, 1952, 211 ("Ancient Indian Geography," 205–14).

74. JESI 2, 1976, 108; see also Srivastava's *Kapilavastu in Basti District of U.P. (A Reply to the Challenge to the Identification of Kapilavastu)* (Nagpur: Nagpur Buddhist Centre, 1978).

75. For further examples of such identifications, see D. C. Sircar, *Cosmology and Geography in Early Indian Literature*, Appendix V: "Cosmography and Geography in Inscriptions," 161–5.

76. P. Gupta, *Geography in Ancient Indian Inscriptions*, 59; for other examples, see RIE 141ff. and IESIS 2.

77. In P. J. Chinmulgund and V. V. Mirashi, eds., *M. M. Chitraoshastri Felicitation Volume* (see ch. 8 n. 15 for reference), 248–88.

cipal general work on this field (now outdated but still unsuperseded), Alfons Hilka's *Die altindischen Personennamen*,[78] makes extensive use of inscriptional evidence along with literary sources. The only major recent study in this field is Tej Ram Sharma's *Personal and Geographical Names in the Gupta Inscriptions*.[79]

The study of *law*, which is constricted by the theoretical and normative character of the textual sources, is supplemented by occasional inscriptional records attesting to the dispensation of actual cases, which are practically never cited in the texts. Thus certain inscriptions describe the resolution of disputes over land tenure; see, for example, SII 20, xxiv and 282–4 (no. 232).[80] A rare document testifying to the enforcement of criminal law is provided by the Lāhaḍapura inscription (EI 32, 305–9), recording a *saṃvid* (decree) declaring the penalties imposed on thieves by a council of Brahmans. The charter of Viṣṇuṣeṇa (EI 30, 163–81) provides an interesting list of seventy-two *ācāras*, or customary laws, which were current in western India in the sixth century. The Jaunpur brick inscription (JUPHS 18, 196–201) records a loan by two bankers.[81]

The latter inscription (op. cit., 200–1) also provides the name of an otherwise unknown coin type (the *ṣaḍboddika-dramma*), as do several other inscriptions, notably Sīyaḍoṇī (EI I, 162–79),[82] which thereby constitute useful supplements for the study of *numismatics*. Several references to coin types in Karnataka inscriptions are compiled and discussed by A. V. Narasimha Murthy in "The Role of Epigraphy in the Study of South Indian Numismatics" (IVMD, 77–85).

78. *Indische Forschungen 3: Beiträge zur Kenntnis der indischen Namengebung* (Breslau: M. & H. Marcus, 1910).

79. For an example of a detailed onomastic study based on epigraphic data, see I. K. Sarma, "Significance on Gotras and Matronymics in Some Early Inscriptions," JESI 8, 1981, 67–75.

80. See also Kishori Mohan Gupta, "Land System in Accordance with Epigraphic Evidence with Notes on Some of the Inscriptions and on Some Terms Used in Them," IA 51, 1922, 73–9.

81. For further examples of data on law (including criminal law) in inscriptions, see J. F. Fleet, "The Present Position of Indian Historical Research" (IA 30, 1901), 18–20; J. Duncan M. Derrett, *Religion, Law and the State in India* (New York: The Free Press, 1968), 168, 188–91; and Derrett, *History of Indian Law (Dharmaśāstra)*, Handbuch der Orientalistik II.3 (Leiden/Köln: E. J. Brill, 1973), 21–3.

82. Cf. D. C. Sircar, *Studies in Indian Coins* (Delhi: Motilal Banarsidass, 1968), 299–303.

8

Bibliographic Survey

8.1 Primary Sources: Notices and Editions of Inscriptions

8.1.1 Periodicals

8.1.1.1 Exclusively or primarily epigraphic periodicals

Epigraphia Indica [EI]:[1] Vols. 1 (1892) to 42 (1977–78). From vol. 3, published by the Archaeological Survey of India under the editorship of the chief epigraphist (formerly government epigraphist for India) biennially in eight parts issued quarterly (but no issues for 1904 and 1943–46). An Index to vols. 1–34 by A. N. Lahiri was published as Appendix to vols. 34–36. Vols. 1–34 were issued in reprint editions by the ASI, New Delhi (vol. 2 by Motilal Banarsidass, Delhi), 1960–87. Actual publication dates of the newer volumes have lagged behind the ostensible dates; vol. 42 (1977–78) was issued in 1989.[2] Inscriptions are published in Devanāgarī or Roman transliteration with detailed introduction on historical, paleographic, and linguistic matters, with or without translation (generally without in recent volumes). EI is traditionally the principal organ for the publication of inscriptions in Indo-Aryan as well as Dravidian and other languages. In recent volumes, the proportion of Dravidian language inscriptions has increased.

Islamic (i.e., Arabic, Persian, and Urdu) inscriptions are published in the companion series *Epigraphia Indo-Moslemica* (biennial, 1907–8 to 1949–50), which was superseded by *Epigraphia Indica: Arabic and Persian Supplement* (1951–52 to 1975++ [actually published 1983]; issued annually since 1961). These occasionally also include Sanskrit inscriptions as part of bilinguals with Arabic or Persian (see 3.5.2 and 3.6).

Journal of the Epigraphical Society of India [JESI] (alternate titles: *Studies in Indian Epigraphy* and *Bharatiya Purabhilekha Patrika*): Vols. 1–19, 1975–92. Published annually by the Epigraphical Society of India, Dharwar or Mysore. Contains

1. The full title for vols. 3–24 is *Epigraphia Indica and Record of the Archaeological Survey of India*.

2. For further details of the publication history of EI, see section 6.3.

texts of inscriptions in Roman transliteration with introduction and translation. In recent years, especially with the tardy and sporadic publication of EI, JESI has become de facto the principal epigraphic periodical in India.

Annual Report on Indian Epigraphy [ARIE]: (Successor to *Annual Report on South Indian Epigraphy*,)[3] published annually by the Government of Madras, 1921–44/45; this, in turn, succeeded a series of reports entitled "Epigraphy" issued as Government Orders by the Government of Madras since 1891.[4] Published biennially by the Archaeological Survey of India under the editorship of the chief epigraphist since 1945–46 (latest volume: 1985–86, issued 1993). (A reprint edition of reports for 1911–56 in eight volumes was published by the ASI, 1986.) Contains reports on inscriptions, both new and previously published, reported or examined by the officers of the Archaeological Survey during the year of issue, with brief description and summary of each inscription. ARIE is an important source for information on new inscriptions as well as on minor or fragmentary inscriptions often not published elsewhere.

8.1.1.2 General Indological periodicals with substantial epigraphic content

Major Indological journals with a large proportion of epigraphic articles include *Indian Antiquary**,[5] *New Indian Antiquary**, *Indian Historical Quarterly*, and the *Journal of Ancient Indian History*. Journals of local historical societies in India, such as the *Journal of the Andhra Historical Research Society*, *Journal of the Bihar (and Orissa) Research Society*, and *Journal of the United Provinces Historical Society**, often publish inscriptional materials. Various periodical publications of the Archaeological Survey of India (besides EI, discussed in the preceding section) are important sources of epigraphic data: these include the [*Annual*] *Reports* (Old Series, vols. 1–23, 1871–87; New Series, 1902/3–1936/37); the [*Reports*], *New Imperial Series* (vols. 1–54, 1874–1937); the *Memoirs* [MASI] (issued serially; vols. 1–86, 1919–87; and *Indian Archaeology: A Review* [IAAR] (1953/54–1984/85; important for reports of current projects and new discoveries).

Inscriptions are also published with varying degrees of frequency in many other current general Indological journals, notably the *Bulletin of the School of Oriental and African Studies*, *Indo-Iranian Journal*, *Journal Asiatique*, *Journal of the American Oriental Society*, *Journal of the Asiatic Society* (*of Bengal*), *Journal of the Bombay Branch of the Royal Asiatic Society*, *Journal of the Royal Asiatic Society*, and *Journal of the Oriental Institute* [Baroda]. The *Bulletin de l'École Française d'Extrême-Orient* has been an important vehicle for the publication of Southeast Asian inscriptions in particular, and more recently for Kharoṣṭhī inscriptions from Pakistan and Afghanistan, in a series of articles by Gérard Fussman.

3. The single issue for 1921–22 is entitled *Annual Report on Indian Epigraphy*.

4. Note also the similar reports entitled "Archaeology" for 1887–90, containing mostly epigraphic information.

5. In this section * indicates a defunct periodical. On the publication of *Indian Antiquary*, see section 6.3.

8.1.2 Epigraphic serial publications

Corpus Inscriptionum Indicarum [CII; see also 6.3]: Presents collections for particular dynasties or classes of inscriptions in Devanāgarī or Roman transliteration, with extensive introduction and translation. The following volumes have been issued to date:

1: *Inscriptions of Asoka*, by Alexander Cunningham, 1887; superseded by New Edition by E. Hultzsch, 1925.
2, part 1: *Kharoshṭhī Inscriptions with the Exception of Those of Aśoka*, by Sten Konow, 1929.
2, part 2: *Bhārhut Inscriptions*, by H. Lüders (revised by E. Waldschmidt and M. A. Mehendale), 1963.
3: *Inscriptions of the Early Gupta Kings and Their Successors*, by John Faithfull Fleet, 1888. Revised ed., *Inscriptions of the Early Gupta Kings*, by Devadatta Ramakrishna Bhandarkar, 1981[6] (ed. Bahadurchand Chhabra and Govind Swamirao Gai). Fleet's original edition contained sixteen inss. of the Guptas and sixty-five inss. of related dynasties, while Bhandarkar's revised edition has forty-eight Gupta inss. but excludes those of contemporary and succeeding kings.
4, parts 1 and 2: *Inscriptions of the Kalachuri-Chedi Era*, by Vasudev Vishnu Mirashi, 1955.
5: *Inscriptions of the Vākāṭakas*, by Vasudev Vishnu Mirashi, 1963.
6: *Inscriptions of the Śilāhāras*, by Vasudev Vishnu Mirashi, 1977.
7: *Inscriptions of the Paramāras, Chandēllas, Kachchhapaghātas and Two Minor Dynasties*, by Harihar Vitthal Trivedi: part 1, *Introduction*, 1991; part 2, *Inscriptions of the Paramāras*, 1978; part 3, *Inscriptions of the Chandēllas, Kachchhapaghātas, etc.*, 1989.

South Indian Inscriptions [SII]: Vols. 1–24++[7] (1890–1982), by various editors, published by the ASI. Contains mostly inscriptions in Dravidian languages, but also some Sanskrit, Prakrit, and other Indo-Aryan inscriptions, especially in the earlier volumes. Texts are given in the appropriate Indian scripts (Tamil, Kannada, Telugu, Devanāgarī). English translations are given in vols. 1–3 only; the remaining volumes contain texts only.

Epigraphia Carnatica [EC]: Original series by B. Lewis Rice and others, published by Mysore Government/Mysore Archaeological Survey; vols. 1–17, 1886–1965 [vols. 13–17 are supplementary volumes]. Texts presented in Kannada script and Roman transliteration, with translation. Mostly Dravidian language inscriptions, but also several Sanskrit and bilingual (Sanskrit and Kannada) records, usually copper plate grants.

New edition: Vols. 1–8++, 1972–84, published by Institute of Kannada Studies, University of Mysore. Completely revised and expanded; in English and Kannada, with translations.

Archaeological Series and *Epigraphical Series* of the Government of Andhra Pradesh:[8] Both of these series, published since 1960 and 1965, respectively, include

6. The revised edition consists principally of an edited version of Bhandarkar's manuscript, completed in 1949, with the addition of four inscriptions discovered subsequently.

7. In this section the symbol ++ indicates an ongoing series, incomplete as of this writing.

8. The former supersedes the Hyderabad Archaeological Series of the Archaeological Department of Hyderabad.

several important epigraphic publications. While most of them are principally concerned with Dravidian inscriptions, there is also much Sanskrit, Sanskrit/Dravidian bilingual, and Prakrit material. Among the most noteworthy publications in the *Archaeological Series* on epigraphic subjects are no. 5, *Copper Plate Inscriptions of Andhra Pradesh Government Museum* by N. Ramesan (nos. 6 and 28); *Salihundam, A Buddhist Site in Andhra Pradesh* by R. Subrahmanyam (no. 17); and *Select Epigraphs of Andhra Pradesh* by P. V. Parabrahma Sastry (no. 31). In the Epigraphy series, besides the publications cited in section 8.1.3.2 (under Andhra Pradesh), particularly useful is the *Annual Report on Epigraphy in Andhra Pradesh* for 1965–67 (nos. 1, 4, 10; published 1965, 1972, 1974).

8.1.3 Anthologies of inscriptions

8.1.3.1 General anthologies

The largest, most complete, and most reliable anthology is Dinesh Chandra Sircar's *Select Inscriptions Bearing on Indian History and Civilization* [SI], in two volumes. SI is unquestionably the authoritative collection of inscriptions in the Old and Middle Indo-Aryan languages,[9] and Sircar's selections have virtually defined the scope of the field for students and nonspecialists. Subsequent anthologies, such as Sadhu Ram's *Some Important Inscriptions of Asoka, The Guptas, The Maukharis and Others*, Raj Bali Pandey's *Historical and Literary Inscriptions*, Śrīrāma Goyala's *Prācīna Bhāratīya Abhilekha Saṃgraha*, Parameśvarīlāla Gupta's *Prācīnā Bhārata ke Pramukha Abhilekha*, Vāsudeva Upādhyāya's *Prācīna Bhāratīya Abhilekha* (vol. 2), and Radhakrishna Chaudhury's *Inscriptions of Ancient India*, are more or less derivative of SI. K. G. Krishnan's *Uṭṭaṅkita Sanskrit Vidyā Araṇya Epigraphs*. Vol. 2: *Prakrit and Sanskrit Epigraphs 257 B.C. to 320 A.D.* is a more extensive anthology (218 inscriptions) than most of the others, and seven further volumes of Sanskrit inscriptions up to A.D. 1600 are planned (foreword, v–vi). Jan Gonda's *Twenty-five Sanskrit Inscriptions for Use in Universities* presents an interesting selection in a small pamphlet, including several little-known late inscriptions. G. S. Gai's recent book *Some Select Inscriptions* consists of reprints of his articles from EI.

There are also several anthologies which are primarily oriented toward inscriptions as literary specimens. These include Bhavadatta Śāstrī and Kāśīnātha Pāṇḍuranga Paraba's *Prâcîna-lekha-mâlâ*, Bahadur Chand Chhabra's *Abhilekhasaṃgrahaḥ*, and D. B. Diskalkar's *Selections from Sanskrit Inscriptions*.

8.1.3.2 Regional anthologies

8.1.3.2.1 Anthologies arranged according to modern Indian states

Andhra Pradesh: P. V. Parabrahma Sastry, *Inscriptions of Andhra Pradesh*; P. Sreenivasachar, *A Corpus of Inscriptions in the Telingana Districts of H.E.H. the Nizam's Dominions*. See also *Epigraphia Andhrica*, vols. 1–4 = Andhra

9. SI contains, however, almost no Dravidian material. The only general anthology of Dravidian inscriptions is V. R. Ramachandra Dikshitar's *Selected South Indian Inscriptions (Tamil, Telugu, Malayalam, and Kannada)*.

Pradesh Epigraphical Series, nos. 4a–6, 11 (1974). For list and summaries, see M. Rama Rao, *Inscriptions of Āndhradēśa.*

Assam: Padmanātha Bhaṭṭācārya, *Kāmarūpaśāsanāvalī*; Dimbeswar Sarma, *Kāmarūpaśāsanāvalī*; Mukunda Madhava Sharma, *Inscriptions of Ancient Assam.*

[West] Bengal: Akshaya Kumara Maitra, *Gauḍalekhamālā*; N. G. Majumdar, *Inscriptions of Bengal*, vol. 3; Ramaranjan Mukherjee and Sachindra Kumar Maity, *Corpus of Bengal Inscriptions Bearing on History and Civilization of Bengal.*

Bihar: Radha Krishna Choudhary, *Select Inscriptions of Bihar*; Bhagwant Sahai, *The Inscriptions of Bihar.*

Gujarat: Acharya Girishankar Vallabhaji, *Historical Inscriptions of Gujarat (From Ancient Times to the End of Vaghela Dynasty)*. See also the "List of Inscriptions from Gujarat" in H. D. Sankalia, *The Archaeology of Gujarat (Including Kathiawar)*, Appendix A. For recent discoveries, see "Post-Independence Epigraphical Discoveries in Gujarat," ch. III (20–35) of Ramlal Parikh and Rasesh Jamindar, *Epigraphic Resources in Gujarat.*

Haryana: S. R. Phogat, *Inscriptions of Haryana.*

Kashmir: B. K. Kaul Deambi, *Corpus of Śāradā Inscriptions of Kashmir.*

Maharashtra: Śāṃtārāma Bhālacaṃdra Deva, *Mahārāṣṭra va Gove Śilālekha-Tāmrapaṭāṃcī Varṇanātmaka Saṃdarbha Sūcī* [summaries only].

Orissa: Satyanarayan Rajaguru, *Inscriptions of Orissa.*

Rajasthan: Māṅgīlāl Vyās ("Mayaṅk"), *Rājasthāna ke Abhilekha* [summaries only].[10]

8.1.3.2.2 Anthologies by old (preindependence) states or kingdoms, and other regional collections. Notable collections in this class include *Antiquities of Chamba State* by J. Ph. Vogel (part 1) and B. Ch. Chhabra (part 2); [V. G. Oza?], *Bhāvanagara Prācīna Śodhasaṃgraha*; [Peter Peterson], *A Collection of Prakrit and Sanskrit Inscriptions*; A. S. Gadre, *Important Inscriptions from the Baroda State*; and D. B. Diskalkar, *Inscriptions of Kathiawad.* An especially important regional collection is Heinrich Lüders' *Mathurā Inscriptions.*

8.1.3.3 Dynastic anthologies

Besides the anthologies of inscriptions by dynasties included in CII (see 8.1.2) and several other dynastic anthologies cited elsewhere (4.3), recent publications of this class include A. C. Mittal, *The Inscriptions of Imperial Paramāras*; K. V. Ramesh, *Inscriptions of the Western Gaṅgas*; Kiran Kumar Thaplyal, *Inscriptions of the Maukharīs, Later Guptas, Puṣpabhūtis and Yaśovarman of Kanauj*; V. V. Mirashi, *The History and Inscriptions of the Sātavāhanas and the Western Kṣatrapas*; R. Subrahmanyam, *Inscriptions of the Sūryavaṃśi Gajapatis of Orissa*; and Vasundhara Filliozat, *L'Épigraphie de Vijayanagara du début à 1377.*

10. References to anthologies and other publications on extra-Indian inscriptions are given in section 4.3.7.

8.1.3.4 Anthologies by religion

Inscriptional anthologies by religion are mostly limited to Jaina inscriptions, which are much better documented than most others. The principal Jaina anthologies[11] are A. Guérinot, *Répertoire d'épigraphie Jaina* [summaries only]; Puran Chand Nahar, *Jain Inscriptions* (*Jaina Lekha Saṃgraha*); Muni Jinavijaya, *Prācīnajainalekha-saṃgraha*; Hīralāla Jaina et al., *Jaina-śilālekhasaṃgrahaḥ*; and Ram Vallabh Somani, *Jain Inscriptions of Rajasthan* [study with texts of inss. in appendix].

An anthology of Buddhist inscriptions, though sorely needed, is yet to appear. An extensive list with summaries of Indian Buddhist inscriptions is, however, available in Masao Shizutani's *Indo Bukkyō Himei Mokuroku.*

8.1.4 Separate monographs

Monographs on particular inscriptions or groups of inscriptions are too numerous to be listed completely here. A few examples of important or model monographs are Benimadhab Barua, *Old Brāhmī Inscriptions in the Udayagiri and Khaṇḍagiri Caves*; D. C. Sircar, *Epigraphical Discoveries in East Pakistan* and *Some Epigraphical Records of the Medieval Period from Eastern India*; and R. L. Turner, *The Gavīmaṭh and Pālkīguṇḍu Inscriptions of Aśoka.* Important new additions to this group are Shobhana Gokhale's *Kanheri Inscriptions* and I. K. Sarma and J. Varaprasada Rao's *Early Brahmi Inscriptions from Sannati.*

8.2 Secondary Sources: Handbooks and Reference Works

8.2.1 Handbooks of epigraphy and paleography

The only truly authoritative handbook of Indian epigraphy (as opposed to paleography) is D. C. Sircar's *Indian Epigraphy* [SIE]. Though not comprehensive in all respects, this is the definitive work on the subject to date. Technical matters such as dating systems and official and legal terminology are treated in particular detail. Also useful, though partly overlapping, is Sircar's "Introduction to Indian Epigraphy and Palaeography" [IIEP] in JAIH 4, 72–136. K. V. Ramesh's *Indian Epigraphy* [RIE] is not a comprehensive handbook but rather a collection of essays on various epigraphic subjects. G. S. Gai's *Introduction to Indian Epigraphy* [*with Special Reference to the Development of the Scripts and Languages*] [IIE] provides a brief general survey of the subject from a primarily southern Indian point of view.

A useful though outdated general survey is found in ch. 1, "Epigraphy," by J. F. Fleet, of vol. 2 of *The Imperial Gazetteer of India*, 1–88 [IGI].[12] Also useful is Fleet's survey of "Indian Inscriptions" in the 11th edition (1910–11) of the *Encyclopaedia Britannica* (s.v. "Inscriptions," vol. 14, 621–6). More up to date, but briefer, is the section on epigraphy (I.156–72) in L. Renou and J. Filliozat, *L'Inde classique* [IC].

11. For further references, see IIEP, bibliography, 134, s.v. "Jain Inscriptions."

12. Fleet's essay "The Present Position of Indian Historical Research" (IA 30, 1901, 1–27; see also 7.1.1) is essentially a briefer version of the same work.

An excellent brief summary of southern Indian materials is to be found in K. A. Nilakanta Sastri's *History of South India from Prehistoric Times to the Fall of Vijayanagara*, 13–9.

Despite its title, Raj Bali Pandey's *Indian Palaeography* [PIP] is not strictly speaking a work of paleography but more a general study of epigraphy. It generally reflects a traditionalist point of view, as manifested, for instance, in Pandey's arguments in favor of an indigenous Indian origin for both Brāhmī and Kharoṣṭhī scripts. The first volume of Vāsudeva Upādhyāya's *Prācīna Bhāratīya Abhilekha*[13] discusses Indian inscriptions in general terms and with reference to their importance for the study of Indian history and culture. A series of articles published by D. B. Diskalkar in JIH 32–38 constitutes in effect a general introduction to the field; although deficient in some respects, this work has the merit of covering a broader range than the other general works, including surveys of inscriptional materials in all languages (including European and other non-Indic languages) from all periods.[14] The chapter on "South Indian Epigraphy" in T. N. Subramanian's *South Indian Temple Inscriptions* [SITI] (III.2, 161–251) also gives a useful overview of the subject and is not strictly limited to southern India. V. V. Mirashi's brief survey of "Epigraphical Research"[15] concentrates on dating systems and eras.

Most other standard works on the study of Indian inscriptions are primarily or exclusively paleographic, rather than epigraphic, studies. Outdated but in some respects still the standard and model for later works is Georg Bühler's *Indische Palaeographie von circa 350 A. Chr.–circa 1300 P. Chr.* [BIP], more usually cited from J. F. Fleet's English translation (*Indian Paleography from About* B.C. *350 to About* A.D. *1300*). Gaurīśaṃkara Hīrācaṃda Ojhā's *Bhāratīya Prācīna Lipimālā*, though also outdated, includes useful plates with specimens of various scripts in facsimile. The most important recent paleographic study is Ahmad Hasan Dani's *Indian Palaeography* [DIP], which significantly refines and revises the standard terminology and understanding of the development of Brāhmī script and it derivatives. Also useful are the sets of script charts for "Ancient Indian Alphabets," "Medieval Indian Alphabets," "Indian Alphabets Abroad," and "Ancient Indian Numerals," prepared under the supervision of P. L. Gupta.

Harry Falk's *Schrift im alten Indien* [SAI] is, as the title indicates, strictly speaking neither a study of epigraphy nor of paleography as such, but rather of the origin, history, and cultural position of writing, epigraphic and otherwise. Nonetheless it contains a wealth of information on epigraphic and paleographic materials, including an extensive bibliography (15–66).

Besides these general texts, there are numerous specific studies of various aspects of Indian epigraphy and paleography, such as Chandrika Singh Upasak's *History and Palaeography of Mauryan Brāhmī Script* and Thakur Prasad Verma's *The Palaeography of Brāhmī Script in North India*. Southern scripts are covered in Arthur

13. On vol. 2 of this work, which contains an anthology of Sanskrit and Prakrit inscriptions, see section 8.1.3.1.

14. See the bibliography, s.v. Diskalkar, for details.

15. In P. J. Chinmulgund and V. V. Mirashi, eds., *M. M. Chitraoshastri Felicitation Volume: Review of Indological Research in Last 75 Years* (Poona: M. M. Chitraoshastri Felicitation Committee and Bharatiya Charitrakosha Mandal, [1967]), 505–29.

Coke Burnell, *Elements of South-Indian Palaeography*, C. Sivaramamurti, *Indian Epigraphy and South Indian Scripts* [IESIS], and T. V. Mahalingam, *Early South Indian Palaeography* [ESIP]. The paleography of Kharoṣṭhī is treated in Charu Chandra Das Gupta, *The Development of the Kharoṣṭhī Script* [DKS]. Brāhmī script as found in central Asian manuscripts is analyzed in detail in Lore Sander, *Paläographisches zu den Sanskrithandschriften der Berliner Turfansammlung*. There are also some monographs discussing the development of modern scripts, such as R. D. Banerjee's *Origin of the Bengali Script* and Kunjabihari Tripathi's *Evolution of Oriya Language and Script.*

In the literature on Indian paleography in general, documentation for the older scripts is relatively stronger, while documentation of the medieval and late premodern scripts is very sparse; a basic study of later Indian paleography is sorely needed. But even for early Indian paleography, much remains to be done. Many of the basic sources are badly outdated (e.g., Bühler's *Indische Palaeographie*), while many of the more recent works are not up to the highest technical and scholarly standards. Sander's *Paläographisches zu den Sanskrithandschriften der Berliner Turfansammlung* is a happy exception, presenting the central Asian varieties of Brāhmī in a fashion which could provide a model for similar updated studies of the Indian scripts. The definitive study of Kharoṣṭhī paleography also remains to be written; the closest approach, Das Gupta's *Development of the Kharoṣṭhī Script*, is useful but by no means fully reliable, and also by now is largely outdated in view of the very large amount of new material found in recent years.

8.2.2 Reference works, bibliographies, and lists

The single most important reference work for epigraphic studies is D. C. Sircar's *Indian Epigraphical Glossary* [IEG], which provides definitions and references for technical and other special terminology found in inscriptions. Comprehensive bibliographies are in general lacking; one exception is Sibadas Chaudhuri's *Bibliography of Studies in Indian Epigraphy (1926–50)*, which contains author and subject indices for journal articles on epigraphic subjects. For a general bibliography, see the bibliography to Sircar's IIEP, 133–6. Also useful is the bibliographic and historical survey by Hermann Kulke et al. in *Indische Geschichte vom Altertum bis zur Gegenwart* (*Historische Zeitschrift*, Sonderheft 10), 36–7 and 98–101. A good general bibliography for southern (Dravidian) inscriptions is provided in Noboru Karashima's *South Indian History and Society*, 197–207. Other than these, epigraphic bibliographies and indices are mainly limited to those in the various publications mentioned earlier, especially the indices at the end of each volume and the comprehensive index to vols. 1–34 of the EI, and the indices to each volume of CII. Convenient though not necessarily comprehensive bibliographic references for important inscriptions are given in the introductory material for each inscription in Sircar's SI.

In practice, the most important reference materials for epigraphic studies are the various lists (generally with dates, brief summaries, and bibliography for each inscription) of inscriptions. The most important among these are those published as supplements and appendices to EI: F. Kielhorn, *A List of the Inscriptions of Northern India from About* A.D. *400* in EI 5 and 8, and *A List of Inscriptions of Southern*

India from About A.D. *500* in EI 7 and 8; H. Lüders, *A List of Brahmi Inscriptions from the Earliest Times to About* A.D. *400* in EI 10; and D. R. Bhandarkar, *A List of the Inscriptions of Northern India in Brahmi and Its Derivative Scripts, from About 200 A.C.* in EI 19–23 [revision of Kielhorn's list in EI 5].

Other important lists[16] include: Hira Lal, *Inscriptions in the Central Provinces and Berar*; Hariharanivāsa Dvivedī, *Gvāliyara Rājya ke Abhilekha*; A. V. Naik, "Inscriptions of the Deccan: An Epigraphical Survey" (*Bulletin of the Deccan College Research Institute* 9; contains an extensive and useful introduction as well as relatively detailed descriptions of each inscription); Robert Sewell, *The Historical Inscriptions of Southern India . . .* ; and T. V. Mahalingam, *A Topographical List of Inscriptions in the Tamil Nadu and Kerala States.* For Kharoṣṭhī inscriptions, N. G. Majumdar, "A List of Kharoṣṭhī Inscriptions" in JASB, n.s. 20, 1924, 1–39, is by now outdated and superseded by Konow's *Kharoshṭhī Inscriptions* (CII 2.1). The latter, in turn, is now extensively supplemented by the references provided in Gérard Fussman's "Gāndhārī écrite, Gāndhārī parlée" (see the bibliography), 444–51 and 488–98.

Lists of inscriptions of particular dynasties are also to be found as appendices to some dynastic histories; for instance, "Inscriptions of the Candellas" (Appendix A) in R. K. Dikshit, *The Candellas of Jejākabhukti*; "List of Pratihāra Inscriptions of Kanauj" (Appendix A) in B. N. Puri, *The History of the Gurjara-Pratihāras*; and "Important Inscriptions of the Vātāpi Chalukyas and Their Contemporaries" in K. V. Ramesh's *Chalukyas of Vātāpi.*

For information on provenance of inscriptions, see R. Stroobandt's atlas of *Epigraphical Find-spots.* Toponyms mentioned in inscriptions are collected and identified in Parmanand Gupta's *Geography in Ancient Indian Inscriptions.*[17]

8.2.3 Miscellaneous studies and collections

Important recent collections of epigraphic essays by different authors include Noboru Karashima, ed., *Indus Valley to Mekong Delta: Explorations in Epigraphy* [IVMD], and Frederick M. Asher and G. S. Gai, eds., *Indian Epigraphy: Its Bearing on the History of Art* [IEBHA]. Also useful for epigraphic researches are the collected papers of various specialists in the field. Particularly important are the *Kleine Schriften* of Franz Kielhorn and Heinrich Lüders, and also Lüders' *Philologica Indica.* The collections of D. C. Sircar's essays on epigraphic and related subjects are indispensable: *Early Indian Numismatic and Epigraphical Studies* [EINES], *Studies in the Geography of Ancient and Medieval India, Studies in the Political and Administrative Systems in Ancient and Medieval India, Studies in the Religious Life of Ancient and Medieval India,* and *Studies in the Society and Administration of Ancient and Medieval India.* Other recent collections with large epigraphic content are V. V.

16. For further references, mostly to lists of primarily local interest and of non-Indo-Aryan inscriptions, see the bibliographic accounts in SIE 10 n. 2; IIEP, 134–5 (s.v. "Lists of Inscriptions"); and EINES, 89. See also the references given in section 8.1.3. For lists of Indic inscriptions from Southeast Asia, see sections 4.3.7.5–4.3.7.11.

17. For further information, see section 7.6.

Mirashi's *Studies in Ancient Indian History* and *Studies in Indology*, Jagannath Agrawal's *Researches in Indian Epigraphy and Numismatics*, and G. S. Gai's *Studies in Indian History, Epigraphy and Culture*.

Festschrifts in honor of epigraphic specialists are also useful, both for articles on epigraphic matters and for bibliographies and biographies of the honorees. Recent publications of this class include volumes in honor of D. C. Sircar (B. N. Mukherjee et al., eds., *Sri Dinesacandrika* [includes biography and bibliography of Sircar, part I, 1–63], and Gouriswar Bhattacharya, ed., *Deyadharma*); B. Ch. Chhabra (K. V. Ramesh et al., eds., *Svasti Śrī*); and G. S. Gai (K. V. Ramesh et al., eds., *Indian History and Epigraphy*).

In recent years several studies of various corpora or of particular aspects of Indic inscriptions have been published in India, mostly following a more or less standard format compiling data on political, administrative, religious, economic, and social life. Examples of recent studies of this kind are Haripada Chakraborti, *Early Brahmi Records in India (c.300 B.C.–c.300 A.D.)* and *India as Reflected in the Inscriptions of the Gupta Period*; Kalyani Das (Bajpayee), *Early Inscriptions of Mathurā—A Study*; and Rāmaprakāśa Ojhā, *Uttarī Bhāratīya Abhilekhoṃ kā eka Sāṃskṛtika Adhyayana*.

Appendix
Selection of Typical Inscriptions

This appendix presents a brief sampling of representative specimens of the most important and common types of inscriptions discussed in this book, particularly in the typological survey (4.1). An attempt has been made, insofar as limitations of space permit, to include inscriptions reflecting diverse geographical regions (both within and outside of India), periods, languages, scripts, types and contents, styles, religious traditions, and so on. In general, inscriptions which are complete and relatively well preserved have been chosen; but it should be understood that in this respect they are not entirely representative, since in actual practice many inscriptions are incomplete and/or otherwise defaced. The conventions of transliteration and punctuation followed here are explained in section 5.1.2.

---

1. Rummindeī Minor Pillar Edict of Aśoka (fig. 11)

Location	Rummindeī, near Paṛariyā, Bataul Dist., Nepal
Script	Early Brāhmī
Language	Aśokan Prakrit, eastern (Ardha-Māgadhī) dialect (prose)
Type and format	Stone pillar inscription; royal edict
Purpose	Records the king's visit to Luṃmini (= Lumbinī, modern Rummindeī) and his erection of the pillar there
Date	Twentieth year after Aśoka's consecration = ca. 252 B.C.
References	G. Bühler, "The Asoka Edicts of Paderia and Nigliva," EI 5, 1898–99, 1–6; E. Hultzsch, CII 1, 164–5; D. C. Sircar, SI I.67–8.

Text

1. devānapiyena piyadasina lājina vīsativasābhisitena
2. atana āgāca mahīyite hida budhe jāte sakyamunī ti

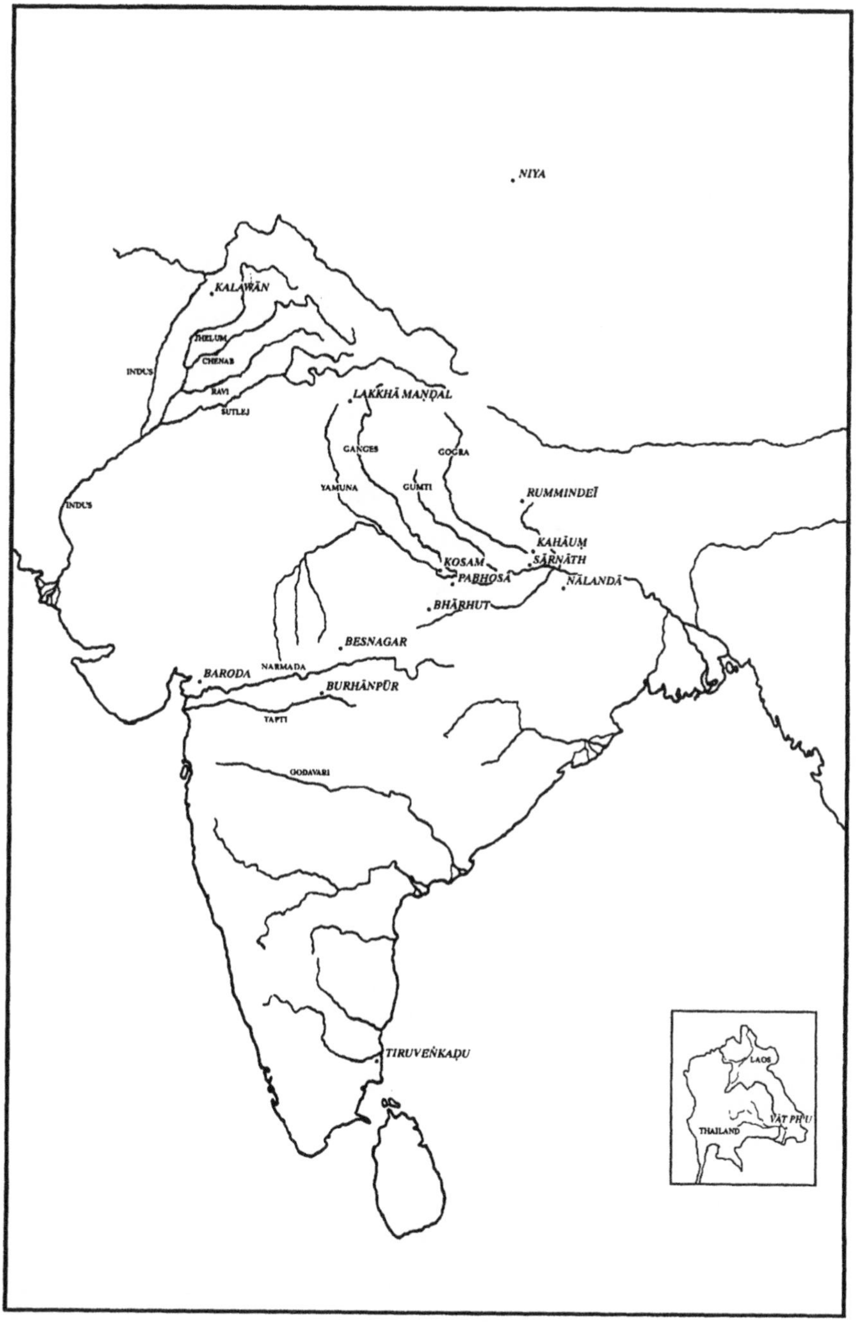

Map 4
Locations of Inscriptions in the Appendix

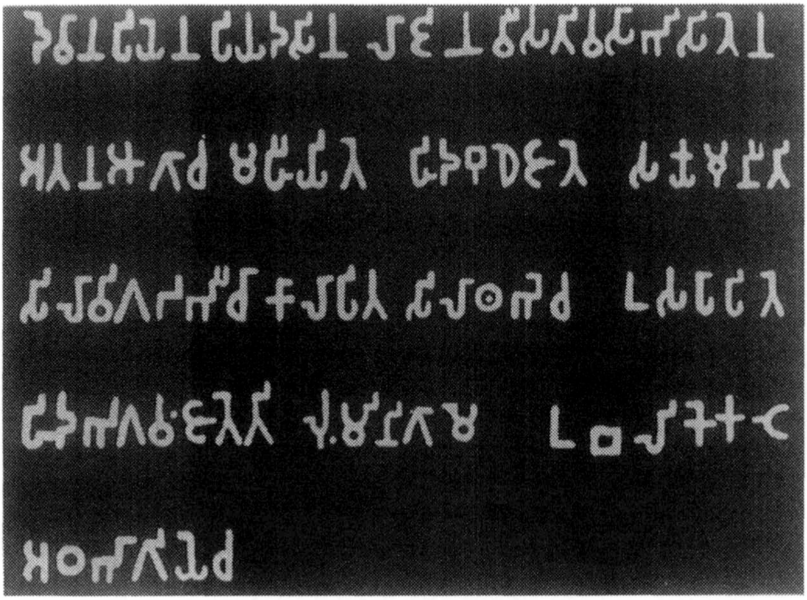

FIGURE 11. Rummindeī minor pillar edict of Aśoka. From D. C. Sircar, *Inscriptions of Aśoka*, plate between pp. 48 and 49; copyright, Archaeological Survey of India.

3. silāvigaḍabhīcā kālāpita silāthabhe ca usapāpite
4. hida bhagavaṃ jāte ti luṃminigāme ubalike kaṭe
5. aṭhabhāgiye ca

Translation

1. The King, Beloved of the Gods, of Loving Regard, when he had been anointed twenty years,
2. came in person and worshiped, because the Buddha Śākyamuni was born here.
3. He had constructed walls inlaid with stone (?) and had erected [this] stone pillar,
4. because [i.e., to proclaim that] the Lord was born here. The village of Lummini was made exempt from taxation
5. and [subject to paying only] a one-eighth share [of its produce].

Notes

Line 3: "walls inlaid with stone": This follows Sircar's interpretation (*silāvigaḍabhīcā* = Skt. *śilā-vikṛta-bhittikāḥ* = *prastara-khacitāḥ iṣṭaka-prākārāḥ*), after Fleet and Bhandarkar (for references see Hultzsch, 164 n. 3). Although as noted by Hultzsch (ibid.) the equation of *bhīcā* with **bhittikā* is problematic, this interpretation seems better than Hultzsch's "a stone bearing a horse (?)", reading *silā vigaḍabhī cā* as separate words. In this inscription the words are often (though not always) separated by spaces, but there are no spaces in the phrase in question, which would support the interpretation preferred here. But the phrase remains highly uncertain, and several other interpretations have been proposed (see, e.g., Bühler, 5). See also Kenneth R. Norman, "A Note on *śilavigaḍabhīcā* in Aśoka's

Rummindei Inscriptions," in *The Buddhist Forum* 3, 1991–93 (London: School of Oriental and African Studies, 1994), 227–37.

Line 4: "because the Lord was born here": this phrase could also be taken with the following sentence: "Because the Lord was born here, the village of Luṃmini was made . . ." (so Bühler, Sircar).

Line 4: "exempt from taxation": *ubalike* = Skt. **udbalikaḥ*.

Line 5: "a one-eighth share": instead of the standard one-sixth share of all produce to be paid to the king.

---

2. Besnagar Pillar Inscription of Hēliodōros (fig. 12)

Location	Besnagar, Vidisa Dist., MP
Script	Brāhmī of the Śuṅga period
Language	Central-western epigraphic Prakrit, with some Sanskritic spellings (prose [possibly verse in ins. B; cf. JRAS 1909, 1093])
Type and format	Stone pillar inscription; private religious dedication

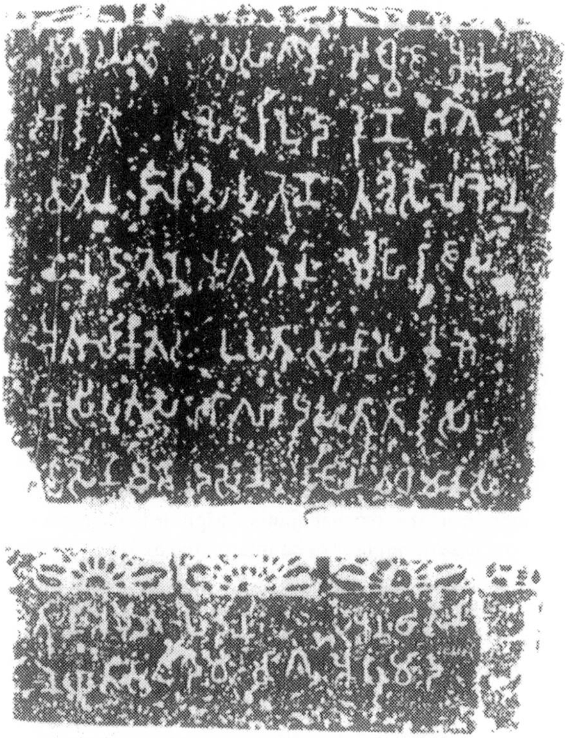

FIGURE 12. Besnagar pillar inscription of Hēliodōros. From ASIAR 1908–9, pl. XLVI; copyright, Archaeological Survey of India.

Purpose	Records the erection of the pillar by Hēliodōros the Greek from Takhkhasilā (= Takṣaśilā, i.e. Taxila), ambassador from King Aṃtalikita (Antialkidas)
Date	Fourteenth regnal year of King Kāśīputra Bhāgabhadra; late second century B.C.?
References	J. F. Fleet, "An Inscription from Besnagar," JRAS 1909, 1087–92; L. D. Barnett, "The Besnagar Inscription B," JRAS 1909, 1093–4; J. Ph. Vogel, "The Garuda Pillar of Besnagar," ASIAR 1908–9, 126–9; Fleet, "The Besnagar Inscription A," JRAS 1910, 141–2 and 815–7; D. C. Sircar, SI I.88–9; H. Lüders, *List of Brāhmī Inscriptions* (EI 10), no. 669, for further refs.

Text

Inscription A

1. [de]vadevasa v[ā][*sude]vasa garuḍadhvaje ayaṃ
2. kārit[e] i[a?] heliodoreṇa bhāga-
3. vatena diyasa putreṇa ta[khkha]silākena
4. yonadūtena āgatena mahārājasa
5. aṃtalikitasa upa[ṃ]tā sakāsaṃ raño
6. kāsīput[r]asa bhāgabhadrasa trātārasa
7. vasena ca[tu]dasena rājena vadhamānasa

Inscription B (on the other side of the pillar)

1. trini amutapād[ā]ni [i][me?] [su]anuṭhitāni
2. neyaṃti sva[gaṃ] dam[e] cāga apramāda

Notes

Line A1: *[de]vadevasa*: Here, as in many other places in the inscription, the reading is uncertain due to the wear on the stone. The vowel signs in particular are often unclear, and the different editions vary slightly in their readings of several words.

Line A1: *garuḍadhvaje*: Note the Sanskritized spelling here, as also in *putreṇa* (A.3) and elsewhere; see section 3.2.3.2.

Line A3: *ta[khkha]silākena*: The second syllable was read as a single *kha* by Fleet and others. There is, however, a clear projection to the left at the middle of the letter, which is perhaps meant to indicate the unusual doubled aspirate consonant; I here follow Sircar's reading, though the *akṣara* might also be interpreted as *kkha*.

Translation

Inscription A

1. This Garuḍa-pillar of Vāsudeva, the god of gods,
2. was constructed here by Heliodora [Hēliodōros], the Bhāgavata,
3. son of Diya [Diōn], of Takhkhasilā (Taxila),
4. the Greek ambassador who came from the Great King

5. Aṃtalikita [Antialkidas] to King
6. Kāsīputra [Kāśīputra] Bhāgabhadra, the Savior,
7. prospering in (his) fourteenth regnal year.

Inscription B

1. (These?) three steps to immortality, when correctly followed,
2. lead to heaven: control, generosity, and attention.

Notes

Line A5: Aṃtalikita: The Indo-Greek king Antialkidas, otherwise known from coins, who probably ruled in the middle or late second century B.C.

Line A6: Kāsīputra Bhāgabhadra: Possibly to be identified with Bhadraka, the fifth Śuṅga king according to some versions of the Purāṇic dynastic lists.

Line A7: "in (his) fourteenth regnal year": Instrumental of time or date, "strange" according to Fleet (1910, 815) but paralleled in several other inss.; cf. Vogel, 128, and *imeṇa kṣuṇeṇa* in the Kalawān inscription (Appendix, no. 4, l. 1).

Lines B1–2: Similar proverbial expressions have been cited from the Dhammapada (2.1; JRAS 1910, 1093) and the Mahābhārata (Udyoga-parvan 42.22 and 44.7; Arthur Venis, JRAS 1910, 815); e.g., Udyoga 42.22ab, *damas tyāgo 'pramādaś ca eteṣv amṛtam āhitam.*

---

3. Bhārhut Label Inscriptions (fig. 13)

Location	Bhārhut, Satna Dist., MP (now in the Indian Museum, Calcutta)
Script	Brāhmī of the Śuṅga period
Language	Central-western epigraphic Prakrit (prose)
Type and format	Label inscriptions, on a stone railing pillar from the south-east quadrant of the Buddhist *stūpa*
Purpose	Explanatory labels for the accompanying sculptured scene
Date	None given; ca. second century B.C.
References	Lüders, *Bhārhut Inscriptions* (CII 2.2), nos. B 32–4, pp. 105–9 + plates XIX and XXXVIII; B. Barua and K. G. Sinha, *Barhut Inscriptions*, nos. II.5a–c, pp. 59–61.

Text

Inscription A (below the sculptured medallion)

jetavana anādhapeḍiko deti kotisaṃthatena ketā

Inscription B (on the left rim of the medallion)

ko[saba]k[ū]ṭi

Inscription C (on the upper rim of the medallion)

gadhakuṭi

Translation

Inscription A

Anādhapeḍika (Anāthapiṇḍika) gives the Jetavana after buying (it) with a layer of crores.

Inscription B

The hut of the Kosabas (Kauśāmbas).

Inscription C

The perfumed hut.

FIGURE 13. Bhārhut label inscriptions. From H. Lüders, CII II.2, pl. XXXVIII; copyright, Archaeological Survey of India.

Notes

A: Anādhapeḍika: The subject is the well-known Buddhist legend of the merchant Anāthapiṇḍika who purchased the Jetavana park in Śrāvastī by covering it with a layer of coins and presented it to the Buddhist *saṃgha*.

A: "after buying": *ketā* < **krayitvā* = Skt. *krītvā*.

4. Kalawān Copper Plate Inscription (fig. 14)

Location	Kalawān, near Taxila, Rawalpindi Dist., NWFP, Pakistan
Script	Kharoṣṭhī of the middle (Kuṣāṇa) period
Language	Northwestern or Gāndhārī Prakrit (prose)
Type and format	Reliquary deposit inscription on a copper plate placed in the foundation of a *stūpa*
Purpose	Records the dedication of bodily relics [of the Buddha] in the *stūpa* at Chaḍaśilā by the lay follower Caṃdrabhi
Date	134 of the Azes [= Vikrama] year, 23rd day of Śrāvaṇa = A.D. 77
References	S. Konow, "Kalawān Copper-plate Inscription of the Year 134," JRAS 1932, 949–65; Konow, "Kalawan Copper-plate Inscription of the Year 134," EI 21, 1931–32, 251–9; J. Marshall, *Taxila*, I.327; D. C. Sircar, SI I.131–2.

Text

1. saṃvatśaraye 1-100-20-10-4 ajasa śravaṇasa masasa divase treviśe 20-1-1-1 imeṇa kṣuṇeṇa caṃdrabhi uasia
2. dhraṃmasa grahavatisa dhita bhadravalasa bhaya chaḍaśilae śarira praïstaveti gahathu-
3. bami sadha bhraduṇa ṇaṃdivaḍhaṇeṇa grahavatiṇa sadha putrehi śameṇa śaïteṇa ca dhituṇa ca

FIGURE 14. Kalawān copper plate inscription. From EI 21, plate facing p. 259; copyright, Archaeological Survey of India.

4. dhramae sadha ṣṇuṣaehi rajae idrae ya sadha jivaṇaṃdiṇa śamaputr[e]ṇa ayarieṇa ya sa[rva]sti-
5. vaaṇa parigrahe raṭhaṇikamo puyaïta sarva[sva]tvaṇa puyae ṇivaṇasa pratiae hotu.

Notes

Line 1: *saṃvatśaraye*: The ligature in the third *akṣara* may also be read as *tsa* (cf. section 2.3.4); Sircar so reads.

Line 4: *ṣṇuṣaehi*: The consonantal portion of the first syllable is written as *ṣ* with a diacritic line above, representing *ṣṇ* (see 2.3.8).

Line 4: *ayarieṇa*: Perhaps to be corrected to *ayariaṇa* = *ācāryāṇām* (Konow, EI 21, 253); or possibly the original draft had *ayarieṇa ayariaṇa ya* . . . , and the engraver omitted the second word haplographically.

Line 5: *sarva[sva]tvaṇa*: Evidently miswritten for *sarvasatvaṇa*; the third *akṣara* appears blurred in the photograph, perhaps as a result of an attempt to correct it.

Translation

1. In the year 134 of [the era of] Aja [= Azes I], the twenty-third (23) day of the month Śrāvaṇa; at this time the lay follower Caṃdrabhi,
2. daughter of the householder Dhraṃma [= Dharma] [and] wife of Bhadravala [= Bhadrabala or Bhadrapāla], establishes at Chaḍaśila [= Chaṭaśilā?] bodily relics (*śarīra*) in the chapel-*stūpa*,
3. together with her brother Ṇaṃdivaḍhaṇa [Nandivardhana], the householder, [and] with her sons Śama and Śaïta [Sacitta?], and her daughter
4. Dhrama [Dharmā], [and] with her daughters-in-law Raja [Rajā?] and Idra [Indrā], with Jivaṇaṃdi [Jivanandin], son of Śama, and [her?] teacher;
5. for the acceptance of the Sarvāstivādins. The country and the town are [hereby] honored; [and] it is for the honor of all beings. May it lead to [their] attainment of Nirvāṇa.

Notes

Line 1: [the era of] Aja: This is the era of 58/57 B.C., later known as the Vikrama era; see section 5.5.1.3.

Line 1: "lay follower": *uasia* = Skt. *upāsikā*.

Lines 4–5: "and [her?] teacher; for the acceptance of the Sarvāstivādins": According to the suggestion proposed in the text note, the intended meaning may have been ". . . and with [her] teacher; for the acceptance of the Sarvāstivādin teachers."

Line 5: "The country and the town": Following Sircar, who takes *raṭhaṇikamo* as a *dvandva* compound = Skt. *rāṣṭra-nigamau* (= *janapadaṃ nagaraṃ ca*). Konow, taking it as a *karmadhāraya*, translates "the country-town."

---

5. Sārnāth Umbrella Shaft Inscription of the Time of Kaniṣka (fig. 15)

Location	Sārnāth, near Vārāṇasī (Benares), Varanasi Dist., UP
Script	Middle Brāhmī of the Kuṣāṇa period
Language	Mixed dialect, or "Epigraphical Hybrid Sanskrit" (prose)

Type and format	Dedicatory inscription on a stone umbrella shaft, originally connected with a colossal Bodhisattva statue (the statue itself bears two shorter dedicatory inscriptions of similar content)
Purpose	Records the dedication of the umbrella and shaft by the Buddhist monk Bala
Date	Year 3 of the Great King Kaniṣka = ca. A.D. 81 (if Kaniṣka's era is taken as equal to the Śaka era of A.D. 77/78; otherwise probably sometime in the second quarter of the second century A.D. (see 5.5.1.4); third month of winter (i.e., Māgha), day 22
References	J. Ph. Vogel, "Epigraphical Discoveries at Sarnath," EI 8, 1905–6, 166–79 (ins. III.a, 176–7); D. C. Sircar, SI I.136–7; Gregory Schopen, "On Monks, Nuns and 'Vulgar' Practices: The Introduction of the Image Cult into Indian Buddhism," *Artibus Asiae* 49, 1988–89, 153–68.

FIGURE 15. Sārnāth umbrella shaft inscription of the time of Kaniṣka. From EI 8, plate facing p. 176; copyright, Archaeological Survey of India.

Text

1. mahāra[*sic*]jasya k[ā]ṇiṣkasya saṃ 3 he 3 di 20-2
2. etāye pūrvaye bhikṣusya puṣyavuddhisya saddhyevi-
3. hārisya bhikṣusya balasya tr[e]pi[ṭa]kasya
4. bodhisatvo chatrayaṣṭi ca pratiṣṭhāpit[o]
5. bārāṇasiye bhagavato ca[ṃ]k[r?]ame sahā māta-
6. pitihi sahā upaddhyāyāca[rye]hi saddhyevihāri-
7. hi aṃtevāsikehi ca sahā buddhamitraye trepiṭika-
8. ye sahā kṣatra[pe]na vanasparena kharapall[ā]-
9. nena ca sahā ca[tu]hi pariṣāhi sarvasatvanaṃ
10. hitā[*sic*]sukhārtthaṃ

Notes

Line 1: *k[ā]ṇiṣkasa:* Vogel and Sircar read *kaṇiṣkasya.* Here and in several other places the reading (especially of the vowel signs) is uncertain due to wear on the stone surface. Sircar's readings are generally more accurate than Vogel's.

Translation

1. In the year 3 of the Great King Kāṇiṣka, [month] 3 of winter, day 22:

2–3. on this aforementioned [date], [as the gift] of the Monk Bala, Tripiṭaka Master and companion of the Monk Puṣyavuddhi [= Puṣyavṛddhi or Puṣyabuddhi?],

4. this Bodhisattva and umbrella-and-staff was established
5. in Vārāṇasi, at the Lord's promenade, together with [Bala's] mother
6. and father, with his teachers and masters, his companions
7. and students, with the Tripiṭaka Master Buddhamitrā,
8. with the Kṣatrapa Vanaspara and Kharapallāna,
9. and with the four communities,
10. for the welfare and happiness of all beings.

Notes

Line 1: "winter": *he* = *hemanta*; "day": *di* = *divase* (cf. 5.4.2.2).

Line 8: "and Kharapallāna": In one of the accompanying inscriptions on the Bodhisattva statue Kharapallāna is entitled *mahākṣatrapa*; perhaps his title has been inadvertently omitted here.

---

6. Niya (Central Asian) Kharoṣṭhī Document (fig. 16)

Location	Niya, on the Niya River on the southern rim of the Takla Makan Desert, Minfeng County, Xinjiang-Uighur Autonomous Region, China
Script	Kharoṣṭhī (central Asian variety)

Language "Niya Prakrit," i.e., the central Asian dialect of Gāndhārī (prose)
Type and format Ink on wooden wedge under-tablet
Purpose Gives an official order for an inquiry into a protest lodged by one Sucaṃma
Date None given; ca. third century A.D.
References A. M. Boyer, E. J. Rapson, and É. Senart, *Kharoṣṭhī Inscriptions Discovered by Sir Aurel Stein*, part II, 240, no. 638, and plate XI; translation in T. Burrow, *A Translation of the Kharoṣṭhi Documents from Chinese Turkestan*, 133.

Text

Obverse

1. mahanuava maharaya lihati cojhbo kranaya ṣoṭhaṃga lýipes̱a ca
2. maṃtra deti [/*] s̱a ca ahuno iśa sucaṃma viṃñav́eti yatha edas̱a purva eka urina huati [/*] ahuno dui urina prochaṃti [/*] yahi eda kilamudr[e?] atra eśati praṭha atra samuha anada pro-
3. chidavo [/*] yatha edas̱a purva eka urina huati iṃthuami ahuno eka urina prochidavo [/*] eṣa navaǵa goṭha saṃña [/*] adham̄ena rajadham̄a na prochidavo [/*]

Reverse

1. sucaṃmas̱a urinas̱a

Translation

Obverse

1. His Majesty the King writes to the Cojhbo Kranaya and the Ṣoṭhaṃga Lýipe,
2. he gives (them the following) instruction: Now there is this Sucaṃma, (who) announces that formerly he had one *urina*. Now they demand (of him) two *urina*. When this wedge tablet shall arrive there, immediately you must investigate this matter in person and carefully.
3. Just as formerly he had one *urina*, so now one *urina* is to be demanded (of him). He is newly designated a householder. The royal law must not be administered unlawfully.

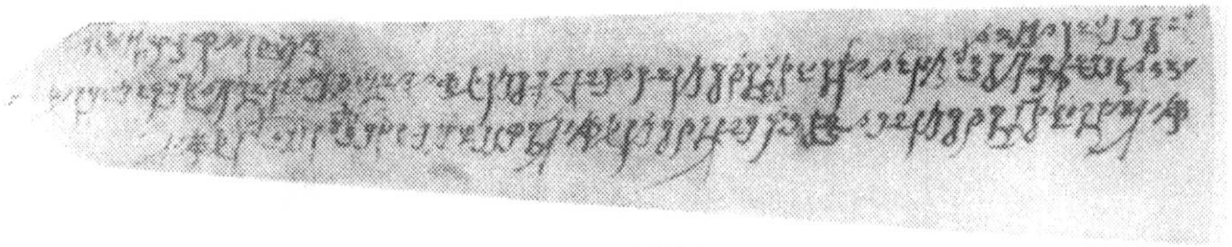

FIGURE 16. Niya (central Asian) Kharoṣṭhī document. From Boyer, Rapson, and Senart, *Kharoṣṭhī Inscriptions* II, pl. XI; reprinted by permission of Oxford University Press.

Reverse

1. [Concerning] the *urina* of Sucaṃma.

Notes

Obverse line 2: *urina*: The meaning of the word is unknown. Perhaps connected with sheep (cf. Skt. *ūrṇa* 'wool')?

---

7. Kahāuṃ Pillar Inscription of the Time of Skandagupta (fig. 17)

Location	On a stone pillar at Kahāuṃ, Gorakhpur Dist., UP
Script	Eastern Brāhmī of the Gupta period
Language	Sanskrit (verse)
Meter	*Sragdharā* (vv. 1–3)
Type and format	Dedicatory stone pillar inscription
Purpose	Records the erection by Madra, son of Rudrasoma, of the pillar with five images of Jaina saints
Date	Gupta year 141, month of Jyeṣṭha (day not specified) = A.D. 460
References	J. F. Fleet, CII 3, 65–8; D. R. Bhandarkar, CII 3 (rev. ed.), 305–8; D. C. Sircar, SI I.316–7.

Text

[*In upper left margin*:] siddham

1. yasyopasthānabhūmir nṛpatiśataśiraḥpātavātāvadhūtā
2. guptānāṃ vanśajasya p[r]avisṛtayaśasas tasya sarvvottamarddheḥ [*/]
3. rājye śakropamasya kṣitipaśatapateḥ skandaguptasya śānte
4. varṣe ttrinśaddaśaikottarakaśatatame jyeṣṭhamāsi prapanne /[*/ 1]
5. khyāte smin grāmaratne kakubha iti janais sādhusaṃsargapūte / [*sic*]
6. puttro yas somilasya pracuraguṇanidher bhaṭṭisomo mahāt[m]ā [*/]
7. tatsūnū rudrasoma[*ḥ] pṛthulamatiyaśā vyāghra ity anyasaṃjño [*sic*] /
8. madras tasyātmajo bhūd dvijaguruyatiṣu prāyaśaḥ prītimān yaḥ /[*/ 2]
9. puṇyaskandhaṃ sa cakkre jagad idam akhilam saṃsarad vīkṣya bhīto
10. śreyortthaṃ bhūtabhūtyai pathi viyamavatām arhatām ādikarttṛn [*/]
11. pañcendrāṃ sthāpayitvā dharaṇidharamayān sannikhātas tato yam
12. śailastambhaḥ sucārur girivaraśikharāgropamaḥ kīrttikarttā [*// 3]

Notes

Line 2: *vanśa*-, [4] *ttrinśad*-, [11] *pañcendrāṃ*: for *vaṃśa*-, *t*(*t*)*triṃśad*-, and *pañcendrān*. The loose application of nasal sandhi and orthographic rules is typical of inscriptional usage (see 3.3.2 and 3.3.8.1).

Line 10: *viyamavatām:* Read *niyamavatām.*

Line 10: *ādikarttṛn*: Read *ādikarttṝn.*

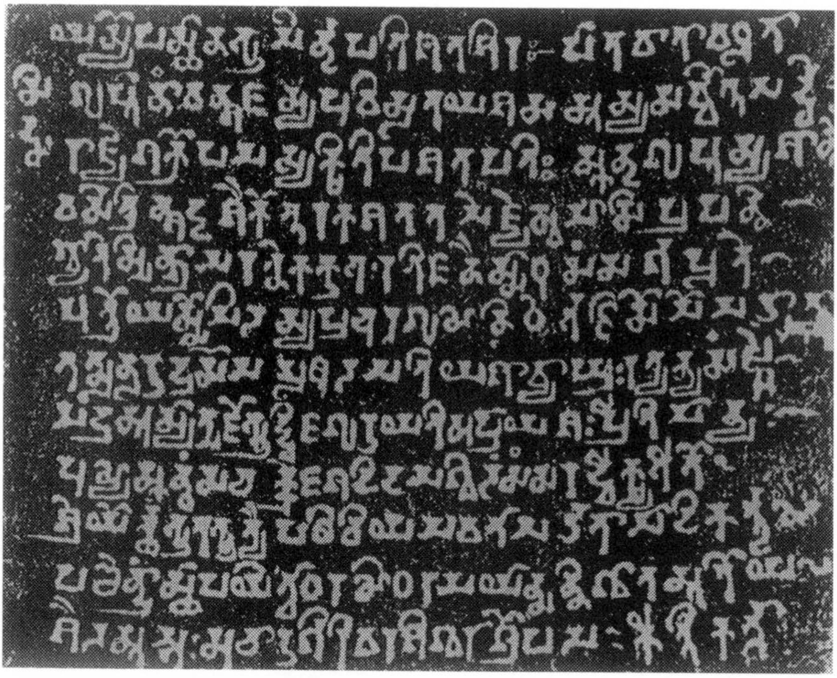

FIGURE 17. Kahāuṃ pillar inscription of the time of Skandagupta. From Fleet, CII III, pl. ix.A; copyright, Archaeological Survey of India.

Translation

Verse 1. Success! During the peaceful reign of Skandagupta, Lord over a hundred kings, who is like Śakra (Indra), whose audience hall is fanned by the breeze from the bowing of the heads of a hundred kings, who was born in the lineage of the Guptas, whose glory has spread afar, and who prospers above all others; in the hundredth year, plus thirty and ten and one [i.e., 141], when the month of Jyeṣṭha had arrived;

Verse 2. In this jewel of a village known among the people as Kakubha, which is sanctified by the presence of good men, [there dwelt] the noble Bhaṭṭisoma, who was the son of Somila, a mine of many virtues; his son was Rudrasoma, also known as Vyāghra, of great intelligence and glory; [and] his son was Madra, who was ever affectionate toward Brahmans, *gurus*, and ascetics;

Verse 3. He [Madra] perceived that all this world is transitory, and being [thus] afraid, he created a mass of merit for [his own] benefit [and] for the well-being of [all] creatures, [by] setting up in stone (these) five Lords, the leaders on the path of the self-restraining *Arhats*. Then [he] erected this very beautiful stone pillar, which is like the highest peak of a mighty mountain, and which confers fame [upon him].

Notes

Verse 2: Kakubha: This provides the original form of the name of the modern village Kahāuṃ (Kahāwaṃ, Kahaon, etc.).
Verse 3: "five Lords": *pañcendrāṃ* refers to the five Tīrthaṅkaras sculpted on the pillar. Cf. SI I.317 n. 3.

---

8. Lakkhā Maṇḍal *praśasti* (fig. 18)

Location	Lakkhā Maṇḍal Temple, at Maḍhā on the upper Yamuna River in Dehra Dun Dist., UP
Script	Siddhamātṛkā
Language	Sanskrit (verse)
Meters	*Āryā* (vv. 1–22); *anuṣṭubh* (23)
Type and format	Donative stone *praśasti*
Purpose	Records the dedication of a temple of Bhava (Śiva) by the Princess Īśvarā in memory of her late husband Candragupta of Jālandhara; the bulk of the text (vv. 2–18) is taken up by a eulogistic genealogy of Īśvarā's family of kings of Siṃghapura
Date	None given; seventh or eighth century A.D.
References	G. Bühler, "The Praśasti of the Temple of Lakkhâ Maṇḍal at Maḍhā, in Jaunsâr Bâwar," EI 1, 1892, 10–15.

Text

1. siddham [*symbol*]
sarggasthitilayahetor vviśvasya [brahma]viṣṇurudrāṇāṃ /
mūrttittrayaṃ pradadhate saṃsārabhide namo vibhave // [*1]
yaduvaṅśabhuvāṃ rājñāṃ saiṅghapuraṃ rājyam ā yugād dadhatām [*/]
2. śrīsenavarmmanāmā rājarṣiẖ prakrameṇās[ī]t // [*2]
tanayas tasya śrīmān nṛpatir abhūd āryavarmmanāmnaiva /
āryavratatāṃ prathamaṃ khyāpitavāṅs tadanu yas caritai[ḥ] // [*3]
śrī[datta]varmma-
3. nāmā dattābhayavibhavavijayavidhva[ṅ]saḥ [*/]
bhītārtthikulāribhyo vabhūva tasyātmajo nṛpatiḥ // [*4]
sūnur abhūt tasya mahān bhūpālaś śrīpradīptavarmmeti /
darppāndhaśattrupṛtanā-
4. pataṅgapaṭalīpradīptāgniḥ // [*5]
śrīśvaravarmmeti sutas tasyābhūd bhūpatiẖ pradānena [*/]
aiśvaryaṃ yaẖ kritavān bhava iva nicaye [bhavā]rtthānāṃ // [*6]
śrīvṛddhivarmmasaṃjñas tasya vabhūvātmajaḥ
5. pravṛddhaśrīḥ [*/]
candra iva tāpahārī nayanānāṃ nandano rājā // [*7]

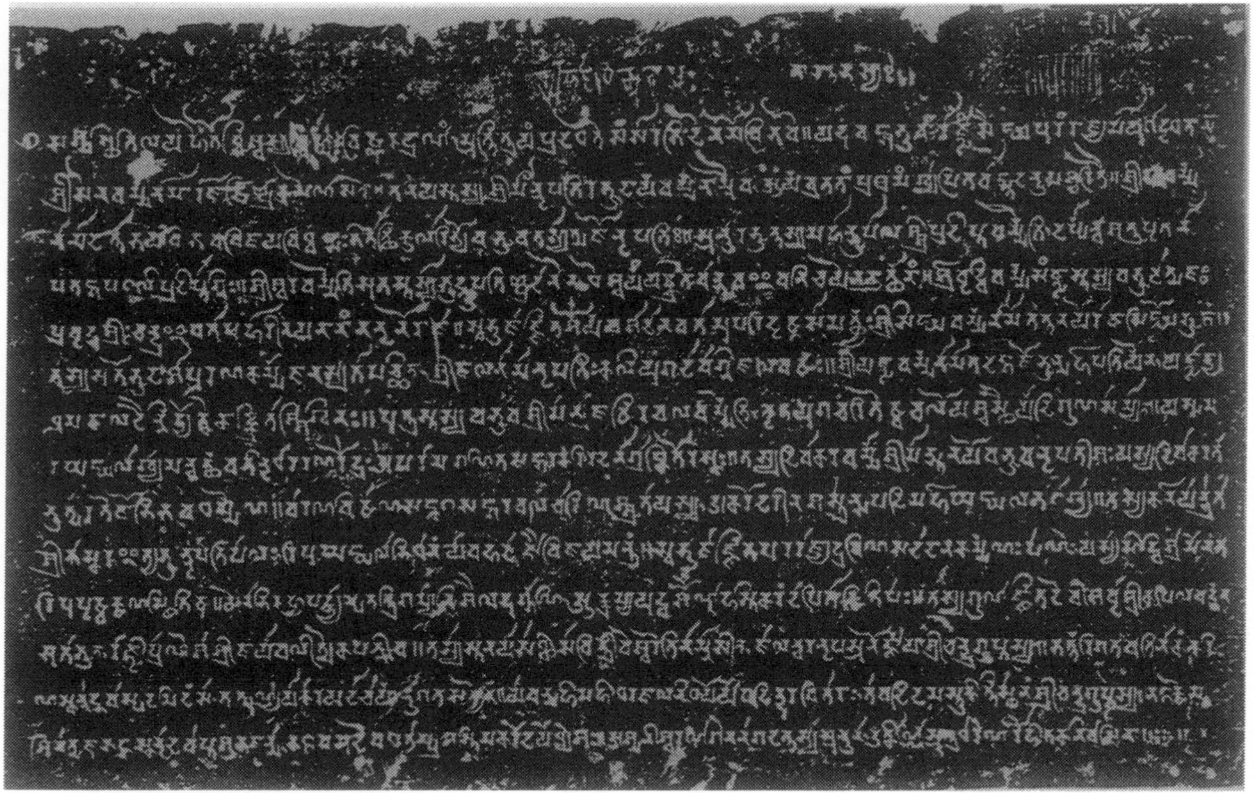

FIGURE 18. Lakkhā Maṇḍal *praśasti*. From EI 1, plate facing p. 12; copyright, Archaeological Survey of India.

svabhujārjjitaśaurya[ya]śā dānavatām upari dṛṣṭasāmartthyaḥ [*/]
śrīsiṅghavarmmanāmā tattanayo rājasiṅgho bhūt // [*8]
6. tasya s[u]to bhūd āśāpūraṇakarmmā janasya tāpacchit /
śrījalanāmā nṛpatiḥ kaliyugadāvāgnijalavarṣaḥ // [*9]
śrīyajñavarmmanāmā tadaṅgajo bhūn mahīpatir yena /
yajñājya-
7. dhūmajaladair nnityotkekāḫ kritāś śikhinaḥ // [*10]
puttras tasya vabhūva śrīmān rājarṣir acalavarmmeti /
kṛtayugacariteṣv acalo yaś ca sthairyādiguṇasāmyāt // [*11]
yas sama-
8. raghaṅghalākhyām anvartthavatīn dadhāra raṇaraudraḥ [*/]
aparām agaṇitasaṅgarakariradanāgrāṅkitoraskaḥ // [*12]
tasya divākaravarmmā śrīmāns tanayo vabhūva nṛpatīśaḥ [*/]
yasya divākaratā-
9. bhūt paratejobhibhavadharmmeṇa // [*13]
vāraṇaviṣāṇasaṅkaṭasaṅgaracalacāriṇaś śrutā yasya /
akarod arīn aśastrān sapadi mahāghaṅghalabhaṭākhyā // [*14]
tasya kanīyān bhrātā
10. śrībhāskara ity abhūn nṛpatipālaḥ /
ripughaṅghalābhidhānaṃ yo vahad ājau vijayamantraṃ // [*15]
svabhujārjjitapararājyadraviṇasadādānakarmmaṇaḥ pāṇeḥ [*/]
yasyāsīd viśrāmo nata-
11. ripupṛṣṭhakṣaṇasthitiṣu // [*16]
yenābhiruhya padbhyām patatrigamyāni śailadurggāṇi [*/]
ākkramya yuddhaśauṇḍā hastikaraṃ dāpitā[*sic*] kṣitipāḥ // [*17]
tasya guṇārjjitadevīśavdā śrīkapilavarddhana-
12. sutābhūt /
rājñī prāṇeśā śrījayāvalīty ekapatnī ca // [*18]
tasyās tanayā sādhvī sāvittrīveśvareti nāmnāsīt /
jālandharanṛpasūnor jjāyā śrīcandraguptasya // [*19]
bharttari gatavati nākaṃ kari-
13. ṇa[*sic*] skandhād bhavāspadam idaṃ sā /
tatpuṇyāyākārayad ācāryānugatasatyena // [*20]
yāvan mahīmahīdharajalanidhayo yāvad induravitārāḥ /
tāvad idam astu kīrttisthānaṃ śrīcandraguptasya // [*21]
bhaṭṭakṣema-
14. śivātmajabhaṭṭaskandād avāptaśubhajanmā /
bhaṭṭavasudeva etām praśastim akarod ayodhyeśaḥ // [*22]
aśmanīśvaraṇāgena nāgadattasya sūnunā /
utkīrṇṇā sūtradhāreṇa rauhitakanivāsinā // [*symbol*] // [*23]

Notes

Line 3: *vabhūva*: i.e., *babhūva* (also lines 4, 7, etc.); the script of this inscription does not have a separate character for *b* but uses only *v*.

Line 4: *kritavān*: for *kṛtavān*; *kri* is a common misspelling for *kṛ* in Sanskrit inscriptions; see 3.3.8.1. Likewise, *kritāś*, line 7.

Translation (arranged by verse number)

1. Success! Homage to God (Vibhu) who breaks the cycle of existences, and who takes on the three forms of Brahmā, Viṣṇu, and Śiva in order to create, preserve, and destroy [respectively] the universe.
2. Among the kings of the Yadu line who have ruled the kingdom of Siṅghapura since the [beginning of] the aeon, there was in the course of time a sage-king named illustrious Senavarman.
3. His son was the illustrious King Āryavarman by name, who first after him (Senavarman) proclaimed through his deeds noble piety.
4. His son was the illustrious King Dattavarman, who gave protection, riches, conquest, and destruction to the frightened, to supplicants, to his family, and to his enemies [respectively].
5. His son was the great king, the illustrious Pradīptavarman, who was a blazing (*pradīpta*) fire to the swarm of moths who were his enemies' army, blinded by their arrogance.
6. His son was the illustrious king Īśvaravarman, who by his generosity attained, like Bhava (Śiva), mastery over the aggregation of worldly matters [/of the elements of existence].
7. His son was named the illustrious Vṛddhivarman, of great fortune [/beauty], a king who, like the moon, was a delight to the eyes and a remover of affliction [/heat].
8. His son was the illustrious Siṅghavarman by name, who earned glory and valor by his own arm; a lion of a king, he demonstrated his powers superior to [those of other] donors [/on the backs of rutting elephants].
9. His son was the illustrious King named Jala, who was a shower of rain on the forest fire of the Kali age; his actions fulfilled the people's wishes [/filled the directions] and removed their afflictions [/heat].
10. His son was the illustrious King named Yajñavarman, who by the clouds of smoke from his sacrificial oblations made the peacocks cry out constantly.
11. His son was the illustrious Sage-king called Acalavarman; in his deeds (worthy of) the Kṛta age he was unwavering [/a mountain] (*acala*), which he resembled in stability and other virtues.
12. He bore a second name, Samaraghaṅghala ("Conqueror in Battle" [?]), which was appropriate to him, as he was terrible in war and his chest was marked by the sharp tusks of innumerable battle elephants.
13. His son was the illustrious Divākaravarman, Lord of Kings; he was [like] the sun (*divākara*) in that he overcame the power of his enemies [/outshone other sources of light].
14. His title of Mahāghaṅghalabhaṭa ("Great Conquering Warrior" [?]) rendered his enemies weaponless the moment they heard it, as they ran in panic over the battle ground that was thick with [severed] elephants' tusks.
15. His younger brother was the illustrious Lord of Kings called Bhāskara, who bore the (second) name Ripughaṅghala ("Conqueror of Enemies" [?]) as a victory-spell in battle.
16. His hand, which was constantly engaged in giving away the wealth of his en-

emies' kingdoms which he had won by his own arm, found rest (only) in the moments when it lay upon the backs of his bowing foes.

17. He climbed on foot mountain fortresses which (only) birds could reach and attacked the battle-hardened kings (there), forcing them to pay him tribute of elephants.
18. His queen, sole wife, and lady of his life was the illustrious Jayāvalī, daughter of the illustrious Kapilavardhana, who by her virtues earned the title of Queen (*devī*).
19. Her daughter, Īśvarā by name, was as virtuous as Sāvitrī. She was the wife of the illustrious Candragupta, son of the King of Jālandhara.
20. When her lord had gone to heaven from his elephant's shoulder, she had constructed this abode of Bhava (Śiva) for the sake of his merit, as an (act of) truth (*satyena*) approved by her teacher.
21. As long as the earth and the mountains and the oceans (shall remain), and as long as the moon and sun and stars (shall shine), so long may this memorial of the illustrious Candragupta remain.
22. Bhaṭṭavasudeva, the Lord of Ayodhyā, who attained his fortunate birth from Bhaṭṭaskanda, the son of Bhaṭṭakṣemaśiva, composed this eulogy.
23. It was engraved on [this] stone by the engraver Īśvaraṇāga, son of Nāgadatta and a resident of Rauhitaka.

Notes

Verse 3: "noble piety" (*āryavratatāṃ*): The phrase plays on the king's name, Āryavarman. The same device is used throughout the genealogical portion of the record; for example, in the following verse, "who gave . . ." refers to the name *Datta*varman.

Verse 8: "superior to [those of other] donors [/on the backs of rutting elephants]": *danavatām* has a double meaning with reference to the "lion of a king." With respect to the lion, it refers to the rutting elephants upon whose backs he demonstrates his strength; with respect to the king, it refers to other benefactors whose generosity he exceeds.

Verse 9: "fulfilled the people's wishes [/filled the directions] and removed their afflictions [/heat]": These epithets too apply punningly to both the king himself and the rain-shower to which he is metaphorically compared.

Verse 10: "made the peacocks cry out constantly": The smoke from Yajñavarman's frequent sacrifices deluded the peacocks, who thought that it was always the rainy season.

Verse 12: "'Conqueror in Battle' [?]": The word *ghaṅghala* here and in vv.14 and 15 is uncertain. Bühler (15 n. 18) notes: "I am unable to find in the *Koshas* and dictionaries accessible to me the word *ghaṅghala*. . . . [It is] probable that its meaning is 'the conqueror:' very likely it is a Deśi word."

Verse 14: "they ran in panic (*-calacāriṇas*) over the battle ground that was thick with [severed] elephants' tusks": *vāraṇaviṣāṇasaṅkaṭasaṅgaracalacāriṇaś* can also be interpreted as modifying *yasya* (instead of *arīn*); thus Bühler, "when he nimbly strode over the battle (*-field*) . . ."

Verse 20: "had gone to heaven from his elephant's shoulder": This euphemistically means that he died in battle (not, as Bühler 15 n. 20, "that he fell from his elephant and broke his neck, or merely that he exchanged his princely pomp for a residence in heaven").

Verse 22: "the Lord of Ayodhyā": Bühler (15 n. 22) remarks that this "means, I suppose, only that Vasudeva was the owner of some village called Ayodhyā."

9. Văt Ph'u Stone Inscription of Jayavarman [I] (fig. 19)

Location	Văt Ph'u, Basăk, Laos
Script	Cambodian derivative of (southern?) Brāhmī
Language	Sanskrit (verse)
Meters	*Śārdūlavikrīḍita* (vv. 1, 3–5); *sragdharā* (2)
Type and format	Stone stele; royal administrative order
Purpose	Records the king's order prohibiting the killing of animals within the sacred precincts of the Liṅgaparvata
Date	None given; ca. second half of seventh century A.D.
References	A. Barth, "Stèle de Vat Phou," BEFEO 2, 1902, 235–40; L. Finot, *Inscriptions du Cambodge*, II, pl. XL (K.367); G. Coedès, *Inscriptions du Cambodge*, II.78; Claude Jacques, *Corpus des inscriptions du pays Khmer*, I.122 + pl. 43.

Text

1. śakrādir vvijito mayā mama śarā moghaṃ gatā na kvacit
   sovaddhyaś ca madhus sakhā mama sadā vaśyañ ca nṛṇāṃ manaḥ [/*]
2. ity evaṃ vigaṇayya mānasabhavo vyaddhuṃ gatas tatkṣaṇaṃ
   yadroṣekṣaṇajātabhasmanicayo rudreṇa jejīyatām [//1//*]
3. yenākṛṣṭaṃ dvibhāraṃ saśaravaradhanur yyogyayāpāstam astaṃ
   mātaṅgāśvīyamartyaprajavavalamanoyuddhaśikṣāvidagryaḥ [/*]
4. sadgītātodyanṛttādyanupamadhiṣaṇā[śās?]tasūkṣmārthacintā-
   ratnaprajñātitikṣāvinayanayamatityāgaratnāmvudhir yyaḥ [//2//*]
5. nānāśastakṛtābhiyogajanitavyāyāmakāṭhinyava-
   tkamvugrīvamahorusaṃhatavṛhatpīnāṅsavakṣastanuḥ [/*]
6. ājānupravilamvahemaparighaprasparddhivāhudva[yo]
   yas sampūrṇṇanarendrasiṅhavalavadrūpābhirūpo bhuvi [//3//*]
7. tasya śrījayavarmmabhūpati[pate]r ājñānubhāvoda[yā]-
   d atra śrīmati liṅgaparvva[tava]re ye sthāyinaẖ prāṇi[naḥ] [/*]
8. vaddhyantān na janena kenacid api prāptāparādhāẖ kadā
   devāya pratipāditaṃ yad iha taddhemādikaṃ siddhyatu [//4//*]
9. devasyāsya yathābhilāṣagamanā gacchantu naivāśra[me]
   yānārohadhṛtātapatraracanābhyutkṣiptasaccāmaraiḥ [/*]
10. poṣyāḥ kukkurakukkuṭā na ca janair ddevasya bhūmaṇḍale-
    ṣv ity ājñāvanipasya tasya bhavatu kṣmāyām alaṅghyā nṛṇām [//5//*]

Notes

Line 2: *mānasabhavo*: Barth reads *mānasabhuvo*.
Line 3: *dvibhāraṃ*: The intended reading may be *dvivāraṃ*. Barth reads *dvibharaṃ*.
Line 4: -[*śās?*]*ta*-: So read by Barth. The intended reading may have been -[*ā*]*vāpta*-.
Line 8: *-āparādhāẖ kadā*: Possibly *-āparādhās tadā*.

FIGURE 19. Văt Ph'u stone inscription of Jayavarman [I]. From BEFEO 2, plate facing p. 230; reprinted by permission of the École Française d'Extrême-Orient.

Translation (arranged by verse number)

1. May that Rudra be eternally victorious, by whose angry eye the Mind-Born One (Kāma) was reduced in an instant to a heap of ashes when he (Kāma) approached to shoot him, disregarding him with the thoughts "I have conquered Śakra (Indra) and other (gods); my arrows never miss their mark; my companion Madhu (Springtime) is invincible; and the hearts of men are always subject to my power."
2. He who cast away the bow, along with its excellent arrows, which he had strung (despite its) double weight, as (useful only) for exercise; who is the foremost among those who have studied the techniques of battle by speed, by power, and by the mind (against) elephants, horses, and men [respectively (?)]; who was an ocean of the jewels of wisdom, patience, humility, tact, intelligence, and generosity, and

who had won [?] the magic gem of understanding of subtle matters through his unequaled knowledge (*dhīṣaṇā* [?]) of fine song, music, dance, etc.;

3. Whose body had a strong, broad, and thick chest and shoulders, great thighs, and a conch shell–like neck, hardened by exercise carried out with practices performed according to various prescriptions; whose two arms, hanging down to his knees, rivaled bars of gold; who was a full moon upon the earth in the mighty form of a lion among kings;
4. By force of the authority of the command of this Lord of Kings, the illustrious Jayavarman, the creatures which dwell on this beautiful and excellent Liṅgaparvata must never be slain by any person, even if they have committed an offense. May gold and whatever is provided to the God here (thereby) achieve its purpose.
5. In the *āśrama* of this god (people) may go at will, (but) they must not go mounted on vehicles, holding opened umbrellas, or with fine chowries held up; and people must not feed dogs and cocks within the boundaries of the land of the God. May this command of the king be inviolable for (all) men on the earth!

Notes

Verse 2: "(despite its) double weight": Following Barth, who translates "malgré son double poids." Alternatively, following the emendation proposed above in the text notes, ". . . discarded his bow after he had strung it (only) twice." Cf. the following note.

Verse 2: "(useful only) for exercise" (*yyogyayā*): The idea seems to be that he had no more use for his bow, as he had already conquered all his enemies after stringing it only twice (i.e., after conducting only two battles or campaigns), if the interpretation proposed in the preceding note is correct. The phrasing, however, is rather obscure. Barth translates "après ses (longues) campagnes, il les a déposés comme inutiles."

Verse 2: "battle by speed, by power, and by the mind (against) elephants, horses, and men [respectively (?)]": If this interpretation of the subcompound *mātaṅgā . . . mano-yuddha-* as an instance of the figure *yathāsaṃkhya* (respective enumeration) is correct, one would have expected the words *-prajava-vala-* to have been reversed. Barth (239 n. 1) attributes this apparent poetic defect to metrical necessity.

Verse 2: "who had won [?]": Translated according to the suggested emendation (*-avāpta-*) given in the text notes. Barth, in his translation and note (239 n. 2), suggests other possible interpretations. Here, as elsewhere in the inscription, the long compounds are highly ambiguous and subject to various interpretations (cf. Barth, 239 n. 1).

Verse 3: "with practices performed according to various prescriptions": Or, reading *nānā+[a]śasta . . .* , "by attacks (*abhiyoga*) made upon the various things which are not recommended" (cf. Barth 239 n. 5). The ambiguity may have been intentional. (Or might the intended reading have been *nānāśāstra . . .* , in which case the sense is "by practices performed [according to] the various textbooks"?)

Verse 3: "moon": Translated according to Barth's suggestion (239 n. 8) that *-abhirūpo* here means 'moon'. As he notes, *saṃpūrṇṇa-* at the beginning of the compound does suggest this interpretation, though the construction here (as in several other places) is rather clumsy.

Verse 4: "never": *kadā* here evidently has to be construed with the preceding *api*, which I interpret (with Barth) as governing *prāptāparādhāḥ* (rather than *kenacid*). Or *kadā* may be construed in an expletive sense ("at any time"), somewhat like *kiyad* 'so many times', in the Nālandā inscription (Appendix, no. 12, l. 1). (But note also the possible alternative reading given in the text notes, and Barth's comments thereon, 239 n. 11.)

Verse 5: "(people) may go at will, (but) they must not go . . .": Following Barth's (240 n. 1) suggested alternative translation.

---

10. Baroda Copper Plate Inscription of Rāṣṭrakūṭa Karkkarāja [II] (fig. 20)

Location	Baroda, Baroda Dist., Gujarat. Now in the British Library, London
Script	Proto-Kannada
Language	Sanskrit (verse and prose)
Meters	*Anuṣṭubh* (vv. 1, 29, 30, 32, 34); *upajāti* (2, 5, 6, 8, 10, 11, 18, 19); *vasantatilakā* (3, 4, 12, 13, 14, 16, 20, 21, 23, 25, 27); *indravajrā* (7, 9, 22, 31, 33); *upendravajrā* (15); *śārdūlavikrīḍita* (17, 24, 26); *āryā* (28); *puṣpitāgra* (35); *śālinī* (36)
Type and format	Copper plate land grant; three plates, approximately 11" × 8"; first side of first plate and second side of last plate (except for codicil) not inscribed
Purpose	Records the grant of the village of Vaḍapadraka to Bhānu, son of Bhaṭṭasomāditya, by Karkkarāja [II] Suvarṇavarṣa, the Rāṣṭrakūṭa king of Gujarat
Date	New moon day of Vaiśākha (*mahāvaiśākhī*), Śaka 734 = A.D. 812 (l. 52)
References	H. T. P[rinsep], "Account of Tamba Patra Plates dug up at Baroda in Goojrat; with Facsimile and Translation," JASB 8, 1839, 292–303 [text transcribed by Kamlakanta; translation by Saroda Prashad Chakravarti]; J. F. Fleet, "Sanskrit and Old-Canarese Inscriptions, No. CXXVII," IA 12, 1883, 156–65; Ramchandra Gopal Bhandarkar, "The Râshṭrâkûṭa [*sic*] King Kṛishṇarâja I and Êlâpura," IA 12, 1883, 228–30.

Text

[Plate 1, side 2]

1. siddhaṃ [*symbol*]
sa vo vyād vedhasā yena yannābhikamalaṅ kṛtaṃ /
haraś ca yasya kāntendukalayā samalaṃkṛtaṃ // [*1]
svasti svakīyānva-
2. yavaṅśakarttā śrīrāṣṭrakūṭāmalavaṅśajanmā /
pradānaśūraḥ samaraikavīro govindarājaḥ kṣitipo babhūva // [*2]
yasyā-
3. [ṅga]mātrajayinaḥ priyasāhasasya /
kṣmāpālaveṣaphalam eva babhūva sainyaṃ /

FIGURE 20. Baroda copper plate inscription of Rāṣṭrakūta Karkkarāja [II], plate 1, side 2. From IA 12, plate facing p. 158; copyright, the British Library.

muktvā ca śaṅkaram adhīśvaram īśvarāṇāṃ /
nāvandatā-
4. nyam amareṣv api yo manasvī // [*3]
putrīyataś ca khalu tasya bhavaprasādāt [*/]
sūnur bbabhūva guṇarāśir udārakīrttiḥ /
5. yo gauṇi[*read* ṇa?]nāmaparivāram uvāha mukhyaṃ /
śrīkarkkarājasubhagavyapadeśam uccaiḥ // [*4]
saurājyajalpe patite prasaṅgā-
6. n [*/]
nideśanaṃ viśvajanīnasaṃpat /
rājyaṃ baleḥ pūrvvam aho babhūva /
kṣitāv idānīn tu nṛpasya yasya // [*5]
atyadbhu-
7. tañ cedam amaṃsta lokaḥ [*/]
kaliprasaṅgena yad ekapādaṃ /
jātaṃ vṛṣaṃ yaḥ kṛtavān idānīṃ /
bhūyaś catuṣpādam avighnacā-
8. [raṃ] /[*/] [*6]
citraṃ na cedaṃ yad asau yathāvac
cakre prajāpālanam etad eva /
viṣṇau jagat[*t]rāṇapare manassthe
tasyoci-

9. ta[ṃ] tanmayamānasasya // [*7]
dharmmātmanas tasya nṛpasya jajñe /
sutaḥ sadharmmā khalu kṛṣṇarājaḥ /
yo vaṅśya-
10. m unmūlya vimārggā[*read* a]bhājaṃ [*/]
rājyaṃ svayaṃ gotrahitāya cakkre // [*8]
brahmaṇyatā tasya ca kāpi sābhūd [*/]
viprā yayā /[*sic*] ke-
11. valajātayo pi /
śreṣṭhadvijanmocitadānalubdhāḥ /
karmmāṇy anūcānakṛtāni cakkruḥ // [*9]
icchātirekeṇa
12. kṛṣībalānāṃ /
payo yathā muñcati jātu meghe [*/]
bhaven manas tadviratau tathābhūd [*/]
yasmin dhanaṃ varṣṣati sevakānāṃ // [*10]
13. yo yuddhakaṇḍūtigṛhītam uccaiḥ /
sau[*read* śau]ryyoṣmasaṃdīpitam āpatantaṃ /
mahāvarāhaṃ hariṇīcakāra /
prājyaprabhāvaḥ
14. khalu rājasiṅghaḥ[*read*-siṃhaḥ] /[*/11]
elāpurācalagatādbhutasanniveśaṃ /
yad vīkṣya vismitavimānacarāmarendrāḥ /
eta-
15. [*t] svayambhu śivadhāma na kṛtrime śrīr [*/]
dṛṣṭedṛśīti satataṃ bahu carccayanti // [*12]
bhūyas tathāvidhakṛtau vyava-
16. sāyahāni[r] [*/]
etan mayā katham aho kṛtam ity akasmāt /
karttāpi yasya khalu vismayam āpa śi-
17. lpī /
tannāma kīrttanam ā[*read* a]kāryyata yena rājñā /[*/13]
gaṅgāpravāhahimadīdhitikālakū-
[Plate 2, side 1]
18. ṭair [*/]
atyudbhutābharaṇakaiṣ kṛtamaṇḍano pi /
māṇikyakāñcanapurassarasarvvabhū-
19. tyā /
tatra sthitaḥ punar abhūṣyata yena śambhuḥ // [*14]
nṛpasya tasya dhruvarājanāmā /
20. mahānubhāvas tanayo babhu(ū)va /
tṛṇīkṛtān yasya parākrameṇa [*/]
pratāpavahnir dviṣato dadā-
21. ha // [*15]
lakṣmīprasādhanavidhāv upayogi kṛtyaṃ /

yaś cintayan svayam abhūd aniśam kṛtārtthaḥ /
kiṃ vātra citram a-
22. napekṣya sahāyam īśaḥ [*/]
sarvvaḥ pumān nijadha[*read* va]dhūṃ svavaśāṃ vidhātuṃ // [*16]
yo gaṅgāyamune taraṅgasu-
23. bhage gṛhṇan parebhyaḥ samaṃ /
sākṣāc cihnanibhena cottamapadaṃ tat prāptavān aiśvaraṃ /
dehāsammitavaibha-
24. vair iva guṇair yyasya bhramadbhir ddiśo /
vyāptās tasya babhūva kīrttipuruṣo govindarājaḥ sutaḥ // [*17]
25. pradeśavṛttivyavasāyabhājāṃ [*/]
purātanānām api pārtvi[*read* rtthi]vānāṃ /
yaśānsi [*sic*] yo nāma jahāra bhūpo [*/]
bhagnapraca-
26. ṇḍākhilavairivīraḥ /[*/18]
unmūlitottuṅganarendravaṅśo [*/]
mahānarendrīkṛtatucchabhṛtyaḥ [*/]
svecchāvidhāyī caritānukāraṃ [*/]
27. cakāra yo nāma vidheḥ kṣitīśaḥ // [*19]
hiñjīraśiñjitaraṇaccaraṇān arātīn [*/]
kurvann kṣaṇena vidadhe dbhutakarmma yaś ca /
28. cakre tathā hi na tathāśu vadham pareṣāṃ /
pārttho pi nāma bhuvanatṛ[*read* tri]tayaikavīraḥ // [*20]
kalpakṣayakṣaṇasamudbhava-
29. vātahelā- [*/]
dolāyamānakulaśailakulānukāraṃ /
yanmuktacaṇḍaśarajālajavapraṇunnā /
yuddhāgatā ripu-
30. gajendraghaṭā cakāra // [*21]
bhrātā tu tasyendrasamānavīryyaḥ /
śrīmān bhuvi kṣmāpatir indrarājaḥ [*/]
śāstā babhūvā-
31. dbhutakīrttisūtis [*/]
tad[*d]attalāṭeśvaramaṇḍalasya // [*22]
adyāpi yasya surakinnarasiddhasādhya- [*/]
vidyā-
32. dharādhipatayo guṇapakṣapātāt /
gāyanti kundakusumaśri yaśo yathāsva- [*/]
dhāmasthitā[*s] sa-
33. hacarīkucadattahastāḥ // [*23]
yenaikena ca gūrjjareśvarapatir yyoddhuṃ samabhyudyataḥ [*/]
śauryya-
34. proddhatakandharo mṛga iva kṣipraṃ diśo grāhitaḥ [*/]
bhītāsaṃṅ[*sic*]hatadakṣiṇāpathama-
[Plate 2, side 2]

35. hāsāmantacakra(ṃ) yato [*/]
rakṣām āpa viluṇṭyamānavibhavaṃ śrīvallabhenādarāt // [*24]
tasyātmajaḥ prathita-
36. vikramavairivargga- [*/]
lakṣmīhaṭhāharaṇasantatalabdhakīrttiḥ /
śrīkakkarāja iti [saṃśritapūritāśaḥ?] [*/]
śāstrārtthabodha-
37. paripālitasarvvalokaḥ // [*25]
rājye yasya na taskarasya vasatir vyādheḥ prasūtir mṛtā [*/]
durbhikṣaṃ na ca vibhramasya mahimā
38. naivopasargodbhavaḥ [*/]
kṣīṇo doṣagaṇaḥ pratāpavinatāśeṣārivarggas tathā [*/]
no vidvatparipanthinī prabhavati krū-
39. rā khalānāṃ matiḥ // [*26]
gauḍendravaṅgapatinirjjayadurvvidagdha- [*/]
sadgūrjjareśvaradigarggalatāṃ ca yasya /
nītvā bhujaṃ vihata-
40. mālavarakṣaṇārtthaṃ [*/]
svamī tathānyam api rājyacha[*read* pha]lāni bhū[*read* bhu]ṅkte /[*/27]
tenedaṃ [*anila]vidyuccañcalam ālokya jīvitaṃ [*asāram] [*/]
kṣitidāna-
41. ñ ca paramapuṇyaṃ pravarttito yaṃ dharmmadāyaḥ [*//28]
sa ca lāṭeśvaraḥ samadhigatāśeṣamahāśabdamahāsāmantā-
42. dhipatisuvarṇṇavarṣaśrīkarkkarājadevo yathāsambadhyamānakān
rāṣṭrapativiṣayapatigrāmakūṭādhi-
43. kārikamahattarādīn samanubodhayaty [*/] astu vaḥ saṃviditaṃ / yathā
mayā śrīsiddhaśamīsamāvāsitena mā-
44. tāpitror ātmanaś caihikāmuṣmikapuṇyayaśobhivṛddhaye śrīvalabhī-
vinirggatataccāturvvidyasāmānya-
45. vāstyā[*read*tsyā]yanasagotramādhyandinasabrāhmacāribrāhmaṇabhānave
bhaṭṭasomādityaputrāyā-
46. ṅkoṭṭakacaturaśītyanna[*read* nta]rggatavaḍapadrakābhidhānagrāmeḥ
[*read* maḥ] yasyāghāṭanāni pūrvvato jambu-
47. vāvikāgrāmas tathā dakṣiṇato mahāsenakākhyaṃ taḍāgaṃ / tathā
paścimato ṅkoṭṭakaṃ / tathotta-
48. rato vagghācchagrāma [*/] evam asau caturāghāṭanopalakṣitaḥ
sodraṅgaḥ sa[*read* so]parikaraḥ sabhūta-
49. vātapratyāyaḥ sadaṇḍadaśāparadhaḥ sotpadyamānaviṣṭikaḥ sadhānya-
hiraṇyādeyaḥ sarvva-
50. rājakīyānām ahastapraksepaṇīya ācandrārkkārṇṇavasaritparvvata-
samakālīnaḥ putrapau-
51. trānvayabhogyaḥ pūrvvapradattadevadāyabrahmadāyarahito
bhūmicchidranyāyena
52. śakanṛpakālātītasaṃvatsaraśateṣu saptasu śca[*read*
ca]tustriṃśada[dhike]ṣu mahāvaiśākhyāṃ snātvoda-
53. kātisarggeṇa balicaruvaiśvadevāgnihotrātithipañcamahā-

[Plate 3, side 1]

54. yajñakratukriyādyutsarppaṇārtthaṃ pratipāditaḥ / yato syocitayā brahmadāyasthityā bhuñjato bho-
55. jayataḥ pratidiśato vā kṛṣataḥ karṣṣayataś ca na kenaca[*read* ci]t paripanthanā kāryyā [*/] tathāgāmi-
56. [*nṛpati]bhir asmadvaṅśyair anyair vvā sāmānya[*ṃ] bhūmidāna[*phala]m avagacchadbhir vvidyullolāny anityāni aiśvaryāṇi tri[*read* tṛ]ṇāgralagnajala-
57. binducañcalañ ca jīvitam āna[*read* ka]layya svadāyanirvviśeṣo yam asmaddāyo numantavyaḥ pāl[*ay]itavyaś ca / yaś cājñānatimi-
58. rapaṭalāvṛtamatir ācchi[*n]dyā[*d ā]cchidyamānañ cānumodate [*read* deta] / sa pañcabhir mmahāpātakair upapātakaiś ca yuktas syā-
59. d [*/] ity uktaṃ ca /[*sic*] bhagavatā vedavyāsena vyāsena /
ṣaṣṭiṃ varṣṣasahasrāṇi svargge tiṣṭhati bhūmidaḥ /
ācchettā
60. cānumantā ca tāny eva narake vaset // [*29]
vindhyāṭaviṣv atoyāsu śuṣkakoṭaravāsinaḥ [*/]
kṛṣṇāhayo hi jāyante
61. bhūmidāyāpahāriṇaḥ /[*/ 30]
agner apatyaṃ prathamaṃ suvarṇṇaṃ [*/]
bhūr vvaiṣṇavī sūryyasutāś ca gāvaḥ [*/]
lokatrayaṃ
62. tena bhavec ca dattaṃ [*/]
yaḥ kāñcanaṃ gāñ ca mahīñ ca dadyāt // [*31]
bahubhir vvasudhā bhuktā rājabhiḥ sagarādibhiḥ /
yasya ya-
63. sya yadā bhūmis tasya tadā phalaṃ // [*32]
yānīha dattāni purā narendrair [*/]
ddānāni dharmmārtthayaśaskarāṇi /
nirmmālya-
64. vāntapratimāni tāni [*/]
ko nāma sādhuḥ punar ādadīta // [*33]
svadattāṃ paradattāṃ vā yatnād rakṣa narādhipa /
mahī[*ṃ]
65. mahībhṛtāṃ śreṣṭha dānāc chreyo nupālanaṃ // [*34]
iti kamaladalāmbu[*bindu]lolāṃ
śriyam anucintya manuṣyajīvitañ ca [*/]
66. ativimalamanobhir ātmanīne[*read* nai]r
nna hi puruṣaiḥ parakīrttayo vilopyāḥ // [*35]
uktañ ca bhagavatā rāmabhadreṇa /
67. sarvvān etān bhāvinaḥ partthivendrān
bhūyo bhūyo yācate rāmabhadraḥ [*/]
sāmānyo yaṃ dharmmasetur nṛpāṇāṃ
68. kāle kāle pālanīyo bhavadbhiḥ // [*36]
dūtakaś cātra rājaputraśrīdantivarmmā // svahasto yaṃ mama śrīkakkarājasya

69. śrīmadindrarājasutasya // likhitañ caitan mayā mahāsandhivigrahādhikṛta-kulaputrakadurggabhaṭasūnunā
70. nemādityeneti / ayaṃ ca grāmo tītanarapatiparīkṣiṇāṃkoṭṭaka-śrīcāturvvidyāya datto bhūt [*/] tenāpi
71. [kurā]jā[*read* ja]nitavilā[*read* lo]pavicchinnaparibhogaṃ vī[*read* vi]jñānavaramānyaśya[*read* sya] vā viśiṣṭasya kaśya[*read* sya]cit bhavatu dvijā[*read* ja]nmana iti niścitya
72. śu[*read* su]varṇṇavarṣadīpa[*read* ya]māna[*ḥ] [va]ṭa[*pu?]ra[vā?]sine bhānubhaṭṭāyānumoditaḥ [*/] śālātāpyaṃ gṛhītvā tālāvārikādi[gaṇañ co?]ddi-
73. śya tāṃbūlapradānapūrvvā[*read* a]kaṃ yathālābha[sevanañ cāśādiśya?] prakṛtikam api puraṃ [i?]ti

[Plate 3, side 2]

74. tathā śrīyāgeśvarapra[*read* pa]ramadhi[*read* ī]śapādamūlaṃ jānātīti//

Notes

Line 1: *yena*: Read *dhāma*, as found in this verse in other Rāṣṭrakūṭa grants.

Line 1: *samalaṃkṛtaṃ*: Read *kam alaṃkṛtaṃ*, as in other inscriptions.

Line 6: *nideśanaṃ*: The intended reading is probably *nidarśanaṃ*, as in other Rāṣṭrakūṭa grants (e.g., EI 35, 278, l. 49).

Line 9: *sadharmmā*: Fleet reads *sudharmmā*; Prinsep, correctly, has *sadharmmā*.

Line 15: *kṛtrime*: Fleet corrects this to *kṛtrimaṃ*, but the emendation does not seem necessary.

Line 16: *vyavasāyahani*[*r*]: The intended reading may have been *-hāner;* R. G. Bhandarkar (IA 12, 229) so reads.

Line 36: *śrīkakkarāja iti* [*saṃśritapūritāśaḥ?*]: This passage has been written over another text, by way of a correction, so that neither is clearly legible. The engraver of the plate appears to have skipped back and forth between this line and the next line in the archetype from which he was copying; traces of the phrase *prasūtir mṛtā durbhikṣaṃ* from l. 37 seem to be visible under the revised text. The reading *saṃśritapūritāśaḥ* is confirmed by the same verse in another Rāṣṭrakūṭa grant (EI 35, 278, v. 46).

Line 38: *pratāpavinatāśeṣārivarggas tathā*: Fleet corrects to *-vinato śeṣāri-*, but this is not absolutely necessary.

Line 40: *tathānyam*: The *akṣara nya* was added below the *thā*.

Line 40: [**anila*], [**asāram*]: These words, which are metrically necessary, are supplied from the usual form of the same verse in other Rāṣṭrakūṭa records; cf. EI 35, 279, v. 41 and n. 2. (Similarly below for *nṛpati* and *phala*, l. 56, and **bindu*, l. 65.)

Line 50: *rājakīyānām*: *kī* was apparently corrected for an original *nī*.

Lines 68–69: *svahasto . . . sutasya*: This portion is in a different hand, representing the king's own signature.

Lines 70–74: *ayaṃ ca . . .* : The text from here to the end of the inscription is a later addition, written in very carelessly, so that the reading is uncertain in many places. (See also the translation notes on this portion.)

Translation

1. Success! May he [i.e., Viṣṇu] protect you, the lotus of whose navel was chosen by the Creator [i.e., Brahmā] as his dwelling [*dhāma*; see text notes]; and [may]

Hara [Śiva], whose head (*kam*) is adorned by the beautiful crescent moon, also [protect you]. [verse 1]
May it be well! There was

2. King Govindarāja, the founder of his own family and lineage, born in the immaculate line of the Rāṣṭrakūṭas, a master of generosity and a unique hero in battle. [v. 2]
His
3. army served merely for the trappings of a king, since he loved adventure and conquered with his own body alone. A wise man, he never bowed before any other, even among the immortals,
4. except for Śaṅkara, the Lord of all the gods. [v. 3]
As he desired a child, by the grace of Bhava (Śiva) was born to him a son who was a store of virtues, of noble repute,
5. and who bore, along with a multitude of nicknames, above all the beautiful principal appellation of "illustrious Karkkarāja." [v. 4]
When conversation happens to turn to ideal kingship,
6. Bali's used to be the model [*nidarśanaṃ;* see text notes] of a kingdom that brought fortune to all the people; but now on earth [the model of a kingdom] is this king's [Karkkarāja's]. [v. 5]
The people of the world thought it to be a great wonder,
7. that he has made the bull [of Dharma], which had become one-footed due to the Kali age, now once again four-footed and roaming
8. freely. [v. 6]
Nor is it any wonder that this he properly protected his subjects; for this was only to be expected of him, since Viṣṇu, who assiduously protects the world was always on his mind,
9. (and thus) his [Karkkarāja's] mind was the same as [Viṣṇu's]. [v. 7]
To that king who was the embodiment of the Dharma was born a son, Kṛṣṇarāja, who was just like him (*sadharmmā*). He
10. overthrew his kinsman who had taken to the wrong path, and ruled the kingdom himself for the benefit of his family. [v. 8]
Such was his piety for Brahmans that it caused even those who were Brahmans
11. by birth only to perform rites which were (previously) done (only) by those learned in the Veda, because of their desire for his gifts suitable for true Brahmans. [v. 9]
Just as, when a cloud gives forth rain beyond the wishes of the farmers,
12. they begin to wish for it to stop, so it was when he rained money on his servants. [v. 10]
13. This lion of a king, of mighty power, turned the great attacking boar, which was seized by a violent lust for battle and burning with the fire of bravery, into a deer. [v. 11]
14. That king caused to be constructed a temple [*kīrttanam*] of marvelous construction on Mount Elāpura, and named it thereafter [*tannāma*]. When the astonished gods behold it as they fly by in their aerial chariots,
15. they always speculate upon it at length, saying "This must be a natural abode of Śiva; for such beauty is never seen in an artificial (construction)";

16. even the artisan who created it was (himself) suddenly amazed, and said: "I cannot bring myself to endeavor to create such a thing again; how is it that I made this?" [vv. 12–13]
17. Although he was already adorned by such supremely marvelous ornaments as the stream of the Gaṅgā, the cool-rayed moon
18. and the Kālakūṭa poison, the (image of) Śambhu (Śiva) who stood there was further ornamented
19. by that (king) with all manner of wealth in rubies, gold, and the like. [v. 14]
    The noble son of that king was named Dhruvarāja,
20. the flame of whose might burned up his enemies with its power as if they had been turned into straw. [v. 15]
21. He always attained his ends by thinking for himself of productive ways to court the favor of Lakṣmī. But really, what is surprising about this?;
22. any man can keep his own wife under his control without the help of others. [v. 16]
    His son was Govindarāja, the very personification of Fame. By seizing from his enemies the Gaṅgā and Yamunā together, charming with their waves,
23. he attained to that supreme sovereignty (/to the head of the Lord [Śiva]) [both] in person and through a symbol;
24. and he filled the directions with his virtues which spread about (as if) their powers were not limited by a physical body. [v. 17]
25. When he smashed the fierce forces of all his enemies, this king stole away the glory even of the kings of old, whose endeavors had their influence in (only certain) regions. [v. 18]
26. In uprooting proud dynasties of kings and turning petty servants into mighty kings,
27. this emperor seemed to emulate the works of Fate, as he disposed according to his whim. [v. 19]
    In setting in an instant his enemies' feet in jangling elephant chains, he accomplished an amazing deed;
28. for not even Pārtha (Arjuna), the unique hero in the three worlds, slew his enemies so quickly. [v. 20]
29. The troop of elephants of his enemies which attacked him in battle were driven away by the many sharp swift arrows he shot at them, so that they imitated the continental mountains, swinging wildly in the winds that blow at the time of the destruction of an aeon. [v. 21]
30. His brother was the illustrious Indrarāja, King of the Earth, whose valor was equal to Indra's. The source of amazing glory, he was the ruler
31. of the territory of the King of Lāṭa which had been given to him by [Govindarāja]. [v. 22]
    Even today, out of fondness for his merits, the Gods, Kinnaras, Siddhas, Sādhyas, and
32. Vidyādhara lords sing of his glory which is as bright as the jasmine flower, each in their own abodes
33. with their hands placed on their consorts' breasts. [v. 23]

When the Gūrjjara king, with neck held high in his vainglory, attempted to attack him,

34. he [Indrarāja] singly sent him quickly fleeing in all directions like a deer; wherefore the circle of the great feudatories of the south, frightened and in disarray,
35. respectfully sought (his) protection when their wealth was being looted by Śrīvallabha. [v. 24]
His son is
36. the illustrious Kakkarāja, who has ever won renown for forcibly seizing the fortunes of all his vastly powerful enemies, who fulfills the wishes of his supplicants, and who
37. protects all the people of the world through his understanding of the meaning of the *śāstras*. [v. 25]
In his kingdom there dwells no thief; affliction by disease has died; there is no famine; delusion has (lost) its power;
38. disasters have ceased to occur; all evils have been wiped out; and every enemy has been chastened by his power. The cruel minds of the wicked, which are the curse of the learned man, no longer prevail. [v. 26]
39. Setting his [Karkkarāja's] (one) arm as a bar to the door of the directions against the powerful Gūrjjara Lord who has become overly proud because of his conquests of the King of Vaṅga and the Lord of Gauḍa,
40. and his other (arm) to protect the stricken Mālava, his Master enjoys the fruits of sovereignty. [v. 27]
Realizing that this life is [*empty] and as fleeting as the lightning [*and the wind], and that a gift of land
41. is the highest virtue, he [Karkkarāja] has instituted this pious donation. [v. 28]
And (so) this Lord of Lāṭa, the illustrious Karkkarājadeva Suvarṇavarṣa, who has won all the great titles and is master of great feudatories,
42. informs the provincial governors, territorial governors, village headmen, superintendents,
43. elders, and others, as far as they are concerned in the matter: Be it known to you, that from my residence at Siddhaśamī I have granted (*pratipāditaḥ*, l. 54),
44. in order to increase the glory and merit of my parents and myself in this and the next life, to the Brahman Bhānu, who has emigrated from Valabhī and who is a member of the *caturvedin* community there,
45. who belongs to the Vātsyayana *gotra* and is a student of the Mādhyandina (*śākhā*), and who is the son of Bhaṭṭasomāditya,
46. the village called Vaḍapadraka within the Aṅkoṭṭaka "Eighty-four," whose boundaries are (as follows): to the east,
47. Jambuvāvikā village; to the south, the tank called Mahāsenaka; to the west, Aṅkoṭṭaka; and to the north,
48. Vagghāccha village. This (village), so demarcated by these four boundaries, (is granted) together with the fixed tax, the additional tax,
49. the income resulting from storms and earthquakes, the fines for the ten offenses, the (right to) forced labor as the occasion may arise, and the tax in crops and cash;

50. it is free from interference by all royal officers, and is to remain (his property) as long as the moon and sun, the oceans and rivers and mountains (remain);
51. it is to be enjoyed by his sons and grandsons and their line, excepting (only) previous grants to gods and Brahmans, according to the law of the expropriation of land;
52. (dated) in the expired years of the Śaka kings, seven hundred plus thirty-four, on the full-moon day of the month of Vaiśākha, after bathing
53. and pouring out water. (The grant is made) for the continued performance (by the donee) of the five great sacrificial rites of *bali*, *caru*, *vaiśvadeva*, *agnihotra*, and *atithi*.
54. Wherefore, according to the appropriate law of grants to Brahmans, no one may interfere with anyone who is making use of (this land)
55. or allowing someone else to make use of it, who assigns it (to someone else), who plows it or causes anyone else to plow it. And future
56. [*kings] of our dynasty or of other (dynasties), recognizing that the [*fruits of] a gift of land are common (to all), and bearing in mind that riches are impermanent and as fleeting as lightning, and that life is as unstable as a drop of water on the tip of a blade of grass,
57. must respect and protect this grant of ours exactly as if it were their own. And anyone who, his mind being covered by the dark veil of ignorance,
58. might revoke or allow someone else to revoke [this grant], would be guilty of the five great sins and the five minor sins.
59. For thus it has been said by the Lord Vyāsa, the compiler of the Vedas:
"A giver of land dwells in heaven for sixty thousand years; [but] he who revokes it
60. or allows [another to revoke it] dwells for the same period in hell. [v. 29]
Those who revoke a grant of land are born as black snakes living in dry holes in the waterless wilderness of the Vindhya mountains. [v. 30]
61. Gold is the first child of Agni; Land is (born) of Viṣṇu; and cows are the offspring of Sūrya.
62. Therefore whoever would give gold, a cow, and land would give the three worlds. [v. 31]
The earth has been possessed by many kings from Sagara onward;
63. whomever the land belongs to at any time, his is its fruits at that time. [32]
The gifts that were given by kings of old produce glory, wealth, and righteousness;
64. (but) they are like the vomited leftovers of offerings; what righteous man would take them back? [v. 33]
O king, zealously protect the land which was given by you or by others;
65. O best of protectors of the earth, protection is (even) greater than giving. [v. 34]
Thus realizing that wealth and human life are as unstable as [*a drop of] water on a lotus leaf,
66. self-controlled men with completely pure hearts would not violate the glories [i.e., gifts] of others." [v. 35]
And also the Lord Rāmabhadra said:
67. "Over and over Rāmabhadra begs all the future kings: this bridge to the Dharma, which is common to all kings,

68. you must protect at all times." [v. 36]
The envoy in this [transaction] was the Rājaputra Dantivarman. Signed by me, the illustrious Kakkarāja, son of the illustrious Indrarāja, in my own hand.
69. This was written by me, Nemāditya, superintendent of the Office of the Supreme Commander of War and Peace, son of the noble Durgabhaṭa.
70. [Codicil:] This village [Vaḍapadraka] has been granted according to [the judgment of] the examiner [the records of?] of former kings to the *caturvedin* community of Aṃkoṭṭaka. The same person
71. has decided that, possession having been broken by an interruption caused by evil kings, it should be (granted) to some distinguished Brahman or other who is revered for his exceptional wisdom;
72. and he has [therefore] awarded [the village] which is being given [in this grant] by Suvarṇavarṣa [Govindarāja] to Bhānubhaṭṭa who resides in Vaṭapura (?). Taking *śālātāpya* (?) designated for the community of Tālāvarikas and others,
73. together with a gift of betel, the original town too (. . . designated ?) is to be used as it was obtained (?).
74. The foot of the supreme lord Śrīyāgeśvara knows that it is so.

Notes

Line 10: "his kinsman who had taken to the wrong path": The reference is to Kṛṣṇarāja's nephew Dantidurga, whom he overthrew.

Lines 10–11: "those who were Brahmans by birth only": For *viprā . . . kevalajātayo*, which Fleet renders as "those who were (*only*) once-born, (*becoming as it were*) *Brāhmaṇs*." This seems unlikely, as it would hardly be to Kṛṣṇārāja's credit that Brahmanical rites were performed by non-Brahmans under his auspices; while the restoration of fallen Brahmans to their former status was considered a highly virtuous act. Here, as occasionally elsewhere, Prinsep's (actually Chakravarti's) translation is more accurate: "those who were only nominally Bráhmanas."

Line 13: "the great . . . boar": The reference is to a king of the Cālukya line, hereditary enemy of the Rāṣṭrakūṭas, whose family crest was the boar.

Lines 14–16: "That king caused to be constructed . . .": I mostly follow the corrections of Fleet's translation suggested by Bhandarkar, taking *kīrttanam* as 'temple' and reading verses 12 and 13 together as a *yugalaka*, with *yad* and *yasya* referring to *kīrttanam*. Unlike Bhandarkar, however, I take *nāma* not as an adverb ('verily'), but as a noun referring to the temple which, it seems to be implied, was named after Elāpura (or perhaps after the architect?).

According to Bhandarkar (229), Elāpura is Elurā (Ellora) and the construction described here is "very likely" the famous Kailāsa temple there.

Line 19: "by that (king)": *yena*; Fleet translates "by means of it," evidently taking the relative pronoun to refer to the palace.

Line 23: "through a symbol" (*cihnanibhena*): Ronald Inden (*Imagining India* [Oxford: Basil Blackwell, 1990], 259) suggests that this refers to Dhruvarāja's [*sic;* actually Govindarāja's] bringing jars of water from the Gaṅgā and Yamunā back to his capital as an emblem of his universal sovereignty.

Line 25: "whose endeavors had their influence in (only certain) regions" (*pradeśavṛttivyasāyabhājāṃ*): Fleet translates "who applied themselves to travelling in foreign countries," which seems to miss the point. Unlike earlier kings whose influence extended over only certain regions (*pradeśa*), Govindarāja, in conquering *all* of his enemies, ruled over the entire world.

Line 35: "Śrīvallabha": According to Fleet (158) and Sircar (EI 35, 275) the reference is to the ruler of the principal Rāṣṭrakūṭa line of Mānyakheṭa, i.e., Karkkarāja's uncle Govinda III (l. 24).

Line 36: "fulfills the wishes of his supplicants": or perhaps "whose supplicants fill all the directions."

Line 40: "his Master": Probably his uncle Govindarāja [III] of the main Rāṣṭrakūṭa line (see note above on l. 35).

LIne 46: Vaḍapadraka: Modern Baroda (Vāḍodara); see EI 22, 80. "Aṅkoṭṭaka" is modern Akola, a part of Baroda (EI 38, 268).

Lines 48ff: "the fixed tax, the additional tax, the income resulting from storms and earthquakes," etc.: For the interpretation of these technical terms (*sodraṅgaḥ soparikaraḥ sabhūtavātapratyāyaḥ* . . .) see the entries in Sircar's *Indian Epigraphical Glossary*.

Line 70: "The same person" (*tenāpi*): Fleet translates "Therefore, also."

Line 71: "some distinguished Brahman or other": This translation is based on the assumption that the word "other" (*anyasya*) has been haplographically omitted; i.e., I read *vijñānavaramānyasy[*ānyasya] vā.* . . . Fleet, reading *vijñānavaram anyasya* . . . , translates "it should be the reward of learning of some excellent twice-born man." Note also the Marathi term *śrotriyamānya* 'Brahman land-grant' (BSOAS 20, 427), which may be related to this term. The translation of this passage, and of the codicil as a whole, is highly uncertain due to the very corrupt text.

Line 72: "Taking *śālātāpya* (?)": The meaning of this word is unknown; Fleet leaves it untranslated, commenting (165 n. 37), "The meaning of *śālātāpya* is not apparent." It could be a toponym, in which case we should perhaps read *śālātāpyāṃ* 'at Śālātapī.'

Line 72: Tālāvarikas: An official of some sort, probably a town superintendent or the like. See IEG s.v. *talavara*, *tālāvārika*, etc.

---

11. Tiruveṅkāḍu Temple Inscription (fig. 21)

Location	South wall of the shrine of the Śvetāraṇyeśvara temple at Tiruveṅkāḍu, Tanjore Dist., Tamil Nadu
Script	Grantha
Language	Sanskrit (verse)
Meter	*Sragdharā* (v. 1)
Type and format	Donative stone inscription
Purpose	Records the dedication by Mahādeva of a permanent lamp in the temple
Date	Thirty-ninth regnal year of Kullotuṅga Coḷa [I?] = A.D. 1108–9
Reference	E. Hultzsch, "Four Inscriptions of Kulottunga-Chola," EI 5, 1898–99, 103–6 (ins. B, 104).

Text

1. svast[i] śrīḥ / ā setor ā h[i]mādrer avati vasumatīṃ śrīkulo-
2. ttuṃgacoḷe nissīmnas tanmahimno jagati vitataye ta-
3. nnavattriṃśavarṣe [*/] saṃskṛtyājyārtham urvvīn dvijakulatila-
4. ko nittyadīpan nyadhatta śvetāraṇye śivāya kṣitividita-
5. mahādevanāmā vipaścit // maṅgalam mahāśrīḥ //

FIGURE 21. Tiruveṅkāḍu temple inscription. From EI 5, plate facing p. 104; copyright, Archaeological Survey of India.

Translation

1–5. Good luck [and] fortune! While the illustrious Kulottuṅga Coḷa was ruling the earth from Setu to the Himālayas, in order to spread his boundless grandeur in the world, in his thirty-ninth [regnal] year, the world-renowned wise man named Mahādeva, an ornament to the family of Brahmans, dedicated to Śiva in the Śvetāraṇya [temple] an eternal lamp, after consecrating land for the (supply of) ghee. [May it be] auspicious [and] most fortunate!

Notes

Line 1: Setu: "The Bridge," i.e., "Adam's Bridge" between India and Sri Lanka.

Line 3: "after consecrating land for the (supply of) ghee": I.e., the donor also granted an area of land as a permanent endowment providing revenue to pay for the ghee to be burned in the lamp.

Line 4: Śvetāraṇya: This is the Sanskrit equivalent of the Tamil Tiruveṅkāḍu, "the White Forest."

---

12. Nālandā Inscription of Vipulaśrīmitra (fig. 22)

Location	Monastery no. VII at Nālandā, Patna Dist., Bihar
Script	Proto-Bengali
Language	Sanskrit (verse)

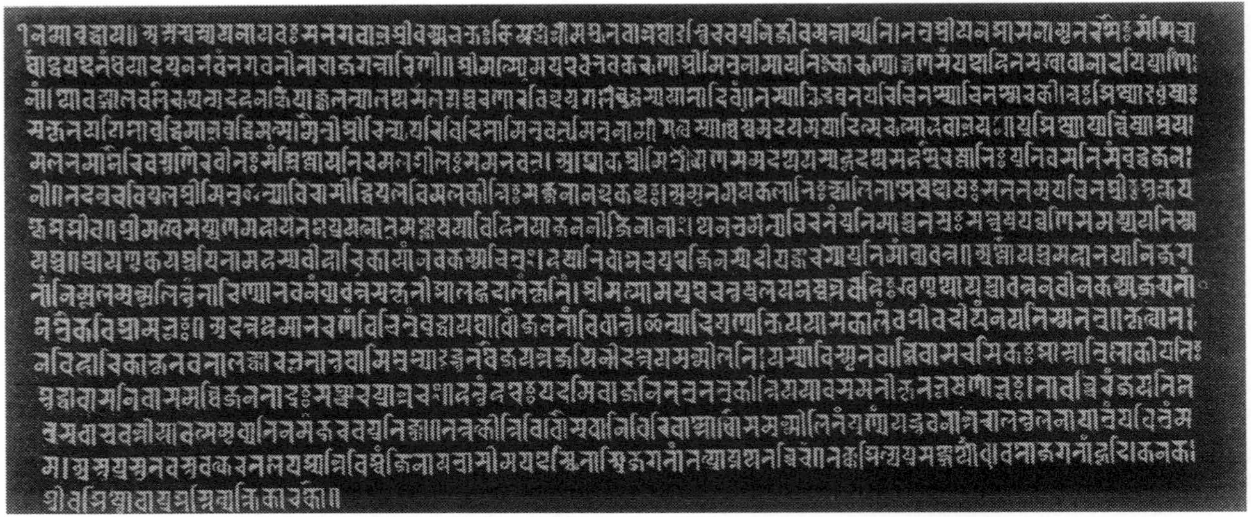

FIGURE 22. Nālandā inscription of Vipulaśrīmitra. From EI 21, plate facing p. 98; copyright, Archaeological Survey of India.

Meters *Śārdūlavikrīḍita* (vv. 1, 2, 8, 10, 12); *mandākrāntā* (3); *śikhariṇī* (4); *mālinī* (5); *vasantatilakā* (6, 11); *indravajrā* (7); *upajāti* (9); *anuṣṭubh* (13)

Type and format Donative stone *praśasti*

Purpose Records the foundation of a monastery and various other pious donations by the Buddhist monk Vipulaśrīmitra

Date None given; ca. first half of twelfth century A.D. on paleographic grounds according to Majumdar (97), but ca. 1060 according to Ghosh

References N. G. Majumdar, "Nalanda Inscription of Vipulasrimitra," EI 21, 1931–32, 97–101; Jogendra Chandra Ghosh, "The Date of the Nālandā Inscription of Vipulaśrīmitra," *Indian Culture* 1, 1934, 291–2.

Text

1. Oṃ namo buddhāya //
astu svastyayanāya vaḥ sa bhagavān śrīdharmmacakraḥ kiyad
yannāma śrutavān bhavo 'sthiravapur nirjīvam uttāmyati /
tatra śrīghanaśāsanāmṛtarasaiḥ saṃsicya
2. bauddhe pade
taṃ dheyād apunarbhavaṃ bhagavatī tārā jagattāriṇī // [*1]
śrīmatsomapure vabhu[*read* bhū]va karuṇāśrīmitranāmā yatiḥ
kāruṇyād guṇasampado hitasukhādhānād api prāṇi-
3. nāṃ /
yo vaṅgālavalair upetya dahanakṣepāj jvalaty ālaye
saṃlagnaś caraṇāravindayugale buddhasya yāto divam // [*2]
tasyācchidravrataparicitasyocitasmerakīrtteḥ
śiṣyo 'dhṛṣyaḥ
4. sukṛtaghaṭito buddhimān buddhimatsu /
maitrīśrīr ity upari vidito mitravat[*sic*] mitranāmā
[sa]tvasyārthe svam udayam upāditsur utsāhavān yaḥ // [*3]
praśiṣyo py anviṃ[*read* nvi]ṣyāśraya-
5. m alabhamānair iva guṇair
adhītaḥ saṃśliṣṭo yatir amalaśīlaḥ samabhavat /
aśokaśrīmi[tro] guṇasamudaye yasya hṛdaye
sahasrair aṣṭābhiḥ prativasati saṃbuddhajana-
6. nī // [*4]
tadanu ca vipulaśrīmitra ity āvirāsīd
vipulavimalakīrttiḥ sajjanānandakandaḥ /
amṛtamayakalābhiḥ kṣālitāśeṣadoṣaḥ
satatam upacitaśrīḥ śuklapa-
7. kṣe śaśīva // [*5]
śrīmatkhasarppaṇamahāyatane prayatnāt[*sic*]
mañjūṣayā vihitayā jananī jinānāṃ /
yena bhramaty aviratam pratimāś catasraḥ
sattreṣu parvvaṇi samarppayati sma

8. yaś ca // [*6]
coyaṇḍake yaś ca pitāmahasya
vīhārikāyāṃ navakarmma citraṃ /
harṣābhidhāne ca pure jinasya
dīpaṅkarasya pratimāṃ vyadhatta // [*7]
aṣṭau yaś ca mahābhayāni jaga-
9. tāṃ nirmūlam unmūlituṃ
tāriṇyā bhavanaṃ vyadhatta sukṛtī śālahradālaṃkṛtiṃ /
śrīmatsomapure caturṣu layaneṣv antarvahiḥkhaṇḍayor
yaś cādhatta navīnakarmma jagatāṃ
10. netraikaviśrāmabhūḥ // [*8]
adatta hemābharaṇaṃ vicitraṃ
buddhāya bodhau janatāṃ vidhātuṃ /
ityādipuṇyakriyayā sa kālaṃ
vaśīva dīrghaṃ nayati sma tatra // [*9]
kṛtvā te-
11. na vihārikā kṛtavatālaṃkārabhūtā bhuvo
mitrebhyo 'dbhutavaijayantajayinī datteyam unmīlati /
yasyāṃ vismṛtavān nivāsarasikaḥ śāstā trilokīpatiḥ
12. śuddhāvāsanivāsam arthijanatāduḥsañcaraprāntaraṃ // [*10]
hartuṃ hareḥ padam ivājani tatra tatra
kīrttir yayā vas[u]matī kṛtabhūṣaṇā bhūḥ /
tāvac ciraṃ jayati ne-
13. trasudhā sravantī
yāvat samṛdhyati na maṃjuravapratijñā // [*11]
tattatkīrttividhau sudhānidhir ivāmbodhau samunmīlitaṃ
puṇyaṃ yad bhuvanāntarālatulanāpātraṃ pavitraṃ ma-
14. ma /
astu prastutavastuvat karatale paśyanti viśvaṃ jinā
yatrāsīmapade sthitās trijagatāṃ tatprāptaye tac ciraṃ // [*12]
tarkkaśilpaprasaṅge yau dhāvato jagatāṃ hṛdi /
kanaka-
15. śrīr vaśiṣṭho vā praśastivyaktikārakau // [*13]

Notes

Line 2: *prāṇi-*: The division of the word at the end of the line is indicated by two short vertical lines, one above the other. Similarly at the ends of lines 4, 5, 10, and 14; but word breaks are not indicated in lines 6, 8, 12, and 13.

Line 9: *bhavanaṃ . . . śālahradālaṃkṛtiṃ*: *bhavana-* is evidently treated here as masculine, which is permissible by Pāṇini 2.4.31 (*ardharcādigaṇa*, no. 203).

Translation

1. Oṃ! Homage to the Buddha.
May that Glorious Lord, (who is) the Wheel of the Dharma, provide for your well-being: hearing his name so many times, the body of Saṃsara (*bhava*) grows

weak and he swoons lifelessly. There at the Buddha's foot let the Lady Tārā, Savior of the world, besprinkle him with drops of the elixir of Śrīghana's (Buddha's) teaching,

2. and thus render him free of future births (*apunarbhavaṃ*). [verse 1] There was in the excellent Somapura an ascetic who was known as Karuṇāśrīmitra on account of his compassion, his wealth of virtues, and his bestowal of happiness and benefit upon (all) creatures.
3. When the armies of Bengal came and set fire to his residence, even as it burned he clung to the lotus-feet of the Buddha, and (so) went to heaven. [v. 2] He who was known for his unbroken vows [Karuṇāśrīmitra] had a disciple called Maitrīśrī, known on high, like the Sun, by the name Mitra [i.e., Maitrīśrīmitra]. He was unshakable; his glory was fittingly bright;
4. he was engaged in good deeds; he was a wise man among the wise; and he energetically undertook his own rising for the sake of (all) being(s). [v. 3] And his [Karuṇāśrīmitra's] disciple's disciple was Aśokaśrīmitra, an ascetic of unblemished character;
5. the virtues, so it seemed, seeking but not finding a resting place, (finally) learned of him and embraced him. In his heart, which was (thus) a storehouse of virtues, dwells the Mother of the Buddhas in eight thousand (verses). [v. 4]
6. After him there appeared Vipulaśrīmitra of vast (*vipula*) and immaculate glory, a source of joy to good people. Like the moon in the bright fortnight, his fortunes increased steadily as he wiped away all sins (/eliminated all darkness) with his divine talents (/digits made of nectar). [v. 5]
7. In the casket which he piously provided, the Mother of the Jinas turns unceasingly in the great temple of the illustrious Khasarpaṇa; and he donated four images for the alms-houses on the occasion of a festival. [v. 6]
8. He also endowed excellent repairs in the monastery of Pitāmaha (Buddha) at Coyaṇḍaka, and an image of the Jina Dīpaṇkara in the town called Harṣa. [v. 7] And in order to tear out by the roots the eight great terrors of the world,
9. this doer of good deeds endowed a temple of Tāriṇī (Tārā) ornamented with a courtyard and a tank; and at Somapura he who was the sole cynosure for the eyes of the world endowed renovations of the inner and outer sections of the four dwelling areas. [v. 8]
10. In order to turn the populace toward enlightenment, he gave to the Buddha a wondrous gold ornament. Like an ascetic, he passed a long time there [at Somapura] in these and other such pious acts. [v. 9]
11. This monastery which this accomplished man built and dedicated to the Mitras blazes forth as an ornament of the world, outshining the marvelous Vaijayanta [Indra's palace]. In it, the Teacher, Lord of the Three Worlds [i.e., the Buddha], who cherishes (a proper) residence, forgot
12. his dwelling in the Śuddhāvāsa heaven, the long road to which is hard for his supplicants to traverse. [v. 10] (His) glory was born in these various places, as if to steal away the rank of Hari; and the Earth with all its riches is decorated by it.
13. It (will) continue to spread victoriously, a salve to the eyes, until the vow of Mañjurava shall be fulfilled. [v. 11]

The pure merit which accrued to me [i.e., Vipulaśrīmitra] from these various acts of glory, like a flood of nectar from the ocean, can be measured [only] by comparison with the distances between the worlds;

14. may it be for the attainment by the three worlds of that infinite place where the Jinas sit and behold the universe as if it were in the palm of their hands (*prastutavastuvat*). [v. 12]

Kanakaśrī and Vaśiṣṭha, who distinguish themselves (*dhāvato*, lit. 'run') in the hearts of men in matters of logic and the arts, are [respectively] the composer and presenter [i.e., engraver] of (this) eulogy. [v. 13]

Notes

Line 1: "Saṃsāra (*bhava*)": *bhava* alternatively (or simultaneously) might be taken as referring to Śiva; cf. the polemic reference to Hari (Viṣṇu) in v. 11. Note also the *virodhābhāsa* (rhetorical contradiction) in *bhavo . . . apunarbhavaṃ*.

Line 2: "known as Karuṇāśrīmitra . . .": The three ablative phrases in *pāda* b of v. 2 provide etymological explanations for the three parts of his name, *karuṇā* 'compassion', *śrī* 'wealth/glory', and *mitra* 'friend', respectively.

Line 3–4 [v. 3]: "like the Sun . . . unshakable . . . ," etc.: *[a]dhṛṣyaḥ*, like all the adjectives in this verse, is doubly applicable to Maitrīśrīmitra and to the sun. For example, *sukṛtaghaṭito* with reference to the Sun means "created by a skillful act," referring to the myth of Viśvakarma's fashioning the Sun on his lathe; *buddhimān buddhimatsu* may be rendered as "he who is awake among those who are awake(ned)," and so on.

Line 5: "In his heart . . . dwells the Mother of the Buddhas in eight thousand (verses)": That is to say, he had memorized the *Aṣṭasāhasrikā Prajñāpāramitā*, known as "Mother of the Buddhas."

Line 6: "Like the moon in the bright fortnight": all the epithets in the verse apply punningly to both Vipulaśrīmitra and to the waxing moon.

Line 7: "the Mother of the Jinas turns unceasingly": the reference is evidently to a ritual turning or procession of the *Prajñāpāramitā* manuscript (contra Majumdar, 100 n. 3).

Line 9: "he who was the sole cynosure for the eyes of the world": Majumdar takes the epithet *jagatāṃ netraikaviśrāmabhūḥ* (ll. 9–10) as referring to the renovation: "—(*a work*) in which alone the eyes of the world found repose." But this is grammatically impossible, as the epithet must refer to the subject, namely, the donor Vipulaśrīmitra.

Line 11: "dedicated to the Mitras": This presumably refers to a declaration by Vipulaśrīmitra of his intention to share the merit of his foundation with the other members of the Mitra lineage.

Line 13: "the vow of Mañjurava": I.e., Mañjurava's (Mañjuśrī) vow to remain a Bodhisattva until all beings are enlightened.

Line 14: "that infinite place": I.e., *Sukhāvatī* (Majumdar, 101 n. 5).

---

13. Pilgrim Inscription on the Kosam Pillar (fig. 23)

Location On the Mauryan pillar at Kosam (Kauśāmbī), Allahabad Dist., UP

Script Devanāgarī with informal orthography (e.g., *ṣ* regularly written for *kha*)

Language: Eastern Hindi (prose)

Type and format: Stone pilgrims' record

Purpose: Records the names of some goldsmiths and invokes the blessing of Bhairava (Śiva) upon them

Date: [Vikrama] Saṃvat 1621, fifth day of the dark half of Caitra, probably = February 20, A.D. 1565

Reference: F. E. Pargiter, "Two Records on the Pillar at Kosam," EI 11, 1911–12, 87–92 (ins. B, 89–92).

Text

1. Śrīgaṇesaḥ vānāna ya nāgarika sonī
2. muṣadarpana darpana sonīnha kau

FIGURE 23. Pilgrim inscription on the Kosam pillar. From EI 11, plate facing p. 87; copyright, Archaeological Survey of India.

3. [deva] bhairava
4. saṃbata 1621 samaai nāma cai[tra] va[dī]
5. paṃcami liṣīte laṣimnu [sonā]rā
6. vaiïsnava[*sic*] a[*sic*]na[nda]suta virti
7. kausaṃvipurī la[kh?]imīdāsa tathā
8. ṣemakrapana laghu bhāï
9. te[nha] ke puruṣa pachīle
10. [nanīgu] sonī
11. mahesada[*sic*]sa sonī
12. [ho]rīla sonī
13. camanda sonī
14. ratanu sonī
15. caṃdile sonī ke put   4   dhane vaisnava
16. ama[du] rāmadāsa   karame vaisna[va]
17. laṣimī[d]āsa   manā vaisnava
18. [vasaṃ]tarāma   anadu vaisnava

Notes

Line 1: *vānāna*: Here as throughout the inscription the character for *va* is written, although the pronunciation was probably *ba*. The final *a*-s were probably not pronounced.

Lines 1–3: The entire passage (expect perhaps for *Śrīgaṇesaḥ*) appears to have been added later, above the rest of the inscription, as the lines curve up toward the right.

Line 2: *muṣa-*: I.e., *mukha-*. (See also translation notes.)

Line 3: *[deva] bhairava*: Here and elsewhere the word-final *va* is marked with a diacritic dot below, presumably indicating a pronunciation as *w* or *o* rather than *b* (cf. note 1 here, and Pargiter, 90).

Line 7: *la[kh?]imīdāsa*: The second syllable is evidently neither the expected *ṣa* nor the Sanskritic *kṣa*. Pargiter (90) notes that it resembles a Bengali *kha*.

Line 10: *[nanīgu]*: The reading is uncertain; Pargiter reads *nalīgu*, but suggests this reading and other possibilities in his note (92 n. 9).

Line 15: *4 dhane vaisnava*: This and the three names below it in the following lines appear to have been added to the original list of names. They seem to specify the names of the four sons of Caṃdila.

Translation

1. Lord Gaṇeśa. The goldsmiths of the city made this.

2–3. May the God Bhairava show his mirror-like [?] face to the goldsmiths.

4–6. Saṃvat 1621; at this time, namely, the fifth of the dark half of Caitra, [this was] written [by] the goldsmith Laṣimnu Vaisnava [i.e., Lakṣmaṇa Vaiṣṇava], Virti son of Ananda [i.e., Ānanda],

7. Lakhimīdāsa [Lakṣmīdāsa] of the town of Kauśāmbī, and

8. Ṣemakrapana [Kṣemakṛpaṇa?] his younger brother.

9. Their fellows after (them):

10. the goldsmith Nanīgu(?),

11. the goldsmith Mahesadasa [Maheśadāsa],

12. the goldsmith Horīla,

13. the goldsmith Camanda,
14. the goldsmith Ratanu,

15–18. the four sons of the goldsmith Caṃdila (Dhane Vaisnava, Karame Vaisnava, Manā Vaisnava, Anadu Vaisnava), Amadu, Rāmadāsa, Laṣimīdāsa [Lakṣmīdāsa], [and] Vasaṃtarāma (?).

Notes

Line 2: "May the God Bhairava show his mirror-like [?] face": The precise sense here is unclear. I tentatively follow Pargiter (90) in taking the second *darpana* as a dittographic error for *darśān* (imperative), = Hindi *darśāẽ*.

Line 5: "[this was] written": *liṣīte* = Skt. *likhita[m]*. Pargiter (90) takes the word as = Hindi *likhte* used for the present plural.

Lines 5–6: "the goldsmith Laṣimnu Vaisnava": The connections of the epithets with the names in this and the following passage are often uncertain; Pargiter takes *vaisnava* with Virti.

Lines 7–8: "and Ṣemakrapana his younger brother": Pargiter translates "of the same town the brothers Khēma-kṛipaṇ (*and*) Laghu."

---

14. Burhānpūr Inscription of Edala-Śāha (Ādil Shāh) (fig. 24)

Location	In the Jum'a Masjid, Burhānpūr, Nimar Dist., MP
Script	Devanāgarī
Language	Sanskrit (verse and prose)
Meters	*Anuṣṭubh* (vv. 1–2); *upajāti* (3–4); *śārdūlavikrīḍita* (5)
Type and format	Donative stone inscription; written in raised letters, in the Islamic fashion, rather than incised as in most Indic inscriptions
Purpose	Records the construction of the Mosque by Ādil Shāh
Date	[Vikrama] Saṃvat 1646/Śāka 1511, cyclical year Virodhin, eleventh day (*tithi*) of the bright half of Pauṣa, Monday, = January 5, A.D. 1590
Reference	Hira Lal, "Burhanpur Sanskrit Inscription of Adil Shah. Samvat 1646," EI 9, 1907–8, 306–10.

Text

1. Śrīsṛṣṭikartre nra[*read* na]maḥ /
avyatka[*read* kta]ṃ vyāpakaṃ nityaṃ guṇātītaṃ cidātmakaṃ [/*]
dyatka[*read* vyakta]sya kāraṇaṃ vaṃde vyaktāvyaktaṃ tam īśvaraṃ // 1 //
yāvaccandrārkkatārā-

2. disthitiḥ syād aṃbarāṃgaṇai[*read* ṇe] [/*]
tāvat phārukivaṃśo sau ciraṃ naṃdatu bhūtale // 2 //
vaṃśe tha tasmin kila phārukīṃdro
vabhūva rājā malikābhidhānaḥ [/*]
tasyābhavat sūnu-

FIGURE 24. Burhānpūr inscription of Edala-Śāha (Ādil Shāh). From EI 9, plate facing p. 308; copyright, Archaeological Survey of India.

3. r udāracetāḥ
kulāvataṃso gajanīnareśaḥ // 3 //
tasmād abhūt kesarakhānavīraḥ
putras tadīyo hasanakṣitīśaḥ [/*]
tasmād abhūd edalaśāhabhūpaḥ
putro bhavat tasya mubārakheṃdraḥ // 4 //
4. tatsūnuḥ kṣitipālamaulimukuṭavyāghṛṣṭapādāmbujaḥ
satkīrttir vilasatpratāpavaśagāmitraḥ kṣitīśeśvaraḥ [/*]
yasyāharniśam ānatir guṇagaṇātīte pare vrahmaṇi
śrīmān edalabhūpati-
5. r vijayaṃ[*read* ya]te bhūpālacūḍāmaṇiḥ // 5 //
svasti śrī saṃvat 1646 varṣe śākre[*read* ke] 1511 virodhisaṃvatsare

pauṣamāse śuklapakṣe 10 ghaṭī 23 sahaikādaśyāṃ tithau some [kṛ]ttikā ghaṭī 33 rāha [*read* saha?] rohi-

6. ṇyāṃ śubha ghaṭī 42 yoge vaṇijakaraṇe smin dine rātrigataghaṭī 11 samaye kanyālagna śrīmubārakhaśāhasutaśrī 7 edalaśāha-rājñī[*read* jñā?] masītir iyaṃ nirmitā svadharmapālanārthaṃ //

Notes

Line 2: *-ādisthitiḥ*: Hira Lal reads *-ādi kṣitiḥ*.

Line 6: *-rājñī*: This is the reading in Hira Lal's text (perhaps a misprint?); the photograph is not sufficiently clear to check it, but the context seems to demand *-rājñā* (though this is not strictly correct grammatically, *-rājena* being the preferred form).

Translation

1. Homage to the Holy Creator.
   I praise that Lord, who is both manifest and unmanifest: (who, as) the unmanifest, is pervasive, eternal, beyond all qualities, and composed of consciousness, and [yet is] the cause of what is manifest. [v. 1]
   As long as the moon and sun and stars shall stand
2. in the firmament of the heavens, so long may this Phāruki [Fārūqī] dynasty rejoice upon the earth. [v. 2]
   In this line there was a Phāruki Lord named Rājā Malika. His son was
3. the noble-minded King Gajanī [Ghaznī], an ornament to his family. [v. 3]
   From him was born the mighty Kesarakhāna [Kaisar Khān]. His son was King Hasana [Hasan Khān]. From him was born King Edala-Śāha [Ādil Shāh], and his son was Lord Mubārakha [Mubārak]. [v. 4]
4. His son was the glorious Lord of Kings, King Edala, of great fame, whose lotus-feet are rubbed by the crowns on the heads of kings, and whose enemies are under the sway of his glorious might. Day and night he bows before the Supreme Brahmā, beyond all qualities;
5. victorious is this crown jewel among lords of the earth! [v. 5]
   Good luck [and] fortune! In the [Vikrama] Saṃvat year 1646, the Śaka [year] 1511, the Virodhin year [of the cycle of Jupiter], in the bright half of the month of Pauṣa, [*tithi*] 10 [for] 23 *ghaṭī*s, and on the eleventh *tithi*, a Monday, [in] Kṛttikā, [for] 33 *ghaṭī*s together with (?)
6. Rohiṇī [in] the Śubha *yoga* [for] 42 *ghaṭī*s, in the Vaṇija *karaṇa*; on this day, at the moment of the 11th *ghaṭī* of the night, [in] the Kanyā *lagna*, this mosque was constructed by the seven-times illustrious King Edala-Śāha, son of the illustrious Mubārakha Śāha, for the protection of his religion.

Notes

Line 1: "I praise that Lord," etc.: Note that this invocatory verse is so phrased as to be acceptable to both Muslim and Hindu beliefs.

Line 5: *ghaṭī*: A measure of time, equivalent to 24 minutes.

15. Pabhosā Jaina Inscription (fig. 25)

Location	In the Dharmaśālā in Pabhosā, Allahabad Dist., UP
Script	Devanāgarī
Language	Sanskrit (prose)
Type and format	Dedicatory stone inscription (Jaina)
Purpose	Records the dedication of a Jaina image by one Hīrālāl
Date	[Vikrama] Saṃvat 1881, Friday, sixth day of the bright half of Mārgaśīrṣa = November 26, A.D. 1824
Reference	A. Führer, "Pabhosâ Inscriptions," EI 2, 1894, 240–4 (no. III, 243–4).

Text

1. saṃvat 1881 mite mārgaśīrṣaścu[*read* śu]klasaṣṭhyāṃ śru[*read* śu]kravāsa-
2. re kāṣṭhāsaṃghe māthuragache puṣkaragaṇe lohācāryāmnāye

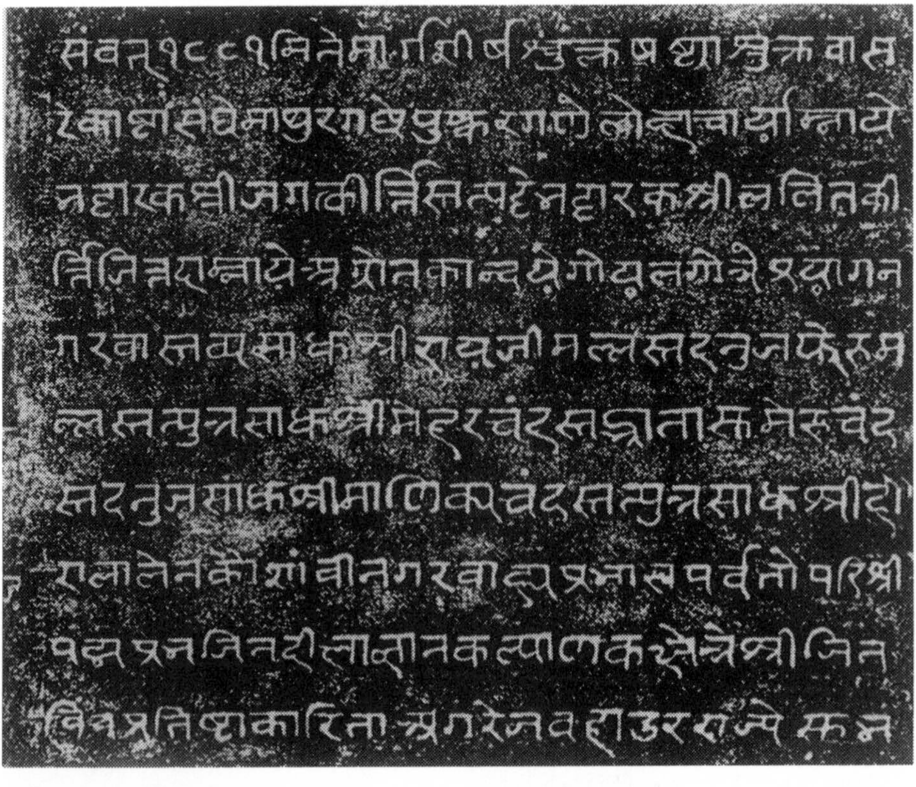

FIGURE 25. Pabhosā Jaina inscription. From EI 2, plate facing p. 244; copyright, Archaeological Survey of India.

3. bhaṭṭārakaśrījagatkīrttis [/*] tatpaṭṭe bhaṭṭārakaśrīlalitakī-
4. rttijit [*/] tadāmnāye agrotakānvaye goyalagotre prayāgana-
5. garavāstavyasādhuśrīrāyajīmallas [/*] tadanujapheruma-
6. llas [/*] tatputrasādhuśrīmeharacaṃdas [/*] tadbhrātā sumerucaṃda-
7. s [/*] tadanujasādhuśrīmāṇikyacaṃdas [/*] tatputrasādhuśrīhī-
8. rālālena kauśāṃvīnagarabāhyaprabhāsaparvatopariśrī-
9. padmaprabhajinadīkṣājñā(?)nakalpā[*read* lyā]ṇaka[kṣe]tre śrījina-
10. viṃvapratiṣṭhā kāritā aṃgarejavahādurarājye [*/] su[*read* śu]bhaṃ [//*]

Translation

1. Year 1881, dated (*mite*) the sixth (*tithi*) of the bright fortnight of Mārgaśīrṣa, Friday:

2–3. In the Puṣkara group of the Māthura branch of the Kāṣṭhā community (which is) in the tradition of Lohācārya, [there was] the illustrious cleric Jagatkīrti;

3–5. in his line was the illustrious cleric Lalitakīrttijit; in his tradition (and) in the Agrotaka lineage (and) Goyala *gotra* was the illustrious worthy Rāyajī Malla, a resident of the city of Prayāga; his younger brother was Pheru Malla;

6. his son was the illustrious worthy Meher Cand; his brother was Sumeru Cand;

7. his younger brother was the illustrious worthy Māṇikya Cand; his son, the illustrious worthy Hīrā Lāl,

8–9. in the place of the auspicious event (*kalyāṇaka*) of the consecration and omniscience (?) of the illustrious Jina Padmaprabha atop Mount Prabhāsa outside the city of Kauśāṃbi,

10. dedicated an image of the illustrious Jina, during the reign of the mighty British (*aṃgareja-vahādura-*). May it be well!

Bibliography

This bibliography includes all books and monographs cited in this book that are primarily or significantly concerned with epigraphic and related matters. A selection of other important epigraphic works is also included, in the interests of presenting an overall summary of available materials. (Cf. "Note on Citation and Bibliographic Form," p. xxi). This bibliography is not, however, intended to be comprehensive, as such a compilation would go far beyond the limits of space available here.

For the most part, journal articles and other nonindependent publications are not included, but some exceptions have been made for items of special significance.

As far as possible, full bibliographic citation is given for each item. In certain cases, however, such as books which have had several editions or printings, only the principal publications are given. Recent reprint editions, mostly from India, of earlier publications are listed insofar as the data are readily available, but due to the difficulties of access and documentation for such publications the listings may not be complete.

Abhilekha-saṃgraha. 12 parts. Kāṭhmāṇḍaū: Saṃśodhana Maṇḍala, Vikrama 2018–20.

Agrawal, Jagannath. *Researches in Indian Epigraphy and Numismatics.* Delhi: Sundeep Prakashan, 1986.

Alsdorf, Ludwig. *Aśokas Separatedikte von Dhauli and Jaugaḍa.* Abhandlungen der Akademie der Wissenschaften und der Literatur, Mainz, Geistes- und Sozialwissenschaftlichen Klasse, 1962.1. Wiesbaden: Franz Steiner Verlag, 1962.

———. *Kleine Schriften.* Edited by Albrecht Wezler. Glasenapp-Stiftung, vol. 10. Wiesbaden: Franz Steiner Verlag, 1974.

Andersen, Paul Kent. *Studies in the Minor Rock Edicts of Aśoka.* Vol. 1: *Critical Edition.* Freiburg: Hedwig Falk, 1990.

Asher, Frederick M., and G. S. Gai, eds. *Indian Epigraphy: Its Bearing on the History of Art* [IEBHA]. New Delhi: Oxford University Press and IBH/American Institute of Indian Studies, 1985.

Bahadur, Mutua, and Paonam Gunindra Singh. *Epigraphical Records of Manipur.* Vol. 1. Imphal: Mutua Museum, 1986.

Banerjee, R. D. *The Origin of the Bengali Script.* Calcutta: University of Calcutta, 1919. Reprint, Calcutta: Nababharat, 1973.

Barth, A., and Abel Bergaigne. *Inscriptions sanscrites du Cambodge.* 2 fascicles. Notices et Extraits des Manuscrits de la Bibliothèque Nationale et autres Bibliothèques, vol. 27, part 1 (pp. 1–180 and 293–588). Paris: Imprimerie Nationale, 1885–93.

Barua, Benimadhab. *Old Brāhmī Inscriptions in the Udayagiri and Khaṇḍagiri Caves.* Calcutta: University of Calcutta, 1929.

Barua, Benimadhab, and Kumar Gangananda Sinha. *Barhut Inscriptions.* Calcutta: University of Calcutta, 1926.

Basham, A. L., ed. *Papers on the Date of Kaniṣka Submitted to the Conference on the Date of Kaniṣka, London, 20–22 April, 1960.* Australian National University Centre of Oriental Studies Oriental Monograph Series, vol. 4. Leiden: E. J. Brill, 1968.

Bemmann, Martin and Ditte König. *Die Felsbildstation Oshibat.* Materialen zur Archäologie der Nordgebiete Pakistans 1. Mainz: Philipp von Zabern, 1994.

Bendrey, V. S. *A Study of Muslim Inscriptions with Special Reference to the Inscriptions Published in the Epigraphia Indo-Moslemica 1907–38 Together with Summaries of Inscriptions Chronologically Arranged.* Bombay: Karnataka Publishing House, 1944. Reprint, Delhi: Anmol, 1985.

Bergaigne, Abel. *Inscriptions sanscrites de Campā.* Edited by A. Barth. Notices et Extraits des Manuscrits de la Bibliothèque Nationale et autres Bibliothèques, vol. 27, part 1, fasc. 2 (pp. 181–292). Paris: Bibliothèque Nationale, 1893.

Bhandarkar, Devadatta Ramakrishna. *Inscriptions of the Early Gupta Kings.* Edited by Bahadurchand Chhabra and Govind Swamirao Gai. Corpus Inscriptionum Indicarum, vol. 3 (revised). New Delhi: Archaeological Survey of India, 1981.

———. *A List of the Inscriptions of Northern India in Brahmi and Its Derivative Scripts, from About 200 A.C.* Appendix to EI 19–23, 1927/28–1935/36.

Bhaṭṭācārya, Padmanātha. *Kāmarūpaśāsanāvalī.* Raṅgpur: Raṅgapura Sāhitya Pariṣat, 1931.

Bhattacharya, Gouriswar, ed. *Deyadharma. Studies in Memory of Dr. D. C. Sircar.* Sri Garib Dass Oriental Series, no. 33. Delhi: Sri Satguru Publications, 1986.

Bhattacharya, Kamaleswar. "Recherches sur le vocabulaire des inscriptions sanskrites du Cambodge." BEFEO 52, 1964, 1–72 + supplements in BEFEO 53, 1966, 273–7, and 55, 1969, 145–51. Revised ed.: Publications de l'École Française d'Extrême-Orient 167. Paris: École Française d'Extrême-Orient, 1991.

———. *Les Religions brahmaniques dans l'ancien Cambodge d'après l'épigraphie et l'iconographie.* Publications de l'École Française d'Extrême-Orient, vol. 49. Paris: École Française d'Extrême-Orient, 1961.

Bhattacharyya, A. K. *A Corpus of Dedicatory Inscriptions from Temples of West Bengal (c. 1500 A.D. to c. 1800 A.D.).* Calcutta: Navana, 1982.

Bloch, Jules. *Les Inscriptions d'Asoka.* Collection Emile Senart, vol. 8. Paris: Société d'Édition "Les Belles Lettres," 1950.

Boyer, A. M., E. J. Rapson, and E. Senart. *Kharoṣṭhī Inscriptions Discovered by Sir Aurel Stein in Chinese Turkestan* [KI]. 3 parts (part 3 by Rapson and P. S. Noble). Oxford: Clarendon Press, 1920/1927/1929.

Brough, John. *The Gāndhārī Dharmapada* [GD]. London Oriental Series, vol. 7. London: Oxford University Press, 1962.

Bühler, Georg. *Die indische Inschriften und das Alter der indischen Kunstpoesie.* Sitzungsberichte der kaiserlichen Akademie der Wissenschaften, Wien, Philologisch-historische Classe 122, no. 11, 1890. English translation: V. S. Ghate, "The Indian Inscriptions and the Antiquity of Indian Artificial Poetry," IA 42, 1913, 29–32, 137–48, 172–9, 188–93, 230–4, 243–9. Reprint of English translation, Calcutta: University of Calcutta, 1970.

———. *Indische Palaeographie von circa 350 A. Chr.–circa 1300 P. Chr.* [BIP]. Grundriss der indo-arischen Philologie und Altertumskunde, I.2. Strassburg: K. J. Trübner, 1896. English translation by J. F. Fleet, *Indian Paleography from About B.C. 350 to About A.D. 1300:* Appendix to *Indian Antiquary* 33, 1904. [Page citations in this book refer to this edition.] Several reprints of English version: Calcutta: Indian Studies Past and Present, 1962; New Delhi: Today & Tomorrow's Printers and Publishers, 1973; New Delhi: Orient Books, 1980.

———. *On the Origin of the Indian Brāhma Alphabet* (*Indian Studies No. III*) [OIBA]. Sitzungsberichte der kaiserlichen Akademie der Wissenschaften, Wien, Philologisch-historische Classe 132, no. 5, 1895. 2d rev. ed.: Strassburg: Karl J. Trübner, 1898. Reprint, The Chowkhamba Sanskrit Studies, vol. 33. Varanasi: The Chowkhamba Sanskrit Series Office, 1963.

———. "The Origin of the Kharoṣṭhī Alphabet" [OKA]. *Wiener Zeitschrift für die Kunde des Morgenlandes* 9, 1895, 44–66. Reprinted in IA 24, 1895, 285–93, 311–16, and in OIBA, Appendix 1, 92–114.

Burgess, Jas. *The Buddhist Stupas of Amaravati and Jaggayyapeta in the Krishna District, Madras Presidency, Surveyed in 1882.* Archaeological Survey of Southern India, vol. 1, 1887 = Reports, New Imperial Series 6. Reprint, Varanasi: Indological Book House, 1970.

Burgess, Jas., and Bhagwanlal Indraji. *Inscriptions from the Cave-Temples of Western India with Descriptive Notes, &c.* [ICTWI]. Archaeological Survey of Western India, Reports, Old Series no. 10, 1881. Reprint, Delhi: Indian India, 1976.

Burnell, A. C. *Elements of South-Indian Palaeography from the Fourth to the Seventeenth Century* A.D. *Being an Introduction to the Study of South-Indian Inscriptions and Mss.* [SIP]. London: Trübner & Co., 1874. Reprint, Varanasi: Indological Book House, 1968.

Burrow, T. *The Language of the Kharoṣṭhi Documents from Chinese Turkestan.* Cambridge: Cambridge University Press, 1937.

———. *A Translation of the Kharoṣṭhi Documents from Chinese Turkestan.* James G. Forlong Fund, vol. 20. London: Royal Asiatic Society, 1940.

Caillat, Colette, ed. *Dialectes dans les littératures indo-aryennes: Actes du colloque international organisé par l'UA 1058 sous les auspices du C.N.R.S.* Publications de l'Institut de Civilisation Indienne, série in–8°, fasc. 55. Paris: Collège de France, Institut de Civilisation Indienne, 1989.

Chakraborti, Haripada. *Early Brahmi Records in India* (*c. 300* B.C.*–c. 300* A.D.). *An Analytical Study: Social, Economic, Religious, and Administrative.* Calcutta: Sanskrit Pustak Bhandar, 1974.

———. *India as Reflected in the Inscriptions of the Gupta Period.* New Delhi: Munshiram Manoharlal, 1978.

Chakravarti, Adhir. *The Sdok Kak Thoṃ Inscription: A Study in Indo-Khmèr Civilization.* 2 vols. Calcutta Sanskrit College Research Series, nos. 111–2. Calcutta: Sanskrit College, 1978–80.

Čhārụk nai Prathēt Thai [Inscriptions in Thailand]. 5 vols. Krungthēp: Hosamut Hāeng Chāt, Krom Sinlapākōn, 1986.

Čhārụk Samai Sukhōthai [Inscriptions of the Sukhothai Period]. Krungthēp: Krom Sinlapākōn, 1983.

Chatterjee, Asim Kumar. *A Comprehensive History of Jainism.* 2 vols. Calcutta: Firma KLM Private Limited, 1978–84.

Chatterjee, Bijan Raj. *India and Java.* Greater India Society Bulletin, no. 5, 2d ed. Calcutta: Greater India Society, 1933.

Chaudhuri, Sibadas. *Bibliography of Studies in Indian Epigraphy* (*1926–50*). The M.S. University Oriental Series, no. 6. Baroda: Oriental Institute, 1966. (Originally published in installments as supplement to JOI 10.1–3, 1960–61; 11.1, 1961; and 15.1, 1965.)

Chaudhury, Radhakrishna. *Inscriptions of Ancient India.* Meerut: Meenakshi Prakashan, 1983.

Chhabra, Bahadur Chand. *Abhilekhasaṃgrahaḥ: An Anthology of Sanskrit Inscriptions.* Sāhityaratnakośa, vol. 6. New Delhi: Sahitya Akademi, 1964.

———. *Antiquities of Chamba State.* Part II: *Medieval and Later Inscriptions.* MASI 72. New Delhi: Archaeological Survey of India, 1957. [Part I by J. Ph. Vogel, q.v.]

———. "Diplomatic of Sanskrit Copper-Plate Grants." *The Indian Archives* 5, 1951, 1–20. Reprint, New Delhi: National Archives of India, [1961?].

———. *Expansion of Indo-Aryan Culture During Pallava Rule (as Evidenced by Inscriptions).* Delhi: Munshi Ram Manohar Lal, 1965. (Originally published in *Journal of the Asiatic Society of Bengal, Letters,* 1, 1935, 1–64.)

Choudhary, Radha Krishna. *Select Inscriptions of Bihar (Introduction and Appendix in English and Text in Sanskrit).* Patna: Smt. Shanti Devi, 1958.

Coedès, G[eorge]. *Inscriptions du Cambodge.* 8 vols. Collection de textes et documents sur l'Indochine 3. Hanoi and Paris: École Française d'Extrême-Orient, 1937–66.

———. *Liste générale des inscriptions du Champa et du Cambodge.* Hanoi: École Française d'Extreme-Orient, 1923. [Revised version in Coedès' *Inscriptions du Cambodge,* vol. 8, 73–255; see 4.3.7.7 n. 44.)

———. *Recueil des inscriptions du Siam* [in Thai and French]. 2 vols. Bangkok: Bangkok Times Press, 1924; 2d ed., [1960?].

Corpus Inscriptionum Indicarum [CII]. [Volumes listed separately under individual authors; see 8.1.2.]

Cunningham, Alexander. *The Bhilsa Topes; or, Buddhist Monuments of Central India.* London: Smith, Elder, and Co., 1854. Reprint, Varanasi: Indological Book House, 1966.

———. *Book of Indian Eras, with Tables for Calculating Indian Dates.* Calcutta: Thacker, Spink and Co., 1883. Reprint, Varanasi: Indological Book House, 1970.

———. *Inscriptions of Asoka.* Corpus Inscriptionum Indicarum, vol. 1. Calcutta: Office of the Superintendent of Government Printing, 1877. Reprint, Varanasi: Indological Book House, 1961.

———. *Mahâbodhi, or the Great Buddhist Temple Under the Bodhi Tree at Buddha-Gaya.* London: W. H. Allen & Co., 1892. Reprint, Varanasi: Indological Book House [n.d.].

———. *The Stûpa of Bharhut: A Buddhist Monument Ornamented with Numerous Sculptures Illustrative of Buddhist Legend and History in the Third Century* B.C. London: W. H. Allen & Co., 1879. Reprint, Varanasi: Indological Book House, 1962.

Damais, Louis-Charles. "Liste des principales inscriptions datées de l'Indonesie." BEFEO 46, 1952, 1–105.

Damsteegt, Th. *Epigraphical Hybrid Sanskrit: Its Rise, Spread, Characteristics and Relationship to Buddhist Hybrid Sanskrit.* Orientalia Rheno-Traiectina, vol. 23. Leiden: E. J. Brill, 1978.

Dani, Ahmad Hasan. *Chilas: The City of Nanga Parvat (Dyamar).* Islamabad: [by the author], 1983.

———. *Indian Palaeography* [DIP]. Oxford: Clarendon Press, 1963. 2d ed., Delhi: Munshiram Manoharlal, 1986.

Das (Bajpayee), Kalyani. *Early Inscriptions of Mathurā—A Study.* Calcutta: Punthi Pustak, 1980.

Das Gupta, Charu Chandra. *The Development of the Kharoṣṭhī Script* [DKS]. Calcutta: Firma K. L. Mukhopadhyay, 1958.

de Casparis, J. G. *Indonesian Palaeography: A History of Writing in Indonesia from the Beginnings to* c. A.D. *1500.* Handbuch der Orientalistik, Abteilung 3, Band 4. Leiden: E. J. Brill, 1975.

———. *Prasasti Indonesia.* Vol. 1: *Inscripties uit de Çailendra-Tijd.* Bandung: A. C. Nix & Co., 1950. Vol. 2: *Selected Inscriptions from the 7th to the 9th Century* A.D. Bandung: Masa Baru, 1956.

Deo, Shantaram Bhalchandra. *History of Jaina Monachism from Inscriptions and Literature.* Deccan College Dissertation Series 17. Poona: Deccan College, 1956.

———. *Mahārāṣṭra va Gove Śilālekha-Tāmrapaṭāṃcī Varṇanātmaka Saṃdarbha Sūcī.* Muṃbaī: Mahārāṣṭra Rājya, 1984.

Deo, Shantaram Bhalchandra, and Jagat Pati Joshi. *Pauni Excavation (1969–70).* Nagpur: Archaeological Survey of India and Nagpur University, 1972.

Desai, P. B. *Jainism in South India and Some Jaina Epigraphs.* Jīvarāja Jaina Granthamālā, no. 6. Sholapur: Jaina Saṃskṛti Saṃrakshaka Sangha, 1957.

Dikshit, R. K. *The Candellas of Jejākabhukti.* New Delhi: Abhinav Publications, 1977.

Dikshitar, V. R. Ramachandra. *Selected South Indian Inscriptions (Tamil, Telugu, Malayalam, and Kannada).* Madras: University of Madras, 1952.

Diringer, David. *The Alphabet: A Key to the History of Mankind.* New York: Philosophical Library, 1953.

Diskalkar, D. B. *Inscriptions of Kathiawad.* Bombay: Karnatak Publishing House, [1941?]. (Originally published in *New Indian Antiquary* 1, 1938–39, 576–90, 686–96, 724–39; 2, 1939–40, 25–41, 591–606; 3, 1940–41, 111–27, 193–210, 273–88, 338–53, 371–82, 398–410.)

———. *Materials Used for Indian Epigraphical Records.* Bhandarkar Oriental Series, no. 13. Poona: Bhandarkar Oriental Research Institute, 1979. [See also under Diskalkar, "Series of articles"]

———. *Selections from Sanskrit Inscriptions (2nd cent. to 8th cent.* A.D.*): Text, Complete Translation into English, Historical, Literary Importances, Introductory and Literary Notes.* Rajkot: [by the author], 1925. Reprint, New Delhi: Classical Publishers, 1977.

———. [Series of articles in *Journal of Indian History* based on lectures on Indian epigraphy at Bombay University in 1953 under the auspices of the Bhaganvanlal Indraji Lecture Series.] "Origin of Indian Epigraphy," JIH 32, 1954, 291–307; "The Progress and Future of Indian Epigraphical Studies," 33, 1955, 131–53; "Development and Decline of Indian Epigraphy," 33, 289–311; "Inscriptions of Foreign Settlers in India," 34, 1956, 39–52; "Dravidian or South Indian Inscriptions," 34, 173–82; "Classification of Indian Epigraphical Records," 35, 1957, 177–220; "Materials Used for Indian Epigraphical Records," 35, 289–307, and 36, 1958, 43–72 [also separately published in revised form; see above]; "Indian Epigraphical Literature," 37, 1959, 319–39; "The Influence of Classical Poets on the Inscriptional Poets," 38, 1960, 285–302.

Dobbins, K. Walton. *Śaka-Pahlava Coinage.* Memoirs, no. 5. Varanasi: Numismatic Society of India, 1973.

Dundas, Paul. *The Jains.* The Library of Religious Beliefs and Practices. London and New York: Routledge, 1992.

Duroiselle, Chas. *A List of Inscriptions Found in Burma.* Part I: *The List of Inscriptions Arranged in the Order of Their Dates.* Rangoon: Archaeological Survey of Burma, 1921.

Dvivedī, Hariharanivāsa. *Gvāliyara Rājya ke Abhilekha.* Gvāliyara: Madhya Bhārata Purātatva Vibhāga, 1947.

Epigraphia Birmanica. 4 vols. Rangoon: Archaeological Survey of Burma, 1919–28.

Epigraphia Carnatica [EC]. 17 vols., ed. B. Lewis Rice et al. Mysore Archaeological Survey, 1885–1965. New ed.: 8++ vols.: University of Mysore, 1972–84. [See 8.1.2 for further details.]

Epigraphia Indica [EI]. 42++ vols. Archaeological Survey of India, 1892–1992. [See 6.3 and 8.1.1.1 for further details.]

Epigraphia Zeylanica [EZ]. Archaeological Survey of Ceylon. Vol. 1: 1904–12; 2: 1912–27; 3: 1928–33; 4: 1934–41; 5: 1955–65; 6, part 1: 1973; 7 ["Special Volume on the Brahmi Inscriptions of Ceylon," ed. Saddhamangala Karunaratne]: 1984.

Falk, Harry. *Schrift im alten Indien: Ein Forschungsbericht mit Anmerkungen* [SAI]. Script-Oralia 56. Tübingen: Gunter Narr Verlag, 1993.

Filliozat, Vasundhara. *L'Épigraphie de Vijayanagara du début à 1377*. Publications de l'École Française d'Extrême-Orient, vol. 91. Paris: École Française d'Extrême-Orient, 1973.

Finot, Louis. *Inscriptions du Cambodge*. 6 vols. Paris/Hanoi: Academie des Inscriptions et Belles-lettres, 1926–37.

Fleet, J[ohn] F[aithfull]. "Epigraphy," ch. 1 of vol. 2 ("Historical") of *The Imperial Gazetteer of India* (Oxford: Clarendon Press, 1909), 1–88. Reprinted in Vincent A. Smith, James Burgess, and J. F. Fleet, *India Its Epigraphy, Antiquities, Archaeology, Numismatics and Architecture*. Delhi: Ess Ess Publications, 1975.

———. *Inscriptions of the Early Gupta Kings and Their Successors*. Corpus Inscriptionum Indicarum, vol. 3. Calcutta: Superintendent of Government Printing, 1888. Reprint, Varanasi: Indological Book House, 1963 and 1970. (Some copies of the "Third Revised Edition" of 1970 include at the end an additional bibliography (no title), which is the same as parts 1 through 5 of Ram Swaroop Mishra's *Supplement to Fleet's Corpus*, q.v.)

Fussman, Gérard. "Gāndhārī écrite, Gāndhārī parlée." In Collette Caillat, ed., *Dialectes dans les littératures indo-aryennes*, 433–501.

———, ed. *Antiquities of Northern Pakistan: Reports and Studies*. Vol. 3. [See s.v. Karl Jettmar.]

Fussman, Gérard and Ditte König. *Die Felsbildstation Shatial*. Materialen zur Archäologie der Nordgebiete Pakistans 2. Mainz: Philipp von Zabern, 1997.

Gadre, A. S. *Important Inscriptions from the Baroda State*. Vol. 1. Śrī-Pratāpasiṃha Mahārāja Rājyābhiṣeka Grantha-mālā, Memoir no. 2. Baroda: Archaeological Department, 1943.

Gai, G. S. *Inscriptions of the Early Kadambas*. New Delhi/Delhi: Indian Council of Historical Research and Pratibha Prakashan, 1996.

———. *Introduction to Indian Epigraphy* [*with Special Reference to the Development of the Scripts and Languages*] [IIE]. Central Institute of Indian Languages Occasional Monographs Series 32. Mysore: Central Institute of Indian Languages, 1986.

———. *Some Select Inscriptions*. Delhi: Agam Kala Prakashan, 1990.

———. *Studies in Indian History, Epigraphy and Culture*. Dharwad: Shrihari Prakashana, 1992.

Gaur, Albertine. *Indian Charters on Copper Plates in the Department of Oriental Manuscripts and Printed Books*. London: The British Library, 1975.

Gazetteer of the Bombay Presidency. Vol. 1 (2 parts). Bombay: Government Central Press, 1896.

Gnoli, Raniero. *Nepalese Inscriptions in Gupta Characters*. 2 vols. Serie Orientale Roma 10; Materials for the Study of Nepalese History and Culture 2. Rome: Istituto Italiano per il Medio ed Estremo Oriente, 1956.

Gokhale, Shobhana Laxman. *Indian Numerals*. Deccan College Building Centenary and Silver Jubilee Series 43. Poona: Deccan College Postgraduate and Research Institute, 1966.

———. *Kanheri Inscriptions*. Pune: Deccan College Post Graduate and Research Institute, 1991.

Gonda, Jan. *Twenty-five Sanskrit Inscriptions for Use in Universities* ... Textus Minores, vol. 4. Leiden: E. J. Brill, 1948.

Gopal, B. R. *Vijayanagara Inscriptions.* Vol. 1. Centenary Publication, no. 3. Mysore: Directorate of Archaeology and Museums, Government of Karnataka, 1985.

[Gopal, L., et al.] "Writing." Chapter 20 of A. Ghosh, ed., *An Encyclopedia of Indian Archaeology.* 2 vols. (New Delhi, Munshiram Manoharlal, 1989), I.359–70.

Goris, Roelof. *Prasasti Bali.* Vol. 1: *Inscripties voor Anak Wungçu.* Bandung: Masa Baru, 1954.

Goyala, Śrīrama. *Prācīna Bhāratīya Abhilekha Saṃgraha, Khaṇḍa I* [*Prāk Guptayugīna*]. Jaypura: Rājasthāna Hindī Grantha Akādami, 1982.

Guérinot, A. *Répertoire d'épigraphie Jaina, précédé d'une esquisse de l'histoire du jainisme d'après les inscriptions.* Paris: Imprimerie Nationale, 1908.

Gupta, Parmanand. *Geographical Names in Ancient Indian Inscriptions: A Companion Volume to Geography in Ancient Indian Inscriptions up to 650 A.D.* Delhi: Concept Publishing Company, 1977.

———. *Geography in Ancient Indian Inscriptions (up to 650 A.D.).* Delhi: D. K. Publishing House, 1973.

Gupta, P[armeshwari] L[al] ("Supervised by"). Sets of script charts entitled "Ancient Indian Alphabets," "Medieval Indian Alphabets," "Indian Alphabets Abroad," and "Ancient Indian Numerals." Delhi: All India Educational Supply Company, [n.d.].

———. *Prācīna Bhārata ke Pramukha Abhilekha.* 2 vols. Vārāṇasī: Annapūrṇā Prakāśana, 1979–83.

Gupta, S. P., and K. S. Ramachandran, eds. *The Origin of Brahmi Script* [OBS]. History and Historians of India Series, vol. 2. Delhi: D. K. Publications, 1979.

Hall, Kenneth R. *Trade and Statecraft in the Age of Cōlas.* New Delhi: Abhinav, 1980.

Hinüber, Oskar von. *Der Beginn der Schrift und frühe Schriftlichkeit in Indien* [BS]. Akademie der Wissenschaften und der Literatur [Mainz], Abhandlungen der Geistes- und Sozialwissenschaftliche Klasse, 1989, no. 11. Mainz: Akademie der Wissenschaften und der Literatur, 1990.

Hira Lal. *Inscriptions in the Central Provinces and Berar.* 2d ed. Nagpur: Government Printing, C.P., 1932. Reprint, Patna: Eastern Book House, 1985.

Hultzsch, E. *Inscriptions of Aśoka. New Edition.* Corpus Inscriptionum Indicarum, vol. 1. Oxford: Clarendon Press, for the Government of India, 1925. Reprint, Delhi: Indological Book House, 1969.

Jacques, Claude. *Corpus des inscriptions du pays khmer.* Vol. 1. Sata-Piṭaka Series, vol. 341. New Delhi: International Academy of Indian Culture, 1980.

Jain, Muni Uttam Kamal. *Jaina Sects and Schools.* Delhi: Concept Publishing Company, 1975.

Jaina, Hīrālāla [vol. 1], Vijayamūrti Śāstrācārya [vols. 2, 3], and Vidyādhara Joharāpurakar [vol. 4]. *Jaina-śilālekhasaṃgrahaḥ.* 4 vols. Māṇikacandra-digambara-jainagranthamālā, *puṣpa* 28, 45, 46, 48. Bambaī: Māṇikacandra-digambara-jainagranthamālāsamiti, 1928, 1952, 1957/Kāśī: Bhāratīya Jñānapīṭha, Vīra Nirvāṇa Saṃvat 2491.

Jayasuriya, M. H. F. *The Jetavanārāma Gold Plates: Being a Fragmentary Sri Lankan Recension of the Pañcaviṃśatisāhasrikā Prajñāpāramitā Sūtra.* [Kelaniya:] University of Kelaniya, 1988.

Jettmar, Karl, ed. (vol. 1, in collaboration with Ditte König and Volker Thewalt; vol. 2, with Ditte König and Martin Bemmann; vol. 3, edited by Gérard Fussman and Jettmar). *Antiquities of Northern Pakistan: Reports and Studies.* 3 vols. Mainz: Heidelberger Akademie der Wissenschaften/Philipp von Zabern, 1989/1993/1994.

Jinavijaya, Muni. *Prācīnajainalekhasaṃgraha* [in Gujarati]. 2 vols. Bhāvnagar: Śrījaina Ātmānanda Sabhā, 1917–21.

Jośī, Harirāma. *Nepāla ko Prācīna Abhilekha.* Kāṭhmāṇḍaū: Nepāla Rājakīya Prajñā-pratiṣṭhāna, Vikrama 2030.

Kane, P. V. *History of Dharmaśāstra (Ancient and Mediaeval Religious and Civil Law in India).* Government Oriental Series, Class B, no. 6. Revised and enlarged ed.; 5 vols. in 7 parts. Poona: Bhandarkar Oriental Research Institute, 1968–74.

Karashima, Noboru. *South Indian History and Society: Studies from Inscriptions A.D. 850–1800.* Delhi: Oxford University Press, 1984.

———, ed. *Indus Valley to Mekong Delta: Explorations in Epigraphy* [IVMD]. Madras: New Era Publications, 1985.

Kaul Deambi, B. K. *Corpus of Śāradā Inscriptions of Kashmir with Special Reference to Origin and Development of Śāradā Script.* Delhi: Agam Kala, 1982.

Kern, H. *Verspreide Geschriften onder zijn Toezicht Verzameld.* 15 vols. 's-Gravenhage: Martinus Nijhoff, 1913–28.

Ketkar, Venkatesh Bapuji. *Indian and Foreign Chronology with Theory, Practice and Tables, B.C. 3102 to 2100 A.D. and Notices of the Vedic, the Ancient Indian, the Chinese, the Jewish, the Ecclesiastical and the Coptic Calendar.* JBBRAS, Extra Number, no. LXXV-A, 1923.

Khan, Abdul Waheed. *A Monograph on an Early Buddhist Stupa at Kesanapalli.* Andhra Pradesh Government Archaeological Series, no. 27. Hyderabad: Government of Andhra Pradesh, 1969.

Kielhorn, Franz. *Bruchstücke indischer Schauspiele in Inschriften zu Ajmere.* In *Festschrift zur Feier des Hundertfünfzigjähringen Bestehens der königlichen Gesellschaft der Wissenschaften zu Göttingen (Abhandlungen der philologisch-historischen Klasse).* Berlin: Weidmannsche Buchhandlung, 1901.

———. *Kleine Schriften mit einer Auswahl der epigraphischen Aufsätze* [KS]. Edited by Wilhelm Rau. 2 vols. Glasenapp-Stiftung, vol. 3. Wiesbaden: Franz Steiner Verlag, 1969.

———. *A List of the Inscriptions of Northern India from About A.D. 400.* Appendix to EI 5, 1898–99. Supplement: Appendix I to EI 8, 1905–6.

———. *A List of Inscriptions of Southern India from About A.D. 500.* Appendix to EI 7, 1902–3. Supplement: Appendix II to EI 8, 1905–6.

Konow, Sten. *Kharoshṭhī Inscriptions with the Exception of Those of Aśoka.* Corpus Inscriptionum Indicarum, vol. 2, part 1. Calcutta: Government of India, 1929. Reprint, Varanasi: Indological Book House, 1969.

Krishnan, K. G. *Karandai Tamil Sangam Plates of Rajendrachola I.* MASI 79. New Delhi: Archaeological Survey of India, 1984.

———. *Uṭṭaṅkita Sanskrit Vidyā Araṇya Epigraphs.* Vol. 2: *Prakrit and Sanskrit Epigraphs 257 B.C. to 320 A.D.* Mysore: Uṭṭaṅkita Vidyā Araṇya Trust, 1989.

Kulke, Hermann et al. *Indische Geschichte vom Altertum bis zur Gegenwart. Literaturbericht über neuere Veröffentlichung. Historische Zeitschrift,* Sonderheft 10. Munich: R. Oldenbourg, 1982.

Lamotte, Étienne. *Histoire du bouddhisme indien: Des origines à l'ère Śaka* [HBI]. Bibliothèque du *Muséon,* vol. 43. Louvain: Université de Louvain, 1958. (English translation by Sara Webb-Boin: *History of Indian Buddhism from the Origins to the Śaka Era.* Publications de l'Institut Orientaliste de Louvain, 36. Louvain-la-Neuve: Université catholique de Louvain, Institut Orientaliste, 1988.)

Lassen, Christian. *Indische Altertumskunde.* 4 vols. Bonn/Leipzig: H. B. Koenig/L. A. Kittler, 1847–62.

———. *Zur Geschichte der griechischen und indoskythischen Könige in Baktrien, Kabul und Indien durch Entzifferung der altkabulischen Legenden auf ihren Münzen.* Bonn: H. B. König, 1838. (English translation by T. H. Edw. Roer, "Points in the History of the Greek, and Indo-Scythian Kings in Bactria, Cabul, and India, as Illustrated by Decyphering the Ancient Legends on Their Coins," in JASB 9, 1840, 251–76, 339–78, 449–88, 627–76, 733–65; reprinted as *Greek and Indo-Scythian Kings and Their Coins*, Delhi: Indological Book House, 1972.)

Lévi, Sylvain. *Le Nepal: Étude historique d'un royaume hindou*, vol. 3. Annales du Musée Guimet, Bibliothèque d'Études 19. Paris: Ernest Leroux, 1908.

Lohuizen-de Leeuw, Johanna Engelberta van. *The "Scythian" Period: An Approach to the History, Art, Epigraphy and Palaeography of North India from the 1st Century B.C. to the 3rd Century A.D.* Leiden: E. J. Brill, 1949.

Luce, G. H., and Pe Maung Tin, eds. *Inscriptions of Burma*. University of Rangoon Oriental Studies Publications, nos. 2–6. London: Oxford University Press, 1934–56. (5 portfolios of facsimiles of inscriptions.)

Lüders, H. *Bhārhut Inscriptions*. Revised by E. Waldschmidt and M. A. Mehendale. Corpus Inscriptionum Indicarum, vol. 2, part 2. Ootacamund: Government Epigraphist for India, 1963.

———. *Kleine Schriften*. Edited by Oskar von Hinüber. Glasenapp-Stiftung, vol. 7. Wiesbaden: Franz Steiner Verlag, 1973.

———. *A List of Brahmi Inscriptions from the Earliest Times to About A.D. 400 with the Exception of Those of Asoka*. Appendix to EI 10, 1912.

———. *Mathurā Inscriptions* (*Unpublished Papers Edited by Klaus L. Janert*) [MI]. Abhandlungen der Akademie der Wissenschaften in Göttingen, Philologisch-Historische Klasse, Dritte Folge, no. 47. Göttingen: Vandenhoeck & Ruprecht, 1961.

———. *Philologica Indica. Ausgewählte kleine Schriften von Heinrich Lüders. Festgabe zum siebstigsten Geburtstage am 25. Juni 1939 dargebracht von Kollegen, Freunden, und Schülern*. Göttingen: Vandenhoeck & Ruprecht, 1940.

Mahalingam, T. V. *Early South Indian Palaeography* [ESIP]. Madras University Archaeological Series, no. 1. Madras: University of Madras, 1974.

———. *Inscriptions of the Pallavas*. New Delhi/Delhi: Indian Council of Historical Research, 1988.

———. *A Topographical List of Inscriptions in the Tamil Nadu and Kerala States*. Vol. 1: *North Arcot District*. New Delhi: Indian Council of Historical Research/S. Chand & Company, 1985.

Maitra, Akshaya Kumara. *Gauḍalekhamālā* [*A Work on the Ancient Inscriptions of Gaur*]. 2d ed., Calcutta: [?], 1914.

Majumdar, N. G. *Inscriptions of Bengal*, vol. 3, "Containing Inscriptions of the Chandras, the Varmans and the Senas and of Isvaraghosha and Damodara." Rajshahi: The Varendra Research Institute, 1929. [Vol. 1 of *Inscriptions of Bengal* is A. K. Maitra's *Gauḍalekhamālā*, q.v.; vol. 2 was apparently not published; vol. 4 is by Shamsuddin Ahmed, "Being a Corpus of Inscriptions of the Muslim Rulers of Bengal from 1233 to 1855 A.C.," containing Arabic and Persian inscriptions.]

Majumdar, R. C. *Champa*. Ancient Indian Colonies in the Far East, vol. 1; Punjab Oriental (Sanskrit) Series, no. 16. Lahore: The Panjab Sanskrit Book Depot, 1927. Reprint (*Champā: History & Culture of an Indian Colonial Kingdom in the Far East 2nd–16th Century A.D.*), Delhi: Gian, 1985.

———. *Inscriptions of Kambuja*. The Asiatic Society Monograph Series, vol. 8. Calcutta: The Asiatic Society, 1953.

———. *Suvarnadvipa. Ancient Indian Colonies in the Far East*, vol. 2. Dacca: Asoke Kumar Majumdar, 1937.

———, ed. *The Age of Imperial Kanauj. The History and Culture of the Indian People*, vol. 4. 2d ed. Bombay: Bharatiya Vidya Bhavan, 1964.

———, ed. *The Struggle for Empire. The History and Culture of the Indian People*, vol. 5. 3d ed. Bombay: Bharatiya Vidya Bhavan, 1979.

Mangalam, S. J. *Kharoṣṭhī Script*. Delhi: Eastern Book Linkers, 1990.

Marshall, John. *Taxila: An Illustrated Account of Archaeological Excavations Carried out at Taxila Under the Orders of the Government of India Between the Years 1913 and 1934*. Cambridge: Cambridge University Press, 1951. Reprints, Varanasi: Bhartiya Publishing House, 1975; Delhi: Motilal Banarsidass, 1975.

Marshall, John, and Alfred Foucher. *The Monuments of Sanchi*. Inscriptions edited, translated, and annotated by N. G. Majumdar. 3 vols. Calcutta: Government of India, 1940. Reprint, Delhi: Swati, 1982.

Mehendale, M[adhukar] A[nant]. *Aśokan Inscriptions in India (A Linguistic Study, Together with an Exhaustive Bibliography)*. Bombay: University of Bombay, 1948.

———. *Historical Grammar of Inscriptional Prakrits* [HGIP]. Deccan College Dissertation Series 3. Poona: Deccan College Postgraduate and Research Institute, 1948.

Mehta, R. N., and A. M. Thakkar. *M.S. University Copper Plates of the Time of Toramana*. Maharaja Sayajirao University Archaeological Series, no. 14. Vadodara: Department of Archaeology and Ancient History, M.S. University of Baroda, 1978.

Mirashi, Vasudev Vishnu. *The History and Inscriptions of the Sātavāhanas and the Western Kṣatrapas*. Bombay: Maharashtra State Board for Literature and Culture, 1981. (Originally published in Marathi as *Sātavāhana āṇi Paścimī Kṣatrapa yāṃcā Itihāsa āṇi Korīva Lekha*. Muṃbaī: Mahārāṣṭra Rājya Sāhitya Saṃskṛtī Maṃḍala, 1979.)

———. *Inscriptions of the Kalachuri-Chedi Era*. Corpus Inscriptionum Indicarum, vol. 4, parts 1 and 2. Ootacamund: Government Epigraphist for India, 1955.

———. *Inscriptions of the Śilāhāras*. Corpus Inscriptionum Indicarum, vol. 6. New Delhi: Director General, Archaeological Survey of India, 1977.

———. *Inscriptions of the Vākāṭakas*. Corpus Inscriptionum Indicarum, vol. 5. Ootacamund: Government Epigraphist for India, 1963.

———. *Studies in Ancient Indian History*. Bombay: Maharashtra State Board for Literature and Culture, 1984.

———. *Studies in Indology*. 2 vols. Nagpur: Vidarbha Samshodhana Mandal, 1960 and 1961.

Mishra, Ram Swaroop. *Supplement to Fleet's Corpus Inscriptionum Indicarum, Vol. III (1888): Inscriptions of the Early Gupta Kings and Their Successors*. Part 1: Bibliography. Monographs of the Departments of Ancient Indian History, Culture and Archaeology, no. 6. Varanasi: Banaras Hindu University, 1971.

Mitra, Debala. *Ratnagiri (1958–61)*. 2 vols. MASI 80. New Delhi: Archaeological Survey of India, 1981–83.

Mittal, A. C. *The Inscriptions of Imperial Paramāras (800* A.D. *to 1320* A.D.*) / Paramāra Abhilekha* [in Hindi]. L. D. Series 73. Ahmedabad: L. D. Institute of Indology, 1979.

Mukherjee, B. N. *Central and South Asian Documents on the Old Śaka Era*. Varanasi: Bharat Bharati, 1973.

———. *Studies in the Aramaic Inscriptions of Aśoka*. Calcutta: Indian Museum, 1984.

———, et al., eds. *Sri Dinesacandrika: Studies in Indology. Shri D.C. Sircar Festschrift*. Delhi: Sundeep Prakashan, 1983.

Mukherjee, Ramaranjan, and Sachindra Kumar Maity. *Corpus of Bengal Inscriptions Bearing on History and Civilization of Bengal*. Calcutta: Firma K. L. Mukhopadhyay, 1967.

Müller, Edward. *Ancient Inscriptions in Ceylon*. 2 vols. London: Trübner & Co., 1883. Reprint, New Delhi: Asian Educational Services, 1984.

Nagaraja Rao, M. S., and K. V. Ramesh. *Copper Plate Inscriptions from Karnataka: Recent Discoveries*. Centenary Publication no. 2. Mysore: Government of Karnataka, 1985.

Nagaswamy, R. *Thiruttani and Velanjeri Copper Plates.* T.N.D.S.A. Publication no. 55. [Madras]: State Department of Archaeology, Government of Tamil Nadu, 1979.

Nahar, Puran Chand. *Jain Inscriptions* (*Jaina Lekha Saṃgraha*) [in Hindi]. 3 vols. Jaina Vividha Sâhitya Shâstra Mâlâ no. 8. Calcutta: Published by the Compiler, 1918/1927 /1929. Reprint, Delhi: Indian Book Gallery, 1983.

Naidu, Venkata Narayanaswami, Srinivasulu Naidu, and Venkata Rangayya Pantulu. *Tāṇḍava Lakṣaṇam or The Fundamentals of Ancient Indian Dancing.* Madras: G. S. Press, 1936. Reprint, New Delhi: Munshiram Manoharlal, 1971.

Naik, A. V. "Inscriptions of the Deccan: An Epigraphical Survey (*Circa* 300 B.C.–1300 A.D.)." *Bulletin of the Deccan College Research Institute* 9.1–2, 1948, 1–160.

Narain, A. K. *The Indo-Greeks.* Oxford: Oxford University Press, 1957.

Niklas, Ulrike. *Die Editionen der Aśoka-Inschriften von Eṟṟaguḍi.* Schriftenreihe des Caulfield-Meisezahl Instituts fur Hochasienforschung 1. Bonn: VGH Wissenschaftsverlag, 1990.

Nilakanta Sastri, K. A. *A History of South India from Prehistoric Times to the Fall of Vijayanagara.* 4th ed. Madras: Oxford University Press, 1976.

Norman, K. R. *Collected Papers.* 6 vols. Oxford: The Pali Text Society, 1990–96.

Nowotny, Fausta. "Schriftsysteme in Indien." *Studium Generale* 20, 1967, 527–47.

Ojhā, Gaurīśaṃkara Hīrācaṃda. *Bhāratīya Prācīna Lipimālā* [in Hindi] [BPLM]. 2d ed. Ajmer: Scottish Mission Industries Company, 1918. Reprint, with English title (*The Palaeography of India*), New Delhi: Munshiram Manoharlal, 1971.

Ojhā, Rāmprakāśa. *Uttarī Bhāratīya Abhilekhoṃ kā eka Sāṃskṛtika Adhyayana* (*Ī. pū. 232 se Ī. san 161 tak*). Lakhnaū: Prakāśana Kendra, 1971.

[Oza, V. G.?]. *Bhāvanagara Prācīna Śodhasaṃgraha* (*Bhāga Pehelo*). Bhavnagar: Darvārī Chāpakhānā, 1885.

Pandey, Raj Bali. *Historical and Literary Inscriptions.* The Chowkhamba Sanskrit Studies, vol. 23. Varanasi: Chowkhamba Sanskrit Series Office, 1962.

———. *Indian Palaeography*, part I [PIP]. 2d ed. Varanasi: Motilal Banarasi Das, 1957.

Pant, Mahes Raj, and Aishvarya Dhar Sharma. *The Two Earliest Copper-plate Inscriptions from Nepal.* Nepal Research Centre Miscellaneous Papers, no. 12. Kathmandu: Nepal Research Centre, 1977.

Parabrahma Sastry, P. V. *Inscriptions of Andhra Pradesh.* Government of Andhra Pradesh Epigraphical Series, nos. 12, 13, 15. Hyderabad: Government of Andhra Pradesh, 1977/1978/1981.

———. *Select Epigraphs of Andhra Pradesh.* Government of Andhra Pradesh Archaeological Series, no. 31. Hyderabad: Government of Andhra Pradesh, 1970.

Paranavitana, S. *Inscriptions of Ceylon.* Vol. 1: *Containing Cave Inscriptions from 3rd Century B.C. to 1st Century A.C. and Other Inscriptions in the Early Brāhmī Script.* Ceylon: Department of Archaeology, 1970. Vol. 2, part 1: *Late Brāhmī Inscriptions, Containing Rock and Other Inscriptions from the Reign of Kuṭakaṇṇa Abhaya* (*41 B.C.–19 B.C.*) *to Bhātiya II* (*140–164 A.D.*). Sri Lanka: Department of Archaeology, 1983.

———. *Sigiri Graffiti: Being Sinhalese Verses of the Eighth, Ninth and Tenth Centuries.* 2 vols. London: Oxford University Press, for the Archaeological Survey of Ceylon, 1956.

Parikh, Ramlal, and Jamindar, Rasesh. *Epigraphic Resources in Gujarat.* Delhi/Baroda: Butala & Company, 1981.

Pathak, V. S. *History of Śaiva Cults in Northern India from Inscriptions* (*700 A.D. to 1200 A.D.*). Studies in History, Culture and Archaeology, vol. 2. Allahabad: University of Allahabad, 1980.

[Peterson, Peter]. *A Collection of Prakrit and Sanskrit Inscriptions.* Bhavnagar: Bhavnagar Archaeological Department, [n.d.].

Phogat, S. R. *Inscriptions of Haryana.* Sources of Haryana History Series. Kuruksetra: Vishal Publications, 1978.

Prachum Silā Čhāruk [Collection of Stone Inscriptions]. 6 vols. Krungthēp: Samnak Nāyok Ratthamontrī, 1978.

Prasad, Pushpa. *Sanskrit Inscriptions of Delhi Sultanate 1191–1526.* Delhi: Oxford University Press, 1990.

Premalatha, V. *A Monograph on Kudumiyanmalai Inscription on Music.* Madurai: [by the author], 1986.

Prinsep, James. *Essays on Indian Antiquities, Historic, Numismatic, and Palaeographic, of the Late James Prinsep, F. R. S.* Edited by Edward Thomas. 2 vols. London: J. Murray, 1858. Reprint, Varanasi: Indological Book House, 1971.

Puri, B. N. *The History of the Gurjara-Pratihāras.* 2d ed. New Delhi: Munshiram Manoharlal, 1986.

Rajaguru, Satyanarayan. *Inscriptions of Orissa.* 6 vols. in 10 parts (vol. 6 by Snigdha Tripathy). Bhubaneswar: Government of Orissa/Orissa State Museum, 1952–74.

———. *Invocatory Verses from Inscriptions.* 2 vols. Bhubaneswar: [by the author], 1971–73.

Ram, Sadhu. *Some Important Inscriptions of Asoka, the Guptas, the Maukharis and Others.* Part 1: *Texts.* Delhi: Munshi Ram Manohar Lal, [1962].

Rama Rao, M. *Inscriptions of Āndhradēśa.* 2 vols. Sri Venkatesvara University Historical Series, nos. 5, 9. Tirupati: Sri Venkatesvara University, 1967–68.

Ramesan, N. *Copper Plate Inscriptions of Andhra Pradesh Government Museum, Hyderabad.* 2 vols. Andhra Pradesh Government Archaeological Series, nos. 6, 28. Hyderabad: Government of Andhra Pradesh, 1962–70.

Ramesh, K. V. *Chalukyas of Vātāpi.* Delhi: Agam Prakashan, 1984.

———. *Indian Epigraphy,* vol. 1 [RIE]. Delhi: Sundeep Prakashan, 1984.

———. *Inscriptions of the Western Gaṅgas.* New Delhi/Delhi: Indian Council of Historical Research/Agam Prakashan, 1984.

Ramesh, K. V., Agam Prasad, and S. P. Tewari. *Svasti Śrī. Dr. B. Ch. Chhabra Felicitation Volume.* Delhi: Agam Kala, 1984.

Ramesh, K. V., S. P. Tewari, and M. J. Sharma. *Indian History and Epigraphy. Dr. G. S. Gai Felicitation Volume.* Delhi: Agam Kala Prakashan, 1990.

Rastogi, Naresh Prasad. *Origin of Brāhmī Script: The Beginning of Alphabet in India.* Krishnadas Sanskrit Studies, vol. 1. Varanasi: Chowkhamba Saraswatibhawan, 1980.

Regmi, D. R. *Inscriptions of Ancient Nepal.* 3 vols. New Delhi: Abhinav, 1983.

———. *Medieval Nepal.* Part 4: *Select Inscriptions, 1524–1768 A.D. with Verification and Corresponding Dates in C.E.* Patna: [by the author], 1966.

Renou, Louis, and Jean Filliozat. *L'Inde classique: Manuel des études indiennes* [IC]. Vol. 1: Paris: Payot, 1947. Vol. 2: (Bibliothèque de l'École Française d'Extrême-Orient, vol. 3). Hanoi: École Française d'Extrême-Orient, 1953. Reprint, Paris: Adrien Maisonneuve, 1985.

Rice, [B.] Lewis. *Mysore Inscriptions.* Bangalore: Mysore Government Press, 1879. Reprint, New Delhi: Navrang, 1983.

Roy, Sourindranath. *The Story of Indian Archaeology 1784–1947.* New Delhi: Archaeological Survey of India, 1961.

Sachau, Eduard C. *Alberuni's India: An Account of the Religion, Philosophy, Literature, Geography, Chronology, Astronomy, Customs, Laws and Astrology of India About A.D. 1030.* Popular edition, London: Kegan Paul, Trench, Trübner & Co., [1914].

Sahai, Bhagwant. *The Inscriptions of Bihar (from Earliest Times to the Middle of 13th Century A.D.).* The Heritage of India, no. 3. New Delhi: Ramanand Vidya Bhavan, 1983.

Sahai, Sachchidanand. *Les Institutions politiques et l'organisation administrative du Cambodge ancien (VIe–XIIIe siècles)*. Publications de l'École Française d'Extrême-Orient, vol. 75. Paris: École Française d'Extrême-Orient, 1970.

Sander, Lore. *Paläographisches zu den Sanskrithandschriften der Berliner Turfansammlung*.Verzeichnis der Orientalischen Handschriften in Deutschland, Supplementband 8. Wiesbaden: Franz Steiner Verlag, 1968.

Sankalia, H. D. *The Archaeology of Gujarat (Including Kathiawar)*. Bombay: Natwarlal & Co., 1941.

Sarkar, Himansu Bhusan. *Corpus of the Inscriptions of Java* (*Corpus Inscriptionum Javanicarum*) (*up to 928 A.D.*). 2 vols. Calcutta: Firma K. L. Mukhopadhyay, 1971–72.

Sarma, Dimbeswar, ed. *Kāmarūpaśāsanāvalī*. Gauhati: Publication Board, Assam, 1981.

Sarma, I. K. *Studies in Early Buddhist Monuments and Brāhmī Inscriptions of Āndhradēśa*. Nagpur: Dattsons, 1988.

Sarma, I. K., and J. Varaprasada Rao. *Early Brahmi Inscriptions from Sannati*. New Delhi: Harman Publishing House, 1993.

Śāstrī, Bhavadatta, and Kāśīnātha Pāṇḍuranga Paraba. *Prâcîna-lekha-mâlâ* (*A Collection of Ancient Historical Records*). 3 vols. (Vol. 2 by Pandit Śivadatta and K. P. Parab.) Kâvyamâlâ, nos. 34, 64, 80. Bombay: Nirṇaya-Sâgara Press, 1892–1903.

Sastry, Sadhu Subrahmanya [vol. 1], and V. Viyayaraghavacharya [vols. 2–6], eds. *Tirumalai-Tirupati Devasthanam Epigraphical Series*. 6 vols. in 7 parts. Madras: Tirumalai-Tirupati Devasthanams Committee, 1931–38.

Sathyanarayana, R. *The Kuḍimiyāmalai Inscription on Music*. Vol. 1: *Sources*. Sri Varalakshmi Academy Publication Series, no. 3; Bulletin of the Board of Research, no. 2. Mysore: Sri Varalakshmi Academies of Fine Arts, 1957.

Satya Murty, K. *Textbook of Indian Epigraphy*. Delhi: Low Price Publications, 1992.

Schneider, Ulrich. *Die Grossen Felsen-Edikte Aśokas. Kritische Ausgabe, Übersetzung und Analyse der Texte*. Freiburger Beitrage zur Indologie 11. Wiesbaden: Otto Harrassowitz, 1978.

Senart, Émile. *Les Inscriptions de Piyadassi*. 2 vols. Paris: Imprimerie Nationale, 1881. English translation by G. A. Grierson: IA 9, 1880, 282–7; 10, 1881, 83–5, 180–2, 209–11, 269–73; 17, 1888, 303–7; 18, 1889, 1–9, 73–80, 105–8, 300–9; 19, 1890, 82–102; 20, 1891, 154–70, 229–66; 21, 1892, 1–13, 85–92, 101–6, 145–55, 171–7, 203–10, 243–50, 258–76.

Settar, S. *Inviting Death: Historical Experiments on Sepulchral Hill*. Dharwad: Institute of Indian Art History, Karnatak University, 1986. (Reissued as *Inviting Death: Indian Attitudes Toward the Ritual Death*. Monographs and Theoretical Studies in Sociology and Anthropology in Honour of Nels Anderson, Publication 28. Leiden: E. J. Brill, 1989.)

Settar, S., and Gunther D. Sontheimer, eds. *Memorial Stones: A Study of Their Origin, Significance and Variety*. I.A.H. Series no. 2/South Asian Studies no. 11.ii. Dharwar: Institute of Indian Art History/Heidelberg: South Asia Institute, University of Heidelberg, 1982.

Sewell, Robert. *The Historical Inscriptions of Southern India* (*Collected Till 1923*) *and Outlines of Political History*. Edited by S. Krishnaswami Aiyangar. Madras University Historical Series, no. 5. Madras: Diocesan Press, 1932.

———. *Indian Chronography: An Extension of the "Indian Calendar" with Working Examples*. London: George Allen and Company, 1912.

———. *The Siddhāntas and the Indian Calendar: Being a Continuation of the Author's "Indian Chronography" with an Article by the Late Dr. J. F. Fleet on the Mean Place of the Planet Saturn*. (Reprint of a series of articles published in EI 13, 1915–16, 61–103; 14, 1917–18, 1–67; 15, 1919–20, 159–245; 16, 1921–22, 100–221; 17, 1923–24, 17–104, 123–87, 205–90.) Calcutta: Government of India, 1924.

Sewell, Robert, and Śankara Bâlkṛishṇa Dîkshit. *The Indian Calendar, with Tables for the*

Conversion of Hindu and Muhammadan into A.D. *Dates, and Vice Versa with Tables of Eclipses Visible in India.* London: Swan Sonnenschein & Co., 1896.

Shah, Umakant P. *Akota Bronzes.* State Board for Historical Records and Ancient Monuments Archaeological Series, no. 1. Bombay: Department of Archaeology, 1959.

Sharan, Mahesh Kumar. *Select Cambodian Inscriptions (The Mebon and Pre Rup Inscriptions of Rajendra Varman II).* Delhi: S. N. Publications, 1981.

———. *Studies in Sanskrit Inscriptions of Ancient Cambodia on the Basis of First Three Volumes of Dr. R. C. Majumdar's Edition.* New Delhi: Abhinav, 1974.

Sharma, G. R. *The Reh Inscription of Menander and the Indo-Greek Invasion of the Gaṅgā Valley.* Studies in History, Culture and Archaeology, vol. 1. Allahabad: Abinash Prakashan/Centre of Advanced Study, Department of Ancient History, Culture and Archaeology, University of Allahabad, 1980.

Sharma, Mukunda Madhava. *Inscriptions of Ancient Assam.* Gauhati: Gauhati University, 1978.

Sharma, R. K. *The Temple of Chaunsathyogini at Bheraghat.* Delhi: Agam Kala, 1978.

Sharma, Tej Ram. *Personal and Geographical Names in the Gupta Inscriptions.* Delhi: Concept Publishing Company, 1978.

Shastri, Ajay Mitra. *Inscriptions of the Śarabhapurīyas, Pāṇḍuvaṃśins and Somavaṃśins.* 2 vols. New Delhi/Delhi: Indian Council of Historical Research/Motilal Banarsidass, 1995.

———. *An Outline of Early Buddhism (A Historical Survey of Buddhology, Buddhist Schools & Sanghas Mainly Based on the Study of Pre-Gupta Inscriptions).* Varanasi: Indological Book House, 1965.

Shizutani, Masao. *Indo Bukkyō Himei Mokuroku* [Catalogue of Indian Buddhist Inscriptions]. Kyoto: Heirakuji shoten, 1979.

Sims-Williams, N. *Sogdian and Other Iranian Inscriptions of the Upper Indus.* Corpus Inscriptionum Iranicarum, part 2, vol. 3, no. 2. London: School of Oriental and African Studies, 1989.

Singh, Jai Prakash. *Aspects of Early Jainism [As Known from the Epigraphs].* Monographs of the Department of Ancient Indian History Culture and Archaeology, no. 7. Varanasi: Banaras Hindu University, 1972.

Sircar, D[inesh] C[handra]. *Aśokan Studies.* Calcutta: Indian Museum, 1979.

———. *Cosmology and Geography in Early Indian Literature.* Calcutta: Indian Studies Past & Present, 1967.

———. *Early Indian Numismatic and Epigraphical Studies* [EINES]. Calcutta: Indian Museum, 1977.

———. *Epigraphic Discoveries in East Pakistan.* Calcutta Sanskrit College Research Series, no. 80; Studies, no. 56. Calcutta: Sanskrit College, 1973.

———. *Indian Epigraphical Glossary* [IEG]. Delhi: Motilal Banarsidass, 1966.

———. *Indian Epigraphy* [SIE]. Delhi: Motilal Banarsidass, 1965.

———. *Inscriptions of Aśoka.* Revised ed. Delhi: Government of India, 1967.

———. "Introduction to Indian Epigraphy and Palaeography" [IIEP]. JAIH 4, 1970–71, 72–136.

———. *Select Inscriptions Bearing on Indian History and Civilization* [SI]. Vol. 1: *From the Sixth Century* B.C. *to the Sixth Century* A.D. Calcutta: Calcutta University, 1942; 2d ed., revised and enlarged, 1965. Vol. 2: *From the Sixth to the Eighteenth Century* A.D. Delhi: Motilal Banarsidass, 1983.

———. *Some Epigraphical Records of the Medieval Period from Eastern India.* New Delhi: Abhinav, 1979.

———. *Studies in the Geography of Ancient and Medieval India.* 2d ed. Delhi: Motilal Banarsidass, 1971.

———. *Studies in the Political and Administrative Systems in Ancient and Medieval India.* Delhi: Motilal Banarsidass, 1974.

———. *Studies in the Religious Life of Ancient and Medieval India.* Delhi: Motilal Banarsidass, 1971.

———. *Studies in the Society and Administration of Ancient and Medieval India.* Vol. 1: *Society.* Calcutta: K. L. Mukhopadhyay, 1967.

———, ed. *Land System and Feudalism in Ancient India.* Centre of Advanced Study in Ancient Indian History and Culture, Lectures and Seminars, no. 1-B (Seminars). Calcutta: University of Calcutta, 1966.

Sivaramamurti, C. *Indian Epigraphy and South Indian Scripts* [IESIS]. Bulletin of the Madras Government Museum, New Series, General Section, vol. 3, no. 4. Madras: Government of Madras, 1948. Reprint, 1966.

Slusser, Mary. *Nepal Mandala: A Cultural Study of the Kathmandu Valley.* 2 vols. Princeton: Princeton University Press, 1982.

Somani, Ram Vallabh. *Jain Inscriptions of Rajasthan.* Prakrit Bharati Puspa 11. Jaipur: Rajasthan Prakrit Bharati Sansthan, 1982.

South Indian Inscriptions [SII]. 24++ vols. Archaeological Survey of India, 1890–1982. (Vols. 1–8 of SII = vols. 9–10, 29, 44, 49, and 52–4 of ASI, New Imperial Series). [See 8.1.2 for further details.]

Sreenivasachar, P. *A Corpus of Inscriptions in the Telingana Districts of H.E.H. the Nizam's Dominions.* Parts 1–3: Hyderabad Archaeological Series, nos. 13 and 19. Hyderabad: The Nizam's Government, 1942, 1940 [*sic*], 1956. Part 4 (ed. P. V. Parabrahma Sastry): Andhra Pradesh Archaeological Series, no. 32. Hyderabad: Government of Andhra Pradesh, 1970.

Srinivasachari, V., and S. Gopalan. *Bhoṃsle Vaṃśa Caritra: Being the Marathi Historical Inscription in the Big Temple, Tanjore on the History of the Mahratta Rajas of Tanjore.* Tanjore Sarasvati Mahal Series, no. 46. Thanjavur: Tanjore Maharaja Serfoji's Sarasvati Mahal Library, 1951. Reprint, 1980.

Srinivasan, P. R., and S. Sankaranarayanan. *Inscriptions of the Ikshvāku Period.* Government of Andhra Pradesh Epigraphical Series, no. 14. Hyderabad: Government of Andhra Pradesh, 1979.

Stein, Burton. *Peasant State and Society in Medieval South India.* Delhi: Oxford University Press, 1980.

Stein, Marc Aurel. *Serindia. Detailed Report of Exploration in Central Asia and Westernmost China Carried Out and Described Under the Orders of H.M. Indian Government.* 5 vols. Oxford: Clarendon Press, 1921. Reprint, Delhi: Motilal Banarsidass, 1980.

Sternbach, Ludwik. *Poésie sanskrite conservée dans les anthologies et les inscriptions.* 3 vols. Publications de l'Institut de Civilisation Indienne, série in-8°, fasc. 46. Paris: Institut de Civilisation Indienne, 1980–85.

Stroobandt, R. *Epigraphical Find-spots.* (Part I of *Corpus Topographicum Indiae Antiquae.*) Gent: Universitas Gandavensis, 1974.

Stutterheim, W. F. *Oudheden van Bali I: Het Oude Rijk van Pedjeng.* Publicaties der Kirtya Liefrinck-van der Tuuk, part 1. Singaradja, Bali: Kirtya Liefrinck-van der Tuuk, 1929.

Subrahmanyam, R. *Inscriptions of the Sūryavaṃśi Gajapatis of Orissa.* New Delhi/Delhi: Indian Council of Historical Research/Agam Kala, 1986.

———. *Salihundam, A Buddhist Site in Andhra Pradesh.* Andhra Pradesh Government Archaeological Series, no. 17. Hyderabad: Government of Andhra Pradesh, 1964.

Subramaniam, T. N. *South Indian Temple Inscriptions* [SITI]. 3 vols. in 4 parts. Madras Government Oriental Series, nos. 104, 121, 131, and 157. Madras: Government Oriental Manuscripts Library, 1953–57.

Sundaram, K. *Studies in Economic and Social Conditions of Medieval Andhra* (A.D. *1000–1600*). Machilipatnam and Madras: Triveni Publishers, 1968.

Swamikannu Pillai, L. D. *Indian Chronology (Solar, Lunar and Planetary): A Practical Guide to the Interpretation and Verification of Tithis, Nakshatras, Horoscopes and Other Indian Time-records,* B.C. *1 to* A.D. *2000.* Madras: Grant & Co., 1911. Reprint, New Delhi: Asian Educational Services, 1982.

———. *An Indian Ephemeris,* A.D. *700 to* A.D. *1799.* 7 vols. in 8 parts. Madras: Government of Madras, 1922–23.

Tarn, W. W. *The Greeks in Bactria and India.* 2d ed. Cambridge: Cambridge University Press, 1951.

Taw Sein Ko. *The Kalyāṇī Inscriptions Erected by King Dhammacetī at Pegu in 1476* A.D.*: Text and Translation.* Rangoon: Superintendent, Government Printing, Burma, 1892.

Taylor, Isaac. *The Alphabet: An Account of the Origin and Development of Letters.* 2 vols. London: Kegan Paul, Trench & Co., 1883.

Tewari, S. P. *Contributions of Sanskrit Inscriptions to Lexicography.* Delhi: Agam Kala, 1987.

Thaplyal, Kiran Kumar. *Inscriptions of the Maukharīs, Later Guptas, Puṣpabhūtis and Yaśovarman of Kanauj.* New Delhi/Delhi: Indian Council of Historical Research/ Agam Prakashan, 1985.

———. *Studies in Ancient Indian Seals: A Study of North Indian Seals and Sealings from Circa Third Century* B.C. *to Mid-seventh Century* A.D. Lucknow: Akhila Bharatiya Sanskrit Parisad, 1972.

Tod, James. *Annals and Antiquities of Rajasthan or the Central and Western Rajpoot States of India.* 2 vols. London: Smith, Elder, and Co., 1829–32. (Many subsequent editions and reprints.)

Tripathi, Kunjabihari. *The Evolution of Oriya Language and Script.* Cuttack: Utkal University, [1962].

———. *Prācīna Oṛiā Abhilekha* [in Oriya]. Bhuvaneśvara: Oṛiśā Sāhitya Ekāḍemī, [1960].

Trivedi, Harihar Vitthal. *Inscriptions of the Paramāras, Chandēllas, Kachchhapaghātas and Two Minor Dynasties.* Corpus Inscriptionum Indicarum, vol. 7, parts 1–3. New Delhi: Director General, Archaeological Survey of India, 1991/1978/1989 [*sic*].

Tuḷpuḷe, Śaṃ. Go. *Prācīna Marāṭhī Korīva Lekha.* Puṇē: Puṇē Vidyāpīṭha Prakāśana, 1963.

Turner, R. L. *The Gavīmaṭh and Pālkīguṇḍu Inscriptions of Aśoka.* Hyderabad Archaeological Series, no. 10. Hyderabad: Department of Archaeology, Government of Hyderabad, 1952.

Upādhyāya, Vāsudeva. *Prācīna Bhāratīya Abhilekha* [in Hindi; English title, *A Study of Ancient Indian Inscriptions*]. 2 vols. Paṭnā: Prajñā Prakāśana, 1970.

Upasak, Chandrika Singh. *The History and Palaeography of Mauryan Brāhmī Script.* Nalanda: Nava Nālandā Mahāvihāra, 1960.

Vajrācārya, Dhanavajra. *Licchavikālakā Abhilekha (Anuvāda, Aitihasika Vyākhyāsahita).* Nepāla ra Eśiyālī Adhyayana Samiti, Aitihāsika Sāmagrī Mālā 6. Kāṭhmāṇḍaū: Tribhuvana Viśvavidyālaya, [Vikrama] 2030.

Vajrācārya, Dhanavajra, and Ṭekbahādura Śreṣṭha. *Śāhakālakā Abhilekha* [*Pahilo Bhāga*]. Kāṭhmāṇḍaū: Tribhuvana Viśvavidyālaya, [Vikrama] 2037.

Vallabhaji, Acharya Girishankar. *Historical Inscriptions of Gujarat (from Ancient Times to the End of Vaghela Dynasty)* [in Gujarati]. 4 parts. (Part 4, *The Sultanate Period,* by Hariparasad Gangashankar Shastri). Shree Forbes Gujarati Sabha Series, no. 15. Bombay: The Forbes Gujarati Sabha, 1933–79.

Venkatasubbiah, A. *Some Śaka Dates in Inscriptions: A Contribution to Indian Chronology.* Mysore: N. Subramanian & Co., 1918.

Verma, Thakur Prasad. *The Palaeography of Brāhmī Script in North India (from c. 236 B.C. to c. 200 A.D.)*. Varanasi: Siddharth Prakashan, 1971.

Vertogradova, V. V. *Indiiskaia Epigrafika iz Kara-tepe v Starom Termeze: Problemy Deshifrovki i Interpretatsii* [Indian Epigraphy from Kara-tepe in Old Termez: Problems of Decipherment and Interpretation]. Moscow: Vostochnaia Literatura, 1995.

Vogel, J. Ph. *Antiquities of Chamba State*. Part 1: *Inscriptions of the Pre-Muhammadan Period.* ASIR, New Imperial Series 36, 1914. [Part 2 by B. Ch. Chhabra, q.v.]

———. "The Earliest Sanskrit Inscriptions of Java." *Publicaties van den Oudheidkundigen Dienst in Nederlandsch-Indië* 1, 1925, 15–35.

Vorob'eva-Desiatovskaia, M. I. "Pamiatniki pis'mom kxaroshtxi i braxmi iz sovetskoi Srednei Azii" [Kharoṣṭhī and Brāhmī Documents from Soviet Central Asia], in G. M. Bongard-Levin et al., eds., *Istoriia i Kul'tura Tsentral'noi Azii* (Moscow: Akademiia Nauk SSSR, 1983), 22–96.

Vyās, Māṅgīlāl ("Mayaṅk"). *Mārvāṛa ke Abhilekha*. Jodhpur: Hindī Sāhitya Mandira, 1973.

———. *Rājasthāna ke Abhilekha* [*Prathama Khaṇḍa*]. Jodhpur: Rājasthāna Sāhitya Mandira, 1980.

Willis, Michael D. *Inscriptions of Gopaksetra: Materials for the History of Central India.* London: British Museum Press, 1996.

Wilson, Horace Hayman. *Ariana Antiqua: A Descriptive Account of the Antiquities and Coins of Afghanistan with a Memoir on the Buildings Called Topes, by C. Masson, Esq.* London: East India Company, 1841. Reprint, Delhi: Oriental Publishers, 1971.

Windisch, Ernst. *Geschichte der Sanskrit-Philologie und Indischen Altertumskunde.* Grundriss der indo-arischen Philologie und Altertumskunde I.1.B. Strassburg: Karl J. Trübner, 1917–20.

———. *Philologie und Altertumskunde in Indien. Drei nachgelassene Kapitel des III. Teils der Geschichte der Sanskrit-Philologie und Indischen Altertumskunde.* Abhandlungen für die Kunde des Morgenlandes 15.3. Leipzig: Deutsche Morgenländische Gesellschaft, 1921.

Woodhead, A. G. *The Study of Greek Inscriptions.* 2d ed. Cambridge: Cambridge University Press, 1981.

Woolner, A. C. *Aśoka Text and Glossary.* 2 parts. Panjab University Oriental Publications. London: Oxford University Press for the University of the Panjab, Lahore, 1924.

Index of Inscriptions Cited

All individual inscriptions cited (with brief bibliographic reference) in the text of this book are listed here with fuller citation. Reference is generally given to the most recent, authoritative, and/or accessible edition. Exhaustive references for all inscriptions are not practically feasible, but in some cases further references are given to other edition(s) where they are deemed to be of particular importance. In general, editions in the volumes of the Corpus Inscriptionum Indicarum (CII) and in Lüders' *Mathurā Inscriptions* (MI) are taken as "authoritative." For inscriptions not published in these collections, preference is usually given to editions in standard epigraphic journals, especially *Epigraphia Indica* (EI) and *Indian Antiquary* (IA). References are also given to D. C. Sircar's *Select Inscriptions* (SI) for inscriptions which are included therein. In most if not all cases, the references given will enable the reader to easily trace all other editions of the inscriptions.

Inscriptions are cited by their generally accepted designations, normally referring to their original findspot,[1] if known, or sometimes to a geographical name in the inscription itself (typically the name of a village granted in a copper plate charter, e.g., "Marmuri copper plate ins."). Inscriptions whose provenance is unknown are usually designated by their present location (e.g., "Bombay Royal Asiatic Society copper plate ins.") or by the name of the issuing authority (e.g., "Indravarman relic casket ins."). For each inscription is listed the findspot, located by district and state, or country if other than India; type of record (pillar inscription, copper plate inscription, etc.); issuing authority or current ruler (dynasty or geographical identification and personal name), if cited; date in the era of the inscription and A.D. equivalent, if given; and bibliographic citation (author, journal or other publication, date, pages). Unless otherwise indicated (e.g., "Kharoṣṭhī"), the script is Brāhmī or a derivative thereof, and the language is Sanskrit or Prakrit.

Abhayagiri (Anuradhapura Dist., North Central Province, Sri Lanka) copper plate Pāli ins.: D. M. de Zilva Wickremasinghe, EZ 1, 1904–12, 39–40; S. Paranavitana, EZ 3, 1928–33, 169–71. **151**

1. For the method of transliteration of toponyms, see "Note on Citation and Bibliographic Form," p. xxi.

Hashtnagar (Peshawar Dist., NWFP, Pakistan) Kharoṣṭhī pedestal ins., [Old Śaka?] 384 = ca. A.D. 234?: S. Konow, CII 2.1, 117–9. **46**

Hāthībāḍā (Chitorgarh Dist., Rajasthan) stone ins. of Gājāyana Pārāśarīputra Sarvatāta: D. R. Bhandarkar, EI 22, 1933–34, 198–205. **86, 87, 141, 239, 240**

Hāthīgumphā (Puri Dist., Orissa) cave ins. of Ceti Khāravela: K. P. Jayaswal and R. D. Banerji, EI 20, 1929–30, 71–89; SI I.213–21. **31, 34, 67, 77, 111, 142, 164, 171n. 26, 208**

Hīrahaḍagalli (Bellary Dist., Karnataka) copper plate ins. of Pallava Śivaskandavarman, regnal year 8: G. Bühler, EI I, 1892, 2–10; 2, 1894, 485–6; SI I.461–6. **91**

Hisse-Borālā (Akola Dist., Maharashtra) ins. of Vākāṭaka Devasena, Śaka 380 = A.D. 458/59: S. Gokhale, EI 37, 1967–68, 1–4; G. S. Gai and S. Sankaranarayanan, EI 37, 1967–68, 5–8; J. E. Mitchiner, JAIH 10, 1976–77, 52–95 (esp. 90–1); B. N. Mukherjee, JESI 7, 1980, 3–5. 4.3. **146, 183n. 83, 196n. 168**

Hmawza (Bago Dist., Burma [Myan Mar]) Sanskrit and Pāli Buddhist inss.: C. Duroiselle, ASIAR 1926–27, 171–80; 1927–28, 127–8, 145; 1928–29, 105–9. **154**

Hmawza Pāli terra cotta ins.: L. Finot, JA, ser. 11, vol. 2, 1913, 193–5. **242**

Honnehaḷḷi (North Kanara Dist., Karnataka) stone ins. of Arasappa-Nāyaka [II], Śaka 1478 = A.D. 1555: M. S. Bhat, EI 34, 1960–61, 205–6. **173n. 32**

Hūli (Belgaum Dist., Karnataka) ins. of the reign of Cālukya Vikramāditya VI, Śaka 1029 = A.D. 1107: L. D. Barnett, EI 18, 196–9 (Ins. F). **234**

Indikaṭusäya (Mihintalē, Anuradhapura Dist., North Central Province, Sri Lanka) copper plaque inss.: S. Paranavitana, EZ 3, 1928–33, 199–212; 4, 1934–41, 238–42. **151**

Indravarman (findspot unknown) Kharoṣṭhī relic casket ins., Azes [=Vikrama] 63 = A.D. 6: R. Salomon, JAOS 102, 1982, 59–68; Salomon and G. Schopen, JIABS 7, 1984, 11–20. **143, 182, 242**

Īsāpur (Mathurā; Mathura Dist., UP) *yūpa* ins. of the time of Vasiṣka, [Kaniṣka] 24 = A.D. 102?: H. Lüders, MI §94; SI I.149–50. **88**

Jagatpur (or Jagatgrām; Dehradun Dist., UP) *aśvamedha* brick inss. of King Śīlavarman: T. N. Ramachandran, *Journal of Oriental Research* [Madras] 21, 1951–52, 1–31; 22, 1952–53, 100; SI I.98–9. **92, 131, 239**

Jāgeśvar (Almora Dist., UP) pilgrim record inss.: D. C. Sircar, EI 34, 1960–61, 249–53. **122**

Jagjībanpur (Malda Dist., West Bengal) copper plate of Pāla Mahendrapāla, regnal year 7: G. Bhattacharya, *South Asian Studies* 4, 1988, 70–2. **148**

Jalālābād (Nangarhar Province, Afghanistan; now in Kabul Museum) stone ins. of Kṣatrapa Tiravharṇa, [Old Śaka?] 83 = ca. 67 B.C.?: S. Konow, *Acta Orientalia* 16, 1937, 234–40; G. Fussman, BEFEO 57, 1959, 43–51; G. Dj. Davary, *Studia Iranica* 10, 1981, 53–5. **153**

Jamālgaṛhī (Mardan Dist., NWFP, Pakistan) Kharoṣṭhī stone ins., [Old Śaka?] 359 = ca. A.D. 209?: S. Konow, CII 2.1, 110–3. **46**

Jamālpur (Mathurā) pillar-base inss.: H. Lüders, MI §47–9 and 53. **88**

Jaṭiṅga-Rāmeśvara (Chitradurga Dist., Karnataka) minor rock edicts of Aśoka: E. Hultzsch, CII 1, 179–80. **136n. 67, 138**

Jaugaḍa (Ganjam Dist., Orissa) rock edicts of Aśoka, regnal years 10, 12, 13: E. Hultzsch, CII 1, 101–18. **73, 137, 219**

Jauliāñ (Rawalpindi Dist., NWFP, Pakistan) Kharoṣṭhī image inss.: S. Konow, CII 2.1, 92–7. **17, 47**

Jaunpur (Jaunpur Dist., UP; now in British Museum) brick ins., [Vikrama] 1273 = A.D. 1217: V. S. Agrawal, JUPHS 18, 1945, 196–201. **131, 251**

Jetavanārāma (Anurādhapura Dist., North Central Province, Sri Lanka) stone ins.: S. Paranavitana, EZ 1, 1904–12, 1–9. **151**

Kāṇherī Pahlavi inss.: E. W. West, IA 9, 1880, 265–8 (= ICTWI 62–6). **107**

Kāṇherī stone ins. of the time of Vāsiṣṭhīputra Śrī-Sātakarṇi: G. Bühler, IA 12, 1883, 272–4. **90**

Kanhiāra (Kāngrā Dist., Himachal Pradesh) biscript (Kharoṣṭhī and Brāhmī) stone ins.: S. Konow, CII 2.1, 178–9. **70, 215**

Kaṅkālī Ṭīlā (Mathurā; Mathura Dist., UP) stone ins.: H. Lüders, MI §21. **88, 94**

Kaṅkālī Ṭīlā (Mathurā) *toraṇa* ins.: H. Lüders, MI §20. **81**

Kānukollu (Krishna Dist., AP) copper plates of Śālaṅkāyana Nandivarman, regnal year 14: B. V. Krishna Rao, EI 31, 1955–56, 1–7. **91**

Kānukollu copper plates of Śālaṅkāyana Skandavarman, regnal year 1: B. V. Krishna Rao, EI 31, 1955–56, 7–10. **91**

Kara (Allahabad Dist., UP) Buddhist copper plate ins.: N. P. Chakravarti, EI 22, 1933–34, 37–9. **129n. 44**

Kara Tepe (Termez [q.v.], Uzbekistan) bowl ins.: O. von Hinüber, *Studies in Indo-Asian Art and Culture* 6, 1980, 123–5. **154**

Kara Tepe Brāhmī and Kharoṣṭhī inss.: M. I. Vorob'eva-Desiatovskaia, "Pamiatniki pis'mom kxaroshtxi i braxmi iz sovetskoi Srednei Azii" [see bibliography]. **154**

Karandai Tamil Sangam (originally from Puttūr, Tanjavur Dist., Tamil Nadu) copper plate ins. of Rājendra Coḷa I, regnal year 8: K. G. Krishnan, *Karandai Tamil Sangam Plates of Rajendrachola I*. **116, 150**

Kārle (Pune Dist., Maharashtra) cave ins. of Sātavāhana Vāsiṣṭhīputra Puḷumāvi, regnal year 24: E. Senart, EI 7, 1902–3, 71–3 (ins. no. 20); SI I.210–1. **174**

Kārle cave ins. of the time of Nahapāna: E. Senart, EI 7, 1902–3, 57–61 (ins. no. 13); SI I.171–2. **89**

Karnāl (Karnal Dist., Haryana; now in Lahore Museum) Kharoṣṭhī stone ins.: S. Konow, CII 2.1, 179. **44n. 122**

Kasiā (Gorakhpur Dist., UP) copper plate ins.: F. E. Pargiter, ASIAR 1910–11, 73–7. **65**

Kaṭrā (Mathurā; Mathura Dist., UP) Jaina pedestal ins., [Gupta] 280 (?) = A.D. 599/600 (?): J. F. Fleet, CII 3, 273–4; H. Lüders, MI §8. **84**

Kauśāmbī (= Kosam, Allahabad Dist., UP) ivory seal ins.: IAAR 1958, 76. **132**

Khajurāho (Chhatarpur Dist., MP) stone ins. of Candella Yaśovarman, Vikrama 1011 = A.D. 953/54: F. Kielhorn, EI 1, 1892, 122–35 (ins. no. II). **229**

Khalatse (Ladakh Dist., Jammu and Kashmir) Kharoṣṭhī stone ins., [Old Śaka?] 187(?) = ca. 37 B.C.?: S. Konow, CII 2.1, 79–81. **44**

Khăn Thevăda (Ubon Ratchaburi Province, Thailand) stele ins.: E. Seidenfaden, BEFEO 22, 1922, 57–60. **155**

Khoh (Satna Dist., MP) copper plate ins. of Śarvanātha of Uccakalpa, [Gupta] 214 = A.D. 533/34: J. F. Fleet, CII 3, 135–9. **97**

Kirārī (Chattisgarh Dist., MP) wooden pillar ins.: H. Sastri, EI 18, 1925–26, 152–7. **131**

Kosam (Allahabad Dist., UP) pillar Hindi ins., [Vikrama] 1621 = A.D. 1565: F. E. Pargiter, EI 11, 1911–12, 89–92. **302–5, 303f**

Kosam pillar ins. of Vaiśravaṇa, [Śaka?] 107 = A.D. 185?: N. G. Majumdar, EI 24, 1937–38, 146–8. **82, 139**

Kosambi (= Kosam) brass seal ins.: A. Cunningham, ASIR 10, 1874–75 and 1876–77, 4 + pl. II no. 4. **139**

Koṭṭayam (Kottayam Dist., Kerala) Pahlavi and Syriac inss.: A. C. Burnell, IA 3, 1874, 308–16; E. W. West, EI 4, 1896–97, 174–6. **107**

Kuḍumiyāmalai (Pudukottai Dist., Tamil Nadu) ins.: P. R. Bhandarkar, EI 12, 1913–14, 226–37; V. Premalatha, *A Monograph on Kudumiyanmalai Inscription on Music*; R. Sathyanarayana, *The Kuḍimiyāmalai Inscription on Music*. **248**

Mahāsthān (Bogra Dist., Bangladesh) stone plaque ins.: D. R. Bhandarkar, EI 21, 1931–32, 83–91; SI I.79–80. **12, 31, 76, 111, 124, 140**

Mamāne Ḍherī (Peshawar Dist., NWFP, Pakistan) Kharoṣṭhī pedestal ins., [Kaniṣka (?)] 89 = A.D. 166/67?: S. Konow, CII 2.1, 171–2; EI 22, 1933–34, 14–5. **69n. 223**

Mandāsā (Ganjam Dist., Orissa) plates of Gaṅga Anantavarmadeva, Śaka 913 = A.D. 995: G. Ramadas, JBORS 17, 1931, 175–88. **187**

Mandasor (Mandasor Dist., MP) pillar ins. of Yaśodharman: J. F. Fleet, CII 3, 142–8; SI I.418–20. **66, 111**

Mandasor stone ins. of the time of Aulikara Naravarman, Mālava [= Vikrama] 461 = A.D. 404: H. Shastri, EI 12, 1913–14, 315–21; SI I.397–8. **96**

Mandasor stone ins. of the time of Gupta Kumāragupta and Aulikara Bandhuvarman, Mālava [= Vikrama] 493 and 529 = A.D. 436 and 473: J. F. Fleet, CII 3, 79–88; D. R. Bhandarkar, CII 3 (rev. ed.), 322–32; SI I.299–307. **118, 182, 229, 233n. 16, 236**

Māṇḍhal (Nagpur Dist., Maharashtra) copper plate ins. of Vākāṭaka Pravarasena II, regnal year 17: A. M. Shastri, EI 41, 1975–76, 68–76. **146n. 91**

Māṇḍhal copper plate inss. of Vākāṭaka Pṛthivīṣeṇa II, regnal years 2 and 10: A. M. Shastri, EI 41, 1975–76, 159–80. **146n. 91**

Māndhātā (Nimar Dist., MP) *Halāyudha-stotra* ins., Vikrama 1120 = A.D. 1063: P. P. Subrahmanya Sastri, EI 25, 1939–40, 173–82; N. P. Chakravarti, ibid., 183–5. **122, 237, 238**

Māṇikiāla (Rāwalpiṇḍī Dist., NWFP, Pakistan) Kharoṣṭhī bronze casket ins.: S. Konow, CII 2.1, 150–1. **214**

Māṇikiāla Kharoṣṭhī silver disk ins.: S. Konow, CII 2.1, 151. **130, 214**

Māṇikiāla Kharoṣṭhī stone ins., Kaniṣka 18 = A.D. 95/96?: S. Konow, CII 2.1, 145–50; SI I.142–3. **78, 215**

Māṅkaṇī (or "Saṅkheḍā"; Baroda Dist., Gujarat) [spurious (?)] copper plate ins. of Taralasvāmin, [Kalacuri] 346 = A.D. 594/95 or 595/96: V. V. Mirashi, CII 4.1, 161–5. **61**

Mānsehrā (Hazara Dist., NWFP, Pakistan) rock edicts of Aśoka, regnal years 8, 10, 12, 13: E. Hultzsch, CII 1, 71–84. **46, 74–75, 136, 222**

Marmuri (originally from Maṇṭur, Bijapur Dist., Karnataka?) copper plate ins. of Western Cālukya Satyāśraya, Bhāva Saṃvatsara = probably A.D. 974: K. G. Kundangar, *Journal of the Bombay Historical Society* 2, 1929, 209–19. **100n. 69**

Maski (Raichur Dist., Karnataka) minor rock edict I of Aśoka: CII 1, 174–5. **73n. 5, 138**

Masoda (Nagpur Dist., Maharashtra) copper plate ins. of Vākāṭaka Pravarasena [II], regnal year 29: A. M. Shastri and C. Gupta, JESI 10, 1983, 108–16. **146n. 91**

Māṭ (Mathurā; Mathura Dist., UP) portrait statue label inss.: H. Lüders, MI §97–8, 100. **84, 120, 121f**

Mathurā (Mathura Dist., UP) biscript (Kharoṣṭhī and Brāhmī) pedestal ins., [Kaniṣka] 46 = A.D. 123/24?: G. Bhattacharya, *Indian Museum Bulletin* 19, 1984, 27–30; S. Subramonia Iyer, EI 40, 1973–74 [actually published 1986], 168–9. **44, 51, 143**

Mathurā coping-stone ins.: H. Lüders, MI §162. **88, 144**

Mathurā Jaina image ins. of the time of Kuṣāṇa Huviṣka, [Kaniṣka] 44(?) = A.D. 122?: R. D. Banerji, EI 10, 1909–10, 113–4; SI I.155–6. **174**

Mathurā Jaina ins., [Old Śaka?] 299 = ca. A.D. 149?: R. D. Banerji, IA 37, 1908, 33–4. **181**

Mathurā lion capital Kharoṣṭhī inss. of the time of Mahākṣatrapa Rajula: S. Konow, CII 2.1, 30–49; SI I.114–9. **51, 143**

Mathurā Nāga statue ins.: H. Lüders, MI §161. **84**

Mathurā (Govindnagar) pedestal ins., [Gupta] 121 = A.D. 440/41 and [regnal] year [of Kumāragupta?] 15: S. Subramonia Iyer, EI 40, 1973–74, 20–2. **172n. 29**

Nidhanpur (Sylhet Dist., Bangladesh) copper plate ins. of Bhāskaravarman of Kāmarūpa: P. Bhattacharya Vidyavinoda, EI 12, 1913–4, 65–79. **166**

Nigālī Sāgar (Bhairwa Dist., Nepal) minor pillar edict of Aśoka, regnal year 20: E. Hultzsch, CII 1, 165; SI I.68.**140, 152n. 101, 222**

Nirmaṇḍ (Mandi Dist., Himachal Pradesh) mask inss., [Laukika] 2 = A.D. 826?: J. Ph. Vogel, *Acta Orientalia* 1, 1922, 230–4. **129**

Niṭṭūr (Bellary Dist., Karnataka) minor rock edicts of Aśoka: P. R. Srinivasan, EI 39, 1971–72, 111–6. **138**

Niya (Xinjiang-Uighur Autonomous Region, China) Kharoṣṭhī wood document ins.: A. M. Boyer, E. J. Rapson, and E. Senart, *Kharoṣṭhī Inscriptions* . . . II.240, no. 638. **272–74, 273f**

Nūtimaḍugu (Anantpur Dist., AP) palimpsest copper plate ins. of Saṃgama (Vijayanagara) Triyambaka, Śaka 1377 = A.D. 1455: N. Lakshminarayan Rao, EI 25, 1939–40, 186–94. **118**

Pabhosā (Allahabad Dist., UP) cave ins. of the time of Ūdāka, regnal year 10: A. Führer, EI 2, 1894, 242 (ins. no. 1); SI I.95–7. **84, 171**

Pabhosā Jaina stone ins., [Vikrama] 1881 = A.D. 1824: A. Führer, EI 2, 1894, 243–4 (ins. no. 3). **308–9, 308f**

Pagàn (Mandalay Dist., Burma [Myan Mar]) Sanskrit and Pāli Buddhist inss.: C. Duroiselle, ASIAR 1926–27, 161–71. **155**

Pagàn stone ins. in Sanskrit and Tamil: E. Hultzsch, EI 7, 1902–3, 197–8. **155**

Paiṭhāṇ (Aurangabad Dist., Maharashtra) plates of Rāṣṭrakūṭa Govinda III, Śaka 716 = A.D. 794: F. Kielhorn, EI 3, 1894–95, 103–13; SI II.457–68. **166**

Pālkīguṇḍu (Raichur Dist., Karnataka) minor rock edict I of Aśoka: R. L. Turner, *The Gavīmaṭh and Pālkīguṇḍu Inscriptions of Aśoka*, 17. **138**

Pāṇḍaraṅgapallī (Kolhapur Dist. [?], Maharashtra) copper plate ins. of Rāṣṭrakūṭa (Mānapura) Avidheya, regnal year 15: V. V. Mirashi, *Annals of the Bhandarkar Oriental Research Institute* 25, 1944, 40–2. **197n. 173**

Pāṅguṛāriā (Sehore Dist., MP) minor rock edict I of Aśoka: D. C. Sircar, EI 37, 1971–72, 1–8 = *Aśokan Studies*, 94–103. **138**

Pāṅguṛāriā umbrella shaft ins.: S. Subramonia Iyer, EI 40, 1973–74, 119–20. **142**

Pañjaur (/Pinjaur, etc.; Ambala Dist., Haryana) ins., Harṣa 563 = A.D. 1168: F. Kielhorn, IA 26, 1897, 31–2. **188**

Paraśurāmeśvara temple (Bhubaneswar, Puri Dist., Orissa) ins.: A. Ghosh, EI 26, 1941–42, 126–7. **97**

Paris (findspot unknown) Kharoṣṭhī carnelian seal ins.: S. Konow, CII 2.1, 7. **132**

Pathārī (Vidisha Dist., MP) pillar ins. of Rāṣṭrakūṭa Parabala, [Vikrama] 917 = A.D. 861: F. Kielhorn, EI 9, 1907–8, 248–56. **234**

Pāṭhyār (Kangra Dist., Himachal Pradesh) biscript (Kharoṣṭhī and Brāhmī) stone ins.: S. Konow, CII 2.1, 178. **70**

Patna (Patna Dist., Bihar) glass seal inss.: K. P. Jayaswal and M. Ghosh, JBORS 10, 1924, 189–201. **128, 131**

Patna *yakṣa* image ins.: K. P. Jayaswal, JBORS 5, 1919, 88–106, 214–5, 516–49; R. D. Banerji, ibid., 210–4.; V. A. Smith and [L. D.] Barnett, ibid., 512–6; H. P. Sastri, ibid., 552–63; SI I.93–4. **128, 241, 248**

Paṭṭadakal (Bijapur Dist., Karnataka) pillar ins. of the time of Cālukya Kīrttivarman II [A.D. 754]: J. F. Fleet, EI 3, 1894–95, 1–7. **39, 71**

Pattana (Aṇhilvāḍ-Pattana; Mahsana Dist., Gujarat) *praśasti*, [Vikrama] 1652 / Allāī [Ilāhī] 41 = A.D. 1596: G. Bühler, EI 1, 1892, 319–24. **195, 243**

Pauni (Bhandara Dist., Maharashtra) Buddhist inss.: S. B. Deo and J. P. Joshi, *Pauni Excavation (1969–70)*, part I, ch. XI, 37–43. **142**

Reh (Fatehpur Dist., UP) stone *liṅga* ins., supposedly of the time of Menander: G. R. Sharma, *The Reh Inscription of Menander*; B. N. Mukherjee, JAIH 12, 1978–79, 150–5 [refutes attribution to Menander]. **141**

Rīsthal (Mandasor Dist., MP) stone ins. of Aulikara Prakāśadharman, [Vikrama] 572 = A.D. 515: R. Salomon, IIJ 31, 1989, 1–36. **146**

Rummindeī (Bhairwa Dist., Nepal) minor pillar edict of Aśoka, regnal year 20: E. Hultzsch, CII 1, 164–5; SI I.67–8. **140, 152n. 101, 222, 250, 262–65, 264f**

Rupar (Ludhiana Dist., Punjab) ivory seal inss.: IAAR 1953, 123 + pl. XLVIII-A. **132**

Rūpnāth (Jabalpur Dist., MP) minor rock edict I of Aśoka: E. Hultzsch, CII 1, 166–9. **138, 219**

Sahasrām (Rohtas [formerly Shahabad] Dist., Bihar) minor rock edict I of Aśoka: E. Hultzsch, CII 1, 169–1. **138, 219**

Sai Fong (Vientiane Province, Laos) stele ins. of Jayavarman VII, Śaka 1108 = A.D. 1186: K 368; L. Finot, BEFEO 3, 1903, 18–33; A. Barth, ibid., 460–6. **158**

Sakrāī (Jhunjhunun Dist. [?], Rajasthan) stone ins., Vikrama 699 (?) = A.D. 643 (?): B. Ch. Chhabra, EI 27, 1947–48, 27–33. **61, 97**

Sālihuṇḍam (Srikakulam Dist., AP) conch shell inss.: IAAR 1958–59, 8 + pl. V-B. **132**

Sālihuṇḍam pot ins.: T. N. Ramachandran, EI 28, 1949–50, 135–7. **131n. 57**

Sāmangaḍ (Kolhapur Dist., Maharashtra) copper plate ins. of Rāṣṭrakūṭa Dantidurga, Śaka 675 = A.D. 753/54: J. F. Fleet, IA 11, 1882, 108–15. **62n. 201, 166**

Sāñcī (Raisen Dist., MP) minor pillar edict of Aśoka: E. Hultzsch, CII 1, 160–1. **140**

Sāñcī *stūpa* inss.: J. Marshall and A. Foucher, *The Monuments of Sanchi*, vol. 1, part 4 (261–396; by N. G. Majumdar). **141, 207–8**

Sāñcī *stūpa* ins. no. 25: J. Marshall and A. Foucher, *The Monuments of Sanchi*, I.302. **207–8**

Sāncor (Jalor Dist., Rajasthan) inss. of Cāhamāna Pratāpasiṃha, [Vikrama] 1444 = A.D. 1388: D. R. Bhandarkar, EI 11, 1911–12, 64–7. **343**

Sāngsi (Kolhapur Dist., Maharashtra) memorial ins.: P. B. Desai, EI 28, 1949–50, 129–33. **120**

Sanjeli (Panch Mahal Dist., Gujarat) copper plates of the time of Hūṇa Toramāṇa, regnal years 3, 6, and 19: R. N. Mehta and A. M. Thakkar, *M. S. University Copper Plates of the Time of Toramana*; K. V. Ramesh, EI 40, 1973–74, 175–86. **146**

Śaṅkarpur (Sidhi Dist., MP) copper plate ins. of the time of Budhagupta and Harivarman, [Gupta] 168 = A.D. 487/88: B. Jain, JESI 4, 1977, 62–6. **145**

[Saṅkheḍā: see Māṅkaṇī.]

Sannati (Gulbarga Dist., Karnataka) rock edicts of Aśoka: K. R. Norman, *South Asian Studies* 7, 1991, 101–10; I. K. Sarma and J. Varaprasada Rao, *Early Brāhmī Inscriptions from Sannati*, 3–56. **137**

Sānta Bommāli (also referred to as Simhipura or Simhapura; Ganjam Dist., Orissa) copper plate ins. of the time of Gaṅga Devendravarman, Gaṅga 520 = ca. A.D. 1018: S. Rajaguru, JAHRS 3, 1928, 171–80. **187**

Sārnāth (Varanasi Dist., UP) minor pillar edict of Aśoka: E. Hultzsch, CII 1, 161–4. **140, 222**

Sārnāth Pali stone inss.: S. Konow, EI 9, 1907–8, 291–3; D. Kosambi, IA 39, 1910, 217 (identifying textual source of the Four Noble Truths ins.). **81**

Sārnāth umbrella shaft ins., Kaniṣka 3 = A.D. 80/81?: J. Ph. Vogel, EI 8, 1905–6, 176–7. **144, 270–72, 271f**

Satyanārāyaṇa temple (Harigaon, Nepal) pillar ins.: R. Gnoli, *Nepalese Inscriptions in Gupta Characters*, I.14–7; D. R. Regmi, *Inscriptions of Ancient Nepal*, no. 27, I.26–30. **122**

Sdok Kak Thoṃ (Pracinburi Province, Thailand) Sanskrit and Khmer stele ins. of Udayādityavarman [II], Śaka 974 = A.D. 1052: A. Chakravarti, *The Sdok Kak Thoṃ Inscription*. **155**

General Index

abbreviations, 67, 98, 176
Abhijñāna-śākuntala (Kālidāsa), 234
Ābhīras, 183n.83, 185
ācāras (customary laws), 240, 251
Achaemenian empire, 13, 28, 46, 52, 210n.66
acute-angled script. *See* Siddhamātṛkā
"Additions to Bactrian Numismatics, and Discovery of the Bactrian Alphabet" (Prinsep), 211
additive/multiplicative system of numerical notation, 56–57, 61n.193, 63–64, 217
adhika-māsa (intercalary month), 178
adhika-tithi (intercalary day), 178
Ādil Shāhis [Ādil Shāh/Ādil Shāhis], 100
administrative documents, 123, 124, 159–60, 231–32
Adzhina Tepe, 153
Afghanistan, 142, 152–53
  Greek and Aramaic inscriptions, 107, 108
  Kharoṣṭhī inscriptions, 44, 45, 78, 211
  pottery inscriptions, 131
  undeciphered script, 71
Africa, 5
Agathocles (Indo-Greek king), 206
Agra inscription, 144
Agrawal, Jagannath, 261
Agrawal, V. S., 250
agriculture, 232
Āguptāyika era, 194
Ahom, 108
Ahom kings, 104, 108
Airikiṇa (Eraṇ), 250
Ajaṇṭā, 246
Ajayapaladeva (Cāhamāna king), 120
Ājīvikas, 138, 140, 243–44
ājñā/ājñapti, 117
Akbar (Mughal emperor), 195, 243
ākhyāyikā, 236
akṣara, 15, 16n.34, 46n.132, 163, 212n.72
Alam Bridge, 143
alaṃkāras, 238
Al-Bīrūnī, 39n.111, 184, 186, 188
Alexander the Great, 22
Allchin, F. R., 133
alphabetic script type, 15
alphabetic syllabary, 20
alphabets. *See specific languages and scripts*
Alsdorf, Ludwig, 133
altered plates. *See* spurious inscriptions
amānta months, 177, 182, 184, 186–87, 188, 191, 193
Amareśvara temple, 237
Amlī era, 195
Amoghavarṣa (Rāṣṭrakūṭa king), 148
Amṛta (sculptor), 247
Aṃśuvarman (king of Nepal), 191
Aṃtalikita (king). *See* Antialkidas
Ānandacandra (king of Arakan), 154
Anantavarman (Eastern Gaṅga king), 62, 187

Ingram Content Group UK Ltd.
Milton Keynes UK
UKHW010118010623
422694UK00001B/18

9 780195 099843